A
Century
of Spies

A
Century
of Spies

Intelligence in the
Twentieth Century

JEFFREY T. RICHELSON

New York   Oxford
Oxford University Press
1995

Oxford University Press

Oxford   New York
Athens   Auckland   Bangkok   Bombay
Calcutta   Cape Town   Dar es Salaam   Delhi
Florence   Hong Kong   Istanbul   Karachi
Kuala Lumpur   Madras   Madrid   Melbourne
Mexico City   Nairobi   Paris   Singapore
Taipei   Tokyo   Toronto

and associated companies in
Berlin   Ibadan

Copyright © 1995 by Jeffrey T. Richelson

Published by Oxford University Press, Inc.,
198 Madison Avenue, New York, New York 10016

Oxford is a registered trademark of Oxford University Press

Library of Congress Cataloging-in-Publication Data
Richelson, Jeffrey.
A century of spies : intelligence in the twentieth century /
Jeffrey T. Richelson.
p.   cm.
Includes index.
ISBN 0–19–507391–6
1. Espionage—History—20th century.
2. Intelligence service—History—20th century.
3. World politics—20th century.
I. Title.
JF1525.I6R52   1995
327.12—dc20   94–35576

1 3 5 7 9 8 6 4 2

Printed in the United States of America
on acid-free paper

Preface

The twentieth century has seen revolutionary change occur in a variety of fields—none more so than intelligence and espionage. At the beginning of the century most intelligence operations of importance emanated from Europe and involved, at most, a small number of agents spread over the continent, spying on military and foreign policy developments. No more than several thousand people were involved in all aspects of intelligence operations.

Today, major intelligence establishments are supported by governments from Washington to Moscow and London to Canberra. In addition, intelligence, is no longer a world of spies, counterspies, political operatives, defectors, and dark alleys. It is that and much more—a world of thirty thousand-pound spy satellites, aircraft packed with cameras and electronic equipment, bristling antenna farms, ultra-high-speed computers, and analysts with advanced degrees in mathematics, physics, foreign languages, economics, engineering, and political science. It is a world with over a million inhabitants that costs more than a hundred billion dollars a year. And despite the end of the Cold War, it is a world that will continue to flourish for a long time to come.

The transformation of the world in the twentieth century—the growth of complex societies, the all-encompassing nature of war, the development of advanced technology, and the emergence of new nations—is reflected in the transformation of the world of intelligence and espionage. The need for information about all aspects of foreign societies, including sophisticated weapons systems, helped transform intelligence into today's multibillion-dollar enterprise, which requires both high-tech collection systems and individuals with advanced training in the social and natural sciences as well as arcane fields such as photographic interpretation.

At the same time, intelligence successes and failures have had a significant impact on world events. Codebreaking helped propel the United States into World War I and ensure an Allied victory. The failure to act on or properly interpret intelligence prior to World War II permitted Hitler to take his first steps toward conquest and led to Hitler's initial successes on the Eastern front. Later in the century the CIA failed to predict the Soviet installation of missiles in Cuba, while the Israeli military intelligence department ignored numerous warning signs prior to the Egyptian attack in October 1973.

On the other hand, there have been important intelligence successes. The gradual development of technical intelligence capabilities from World War I to the Cold War ultimately helped to limit the fear of enemy superiority and surprise attack, permitted the verification (and thus the negotiation) of arms control treaties, and aided crisis-monitoring. And human agents—from Richard Sorge in World War II to Eli Cohen and Oleg Penkovskiy in the 1960s to Oleg Gordievsky—have also had an impact. They have affected the outcome of battles and crises and altered diplomatic strategies.

Alexandria, Va.   J. T. R.
October 1994

Acknowledgments

This book could not have been written without the help of numerous individuals. John Taylor and Wilbert Mahoney of the Military Research Branch of the National Archives and Records Administration helped in identifying and locating relevant documents. Helen Wilson of the Australian National University visited the Australian Archives in Canberra on my behalf on several occasions.

Bill Burr of the National Security Archive provided several significant documents, including many concerning the Penkovskiy case. Others who provided information and documents include Matthew Aid, William Arkin, Desmond Ball, Bill Robinson, Robert Windrem, and several sources who must remain anonymous. Dan Halpin of Cloak and Dagger books was able to quickly satisfy repeated requests for hard-to-find volumes.

I would especially like to thank David Kahn and William Burrows, who read portions of the manuscript and offered helpful advice and crucial corrections. I also owe a great debt to Marjorie Robertson for her valuable research assistance and translation services.

In addition, I am extremely grateful to a large number of authors, whose identity will be apparent in the notes, for their research. A book of this scope must be built, in part, upon the work of others if it is to be completed in any reasonable length of time. Without the research of other authors, who have spent thousands of hours combing the files of the British Public Record Office or reading German documents from World War II, my task would have been completely unmanageable.

Gail Ross, of Lichtman, Trister, Singer, and Ross, is an incomparable agent, and without her perserverance and counsel this book would not have been possible.

Contents

I

1900–1939

1

A Shady Profession

In 1800 a Londoner had the distinction of living in the most populous city in Europe, as one of 900,000 residents. London and Paris, with 600,000 residents, were the only European cities with more than a half million inhabitants. By 1900 they had grown to metropolises of 4.7 and 3.6 million citizens respectively, and sixteen additional cities had populations of a half million or more. Berlin, Glasgow, Moscow, St. Petersburg, and Vienna all had over a million residents.[1]

The urbanization that changed the face of Europe was the product of two factors, the overall population explosion and industrialization. Between 1821 and 1871 the population of Britain nearly doubled, from 14 to 26 million. From 1900 to 1913, the German population grew by the rate of 1 million per year.[2] The wealth and employment generated by industrial enterprise drew men from the countryside to the cities. They manned the factories which produced consumer and capital goods, worked in the steel mills, and were employed by service industries.

The nineteenth century also saw dramatic developments in the means of transportation and communications, developments which contributed to urbanization and industrialization. The telegraph first appeared in the 1840s. Steam-driven railways and ships came into service in growing numbers after 1860, driving down transportation costs. In 1876 Alexander Graham Bell invented the telephone.[3]

The telegraph and telephone had dramatically changed the nature of communications. Until the middle of the nineteenth century, couriers, postal services, and diplomatic bags represented the major means of communication. Visual signals could be sent by semaphore flags or heliograph mirrors. The introduction of the telegraph (at midcentury) and the telephone (during the later part of the century) made it possible to communicate over great distances in short periods of time.[4]

By 1900 urbanization, industrialization, and technological advances had already had a dramatic impact on the way people lived. These forces would also have a dramatic impact on how nations fought wars and how they spied on each other.

Marconi and the Wright Brothers

Telegraphs and telephones had their limitations. Telegraphy required specially laid land lines to carry the Morse signals, while telephone systems required wires to carry voice communications. This precluded communications with ships out of sight of land or each other, except through scouting vessels. It also limited communications to points with already established telegraph or telephone connections. Guglielmo Marconi would remove those limitations.

During an 1895 vacation in the Italian Alps Marconi read a scientific paper which suggested to him that it might be possible to transmit signals through the air, rather than through wires. His enthusiasm for the idea led him to cut short his holiday and return to his top-floor laboratory—a spare room—at the Villa Griffone.[5]

Initial experiments seemed to indicate that while communication was possible, the range was limited to 100 yards or so at most. But Marconi discovered that raising the antenna to new heights resulted in a dramatic extension of range. On June 2, 1896, Marconi applied for the world's first patent for wireless telegraphy, which was quickly granted. On March 2, 1897, he filed the complete specifications and less than five months later the Wireless Telegraph and Signal Company opened, with the objective of developing the Marconi device commercially. A successful demonstration in August, witnessed by the king and queen of Italy, led to the Italian navy's adoption of Marconi's system. In October, he was able to establish communications between Salisbury and Bath, thirty-four miles apart.[6]

Just as Marconi would have a dramatic impact on the new century, so would two brothers born in Ohio in the second half of nineteenth the century. Whereas Marconi sought to send voices and signals through the air, Wilbur and Orville Wright sought to send men through the air.[7]

As a result of their research and discussions Orville and Wilbur became convinced that human flight was possible—and they wanted to play some role in achieving it. They began by exploring the problems involved in controlling a vehicle in the air. Based on wind current data they chose Kitty Hawk, North Carolina, as their testing ground.[8]

After more than three years of effort, at 10:35 A.M. on December 17, 1903, the historic first flight took place. With Orville Wright on board, the *Flyer* rose by its own power into the air and, for about 12 seconds and 120 feet, engaged in full flight. The brothers made three more flights that day. The final flight, with Wilbur on board, lasted 59 seconds and traveled 852 feet.[9]

In the Beginning

When Marconi and the Wright brothers began their scientific work few, if any, in the intelligence world took notice. Indeed, in 1900 the world of intelligence was a very small world. While the governments of Europe maintained organizations to gather political and military intelligence about their enemies and potential enemies, those organizations generally existed on the periphery of government, understaffed and underfunded. They did not regularly brief their prime ministers or chancellors on world events, and their work did not often affect the day-to-day foreign and defense policies of their governments.

Although Great Britain was reputed to have a wide network of spies operating across the continent, the truth was far different. In 1873 the War Office had established an Intelligence Branch, staffed by twenty-seven military and civilian personnel. By that time the increased technological sophistication of armies and navies had become evident, with their use of breech-loading rifles, rifled breech-loading artillery, and armored ships. The scope of military intelligence encompassed not only weapons, tactics, and troop numbers, but technical information.[10]

In 1882 the Admiralty followed suit, organizing a Foreign Intelligence Committee (renamed the Naval Intelligence Department in 1887). The committee received reports from the Royal Navy on the dispositions and activities of foreign warships and merchant vessels on the high seas. Port visits produced useful economic intelligence on the destinations and cargoes of foreign merchant ships.[11]

British military attachés in Berlin, Vienna, and St. Petersburg reported on military developments in their host countries. But they did so in a gentlemanly and honorable fashion. They were not expected to engage in "secret service" and were discouraged from even the slightest involvement in such activities. One attaché remarked:

> I would never do any secret service work. My view is that the Military Attaché is the guest of the country to which he is accredited, and must only see and learn that which is permissible for a guest to investigate. Certainly he must keep his eyes and ears open and miss nothing, but secret service is not his business, and he should always refuse a hand in it.[12]

Nor did France have much in the way of an intelligence establishment. After France's disastrous 1870 war with Germany, which resulted in the loss of Alsace-Lorraine, a Statistical and Military Reconnaissance Section was established and given the task of collecting intelligence on the German troops occupying France's former province.[13]

After the occupation ended in 1873 the section grew and was alternately known as the Information Service (Service de Renseignement, SR) or Special Service. By 1880 the SR had agents in Berlin, Vienna, Dresden,

Leipzig, Frankfurt, Cologne, and Mannheim. Among their accomplishments was the acquisition of German mobilization plans.[14]

However, the involvement of certain members of the SR in the Dreyfus Affair resulted in the SR's abolition as a separate entity in 1899. Its counterespionage functions were assigned to the Sûreté Générale of the Interior Ministry, while its foreign intelligence role was reduced. The Service de Renseignement became the Section de Renseignement, subordinate to the Deuxième Bureau (Second or Intelligence Department) of the General Staff.[15]

The most elaborate intelligence network at the turn of the century was that of Imperial Germany. On June 23, 1866, just ten days prior to the beginning of war with Austria, a royal decree established the Foreign Office Political Field Police (subsequently the Secret Field Police), run by Wilhelm Stieber, whose mission included "support of military authorities by procuring intelligence about the enemy army." When the war ended Stieber expanded his secret service and renamed it the Central-Nachrichtenbüro (Central Intelligence Bureau). In addition to hounding opponents of the regime, the bureau maintained agents in Paris, London, and Vienna.[16]

Stieber believed that a massive espionage network was necessary to produce a complete picture of a potential enemy. He explained:

> The type of isolated observation, involving only a few spies, which has traditionally been employed to spy on other nations, has produced very limited results. . . . [A] multiplicity of spies will enable us to penetrate to the best-protected secrets. . . . Moreover, the importance and accuracy of each piece of information collected by an army of agents can be more carefully analyzed in terms of the other pieces of information which verify or contradict it.[17]

The chief of the Prussian General Staff, Helmuth von Moltke, considered Stieber's successes and the inability of the army to procure its own intelligence to be an unworthy reflection on the army. On February 11, 1867, von Moltke established a permanent competitive service, the Intelligence Bureau.[18]

Stieber's ill-health, which forced him to resign in the mid-1870s and killed him in 1882, permitted the generals to seize control of military intelligence. By the late 1880s the Intelligence Bureau possessed a small but solid network of agents in Paris, Brussels, Luxembourg, Belfort, and other French cities. Seventy-five agents and informants operated in Russia. From 1889 on they furnished various details of the mobilization plans and deployment of the czar's armies.[19]

In 1889 a layer of deputy chiefs of staff, or Oberquartiermeisters, was established and the Intelligence Bureau was subordinated to the IIIrd Oberquartiermeister (O. Qu. III). From that point on it became known as IIIb.[20]

Over the remainder of the century its funding increased, steadily, resulting in a budget greater than that of any other European intelligence service, excluding Russia. As a result, what was initially a tiny office had expanded, by 1901, to 124 officers directing agent activities from war intelligence posts in Belgium, Switzerland, England, Italy, Spain, Luxembourg, Denmark, Sweden, and Romania.[21]

The primary mission of the Russian intelligence establishment was not the collection of foreign intelligence but the monitoring of opponents to the czarist regime—whether they operated inside or outside the country. In 1900 the Special Department, commonly referred to as the Okhrana, became the successor to a series of secret police organizations. The Special Department's Foreign Agency operated mainly in France, Switzerland, and Britain, where Russian revolutionaries and dissidents congregated.[22]

Military intelligence was the responsibility of the Russian Army's General Headquarters. The Fifth Bureau of the First Department of the Operations Directorate was entrusted with intelligence collection and analysis. A variety of subsections studied the military forces and capabilities of Germany, Austria-Hungary, the Balkan states, Scandinavia, Turkey, and Persia. Military attachés reported directly to the Fifth Bureau.[23]

In contrast to Russia and Germany, at the turn of the century the United States had neither an extensive domestic intelligence operation nor an extensive foreign intelligence network. As was the case with Britain, the first permanent intelligence organizations established in the United States were those organized by the U.S. Army and Navy. In this case the Navy was first, establishing the Office of Naval Intelligence in 1882. Under the provisions of General Order No. 292, the ONI was "to collect and record such naval information as may be useful to the Department in wartime as well as peace." To provide intelligence for ONI the commanding officer of every ship was ordered to appoint an intelligence officer to report to ONI on harbors, fortifications, and foreign vessels.[24]

In 1885 Secretary of War William C. Endicott is said to have requested information on the military of a European nation, possibly Germany or Russia, from Adjutant General R. C. Drum. Endicott was surprised to discover that Drum had neither the information nor the means of obtaining it. The result, as the story goes, was that Drum established a Military Information Division (MID) to collect "military data on our own and foreign services which would be available for the use of the War Department and the Army at large." The entire division consisted of a single officer and a single clerk.[25]

Subsequent years saw each organization deploy a network of attachés. ONI representatives established themselves in Paris, Berlin, Rome, Vienna, and St. Petersburg. In 1887 Army attachés were posted to Berlin, Paris, London, Vienna, and St. Petersburg. The Army's attachés contributed to the MID's ability, in 1891, to summarize the numbers and types of arms in the arsenals of eleven European countries.[26]

But by 1900 one of the new intelligence organizations was in disarray. When Captain Charles D. Sigsbee became head of ONI in February 1900 he sent a memo to his immediate superior in which he claimed that ONI was in a shambles. According to Sigsbee's memo the forms sent to officers at sea were outdated, and the information sought would not allow ONI to answer broad tactical or strategic questions. In addition, the officers themselves had received little specific intelligence training. Things did not improve in the next few years. In 1903, near the end of Sigsbee's tenure, the Navy reduced the number of professional naval officers assigned to ONI—from seven to five.[27]

His Majesty's Secret Service

Before the first decade of the new century was over the intersecting fears of war and foreign spies would contribute to the expansion of many nations' espionage operations. Britain's policy of "splendid isolation" fell to the pressures of international politics. The 1900 German Navy Law was an explicit challenge to British naval supremacy, providing for the construction of nineteen new battleships and twenty-three cruisers over the next twenty years. Britain settled its colonial problems with France in 1904. The Anglo-French Entente was followed in 1907 by the Anglo-Russian Entente, along similar lines. Meanwhile, France and Germany confronted each other over Morocco in 1905. The alliances that would face each other in the first world war had started to come together.

February 1904 marked the beginning of a series of changes in British intelligence. The Intelligence Department, minus its Mobilization Division, was rechristened the Directorate of Military Operations. Intelligence, in one form or another, was the responsibility of three of the four sections of the new directorate. MO2 was the Foreign Intelligence Section, MO3 the Administration and Special Duties Section, MO4 the Topographical Section.[28]

The Foreign Intelligence Section began expanding almost as soon as it was formed, experiencing the largest increases in officers and total personnel of all the sections. Before the year was out two further subsections were added to cover the United States and the Far East. "Special Duties" included censorship, counterintelligence, and, apparently, clandestine intelligence collection.[29]

The concern of many British officials with collecting foreign intelligence was more than matched by the fear of foreign spies. From the beginning of the century Britain was the subject of a variety of invasion and spy scares—often promoted by novelists and journalists to whom such scares meant good business. Whereas France was perceived as the likely enemy in 1900, after 1904 Germany was seen as the prime menace. Not surprisingly, in 1905 author William LeQueux "discovered" a "great network of German espionage spread over the United King-dom."[30]

Fear of a Hun invasion was further exacerbated by advances in battle-ship technology and the November 1907 announcement of an accelerated German naval building program. Those fanning the flames in the autumn of 1907 included Leo Maxse, editor and owner of the influential *National Review*, and Colonel Charles Repington, the military correspondent of *The Times*. With support of some of the Tory leadership, they convinced the government to establish a subcommittee of the Committee of Impe-rial Defence (CID) to study the invasion threat. The result was not what Maxse and his allies expected: the study showed surprise attack to be impossible.[31]

The conclusions of the CID neither convinced ardent proponents of the invasion threat nor eliminated fears of a German espionage network operating across Britain. Among those convinced of massive German in-filtration of Britain was a friend of LeQueux, Lieutenant-Colonel James Edmonds, who became responsible in 1907 for counterintelligence and the organization of an espionage network in Germany.[32]

Edmonds took his conclusions to R. B. Haldane, the secretary of state for war, who in March 1909 established and chaired a new CID subcom-mittee to examine "the nature and extent of the foreign espionage that is at present taking place within this country and the danger to which it may expose us." The subcommittee membership was composed of eleven other high-ranking officials, including the First Lord of the Admiralty, the Home Secretary, the permanent undersecretaries of the Treasury and the Foreign Office, the Commissioner of Metropolitan Police, the Director of Military Operations, and the Director of Naval Intelligence.[33]

Edmonds presented to the subcommittee a variety of evidence con-cerning German espionage in Britain, much of it misinterpreted or fabri-cated. However, at the third meeting of the subcommittee Haldane sug-gested that there was sufficient evidence to issue a report. The rest of the committee agreed:

> The evidence which was produced left no doubt in the minds of the subcom-mittee that an extensive system of German espionage exists in this country, and that we have no organization for keeping in touch with that espionage and for accurately determining its extent or objectives.[34]

The committee also concluded that Britain's foreign intelligence sys-tem was inadequate. The Director of Military Operations, Major-General John Ewart, admitted during the meetings of the invasion subcommittee in 1908 that "the existing machinery for obtaining information from Ger-many and the Continent generally during peace or war" was seriously deficient. General Staff assessments of probable German invasion plans were based on "hypothetical assumptions." The Naval Intelligence Divi-sion (NID) agreed. When Rear-Admiral Esmond Slade became Director of

Naval Intelligence in October 1907 he discovered that the naval "secret service . . . was not organized in any way."[35]

Attempts had been made by military and naval intelligence to develop some agents, but they did not amount to much. At the beginning of 1907 there was not a single British agent operating in Europe. Before the end of the year Edmonds had received approval from the Director of Military Operations to organize an espionage network in Germany. The initial attempts were highly amateurish. Edmonds asked friends visiting Germany to ask the local police for the names of British residents. His first agent was provided by Courage and Company brewers, which pressured its Hamburg representative to gather "information as to naval and military matters in connection with harbor works, number of ships, railway arrangements, movement of troops, etc." Over the next two years the reluctant spy was never given a specific assignment. After his trips in 1908 and 1909 he simply invented whatever he thought would please the War Office.[36]

Slade's NID was also active in the espionage arena. In March 1908 Slade sent an NID officer into Germany to make contact with a potential spy. A year later, he reported that there were "three or four agents in our employ, most of whom work for the War Office and Admiralty jointly."[37]

The War Office and Admiralty networks were not adequate in the eyes of the foreign espionage committee. The Admiralty was suspicious that the Germans were secretly accelerating their shipbuilding program— stockpiling guns, turrets, and armor well in advance of actually building the hulls. Since building the guns, gun mountings, and armor was more time-consuming than building the hulls, such a stockpiling effort could cut the three years required to build a ship to two and a half or two. In addition, it was suspected that construction was being started in advance of the dates scheduled by the German Navy Law—in advance even of the authorization of funds by the Reichstag. The consequence of such subterfuge could be dramatic: instead of a 16:13 battleship ratio in favor of Britain in 1912, Britain was facing the possibility of a ratio anywhere from 17:16 to 21:16 in favor of Germany.[38]

It was in this atmosphere that the CID's espionage committee recommended the formation of a secret service bureau to serve three purposes: to serve as a barrier between the military services and foreign spies; to act as the intermediary between the military service departments and British agents abroad; and to take charge of counterespionage.[39]

The Secret Service Bureau began operations on October 1, 1909, under the nominal supervision of the War Office. Originally organized into a Military Branch and Naval Branch, within a month the Secret Service had undergone an internal reorganization, with home and foreign sections replacing the military and naval sections, respectively—possibly because the Military Branch was primarily concerned with counterespionage while Britain's foreign agents were primarily operating in ports and dockyards and reporting naval intelligence. In 1910 its two sections separated, with the Home Section being placed under the Home Office and the Foreign Section under the Admiralty, then its chief customer.[40]

Selected to head the Secret Service's foreign section was a short, thick-set naval officer, Commander (later Captain Sir) Mansfield George Smith-Cumming. Born on April 1, 1859, Cumming served on patrol in the East Indies, took part in operations against the Malay pirates, and was decorated for his role in the Egyptian campaign of 1882. According to his naval record, he was "a clever officer with great taste for electricity," who had "a knowledge of photography," "speaks French," and "draws well."[41]

However, Cumming not only had health problems, but he increasingly suffered from severe seasickness—a rather unfortunate malady for a sailor. In 1885 he was placed on the retired list as "unfit for service."[42]

Cumming established both the Secret Service Bureau foreign department and his own London flat at the top of 2 Whitehall Court in "a regular maze of passages and steps, and oddly shaped rooms," which could be reached only by a private elevator. In Cumming's office was a plain work table, a big safe, some maps and charts on the walls, a vase of flowers, one or two seascapes, and various mechanical gadgets, including a patent compass and a new sort of electric clock.[43]

Cumming himself could have emerged from the pages of a novel. Known as "C," as the chief of the secret service is still known, he wrote only in green ink. Having lost a leg in an accident, he got around the corridors by putting his wooden leg on a child's scooter and propelling himself vigorously with the other. Visitors were treated to the spectacle of Cumming stabbing his wooden leg with his paper knife to emphasize the point of an argument. By his own admission, he considered secret service work "capital sport."[44]

Cumming's priorities were naval, his resources limited. As a postwar report admitted, the Foreign Section was unable to employ full-time agents and was forced to rely on "casual agents"—agents whose performance was unsatisfactory.[45]

The most productive of the part-time agents were a small group of men in the shipping or arms industries who either regularly traveled to or resided in Germany and combined their business travels with part-time intelligence work. Much of that intelligence work did not involve actual espionage. Instead, Cumming's part-timers collected a wide assortment of newspapers and journals published in Kiel, Wilhelmshaven, Danzig, and Berlin. They also observed the harbors and waterfronts of Hamburg and Bremen, homes to major shipyards, and of Kiel.[46]

The most successful of Cumming's known networks was run by Max Schultz, a naturalized Southampton ship-dealer. During his travels in Germany in 1910–11 Schultz recruited four informants, the most important being an engineer named Hipsich, in Bremen's Weser shipyards. In the two years Hipsich operated before being detected he had the opportunity to inform the British about Germany's battleship plans and apparently handed over a large collection of drawings.[47]

Cumming's German network provided an abundance of technical intelligence on the German navy—on topics from fire control to range finders. While the bulk of reports were based on published information, that information would not have been noticed except for Cumming's network. Agent reports proved to be of great value in keeping the Naval Intelligence Division informed of the status of the Hochseeflotte (High Seas Fleet) and U-boat construction programs. They often provided the only data on the final stages of battleship construction or U-boat speed and endurance trials. In early 1911 agents provided the Admiralty with "a full and illustrated description" of the new heavy shell introduced a year earlier, as well as "an account of its [impressive] performance against many varieties of armoured targets."[48]

In addition to Germany, Rotterdam, Brussels, and St. Petersburg were targets of Cumming's spies. Richard Tinsley, code-named T, headed Cumming's operations in Rotterdam. Tinsley had developed a successful shipping business, which he used as a cover for his intelligence work. But Ivone Kirkpatrick, a future permanent undersecretary at the Foreign Office, found T "a liar and a first-class intriguer with few scruples."[49]

Cumming's Belgian network was both larger and more disreputable than the Dutch network. Henry Dale Long, code-named L, served as chief of operations in Brussels from 1910. However, the Brussels network did business with a free-lance Brussels intelligence service that sometimes sold fabricated intelligence, including bogus German invasion plans. Cumming was persuaded to spend £600 to purchase an alleged German codebook which a wartime cryptanalyst later showed to be a "pup of the poorest class."[50]

Sidney Reilly

While the names of Richard Tinsley and Henry Dale Long are relatively unknown, the chief British agent in St. Petersburg became the inspiration for numerous books and a twelve-part television series. Much of what has been written by or about Sidney Reilly is myth. Reilly, it has been claimed, "wielded more power, authority and influence than any other spy," was an expert assassin "by stabbing and shooting and throttling," and possessed "eleven passports and a wife to go with each."[51]

Reality was less sensational. Born Sigmund Georgievich Rosenblum in 1874, Reilly was the only son of a rich Russian Jewish father. Sometime in the 1890s he emigrated to London, breaking off all contact with his family in the process, and changing his name to Sidney Reilly. At the beginning of the new century he moved to Port Arthur, headquarters of the Russian Far Eastern Fleet, where he worked as a partner in a timber sales company. By the time Reilly returned to London, on the eve of the Russo-Japanese War in 1904, he had become an international adventurer, fluent in several languages. It is possible, although by no means certain, that

Reilly provided the Naval Intelligence Division with intelligence on the Russian Far Eastern Fleet during his years in Port Arthur.[52]

After completing a course in electrical engineering at the Royal School of Mines he entered Trinity College, Cambridge, in October 1905 as an advanced student, using a fake certificate from Roorkee University in India. Reilly left Cambridge after two or three years and proceeded to invent a different postgraduate career, boasting that he had a doctorate from Heidelberg. That was only one of many personal fantasies, some of which he began to believe. Eleanor Toye, one of his secretaries, claimed that "Reilly used to suffer from severe mental crises amounting to delusion. Once he thought he was Jesus Christ."[53]

But Reilly's aptitude for intelligence work won him the admiration of both C and Winston Churchill, undersecretary for colonies in 1905 and subsequently Home Secretary and First Lord of the Admiralty (in 1911). The first British diplomat to arrive in Soviet Russia, Robert Bruce Lockhart, while not having a particularly high opinion of Reilly's intelligence, found his courage and indifference to danger "superb." It was probably soon after the creation of the Secret Service Bureau that Reilly established himself as a successful commission agent for the Hamburg shipbuilders Blohm and Voss. It is unlikely that Reilly provided Cumming and the British Admiralty with information on every new design or modification in the German fleet, as has been claimed, but his performance did not prevent his being rehired in the midst of the First World War.[54]

The Kaiser's Spies

While British agents sought to uncover German capabilities and intentions, German agents were operating in Britain, France, and Russia. In France, Germany had a long-standing agent whose service had begun in 1866. In June 1866 Baron August Schluga brought to Berlin the order of battle of the Austrian army, along with the profiles of some of the more important Austrian army commanders.[55]

Schluga, then twenty-five was a slim, blue-eyed blond, born in Zsolna, Hungary. He had joined the Austrian infantry and fought "very bravely" at Magenta and Solferino in 1859. Although described as a capable officer suited for a general staff post, he resigned in 1863, just before taking the examination for the Austrian War School, claiming that he would manage the estates he would acquire through marriage. His credentials as a former officer apparently allowed him to penetrate the Austrian army headquarters and gather the information he brought to Berlin.[56]

After the war of 1866 Schluga journeyed to Paris, where he delivered information to the Prussian military attaché. Designated by IIIb as "Agent 17," he came to be regarded by the Germans as an ideal agent. He was charming, well-educated, aristocratic, and a mystery to his German spymasters. They never knew his sources, his other activities, or even whether he lived in Paris under his own name or a pseudonym. He deflected IIIb's inquiries, arguing that their only concern should be his performance.[57]

For the forty years between the wars of 1870 and 1914, IIIb rarely called on Schluga, protecting him from suspicion and preserving him for use in a crisis. IIIb's restraint paid off, for before the outbreak of the world war, Schluga delivered a document of enormous value. It specified how the French would deploy some of their troops on the fifth day of their mobilization. That document alone justified IIIb's existence and all the money it had spent, for it gave Germany the apparent key to defeat a French counterattack in the forthcoming war. But it would become one of many examples of intelligence not properly used by its customers.[58]

While the IIIb networks in France and Russia were extensive, the network in Britain was not. It included Dr. Max Schultz (not to be confused with the naturalized Max Schultz) and Armgaard Karl Graves. Schultz operated from a houseboat near Plymouth. He flew a German flag from the boat and threw parties where he tried to turn the conversation to naval matters. Graves was a con man who victimized the British and German intelligence services. Far better at requesting money than acquiring secret intelligence, he was subsequently fired by the head of German naval intelligence in Britain, who described him as "a double-dyed rascal."[59]

In addition to actual spies, Germany maintained the standard network of military attachés, whose sources included the daily press, parliamentary records, service journals, cartographic publications, and even postcards. As a general rule, Germany's military and naval attachés avoided espionage work, preferring to cultivate social contacts. Imperial directives of 1878, 1890, and 1900 cautioned against illegal acts of intelligence gathering. As a result attachés sought to establish personal relationships with foreign officers and politicians, taking part in the social life, especially club life, of their host country.[60]

The Czar's Spies

Russia was also interested in the military plans of its potential enemies and went to great lengths to acquire such information. While most nations' attachés refrained from espionage activities, those of Russia did not. The military attaché in Denmark and Sweden from 1908 to 1912, A. A. Ignat'ev, controlled a large network of agents within Germany. In 1914 Colonel Bazarov was declared persona non grata in Germany after his agents had been detected. Colonel Zankevich, attaché in Vienna, was expelled when Austrian counterespionage unmasked his network, which included a retired sergeant major, a policeman, a lieutenant at the military academy, and other officers.[61]

From 1905 Russia's most productive spy in the Austro-Hungarian military establishment was Colonel Alfred Redl, who also sold information to the French and Italian secret services. From 1900 until his exposure in May 1913 Redl served first as a deputy chief of the Evidenzbüro, the military and counterespionage organization in Vienna, and then as intelligence chief of the Army's VIII Corps, headquartered in Prague. Redl may have been blackmailed over his homosexuality, although the Russians made quite substantial cash payments.[62]

In addition to photographing secret documents for his Russian masters Redl also disclosed the identity of Austrian agents. Redl sold Russian intelligence Plan 3, the Austrian mobilization plan against Russia, and betrayed details concerning a critical network of fortresses along the Galician border with Russia. The Austrian military council concluded that Redl's espionage activities had helped "deal a heavy blow" to Austria's military strength, "destroying the solid constructive work of many years." The secrets Redl betrayed led the Austro-Hungarian general staff to change codes, railway timetables, and other plans on a massive scale.[63]

Redl did not live to see the damage he had done. In the early hours of Sunday morning May 25, 1913, Colonel Alfred Redl blew his brains out in a room at the Hotel Klomser, in the fashionable Herrengasse district of Vienna. He was permitted to "judge himself" after interrogation, during which he claimed to have spied only for a year or so and provided only some manuals and the Army's VIII Corps's mobilization plan. That evening's papers carried an official communiqué which announced Redl's suicide and claimed he had suffered a nervous breakdown. But the next day Berlin and Prague newspapers carried accounts of his espionage activities.[64]

The Codebreakers

In addition to the spies in the field the cryptanalysts at home could be an important source of intelligence. Traditionally the deciphering or decoding of the communications of a foreign government required that a copy of the communications be obtained—by theft, by recruitment of a foreign government source, or by obtaining copies of the cable at the cable or telegraph office. Marconi's invention would dramatically change that.

But that change was not anticipated. And the cryptanalysis of stolen communications was considered of so little importance to most countries that only France, Austria-Hungary, and Russia had fully organized central cryptanalytic bureaus before the war.

France had five cryptanalytic bureaus—in the ministries of war, navy, foreign affairs, interior, and posts and telegraphs. The key bureau was the Foreign Ministry's Cabinet Noir, which had functioned intermittently since the days of Cardinal Richelieu. Revived during the 1880s, by the early 1890s it was able to decrypt a significant number of the English, German, and Turkish diplomatic telegrams transmitted by telegraph cable.[65]

In 1912 the cryptographic and cryptanalytic bureaus of the Ministry of

War were merged and placed directly under the Minister of War. There were only two codebreakers assigned to the bureau in peacetime, but they were not the only military cryptanalysts. By the beginning of the century a Commission de Cryptographie Militaire (Military Cryptographic Commission) had been formed. The approximately ten members of the commission remained in their units and were to devote themselves to cryptology in their spare time.[66]

Work was never lacking. Material came pouring in from a variety of sources. The most important were the telegrams delivered by the Ministry of Posts and Telegraphs. Other sources were the military radiograms sent by the neighboring countries during peace maneuvers and intercepted by special intercept stations on the eastern frontier.[67]

Commission members spent part of their time on general theoretic studies as well as the computation of linguistic statistics. At other times they worked on German radio messages transmitted, and intercepted, during peacetime maneuvers.[68]

The commission members also devoted considerable time to the detailed analysis of cipher systems as they were used during peacetime and might be used during war. They relied not only on statistics concerning frequencies but on information obtained through spies, deserters, members of the Foreign Legion, or from German military manuals. The resulting confidential memoranda described the systems, statistical data, instructions for cryptanalysis, and other necessary instructions to be distributed directly among the mobilized cryptanalysts in the event of war.[69]

Other nations maintained extremely primitive cryptanalytic capabilities. The German Ministry of Foreign Affairs maintained a cryptanalytic bureau, although to a very limited extent, apparently due to a lack of experts.[70] Czarist codebreakers, located in both the foreign and interior ministries, could trace their origins back to at least the first part of the eighteenth century. The bureau apparently had success with the Turkish, British, Austrian, and Swedish codes.[71]

Aerial Reconnaissance

The Wright brothers believed that the monetary rewards for their work would be provided by governments, not the commercial sector. Their flying machines would be of tremendous value, they believed, in time of war. Reconnaissance was the mission they had in mind for the aircraft.[72]

Lieutenant-Colonel David Henderson shared the Wright brothers' vision. Henderson, who served as the third and last director of military intelligence during the Boer War, also wrote *Field Intelligence, Its Principles and Practices* (1904). In 1908 Wilbur Wright surprised Europe with record-setting flights in a power-driven airplane and David Henderson began thinking about the wartime use of airplanes. It was not a coincidence that Henderson, who believed that "reconnaissance is the method of most vital importance," became one of the founding fathers of British military aviation.[73]

In the years leading up to World War I, Henderson's views would be supported by a variety of events. While the first photographs taken from an airplane were probably taken from the plane piloted by Wilbur Wright in the vicinity of Rome in 1909, it was the French who produced the first high-quality stills taken from an airplane, and the Italians who first made use of the airplane for reconnaissance. In October 1911, during the Italo-Turkish War, a Captain Piazza of the Italian army flew a visual reconnaissance mission over Turkish troops near Tripoli in North Africa. On February 24 and 25, 1912, he photographed Turkish positions from his monoplane.[74]

In the years leading up to World War I the majority of British officers, like their French and German colleagues, viewed reconnaissance as the primary mission of military aircraft, balloons, airships/dirigibles, and airplanes in a future war. That airships and airplanes could be employed to attack the enemy was appreciated to some extent, but reconnaissance was viewed as the clear primary mission. A 1912 British War Office memorandum recommended the establishment of a military flying school because of the importance of aerial reconnaissance. The first-priority mission for airplanes in support of ground forces was to be reconnaissance (primarily visual), followed by the prevention of enemy reconnaissance, communications, observation of artillery fire, and attacks on the enemy.[75]

2

The Great War:
Spies and Saboteurs

Despite the repeated crises prior to 1914 Europe had escaped war. But a state visit to Serbia by Archduke Franz Ferdinand, heir apparent of the Austro-Hungarian empire, and his wife, Sophie, the Dutchess of Hohenberg, ended with their assassination and a crisis from which there was no escape.

The assassinations presented the Austro-Hungarian leadership with a golden opportunity to move against Serbia, the nation which provided a home and support for those forces rebelling against the 1908 annexation of Bosnia. On July 23, after nearly a month of increased tension, Austria-Hungary delivered a ten-point ultimatum to Serbia.[1]

Serbia delivered a reply to the Austrian minister in Belgrade ten minutes before the July 25 six o'clock deadline, agreeing, remarkably, to all but one condition. For Austria, which had already decided to crush Serbia, that was a sufficient excuse for action. At six o'clock Vienna broke off diplomatic relations. Austrian troops massed on the border, while the Serbian king, in anticipation of the invasion, moved inland, along with his staff and the national treasury.[2]

On July 27 Austria invaded Serbia. Germany had declared support for Austria-Hungary, Russia for Serbia, and France for Russia. Russian troops began to mobilize and move toward the German border, despite Kaiser Wilhelm's threats. On July 31 a German agent reported that Russia was fully mobilized. The Kaiser ordered Germany's troops mobilized.[3]

On August 1, with the Russian mobilization continuing, Germany invaded neutral Luxembourg as part of its plan to knock France out of the war before the Russians could launch an effective attack. That same day Germany also declared war on Russia. Three days later, Germany invaded Belgium, and England, committed by treaty to Belgium's defense, joined the war. On August 6 Austria-Hungary declared war on Russia.[4]

IIIb

From the time of the assassinations the members of the Triple Entente were concerned with how Austria-Hungary and Germany would react. Meanwhile, Austria-Hungary and Germany were concerned with the reactions of England, France, and Russia to their deeds. However, in accord with the Kaiser's view that war with Russia and France was a possibility but by no means a certainty, IIIb did not immediately go on alert. It was only on July 16, with chief Walter Nicolai on leave, that the acting head of IIIb notified five intelligence posts in the eastern corps districts that it was "desirable to watch developments in Russia more closely." Even then it was noted that there was no need to take "special measures of any kind," and several intelligence officers in the border districts were permitted to remain on leave until July 25.[5]

However, after being briefed on July 23, and in light of an Austro-Hungarian request for information on developments in Russia, Field Marshal Count Alfred von Waldersee ordered that additional measures be taken. Section IIIb immediately notified the five intelligence officers in the eastern corps districts that "increased watchfulness is required" and that Berlin had a "special" and urgent interest in information about all Russian developments. The next day a similar notice was received by the intelligence officers in the western corps districts, informing them that the political situation required a close watch on "all military developments in France".[6]

On July 25 Nicolai returned from leave, and after being briefed on the international situation obtained permission to put his organization on full alert. All personnel were called back to their duty posts, and the eleven intelligence officers in the border districts were instructed to send off their "tension travelers"—volunteers, including army reserve officers, who would enter Russia or France as businessmen or vacationers. The mission for most was simply to make a relatively short round-trip into potential enemy territory to survey the situation. Some, however, were to be sent to rather distant locations, particularly in Russia, and were to communicate their intelligence with coded telegrams or letters. Nicolai soon amended his orders, instructing the intelligence officers to focus on determining *"whether war preparations are taking place in France and Russia."* Even then, Nicolai also noted the officers should not act with "undue haste" or immediately dispatch all of the tension travelers. War was not considered to be either imminent or inevitable.[7]

On the afternoon of that same day IIIb was informed that an unusually long exchange of coded messages between the Eiffel Tower and the Russian wireless station at Bobruysk had been detected the previous evening. The next morning the German military representative to the czarist court reported that Russian troops at a camp near St. Petersburg had been suddenly ordered back to their garrisons, that officer candidates had been commissioned ahead of schedule, and that apparently "all preparations for mobilization against Austria" had been placed in motion.[8]

Section IIIb immediately ordered its eastern corps representatives to determine the location of assorted Russian units which had been observed in training grounds away from their garrisons. To augment the efforts of the border intelligence officers, Nicolai also dispatched his own tension travelers. Wilbert Stratton, a London businessman with an American passport, was ordered to St. Petersburg; Herr Beckers to Moscow, and two additional travelers made shorter trips to Vilna, Minsk, and Warsaw between them.[9]

Several of the telegrams sent by the travelers failed to reach Berlin in time to be of much value. But some did, and along with the oral reports of the returning travelers, the messages made a significant contribution to the early discovery of assorted war preparations in the Russian military districts which were close to the German border.[10]

Meanwhile, the intelligence officers targeted on France were instructed that reports on "all indications of tension" were needed, but that once mobilization occurred "another source" would provide sufficient information and that there would be no need for reports from their agents until deployments of French troops began.[11]

The "other source" was apparently Agent 17, Baron Schluga. And he may have provided the French mobilization plan as well as Plan XVII—General Joseph Joffre's basic strategic concept. But German commanders, uncertain as to whether Plan XVII or a suspected variant had been activated, did not act on the information.[12]

Section IIIb's performance was better with respect to Russia. On the morning of July 27 the intelligence officer at Königsberg warned IIIb that the Russian border guard units on the East Prussian border had been placed on alert, that troop transports from Kovno toward the border had been spotted, and that empty freight trains were being moved to the interior on two Russian rail lines.[13]

Additional reports confirmed the alert of the Russian border guard units, the early departure of Russian army units from their summer training grounds, the arrival of infantry and artillery troops at Vibralis, the assembly of rolling stock at Vilna, and extensive radio traffic between French and Russian stations. At approximately 10 P.M. IIIb heard from a tension traveler that war preparations in Vilna had begun. Further, the Königsberg station reported that martial law had come into effect in the Kovno, Vilna, and Suwalki districts.[14]

By the time the evening reports arrived a newly formed intelligence assessment board—the Nachrichtenabteilung IVK—had concluded that the Russians had begun their premobilization program. A top-secret summary, prepared in the late afternoon, concluded that the "period preparatory to war" had started in Russia. France, however, was assessed as "quiet."[15]

By July 29 some reports from IIIb operatives indicated that in certain areas Russian war preparations were not as extensive as had been believed. The new intelligence meant a small reduction in tension at the General Staff—the late afternoon report prepared by IVK mentioned that the Russians had moved to protect their rail system in the entire border region but stressed that there was no hard evidence that mobilization orders had been issued for the Vilna and Warsaw military districts. Further, the report observed that no significant number of Russian reservists had been called up, although reservists had been notified that they should "hold themselves ready." France also had not resorted to a "general call-up of reservists."[16]

But the next day brought official news from St. Petersburg that a partial mobilization was under way, confirming agent reports that had already arrived at IIIb. The late afternoon intelligence report noted that the "period preparatory to war" had reached a "far advanced" stage in the "German-Russian frontier region." As a result, Germany would have to contend with a more rapid mobilization than expected.[17]

The report was correct. At about 6 o'clock local time, the czar's order for general mobilization was being transmitted by the St. Petersburg telegraph office. Section IIIb apparently received two reports late that evening that Russia was moving from partial to complete mobilization, but the warnings were not considered definitive by the Great General Staff in Berlin. (The Great General Staff was the central headquarters, in contrast to the staffs at corps, regiment, and fortress headquarters, known collectively as Troops General Staff.) Further reports flowed in during the night, but none allowed for a definitive appraisal of the situation in Russia. But between 7 and 8 the next morning it was reported that IIIb agents had seen red posters announcing general mobilization along the Russian border with East Prussia.[18]

Such information proved to be of marginal value. At about 11:45 the German foreign ministry received a telegram from its embassy in St. Petersburg that Russia's general mobilization had begun. At 1 P.M. the German government declared a state of "imminent danger of war" to exist.[19]

Train Watchers

The beginning of the war threw the intelligence establishments of the major combatants into high gear. For Britain the Foreign Section, the Naval Intelligence Division, and the British Expeditionary Force all operated intelligence networks.

Running agents in German-occupied France and Belgium was the responsibility of a Foreign Section network controlled by Cecil Aylmer Cameron, code-named EVELYN, from the Folkestone intelligence station in southern England. Aided by his Belgian-born deputy, Georges Gabain, Cameron also directed two additional stations, one at Rotterdam and the other at Montreuil on the French coast.[20]

The White Lady Intelligence Network, November 1918.

Source: Leon C. Messenger, "The White Lady Intelligence Network," *Studies in Intelligence*, Summer, 1988.

By the end of 1916 the Allied intelligence organizations had established a vast network of train-watchers. German troop movements were routinely noted and the information was transferred over the lines by carrier pigeon. The first of the major train-watching networks was code-named FRANKIGNOUL, after one of its main organizers, Brazil Frankignoul. The network consisted of approximately twenty train-watching posts throughout Belgium and northern France. The Germans closed down the network in the fall of 1916, after discovering its primary means of communication, a train which ran between Lanaken in Belgium and Maastricht in neutral Holland. The train-watchers' reports were intercepted by the Germans until they could identify most of the agents involved in the spy ring. On December 16, 1916, ten members of the network were executed at Hasselt. Subsequently, rather than being permitted to cross the frontier unimpeded the train would be stopped, the passengers would be subjected to a personal search, and then they would be allowed to walk across the border to pick up transportation waiting on Dutch territory.[21]

Britain was not alone in establishing train-watching networks in Holland and Belgium. French and Belgian networks contributed to the overall intelligence picture. The largest Allied network in German-occupied territory, and one that survived till the end of the war, was code-named LA DAME BLANCHE (THE WHITE LADY). Based in Liège, a critical node of the rail network in eastern Belgium and a crucial link in the movement of German troops across the country, LA DAME BLANCHE's cells extended out from Liège along the rail lines like the spokes of a wheel.[22]

At its peak the network consisted of fifty-one train-watching posts, which reported to twelve secretariats, where individual reports were collated, typed, and enciphered for transmission across the front lines. Of the 1,200 individuals recruited for WHITE LADY operations only 45 were arrested by the Germans. Two of them were executed. It has been estimated that WHITE LADY provided 75 percent of the intelligence coming from the occupied territories during the final eighteen months of the war.[23]

Although every train that ran on occupied Belgium's railways was of interest to the Allies and reports were expected on all of them, some merited special attention. The movement of leave trains, hospital trains, or trains carrying trench stores and weapons were of far less importance than those carrying German troops.[24]

Observers were told to identify each segment of rolling stock and given a list of abbreviations which permitted them to provide information on each part of the train in the minutest detail. A model report illustrated their task:

    1735 IVOF/28WSL&CHV
    4W#4CN/5W#12CAIS
    1W#2CUIS/15W#20
    CHR/band noir
    epauliere jaune
    No.15

When translated this read:

    5:35 P.M. One officer's carriage/28 wagons for soliders and horse
    Four wagons with four guns/5 wagons 12 artillery caissons
    One wagon with two field kitchens/15 wagons with 20 trucks
    black capbands
    yellow shoulder straps
    Regiment No. 15.[25]

Such reports provided information on the composition of each train and its cargo, whether human or material, down to the last item. The train and its cargo could then be traced along the route of its destination. The British were able not only to monitor the movement of enemy troops but to identify those troops—which played a crucial role in establishing the enemy order of battle. Thus by the time of the armistice the British Expeditionary Force's General Headquarters knew the precise location of all but two of the German divisions on the western front.[26]

Other British networks performed a variety of intelligence and intelligence-related functions. Five networks were engaged in watching aerodromes, reporting on German aircraft, and aiding downed Allied airmen to escape. Twenty-seven networks smuggled information across the Dutch–Belgian frontier: one was involved in counterespionage and assisting imprisoned agents, three smuggled mail from Belgian soldiers to their families and friends, seven smuggled Allied propaganda and prohibited goods, while another three were involved with customs, historical records, and clandestine payments.[27]

French Spies

French spies also made their contribution to the Allied effort. The activities of agents in Belgium, Holland, and the portions of France under German control were directed by a joint British–French post at Folkestone. To verify all the intelligence and documents arriving from French agents, as well as other intelligence sources, a Bureau d'Exploitation was created soon after the war began.[28]

One agent, who went by the pseudonym Carlos, was an Alsatian mobilized with the German army in 1914. After being wounded early in the war, he was transferred to the Customs Service, where his primary function was managing the supply of wine and liquor for the German officers' mess on the western front. The intelligence that he collected was relayed to the SR via a chemist in Basel who reported to an intelligence outpost at Belfort.[29]

Between 1915 and the end of the war Carlos regularly furnished information on the movements of German divisions. He warned of the German attack on Verdun in February 1916. Erich von Falkenhayn, chief of the German General Staff, believed that the French were at the breaking point; a victory at Verdun would convince the French people that there was no hope for France on the battlefield and that peace talks were necessary.[30]

Carlos reported that:

> The Germans are to launch a serious offensive in the region of Verdun. The troops charged with this offensive will be placed under the orders of the Crown Prince. . . . Numerous guns have been installed in the forest of Gremilly.[31]

Unfortunately, Carlos's report was greeted with skepticism by the French High Command, which failed to act on it—possibly because of previous instances where the Germans had managed to pass on false information. In this case, Joffre believed that the primary objective was Fort Douaumont. When, on February 21, the German army's big guns began raining 100,000 shells every hour on Verdun, Joffre realized he was wrong.[32]

Carlos also provided information concerning the last German offensive. As a result, the SR reported in the *Bulletin de Renseignements* of July 1, 1918, that

[t]he next German offensive will take place to the East of Reims on the front of the 3rd German Army. The last preparation ought to be terminated by 6 July. It is possible that the launching of the attack won't take place until 2 or 3 days later.[33]

This time the French High Command believed the SR, which was proved correct by the July 15 assault on Champagne.[34]

Russian Networks

During the war Copenhagen had become one of those cities where spies could be found everywhere. It had become perhaps the most important center for German espionage directed against Russia. At the same time there was an extensive Russian espionage network operating in the Danish city. The Russians operated three separate organizations for intelligence collection against the German target. The most important was headed by Sokoloff-Rascha, who operated through three chief agents, each in control of three nets. In addition, this organization apparently conducted some limited operations against Austria via Switzerland.[35]

The second Russian network in Denmark was headed by the Russian military attaché, Colonel (later General) Potocki. In addition to its military targets there were some political targets; for example, how did the Germans arrange for the Bolsheviks to receive monetary subsidies? As with the Sokoloff-Rascha network, it consisted of three circuits. The third of the circuits consisted of twelve agents but was the most penetrated of the three.[36]

The Russians also established two sizable networks in Holland, targeted on Germany and particularly the Ruhr. Colonel de Meier, the military attaché, headed one. Below de Meier were five circuits, including a special deserter's circuit, with a combined total of at least twenty-one agents. The agents were located in Hanover, Essen, Aachen, Berlin, and elsewhere. The network, according to Austrian sources, suffered heavy losses.[37]

The second Russian network in Holland had nine agents. In Switzerland there were four distinct Russian circuits. The first circuit was headed by a Major Ivanov, based in Geneva, and largely responsible for liaison with the French and Czech intelligence circuits based there. The second circuit was responsible for propaganda, the third handled "general espionage activity," while the fourth was probably involved in political intelligence collection. [38]

Nicolai's Legions

By mid-December 1915 Nicolai had 337 agents operating in the west. Most of these were run from nine regional war intelligence posts. Of these, the Antwerp post, headed from early 1915 by Elsbeth Schragmuller, was possibly the most effective. By mid-December Antwerp controlled 62 agents, two-thirds of whom were active. Three months later the number had almost doubled and the fraction of active agents had risen to three-quarters.[39]

Germany's best known World War I spy was, of course, Mata Hari, designated H-21. Using the well-known dancer for espionage purposes was the idea of Baron von Mirbach, a IIIb officer stationed in Kleve. IIIb chief Nicolai apparently met her early in 1916 and then put her up at a hotel in Frankfurt-am-Main for her training. Schragmuller briefed her on her trip and explained how to make observations and write reports, while instruction in the use of invisible ink was provided by Herr Habersack of the Antwerp intelligence post. After training she disappeared into enemy territory, where her career was neither long nor illustrious. Two or three letters written in secret ink were received from her at cover addresses but they contained no important information. Early in 1917, French intelligence intercepted and deciphered a message from the German military attaché in Madrid requesting that she be paid. Instead she was arrested and shot at dawn in the courtyard of the Vincennes fortress.[40]

About the time war began the far more valuable Agent 17, then seventy-three years old, began to suffer from poor health. After a rest in Germany, he returned to Paris by May 1915 and resumed his espionage activities. Every second day he transmitted reports via a messenger system tailored to exploit the vulnerabilities in the border controls between France and Switzerland. Usually the reports reached the IIIb Report Collection Station South at Lörrach in southwestern Germany, just across from Basel in Switzerland, within forty-eight hours. Schluga's report of June 9, 1915, which arrived on the June 11, divulged that "[the English are] complaining over lack of munitions. They regret that the promised support of the French attack north of Arras is not possible on account of munition insufficiency."[41]

Schluga was Germany's best source in France, yet even his reporting had its limitations. His sources consisted largely of members of the legislature and personnel in the Ministry of War. Those sources' access to French plans was limited, mainly because the commander-in-chief, Joseph Joffre, and the war minister, Alexandre Millerand, kept their plans secret from the legislature. Generally, Schluga could provide information on tactical matters. Further, the frequently changing views of high French officials meant that information that might be true when first divulged by Schluga's sources might well be false by the time it reached IIIb. Schluga was well informed on the political, economic, and psychological situation. His reports appeared to be accurate—but this very accuracy almost backfired.[42]

Schluga's reputation as a veteran, reliable, and well-placed agent led General Falkenhayn to insist on seeing Schluga's reports himself. Falkenhayn personally analyzed the reports and treated them as the sole source of information on French developments. Since Schluga repeatedly focused on French weaknesses in character and government, the reports strengthened Falkenhayn's inclination to underestimate the French determination and capability to attack. As a result, in the summer of 1915 he discounted clear indications of an imminent offensive: the forward movement of troops, the construction of installations for an attack, and even intelligence derived from prisoner interrogations. The apparent midsummer inaction of the Allies and Schluga's intelligence confirmed Falkenhayn's belief that the Allied situation was hopeless. Continued sole reliance on Schluga's reports may have spelled a serious defeat. The unmistakable sounds of the Allies' heavy guns forced Falkenhayn to take action and move to repel the Allied advance.[43]

Finally ill health forced Schluga to retire from espionage. After his last report arrived on March 5, 1916, he went to Germany. After a year of receiving his well-deserved pension from the intelligence bureau he died—considered by his employers as "the most important phenomenon in the entire history of espionage, so far as that history is known to us."[44]

That assessment may have been excessive. But Schluga was certainly a far better source than any IIIb had in the United States. It had deployed virtually all of its experienced intelligence officers and agents to the major nations expected to be Germany's enemy in any upcoming war—France, Russia, and England. Further, Nicolai held the rather peculiar view that it was "no business of the intelligence service" to obtain information about U.S. capabilities that could influence the outcome of the war. Section IIIb did not even begin to prepare to collect intelligence concerning the United States until several months after the United States entered the war. It was not until U.S. troops began landing at French ports that the intelligence bureau was able to gather any useful intelligence about their strength and capabilities. In the end, its total effort against the United States amounted to seven agents.[45]

Saboteurs

Nicolai's lack of preparation meant that even if trained agents could be mobilized in sufficient quantity the likelihood of infiltrating undetected into the United States was minimal, or so the Germans believed. The alternative was for the German ambassador, Johann von Bernstorff, to direct the German espionage operation in the United States. His associates included Captain Franz von Papen, the military attaché and future chancellor of Germany, who in 1933 would persuade Paul von Hindenburg, field marshal and Weimar Republic president, to install Adolf Hitler as chancellor. Other associates were Captain Karl Boy-Ed, the naval attaché, and Heinrich Albert, the commercial attaché. Albert also served as the paymaster for all German diplomatic activities and became the chief disburser of von Bernstorff's secret funds.[46]

Those secret funds went for more than espionage activities. From almost the instant the war began Ambassador von Bernstorff explored ways of preventing arms produced in the United States from reaching the Allies. Von Bernstorff argued that the emergence of an immense new arms industry in the United States, all of it providing weapons to the Allies—the only side that could safely transport the arms to the front—was unacceptable. Nor was it honorable, since it represented, in his view, a de facto violation of U.S. neutrality.[47]

To stem the flow of U.S. weapons to the Allies, Germany resorted to sabotage, one of the many forms of what has become known as covert action. Several ideas for sabotage proposed by a German intelligence agent, Horst von der Goltz, were apparently rejected by Bernstorff. But a September 1914 proposal to blow up the Welland Canal connecting Lakes Ontario and Erie in Ontario, Canada, was approved. The objective was the disruption of raw materials from Canada, required by United States-based producers of weapons and other war commodities.[48]

Along with some associates, von der Goltz headed for Buffalo, just across the border from Ontario. Following along was a contingent of suspicious U.S. Secret Service agents. One of von der Goltz's conspirators, Friedrich Busse, backed out when von der Goltz ordered him to travel along the Welland Canal as far as St. Catherines and "get all the information I could concerning the shipments of . . . munitions to the Allies, how the canal was guarded, etc." Others backed out of the project also, because the canal was too closely guarded, and the project collapsed.[49]

On November 11, 1914, the German General Staff issued a message to military attachés in some neutral nations, including von Papen, that suggested "hiring destructive agents among members of anarchist organizations." Similarly, seventeen days later the Intelligence Bureau of the High Sea Fleet General Staff instructed all German marine agencies and naval societies to

> mobilize immediately all destruction agents and observers in those commercial and military ports where munitions are being loaded on ships going to England, France, Canada, the United States of North America and Russia, where there are storehouses of such munitions, and where fighting units are stationed.[50]

A number of incidents in 1915 may have represented attempts to implement that order. On the first day of the year a fire of unknown origin broke out at the John A. Roebling wire-cable manufacturing plant in

Trenton, New Jersey. On January 3, an explosion ripped the SS *Orton* in Erie Basin, Brooklyn. Over the following four months fires and explosions damaged New Jersey factories producing weapons or powder. In April an arms-carrying ship caught fire at sea, while bombs were discovered in two others.[51]

Saboteurs acting under the direction of Franz von Bopp, the German consul in San Francisco, placed time bombs on four ships docked at Tacoma, Washington—ships that were to carry gunpowder for Russian forces. The explosions rocked Tacoma and nearby Seattle, destroying the whole cargo of powder. Two of the saboteurs fled east, stopping at the Chicago stockyards and Detroit railroad yards to plan the bombing of trains carrying thousands of horses to ports from which they would be shipped to Europe.[52]

Eight ships caught fire at sea under questionable circumstances between April and July 1915, with bombs being discovered on five others. Explosions tore through arms and powder plants in Wallington, Carney's Point (three times), and Pompton Lakes, New Jersey; Wilmington, Delaware (twice); Philadelphia, Pittsburgh, and Sinnemahoning, Pennsylvania; and Acton, Massachusetts. A train carrying arms was wrecked at Metuchen, New Jersey, while a fire devastated a railroad grain elevator at Weehawken, New Jersey. Some of the operations were the work of Captain Franz von Rintelen, a junior officer of the German admiralty staff who had been dispatched in March 1915 to conduct sabotage operations outside the embassy. Aiding Rintelen was Germany's long-time spy in the United States—Walter Scheele. Scheele provided Rintelen with incendiary bombs the size of cigars. The "cigars" were timed to flame out in fifteen days, a time considered adequate to allow the devices to be loaded on the ships and ignite before the ships arrived at their destination. Furthermore, the "cigars" would burn themselves up, leaving no evidence of sabotage.[53]

The rest of 1915 saw continued successful German sabotage operations. At least thirteen more ships caught fire or suffered explosions while at sea. A similar number of blasts damaged or wrecked arms and powder plants in New Jersey, Pennsylvania, Delaware, and elsewhere in the East.[54]

The year ended, however, with a disruption of the German sabotage network, partly through the carelessness of Albert, who left a portfolio on a train as he hurriedly alighted. It was retrieved by a U.S. Secret Service agent who had been following him. Examination of the papers led, in part, to the indictment of von Rintelen as well as the recall of von Papen and Boy-Ed.[55]

But the disruption did not prevent the Germans from carrying out their biggest and most successful sabotage operation in 1916. The *New York Times* of Sunday, July 30, 1916, headlined:

MUNITIONS EXPLOSIONS SHAKE NEW YORK:
WRECK $7,000,000 JERSEY STORAGE PLANT;
MANY KILLED; ALARM AND DAMAGE HERE

The story began: "A series of explosions, beginning with a terrifying one at 2:08 o'clock this morning, shook New York and New Jersey and spread panic and destruction throughout the city and the suburbs."[56] German agents had successfully blown up Black Tom—the most important center in the United States for shipping arms and gunpowder to the Allied forces.[57]

The explosion caused the entire harbor area to vibrate, as if an earthquake was in progress. Skyscraper windows shattered, hurling splinters of potentially deadly glass to the streets below. Shrapnel pellets ripped into the Statue of Liberty and tore enormous holes in the walls of buildings on nearby Ellis Island, a stopping point for the many European immigrants who had left their homelands to escape the horrors of the war. The force of the explosion was so great that it also shattered the windows of office buildings in Manhattan as far north as Times Square.[58]

In the light of morning it was evident that the damage was extraordinary. Thirteen giant warehouses and six piers were demolished. Fires continued to rage, burning through the remains and destroying hundreds of railway cars and barges tied to the docks. Explosions of approximately eighty-seven dynamite-carrying railroad cars created a crater so deep that it reached below sea level.[59]

Black Tom, the most impressive of the German sabotage operations, was by no means the last. A little over five months later, on January 11, 1917, a fire swept through the Canadian Car and Foundry Company plant in Kingsland, New Jersey. An estimated 500,000 three-inch-high explosive shells were launched into the air as a result. Although the charges for projecting the shells were ignited by the fire, the shells had not been equipped with detonators and therefore did not explode when they hit the ground.[60]

Even so, the Kingsland plant was totally destroyed and damage was estimated at $17 million. An inventory indicated the precise losses involved: 275,000 loaded shells, more than 1,000,000 unloaded shells, almost 500,000 time fuses, 300,000 cartridge cases, 100,000 detonators, vast quantities of TNT. The biggest loser was the Russian government and its troops fighting on the eastern front against Germany.[61]

The United States entered the war on April 6, 1917. Four days later German saboteurs apparently struck again. A large arms plant at Eddystone, Pennsylvania, was blown up. This time the damage went beyond instruments of war and railroad cars. One hundred and twelve workers, mostly women and young girls, were killed in the blast. Not long after, Louis Kopf, a German agent, attempted to destroy the Elephant Butte Dam on the Rio Grande, but he was frustrated and caught.[62]

3

Spies in the Great War: Eyes and Ears

Spies played their role in the Great War, just as they had in earlier wars. However, for the first time in war, technology was a major factor in gathering intelligence. Combatant nations had adopted radio as a major means of communication for diplomatic and military purposes. Intercepting enemy messages often started as the by-product of maintaining antenna systems for the receipt of one's own communications. It soon became clear that the time and resources devoted to eavesdropping on the enemy were well worth it. At the same time, camera-equipped aircraft flew over enemy territory taking photographs.

Intercepts and photographs would prove useful on numerous occasions—and at times crucial—in influencing the course of events. The outcomes of the Battle of the Marne, the Battle of the Somme, Tannenberg, the war at sea, and even the diplomatic war would all be significantly influenced by aerial photography, communications intelligence, or both.

Preparation

France and Germany were the leaders in aerial reconnaissance at the beginning of the war. France began the war with twenty squadrons, and in October 1914 decided to increase the total to fifty. The Germans also expanded their aerial reconnaissance forces in response to demands by corps commanders.[1]

French photographic reconnaissance aircraft were equipped with cameras that could take clear pictures from as high as 3,000 feet. The French camera systems included an automatic or serial camera, which would take pictures at intervals along the airplane's path. The German Air Service had 100 aerial cameras available when war broke out.[2]

Despite the efforts of David Henderson, Britain's Royal Flying Corps

31

lagged behind the two continental powers. The results achieved by Britain's allies and a special study of France's photographic reconnaissance units—their organization, equipment, and methods—were followed by the creation of an RFC experimental photographic section in early 1915. A four-man team designed, in less than two months, a hand-held camera which was more advanced than any other of the time. Further improvements enabled the British, by mid-1915, to mount cameras on the bodies of the airplanes, rather than relying on observers holding the cameras.[3]

Eventually the photographic reconnaissance organizations could supply several varieties of photographs. Vertical photographs, taken with the camera pointed straight down at the target below, allowed measurement of objects and accurate mapping but required interpreters trained to analyze such images since untrained individuals were not accustomed to a direct overhead view. Oblique photographs, taken from in front of or to the side of the target, were more popular because they could be understood by nonspecialists. Stereoscopic photos, produced by taking photos of overlapping target areas, could be used to give a three-dimensional effect to the images, making it easier to determine the dimensions of objects in the photos.[4]

Photographs of the battlefield served as the foundation for extraordinarily detailed maps of the enemy's deployments, which in turn were crucial in preparing the plans for artillery bombardments. After the artillery bombardment ended, planes photographed the resulting damage. Infantry troops were supplied with aerial photographs of their objectives. By 1916 the Italian army was disseminating photographs to division and even brigade headquarters. Before the war was over the troops in the trenches were receiving them.[5]

There were, of course, limitations. Bad weather could impede observation; worse weather could ground aircraft. In the summer of 1917 torrential rains converted the ground chosen for Field Marshal Douglas Haig's Flanders offensive into a quagmire. It also prevented the Royal Flying Corps from providing valuable intelligence on the location of German pillboxes, which explained their high survival rate despite repeated shelling by their enemy.[6]

France was also well-prepared to conduct communications intelligence operations in support of its war effort. The stations that had been intercepting German radio messages in peacetime continued to do so in war. When the German army crossed the border in early August and passed beyond the range of their telegraph network, they were forced to resort to radio communication. And the French were listening.[7]

Within the War Ministry the Bureau de Chiffre employed several dozen cryptanalysts, who sought to unravel enemy diplomatic and naval cryptograms, new military systems, and messages from remote fronts. Meanwhile, the G.H.Q. Service du Chiffre's staff attempted to solve the German army's strategic messages, usually employing the methods and keys provided by the Bureau du Chiffre.[8]

The Battle of the Marne

Within a month after the beginning of the war German armies, following a modified version of the Schlieffen Plan, had swept through Belgium, past the British Expeditionary Force, and had the French army reeling—in what became known as the Battle of the Frontiers.[9]

The commander of the German First Army, Alexander von Kluck, saw victory just ahead. He believed that the British had already been defeated and the only French units left were a uncoordinated group that had been constituted as the French Sixth Army. He had no doubt that his forces could defeat the French forces and take Paris, which would force a French surrender and just as certainly make von Kluck a German national hero.[10]

But von Kluck's vision was never to be realized, in large part because of the RFC's reconnaissance activities. On August 31 the British General Headquarters did not know the precise location of von Kluck's army. During a routine patrol that day Captain E. W. Furse spotted the German general's cavalry corps heading west. Another reconnaissance mission confirmed Furse's discovery. That information was quickly transmitted along telephone lines to GHQ to the commanding generals of the threatened French Fifth and Sixth armies.[11]

Von Kluck, in moving west, was pulling away from the German Second Army on his immediate left, creating a gap between the two German armies on the right of the German line. If the Allies could enter the gap they could attack the undefended flanks of either army. Although the Allies were not in position for such an attack, the French Fifth Army was able to stop the German Second Army at Guise. In response to a call for help from the Second Army commander, von Moltke, chief of the General Staff, agreed to von Kluck's proposal to bring his forces across the front of Paris and to the Second Army's aid. While such a maneuver would prevent the envisioned triumphant entry into Paris, von Kluck bowed to General Staff doctrine—which demanded the destruction of the enemy's armies in the field before all else. With the Fifth Army troops in retreat after their triumph at Guise, and believing that they were in chaos, von Kluck turned away from his prize.[12]

Von Kluck's troops would have to pass across the Allied front, exposing their poorly guarded right flank to the growing strength of the Sixth Army. But in order to take advantage of von Kluck's vulnerability the Sixth Army needed to know when he made the potentially disastrous turn. On September 3, the Royal Flying Corps provided just such knowledge. Director of Military Intelligence George Macdonough was ecstatic: "A magnificent air report was received disclosing the movements of all the Corps of the 1st German Army diagonally South East across the map towards the Marne."[13]

Similarly, French observer reports provided their commanders with a clear understanding of the German movements. Partly as a result, Minister of War (and Chief of the General Staff) General Joseph Joffre could tell his staff on the evening of September 4, "Gentlemen we will fight on the Marne." Meanwhile, the German Second Reserve Corps had no aerial reconnaissance capability and relied on the Fourth Army Corps. However, the Fourth Army Corps's airplanes failed to adequately cover the west, exactly where the French Sixth Army was moving to launch its attack.[14]

Joffre's counteroffensive began on September 6, with the Sixth Army attacking the rear of von Kluck's forces from the west, while the British Expeditionary Force (BEF) and French Fifth Army advanced to the north. With the Schlieffen Plan having been abandoned, the only winning German option was to break through the French center. Von Kluck was instructed to move his army to confront the Sixth Army, while the German Second and Third Armies would attack the French Fourth and Ninth Armies.[15]

By September 8 the German attacks had made some, but not conclusive, progress. Von Kluck had withdrawn a good deal of his forces from the territory of the French Fifth Army and BEF and redeployed it to successfully halt the Sixth Army. As a result a gap opened opposite the French Fifth Army and the BEF, who promptly moved into it. The next day, General Karl von Bülow, commander of the German Second Army, discovered that British infantry and French cavalry were approaching the Marne. By 11 A.M. he had ordered a withdrawal of his forces. Von Kluck's forces were ordered to withdraw by midday.[16]

RFC reconnaissance aircraft provided Sir John French, commander of the BEF, with good information concerning the movements of von Kluck's troops as well as the progress made by the advancing British forces. Reports on September 9 of a large group of enemy forces north of Chateau Thierry caused the French to halt the British advance until afternoon reconnaissance conclusively indicated that the German First Army was leaving the battlefield to the north and northeast.[17]

French information on German movements did not come solely from the RFC. With the war being fought on French soil the French were able to rely on their wire-cable network for tactical communications, leaving French and British radios free to eavesdrop on the heavy radio communications of the invading German armies. And those communications showed little sign of elementary communications security.

Every transmitter associated with a particular army had the same initial letter in its call sign, while call signs and frequencies remained unchanged. Encrypted messages were often followed by questions or answers in the clear. Often, the signature of the commander was also sent in the clear. As a result, after a few days, it was known that a call sign beginning with "S" meant that it was the transmitter of a corps commanded by General Georg von der Marwitz. Sometimes an entire message was sent in plaintext.[18]

The work of the intercept service prior to the war gave the French an advantage once war began. Checking of call signs allowed them to identify the staff transmitters of armies, most cavalry divisions, and some army corps and infantry divisions. Enciphered messages were quickly solved using plaintext references to their content. Over a span of fourteen days the French service intercepted about 350 messages just from cavalry corps under General von der Marwitz. Not only did those messages betray the movement plans and deployments of all of Marwitz's corps, but they exposed those of von Kluck's First Army, to the north, and the Second Army, under von Bülow, to the south.[19]

Following the Battle of the Marne, France and Germany tried to outflank each other to the north, in a series of maneuvers that came to be known as the race to the sea. By winning that race, and seizing control of the French coast all the way to the Somme River, Germany would avoid being outflanked, deprive Britain of ports, and gain bases for future submarine and air attacks against Britain in an attempt to break the looming naval blockade.[20]

The French intercept service detected the movement of the German Sixth and Seventh Armies from the southern front to the extreme north and to the Aisne sector, respectively. The product of the French and British services allowed the identification of the formation of a new German Fourth Army in Belgium and warning of its October 18 offensive in time to stop it at the Yser River in Flanders. The attempt of the redeployed Sixth Army to penetrate toward Ypres was revealed by further intercepts. As a result it failed and, in November 1914, the war of movement in the west came to a halt.[21]

Tannenberg

Germany, victimized by its own poor communications security on the western front, benefited from poor Russian communications security during the early days of the war on the eastern front. The Russians hoped to trap and eliminate the entire German force in East Prussia in a pincer movement, then move on Berlin. The Russian plan called for General Pavel Rennenkampf's First Army to move toward the East Prussian heartland. At the same time, General Aleksandr Samsonov's Second Army would head north to a point northwest of Tannenberg. If the two armies' movements were succesful, they would envelop the German forces.[22]

As the Russian armies advanced they communicated—among themselves, between armies, and with higher headquarters—by radio. But their cipher clerks and radio operators could not transmit messages with any degree of speed or accuracy. Poor cryptographic procedures and the inability to properly use their simple cipher required that messages be repeated over and over. The number of errors was so large that even the intended recipients, armed with the correct keys, had extreme difficulty deciphering the messages.[23]

To ease the burden Russian operators resorted to a number of shortcuts—all examples of poor cryptographic practice. Some messages were sent in the clear. In others only important words and phrases were enciphered. In some cases, upon learning that a unit that had been sent a message in a new key did not possess that key, the message was sent again in the old key.[24]

Listening to the Russians were operators at the German radio station at Thorn. The chief had put the operators, who had long idle periods, to work eavesdropping on the enemy. Intercepted messages were supplied by motorcycle to the front commander and future General Staff chief, Paul von Hindenburg.[25]

The basic Russian objective was first revealed, not by communications intelligence, but by acquisition of a Russian document. An order found on the body of a Russian officer who had been killed in battle on August 20, 1914, spelled out the Russian goals. Almost simultaneously an intercepted Russian radio message mentioned the forthcoming attack.[26]

After a bloody battle with the German I Corps, Rennenkampf's army was headed toward its rendezvous with Samsonov's troops. But communications intelligence would help the Germans turn the tables on the advancing Russian forces. An unenciphered Russian radio message indicated that Rennenkampf had halted to replenish decreasing supplies of ammunition, food, and fodder, did not appear to have any great interest in following up his victory, and would not be a threat until at least August 26. General Erich Ludendorff, deputy chief of the Great General Staff, gambled that he could turn most of the Eighth Army and defeat the Russian Second Army before Rennenkampf realized that only skeletal forces were arrayed against him. Leaving only a cavalry division and a brigade of territorials behind to screen his movement, Ludendorff ordered the rest of his army onto trains that carried them toward Tannenberg and the advancing Russian Second Army.[27]

An intercepted Russian radio message, also transmitted in the clear, revealed the complete organization and destination of Samsonov's army. Thus when General von Hindenburg arrived on August 25 at the General Command Staff of I Corps he was completely informed concerning the plans of the Second Army.[28]

On August 27 the Germans began their offensive. Over the next four days they pounded the Russian forces, guided by their eavesdroppers. Radio intercepts on the 27th indicated that the Russians were expecting or had received reinforcements and provided insight on the mission of the Russian XV Corps. On the 29th a number of intercepts indicated that the Russians were planning to encircle Königsberg from the south. The next day an intercept revealed plans to demolish the railroads and telegraph wires west of the Königsberg–Rastenburg line.[29]

By August 31 Samsonov's Second Army was defeated. Two corps were almost totally destroyed, three corps were shattered, and the remainder of the army was in retreat. Perhaps 30,000 Russians were killed, while 90,000 were taken prisoner.[30]

The Battle of the Somme

Aerial reconnaissance played a significant role in alerting the Germans to the British attack on July 1, 1916, which launched the Battle of the Somme. Signs of the Allied offensive had been detected by German air reconnaissance in the areas behind the Allied front, with fresh hutments being detected as early as February. From March on antiaircraft fire against reconnaissance aircraft flying over the sensitive sector increased. Allied aerodromes and aircraft increased from April, while from May new communication trenches and new batteries appeared in photographs of Allied positions. The only important question left unanswered by German air reconnaissance was when the attack would come. The Allies' prolonged artillery preparation program provided the answer.[31]

In the two days after the initial attack, British infantry mopped up and sought to locate and destroy hostile artillery batteries, with the aid of aerial photographs. Strategic reconnaissance detected the trains that delivered German reinforcements to railheads. On July 12 an observer saw what appeared to be the beginning of covering fire for a German counterassault, identified and located the hostile batteries, and called for retaliatory fire, which proved effective.[32]

Trench warfare followed for the next two months, with visual and photographic reconnaissance of German battery positions being restricted at the end of July by bad weather. Urgent and intense reconnaissance followed the improvement in the weather, the objective being to redraw the counterbattery map. Close tactical reconnaissance and contact patrols were continuous and appear to have been of significant value.[33]

A battle of maneuver resumed in mid-September and continued for another two months. By the time it ended, on November 13, 1916, casualties for each of the main combatants would run into the hundreds of thousands—450,000 for Britain, 340,000 for France, and 530,000 for Germany.[34]

COMINT at Sea

The role of communications intelligence (COMINT) in land warfare was easily matched by its role in sea warfare. Certainly, the best known World War I COMINT organization is Britain's Room 40. According to the standard account of Room 40's origin and purpose, on the day Britain went to war Rear Admiral Henry "Dummy" Oliver, the director of naval intelligence, received a series of coded signals believed to be of enemy origin, intercepted by an Admiralty wireless station. Oliver suggested to Sir Alfred Ewing, Director of Naval Education, who had advanced knowledge of radiotelegraphy and had dabbled in codes and ciphers, that "education would probably be considered of little importance for the next few months" and Ewing might more profitably devote his energies to dealing with the intercepted signals. Ewing agreed.[35]*

The volume of available signals soon increased. On August 5 the British navy cut Germany's overseas cables, forcing Germany to either transmit messages by radio or rely on foreign cables, which could be tapped. In September the first of what would be a wartime network of fourteen listening posts was established at the Hunstanton Coast Guard Station.[36]

But Ewing found himself overmatched by the German cryptologists and turned to the naval colleges of Dartmouth and Osborne. The colleges provided an assortment of volunteers, the ablest being Alastair G. Denniston, who had played on the Scottish Olympic field hockey team and had attended the Sorbonne and Bonn University. Another standout was Dillwyn "Dilly" Knox, two years younger than the thirty-three-year-old Denniston.[37]

The novice cryptographers soon received three remarkable windfalls— the codebooks for the three main German naval codes. At the end of October a copy of the Handelsverkehrsbuch (HVB), which had been seized by an Australian boarding party from a German-Australian steamship, arrived at the Admiralty. The HVB was employed largely to communicate with merchantmen but was also used within the Hochseeflotte itself.[38]†

Even before the HVB arrived another German naval codebook had arrived, courtesy of the Russian navy. On August 26 the German ship *Magdeburg* ran aground on the island of Odensholm off the Estonian coast. Before the personnel and papers could be transferred to a large torpedo boat that came to the assistance of the *Magdeburg* two Russian cruisers intervened. Only part of the crew could be transferred to the torpedo boat before it had to depart. Left behind were the commander, fifty-seven of his men, and the Signalbuch der Kaiserlichen Marine (SKM). The SKM served two purposes. Weather reports were coded in the SKM. Other signals were coded in the SKM and then reciphered.[39]

After "an apparently vain effort to use it," the Russians offered it to the British. A British cruiser was sent to collect it. On October 13 it was

---

* The standard account is disputed by Nicholas Hiley, who writes that in August 1914 there was at already least one officer in the Naval Intelligence Division who had made a special study of German naval signals—the head of the German section, Fleet Paymaster Charles Rotter, who had who apparently started investigating German wireless intercepts shortly after joining the Intelligence Division in 1911.

In addition, Hiley writes that Rotter was initially excluded from the entire cryptographic operation under Ewing. At the same time, he notes that archival material shows that the first intercepted signals were from wavelengths over 1,000 meters, which were reserved for long-distance communications. Based on this and other evidence, Hiley suggests that Ewing was focusing not on naval traffic but on long-range strategic and diplomatic communications emanating from the German transmitter at Nauen. See Nicholas Hiley, "The Strategic Origins of Room 40," *Intelligence and National Security* 2, no. 2 (1987): 245–73. For a comment by David Kahn and Hiley's response see "Correspondence," *Intelligence and National Security* 3, no. 2 (1988): 350–52.

† The HVB was used by German outpost vessels and airships until March 1916.

presented to First Lord of the Admiralty Winston Churchill and the First Sea Lord, Prince Louis of Battenberg.[40] Then, on November 30 a British trawler found in its nets a lead-lined chest from a sunken German destroyer. Inside the chest was a copy of the Verkehrsbuch (VB), the last of the three German naval codes. By December 3 it was in the hands of the Admiralty.[41]

The British naval codebreakers also benefited from the appointment of a new Director of Naval Intelligence after the promotion of Henry Oliver to Chief of Staff. The new DNI was Captain (later Admiral Sir) Reginald Hall, nicknamed Blinker for his pronounced facial twitch and habit of high-speed blinking.[42]

Hall, born in 1870, was the eldest son of the first director of naval intelligence, Captain William Henry Hall. In 1884 he joined the Royal Navy, subsequently specialized in gunnery, and in 1901 was promoted to commander. Four years later he was promoted to captain, and three years after that was placed in charge of the *Cornwall*, a cadet training cruiser. His first taste of covert intelligence work came during a visit to Kiel. The Admiralty wished to know the number of building slips the Germans had, but the Germans denied access to them to foreigners. Hall borrowed a very fast motor boat from a visiting duke and, disguised as a yachtsman, sped up and down Kiel fjord until he managed a convenient "breakdown" just off the building slips. While the boat was being "repaired" two of his officers, hidden in the cabin, photographed the construction area to provide the Admiralty with the desired intelligence.[43]

One of those who served under him, W. F. Clarke, described him as a man who "had a very remarkable and agile brain, a flair for intelligence and a capacity to get the best out of those who worked under him."[44]

Hall came to the aid of the naval cryptographers in two ways. First, he found them working space in Room 40 of the Admiralty Old Building, which was less cramped than their previous working area and subsequently became one of several adjoining rooms from which they worked. The rather eccentric Dilly Knox was given Room 53, much of which was taken up by a bath that had been installed by the Admiralty for use after night duty. Knox claimed that he did his best work in the steamy, soapy atmosphere of a bath. Hall's second contribution came in November when he appointed Commander Herbert W. W. Hope to analyze the steadily increasing number of German intercepts and provide the naval expertise that the cryptographers lacked.[45]

When Room 40 did get into its stride it proved invaluable. At the beginning of the war the Grand Fleet was forced to spend a good portion of its time searching the North Sea for the enemy, fearful of being surprised. But from December 1914 till the end of the war, with the exception of a brief period in 1918, the major movements of the German Hochseeflotte were known to Room 40. A naval staff summary of the situation at the end of 1914 observed that as a result of Room 40 it was no longer necessary for the Grand Fleet . . . to carry on the continual sweeps of the North Sea, as prescribed in a state of complete readiness. It was now possible for rest and training to be looked upon as matters of essential routine. On the whole, the Grand Fleet was less harassed, more secure, and stronger than when war broke out.[46]

Room 40's intelligence was often underutilized or misused. At the Battle of Jutland, Room 40's efforts were again partially neutralized, not by German tactics or communications security, but by the foolishness of senior naval officers. On May 31, 1916, the Battle of Jutland was fought; 248 British and German ships, including 56 dreadnoughts, were engaged.

The chief of the Admiralstab, Admiral Reinhard Scheer, planned to entice the British fleet into a U-boat trap, in which he hoped to cut off one or two isolated British squadrons. Eighteen U-boats, including three minelayers, had been deployed from the Orkneys down to the Dutch coast with offensive and observation missions. Room 40 noted their sailing on May 16 and subsequent absence from the trade routes, concluding that a major operation was imminent.[47]

Intercepts on May 28–31 allowed Room 40 to closely monitor the German fleet and obtain information that could have had great strategic value. However, Oliver and Captain Thomas Jackson, director of operations, misunderstood Room 40's analysis and informed the fleet that there was no sign of the Germans and "[t]hey made all preparations for sailing early this morning."[48]

The misinformation had serious consequences. Admiral of the Fleet John Jellicoe, aware of the need to conserve fuel, made no effort to speed up his rendezvous with Admiral of the Fleet David Beatty and attack the German fleet. As a result the distance between the main part of the Grand Fleet and the battle cruisers was increased. In turn, an hour or two of daylight, which might have made a huge difference to the outcome, was lost. In addition, when Beatty sighted German battle cruisers a little less than three hours after he and Jellicoe had been informed that the Hochseeflotte was still in port, his and Jellicoe's confidence in the intelligence they received from the Admiralty was seriously shaken.[49]

Most significantly, though, the German fleet avoided destruction. The initial misinterpretation of Jackson and Oliver made German escape possible; a second error made it inevitable. At 9:25 P.M. Room 40 provided, on the basis of an intercept from a German destroyer, the position and course of the rear German battleship as of 9:00 P.M. Sent out at 9:58, it was not received by Jellicoe until 10:23 P.M. But Jellicoe considered the information to be obviously wrong. When added to the the earlier signal reporting the Hochseeflotte to still be in the Jade river it destroyed what remaining faith he had in the intelligence provided by the Admiralty.[50]

At five minutes before ten, Room 40 delivered still more vital items of intelligence—that at 9:14 P.M., the German battle fleet, with its battle cruisers bringing up the rear, had been ordered home. The codebreakers also provided the course and speed of the retreating ships. At 10:41 the information was radioed to Jellicoe, information which should have clearly indicated that the German ships were going to pass through the Horns Reef channel. Jellicoe either drew a different conclusion or simply dismissed it on the grounds that Room 40's intelligence was unreliable. He did not alter his course or alter his rear screen in the event that a confrontation with the German Fleet was approaching.[51]

Another item of intelligence provided to the Admiralty by Room 40 might have convinced Jellicoe. At 10:10 Room 40 reported that Zeppelin reconnaissance of Horns Reef had been ordered at 9:06. That intelligence might have led Jellicoe to the proper conclusion, but it was never sent out to him. Indeed, of the no fewer than sixteen decodes provided by Room 40 to the Admiralty between 9:55 P.M. on May 31 and 3:00 A.M. on June 1, all of which would have added to Jellicoe's knowledge, only three were sent to him.[52]

Germany failed to achieve its objectives of destroying or crippling the Grand Fleet and breaking Britain's naval stranglehold. Britain maintained mastery of the North Sea, but the misuse of Room 40's intelligence cost Britain a chance for a tremendous victory. As naval historian Patrick Beesly observed:

> Jutland would have been a crushing victory if only the inestimable advantage of superior intelligence had not been so needlessly dissipated by a faulty system. Room 40 had certainly performed brilliantly. It had forecast the sortie of the Hochseeflotte more than a week before it occurred; it had given warning of its actual departure in time for Jellicoe and Beatty to get to sea before their adversaries had even sailed from the Jade . . . it had provided all the information necessary to enable Jellicoe to renew the battle under highly favorable circumstances [on June 1], if only it had been passed to him.[53]

Russia also found COMINT to be an invaluable aid to its naval strategy. Both the Baltic and Black Sea fleets had effective radio intelligence organizations, each ultimately responsible to its respective fleet headquarters.[54]

The decision to establish these radio intelligence services was a direct result of the Russian recovery of the *Magdeburg* codebooks. Immediately afterwards the commander-in-chief of the Baltic Fleet decided to establish a "special purpose (OZNAZ) radio intercept station" on the southeastern shore of the Gulf of Finland. The station and its activities, which included both interception and cryptanalysis, were treated with the utmost secrecy. The station's location placed it far from populated areas and German espionage activities. Its buildings were hidden from outside view, and station personnel were forbidden to communicate with the outside world. Added protection was provided by guards around the station, while supplies were delivered by car at specified times.[55]

The Baltic Fleet COMINT operation expanded dramatically from that initial station. By the autumn of 1915 the fleet's northern region had five radio direction finding (RDF) posts and five intercept posts operating. Its southern region had also expanded its intercept capability to five RDF and four intercept stations. Earlier in the year a southern-region Radio Intelligence Center had been set up in Revel (now Tallinn). Similar centers may have been established within the other regions to deal solely with COMINT-related information before passing that information on to their respective central radio stations. It is not clear whether the eastern region had any intercept capability.[56]

According to a former high-ranking Baltic Fleet officer, the Russian navy's use of COMINT proved to be highly effective, in large part due to the analytical judgments of the chief of the Baltic Fleet Communications Service, Captain A. I. Nepenin, who was promoted to commander-in-chief of the Baltic Fleet in 1916. According to the officer:

> Nepenin had developed to the highest degree the gift of establishing a complete picture of the movements of enemy ships and from this determining the plans and intentions of the enemy. Nepenin was able to accomplish this task . . . on the basis of decrypted German radiograms and bearings obtained by radio direction finding. His predictions of enemy movements, sometimes very bold and apparently with little basis, almost always were vindicated. . . . Not one operation was undertaken [by the fleet] without first receiving a detailed and almost always correct interpretation (of information) on the requested area from Nepenin.[57]

The first of those operations took place on February 14, 1915. Through COMINT the Russians discovered the arrival and departure schedule for a German cruiser at the port of Libau (now Leipaya). A Russian submarine was immediately dispatched and sank the cruiser as it departed Libau.[58]

On July 1, 1915, a detachment of Russian cruisers, on their way to bombard German targets in Memel, received COMINT-derived information concerning the position of a planned rendezvous between the German cruiser *Augsburg* and other German ships. The Russian detachment was able to force the German ships to retreat, preventing the rendezvous.[59]

Probably the most dramatic use of radio intelligence by the Baltic Fleet took place beginning July 31, 1915. At that time the Russians obtained warning of a planned Germany navy thrust into the Gulf of Riga in conjunction with the German army's seizure of Riga. The information Russian cryptanalysts extracted from German radio messages, when combined with that from aerial reconnaissance and shore-based observation posts, included the proposed date and time of the offensive as well as how enemy forces would be employed. As a result, the Baltic Fleet was in place and able to break up the German navy's August 8 attack.[60]

The Zimmermann Telegram

The greatest intelligence coup of World War I was the British interception, decryption, and subsequent exploitation of the Zimmerman Telegram. By January 1917 the war, which had dragged on for two and a half years without either side gaining the upper hand, was reaching a crucial period. Millions had been killed, wounded, or maimed. The internal situation in all the warring countries was declining rapidly. Meanwhile, the United States was trying to stay out of the war. President Woodrow Wilson had proclaimed U.S. neutrality at the war's start and won reelection in 1916 with the slogan "He Kept Us Out of War." And it appeared to the British that, despite a strident prowar group led by Theodore Roosevelt and Senator Henry Cabot Lodge, America would remain on the sidelines unless something drastic happened to unite the American people and propel the country into the war.

The Zimmermann Telegram was that drastic event. On January 16, 1917, Arthur Zimmermann, the German foreign minister, sent a coded message to Ambassador Johann A. von Bernstorff in Washington to be forwarded to German Minister Heinrich J. F. von Eckhardt in Mexico.[61]

That message had been encoded using Code 7500 for transmission to Washington. However, von Eckardt did not have Code 7500. Upon receipt von Bernstorff decoded it and, after making changes in the date and serial number, recoded it using 13040.[62]

The British interception of the cable was the result of measures taken immediately after the outbreak of the war to restrict German means of long-distance communications. Before the war, German diplomatic communications to the Western Hemisphere were conducted through various transatlantic cables and by radio. Within a few weeks after the war began all of Germany's means of rapid communication other than radio had been severed as a result of British military and diplomatic action.[63]

Other means of communication were available to the Germans, but there were major drawbacks. The powerful radio station at Nauen, just outside Berlin, was a target of four British listening posts. An even less desirable method involved the receiving terminals at Sayville, Long Island, and Tuckerton, New Jersey. In accordance with U.S. neutrality, all messages transmitted or received at the stations had to be submitted to the U.S. government for censorship, along with the code or codes and the plaintext copies of each message.[64]

Another means of communication was provided by the Swedish government. Messages were transmitted from Berlin to Stockholm by radio and then, by cable, to Buenos Aires and on to Washington. The messages appeared as Swedish message traffic, although they were actually in German code to which a superficial encipherment had been added.[65]

The final method available to the Germans for radio communication was through the U.S. government. During some critical periods, encrypted German communications were transmitted from Berlin to Washington and Washington to Berlin by the State Department. The communications, masked as U.S. traffic,were sent without the United States being furnished either plaintexts or the codes. The Germans persuaded the State Department to consent to this method on the grounds that it was the only means to ensure the security of German communications between Berlin and Washington. The German messages, however, were not recoded into the State Department code but simply given the preamble, address, and signature of a U.S. message; since the U.S. code usually consisted of letter groups while the German code consisted of numbers, the British could easily distinguish the German messages from actual U.S. message traffic.[66]

The importance of this message led Zimmermann to take special measures to make sure it reached its destination. Originally it was to be sent via Sweden and by a submarine, the *Deutschland*. The *Deutschland* was, however, delayed and Zimmermann chose as the second route for his message the State Department, sending what appeared to be a revised message concerning his reaction to President Wilson's recent peace proposals.[67]

On the morning of January 17, two days before the message would be relayed from Washington to Mexico, William Montgomery and Nigel de Grey, two cryptanalysts working in Room 40's diplomatic section, handed a partially decoded copy of the telegram using 7500 to Blinker Hall. At the time the British had been working on both codes. While they had solved most of 13040, they had been much less successful with 7500, which was more complex in nature and had been in existence for a much shorter period of time. In addition, traffic sent in 7500 was limited because the code had not been widely distributed.[68]

Room 40's inability to master 7500 was evident by the many unsolved sections in the partial text they produced from the intercepted telegram:

> Most secret for your Excellency's personal information and to be handed on to the Imperial Minister in (Mexico?) with Tel. No. 1 *** by a safe route.
> We propose to begin on 1st February unrestricted submarine warfare. In doing so, however, we shall endeavor to keep America neutral ***? If we should not (succeed in doing so), we propose to (Mexico?) an alliance upon the following basis:
> (joint) conduct of war
> (joint) conduct of peace
> Your Excellency, should for the present inform the President secretly (that we expect) war with the U.S.A. (possibly) (*** Japan) and at the same time to negotiate between us and Japan *** (indecipherable sentence meaning please tell the President) that *** our submarines will compel England to peace in a few months. Acknowledge receipt.
>
> Zimmermann.[69]

Montgomery and de Grey, zealously attempting to uncover the total message, were able to produce only the partial text. The significance of the intercept was immediately understood by Hall. The message, even in its garbled form, might push the United States into war. However, providing the United States with the message would force Hall to reveal how the message was obtained and also constitute an admission that the British were reading the messages of neutral nations, which included the United States. The latter implication might cause resentment and jeopardize Britain's efforts to enlist the United States as an ally. In addition, providing the message in its garbled form could cause doubts about its authenticity and even result in charges that Britain had created the entire telegram.[70]

On the other hand, if Hall could make it appear that the telegram was acquired in Mexico, the Germans might conclude that only the plaintext version delivered to von Eckardt had been uncovered. In that case the Germans would presumably continue to use their current codes and Room 40 could continue reading them. Further, Hall may have known or assumed that Eckardt did not have Code 7500 and that von Bernstorff might be forced to relay Zimmermann's message in a more breakable code, resulting in a complete version of the telegram.[71]

In early February a British official in Mexico, through an agent in the telegraph office in Mexico City, acquired the telegram. And the telegram had indeed been encoded with a code that Room 40 had already solved, Code 13040.[72]

The full telegram read:

> We intend to begin unrestricted submarine warfare on the first of February. We shall endeavor in spite of this to keep the United States neutral. In the event of this not succeeding, we make Mexico a proposal of alliance on the following basis: Make war together, make peace together, generous financial support, and an understanding on our part that Mexico is to reconquer the lost territory in Texas, New Mexico, and Arizona. The settlement in detail is left to you.
>
> You will inform the President [of Mexico] of the above most secretly as soon as the outbreak of war with the United States is certain and add the suggestion that he should, on his own initiative, invite Japan to immediate adherence and at the same time mediate between Japan and ourselves.
>
> Please call the President's attention to the fact that the unrestricted employment of our submarines now offers the prospect of compelling England to make peace within a few months. Acknowledge receipt.
>
> Zimmermann.[73]

Although the British had the full version in hand, with its suggestion of Mexican recovery of Texas, New Mexico, and Arizona, they were still hesitant about passing it to the United States. But even after the early February break in relations with Germany over unrestricted submarine warfare, there were no indications that the United States would enter the war any time soon.[74]

Finally, Britain could delay no longer. On February 22 Hall showed the decoded Bernstorff-to-von Eckhardt telegram to Edward Bell, the American embassy official who handled liaison with the British intelligence services. Two days later Ambassador Walter Hines Page telegraphed the contents to Wilson, with the fanciful explanation of its interception and decipherment that Hall had given Page. As might be expected, the British put no restriction on the publication of the telegram.[75]

The *New York Times* headline on March 1 read: "Germany Seeks An Alliance Against US; Asks Japan and Mexico to Join Her; Full Text of Her Proposal Made Public." The full text of Zimmermann's message was reprinted immediately below the headline. The *Washington Post* headline proclaimed: "German Plot to Conquer United States with Aid of Japan and Mexico Revealed: Details of Machinations, Begun in Berlin January 19, Furthered by Von Bernstorff, in President's Hands."[76]

The impact was predictable and overwhelming. But some senators objected that the authenticity of the telegram had not been fully verified. As a result Secretary of State Robert Lansing telegraphed Page: "This government has not the slightest doubt as to its authenticity, but would be of the greatest service if the British Government would permit you . . . to personally decode the original message which we secured from the telegraph office in Washington. . . . Assure [Foreign Minister Arthur Balfour] that the Department hesitated to make this request but feels that this course will materially strengthen its position and make it possible for the Department to state that it has secured the Zimmerman note from its own people."[77]

On March 2 Page's reply informed Lansing that Bell had personally decoded the Zimmermann telegram and would testify to its legitimacy. As it turned out Bell's testimony was not necessary. On March 3, for reasons that remain unknown, Zimmermann eliminated all doubts when he acknowledged the authenticity of the telegram. A little over a month later, on April 6, 1917, the United States entered the war.[78]

The United States would probably have joined Britain anyway, as a consequence of Germany's unrestricted submarine warfare. However, not everyone was affected by such warfare. Further, by the time the United States would have been ready to enter the war the Central Powers might have been victorious. But the telegram posed the clear threat of the loss of U.S. territory in the Southwest and West, making Germany a concrete menace to the people living there. It also led many to believe that a German victory would mean German annexation of some parts of the country. It clearly indicated German hostility and helped convert "Europe's war" into a "Great War for Democracy."[79]

Secretary of State Lansing concluded that the telegram was more important than Germany's resumption of unrestricted submarine warfare in unifying American public opinion and putting "the people solidly behind the Government" and making war "inevitable, if not popular, because the German Government's sinister intent toward the United States should no longer be doubted."[80]

4

Lenin's Spies

World War I, which so revolutionized intelligence, also produced a revolution in Russia. That revolution resulted, in part, from Russia's military defeats—defeats which in many cases resulted from German communications intelligence successes. But the forced abdication of Czar Nicholas II on March 2, 1917, was also due to the failures of his regime, which was described by one member of the Duma as being "handicapped by incompetence bordering on high treason."[1]

The Russian Revolution, which began with a February 23, 1917, protest by 7,000 female textile mill workers, was more than a coup d'état. Workers, soldiers, and peasants seized factories, emptied prisons, and occupied garrisons and estates. With no political party in control there was a room for an enterprising party to make itself the vanguard of the revolution.[2]

Initially, V. I. Lenin's Bolsheviks were in no position to take advantage of the power vacuum. Lenin was in Switzerland, Leon Trotsky and Nikolay Bukharin were in New York, others were in Paris, and still others, including Josef Stalin, were in exile in Siberia. When word of the revolution reached them they streamed back into Russia and gathered in Petrograd. With Lenin providing the primary ideological and organizational leadership, they began planning for the coup d'état that would put them in power.[3]

The chaos that ensued provided fertile ground for the Bolshevik planners. By the summer of 1917, all traditional forms of authority were crumbling. Defeats on the battlefield were matched by defeats on the home front. Production had come to a halt, food was scarce, and transportation was disorganized. Preserving law and order proved to be beyond the capabilities of the new provisional government. And, despite the hatred of the war by the Russian populace, the provisional government insisted on continued Russian participation. A July uprising in Petrograd was supressed by a cavalry division recalled from the front. But with the provisional government lacking both popular support and political talent to govern effectively, time was running out.[4]

Although the Bolsheviks were a minority party, with fewer than 20,000 members in early 1917, their rivals for power were indecisive and timid. Aided by good luck, Lenin and his allies were able to turn the massive dissatisfaction to their own advantage. The result was the October 25 (November 7) coup,* in which the Bolsheviks claimed power in the name of, but without the support of, the working class.[5]

The Cheka

Following their seizure of power the Bolsheviks attempted to consolidate their power over a backward, chaotic, and war-weary country. Their enemies could be found both outside and within Russian territory. One of the first organizations created by the new Bolshevik government, on December 7 (20), 1917, came to be known as the Cheka. Its formal title was more complex: Vserossiiskaya Chrezvychainanya Kommissiya po Borbe s Kontr-revolyutsiei i Sabotazhem (All-Russian Extraordinary Commission for Combating Counterrevolution, Sabotage, and Speculation). Headquartered first in Petrograd, the Cheka† moved to Moscow, along with the rest of the revolutionary government, in March 1918.[6]

The Cheka's creation was the work of Felix Dzerzhinsky, an ascetic Polish-born revolutionary who flourished on eighteen-hour workdays. By the time of the Cheka's formation he had established himself as an expert on security matters, having initiated the Commission for Combating Counterrevolution and Sabotage, an all-Russian Central Executive Committee, as well as the Commission for Reorganizing the Security of Petrograd. When responsibilities were being allocated to the new members of the NKVD (People's Commissariat of Internal Affairs) Collegium Dzerzhinsky volunteered to make the restoration of order throughout Russia his responsibility. But before he could turn his attention to the country as a whole it was felt he needed to address the problem of restoring order in the capital.[7]

However, before the commission could become operational, the Soviet of People's Comissars (Sovnarkom) received a report indicating the imminence of a general strike of state employees throughout Russia. It then decided "to charge Comrade Dzerzhinsky to establish a special commission to examine the possibility of combating such a strike by the most energetic revolutionary measures, and to determine methods of suppressing malicious sabotage."[8]

---

* The date in parentheses is the date of the event under the Gregorian calendar, used in western Europe. The first date is the date under the Julian calendar, used in Russia until February 1, 1918, when the Gregorian system was adopted.

†The actual acronym for the commission was VECHEKA. Regional components of the VEC-HEKA were known as CHEKAs. The term Cheka came to denote the entire organization both on a national and a regional level.

On December 7 (20) Dzerzhinsky reported to the Sovnarkom on the creation of the new commission. He is reported to have said:

> Our revolution is in clear danger. We have been too complacent in looking at what is going on around us. The opposition is organizing its strength. Counterrevolutionaries are active in the countryside, in some places winning over our own forces. Now the enemy is here, in Petrograd, at our very hearts. We have incontrovertible evidence of this. We must send to this front . . . resolute, steadfast and devoted comrades for the defense of the conquests of the revolution. I propose, I demand the organization of revolutionary violence against the counterrevolutionaries. And we must not act tomorrow but today, immediately.[9]

The committee approved his recommendations and, with the hastily drafted Protocol No. 21, established the Extraordinary Commission for Combating Counterrevolution and Sabotage.* The protocol enumerated the commission's tasks:

1. To surpress and liquidate all attempts and acts of counter-revolution and sabotage throughout Russia, from whatever quarter.
2. To hand over for trial by revolutionary tribunal all saboteurs and counterrevolutionaries, and to work out means of combatting them.
3. The Commission solely carries out preliminary investigation, in so far as this is necessary for surpression.[10]

The Sovnarkom also approved limited measures for use against the counterrevolutionaries: "seizure of property, resettlement, deprivation of [ration] cards, publication of lists of enemies of the people, etc." But the Cheka's main weapon was to be terror. When Lenin saw the massive opposition to Bolshevik rule he concluded that "a special system of violence" would be necessary to establish the dictatorship of the proletariat. It was a decision Dzerzhinsky supported, for as he explained to his wife, he had schooled himself to be "without pity" in defending the revolution.[11]

Felix Dzerzhinsky

Dzerzhinsky was well-suited to lead the Cheka. He was neither Russian nor an intimate Lenin ally, yet his record as a Marxist revolutionary was second to none. Born into the Polish intelligentsia on August 30 (September 11), 1877, in Russian-occupied Poland, Dzerzhinsky continued to speak Russian with a Polish accent.[12]

Felix's upbringing stressed strict Catholicism and Polish patriotism. Although he later abandoned both beliefs, a legacy remained in the inten-

---

* The VECHEKA's official designation underwent various permutations, eventually becoming the All-Russian Extraordinary Commission for Combating Counterrevolution, Speculation, Sabotage and Misconduct in Office.

sity of his convictions and his utter devotion to his cause. He was also schooled in the czarist oppression of the Poles and, like other Poles, he dreamed of revenge. Childhood fantasies included possession of a magic cap that would make him invisible and allow him, in Dzerzhinsky's words, "to slay all the Russians."[13]

In 1894 Dzerzhinsky's German instructor at Vilna Gymnasium, who characterized him as being "dissatisfied" with the existing order, demanded his expulsion. That same year ended with his abandonment of his fanatical religious faith, the result of his association with a Marxist study group organized by the Vilna-based Lithuanian Social-Democratic party. Marxism-Leninism had become Dzerzhinsky's new faith, and Dzerzshinky pledged "to fight against evil to the least breath."[14]

The next year he joined the Social Democratic party of the Kingdom of Poland and Lithuania. His initial assignment was to establish links with the working class. In January 1896 he quit school, at the age of nineteen, to become a full-time professional revolutionary in Vilna.[15]

While he soon earned a reputation as a skillful agitator and organizer, his effectiveness prompted police surveillance. His next assignment was in the small industrial town of Kovno, where he was responsible for printing and distributing a clandestine newspaper as well as organizing local factory workers. Those activities led to his arrest in July 1897, after betrayal by a trusted worker. While awaiting trial he wrote his sister: "Prison is terrible only for those who have a weak spirit."[16]

But, rather than being sent to prison, Dzerzhinsky was sentenced to three years in exile under police scrutiny. In May 1898 he began his journey into exile, to Nolinsk in the Siberian province of Viatka, where he worked in a tobacco factory and dreamed of the time when "I shall be free and they will pay for everything."[17]

Even in exile Dzerzhinsky continued to proselytize, with police noting his efforts "to influence a number of people who were formerly quite reliable." As a result the local authorities ordered him moved from Nolinsk "to such a point in the province where there would be less possibility to spread his influence over those around him." The desolate village of Kiagorodsk, several hundred miles farther north, became his new home until August 1899 when he managed to escape.[18]

But his escape would be only one of several in a sequence of imprisonments and escapes.* Of Dzerzhinsky's twenty years in the revolutionary underground, eleven were spent in prison. He was arrested six times between 1897 and 1912. Three times he was sentenced to Siberian exile and escaped. But his only two significant periods of liberty were June 1902 to July 1905 and late 1909 to September 1912. And although his spirit may have survived, his health did not, for it never recovered from the physical rigors of life in the czar's jails. Even his spirit was tried by his being cut

---

* It was during a period of freedom in 1906 that he first met Lenin and Stalin, at the Fourth Bolshevik Unity Congress in Stockholm.

off from revolutionary work. At times he questioned whether he could remain resolute. After his fifth prison sentence was handed down he wrote:

> When I begin to think about the long days I shall have to live in prison, day after day, hour after hour, I experience a feeling of horror and from the depths of my soul the words break out: I cannot endure it! Still I will find the strength, as others will, just as many more have endured much worse torment and suffering. . . . Should I fail to muster the strength, death will come and rid me of the feeling of helplessness and resolve everything. So I am resigned.[19]

Dzerzhinsky was just as capable of disregarding the sufferings of others. He could be pitiless not only with respect to his enemies but toward those he acknowledged to be the victims of injustice. He could describe the enemy as a social evil that had damned innumerable innocents "to a pitiful and inhuman existence," yet he could write: "The hunger and sufferings of the masses of the people, the weeping of children and the despair of their mothers are the sacrifices which the people must make in order to overcome the enemy and triumph." Dzerzhinsky would take whatever measures were necessary to destroy his enemies. Along with Lenin, he believed that "life is such that it rules out sentiment, and woe to the man who lacks the strength to overcome his feelings."[20]

Dzerzhinsky's sixth and last arrest occurred in Warsaw in September 1912. This time there would be no escape and he remained in prison until the fall of the czar. On March 1, 1917, at age thirty-nine, the February Revolution ended his life as a prisoner. He immediately allied himself with the Bolsheviks and was elected to the Bolshevik Central Committee during the summer party conference.[21]

Internal Enemies

Dzerzhinsky's actions as head of the Cheka indicated he had lost none of his zeal for the cause or his hatred of his enemies. During his first year as secret police chief he worked, ate, and slept in his office in the Lubyanka—the former insurance company headquarters that had been taken over by the Cheka. His ascetic lifestyle and legendary endurance earned him the nickname "Iron Felix."[22]

Under its December 1917 charter the Cheka was limited to "preliminary investigations." But the Cheka soon became more than an investigatory organ. By January 1918, with White Guard and Red armies locked in a civil war, the Cheka was permitted to search, seize, and arrest. A February decree, written by Lenin himself, authorized Cheka reprisals against active counterrevolutionaries. The counterrevolutionaries were to be "mercilessly executed by detachments of the Commission [Cheka]" at the spot of their crimes.[23]

Initially, the Cheka showed considerable restraint in exercising its life-and-death powers. The events of August 1918 altered the situation. The landing of English and French troops at Archangel, along with Western intelligence operations, led the Bolsheviks to conclude that the Allies were plotting to overthrow the Soviet government.[24]

British troops had first landed in Russia at the arctic port of Murmansk on March 6, only three days after the signing of the Brest-Livotsk Treaty, which ended Russian participation in World War I. The troops, a company of marines, were there to prevent the Germans from acquiring the massive quantity of war material shipped to Murmansk for use on the eastern front. At the same time, preparations began for an anti-Bolshevik coup in Moscow.[25]

By mid-July it was believed time to implement those plans. On August 2 a detachment of British marines, a French battalion, and fifty American sailors landed at Archangel, ostensibly to keep war supplies out of German hands. In fact, the landing was timed to coincide with an anti-Bolshevik coup there. Two weeks earlier two groups of Allied agents had secretly landed, only to be apprehended and imprisoned by the Bolsheviks. But on the night of August 1 Captain Georgi Chaplin, a Russian naval officer with Royal Navy connections, did carry out a successful coup. When the Allied troops landed the following day they did so at the request of the anti-Soviet "Supreme Administration of the Northern Region."[26]

Agents from France and the United States were also involved in aiding anti-Bolshevik groups. On August 25 allied agents met in Moscow at the office of De Witt Poole, the U.S. consul general. It was agreed that after the imminent departure of the remaining Allied diplomatic staff, espionage and sabotage would be conducted by stay-behind agents: Britain's Sidney Reilly, France's Colonel Henri de Vertement, and America's Xenophon de Blumental Kalamatiano. Unfortunately for the conspirators, those present at the meeting included René Marchand, a journalist associated with the French mission—and a Cheka informer.[27]

Early on the morning of August 31, according to the Soviet version, "Cheka agents started the liquidation of the . . . conspiracy." The Cheka failed to catch Reilly but did grab Kalamatiano, who had been posing as a Russian engineer. A hollow cane in his apartment yielded a list of agents to whom he had provided money.[28]

The timing of the raid may have been the result of two attempted assassinations the previous day. One attempt killed the head of the Cheka in Petrograd. The other intended victim was none other than Lenin, who was shot and seriously wounded.* To the Bolsheviks, these events signaled the beginning of the counterrevolution and the Cheka was ordered to take appropriate action.[29]

---

* In early 1993 it was reported that "Russian authorities are reopening investigations into a 1918 attempt to kill Vladimir Lenin amid suggestions the whole episode may have been a Bolshevik fabrication." Mark Trevelyan, "Lenin's Shooting Probed," *Washington Times*, February 7, 1993, p. A8.

The September 3 issue of *Izvestia* carried a Cheka declaration which called upon the working class to crush the "hydra of counterrevolution" by applying mass terror. The same issue also contained a telegram from Stalin calling for "open, mass, systematic terror against the bourgeoisie and its agents." Two days later, the "Red Terror" became official government policy, effectively giving the Cheka a mandate to kill. But the Cheka was already hard at work exterminating enemies of the revolution. By September 3, the Petrograd Cheka had executed more than 500 people. During the remainder of the year several thousand more were shot throughout the country.[30]

As the Red Terror grew so did the Cheka, becoming, by early 1919, a major component of Bolshevik power throughout Soviet Russia. More and more responsibilities were assigned to Dzerzhinsky's organization, as Transport and Frontier Chekas were established along with Special Departments in the Red Army (to monitor the loyalty of its troops). By the middle of 1921 Cheka personnel, including armed troops, numbered over 250,000.[31]

The Cheka's brutal methods resulted in protests, but the Party investigated and concluded that the Cheka had properly performed its mission. Despite that finding, the Party warned regional Chekas to focus their attention on real enemies of the people and grant peaceful citizens "the opportunity to be convinced once and for all of the stability and necessity of the existence of the Soviet regime." Such warnings from headquarters counted for little with Cheka units in the field, who continued to kill and torture on a regular basis. By the time the civil war had ended the Cheka was responsible for the deaths of at least 200,000 people.[32]

Civil War COMINT

The Bolshevik effort in the civil war was aided not only by the Cheka's investigative efforts but by Red Army communications intelligence operations. The Bolsheviks's enemies, both White Guardists and foreign troops, made extensive use of fixed and mobile radio sets. Sets were supplied to army, corps, and division headquarters in addition to naval vessels and merchant ships carrying troops, arms, ammunition, and other military supplies. Attached to headquarters of White Army commanders were military-diplomatic representatives from the United States, Britain, and France, with their own radio equipment, employed to maintain contact with London, Paris, Warsaw, and other cities.[33]

Those communications provided an intelligence bonanza for the Bolsheviks, for the White forces took few communications security measures. They transmitted, without encipherment, operational summaries concerning combat operations at the front, and, at times, combat orders. Enemy troop groupings as well as the movements of headquarters could be directly determined by radio messages or radio direction-finding information or, indirectly, by the cessation of a field radio set and its resumption with reduced audibility.[34]

The Red Army began establishing radio intelligence subdivisions in early 1919, under the supervision of the radio department of the Red Army Communications Directorate. It was expected that each front and army headquarters would have one intercept station and one radio direction-finding station. The intercept station targeted foreign newspaper reports and messages broadcast by the enemy's field radio sets. In January 1919 a twenty-two-person radio intercept station was set up at Serpukhovo.[35]

In addition to White Forces communications the radio intelligence service also intercepted the radio tranmissions from foreign telegraph agencies. From 1919 to 1921, approximately 1,000 intelligence summaries were issued, based exclusively on the intercepts of British, German, French, and Italian messages. Summaries of the radio-intercept materials from the foreign press were provided to Lenin.[36]

Intercepted foreign radio messages provided valuable political, economic, and military intelligence. One message, intercepted in early 1919, exposed White General Alexsandr Kolchak's overall strategy for the 1919 spring offensive. The intercepted message specified that "[w]e will attempt to establish contact with Arkhangel'sk, and as soon as we succeed in occupying a line on the Volga, we shall establish contact with the south and General [Anton Ivanovich] Denikin, after which we will change over to the offensive and advance on Moscow. Seizing Moscow is our primary goal."[37]

During Red Army operations against Kolchak's forces in 1918 and 1919, its eastern front radio intelligence service monitored the radio transmissions of Kolchak's Siberian, Western, and Urals White Cossack armies, as well as White Guard radio stations in the Astrakhan, Gur'ev, Krasnovodsk, and Baku areas. Intercept operations also provided evidence of radio contact between Kolchak and foreign interventionist forces. The unenciphered, uncoded radio messages of the White forces made it possible to establish the location of the headquarters of Kolchak, Denikin, the Caspian front, the Caucasian and Don armies, the Astrakhan detachment, and the group of forces in the northern Caucasus.[38]

In 1919 radio stations on the southern and southeastern fronts monitored the mobile stations of Denikin's army and the fixed stations located on the coast of the Black Sea. Southern front stations intercepted a variety of messages transmitted in the clear. The messages revealed a grouping of Denikin's troops in the area, the concentration of the Volunteer Army in the Azov-Donetsk sector, the Third Don Army south of the Don in the Tsaritsyn sector, and the Caucasian Army in the northern Caucasus, and they established the deployment of several White Guard headquarters.[39]

On October 5, 1919, the Ninth Army headquarters intercepted and decrypted a combat order issued by General-Lieutenant A. G. Shkuro, commander of the Voronezh Group, specifying the duties of Shkuro's cavalry troops, who had seized Voronzeh on September 17. The intelligence was transmitted without delay to southeastern front headquarters. Ultimately, the counteroffensive of General Semen Mikhailovich Budennyi drove Shkuro's forces into retreat and opened the way for a larger Bolshevik counteroffensive that drove the armies of General Denikin into retreat.[40]

Communications intelligence also aided the Red Army in its confrontations with the Caucasian Army forces of General Petr Nikolaevich Wrangel. Intercepted messages concerned enemy groupings, the redeployment of headquarters, and the retreat of White Guardists from the Crimea. Starting on August 8, 1920, the radio stations on the Caucasian front detected an unusually heavy volume of radio traffic in the Sea of Azov area, to the northeast of the Crimea. The heavy volume of traffic suggested the possibility of an imminent landing by White forces. On August 14 White forces landed in the Akhtarsk area while front-line intercept stations continuously monitored their communications. The intelligence gleaned from the intercept operations contributed to the landing's defeat.[41]

A little over two months later, on October 16, a Caucasian front headquarters station intercepted an order, sent in the clear, from the commander of the Second Army. That order concerned the planned shift on the following day to the offensive, which would involve an attack against Red Army forces on the Kakhovka bridgehead. Armed with the advance warning, the Red Army was able to destroy the attacking forces.[42]

In the concluding phase of Red Army operations in the Crimea, the White Guardists lacked sufficient time to encrypt their messages, which concerned the evacuation of units from the Crimea. Thus an October 25, 1920, southern front radio intelligence summary noted the removal of "radio station Och, attached to I Army headquarters . . . for transfer to a new location." The summary also noted that the evacuation of Mehtopol, and the transfer of the radio station that served the headquarters of troops operating in the Nikolaev area. Further, it observed that for "the past few days we have observed almost no activity by the enemy's field radio stations. One can assume that the headquarters of the division and corps to which the field stations are attached are being redeployed."[43]

Intercepted communications were also vital in monitoring the enemy's evacuation. Intercepts revealed that General Aleksandr Kutepov had 6,500 officers on board a steamship, without bread or water. Kutepov also reported that "the LAZAR, which was being towed by it," had sunk due to a leak. Meanwhile, the Kronshtadt reported that it had no coal or food supplies, had 5,000 passengers on board, and was towing the Zvonkig.[44]

Relying on that information Commander of the Southern Front Mikhail Frunze demanded, in a November 15, 1920, order, the "development of the most energetic efforts on the part of submarines and the liquidation of the enemy's attempts to use the sea to escape the blows being dealt by our enemies."[45]

Foreign Intelligence

By the end of 1920 the Red Army had won, and external military threats had ended with the conclusion of an armistice with Poland and the end of Allied intervention. In anticipation of victory Dzerzhinsky, in February 1920, addressed a meeting of Cheka personnel. He told them a new era was emerging and it was necessary to change their methods of operation. Terror was no longer appropriate. Instead, it was necessary to place primary emphasis on the collection of information "to nip in the bud the intrigues and evil intentions" of the counterrevolutionaries.[46]

By 1920 it was not the Germans that worried the Soviets, but Russian émigré organizations. Such organizations, occasionally with the aid of their host governments, sought to continue the fight with the Bolsheviks. They trained, equipped, and infiltrated into Soviet territory individuals and groups who disseminated anti-Bolshevik propaganda and attempted to foment uprisings and strikes. If necessary, they would resort to sabotage and terrorist acts, as had the Bolsheviks.[47]

The Cheka assigned a former military man, code-named Comrade Gregory, to monitor the activities of all anti-Soviet organizations operating from Estonia. Comrade Gregory was to provide information on the names and histories of the organizations' leaders as well as lists of their employees and agents. The Cheka also wanted to know when the agents of the anti-Soviet organizations left Estonia for Soviet Russia, the means used in crossing the border, their assignments, and their contacts on each side of the Russia–Estonia border.[48]

In Lenin's view, a more extensive and drastic effort was needed. On December 1 he ordered Dzerzhinsky to develop plans for neutralizing the most dangerous groups and to prevent the creation of combat groups capable of operating inside Soviet territory. Within days Dzerzhinsky had prepared an extremely secret directive which outlined a multiple-track approach for neutralizing the threat. The directive proposed that special detachments be established to carry out acts of terror against émigrés and suggested the creation of front organizations that could infiltrate the most hostile groups and entice their agents back to Russia and destruction.[49]

To conduct such operations Dzerzhinsky established the Foreign Department (INO, Innostranoye Otdel). As relations were established and envoys exchanged with nations throughout the world, the Cheka deployed representatives under the cover of diplomatic and commercial missions.[50]*

In 1920 and 1921 Cheka agents were sent to Estonia to monitor local

---

* It was not until the late 1920s that Cheka representatives and their agents began operating, in some instances, under false foreign identities. Such representatives were known as illegals, in contrast to the legal diplomats and trade representatives, whose presence in the country was legal, although their espionage activity was not.

émigré activities, and agents were deployed to Warsaw and Ankara in 1921. The INO's main diplomatic target was Great Britain, viewed by the Bolshevik leaders as the greatest world power and the key to Russia's acceptance by the capitalist world.[51]

In the early 1920s the Cheka began to build an espionage apparatus to collect political, military, and scientific intelligence. That effort was directed, beginning in August 1921, by Mikhail Abramovich Trilisser. In 1901, the eighteen-year-old Trilisser, a Russian Jew, became a professional revolutionary. In the years before World War I he had worked in counterintelligence, hunting down police agents among the Bolshevik émigrés.[52]

Building an espionage network first required recruiting agents. As a result of their underground struggle there were numerous Bolsheviks experienced in clandestine tradecraft—forging passports, creating codes and ciphers, covert communications, and concealment of identities. But the Bolsheviks who had the clandestine background as well as the knowledge of conditions and language skills to operate abroad constituted a small group. The Cheka therefore turned to the Communist parties in Germany, Poland, Austria, and Hungary. Although the agents recruited from these parties were amateurs, they still played an important role in the early Soviet espionage network.[53]

The Cheka and its successors* often found less difficulty in penetrating European diplomatic missions outside Europe. In the early 1920s the mistress of the British consul at Resht, Persia, provided a Cheka officer with the consul's secret papers. The same officer, after he became the resident at Meshed in 1923, obtained copies of the British consul's reports to the Teheran embassy as well as correspondence between the military attaché in Teheran and the high command in India.[54]

By May 1923 the INO's network of officers and agents abroad was more extensive and more determined than that of Britain's Secret Intelligence Service, whose budget had been sharply reduced after World War I. In a late 1924 report to the Council of People's Commissars, Dzerzhinsky described the creation of "a network of information [and] intelligence agencies in all the large centers of Europe and North America. Responsible workers of the OGPU are detailed to all the diplomatic and trade missions of the Union of Soviet Socialist Republics abroad." Dzerzhinsky added that the OGPU's 1,300-person Foreign Department had "repeatedly rendered service to the Commissariat of Foreign Affairs and the Staff of the Red Army by supplying secret information both of a political and military nature."[55]

---

*On February 6, 1922, the Cheka was renamed, for public relations purposes, the State Political Administration (Gosudarstvennoye Politicheskoye Upravlenie; GPU) and incorporated into the People's Commissariat of Internal Affairs (NKVD). In November 1923, the GPU became the OGPU (United [Obyedinennoye] State Political Administration) and was separated from the NKVD.

Red Army Intelligence

Along with the fall of the czarist regime came the collapse of the Imperial Russian Army and its intelligence service. The Red Army's intelligence service emerged from two sources, the Red Army itself and the Cheka. Except for one short period, Cheka personnel handled intelligence and counterintelligence duties for the Red Army until November 1920, when the civil war concluded. In the early years of the Soviet republic, the Red Army, more than 80 percent of whose commanders were former czarist officers, was not considered of adequate political reliability—and thus was not permitted to operate its own intelligence and counterintelligence organizations.[56]

In February 1918, a month after the establishment of the Red Army, a Registration Directorate (Registrupravlenie) was established to register and control former czarist officers. The officers, while needed because of their skills, were also believed to constitute a serious counterrevolutionary threat.[57]

A battle over control of military intelligence and security ensued and a special commission, chaired by Dzerzhinsky, studied the problem in November 1918. As a result Cheka and Military Council units within the army were consolidated into a single military counterintelligence organization, which facilitated an extensive purge of non-Cheka personnel, so that by the end of 1918 the Cheka was in total control of Soviet intelligence and counterintelligence operations.[58]

In February 1919, following the Cheka takeover, the Party Central Committee and Revolutionary Military Council issued a directive designating the consolidated military counterintelligence unit as the Cheka Special Department (OO). The department was assigned the task of combating counterrevolution and espionage in the army and navy, as well as conducting intelligence operations abroad and in areas occupied by the regime's civil war opponents.[59]

In December 1920 Yan Berzin joined the Registration Directorate. Born Peter Kuzis in November 1889 in Latvia, Berzin began his revolutionary activities early, was wounded and imprisoned in 1907, but was released in 1909. Arrested again in 1911, he spent five years in jail and was then exiled to Siberia. After escape from Siberia he was able to spend several years at a university while also further developing his abilities as a revolutionary.[60]

After a short stint in 1919 as deputy commissar for internal affairs in the short-lived Soviet Latvian Republic, he became a divisional political commissar in the Red Army. From August 1919 to November or December 1920 he served as commander of the Cheka Special Department of the Fifteenth Red Army, which was involved in the Soviet-Polish War.[61]

In December 1920 Berzin was transferred, on Dzerzhinsky's orders, to the Registration Directorate. Possibly Dzerzhinsky envisioned a role for him in intelligence, for at about the time of his joining the directorate it was decided to expand it into a military intelligence service. After serving as chief of the organization's Second Section, he became deputy chief of military intelligence on December 27, 1921. By that point the Registration Directorate may have been officially retitled Intelligence Directorate (RU [Razyedyvatelnoye Upravleniye]). On March 23, 1924, Berzin became chief and remained in that position until April 1935.[62]

Although Berzin would go on to make several important contributions to the development of Soviet military intelligence, the Intelligence Directorate initially developed at a leisurely pace, resulting in relatively few examples of RU operations against the West during the 1920s, most of which took place in France. It was not until the early 1930s that RU began to prepare its officers for operations in the West.*

The Trust

Among the major targets of the INO's anti-émigré operations was Boris Savinkov, a former Socialist revolutionary terrorist who had directed the prewar assassinations of Minister of the Interior V. K. Plehve (1904) and Moscow governor-general Grand Duke Sergei Aleksandrovich (1906). In January 1918 Savinkov established the underground Union for Defense of Country and Freedom (SZRiS). The Cheka soon discovered the organization's existence and in May 1918 arrested thirteen of its members in Moscow. Additional arrests caused Savinkov's organization to unravel, and the remnants mounted three unsuccessful insurrections in July of that year.[63]

During the Soviet-Polish war of 1920, Savinkov chaired the Warsaw-based Russian Political Committee (RPC) and played a key role in raising the Russian People's Army, which fought under Polish command. In January 1921, out of the fragments of the RPC, Savinkov formed a new union, the People's Union for Defense of Country and Freedom (NSZRiS), headquartered in Warsaw (although he chose to reside in Paris). He reached agreements with the émigré Ukrainian government and Cossack and Belorussian groups in Poland to conduct joint operations. The NSZRiS Information Bureau ran a clandestine network of agents on Soviet territory, agents who provided intelligence (shared with the Polish Military Intelligence Service) on military, political, and economic matters and who worked to prepare for uprisings against the Soviet regime.[64]

Once again the Cheka was able to neutralize Savinkov's efforts. In December 1920, Edwards Upeninsh, using the name Aleksandr Eduardovich Opperput, arrived in Poland carrying a suitcase crammed with

---

* After his initial stint as chief of military intelligence, Berzin served from 1935 to 1937 as a Red Army commander in the Far East and as senior Soviet military adviser (under the alias Grishin) to the Republican government in the Spanish civil war. On June 9, 1937, he was recalled and reappointed chief of military intelligence. Before the year was over he had been arrested in Stalin's purge. On July 29, 1938, he was executed. Christopher Andrew and Oleg Gordievsky, *KGB: The Inside Story* (New York: Harper Collins, 1990), pp. 173–75.

secret documents and claimed to be on leave from his post as deputy chief of staff of Internal Service Troops (VNUS) in Gomel. He also claimed to be a member of an anti-Bolshevik underground organization. Quickly recruited by Savinkov, he was returned to his post and became one of Savinkov's most trusted agents in Soviet Russia—providing apparently valuable information on the Red Army.[65]

A CIA study suggested that Opperput was a Chekist at the time he first joined Savinkov's operation. However, according to a 1981 KGB study, Opperput began as a sincere follower of Savinkov but was turned by the Cheka after his arrest in May 1921, becoming a leading agent provocateur for the Cheka and its successors. Whatever the case, in August 1921 *Izvestia* reported on the trial of forty-four Savinkov agents who had been rounded up by the Cheka, possibly with Opperput's help.[66]

The Soviet government, armed with documentary proof of Savinkov's anti-Soviet operations, lodged a protest with the Polish government on July 4, 1921. Three months later the Poles bowed to Soviet pressure, expelling Savinkov's organization. Savinkov moved his organization on to Prague and then Paris.[67]

But the Cheka was not satisfied. Savinkov's expulsion only triggered an operation called SINDIKAT-II, designed to neutralize what remained of Savinkov's movement in both Russia and the West and lure him back to Soviet territory.[68]

In July 1923 Savinkov met in Paris with "A. P. Mukhin," believing he was conferring with one of the leaders of a Moscow underground organization. Mukhin, who was really senior GPU officer A. P. Fyodorov, told him that his leadership was desperately needed by the Moscow underground, which was allegedly deeply split over tactics. But instead of going to Moscow himself Savinkov sent an aide, who was promptly arrested upon arrival. Under pressure the aide agreed to help the GPU by sending a series of messages to Savinkov, urging him to come to Moscow. Finally, in July 1924 Savinkov agreed and on August 15 he crossed the Russian border with some of his supporters, walking straight into an OGPU trap.[69]

On August 27–29 Savinkov stood trial before the Military Collegium of the U.S.S.R. Supreme Court. In the dock he confessed to his anti-Soviet activities and repented. His repentence, as well as cooperation with the OGPU, bought him a little time. His death sentence was immediately commuted to life imprisonment, but on May 7, 1925, he fell to his death from a Lubyanka window. According to the testimony of an OGPU officer at the scene, Savinkov had been involved in a drinking bout with secret police officers and it was not clear whether he fell from the open window or jumped.[70]

Even more successful than the SINDIKAT operation was the Cheka-GPU-OGPU creation and use of the Monarchist Association of Central Russia (MOTSR), better known by its cover name, the Trest (Trust). The Trust operation's two chief targets were the principal White Russian émigré organizations: the Berlin-based Supreme Monarchist Council (VMS) and the Paris-based Russian Combined Services Union (ROVS), headed by General Aleksandr Kutepov.[71]

The operation began in late autumn 1921 when Aleksandr Yakushev, a Cheka officer posing as a Soviet trade representative, traveled to Estonia to contact the VMS representative there, Yuri Artamonov. He then startled Artamonov by disclosing the existence of a clandestine, well-organized monarchist association operating inside the Soviet Union—the Trust. Using Artamonov as a conduit the Cheka was able to contact the VMS. Artamonov moved to Warsaw in 1922 and became the ROVS representative there, thus providing a means of communication with General Kutepov. The next few years saw a stream of Trust representatives, all provided by the Soviet secret police, visiting Germany, France, and Poland and expanding their contacts with the White Russian émigré communities.[72]

Through the Trust the Cheka and its successors were able to thoroughly penetrate the main White Guard émigré groups and identify their sympathizers in Russia. It also, in varying degrees, deceived the intelligence services of Finland, the Baltic states, Poland, Britain, and France. Estonian and Polish diplomats even permitted the Trust to send its messages via their diplomatic bags.[73]

The Trust was used to convince émigré groups that violent actions inside the Soviet Union would only hurt the cause of the monarchist forces. The émigrés were assured that the best chance of achieving their goals was to let the Trust operate quietly to undermine the Soviet regime. It was also employed to feed false information to British and Polish intelligence and to encourage them to send agents to attempt to subvert the Bolsheviks. The Trust also siphoned funds from White émigrés funds that might have been used to support insurrections. Additionally, it was employed to expose and entrap the remaining anti-Soviet underground.[74]

The most sensational aspect of the Trust operation involved luring British "master spy" Sidney Reilly back to Russia. Ever since his 1918 Moscow exploits, Reilly unrealistically saw himself as Russia's savior. And the Bolsheviks saw him, just as unrealistically, as their main nemesis. Reilly actually only had a loose connection with the British Secret Intelligence Service (SIS), having been refused a job on its peacetime staff. But the Bolsheviks saw his peculiar schemes to overthrow their regime as an indication, not that he was living in a fantasy world, but that there was a sophisticated SIS conspiracy approved at the highest level within Whitehall. By 1924 enticing Reilly to enter Russia became a major goal of the OGPU.[75]

Reilly's relationship with the Trust was encouraged by Commander Ernest Boyce, his friend and SIS station chief in Russia during Reilly's escapades. In 1919 Boyce became station chief in Finland, the main base for SIS operations against Soviet Russia. Boyce was a strong believer in both the Trust and Reilly. Even Savinkov's capture did not shake his faith in the Trust, which he believed to be growing in strength and possessing supporters within the Soviet regime.[76]

In January 1925 Boyce requested that Reilly meet with Trust representatives in Paris. Personal business intervened, but on September 3 Reilly was in Paris where he met with Boyce and General Kutepov. He decided to move on to Finland and meet with Trust representatives there. After arriving in Helsinki on September 21, he traveled to Yiborg for a meeting with the Trust's chief foreign representative, OGPU officer Yakushev. Reilly had intended to go no further, but Yakushev convinced him that it was crucial for him to meet the Trust leadership in Moscow. He assured Reilly that he would be back in Finland in sufficient time to catch a boat leaving Stettin on September 30.[77]

Reilly headed for the Russian frontier, leaving behind a letter to his wife, "only for the most improbable case of a mischance befalling me." Even if he were interrogated by the "Bolshies," he assured his wife, it was unthinkable that they would realize that he was Sidney Reilly: "If by any chance I should be arrested in Russia it could be only on some minor, insignificant charge and my new friends are powerful enough to obtain my prompt liberation."[78]

But there were no friends to ensure his freedom. Reilly failed to return from Russia on the night of September 28–29, as was planned. Instead, the OGPU once again deceived Finnish military intelligence and the SIS. That night they heard shots near the village of Allekul on the Soviet side of the border and saw frontier guards carrying away a man on a stretcher. When the Soviet frontier guard—who, operating under OGPU control, had helped czarist sympathizers across the border in apparent collaboration with the Finns—was not heard from again both SIS and the Finns concluded, as the OGPU desired, that he and Reilly had been killed during the return crossing.[79]

But Reilly was still very much alive. After crossing into the Soviet Union on September 26 Reilly, along with his OGPU companions, traveled to Leningrad by train. In Leningrad he met with an OGPU counterintelligence officer who was posing as a Trust representative. That evening Reilly left for Moscow, where he arrived the next morning. After a meeting with Trust "leaders" Reilly got into a car, believing it would take him to October Station to catch the night train to Finland.[80]

Instead he was driven straight to the OGPU's Lubyanka headquarters and prison. At first Reilly turned aside suggestions that he aid his captors, hoping that the British would arrange for his release. But on October 30, believing that the Soviets were ready to carry out his 1918 death sentence, Reilly could resist no longer. At the suggestion of his OGPU interrogator he wrote to Dzerzhinsky stating his "agreement to co-operate in sincerely providing full evidence and information answering the questions of interest to the OGPU relating to the organization and personnel of the British intelligence service."[81]

For the next six days Reilly provided details on various aspects of

British intelligence operations, including his final mission for SIS, as well as what information Britain had on the Soviet Union and the Comintern. On one occasion he was questioned on Special Branch operations directed against the Soviet Trade Delegation in London and whether British counterintelligence had succeeded in penetrating the All-Russian Cooperative Society (ARCOS) in London.[82]

But Reilly's cooperation did not save his life. Much of the information he supplied had already been acquired by OGPU agents in the Trust. The OGPU believed that Reilly was still stalling, waiting for the British to arrange for his release, and feared that any leak that Reilly was alive would compromise the viability of the Trust operation. According to Soviet sources, on the evening of November 5, 1925, Reilly was taken for what he was told was an outing in the woods. When "mechanical trouble" halted the car at a prearranged spot, it was suggested that Reilly and his four OGPU guardians stretch their legs, while the problem was corrected. According to one of those guardians, in his official report: "After walking some 30–40 steps, [OGPU officer] Ibragim, from slightly behind us, shot [Reilly], who let out a deep breath and fell without a cry." Four days later Reilly was secretly buried.[83]

The Soviet Trust operation continued until 1927. Early that year, prompted by the decline in influence of their penetration agents and the increasing influence of General Kutepov, who advocated an aggressive policy of attack, the OGPU chiefs decided to terminate the operation. In April 1927 Opperput crossed into Finnish territory and exposed the whole deception—whether at the behest of the OGPU in order to reap a propaganda victory or in an attempt to personally profit by selling information on the Soviet operation before it was too late is not clear, but the articles Opperput proceeded to write about the Trust operation severely embarrassed the émigré organizations. Either way, the Trust died about a year and a half after Sidney Reilly.[84]

5

Spies Between the Wars:
1919–1929

Intelligence by no means disappeared from the international scene after World War I. In the United States, postwar reductions left the Military Intelligence Division with twenty-five times more personnel than it had in 1916.[1] Even Germany, saddled with an enormous debt and with restrictions on its military, chose to establish a variety of intelligence organizations over the decade.

Not only did many agencies continue to operate behind the scenes, but they often had an impact on the course of international events. This was particularly true with respect to the agencies involved in the interception and decryption of foreign communications, for no form of intelligence had as dramatic an impact on the world in the eleven years between the wars as communications intelligence. The cipher bureaus that proved so important during the war also proved to be of value during peace. British Foreign Secretary George Nathanial, Earl Curzon of Kedleston, considered cryptology during the 1920s as "without exception the cheapest and most reliable form of Secret Service."[2]

Government Code and Cypher School

Many of the postwar communications intelligence organizations were civilian successors to the military COMINT organizations of World War I. Early in 1919 the British cabinet decided that the results obtained during the war by Room 40 and the Army's COMINT organization (MI-1b) justified the formation of a permanent peacetime civilian organization to perform such functions.[3]

On November 1, 1919, Britain established the Government Code and Cypher School (GC&CS), a title selected after much debate. Despite the Foreign Office's attempt to gain control over the new organization the Director of Naval Intelligence, Commodore (later Rear-Admiral) Hugh

"Quex" Sinclair, was assigned responsibility for supervising the new organization and coordinating the activities of the military service units that manned the intercept sites.[4*]

The acknowledged function of the school was "to advise as to the security of codes and cyphers used by all Government departments and to assist in their provision." Its unannounced function, spelled out in a secret directive, was "to study the methods of cypher communications used by foreign powers." Decrypted messages were to be sent to the foreign secretary, who would decide which ones should be distributed to other cabinet members.[5]

Selected as the school's first operational head was Alastair Denniston. Known to his staff as "the little man," he had, according to one of his future subordinates, "little liking for questions of administration" [and] "even less for the ways of bureaucracy and the demands of hierarchy." At the start Denniston had six senior assistants, including Dilly Knox and Oliver Strachey, the best cryptanalysts from Room 40 and MI-1b respectively.[6]

The raw material for Britain's deciphering operations was obtained by intercepting the messages transmitted on telegraph cables and via radio. It was the telegraph cables that provided the bulk of high-grade material in peacetime, although during the 1919–24 period valuable messages were also sent by radio. Acquiring the messages presented no difficulty. The Official Secrets Act of 1920 authorized the British government to obtain copies of any telegrams transmitted by cable on Imperial territory. Inasmuch as most of the world's cables were either owned by British companies or passed through Imperial territory, British codebreakers had easy access to an enormous volume of cable traffic.[7]

The codebreakers examined all cable traffic passing through London, virtually all the traffic between Europe and both South America and East Asia, and a considerable quantity of transatlantic traffic. But they did not have access to cable traffic within continental Asia, Europe, or the United States, between the United States and Asia, or between South America and the United States.[8]

The primary target for GC&CS intercept and cryptanalytical activities was diplomatic traffic, although military traffic, as well as that of Soviet intelligence organizations and selected oil companies, was attacked at times. Italian naval and naval attaché traffic was successfully deciphered in the early 1920s. Until at least 1923 some Soviet and Turkish military communications were also read. Japanese naval and naval attache traffic was also apparently broken throughout most of the interwar period.[9]

The school had little success with Germany's postwar codes, even before Germany's adoption of the Engima machine. But American,

---

*Jurisdictional battles over control of GC&CS would continue for years. The Foreign Office would gain effective control over the organization in 1921 and formal control in 1922. In 1923 operational control over the school was assigned to the Secret Intelligence Service, directed by Sinclair, while the Foreign Office was responsible for the school's administrative needs.

French, and Italian ciphers all fell to the onslaught of British cryptanalysts. GC&CS benefited from the French Foreign Office's distaste for cipher machines and the Italian navy's "delightful . . . habit of enciphering long political stories from the daily press."[10] From October 1923 to January 1924, it solved, on average, twelve important French diplomatic messages a week. According to Denniston, the GC&CS read virtually all French diplomatic traffic from 1919 to 1935, when the French introduced a system that defied solution.[11]

In February 1921 the GC&CS reported that the U.S. government had "instituted a complicated cipher about a year ago which has taken some time to solve but in a month or so these messages will be legible." The school solved at least five American diplomatic telegrams in 1919, six in 1920, two in 1921, two in 1922, and one in 1923. All were broken within one to two weeks. The decryption efforts were considered valuable by the Foreign Office's American Department, which indicated in 1921 that it had learned a great deal from the deciphered American telegrams.[12]

Japanese diplomatic ciphers, when resources permitted, were also attacked and solved by the British codebreakers. To help them Denniston recruited a retired diplomat who had spent twenty years in Japan and "soon acquired a skill in never missing the important." As a result, throughout "the period down to 1931 no big conference was held in Washington, London or Geneva in which he did not contribute all the views of the Japanese Government and of their too verbose representatives."[13]

British cryptanalytical successes helped guide British diplomacy in a variety of areas or situations, including the Middle East during 1920 to 1923. British success in the Lausanne Conference of 1923, which established, among other things, Turkish borders with Bulgaria, Greece, Iraq, and Syria, was, in part, due to penetration of the Turks' telegrams. That penetration, according to one British diplomat, "put us in the position of a man who is playing Bridge and knows the cards in his adversary's hands."[14]

But the GC&CS's greatest victories in the 1920s were against Soviet Russia—at least in part due to the Soviet government's fear of relying on czarist codes and ciphers, which led them to adopt simpler, less secure systems. Just as poor cipher security had plagued the czarist regime during World War I, it compromised Soviet communications. In addition, Soviet traffic was often transmitted along easily intercepted channels. Until the mid-1920s the majority of Soviet diplomatic traffic, as well as internal traffic, was transmitted via radio. The Soviet diplomatic representative in London not only relied on radio to communicate with Moscow but used the British Admiralty's radio. In 1923 the Soviet government began to rely on British cables passing through India when corresponding with its representatives in Afghanistan.[15] Such carelessness helped make possible the enormous success that Britain had against Soviet diplomatic and military communications traffic from 1918 through 1927. Another key factor in Britain's success was E. C. Fetterlein, head of the GC&CS Russian section, who had been one of czarist Russia's leading cryptanalysts. A small, rather solitary man, Fetterlein's social interaction did not go much beyond saying "Good morning" in a thick Russian accent to other members of the school. Denniston, in an attempt to alleviate the Russian's loneliness, invited him and his wife, who spoke little English, to Christmas dinner several times.[16]

By the time that Anglo-Soviet trade negotiations began in May 1920 Britain's most valuable source of intelligence about the Soviets was provided by Fetterlein and his assistants at the GC&CS. For the next seven years, COMINT would be more valuable than human intelligence. Intercepted Soviet communications included letters and dispatches. But the most numerous and valuable intercepts were Soviet coded telegrams and radio communications.[17]

At the beginning of the negotiations Prime Minister David Lloyd George spelled out three main requirements for the resumption of normal trade: termination of all hostile activities and propaganda within the British Empire or on its borders; prompt exchange of all remaining British and Russian prisoners; and recognition "in principle" of czarist Russia's debts to the Allies.[18]

While the initial approach of the Soviet negotiator, Leonid Krasin, was conciliatory, orders to take a tougher approach soon arrived from Foreign Minister Georgi Chicherin:

> You must [not] yield to British blackmailing. The situation that has been created in the East is a difficult one for England. In Persia they are almost helpless in the face of revolution. Disloyalty is increasing amongst the Indian troops. . . . By a policy of capitulation we shall attain nothing. . . .

Lenin, even less diplomatically, advised Krasin: "That swine Lloyd George has no scruples or shame in the way he deceives. Don't believe a word he says and gull him three times as much."[19]

Both messages were intercepted and read by the GC&CS and passed on to Lloyd George and his senior ministers. Thus the prime minister was prepared when Krasin arrived at 10 Downing Street on June 29 and read the text of a long message which Lloyd George characterized as "more in the nature of a lecture than a business reply." The next day Lloyd George sent the Soviet negotiator a formal statement of Britain's conditions for a trade agreement, which included a request for "categorical replies, yes or no" from the Soviet government. On July 1 Krasin left for Russia on a British destroyer to get new instructions. He returned in early August.[20]

In the interval the GC&CS had produced devastating evidence that the Soviet trading delegation was engaging in subversive activities in Britain. The Soviet-funded *Daily Herald* sought, by its slanting and editing of the news, to create the fear that workers were to be conscripted to fight against the Soviets in the Russo-Polish war. A Council of Action was formed by the Labour party and Trade Unions Congress to battle, with violence if necessary, any plans for intervention on the Polish side. According to a memo from the chief of the Imperial General Staff, Sir Henry Wilson, GC&CS decrypts indicated "[t]hat the 'Council of Action' is in the closest touch and collaboration with the Russian Soviet for the downfall and ruin of Britain." The cabinet's inclination, after hearing the GC&CS revelations, was to expel the entire Soviet delegation. Lloyd George managed to talk his fellow ministers out of such drastic action, but only by agreeing to another drastic action. He agreed to make public the intercepts of eight telegrams by providing them to all the national newspapers except the *Daily Herald*.[21]

The telegrams, between Deputy Commissar for Foreign Affairs Maxim Litvinov, and his boss, Georgi Chicherin, concerned the *Daily Herald*'s financial difficulties and the Soviet interest in ensuring its continued operation as a far left newspaper. Thus in a July 11 message Litvinov told Chicherin that

> [i]f we do not support the *Daily Herald*, which is now passing through a fresh crisis, paper will have to turn "Right" trade union. In Russian questions it acts as if it were our organ . . . and decidedly advocates "direct action." . . . I consider work of *Daily Herald* as especially important for us.[22]

Because all the released telegrams were in one cipher it was undoubtedly hoped that the Soviets might not realize that their other ciphers were also vulnerable. The press was asked to contribute to the deception by stating that the messages had been obtained from "a neutral country." However, to Lloyd George's great annoyance, *The Times* story began: "The following wireless messages have been intercepted by the British Government." The indiscretion caused no problem. Either the Soviets did not read the *Times* or they concluded that only the Marta cipher had been compromised.[23]

During the fall of 1920 the trade talks were stalemated. Recriminations over interference in British affairs as well as the time involved in setting up an exchange of prisoners, another of Lloyd's George's preconditions to negotiations, kept the talks in abeyance. On September 30 and October 12 the cabinet delayed the resumption of the negotiations. It was only on November 18, after the release of the last British prisoners from the Soviet jails, that the cabinet agreed to resume negotiations.[24]

The GC&CS was able once again to provide valuable intelligence on the Soviet bargaining strategy. The decrypted messages indicated that only with respect to trade did Krasin have any real flexibility. When it came to the cessation of hostile activities and propaganda as well as the settlement of czarist debts he was under strict Politburo guidance to make "merely a statement of principles." In early January 1921 Krasin headed for Moscow, carrying a draft agreement. By this time, however, Britain's codebreakers had lost their source of intelligence.[25]

A report by Mikhail Frunze, commander of Soviet forces fighting against White Guardist General Wrangel, informed Soviet leaders that "absolutely all our ciphers are being deciphered by the enemy . . . all our enemies, particularly England, have all this time been entirely in the know about our internal work, military-operational and diplomatic."[26]

The Soviets responded a week later by ordering the trade delegation in London to rely on couriers to the maximum extent feasible "until the establishment of new cypher systems." Those new systems were, at first, impenetrable. On March 22 Sinclair informed the cabinet that "although a large number of telegrams are received daily, it is not possible at present to decypher them."[27]

But events in Russia provided the help to the British negotiators that the GC&CS no longer could. The hardships imposed by the Soviet regime resulted in more than 100 uprisings during February, culminating in the Kronstadt rebellion—whose supression required the lives of 10,000 Red Army troops.[28]

The rebellion accelerated the replacement of War Communism by the New Economic Policy. The change in economic policy made the Soviet leaders all the more desirous to successfully conclude the trade negotiations. As a result, when Krasin returned to London he requested only minor modifications in the draft agreement he had taken to Moscow two months earlier. Talks resumed on March 11 and ended on March 14, with the agreement being signed two days later.[29]

The Black Chamber

The United States also converted its military cipher bureau into a civilian organization, headed by Herbert Yardley. Born in Worthington, Indiana, in 1889, Yardley worked from 1907 to 1912 as a telegraph operator at various railroads. Arriving in Washington in 1912, he joined the State Department as a $900 a year telegraph operator and code clerk.[30]

The coded messages that came across his desk led him to wonder why the United States did not have a bureau to attack the ciphers of foreign nations. Turning to the Library of Congress for books on the subject, he began to educate himself. He moved from theory to practice—decoding not only State Department messages but foreign embassy messages that he was able to obtain.[31]

In May 1916 Yardley began working on a treatise describing the poor state of American codes and ciphers. The result, "Solution of American Diplomatic Codes," shocked his superior, David Salmon. Knowing that the British maintained a large codebreaking establishment, Salmon asked Yardley whether he believed that the British could solve the American code. Yardley replied: "I always assume that what is in the power of one man to do is in the power of another."[32]

Yardley's work led to a meeting with General Ralph van Deman, director of military intelligence, shortly after America's April 6 declaration of war. Van Deman had struggled to get the Army's highest officials to recognize the value of intelligence. It must not have been difficult for Yardley to persuade him of the need for a code and cipher section. In June 1917, with the United States having entered the war, Yardley pinned on the gold bars of a second lieutenant and, with the help of two civilians, began setting up MI-8 (Cipher Bureau).[33]

It was not long before Yardley and his staff, which increased to twenty-five, were attacking a variety of codes. Sixty-four messages in one code, transmitted from Nauen to Mexico, were intercepted by U.S. monitoring stations between January 13 and February 2, 1918. In addition to warning against engaging in negotiations with the Japanese, the messages presented a plan for providing Mexico with arms and with machinery and technical staff for the manufacture of weapons, including aircraft. A February 18 message, also transmitted by the Nauen wireless station, authorized the German minister in Mexico to offer ten million pesetas to the Mexican government as a "preliminary amount on supposition that Mexico will remain neutral during war."[34]

Perhaps MI-8's most visible solution was the one that helped convict Lothar Witzke, suspected of setting off the Black Tom explosion. Witzke was captured on February 1, 1918, and the American agent who apprehended him discovered a ciphered letter in his baggage. The cipher reached MI-8 in the spring and was finally solved on May 18.[35]

The document, which identified Witzke as a German secret agent, helped him become the only German spy sentenced to die in the United States during World War I. Witzke did escape the hangman's noose when President Wilson commuted his sentence to life imprisonment on June 4, 1920. Approximately three and a half years later, on November 23, 1923, he was deported to Germany.[36]

Some U.S. codebreaking efforts against Germany were aided by the British. The first German diplomatic code MI-8 attacked was Code 13040, which had figured in the Zimmermann Telegram incident. The British provided Yardley with the result of their work—which amounted to about a 50 percent reconstruction of the code.[37]

The stress of directing the codebreaking effort finally got to Yardley; in July 1918 he was "close to a breakdown and asked to be relieved." He was sent to Europe to visit British and French cryptographers. Once there he was warned by Colonel Tolbert, U.S. military attaché to Copenhagen, of "repeated attempts of the British to plant secret agents in his office." Yardley found that while the British were eager to acquire information about their allies they were, at least initially, less enthusiastic about sharing information.[38]

How much Yardley actually learned about British codebreaking activities is not clear. But he apparently concluded that the British cipher bureaus "had a long and dark history, backed by a ruthless and intelligent espionage," and that Great Britain was a world power due to such activities. For the United States to be a great power MI-8 must survive the war.[39]

Yardley's last stops before returning home were the peace negotiations at Versailles and Paris. At Versailles he was to "organize code and cipher communications between the Peace Conference and the Military Intelligence Division in Washington." By the time the Armistice was signed Yardley was in Paris, attempting to develop closer ties with the French codebreakers. During that time he was ordered by Washington to manage the code bureau of the American Commission to the Peace Conference. From their two rooms in the Hotel Crillon Yardley and his small group encrypted the American delegation's messages and decrypted those of their allies. Many of the intercepted messages concerned the espionage operations that flourished during the conference as each nation tried to uncover the others' objectives.[40]

When Yardley arrived back in the United States he found MI-8 in a shambles. No money was available to pay for the organization's operations. Yardley tried to convince officials "that if the United States was to be placed on an equal footing (with the European powers) it would be necessary to finance a group of skilled cryptographers."[41]

Brigadier General Marlborough Churchill, who succeeded van Deman as Director of Military Intelligence, agreed with Yardley's assessment, believing that irrespective of cost the Code and Cipher Solution Section, at the very least, had to be preserved. On January 28, 1919, Churchill sent a telegram to the Military Staff: "I consider the establishment of M.I. 8 on a permanent peace basis most essential and believe that Yardley . . . should be . . . Chief."[42]

Churchill asked Yardley for an estimate of what it would cost to continue operations. The $100,000 a year that Yardley estimated was more than the War Department had available in secret funds. Churchill turned to Acting Secretary of State Frank L. Polk, who also believed there was a need for a cryptanalytic bureau. On May 16, 1919, Yardley submitted to the Army Chief of Staff a plan for a "permanent organization for code and cipher investigation and attack." On May 17 Polk brown-penciled his "O.K." and his initials on it. On May 19 it was approved by the Secretary of War over the signature of the Chief of Staff. It was agreed that Military Intelligence would pay $60,000 with the State Department providing the remaining $40,000, although expenditures never actually reached that sum and soon fell sharply.* Yardley and his staff of twenty set up shop in New York City, because the State Department money could not be legally spent in Washington, D.C. Locating the organization in New York, perhaps thereby keeping its existence hidden from the eyes of prying foreign governments, was undoubtedly considered a bonus.[43]

---

* The Black Chamber budget for fiscal year 1921 was cut in half to $50,000 when the War Department reduced its contribution to $10,000 on the grounds that the chamber provided information that was useful only to the State Department.

Among the original members of the American Black Chamber, as Yardley's organization came to be known, was Dr. Charles J. Mendelsohn. A holdover from MI-8, Mendelsohn spent his mornings teaching history at City College and his afternoons at the Black Chamber. Another MI-8 holdover was Victor Weiskopf, a former agent and cryptanalyst for the Justice Department, which paid him $200 above his Black Chamber salary to solve ciphers for Justice on the side. Other early members included Frederick Livesey, a Harvard graduate and businessman who worked with Yardley in Paris, and two Japanese specialists, including Edna Ramsaier, who would become the second Mrs. Yardley.[44]

From its inception through at least the early 1920s the Black Chamber briefly focused on the code and cipher systems of a variety of European nations—Austria, Belgium, Denmark, Finland, Greece, Italy, the Netherlands, Norway, Poland, Portugal, Romania, Sweden, and Switzerland—although in most instances this involved no more than filing accidentally obtained intercepts.[45]

The one European nation other than Germany that was a major target of MI-8 and the Black Chamber during their early years was Spain, most likely due to Spain's pro-German sympathies and its serving as a channel through which Germany could maintain contact with agents in Latin America. By 1920 all but three of the twenty-six Spanish systems had been solved. Some of the solutions were advanced by access to Spanish code material, which in two cases were supplied by the British.[46]*

Those in the Black Chamber trained in Spanish were by no means restricted to working on Spanish codes, for the codes of numerous nations in Latin America were attacked by Yardley's organization. A 1919 memo from the Director of Military Intelligence to the Chief of Staff noted that the work of MI-8 had resulted in a "large and constant stream of information . . . in regard to the attitudes, purposes, and plans of our neighbors."[47]

Among the most prominent Latin American targets were Mexico, Chile, and Portuguese-speaking Brazil. In the case of Mexico, no code was solved by MI-8 until the postwar period. The attack on Chilean codes, of which there were three, produced more success.[48]

Other Latin American nations whose codes and ciphers came under American attack between 1917 and 1920 were Argentina, Costa Rica, Panama, Peru, and Uruguay. Results included the solution to the Argentine diplomatic code and the translation of about 300 coded Costa Rican messages (due to compromised code books), as well as the solution of at

---

*In a third instance the son of the Spanish consul in Panama was induced, by some young women, to drink to excess. While he was drunk the key to the office safe was stolen and an impression made. When the consul was away from the office the safe was opened and the code photographed. Since one of the pages was not photographed clearly, the operation had to be repeated. Army Security Agency, *Historical Background of the Signal Security Agency*, vol. 2: World War I (Washington, D.C.: ASA, 1946), p. 91n.

least one Panamanian code, four of eight Peruvian codes, and at least one Uruguayan code.[49]

The prime task for the Black Chamber's codebreakers after World War I was to attack the codes of a nation that would become the major target of American codebreakers for the next twenty-five years—Japan. Friction was already growing between the two Pacific nations. Yardley rashly promised to resign if he didn't produce a solution within a year. It took him five months, until February 1920.[*] Yardley labeled the first code "JA": "J" for Japanese, "A" for the first code.[50]

Yardley's work was far from done. Between 1919 and the spring of 1920, Japan introduced eleven different and complex codes. The codes' complexity was due to Polish expert Jan Kowalefski, who taught the Japanese how to divide their message into two, three, or four parts, rearrange the parts, and then encipher them in transposed order to hide stereotypical beginnings and endings.[51]

By May 4, 1920, Yardley was able to claim the solution of four Japanese codes, JA, plus JB, JC, and JE. In July he reported that there was material available for the solution of other codes, including a diplomatic code (JH) believed to have 100,000 groups, a naval code (possibly JD), and a military attaché code (JF). A thousand groups of the diplomatic code had been identified, making it possible to read some messages. JF was solved that summer but produced little of interest. By mid-September the new military attaché code (JK) was also solved.[52]

During the summer of 1921, the Black Chamber produced the solution to telegram 813 of July 5 from the Japanese ambassador in London to the Foreign Office in Tokyo. It contained the first hints of British and Japanese interest in a conference on naval disarmament, an interest which ultimately resulted in the Washington Naval Conference (November 11, 1921, to February 6, 1922). Another indication was Japanese introduction of a new code, the YU, for their most confidential messages. The new code, designated JP by the Black Chamber, was partially solved, although it is not clear when work had progressed sufficiently to allow a significant unraveling of the messages transmitted using the code.[53]

In the months leading up to the Washington Naval Conference U.S. government decision makers, thanks to Yardley and his staff, were able to read an assortment of Japanese diplomatic messages.[†] Among the telegrams were those between the Japanese ambassador in London and Tokyo

---

[*] According to William F. Friedman, "Yardley's difficulties with these messages were entirely due to his ignorance of the language. As a problem in cryptography, it was of the simplest order. Had he gone about the matter scientifically, he could have accomplished the results in 5 days instead of five months." Army Security Agency, *Historical Background of the Signal Security Agency*, vol. 3 (Washington, D.C.:ASA, 1946), p. 92n.10.

[†] One of the two Japanese naval attaché codes of the time, designated JJ, remained, however, impenetrable during the conference. Army Security Agency, *Historical Background of the Signal Security Agency*, vol. 3 (Washington, D.C.: ASA, 1946), p. 103.

reporting the conversations between British Foreign Minister Curzon and the ambassador on the upcoming naval conference and other subjects.[54]

Among the messages available to U.S. decision makers was London–Tokyo telegram 874 of July 21, 1921, which noted:

> Lord Curzon said that if, before the Japanese Government made any proposal to the American Government concerning the Pacific Conference, the contents of the proposal could be confidentially communicated to the British Government, it would be much appreciated. If the Japanese Government wished the agenda made clear beforehand, plans for this must be devised.[55]

A few days later another decoded Japanese telegram indicated British displeasure with the manner in which the United States was attempting to influence the direction and location of the conference:

> Great Britain had encouraged the Americans to take the initiative in issuing invitations to the conference, but she had not imagined that America would plan the agenda. . . . America did not understand the situation. . . . [Lord Curzon] thought that London would be a more suitable atmosphere for the place of meeting than America. . . .[56]

The same telegram revealed that the Japanese ambassador believed that "it would be an opportune policy to inform Great Britain of the substance of our answer to America, and to work to secure a complete understanding between Great Britain and Japan before the conference."[57]

A few months prior to the November 11, 1921, opening of the Washington conference daily courier service was established between the Black Chamber and the State Department. The upper ranks of State were reported to be delighted with Yardley's work and read the decrypts each morning at breakfast.[58]

Their attitude would certainly not change as a result of the conference. The conference's objective was to limit the tonnage of capital ships of the participants—the United States, Britain, France, Italy, and Japan. Secretary of State Charles Evans Hughes was selected as conference chairman. In his opening address he called for three major naval powers—the United States, Britain, and Japan—to freeze construction of capital ships for ten years and scrap their oldest ships. The United States proposed a $10:10:6:3:3$ tonnage ratio, with the United States and Great Britain each being permitted approximately 500,000 tons of capital ships while Japan would be permitted 300,000 tons. France and Italy, being primarily land powers, would each be allowed 175,000 tons. Japan sought a $10:10:7$ agreement.[59]

The proposed treaty would also limit the size of future ships. Battleships and battle cruisers would be limited to 35,000 tons, aircraft carriers to 27,000 tons, and cruisers to 10,000 tons. The treaty would also prohibit battleships from mounting guns larger than sixteen inches in caliber (the largest that had been deployed) as well as restrict aircraft carriers to mounting guns eight inches in caliber or less.[60]

The participants were surprisingly receptive to Hughes's proposal, while seeking to obtain the most favorable ratio. Japan, harboring naval ambitions and expansionist dreams, continued to seek a 10 : 10 : 7 ratio with the United States and Britain.[61] But the Japanese negotiators would be operating under a tremendous handicap.

A November 28 message from the Japanese Foreign Office to its ambassador in Washington, read by the Black Chamber, stated: "It is necessary to avoid any clash with Great Britain and America, particularly America, in regard to the armament limitation question." Further, it instructed the ambassador:

> You will to the utmost maintain a middle attitude and redouble your efforts to carry out our policy. In case of inevitable necessity you will work to establish your second proposal of 10 to 6.5. If, in spite of your utmost efforts, it becomes necessary in view of the situation and in the interests of general policy to fall back on your proposal No. 3, you will endeavor to limit the power of concentration and maneuver of the Pacific by a guarantee to reduce or at least maintain the status quo of Pacific defenses and to make an adequate reservation which will make clear that [this is] our intention in agreeing to a 10:6 ratio. No. 4 is to be avoided as far as possible.[62]

The difference between Japan's preferred 10 : 7 and America's preferred 10 : 6 was 100,000 tons—about three battleships. The decoded message told American negotiators all they needed to know: if they pressed, Japan would yield. Secretary of State Hughes did just that, and on December 10 Japan yielded to his insistence, cabling its negotiator that "there is nothing to do but accept the ratio proposed by the United States." Not surprisingly, the Five Power Treaty established the ratio of 10 : 10 : 6 : 3.3 : 3.3 for the United States, Great Britain, Japan, France, and Italy. Yardley received a letter of commendation from Hughes.[63]

Japan was not the only Naval Conference participant whose codes were attacked by the Black Chamber. In the fall of 1921, work began on French code systems, which had not been attacked during World War I or its immediate aftermath. French traffic was divided between messages transmitted in letters and those in numbers, with the numerical traffic being further subdivided on the basis of which of three officials signed the message. While the messages transmitted in letters proved immune to the Black Chamber's assault, some success was attained against the numerical traffic—although not during the conference. It would not be until March 1923, a little over a year after the end of the conference, that the

Black Chamber was able to achieve its first breaks into the French codes. Even then it amounted only to the identification of fifteen to twenty words, and work on those codes does not seem to have progressed much beyond that point.[64]*

The conference's conclusion could not have come too soon for Yardley. During the conference he and his staff had produced more than 5,000 solutions and translations. But Yardley came close to a nervous breakdown, and in February he began four months of recuperation in Arizona. Yardley was not the only codebreaker to experience such problems. One member of the Black Chamber dreamed of being chased around the bedroom by a bulldog that had "code" written on its side. Another repeatedly dreamed of carrying an enormous sack of pebbles that could be lightened by finding a matching stone along a deserted beach, which could then be thrown into the sea. A third simply babbled incoherently. All resigned.[65]

The Naval Conference was the high point for the Black Chamber. In 1924 half of Yardley's staff left, although not for psychiatric reasons. A dramatic reduction in its appropriation necessitated the reduction of the Black Chamber to about a dozen employees. By 1927 Japan was the only target of the organization's activities. Despite these cuts, Yardley said that the Black Chamber managed, from 1917 to 1929, to solve more than 45,000 coded telegrams, including those of Argentina, Brazil, Chile, China, Costa Rica, Cuba, France, Germany, Great Britain, Japan, Liberia, Mexico, Nicaragua, Panama, Peru, San Salvador, Santo Domingo (later the Dominican Republic), the Soviet Union, and Spain.[66]

The codes of China at first proved impenetrable, with Yardley writing in July 1922 that he had never read any Chinese messages and would need a large volume of message traffic to break into the system. By early September 1926, he was able to separate the Chinese traffic into six codes, and toward the end of the month he reported that the Black Chamber was able to read practically all the Chinese telegrams.[67]

But in 1929 the Black Chamber fell victim to a new administration. Funding was down to $25,000, of which the State Department paid $15,000. The funding paid for rent, books, postage, travel, transportation, Yardley, a code and cipher expert, one Japanese translator, a secretary, and two clerk-typists. As a result the bureau was solving only occasional Japanese diplomatic messges. The limited funding permitted no cryptanalytical research, training, intercept work, code compilation, and no secret ink work.[68]

Further, the presidents of the Western Union Telegraph and Postal Telegraph companies, who had been cooperative in providing Yardley

---

* Much greater progress would likely have been made if the Black Chamber had more personnel available during the Naval Conference. The priority assigned to breaking Japanese messages was such that the Black Chamber informed the organization that delivered the telegrams to be decoded that they could discontinue providing French messages. With the conclusion of the conference the urgency of decoding the French messages became markedly lower.

with copies of telegrams, became recalcitrant.* Yardley had no Official Secrets Act to force compliance. Indeed, U.S. law had become more restrictive. Whereas the 1912 Radio Act merely prohibited the divulgence of telegrams, the 1927 Radio Act prohibited *interception* as well as divulgence. The administration of Herbert Hoover had just taken office, and Yardley decided to settle the matter with it by presenting Hoover with a memorandum, outlining the history and activities of the Black Chamber and the steps required "if the Government had hoped to take full advantage of the skill of its cryptographers." But before he did Yardley listened to Hoover's first speech as president and concluded that Hoover's ethics would bring the end of the Black Chamber.[69]

It was not Hoover, however, but Secretary of State Henry Stimson who killed the Black Chamber. Yardley thought that after a few months in office Stimson would have lost some of his innocence in dealing with international affairs and might be amenable to the type of help the Black Chamber could provide. To illustrate its value Yardley sent him the solution to an important series of messages. This stratagem worked with previous secretaries but not with Stimson, who was shocked to learn of the Black Chamber and its activities. As he explained many years later, "Gentlemen do not read each other's mail."[70]

The books were officially closed on the Black Chamber on October 31, 1929. Over the decade of its existence it had cost the State Department $230,404 and the War Department $98,808.49 -just under a third of a million dollars.[71]

Statisticians and Volunteers

Germany's defeat in World War I produced the Versailles Treaty, which intended to strip Germany of any true military capability. In the hope of preventing future German aggression, the treaty prohibited such organizations as a general staff. As a result, the German military that was permitted to exist resorted to a series of subterfuges. The General Staff was abolished on September 30, 1919, and recreated the very next day as the Troops Department (Truppenamt). What had been the Foreign Armies Branch analytical unit became the Truppenamt's Third Branch (T3), officially designated the Army Statistical Section. The remains of Section IIIb became the Third Branch's Abwehr (Defense) Group.[72]

At virtually the same time army and navy COMINT organizations were created. The army organization was given the obscure title of Volunteer Evaluation Office of the Army High Command, with the intention of keeping the Inter-Allied Military Control Commission in the dark about its true activities. A Foreign Office organization, Bureau C, was soon established to decipher foreign diplomatic traffic. In a preview of the Nazi

---

* Radio interception had played a minor role in the provision of traffic for the Black Chamber. The first intercept was obtained in 1923, from the Coast Guard. In 1926 only eleven radio intercepts of Japanese messages were received by Yardley's organization.

era, the organizations soon became involved in bitter bureaucratic battles.[73]

In February 1920 the twelve-person Volunteer Evaluation Office was
moved to the Defense Ministry, took the title Cipher Bureau of the Army
High Command, and for a few years also became Group II of the Abwehr.[74]

In their early years the COMINT organizations monitored the Soviet
civil war, the uprisings in Hungary, and the Russo-Polish war. All this
was done surreptitiously to avoid detection by the Inter-Allied Military
Control Commission. In one instance Army Cipher Bureau personnel
posed as a newspaper translation office. By 1926, however, there were six
Fixed Intercept Stations—one each in Königsberg, Frankfurt, Breslau,
Munich, Stuttgart, and Münster—with each station monitoring a specific
target set. The Munich station monitored transmissions from Italy,
Switzerland, Austria, and part of the Balkans, the Stuttgart station focused on France, Spain, and North Africa.[75]

In addition to the establishment of the Beobachtungs Dienst (Observation Service) COMINT service, the navy established several other intelligence units during the same period of time. The Fleet Section produced
overt intelligence, clandestine intelligence, and counterintelligence reports. By 1928 the navy was also operating a Naval Supply Organization
with intelligence functions and the World Intelligence Service.[76]

In 1928 the new defense minister was urged by of one his subordinates,
Kurt von Schleicher, to increase his power by grabbing control of organizations from subordinate services. One area where this could be done was
intelligence. On April 1, 1928, the minister removed the Abwehr Group
from T3 and the World Intelligence Service from the navy's command,
and he merged them with the Defense Ministry's Cipher Center into the
Abwehr Branch, "the "Defense Ministry's sole intelligence-acquistion
post."[77]

The new branch consisted of four sections: Espionage (I), Cipher Unit
(II), Counterespionage (III), and the Navy Group, which incorporated the
World Intelligence Service.[78]

6

Spies Between the Wars: 1930–1939

The Great Depression brought the political, economic, and social turmoil that was instrumental in Hitler's rise to power and the worldwide tragedy that followed. Developments in the world of intelligence reflected these events. German and Japanese intelligence expanded to meet the requirements of their nations' aggressive foreign policies. As Germany and Japan became more obviously a world menace, the intelligence establishments of the United States, Great Britain, and France expanded their operations to cope with the increasingly hostile international environment.

Meanwhile, the Soviet Union's intelligence apparatus had a large variety of targets. Its human intelligence operations in Britain and the United States not only would provide it valuable information during the coming war, but would prove of significant value during the Cold War.

Friedman's SIS

Even before Herbert Yardley's attempt to demonstrate the value of the Black Chamber backfired, the U.S. Army had decided to establish its own centralized COMINT organization, which would absorb Yardley's organization. On April 5, 1929, Secretary of War had directed that "the Signal Corps be charged with the duties, pertaining to the solution of enemy codes and ciphers and the detection of secret inks in war, in addition . . . to the interception of enemy radio and wire traffic in war."[1]

On May 10, the Army established the Signal Intelligence Service, under the direction of the Signal Corps. The new term *signal intelligence*, reflected the fact that the mission of SIS would be broader than extracting intelligence by reading foreign communications. SIS would also be responsible for determining the location of transmitters by detection of the signals emanating from the transmitters.[2]

The new term had been coined only days earlier by the chief of the SIS, William F. Friedman. Born Wolfe Friedman in Kishinev, Russia, on September 24, 1891, he moved with his family to Pittsburgh in 1892. Friedman enrolled in Michigan Agricultural College in 1910 but quickly realized that his future was not in farming. By the end of his first term he was headed for Cornell University to study genetics.[3]

Friedman followed his undergraduate studies at Cornell with a graduate degree, and then a job, starting in June 1915, at Riverbank Laboratories, on the estate of wealthy textile merchant George Fabyan. In addition to his genetics work Friedman aided Fabyan's cryptologists, who were attempting to prove Fabyan's theory that Sir Francis Bacon was the true author of Shakespeare's plays. His abilities soon made him head of the Department of Ciphers as well as the Department of Genetics.[4]

It was in June 1916 that the Department of Ciphers, whose services had been volunteered by Fabyan, began receiving work from the U.S. government. Friedman and his cryptologists set to work solving messages, including Mexican diplomatic messages, for the Departments of State and Justice, among others.[5]

In January 1921 Friedman left Riverbank to become head of the Army Signal Corps's Code and Ciphers Section. After becoming SIS director he quickly recruited a small but highly talented staff. Included among the initial recruits were three mathematicians (Solomon Kullback, Frank Rowlett, and Abraham Sinkov) and a Japanese linguist (John Hurt) who would become prominent in U.S. cryptanalysis during World War II. These four, Friedman, and two others became the entire U.S. Army Signal Intelligence Service. For the next seven years SIS would operate with only seven employees and a budget never greater than $17,400.[6]

To avoid emulating the Black Chamber's dependence on the cooperation of cable companies, several intercept stations were established. A Provisional Radio Detachment was activated at Fort Monmouth, New Jersey, in 1933. In 1935 a radio detachment was established in the Philippines, followed the next year by an intercept station at Quarry Heights in Panama. On January 26, 1938, the Panama station was instructed to begin twenty-four-hour-a-day operations, giving first priority to diplomatic communications between Rome and Tokyo. Traffic between Berlin and Tokyo was the second priority. In addition, it was ordered to monitor diplomatic traffic to and from Japan and Latin America.[7]

By 1938 the SIS also had intercept stations in California, Texas, and Hawaii. The intercept activity was performed under conditions of strict secrecy inasmuch as the Federal Communications Act of 1934 made it illegal to divulge foreign communications.[8]

SIS was not the only U.S. military signals intelligence organization. The Office of the Chief of Naval Operations had established OP-20-G in 1922 as its Research Desk. By the late 1930s it employed, at headquarters and in the field, more than 100 officers and enlisted personnel, and it maintained major intercept facilities in Washington, Maine, Maryland,

Hawaii, Shanghai, and the Philippines. Smaller stations were located in Guam, California, Long Island, and Florida.[9]

The intercepts of Japanese traffic indicated that Japan was employing a minimum of nine different cipher systems. The most significant appeared to be a machine system reserved for high-level diplomatic traffic—the Angooki Taipu A, or Cipher Machine Type A, known within SIS as the RED machine. The system was in use before 1932, was first attacked by SIS in 1935, and was broken in 1936, permitting SIS to read virtually every communication to and from the Japanese Foreign Office.[10]

Codes, Ciphers, and Spies

Britain's COMINT operations were not subject to the organizational turmoil that afflicted those of the United States, but its Government Code and Cipher School was subject to stringent financial limitations. Its operational head, Alastair Denniston, complained that "[GC&CS] became in fact an adopted child of the Foreign Office with no family rights, and the poor relation of the SIS [Secret Intelligence Service], whose peacetime activities left little cash to spare."[11]

The main triumphs of GC&CS in the 1930s included deciphering Japanese, Italian, and Comintern communications. By 1930 Royal Navy ships were intercepting, and GC&CS-trained cryptanalysts were solving, Japanese naval signals. A significant volume of Japanese military and military attaché traffic was also decrypted during and after Japan's September 1931 invasion of Manchuria. Although the British cabinet decided not to respond to the Japanese invasion, the intercepts did allow Britain to track Japanese activities.[12]

On the other hand, GC&CS was less accomplished with the codes and ciphers of the other nations whose activities were of greatest significance to Britain. The intelligence value of French intercepts was erratic. The proximity of London and Paris permitted the French to transmit a good deal of traffic by diplomatic bag rather than wireless. In 1935 the French Foreign Ministry introduced the first interwar French code that proved invulnerable to Britain's codebreakers (although some of the older codes that had proved vulnerable continued in use).[13]

GC&CS also had little success with Soviet and German traffic, particularly diplomatic traffic. In 1927 the British cabinet, to justify its decision to break diplomatic relations, released for publication the decrypted texts of several Soviet diplomatic messages, which demonstrated that Soviet representatives in Britain were engaged in subversive activities. While the Soviets may not have reacted to disclosures in *The Times* in 1920, they did in 1927. After seeing their diplomatic messages in the *The Times*, the Soviets adopted unbreakable one-time pads for their communications. Denniston would remark bitterly that the Conservative government of Stanley Baldwin had "found it necessary to compromise our work beyond question."[14]

The German Foreign Office sent its high-grade communications by one-time pad or a code designated FLORADORA. While the basic FLORADORA code was solved during the 1930s, it was usually reciphered in a form that proved invincible until 1942. Telegrams that were not reciphered could be read but, according to Denniston, they dealt with matters "of little interest or value."[15]

GC&CS had more success against German and Soviet military codes and ciphers. Prior to 1935 little effort was made against German military communications. Until the early 1930s the bulk of German military radio traffic was transmitted in the clear, although the German armed forces regularly broadcast enciphered signals on backup communications links for practice purposes. Since the unenciphered and unencoded signals that Britain could read were considered of little value in London and the transmissions were difficult to intercept from British stations (located in Britain or the Middle East), little effort was made to extract intelligence from these communications.[16]

Things changed somewhat in the 1930s, with the introduction of high frequencies, the acceleration of military preparations, and the resumption of military operations. An ever greater volume of military traffic was intercepted. However, German as well as Soviet high-grade communications remained invulnerable to attack.[17]

Success came against less significant communications. From 1932 enough Soviet military radio traffic was intercepted that GC&CS recruited two cryptanalysts to tackle the traffic. Against low-grade codes they made some headway. German low-grade codes were also attacked with some success after 1934, when regular interception of German military traffic resumed after a fifteen-year hiatus.[18]

German military traffic came from a variety of sources. German air force training activities produced a large volume of tactical traffic. The deciphered communications, along with traffic analysis, contributed significantly to estimates of operational strength and the disposition of German bomber and reconnaissance units. By September 1935 GC&CS was able to confidently identify 60 ground stations and 578 individual aircraft.[19]

Interception and analysis of the German navy's call signs made it possible to determine the number and, combined with direction-finding data, the movements of its U-boats and surface units. However, the navy made virtually no use of medium- or low-grade codes or ciphers. Meanwhile, the German army's minimal use of low- and medium-grade codes helped prevent successful attack.[20]

A major factor in the difficulties presented by the German ciphers was the fact that the German army and navy as well as all other state organizations, such as the railways and the SS, used different variations of the same cipher system for all their tactical communications. The cipher system—the Engima machine—had been commercially available since the 1920s. Progressive German modifications had made it more secure.

The less secure version proved vulnerable to attack in 1937, allowing GC&CS to read some German codes, but otherwise the Engima still proved invulnerable and appeared to be so for the foreseeable future.[21]

Finding out what was going on in the increasingly bizarre Reich was not solely the responsibility of the codebreakers. SIS stations bordering Germany—in Prague, Berne, Paris, Brussels, Copenhagen, and The Hague—were assigned the responsibility of penetrating the Reich.[22]

Inside Germany the SIS network consisted of two senior officers in Berlin and four outstations at Frankfurt, Cologne, Hamburg, and Munich. Among their sources were Ian Colvin and Sefton Delmer, British journalists who had established close ties with both the regime and its opponents. Relying on Colvin and Delmer, the Berlin Station was able to provide detailed assessments of the German political situation and developments within the Nazi party. Another British source was Malcolm Graham Christie, the British air attaché in Berlin from 1927 to 1930, who continued to reside in Germany and had excellent contacts with Hermann Göring, his deputy, Erhard Milch, and the Air Ministry.[23]

Britain did have some valuable German sources. A German diplomat in The Hague, Wolfgang zu Pulitz, began acting as a source for SIS and MI5 in 1934. Otto Krueger, a retired German naval officer living in northern Germany, had been supplying SIS with high-level naval intelligence since the end of World War I.[24]

SIS also benefited from the work of the Czech intelligence service, which passed along information from two major agents. A-52 was a Luftwaffe staff officer who had been recruited by the Czechs in Zurich in late 1934. A-52 had access to a large quantity of secret information concerning Göring's illegal air force, which had been created in violation of the 1919 Versailles Treaty.[25]

Whereas A-52 worked for money, A-54 was a volunteer. In March 1937, General Frantisek Moravec, head of the Czech military intelligence service, received a letter from Paul Thümmel, a senior Abwehr officer and long-time Nazi party member, detailing his responsibilities and offering his services. At their first meeting Thümmel provided Moravec with some secret Czech plans and the identity of the Czech staff officer who had betrayed them to the Abwehr.[26]

Thümmel was also able to provide a wide variety of valuable intelligence on German intelligence services, military capabilities, and intentions. He delivered extraordinarily detailed information on the organization and structure of the Abwehr and Sicherheitsdienst (SD, the Nazi party's Security Service), the near-complete order of battle of the Wehrmacht and Luftwaffe, and German mobilization plans. Later in the decade he gave advanced warnings of the German annexation of the Sudetenland as well as the invasions of Czechoslovakia and Poland. A-54's information was passed on to the Head of Station in Prague, and from there to SIS London.[27]

Hitler's Spies

Hitler's assumption of the chancellorship in 1933 inevitably resulted in an expansion and restructuring of German intelligence operations. A key individual in that expansion was Captain Wilhelm Franz Canaris. On April 1, 1905, three months after his eighteenth birthday, Canaris arrived at Old Warrant Officers' School in Kiel to begin his career as an officer in the Imperial Navy.[28]

In October 1907, Midshipman Canaris was ordered to report to the light cruiser *Bremen*. The next year he helped establish an intelligence network in Argentina and Brazil in support of *Bremen* operations. During World War I Canaris developed a South American intelligence network to support the operations of his ship, the *Dresden*.[29]

Canaris's World War I activities also included a journey to Spain on behalf of the navy's intelligence section. He toured Spanish ports in search of new recruits for the German naval intelligence network, which had been established immediately after the outbreak of the war to provide German warships with supplies and information about the enemy. By early 1916 agents in Spain's principal ports were pumping sailors from Allied ships while Spanish laborers and seamen at Britain's Gibraltar naval base were reporting to Canaris.[30]

On January 28, 1925, Canaris once again left for Spain, where he proceeded to contact his wartime agents and assign them new missions. His new organization was responsible for dispatching agents to France, the establishment of an intelligence center in Spain geared to mobilization, and submission of regular reports on political and economic matters.[31]

A little less than ten years later Canaris found himself about to be assigned a far more ambitious task. By the autumn of 1934 the position of Captain Conrad Patzig as head of the Abwehr had become untenable. Poor performance by Abwehr agents, Patzig's conflicts with Nazi security officials, and his approval of aerial reconnaissance missions that could have threatened the nonagression pact with Poland led to his dismissal. To take his place Patzig nominated Canaris. Patzig recalled that "I nominated Canaris because I knew of no one in the Navy who could have been better suited without a long running-in period."[32]

On January 2, 1935, Canaris took office as head of the Abwehr. "What I want," Hitler told Canaris, "is something like the British Secret Service— an Order doing its work with passion." One former Abwehr officer had his doubts: "compared with the brisk and energetic Captain Patzig he seemed too old and spent for the job." Approximately five feet, three inches, the white-haired Canaris had a slight physique and an aura of fatigue about him, an unmilitary bearing, a reserved manner, and an occasional lisp. He also had the annoying habit of answering one question with another.[33]

Despite appeareances Canaris quickly moved to settle jurisdictional disputes with the leaders of the Gestapo and the Nazi party's SD. On January 17, 1935, Canaris and his new allies signed an agreement defining the responsibilities and powers of their organizations. Abwehr functions included:

1. Military espionage and counterespionage.
2. Intelligence work in the Reichswehr* and in Reichswehr-owned concerns. . . .
3. Supervision and implementation of all regulations enacted as safeguards against espionage. . . .
4. Control and supervision of enrollment [of new officers] in the Wehrmacht.
5. Direction and determination of policy in all matters affecting national defense.[34]

The first test of Canaris and his organization occurred before the spring was out. Less than two months later, on March 16, the cabinet approved Hitler's rearmament manifesto, "Proclamation of German Military Sovereignty," which tripled the size of the army from twelve to thirty-six divisions. Reichswehr leaders feared a fierce reaction from Germany's neighbors. Diplomatic protests were lodged virtually immediately by Britain, France, and Italy. The Abwehr was ordered to determine if any military action was in the works. On March 29, 1935, Canaris made an announcement to his organization: "Times of great international tension are a test of the intelligence service, its organization and mettle. I therefore expect all members of the Abwehr Section to do their utmost to meet the extreme demands of these days for the good of the Fatherland."[35]

Reports that the French, Italian, and British heads of government planned to hold a summit meeting at Stresa on April 11 to plan unified action against Germany further goaded the Abwehr into action. After a few weeks the Abwehr reports landing on Canaris's desk convinced him that Hitler had succeeded, that the major foreign powers would acquiesce. Doubts of top Reichswehr officials were swept away, and Hitler's generals proceeded with his rearmament programs.[36]

Early in 1936 the Abwehr was once again asked to provide intelligence on probable reaction to one of Hitler's gambles. On March 7, 1936, some 40,000 German soldiers—nineteen Wehrmacht battalions and thirteen batteries—crossed into the Rhineland. Operation Winterübung (Winter Exercise) had begun and Hitler and his generals anxiously wondered if the Abwehr's agents would send back word of an impending military response, a response that Germany could not resist.[37]

Messages that soon arrived from France and Belgium contained no information that was not to become public knowledge within a few hours. Information from France indicated that the Maginot line was brought up to wartime strength and leave was canceled for garrison troops in northern and eastern France, while the French General Staff

* The Nazis retained the designation Reichswehr, Republican Armed Forcies, until May 21, 1935 when it was changed to Wehrmacht.

transferred some North Africa divisions from the south of France to the German border. The agents found nothing else, no sign of warlike reaction. In Britain they reported no signs of mobilization measures.[38]

The changes in the Abwehr resulting from Canaris's appointment were preceded and followed by changes in Germany's very diverse COMINT apparatus. In February 1933 a member of the Defense Ministry's Cipher Center, Gottfried Schapper, approached Hermann Göring with a suggestion—the creation of a central German COMINT agency. Schapper had hoped to establish the agency under the Chancellery, but that was ruled out by Hitler's fear of intelligence monopolies. Göring approved Schapper's proposal that the agency be subordinate to Göring as an individual and thus independent of any ministry, including Göring's. He also approved Schapper's proposed name for the agency, the "Forschungsamt" (Research Office) because, as he told Schapper, "You indeed research the truth."[39]

The Forschungsamt began operations on April 10, 1933, in Göring's Air Ministry building. By July it had a staff of about twenty—radiomen, technicians, cryptanalysts, and evaluators. It relied on a postal radio station to intercept wireless transmissions and took over the responsibility for telephone-tapping from the Defense Ministry. By the end of the year it relocated its operations in a former hotel, while in 1934 and 1935 it moved into a converted housing complex. Apartments became offices while the basement was occupied by teleprinters and pneumatic tubes.[40]

While Schapper may have envisioned the Forschungsamt as the central German COMINT agency, it was far from the only one. As was standard in the Nazi intelligence apparatus numerous agencies duplicated the work of other agencies and bitter rivalries were commonplace. The Forschungsamt had several rivals. Canaris's Abwehr controlled the Armed Forces Decipherment Service. The navy continued to operate its own listening service, the B-Dienst. The Foreign Office was also involved in COMINT activities, with its I Z organization, renamed Pers Z in 1936.[41]

To feed its COMINT organizations the Germans maintained a network of listening posts around the periphery of German territory. The central Decipherment Service and its listening posts were located in the Berlin region. The navy's B-Dienst operated a network of intercept stations along the coasts of the Baltic and North seas, which could be used in combination with warships and other vessels at sea. Army intercept facilities were largely made up of fixed stations close to command posts in the military districts and linked to field posts near the frontier, in order to permit information obtained from traffic analysis to be provided to local commanders and army signals headquarters.[42]

The intercept facility at Münster concentrated on British radio signals while Stuttgart monitored French radio transmissions, Munich listened to Italian communications, and Breslau eavesdropped on Czech and Balkan traffic. On occasion Breslau assisted Frankfurt an der Oder (and later Jüterbog) or Königsberg, whose primary target was Soviet espionage networks, in monitoring Polish transmissions.[43]

A combination of circumstances ensured that the German intercept facilities would be kept busy. One was Germany's location in the center of European communication networks—air, cable, rail, and telephone—running on both a north–south axis (Stockholm–Naples) and an east–west axis (Istanbul–Moscow–London–Lisbon), with connections to the Middle East, Asia, and the Western Hemisphere. As a result German authorities were less dependent on extended radio communications abroad, allowing German radio stations to devote more time to acquiring the traffic of nations which were more dependent on overseas radio communications. European nations with colonies increasingly depended on radio, and their communications made an attractive target. Special attention was focused on British diplomatic and military traffic with the outposts of its far-flung empire—in Africa, the Near East, and India. Italian communications to Africa and the Middle East were also major targets. To the east Soviet leaders placed heavy reliance on radio communications as a means of exercising control over their vast country. Soviet diplomatic and armed forces communications were monitored, along with those of the internal security forces, collective farms, and the Comintern. Finally, the U.S. State and War Departments relied on radiograms with increasing frequency for communications with the European continent.[44]

The second factor was Hitler, whose rise to power led to an increase in European diplomatic traffic. A steady flow of French and Italian decrypted messages was equaled by an "extremely successful" interception of British traffic. Likewise, German codebreakers experienced significant success in 1933 with the U.S. State Department messages transmitted in the GRAY and GREEN codes.[45]

And it appears that the flow of intercepts was not short-lived but continued throughout the decade. Scattered documents and references to decrypts found in surviving German archives suggest a steady flow of decrypted French, British, Polish, Italian, Japanese, and Balkan messages reaching Germany's rulers between 1934 and 1939—making it easier to minimize the risk that their dangerous policies would backfire.[46]

Stalin's Spies

The 1930s was a time of turmoil and triumph for the Soviet intelligence apparatus. In 1934 the OGPU was absorbed into the NKVD (People's Commissariat of Internal Affairs) as the GUGB (Glavnoye Upravleniye Gosudarstvennoy Bezopasnosti; Chief Administration of State Security).[47]

Of even more significance for Soviet intelligence operations was the purge unleashed by Stalin in 1936. Before concluding in 1938 it took the lives of millions of Soviet citizens, including important military and intelligence officers. Among those who fell victim to Stalin's paranoia were

Gleb I. Boki, head of the NKVD COMINT unit, Teodor Maly, one of Kim Philby's case officers, and M.A. Trilisser, first head of the INO.[48]

Despite the damage inflicted on the Soviet intelligence services by Stalin and his minions the 1930s saw important gains in both communications and human intelligence operations. A key figure in COMINT developments was General Yan Karlovich Berzin, head of the Fourth Department (military intelligence).[49]

Early in the 1930s Berzin played a key role in establishing a joint OGPU/Fourth Department unit within the OGPU Special Department (Spets-Otdel), responsible for both civilian and military COMINT. The most secret unit in Soviet intelligence, it was housed until 1935 outside the Lubyanka or Fourth Department, in the People's Commissariat of Foreign Affairs.[50]

The Soviet COMINT unit was the world's largest and richest. It also relied more than any other on the assistance that was provided by espionage. While other espionage services occasionally acquired cipher material for their codebreakers, the OGPU/GUGB and Fourth Department made such acquisitions a high priority. They had particular success in acquiring Japanese cipher materials through officials in the Japanese embassies in Berlin and Prague.[51]

In its first years of operation the unit's most significant impact on Soviet policy was with respect to Japan. A decrypted March 1931 telegram from the Japanese military attaché in Moscow to the General Staff, six months prior to the Manchurian Incident,* aroused Soviet fears of war. The telegram read:

> It will be [Japan's] unavoidable destiny to clash with the U.S.S.R. sooner or later. . . . The sooner the Soviet–Japanese war comes, the better for us. We must realize that with every day the situation develops more favorably for the U.S.S.R. In short, I hope the authorities will make up their minds for a speedy war with the Soviet Union and initiate policies accordingly.[52]

In September 1931 the Soviets viewed the Manchurian Incident as a possible prelude to the attack on the Soviet Union advocated in March. Another intercepted telegram contained comments by the Japanese ambassador in Moscow to a visiting Japanese general, further alarming Moscow:

> Putting aside the question of whether or not Japan should make war against the Soviet Union, there is the need to take a strong policy vis-à-vis the Soviet Union, with the resolve to fight the U.S.S.R. at any time necessary. The objective, however, should not be the defense against Communism but, rather, the occupation of Eastern Siberia.[53]

---

* In September 1931 Japanese troops stationed near the Japanese-owned South Manchurian Railway blew up a segment of the track. They then charged Chinese troops with responsibility for the explosion, using the charges as a pretext to invade and occupy Manchuria.

By the winter of 1931–32 the Soviet rulers became so fearful of a Japanese attack that, despite being aware of the possible impact on the Soviet COMINT effort, they resorted to releasing decrypted Japanese messages. In March 1932 Moscow announced: "We are in possession of documents which originate from officials of the most senior military circles in Japan, and contain plans for an attack on the U.S.S.R. and the seizure of its territory." *Izvestia* published extracts of decrypted Japanese telegrams which disclosed the military attaché's plea for a "speedy war" and the ambassador's call for Japanese occupation of Siberia.[54]

During the mid-1930s the joint COMINT unit again produced information of significant value, allowing the monitoring of the prolonged negotiations in Berlin between General Hiroshi Oshima, the Japanese military attaché (and later ambassador), and Joachim von Ribbentrop, which resulted in the November 1936 Anti-Comintern Pact between their countries. COMINT was again aided by human sources. In the summer of 1936 a Berlin-based agent run by the NKVD resident in the Netherlands, Walter Krivitsky, obtained access to the Japanese embassy's codebooks as well as its files on the German–Japanese negotiations. After that time, according to Krivitsky, "all correspondence between General Oshima and Tokyo flowed regularly through our hands." A supplementary source of intelligence was certainly traffic between Tokyo and the Japanese embassy in Moscow, which was decrypted by the joint COMINT unit.[55]

As a result of such activities Stalin and other high Soviet officials knew there was more to the Anti-Comintern Pact than the published version, which simply provided for the exchange of information on Comintern activities and cooperation in taking preventive measures. They knew that a secret protocol specified that if either Germany or Japan became the victim of "an unprovoked [Soviet] attack or threat of attack," both would immediately consult on the appropriate response while neither took any action to "ease the situation of the U.S.S.R."[56]

The Soviets were also scoring dramatic successes in recruiting agents—including spies whose greatest value would come during the first decade of the Cold War. General Berzin again played a crucial role, adapting the methods developed by the Cheka/GPU/OGPU in the 1920s for infiltration of White Guard émigré groups to a different target, foreign government bureaucracies, including their intelligence services. Although the 1930s began with White Guardist and Trotskyist groups being the top priority for the OGPU's Foreign Department (INO), Berzin lobbied to devote greater attention to foreign intelligence collection, a position soon accepted by the OGPU/GUGB.[57]

Berzin's most successful penetration agent was a German, Richard Sorge. Born in 1895 in the Caucasus, he attended school in Berlin, was wounded in World War I, became disillusioned by the devastation, and joined the revolutionary wing of the labor movement. The Bolsheviks' success in Russia convinced him "not only to support the movement theoretically but to become an actual part of it."[58]

After the war he obtained a Ph.D. in political science from Hamburg University. In late 1924 Sorge moved to Moscow, where he soon acquired Soviet citizenship and began work for the International Liaison Department (OMS) of the Communist International. From 1927 to 1929 he was sent on a series of political intelligence missions to Germany and possibly to England and Scandinavia.[59]

In 1929 Berzin recruited Sorge for the Fourth Department and sent him off to Shanghai to consolidate and expand the department's China network. It was there that he recruited Hotsumi Ozaki, the Japanese journalist who would become his most valuable source. Ozaki was the perfect recruit—a young Marxist idealist from a wealthy family, with superb connections with the Japanese government. When Sorge returned to Moscow Berzin personally applauded his accomplishments in China. His next stop was Tokyo, but he first spent several months in Germany, building up his journalistic cover and establishing himself as a genial Nazi party member. So successful was Sorge that those attending his farewell dinner in Berlin included propaganda chief Dr. Josef Goebbels.[60]

When Sorge arrived in Tokyo Stalin was still fearful of a Japanese attack. Its invasion of Manchuria gave Japan control of a long land border with the Soviet Union. As a result Sorge was instructed "to give very careful study to the question of whether or not Japan was planning to attack the U.S.S.R." After his arrest in 1941 he wrote that "[t]his was for many years the most important duty assigned to me and my group; it would not be far wrong to say that it was the sole object of my mission in Japan. . . ."[61]

Sorge made significant use of the German embassy to conduct his espionage operations, ingratiating himself soon after his arrival. Sorge's most important and closest contact within the embassy was Colonel Eugen Ott, military attaché from 1934, and his wife, one of Sorge's many sexual partners. Thanks to Ott, Sorge was able to see a good deal of the information on the Japanese armed forces that Ott passed on to Berlin, along with numerous documents on German policy in the Far East. Beginning in April 1938, when Ott became ambassador, he and Sorge had breakfast each morning, with Sorge briefing him on Japanese affairs and even drafting some of his reports to Berlin.[62]

Meanwhile, Ozaki had increasing access to inside information concerning Japanese policy as a result of his role in the brain trust of Prince Konoye, the leading Japanese statesman. Toward the end of 1935 he was able to provide Sorge with a photographic copy of a planning document for 1936, which indicated that there was no immediate chance that Japan would attack Russia.[63]

With Hozumi's aid, Sorge was able to forecast, several weeks ahead of time, the Japanese military mutiny of February 1936 and the Japanese invasion of China in July 1937, and he reassured Soviet decision makers that the troop movements involved were directed south and not against Siberia. Sorge also forwarded details on the Anti-Comintern Pact a month before its public announcement, complementing the information provided by Soviet COMINT operations.[64]

Sorge was only one of many agents recruited by Soviet intelligence in the 1930s. It was in Britain, as far as is known, that the Soviets had the greatest success. Indeed, even today, the full extent of Soviet penetration of Britain is unknown. Thus the identities of the agents code-named PROFESSOR, BEAR, ATILLA, and SUCCESSOR have never been publicly revealed.[65]

Soviet COMINT operations against Britain received a boost beginning in 1929 when a Foreign Office cipher expert, Ernest Holloway Oldham, walked into the Soviet embassy in Paris and provided the military attaché with a cipher. Oldham would provide further information on Foreign Office ciphers, security procedures, and colleagues in the Communications Department. In September 1933 Oldham died: according to an inquest, he had taken his life by "coal gas suffocation" while of "unsound mind."[66]

Aided by information provided by Oldham, the GUGB, in 1935, was able to recruit Captain John Herbert King, also of the Communications Department. Posing as a representative of a Dutch banker, an NKVD illegal convinced King, who was assigned the code name MAG, that he could make a great deal of money if he would provide inside information on international affairs. Included in the material provided by King were telegrams from the British embassy in Berlin reporting on meetings with Hitler and other Nazi leaders. Some of the documents were considered so significant that they were shown to Stalin.[67]

Oldham and King were mercenary agents. But the NKVD had far more success with ideology, recruiting a group of agents who would go on to penetrate the Foreign Office and intelligence services. The explanation Anthony Blunt offered for his own willingness to serve as a Soviet agent may hold true for the entire group:

> In the mid-1930s it seemed to me . . . that the Communist Party and Russia constituted the only firm bulwark against fascism, since the Western democracies were taking an uncertain and compromising attitude towards Germany. I was persuaded . . . that I could best serve the cause of anti-fascism by [working] for the Russians.[68]

The most famous of the group was Harold Adrian Russell Philby, nicknamed "Kim." Born in India on January 1, 1912, his father, Harry St. John Philby, was a civil servant of the British raj. But that was only one of his many occupations. He wrote for *The Times,* ran for Parliament, was a frequent visitor to London's clubs, and was a devotee of cricket. He was a convert to Islam and his second wife was a Saudi slave girl. He also betrayed British secrets to a foreign power he felt a greater commitment to than Britain—providing Saudi King Ibn Saud with secret documents on the Middle East.[69]

In October 1929 Kim began attending Trinity College of Cambridge University. Soon after arriving he joined the Cambridge University Socialist Society (CUSS), although he did little more for the next two years than attend its meetings. Those two years were also devoted to reading history and doing little actual work.[70]

The Labour party's disastrous showing in the 1931 election led Philby "to thinking about possible alternatives to the Labour Party." He took a more active role in what had become a Communist-dominated CUSS, becoming its treasurer during the 1932–33 academic year, his last at Cambridge. Finally, in his last term at Trinity, in the early summer of 1933, Philby reached the conclusion that "my life must be devoted to Communism." That conclusion may have been helped along by a March 1933 visit to Berlin, where he witnessed Nazi persecution of the German Communist party (KPD) and the establishment of the Nazi police state.[71]

On his final day at Cambridge Philby went to visit Maurice Dobb, an economics don and avowed communist, to ask his advice on how to best serve the antifascist cause. Dobb, according to Philby, provided him with "an introduction to a communist group in Paris, a perfectly legal and open group." The group passed Philby on to an underground communist group in Vienna. Philby's introduction into illegal underground work began when he served as a courier between the outlawed Austrian Communist party and contacts in Hungary, Paris, and Prague. Philby's work in Vienna led to his recruitment by the NKVD.[72] According to Philby: "My work in Vienna must have caught the attention of the people who are now my colleagues in Moscow because almost immediately on my return to Britain I was approached by a man who asked me if I would like to join the Russian intelligence service."[73]

Philby was assigned the code name SYNOK and the task of penetrating the British Foreign Office or SIS. His first attempt quickly ended in failure, due to the doubts of his academic referees. Aware of his communist sympathies while at Cambridge referee Dennis Robertson, Philby's former Trinity director of studies in economics, wrote Philby that while he could praise his energy and his intelligence, he would feel obliged to also mention that "his sense of political injustice might well leave him unfit for administrative work."[74]

Philby then undertook a more indirect route after withdrawing his application. In the fall of 1934 he became a copy editor and writer with the London-based liberal monthly *Review of Reviews*, broke contact with his Cambridge communist friends, and made it apparent that his politics had changed.[75]

The second Cambridge undergraduate to join what the NKVD and its successors would call the "Magnificent Five" was Donald Maclean. Maclean's original plan was to teach English in the Soviet Union or stay at Cambridge for graduate work after obtaining his undergraduate degree. But after his June 1934 graduation with first-class honors in modern languages he began almost a year of preparation for the Foreign Office exams that would be held in August 1935. When Maclean, originally code-named SIROTA (ORPHAN) by the NKVD, entered the Foreign Office in October 1935 he became the first of the Magnificent Five to penetrate the British national security establishment.[76]

Recruited upon the rather lukewarm advice of Philby, who placed him last on his list of suggested recruits, was Donald Burgess. Burgess arrived at Cambridge in 1930, was a Marxist by 1932, and joined the Communist party in 1933. After a visit in the summer of 1934 to both Germany and Russia he was persuaded that the most effective strategy involved going underground and breaking all visible ties to the Communist party. Soon Burgess, who was given the code-name MÄDCHEN (LITTLE GIRL), was comparing Stalin unfavorably with fascist dictators, arguing that they were less reactionary.[77]

The most senior of the Magnificent Five was Anthony Blunt, who had entered Cambridge in fall 1926 with a scholarship in mathematics but switched to modern languages. By the time he graduated in 1930 he already had been elected to the Apostles, a Cambridge intellectual group founded in 1820, had become seriously interested in Marxism, and was a discreet homosexual. It was just as Blunt began postgraduate research that Burgess arrived at Cambridge. Blunt would introduce Burgess into the Apostles while Burgess would convince Blunt, in 1933, that he should actively work for the "Comintern."[78]

It is only recently that the question of the existence and identity of the fifth man has been settled. John Cairncross, who lived to see his role as the fifth man revealed, was born in 1913. At the age of seventeen he entered Glasgow University, where he studied French, German, political economy, and English for two years. By the time he arrived at Cambridge in October 1934 to study French and German he was an avowed communist.[79]

One of Cairncross's supervisors in French literature was Anthony Blunt, by now a faculty member, who introduced him to Donald Burgess. By 1936 Cairncross had broken all open contact with the Communist party and applied to the Foreign Office. In the summer of that year he graduated from Cambridge with first-class honors in modern languages and finished first in the Foreign Office entrance examinations. In the fall he became the third Soviet agent in the British Foreign Office, joining John King and Donald Maclean.[80]

At first Maclean may have had limited access to information of interest to the NKVD. He began in the League of Nations and Western Department, which focused on Dutch, Iberian, Swiss, and League affairs and had easy access to a very limited range of Foreign Office material. But he was able to pass on the complete minutes of the Committee of Imperial Defence meeting on December 20, 1936, which was attended by Prime Minister Stanley Baldwin. That meeting had focused on radio broadcasting during wartime, measures for defending government buildings against air attack, ammunition procurement, fuel supplies, and tanks.[81]

Maclean also passed on information concerning British codebreaking activities. In addition to informing the NKVD that the GC&CS was reading Comintern message traffic, he also indicated that the "school" had obtained some success against American, French, and German diplomatic traffic.* In March 1938 he was recommended by the Foreign Office personnel department to the British ambassador in France as third secretary in the Paris embassy as well as being cited as a future permanent undersecretary.[82]

John Cairncross also had initial problems after entering the Foreign Office in the fall of 1936. Cairncross spent two years moving from one department to another—the American, League of Nations, Western, and Central—without establishing himself. After his first year his controller suggested that he consider transferring to the Treasury, which the NVKD had not penetrated. In October 1938, in the person of Cairncross, it did.[83]

Burgess also had his difficulties. Finally, in late 1936 he began a £500-a-year job as a producer in the BBC Talks Department and began looking for men with past or present intelligence connections.[84]

Nineteen thirty-six was also the year that Philby took his first step toward penetrating SIS. It was in Berlin in July that he heard that the Spanish Civil War had erupted. The war led to his first major intelligence mission, "to get first-hand information on all aspects of the fascist war effort." Arriving in Spain in February 1937 as a free-lance journalist, by May he had become one of two official correspondents for *The Times* in Nationalist Spain. His job gave him comprehensive knowledge about the extent of German and Italian military assistance to Franco's forces—number of aircraft, type, caliber of artillery, number of rounds fired, composition of attacking infantry force—which he then passed on to NKVD officers during meetings across the French border. But one operation he was assigned to participate in—the assassination of Francisco Franco—was never carried out, being abandoned in the summer of 1937 before Philby had ingratiated himself into Franco's inner circle.[85]

Although the United States represented a lower priority for Soviet intelligence in the 1930s, it was not ignored. By the mid-1930s there were varying levels of contact between several influential underground cells of the CPUSA (Communist Party of the United States of America) and Comintern and Soviet intelligence officers. The main connection between the underground CPUSA apparatus and Soviet military intelligence was Whittaker Chambers, a communist journalist who, in 1932, was ordered to break overt contact with the party.[86]

In 1934 Chambers began serving as a courier between the Comintern officer who guided the CPUSA and an underground cell in Washington founded by a Department of Agriculture official. The cell included officials not only from Agriculture, but from the State Department, National Recovery Administration, National Labor Relations Board, and Office of

* As noted previously, successes against German and French traffic were sporadic.

Price Administration. Included in the group was Alger Hiss, then of the Department of Agriculture.[87]*

The next year Chambers instructed Hiss to found a parallel cell. New agents who joined Chambers's network in the 1935–36 period included Harry Dexter White from the Treasury Department, George Silverman (a government statistician later employed by the Pentagon), and the Oxford-educated economist Julian Wadleigh, who transferred in 1936 from the Department of Agriculture to the Trade Agreements Division of the State Department and supplied the Soviets with hundreds of documents from his State Department position.[88]

But Hiss continued to be the star. In fall 1936 he became assistant to Francis B. Sayre, assistant secretary of state, which gave him access to a wide range of telegrams from diplomats and military attachés. By early 1937 he was delivering documents to Chambers every week or ten days. Possibly the most significant were those that concerned Japanese policy during the Sino-Japanese War. A March 2, 1937, cable reported the view of unidentified "Japanese army chiefs . . . that they will be able to wage a successful war against Russia while holding the Chinese in check on their flank with little difficulty."[89]

In April 1938, nine months after he had been ordered to Moscow, Chambers broke off all contact with the Soviets. After spending most of the remainder of the year hiding, he began to tell his story. But it took many years before anyone in Washington listened.

* In 1992 it was reported that Hiss had been cleared of any involvement of espionage by General Dmitri A. Volkogonov, an adviser to President Boris Yeltsin. Volkogonov's statement was allegedly made on the basis of research in Soviet intelligence archives, although apparently not in the GRU military intelligence archives where it would be expected any records on Hiss would be held, given that Chambers was run by that agency. In any case, it soon became apparent that his research was far from thorough. Volkogonov subsequently stated that he was "not properly understood."

The evidence of Hiss's guilt presented in Allen Weinstein, *Perjury: The Hiss–Chambers Case* (New York: Alfred A. Knopf, 1978), remains persuasive. Reports and commentary on the 1992 statements by General Volkogonov include David Margolick, "After 40 Years, a Postscript on Hiss: Russian Official Calls Him Innocent," *New York Times*, October 29, 1992, p. B14; Jeffrey A. Frank, "Stalin Biographer Offers Latest Twist in Hiss Case," *Washington Post*, October 31, 1992, p. A3; Sam Tanenhaus, "The Hiss Case Isn't Over Yet," *New York Times*, October 31, 1992, p. 21; Arnold Beichman, "Verdict Begs Appeal to Yeltsin," *Washington Times*, November 2, 1992, pp. E1, E4; Allen Weinstein, "Reopening a Cold War Mystery," *Washington Post*, November 4, 1992, p. A19; "He Was Never a Soviet Spy," *Newsweek*, November 9, 1992, p. 31; Eric Breindel, "Dimitri's Dubious Research," *Washington Times*, November 15, 1992, p. B4; John Lowenthal, "A Cold War Case Closed," *Washington Post*, November 21, 1992, p. A23; Michael Wines, "Hiss Case's Bogeymen Are Still Not at Rest," *New York Times*, December 13, 1992, p. E6; Serge Schmemann, "Russian General Retreats on Hiss," *New York Times*, December 17, 1992, p. A17; Arnold Beichman, "Changing Hiss-tory Again," *Washington Times*, December 21, 1992, pp. E1, E4. Recent articles offering new information and suggesting Hiss' guilt include Sam Tanenhaus, "Hiss:Guilty as Charged," *Commentary*, April 1993, pp. 32–37; Maria Schmidt, "The Hiss Dossier," *New Republic*, November 8, 1993. pp. 17–20.

Espionage from Above

While communications and human intelligence provided the bulk of intelligence during the 1930s, the development of aerial reconnaissance continued in Britain, France, and Germany. In Germany the driving force was Theodor Rowehl, who began his reconnaissance career in World War I. In 1930 Rowehl was an Abwehr-employed civilian with one chartered plane, a single-engined Junkers W.34 that had set a world altitude record of approximately 41,800 feet in May 1929. With the approval of Abwehr chief Patzig, Rowehl flew reconnaissance missions directed at Poland. On many missions Rowehl stayed inside German territory, flying along the border and taking oblique photographs of fortifications. On others he overflew Polish territory. Those overflights ended, temporarily, in 1934 after Hitler signed a nonaggression treaty with Poland which broke the string of French treaties with states surrounding Germany. Since the Rowehl flights jeopardized the treaty, they were halted.[90]

By that time Rowehl had rejoined the military, had a fleet of five airplanes, and had a group of expert pilots to fly them. He moved his unit, the Experimental Post for High-Altitude Flights, from Kiel to the Staaken airfield in western Berlin. From there Rowehl and his pilots flew, in 1934, their first missions over the Soviet Union. Their twin-engined planes flew over the Kronstadt naval base, over Leningrad, and over the industrial areas of Pskov and Minsk. At approximately the same time, the unit began to photograph the border fortifications being built by Germany's neighbors. To determine what the French were building Rowehl flew along the Rhine, producing oblique photographs that "looked down the throats of the guns in the concrete bunkers of the Maginot line." Over Czechoslovakia, he employed stereophotography to obtain revealing photographs of the deep-set fortifications.[91]

The pictures were distributed to a variety of consumers, including Luftwaffe chief Hermann Göring. And one day in 1936, Canaris took the flyer over to meet Göring. Soon Rowehl and his unit were transferred to the Luftwaffe, subordinated to the Fifth (Intelligence) Branch of the Luftwaffe General Staff, and renamed the Squadron for Special Purposes.[92]

The transfer proved beneficial, for Göring and the Luftwaffe had command of more extensive resources than Canaris and the Abwehr. Requests for high-quality personnel, aircraft, and equipment were quickly filled. The first basic aircraft the unit received from its new masters was an He-111, which could carry a four-man crew to a normal range of 2,000 miles and provide a stable platform for photography. The twelve-inch-square exposures produced by the airplane's cameras were surprisingly detailed.[93]

In the late 1930s the squadron conducted reconnaissance missions against Poland, France, Czechoslovakia, the Soviet Union, and Britain. The primary objective of the missions was the collection of intelligence concerning potential bomber targets. Strategic targets included arma-

ment factories and harbors, including London harbor, while tactical/
operational targets included border fortifications and interior road networks.[94]

If the target was to be a city or some other open area, the planes were
disguised as commercial aircraft, with civilian markings and crews in
mufti. The pilots pretended to be checking out new airline routes for
Deutsche Lufthansa. The phantom air routes they explored in 1938 and
1939 took them over the eastern and southern coast of England, the entire
continental coast of the English Channel and North Sea, and the Baltic
coast all the way into Leningrad. If the target was secret, the planes flew at
sufficiently high altitudes, up to 32,000 feet, to make themselves invisible to ground observers. People might be able to hear the faint drone of the
engines, but the planes were long gone before they could be located with
binoculars. With radar yet to be invented, the planes could be detected
only if they left condensation trails, in which case the mission was usually aborted.[95]

The flights over Czechoslovakia and Britain violated air treaties that
those nations had signed with Germany; neither nation protested. Most
probably they were never detected. If they had been, it is not clear there
would have been any means of establishing their German origin. In addition, it is not clear that the issue would have been raised for fear of
irritating Hitler. Even the loss of an He-111 over Russia, with which
Germany had no treaty, did not result in a diplomatic protest. Perhaps the
fact that the plane was disguised as a passenger plane gave the Soviets an
excuse to look the other way.[96]

The unit's product fed the air force's Main Photo Center, which produced a stream of glossy prints that went into Luftwaffe target folders,
and to the Abwehr's air section, possibly for the Abwehr's spies to provide
more data. The photographs also went to the German army: photographs
of the Czechoslovakian border were assembled into a photomap that the
German forces brought with them when they marched into the Sudetenland in the fall of 1938.[97]

While Germany's aerial spies overflew Britain and France, those two
nations were involved in a cooperative effort aimed at Germany. Their
cooperation was, in part, a result of French initiative. In 1936, the French
undertook, for the first time since 1929, air reconnaissance missions directed against Germany, photographing targets near the border with Germany. The results were made available to SIS.[98]

After 1937, the increasing difficulty of penetrating the "German target" with human agents heightened the value of aerial reconnaissance.
Prior to September 1938 it had been possible to rely on agents to provide
intelligence on the number of aircraft placed on the tarmac outside aircraft factories before being flown to their operational squadrons, permitting informed intelligence estimates of German military aircraft production.[99]

But an increased Nazi emphasis on security eliminated human agents as a steady source. Out of desperation Georges Ronin, of the French Deux-ième Bureau, obtained an old airplane and had it fitted with a large wooden camera. The plane was then flown up and down the Rhine by a civilian pilot, while the camera was operated by a portrait photographer from Paris.[100]

Ronin told Fred Winterbotham of the British SIS Air Section of his project and that it had managed to produce a few good photographs, allow-ing him to keep track of the fortifications on the German side of the river. He also asked Winterbotham whether the operation couldn't profitably be extended.[101]

SIS involvement in aerial reconnaissance would give Britain a means of conducting flights over German territory. The RAF had already, in 1936, flown peripheral reconnaissance missions against targets of the Italian Empire, relying on oblique photography. But such peripheral missions limited the number of targets that could be observed. Direct RAF over-flights of Italian, much less German territory, was something the Air Ministry felt was impossible for international political reasons. However, an intelligence organization operating through a cover organization was not so limited.[102]

At first there appeared to be technical questions concerning the fea-sibility of direct overflights. While camera systems had improved consid-erably since World War I, a nagging problem remained. At altitudes over 8,000 feet camera lenses would be fogged with condensation from the cold air. To fly at even 8,000 feet over Germany in a civilian airplane would be impossible because the Germans would soon discover what was going on. In wartime military reconnaissance at such a low altitude would be suici-dal: German antiaircraft guns and fighter planes would slaughter the pi-lots and the crews.[103]

Winterbotham and Ronin also came to the conclusion that if they could obtain a modern American executive plane with a cabin for four or five people they would at least be able to conduct some experiments and possibly take it into Germany under some commercial cover, perhaps with a hidden camera. In the meantime, they could try to raise the alti-tude at which they could take pictures.[104]

The plane chosen was a Lockheed 12A. Two were ordered, one for the SIS and one for the Deuxième Bureau. Sidney Cotton, an Australian pilot, was hired toward the end of 1938 to serve as pilot for the SIS plane and establish the Aeronautical Research and Sales Corporation to provide cover for the entire operation, which would be conducted from a French base.[105]

The first experiments with photography above 8,000 feet produced a surprise. Cameras were fitted to a special frame, one pointing directly down and another two pointed out to obtain maximum coverage. The developed film included perfectly clear photographs taken from altitudes up to almost 20,000 feet. It was soon discovered that with the engines running the warm air that flowed out of the heated cabin also flowed beneath the camera lenses. Winterbotham later recalled: "It was as simple as that. I find it almost impossible to describe my elation at this chance discovery."[106]

What the photographs did not contain, despite their clarity, was the fine detail required for military intelligence purposes. Winterbotham was able to obtain from the RAF Photographic Department several cameras and lenses. In addition, the RAF supplied a device for automatically timing use of the cameras in response to the plane's height and speed. The opening in the aircraft's belly for the camera was disguised as an emergency fuel release while a special cover, in the form of a spare fuel tank, was made for the cameras. The complete system produced exactly the results that Winterbotham and Ronin desired—absolutely clear detailed pictures taken from 20,000 feet. In addition, the cameras had produced overlapping images that could be used for stereo interpretation.[107]

An early spring 1939 test over the Mediterranean produced, Winterbotham wrote, excellent results:

> Flying almost unnoticed at 20,000 feet Cotton photographed every Italian naval base and air base on the North African coast and then did the same along the northern Mediterranean. Dockyards, harbours, aerodromes— everything was photographed in detail . . . when we got all the photographs back and had them printed . . . I was able to hand over complete sets to the directors of intelligence of all three services. . . . Requests came pouring in from the Admiralty, the War Office, and Air Ministry for photographs of aircraft factories, dockyards, anything we could get over Germany.[108]

By April 1939 Cotton had photographed not only the Mediterranean but large areas of Germany under the cover of commercial flights. At that point cooperation with the French concluded, with Cotton turning his plane over to the Deuxième Bureau and heading back to England. From Heston airfield he began flying a second Lockheed 12A, carrying extra fuel tanks that increased the range from 700 to 1,600 miles, and painted duck-egg green to lessen the chance of detection. The plane could photograph an 11-mile strip from 20,000 feet. Additional hidden cameras were fitted in the wings. During June, July, and August Cotton made several more flights over Germany, photographing units of the fleet for the first time. Flying over the Italian Empire he supplemented previous RAF oblique coverage of key points from Sicily to Rhodes and Italian East Africa with vertical overhead images.[109]

Certainly, the strangest mission occurred during the Frankfurt Air Show in late July. Cotton took the plane to the show to defuse any suspicion about its true role. The plane received a great deal of attention, particularly from General Albert Kesselring, chief of Berlin's Templehof Airport, who made it apparent that he would like to go for a ride. As they were flying over the Rhine Cotton turned the controls over to Kesselring while switching on the cameras—inasmuch as there were various airfields, ammunition dumps, factories, and fortifications close to the Rhine that Cotton thought might be worth photographing. When Kesselring questioned the meaning of the flashing green light, which indicated that photographs were being taken, Cotton told him that the flashing light indicated that fuel was running smoothly to the engines.[110]

II

The Second World War

7

Intelligence and the Onset of War

The intelligence collection operations of the 1930s were intended to provide the basis for an accurate assessment of other nations' political intentions and military capabilities. Another important function was to prevent an enemy from launching a successful surprise attack, one that would leave the victim staggered and susceptible to a knockout blow.

The events of the late 1930s and early 1940s—in central Europe, in the western Soviet Union, and at Pearl Harbor—might seem to suggest that the intelligence operations of several major powers failed, tragically, to accomplish their major peacetime goals. Yet the failures of policy and warning suffered by Great Britain, the Soviet Union, and the United States resulted from a variety of factors, many not under the control of those nations' intelligence establishments.

Intelligence and Appeasement

Of particular importance for Britain and France was intelligence on Hitler's intentions and his ability to achieve his objectives by force. In particular, intelligence before the German seizure of the Rhineland in 1936, leading up to the Munich confrontation in September 1938, and from the Munich agreement to the Nazi–Soviet pact of August 1939 could have played a crucial role in avoiding the cataclysm that Hitler unleashed in September 1939.

Hitler's willingness to brush aside the limitations imposed by the Versailles Treaty and take what he wanted by force was apparent before the end of 1935. On March 9 Reichsmarshall Hermann Göring announced the existence of the Luftwaffe, although an air force had been prohibited by the Versailles Treaty. One week later, Hitler announced further breaches of the treaty: the return of conscription and a "peacetime" army of thirty-six divisions and 500,000 men.[1]

On March 7, 1936, Hitler won an even bigger gamble. His army entered the Rhineland, reestablishing German control. If France had resisted and attacked, Hitler would have withdrawn the troops in humiliation. The resulting failure and loss of popularity might have led to the fall of the Nazi regime.[2]

The German army's entrance into the Rhineland did not, according to a former French intelligence chief, catch France by surprise. General Maurice Gauche, who commanded the Deuxième Bureau in 1935, claimed that his office believed from the beginning that "[w]ith *Mein Kampf* we were *at the very epicenter of Hitler's thought.*"[3]

Mein Kampf may have provided the Deuxième Bureau with the basis for concluding that Hitler would take the Rhineland, but not the specific time period. Britain also foresaw the possibility of Hitler's action in the Rhineland, but not the timing. In fact, Hitler made the final decision to proceed with the Rhineland invasion about two weeks before the action.[4]

The key intelligence question concerning the Rhineland invasion, however, was not the precise timing but the consequences of British and French resistance to Hitler's moves. The Deuxième Bureau estimated that Germany's twenty-nine divisions had a disabling weakness—a severe shortage of trained officers—and that French military action would be successful. Despite such intelligence the French leadership failed to act.[5]

Reacquiring the Rhineland did not satisfy Hitler. In the two years between the Nazi seizure and the Munich agreement, which included the *Anschluss* with Austria, Britain and France sought, without success, to limit Hitler's ambitions. Their intelligence services had two main tasks: to determine the threat from German rearmament and to provide advance warning of any German moves.

Military and air intelligence estimates during the first five years of Hitler's rule followed a similar pattern: an initial underestimation of German military potential, a reversal in autumn 1936, and a subsequent overestimation of the immediate threat. Britain's Military Intelligence Directorate (MID) and Industrial Intelligence Centre (IIC) were misled by the relatively slow start to the German rearmament program. In July 1935 they jointly estimated that the Wehrmacht would grow at a maximum of 8 or 9 divisions a year, reaching a peak of 90 to 100 divisions in 1943. Until September 1936 MID was not particularly concerned about the revival of the German army, viewing it as a moderating influence on Nazi extremists. MID also believed Hitler's declaration that the army would not be expanded beyond a peacetime strength of 36 divisions, a size they considered reasonable.[6]

On May 30, 1938, Hitler approved plans for Operation GREEN, the invasion of Czechoslovakia, giving the Wehrmacht until October to complete the necessary preparations. However, SIS received misleading reports from at least two often valuable human sources, Paul Thümmel and Malcolm Christie, which suggested an imminent attack. On the basis of such reports Britain warned Hitler against any invasion, while Czechoslovakia mobilized 170,000 men. When no invasion materialized, SIS's "timely" intelligence was given credit by British leaders for helping prevent German action and SIS chief Admiral Hugh Sinclair moved closer to the center of policymaking.[7]

It was apparent, though, that Hitler's desire to establish a greater Reich required absorption of at least portions of Czechoslovakia. In July 1938 SIS again received warning of Operation GREEN, possibly from the Czechs. Additional warnings from the private intelligence network of Foreign Office Permanent Under-Secretary Sir Robert Vansittart followed later in the month. Once again the reports were premature. Although Operation GREEN was not scheduled to begin until October 1, the reports pointed to a German attack any time after the end of August. In early August two independent, and probably accurate reports arrived concerning a meeting at Berchtesgaden at which Hitler reaffirmed his decision to attack once the harvest was in, irrespective of any risks or obstacles.[8]

Fear of a German attack on Czechoslovakia was heightened on August 17, when the SIS station chief in Vienna, Captain Thomas Kendrick, was arrested while driving in the vicinity of German troops on maneuvers. Further arrests of individuals accused of spying on German troop movements followed. The arrests seemed to be aimed at gaining a propaganda victory or preventing the collection of intelligence about Operation GREEN.[9]

On September 11 Hitler demanded "self-determination" for the Sudetenland and an "end to slavery" at a Nuremberg rally. The next day SIS reported, incorrectly, that all German missions had been informed that Operation GREEN would begin on the 25th. The Foreign Office concluded an attack might come any time between September 18 and 29.[10]

Prime Minister Neville Chamberlain felt it was urgent to dissuade Hitler from launching an invasion, fearing that if he waited past mid-September, it would be too late. On September 15 he climbed aboard an airplane for the first time in his life to make the flight to Munich in order to consult with Hitler at his mountain retreat.[11]

Poor intelligence undoubtedly influenced Chamberlain's urgency and his actions after he arrived. In early August MID had circulated a study of the German army, which concluded that while Germany's prospects in a war against Britain were poor, she could launch "at will a sudden and overwhelming onslaught on Czechoslovakia without fear of effective interference from the West during this operation." In late August the paper was revised to eliminate consideration of Germany's prospects in a long-term European war. The report ignored the IIC's conclusion that Germany had not accumulated adequate inventories of raw materials to fight a European war. Instead, it concluded that Germany could launch a massive attack on Czechoslovakia and "view with growing equanimity the outcome of an attack delivered against her from the West."[12]

All the key British officials—Chamberlain, Foreign Secretary Viscount

Halifax, the chiefs of staff, and Sinclair—believed that war must be avoided at any cost. Sinclair and SIS insisted that giving up the Sudetenland would actually strengthen Czechoslovak security.[13]

The actual hard intelligence available to SIS did not support a policy of appeasement. The War Office's intelligence indicated that the German army possessed only a limited numerical advantage over the Czechs and was actually badly outnumbered on the border with France.[14]

Such intelligence was subsequently confirmed when General Alfred Jodl, who had been chief of the Wehrmacht Operations Staff, testified during the Nuremberg trials that "[w]ar in 1938 at the time of Munich was out of the question because there were only five fighting divisions and seven reserve divisions on the western fortifications which were nothing but a large construction site to hold out against one hundred French divisions."[15]

The weakness of German forces was not reflected in a key SIS analysis, prepared in response to a request by Chamberlain for a paper on what Britain should or could do short of war to restrain Hitler. The Most Secret "What Should We Do?" was presented to the prime minister on September 18, just eleven days prior to the culmination of the Munich crisis.[16]

The unsigned paper was almost certainly written by Sinclair, deputy chief Stewart Menzies, the head of the SIS political section, and perhaps the section head's deputy. It informed Chamberlain that, in the estimation of the SIS, Hitler was determined to achieve German supremacy in central and southeastern Europe, Belgium, Holland, the Baltic states, and Scandinavia, while promoting the dissolution of the Soviet Union. In addition, the Germans expected to recover their overseas colonies.[17]

To attain such objectives Germany was creating "the strongest possible Armed Forces, sufficient to overcome any combination of Powers and emerge victoriously in any conflagration." Sinclair and his co-authors recommended that in order to gain the time needed to rebuild British military strength, part of Czechoslovakia should be sacrificed to Germany, leaving only "a State which would be literally Czechoslovak—a compact, homogeneous, neutralized State under international guarantee." The Czechs, according to the paper, should be pressured to accept the "inevitable" surrender of the Sudetenland. To ensure such acceptance they should be made to "realise unequivocally that they stand alone if they refuse such a solution." And if it was necessary to sacrifice all of Czechoslovakia to buy time, that was also acceptable to the authors.[18]

Concerning Germany's grievances and claims in general, the SIS memo observed:

> We should not wait until these become, in regular sequence, critical. International steps of some of sort should be taken, without undue delay, to see *what really legitimate* grievances Germany has and what surgical operations are necessary to rectify them. . . . If there are genuine cases for self-determination they should be established and remedied. . . . It may be

argued that this would be giving in to Germany, strengthening Hitler's position and encouraging him to go to extremes. Better, however, that realities be faced and that wrongs, if they do exist, be righted, than leave it to Hitler to do the righting in his own way and time—particularly if, concurrently, we and the French unremittingly build up our strength and lessen Germany's potentialities for making trouble.[19]

SIS did not believe, however, that such a policy would ensure peace. Hitler, it realized, could not be depended on to keep his promises. Nor would Germany be satisfied even if all "legitimate" German grievances were remedied. In addition, SIS believed that British security required comprehensive and rapid rearmament. While, in SIS's view, Britain could not "really trust any foreign country," SIS suggested "a permanent defensive alliance with France in conjunction with pressure on the French to rearm as rapidly as possible."[20]

However, in his meeting with Hitler on September 29 Chamberlain went beyond Sinclair's recommendation by permitting the immediate German occupation of the Sudetenland. In return he received Hitler's worthless assurances in a document that guaranteed, as Chamberlain told British citizens upon his return to London, "peace in our time."[21]

Chamberlain's concession, while going beyond Sinclair's recommendation, was certainly motivated in part by the SIS paper. In addition, there was a lack of intelligence on overall German air capabilities, as opposed to details about the numbers of specific aircraft and their capabilities. The cabinet was provided no detailed estimate of the German capability to use air power against British targets. Well aware that the Royal Air Force was less than combat-ready and air raid defenses were minimal, they imagined the worst. Accurate intelligence would have reported the same conclusion as reached by the German air staff—that a knockout blow against Britain was impossible—although there is no guarantee that leaders such as Chamberlain would have accepted the truth in place of their image of an all-powerful Luftwaffe.[22]

Britain's refusal to fight was matched by a French reluctance, which was reinforced by Deuxième Bureau estimates. Two days before the Munich agreement the Deuxieme Bureau's chief, General Gauche, advised the General Staff that Germany could mobilize 120 divisions and was prepared for "general war." The chief of the General Staff, General Maurice Gamelin, used the figures to rationalize France's refusal to come to Czechoslovakia's defense.[23]

The Pact

The parts of Czechoslovakia that Britain and France did not turn over to Hitler in 1938 were occupied by German forces on March 15, 1939. Hitler's actions were consistent with the darkening view of SIS in the months following Munich. On March 11 SIS predicted an invasion in three days. The Deuxième Bureau fared less well. On March 6 the department's prime secret source, code-named MAD, reported that Hitler would seize Prague on the 15th. But a March 9 report to the General Staff did not mention MAD's information and concluded that no threat was imminent.[24]

The invasion of Czechoslovakia produced a British guarantee to Poland. But it was not a guarantee that Hitler would take seriously, given British performance up to that point. There was a strategy that could have convinced Hitler that further aggression would be dangerous—an alliance among Britain, France, and the Soviet Union, which would confront the Nazi dictator with the prospect of a two-front war.

The British were not immediately convinced of the need or wisdom for such an alliance. The delay in opening negotiations with the Soviets, the inability of the British and French delegations to discuss the military issues the Soviets considered paramount, and Poland's unwillingness to permit Soviet troops to cross its borders to confront Nazi troops doomed any chance the negotiations may have had.

Thus on August 23, 1939, German Foreign Minister Joachim von Ribbentrop and Soviet Foreign Minister Vyacheslav Molotov signed the Nazi–Soviet Non-Aggression Pact. The signing represented a major disaster for British foreign policy and ultimately doomed the world to a second world war.[25]

The signing occurred after years of intermittent rumors, which had resumed after the opening of German–Soviet trade talks in January 1939. In May 1939, after the dismissal of the pro-Western foreign minister, Maxim Litvinov, rumors flooded in. One message that reached the Foreign Office was from a credible source and stated that the "German generals" received a new offer from the Soviet Union which might dramatically change the situation. The French ambassador in Berlin told British ambasssador Sir Neville Henderson that several sources had indicated that Hitler and Stalin had agreed to a nonaggression pact.[26]

The next month information arrived from new and more reliable sources. On June 9 the French Foreign Office passed on information from a previously reliable source who claimed that a major German effort was being made to produce an agreement with the Soviet Union and the effort was expected to succeed. Two days later, the League of Nations High Commissioner in Danzig, a trusted Foreign Office confidant, reported that the Germans were working to guarantee Soviet neutrality in case of war.[27]

On June 16 a German Foreign Ministry source reported that there was definitely contact between the Germans and Soviets. The Soviets were simply listening to German proposals, but the warm reception given to the Germans seemed to indicate that they were encouraged to continue.[28]

From mid-June on Group Captain Christie was sending Under-Secretary Vansittart regular reports on German preparations for war with Poland and alliance with the Soviets. On June 15 the anti-Nazi German diplomats Erich and Theodor Kordt delivered the same message to Vansittart in London. But Vansittart's sources were considered suspect by officials such as Permanent Under-Secretary of the Foreign Office Sir Alexander Cadogan.[29]

In addition, the Military Intelligence Directorate pointed to conflicting evidence, much of which came from SIS. Thus MID noted that

> [a]t least one most secret report indicat[ed] that the Germans held the view that the elimination of Stalin was essential for their plans. Another most secret report from a reliable source on the Russian side stated that Stalin was very bitter on account of German intrigues in the Ukraine and that, so long as he remained, no question of a rapprochement was possible. A further report . . . stated that although certain sections of influential Soviet opinion might be against active cooperation with the Western Powers, yet the feeling against Germany was still very bitter.[30]

At the beginning of July reports indicating a possible German–Soviet rapprochement decreased while some key analysts expressed their skepticism. Foreign Office Northern Department head Lawrence Collier indicated that he refused to believe that a rapprochement was possible as long as Hitler and Stalin remained in power.[31]

Collier's view was supported by a July 4 report by MID which noted that prior to Hitler's ascension to power relations between Germany and the Soviet Union were "comparatively close," with active contact between the two general staffs. However, after 1933, according to the report, the German attitude became abusive and most qualified observers concluded that Hitler was "violently anti-Soviet." The report noted that during the first three months of the year there had been several rumors of an impending rapprochement. However, the report concluded "There seems to be no real circumstantial evidence of negotiations being in progress although a commercial agreement was likely, but the danger of such a rapprochement cannot be discounted and it is still wise to watch the situation very carefully."[32]

Had definitive intelligence been available to the British cabinet, they may have acted far more forcefully to obtain an agreement with the Soviets and block a Nazi–Soviet pact. Several factors contributed to the failure of British intelligence to anticipate the signing of the Nazi–Soviet pact. Information reaching Britain was often confused and incorrect in key areas. Further, the frequency of reports reflected the magnitude of the debate within Germany, which dropped dramatically in mid-June and did not reappear to any meaningful degree between July 30 and August 17, the most active period. Once Hitler made the decision to seriously examine the possibility of a pact with the Soviets, dissenting officials ceased to discuss the subject while others heard no more about it.[33]

On at least one occasion key intelligence was late. In May Hans "Johnnie" von Herwarth, the second secretary of the German embassy in Moscow, informed American diplomat Charles E. "Chip" Bohlen of the seriousness of the Nazi–Soviet talks. Bohlen informed his ambassador, who was reluctant to pass the information on to his British and French counterparts in Moscow for fear of compromising Herwarth. By the time the information was passed on to the State Department in Washington, to the British and French ambassadors there, and on to London and Paris, it was August 18—by which time the military talks among Britain, France, and the Soviet Union had adjourned.[34]

It was also assumed that the ideologies of the Hitler and Stalin regimes made them unrelenting enemies for whom even a short-term alliance was impossible. But a fourth reason also existed for the failure: the GC&CS's inability to read the Soviet diplomatic cipher. Starting in 1927, the GC&CS had suffered severe cuts in expenditure, which were compounded after 1931.[35]

The failure raised concern in Parliament over the capability of the intelligence services. On August 25, R. A. Butler, the Foreign Office representative to Parliament, reported to Cadogan that "[i]n the Commons last night everyone was asking me what our intelligence was up to." A similar question was presented to the Foreign Office by numerous government departments. Lawrence Collier, who had dismissed the possibility of such a pact, presented a paper on "German–Soviet Intrigue," in which he complained that "[i]n general, we find ourselves, when attempting to assess the value of these secret reports, somewhat in the position of the Captain of the Forty Thieves when, having put a chalk mark on Ali Baba's door, he found that Morgiana had put similar marks on all the doors in the street and had no indication to show which mark was the true one."[36]

Hugh Sinclair may have been partly responsible for the failure of the Foreign Office to properly sift through the reports. Although Butler told Cadogan on September 5 that he understood that "the outline terms" of the Nazi–Soviet pact "were known to our intelligence, and reached this office," Sinclair apparently did not give sufficient emphasis to the report when he presented it to the Foreign Office.[37]

Even if more definitive and timely intelligence had been presented to senior officials, it is not clear that it would have had an impact. The preconceptions of national leaders might have again overriden intelligence. At one point that summer Chamberlain joined his foreign secretary in rejecting the intelligence presented to them on a possible Nazi–Soviet alliance, observing that "I cannot bring myself to believe that a real alliance between Russia and Germany is possible."[38]

French intelligence also had its problems, at least initially. A May 10 Deuxième Bureau assessment, written after a May 7 warning from the French embassy in Berlin, rejected the notion that Litvinov's removal as foreign minister indicated Stalin's intention to conclude an agreement with Hitler. According to the assessment, "such a reversal of Soviet policy [was] difficult to reconcile" with a new Soviet–Turkish accord.[39]

However, two weeks later, after a second warning, views had changed. By late June the Deuxième Bureau had concluded that "German diplomacy is actively engaged in sabotaging the Moscow negotiations and even in preparing a German–Soviet entente which could be very rapidly negotiated."[40]

Barbarossa

Three months to the day after the signing of the Nazi–Soviet pact Hitler told a select group of senior military officers that he would turn on his Soviet ally at the first opportunity after the conquest of western Europe. It was not long before that conquest was complete. On June 17, 1940, France sued for peace. On June 22, 1941, 3 million German troops poured across more than 1,000 miles of the Soviet frontier, from the Arctic Circle to the Black Sea.[41]

Operation BARBAROSSA surprised the Soviet political and military leadership. Unprepared, the Soviets met a string of defeats that imperiled the survival of the regime and could have resulted in Hitler gaining control over Soviet weapons and resources.

That Hitler achieved such surprise was not due to an absence of information available to the Soviets. During the period between the signing of the Nazi–Soviet pact and the beginning of BARBAROSSA the Soviet leadership, most particularly Stalin, received a number of intelligence reports, signals, and warnings that should have led them to believe that a Nazi attack was coming.*

Among the signals available to Soviet authorities was the pronounced redeployment of German troops eastward starting in August 1940. Between the end of August and the middle of December the number of Wehrmacht divisions facing Russia grew from 5 to 34. By the end of February the number of divisions had grown to approximately 70. It increased to 87 in May, decreased to 80 by June 1, but then began a steady increase that resulted in 123 German divisions facing the Soviet Union on June 21. These movements were detected by the Soviet intelligence services, as well as by the British, Polish, and Japanese intelligence organizations.[42]

Another signal was extensive aerial reconnaissance missions over Soviet territory. While Hitler had vetoed a request by the army's High Command in September 1940 to begin aerial reconnaisance flights, for fear of disclosing his intentions so early, a month later a secret order from Hitler to Rowehl launched the aerial spy campaign. Initially the planes were restricted in the extent of their overflights—going as far as Lake Ilmen, Minsk, Kiev, and the north coast of the Black Sea. Two weeks before the beginning of BARBAROSSA deep penetration missions began.[43]

---

* For purposes of this section the terms intelligence, signals, and warnings refer to distinct types of information. *Intelligence* refers to information acquired about the plans or intentions of the adversary. *Signals* refers to activities undertaken by an adversary—such as increasing reconnaissance activities, the movement of troops, withdrawing personnel at a foreign embassy, or burning code material—that would indicate an attack is about to take place. *Warnings* refer to judgments passed on by third countries that an attack is to take place.

Even before those missions began the Soviets protested. On April 22, 1941, they charged that there had been no fewer than 80 flights in the period between March 27 and April 18. There could be no doubt that these were spy flights. When one plane made an emergency landing near Rovno in the Ukraine, it was discovered to be carrying topographic maps of sensitive areas of the Soviet Union along with cameras to photograph these areas. The Soviet protest had no effect and another 180 or so spy flights took place before the end of May, allowing the Luftwaffe to complete its survey of every airfield and military base in the western Soviet Union.[44]

The Germans were also busy spying on the ground, probing Soviet border defenses and trying to assess the state of affairs inside the country. In September 1940 Admiral Canaris had been instructed to expand Abwehr coverage of the Soviet Union. Between January and June 1941 there was a steady increase in the number of German agents detected, with the April–June 1941 number being twenty-five to thirty-five times the number for the April–June 1940 period.[45]

A very traditional signal was available to Stalin on June 11. Two days earlier the German embassy in Moscow received instructions from Berlin to secure its secret documents and authorizing the "inconspicuous departure of women and children." On the 11th the NKGB* reported the order to Stalin and reported that the embassy had begun burning documents. Shortly thereafter the evacuation began.[46]

Warnings came from a variety of nations, including the United States and Great Britain. In August 1940 the United States began receiving detailed intelligence on German plans to attack the Soviet Union. When the cumulative reports reached Secretary of State Cordell Hull in late February 1941 he realized the implications and took the matter to President Roosevelt, who agreed that the Soviets should be informed. On March 1 Konstantin Umansky, the Soviet ambassador to Washington, received a summary of the intelligence.[47]

In April Under Secretary of State Sumner Welles again provided Umansky with the product of U.S. intelligence operations—decrypts of Japanese diplomatic communications, including a March 19 telegram from Moscow that reported a dramatic change in Soviet–German relations and two telegrams from Berlin which outlined Germany's "preparations for war with Russia." In addition, he supplied a March 22 Army Signal Intelligence Service memorandum which predicted, based on the decrypts of Japanese traffic, "a German attack on the U.S.S.R. within two months."[48]

Following up on earlier warnings, on June 10, 1941, Permanent Under-Secretary Sir Alexander Cadogan informed Ambassador Ivan Maisky of recent German redeployments of forces eastward, providing the specific dates and places of movement of one division after another. After the

*In February 1941 the GUGB of the NKVD became the People's Commissariat of State Security (NKGB). After the German invasion it once again became the GUGB. In 1943 it became the NKGB again.

briefing Maisky quickly returned to his embassy to transmit the information to Moscow.[49]

On June 13 Foreign Secretary Anthony Eden summoned Maisky and told him that

> in the past forty-eight hours the information reaching us had become more significant. The troop concentrations might be for the purpose of a war of nerves, or they might be for the purpose of an attack on Russia . . . but we were bound to consider in the light of this very formidable build-up, that conflict between Germany and Russia was possible.[50]

Aside from signals and warnings the Soviets benefited from intelligence—in the form of documents, defectors, or reports from some of their top officers and agents. Seven days after Hitler signed the directive authorizing BARBAROSSA an accurate summary of that document was contained in an anonymous letter to the Soviet military attaché in Berlin.[51]

Some time after the German takeover of Czechoslovakia the vice-president of the Skoda Works offered his services to Soviet military intelligence. In April 1941 he reported, based on contacts with senior German officers in Czechoslovakia, the Wehrmacht's massive redeployment toward the Soviet border and that his organization had been ordered to cease delivering arms to the Soviet Union because war had been scheduled for the second half of June.[52]

The most important intelligence concerning German intentions and troop deployments were those provided by Richard Sorge and Soviet networks within the Reich. On May 2 Sorge reported from Tokyo that "Hitler is fully determined to make war upon and destroy the USSR in order to acquire the European area of the USSR as a raw materials and grain base. . . . The decision about hostilities will be taken by Hitler in May."[53]

On May 19, following up two earlier messages which had predicted a German attack at the end of May, Sorge reported: "Nine armies consisting of 150 divisions will be concentrated against the U.S.S.R." He also prepared a message predicting an attack on June 20, although the message may have never reached Moscow.[54]

According to a KGB-approved account, the most important of the last warnings of a Nazi attack were received in Moscow on June 16, 1941, from "two of our intelligence groups in Berlin." These groups, probably those of Arvid Harnack of the Ministry of Economics and Lieutenant Harro Schulze-Boysen of the Air Force Ministry,* reported that "[a]ll Germany's military measures preparatory to an armed attack on the Soviet Union have been fully completed and the blow may be expected at any time."[55]

A last-minute warning was provided by a senior intelligence officer,

---

* See Chapter 8 for details on these groups.

Leopold Trepper, on June 21. He had learned, during a series of drinking bouts with senior SS officers in France about to leave for Poland, that Hitler would strike in June. Early on the 21st, in Paris, he learned that the Wehrmacht would attack that night. Without access to a radio transmitter he was forced to pass his information through the Soviet embassy in Vichy. When he arrived in Vichy that evening Trepper told the military attaché, Major-General I. A. Susloparov, "Here is a message of vital importance, for immediate transmission!" But Susloparov was not convinced, and only at Trepper's insistence did he authorize the message to be sent.[56]

But all the signals, warnings, and intelligence from the Soviet Union's top intelligence officers was to no avail—for a variety of reasons. The Soviets received substantially more signals, warnings, and intelligence reports than those just mentioned. Some were not credible, casting doubt on others. Signals or warnings, particularly warnings in which German officers disclosed or hinted at imminent war, could easily be interpreted as a part of a ploy to extract further concessions from the Soviets.

The Germans also made a significant effort to deceive the Soviets. In 1940 Hitler initiated two major deception themes. The first explained the buildup of German forces in the east as part of preparation for the invasion of England, Operation SEA LION. Movement of the forces to the east was claimed to be for training purposes and to keep them out of range of British bombers and reconnaissance aircraft. Later that year, in September, Hitler instructed the Abwehr to portray eastward troop movements as a contingency against hostile Soviet actions. Closer to the date of the invasion, shortly before May 17, 1941, the Reich Foreign Office trumpeted the message that German actions would be determined by Soviet behavior. The same message was propagated after May 25 by the OKH (Oberkommando des Heeres, German High Command).[57]

An additional factor was the chief of military intelligence, General Filipp Ivanovich Golikov. According to the then chief of staff, Marshal Georgi K. Zhukov, Golikov sent his reports, which Trepper, Sorge, and other key sources contributed to, exclusively to Stalin. Not even Zhukov or the Commissar for Defense received the reports.[58]

Unfortunately for millions of Soviet troops and citizens, Stalin and Golikov were committed to the view that war with Germany was still several years away and reports to the contrary were being engineered by the devious British to involve the Soviets in a war with Hitler that would force Germany to fight a two-front war. A March 21, 1941, report from Golikov to Stalin discussed indications of German plans for a surprise attack but concluded that such an attack was unlikely until the war with Britain had been resolved. In the report Golikov echoed Stalin's line, asserting: "Rumors and documents to the effect that war against the U.S.S.R. is inevitable this spring should be regarded as misinformation coming from the English or perhaps even the German intelligence service."[59]

But it was Stalin who was the key. He selected Golikov as RU chief because he was a reliable Stalinist who shared Stalin's belief in a British plot to start a German–Soviet war. Stalin consistently rejected raw intelligence from his best intelligence officers that suggested Hitler might be planning to attack. This may have partly been due to Soviet access, through John Cairncross, to British intelligence estimates, which until mid-June 1941 did not support the warnings he received from the Churchill government.[60]

But a bigger factor in Stalin's refusal to even consider the possible validity of dramatic signals and reports from trusted sources was his unwillingness to question his own judgment. The RU resident in Prague, based on intelligence from the vice-president of the Skoda Works, transmitted a report on April 17, 1941, warning of a German attack in the second half of June and noting the reliability of the source. Stalin returned the report with his commentary: "English provocation. Investigate! Stalin."[61]

Sorge's May 19 report led Stalin to refer to his star agent in Japan as "a shit who has set himself up with some small factories and brothels in Japan." The June 16 reports from Harnack and Schulze-Boysen brought the response that "there are no Germans who can be trusted, except for Wilhelm Pieck [a member of the German Communist party living in Moscow]."[62]

Trepper's final report also was rejected by Stalin, although he was uncharacteristically polite. When told of the report Stalin observed: "As a rule, OTTO [Trepper's code name] sends us worthwhile material that does credit to his political judgement. How could he fail to detect at once that this was merely a piece of British provocation?"[63]

Pearl Harbor

Less than six months after Hitler's devastating strike into the Soviet Union, his Japanese allies stunned U.S. forces with their December 7 surprise attack at Pearl Harbor. The attack, based on a plan completed in May 1941, implemented a November 5 decision to go to war with the United States, Britain, and Holland barring an unlikely breakthrough in negotiations with the United States over Japanese military actions in Asia and the resulting U.S.–British–Dutch embargo.[64]

On November 26, 1941, a Japanese task force of thirty-three ships rendezvoused in the Kurile Islands and headed out across the North Pacific. Before dawn on December 7 the task force, with a nucleus of six aircraft carriers, reached 220 miles north of Oahu. From that point the task force launched, in two successive waves, 350 aircraft—40 torpedo bombers, 78 fighter aircraft, 103 high-level bombers, and 129 dive bombers.[65]

By the time the raid was over 18 warships had been sunk, capsized, or damaged in varying degrees—8 battleships, 3 light cruisers, 3 destroyers, and 4 auxiliary craft. In addition, 190 Army and Navy airplanes were destroyed or damaged beyond repair. Most tragically, 2,403 Army, Navy, Marine and civilian personnel were killed, missing, or mortally wounded. Another 1,178 were wounded but survived.[66]

As a result, Pearl Harbor has universally been perceived as the greatest strategic intelligence failure in United States history.* While the Military Intelligence Division, Office of Naval Intelligence (ONI), and many leaders were aware of the possibility that Pearl Harbor (or other U.S. naval bases) could become a target in the event of war, no intelligence estimate predicted that Japan's response to the deepening crisis of November and December 1941 would be a strike at the headquarters of the U.S. Pacific Fleet.

Expectations about the *targets* of a Japanese strike remained much the same in late November and early December as they had been earlier in the year. An Office of Naval Intelligence estimate of July 2, 1941, "Possibility of Early Aggressive Action by Japan," observed that "if any sudden aggressive action at all is planned, such action would be in the direction of further minor action against the South China coast or possibly directed towards seizure of additional bases in French Indo-China."[67]

On November 27, three weeks after the Japanese decision to attack Pearl Harbor and a day after Japanese warships had rendezvoused, the Chief of Naval Operations informed the Commander-in-Chief of the Pacific Fleet, Admiral Husband E. Kimmel, that

> [n]egotiations with Japan looking toward the stabilization of conditions in the Pacific have ceased and an aggressive move by Japan is expected within the next few days. The number and equipment of Japanese troops and the organization of naval task forces indicates an amphibious expedition against either the Philippines, Thai or Kra Peninsula or possibly Borneo.[68]

On the same day, MID issued its analysis of "Recent Developments in the Far East," which observed that "it appears evident that the Japanese have completed plans for further aggressive moves in Southeastern Asia. . . . This Division is of the opinion that the initial move will be made against Thailand from the sea and overland through Southern Indochina." On December 1, an ONI "Fortnightly Summaries of Current National Situation," observed that "strong indications point to an early Japanese advance against Thailand."[69]

But the failure of either MID or ONI to provide even minimal strategic warning of the attack may have had less to do with failures of U.S. intelligence analysis than with the limitations of U.S. intelligence collection—limitations imposed, in part, by Japanese security measures.

The earliest warning that the United States could have obtained about

---

*Discussion of Pearl Harbor, particularly the issue of the responsibility for the extent of losses suffered, involves numerous areas in addition to intelligence—national command and control, leadership, preparedness, interservice coordination, information dissemination, the responsiblities of the local commanders, and tactical warning.

the attack plan or the November 5 decision would have come from human intelligence, from a source who had contacts within the Japanese leadership.* But in contrast to the Soviet Union, the United States did not have a Richard Sorge, whose agents could provide intelligence on Japanese intentions.

The MID did not have clandestine sources in Japan or elsewhere. The information its military attaché in Tokyo could provide was, according to Brigadier General Sherman Miles, the head of MID, "very limited; the Japanese being extremely close-mouthed." ONI had several varieties of human sources—attachés, a coast-watching network, and, until October 15, 1941, when it was transferred to the Office of the Coordinator of Information, a clandestine collection section. But none of those capabilities was able to provide advance word of Japanese intentions.[70†]

A third source was Ambassador Joseph C. Grew, but his dispatches generally "included only 'very indefinite and general' information about Japanese military and naval movements." As Japan's internal deadline for resolving the crisis approached, information gathering became more difficult. In a November 17 telegram to the State Department, Grew warned the State Department that it should not place

> the major responsibility in giving prior warning upon the Embassy staff, the naval and military attachés included, since in Japan there is extremely effective control over both primary and secondary military information. We could not expect to obtain any information in advance either from personal contacts or through the press; the observation of military movements is not possible by the few Americans remaining in the country.[71‡]

---

* While training, based on the attack plan, began before November, the pilots and crews were not informed of their ultimate goal. That information was restricted even among top Navy personnel. Robert Wohlstetter, *Pearl Harbor: Warning and Decision* (Stanford, Calif.: Stanford University Press, 1962), p. 368.

† In the ensuing investigation Representative John Coffee of Washington expounded on the failure of U.S. human intelligence: "They [U.S. military intelligence] are as ignorant of life in Japanese slum areas and of the influence of the geisha and Yoshiwara activities upon the soul of Japan as though they were on the planet Mars." But knowledge of Japanese plans was not available in the slums or from geisha girls. The United States needed its own Sorge, with contacts in the Japanese elite. Gordon Prange with Donald M. Goldstein and Katherine V. Dillon, *Pearl Harbor: The Verdict of History* (New York: McGraw Hill, 1986) pp. 285–86.

‡ Grew did report on January 27, 1941, that the Peruvian minister to Japan had informed an American diplomat he had heard credible rumors that the Japanese would launch a massive surprise attack on Pearl Harbor in the event of trouble with the United States. ONI passed on the report to Admiral Kimmel with the comment that "Naval Intelligence places no credence in these rumours. Furthermore, based on known data regarding the present disposition and employment of Japanese naval and army forces, no move against Pearl Harbor appears imminent or planned for in the foreseeable [sic] future."

At the time, Grew did not press for information about the source. If he had, ONI would have undoubtedly placed even less credence in the report; the source was a Japanese employee of the Peruvian embassy who had obtained the information from her boyfriend, a Japanese chauffeur. His source was the war novel he was reading. See Gordon W. Prange, *At Dawn We Slept: The Untold Story of Pearl Harbor* (New York: McGraw-Hill, 1981), p. 33; Wohlstetter, *Pearl Harbor*, p. 386).

One oft-reported source was Dusko A. Popov, a Yugoslavian who had been recruited by the Abwehr but volunteered to serve as a double agent for the British, who code-named him TRICYCLE. Popov arrived in the United States in August 1941, theoretically to establish a new German intelligence network. With him he brought a questionnaire, one-third of which consisted of questions about Hawaii and Pearl Harbor.[72]

The questionnaire was passed to the FBI, but exactly how much of the Hawaii information, and in what context, was passed by J. Edgar Hoover to the military intelligence services has been the subject of substantial controversy.[73]

But even had the full questionnaire been available to the ONI and MID there would have been no reason to conclude that the Japanese were planning an air raid against Pearl Harbor. The nature of the questionnaire did not suggest Pearl Harbor as a *Japanese* target. There was no proof that the questionnaire had been given to Popov at the request of the Japanese. The only certainty was that the Germans were asking questions. Indeed, the numerous mistakes in the questionnaire—such as locating Pearl Harbor on "Kuhusa" rather than Oahu, rendering Hickam Field as "Wicham Field," and using the outdated term "Lukefield" for the Ford Island Naval Air Station—were errors more indicative of a German interest than a Japanese interest. In addition, the questionnaire asked largely about land-based facilities and not about either the Pacific Fleet itself or the numbers and types of aircraft, air scouting patterns, antiaircraft positions, ship types and movements, or mooring details—crucial information for planning an air attack. The only item on the questionnaire that would be significant to air planners concerned torpedo protection nets. The questionnaire, and particularly its focus on fixed facilities, was more consistent with German preparations for possible sabotage operations. And in the absence of bombers that could reach the United States from Europe, sabotage would be the only way in which the Germans could attack the United States.[74]

Communications intelligence provided valuable intelligence on diplomatic and espionage activities, but no clear warning of the forthcoming attack on Pearl Harbor. William Friedman's Army Signal Intelligence Service had reconstructed the code machine, designated PURPLE, used for Japan's highest-grade diplomatic code. The intelligence derived by the decryption activities was given the code name MAGIC.

On September 24, 1941, the Japanese Foreign Ministry, in response to a request from the naval staff's Third (Intelligence) Bureau, requested the consulate in Honolulu to report on vessels in Pearl Harbor using a grid system. The message divided the waters of Pearl Harbor into five areas. It also requested reports on warships and aircraft carriers at anchor, tied up at wharves, buoys, and in docks. The bureau also wanted to know when two or more vessels were moored "alongside the same wharf."[75]

During November, as negotiations between the United States and Japan became critical, there was a sharp rise in the number of MAGIC intercepts—to an average of twenty-six per day. Included was a November 5 message from Tokyo to Ambassador Kichisaburo Nomura in Washington—"Because of various circumstances, it was absolutely necessary that all arrangements for the signing of this agreement to be completed by the 25th of this month"—reflecting the decision taken that day to attack Pearl Harbor in the event negotiations were unsuccessful by that date. November 11 and 15 messages again emphasized that reaching an agreement by November 25 was "absolutely necessary." Both messages were available to MAGIC recipients within twenty-four hours.[76]

A November 15 message to the Honolulu consulate stated: "As relations between Japan and the United States are most critical, make your 'ships in harbor report' irregular, but at a rate of twice a week." This was apparently the only case where consular reports were linked to the state of relations between Japan and the United States. The message also indicated interest in current information on the ships in Pearl Harbor.[77]

On November 19, a message transmitted in the lower-grade J19 diplomatic code established a means of notification if Japan's relations with a variety of potential enemies had reached the breaking point. The message, which was soon decrypted by American cryptanalysts, stated that if Japan–United States relations were in danger, the message HIGASHI NO KAZE AME, or "East Wind Rain," would be transmitted. "North wind cloudy" would indicate that Japan–Soviet Union relations were in danger. "West wind clear" would signify that Japanese–British relations were in trouble. Upon receipt of the message the recipients were to destroy all code papers.[78]

On November 20 Japan had made a final attempt to resolve the crisis with the United States, offering to withdraw from southern Indochina if the United States would unfreeze Japanese assets, provide oil and other strategic materials, and refrain from providing assistance to the Chinese resisting Japan. Six days later the United States responded with a counterproposal: if Japan would withdraw from all of Indochina and China and join in a multilateral nonaggression pact covering eastern Asia, the United States would release Japanese assets and resume trade.[79]

A November 22 message from the Foreign Ministry, in response to pleading by Ambassadors Nomura and Saburo Kurusu, had extended the deadline for completion of negotiations to November 29. The decrypted message stated: "This time we mean it . . . the deadline absolutely cannot be changed. After that things are automatically going to happen."[80]

A November 28 message, intercepted and translated that same day, indicated that negotiations were doomed. The message from Tokyo to Washington referred to the U.S. counterproposal as "humiliating" and stated that the "Imperial Government can by no means use it as a basis for negotiations." Although the ambassadors would be receiving a message that would mean the end of negotiations, they were instructed not to "give the impression that the negotiations had been broken off. Merely say to them that you are awaiting instructions." A December 1 message stated: "To prevent the United States from becoming unduly suspicious we have been advising the press and others that though there were some wide differ·.nces between Japan and the United States, the negotiations are continuing."[81]

Another espionage message was sent on the 28th to consular agent Takeo Yoshikawa in Hawaii. He was instructed by the Third Bureau to "[r]eport upon the entrance or departure of capital ships and the length of time they remain at anchor, from the time of entry into port until departure." The next day the bureau indicated that it wished Yoshikawa to report at regular intervals even if there were no movements, obviously to ensure that none of his reports were missed. The two messages were decrypted on December 5.[82]

A December 1 PURPLE message indicated that Japanese attaché offices in London, Hong Kong, Singapore, and Manila had been instructed to abandon the use of their code machines and destroy them. Another message informed the Washington office of steps to take "when you are faced with the necessity of destroying codes." The implication was that British and Dutch possessions would be the first subjects of attack, not the United States or its possessions.[83]

On December 3 another PURPLE message instructed the Washington embassy to "burn all [codes] but those now used with the machine and one copy each of O code [PA-K2] and abbreviating code [LA]. . . . Stop using one code machine unit and destroy it completely." To Undersecretary of State Sumner Welles it meant that "the chances had diminished from one in a thousand to one in a million that war could then be avoided."[84]

On December 6 the embassy received a communication from Tokyo stating that it was about to transmit a fourteen-part response to Secretary Hull's November 26 counterproposal. The Navy's intercept station at Bainbridge Island, Washington, picked up each part of the message as it was transmitted. From Bainbridge it was transmitted to the Navy's cryptanalysts in Washington. By 8:45 P.M. the first thirteen parts had been intercepted and decrypted by OP-20-G and SIS.[85]

Even before receiving the fourteenth part Roosevelt understood the import. When the first thirteen parts were delivered to the White House after 9 P.M. Roosevelt read them and told aide Harry Hopkins that, in effect, "This means war." But he still did not foresee Pearl Harbor as a likely target.[86]

The fourteenth part was not intercepted until just after midnight of the 6th. The cryptanalysts in Washington soon determined the text of the message, including its conclusion, that "in view of the attitude of the American Government it is impossible to reach an agreement through further negotiations."[87]

The next morning, Captain Theodore S. Wilkinson read the fourteenth part of the message and became alarmed, believing the implications to be "very serious" and that the message contained "fighting words." Around

8:30 that morning Rufus Bratton, Far Eastern Section chief of the Military Intelligence Division, was reading the message in his office when he was handed another MAGIC intercept. The new message instructed Ambassador Nomura to submit "our reply to the United States at 1:00 P.M. on the 7th your time."[88]

When Bratton read the message he understood the significance of the instruction—the message was to be delivered to coincide with the beginning of an attack on an American ship or territory. Given that 1:00 P.M. Washington time was 7:30 A.M. Hawaii time, Pearl Harbor became a highly likely (if not definite) target. But by the time higher officials were informed of the new intelligence and a further warning to the theaters had been drafted and arrived, the attack was under way.[89]

Thus, despite the ability of the United States to break Japan's most secret diplomatic traffic, U.S. intelligence agencies were unable to provide timely warning. The diplomatic and espionage messages provided valuable intelligence, but none of those read before December 7 pointed conclusively toward Pearl Harbor as the most likely of targets.

Messages concerning Japanese intelligence operations in Hawaii were not generally taken by senior officials or analysts as signaling Pearl Harbor as a likely target. The September 24, 1941, espionage message was considered by Bratton as indicating an "unusual interest" in Pearl Harbor. But neither the chief of MID, Brigadier Sherman Miles, Secretary of War Henry Stimson, Army Chief of Staff George Marshall, or the chief of the Army War Plans Division found the message particularly significant. The Office of Naval Intelligence thought the message might indicate an attempt to improve communications efficiency—although one ONI member suggested that the message might be an indication of sabotage planning.[90]

Although requests from Tokyo to Manila and Pearl Harbor increased in the week before the attack, Pearl Harbor and Manila were far from being the only targets of intensive Japanese espionage. Japanese intelligence had also instructed its representatives to collect information on several other key U.S. military and naval installations, including the Panama Canal, San Diego, and Seattle.* The requests concerning Pearl Harbor were part of an overall pattern, and consistent with Japan's "insatiable" appetite "for detail in all respects."[91]

Nor was any intercepted diplomatic message in the days leading up to

---

* The most revealing espionage message, sent on December 2 from the Third Bureau to the Honolulu Consulate, was not read until after December 7. The message read: "In view of the present situation, the presence in port of warships, airplane carriers, and cruisers is of utmost importance. Hereafter, to the utmost of your ability let me know day by day. Wire me in each case whether or not there are any observation balloons above Pearl Harbor or if there are any indications that they will be sent up. Also advise me whether or not the warships are provided with antimine [i.e., antitorpedo] nets." Prange, *At Dawn We Slept*, p. 443.

The last two items were particularly relevant since they were of use only in devising or modifying attack plans. At the same time the request did not indicate an imminent attack. They would also be consistent with a feasibility study and/or long-range planning.

December 7 a clear indication of the planned attack, for the Japanese told not a single one of their diplomatic representatives, including their ambassadors in Washington and Berlin, of the operation. Likewise, messages ordering destruction of codes or evacuation of citizens mirrored U.S. actions taken as result of the growing pessimism about the outcome of the negotiations.[92]

Contributing to the inability of U.S. intelligence to warn of the coming attack were Japanese deception and security measures. The task force rendezvoused at Hitokappu Bay off Etorufu Island, in the remote northern islands, where it was unlikely to be noticed even by Japanese citizens. Intricate measures concealed the purchase of the cold-weather clothing and equipment needed for the planned rendezvous and ensuing journey. Even the dumping of garbage into the Kuriles' waters was prohibited.[93]

Starting on November 10, radio communication between the task force's ships was proscribed, making it impossible to locate them by direction-finding. At the same time deceptive communications were employed to create the impression that the task force was training in Kyushu. Large numbers of seamen from the Yokosuka Naval District were allowed shore leave in Tokyo and Yokohama to reinforce the impression.[94]

To further ensure secure communications, at midnight on December 1 the Imperial Navy changed its 20,000 radio call signs. This extremely premature change—five months before the next change was due—should have been taken as a troubling sign. But the change was consistent with *any* imminent Japanese military action.[95]

In addition, the intelligence updates and commands from the Naval General Staff to the task force were transmitted on a special frequency and in a code, JN25b, which the undermanned U.S. cryptographers had been unable to solve. Only after the war was over would it be discovered that those messages indicated planning for a surprise attack by a naval task force and that such a task force was steaming toward Hawaii. The messages also included the December 2 instruction to "climb Mount Nitaka December 8, Repeat December 8." December 8 in Japan was December 7 in Hawaii.[96]

Intelligence historian David Kahn is certainly partially correct when he observes that:

> Intelligence officers could perhaps have foreseen the attack if the United States, years before, had insinuated spies into high-level Japanese military and naval circles, flown regular aerial reconnaissance of the Japanese navy, put intercept units aboard ships sailing close to Japan to pick up naval messages that a greatly expanded codebreaking unit might have cracked. . . . The intelligence failure at Pearl Harbor was not one of analysis, but of collection.[97]

But there is one respect in which analysis failed. For the result of analysis is dependent not only on the specifics of the information collected but on the assumptions used to analyze it. Comparing U.S. and Japanese capabilities, it was clear to both Japanese and American leaders that Japan could not hope to win a prolonged all-out conflict with the United States. American officials, including those in MID and ONI, therefore tended to dismiss the prospect that Japan would undertake a suicidal direct attack on the United States. But as Ambasssador Joseph Grew had observed: "National sanity would dictate against such an event, but Japanese sanity cannot be measured by our own standards of logic."[98]

8

Spies and Counterspies

In the periods leading up to the Nazi seizure of the Rhineland and invasion of Poland, the signing of the Nazi–Soviet Non-Aggression Pact, the Soviet invasion of Russia, and the surprise attack on Pearl Harbor the spies of Britain, Germany, Japan, the Soviet Union, and other nations were seeking to discover the intentions and capabilities of their nation's potential enemies. But they either proved unable to secure the crucial information or, as in the case of Richard Sorge and several other Soviet agents, their information was ignored by their nation's political leadership. Once war began, the espionage and counterespionage efforts of all the major participants grew dramatically. For some countries these efforts proved of significant value; for others they did more harm than good.

The Red Orchestra

In the summer and fall of 1941 Stalin and the rest of the Soviet leadership were faced with two nightmares. One—the dramatic advance of the German army through the Soviet Union—was already in progress. The other—a Japanese attack against Siberia—was still a possibility. Such an attack was being urged on the Japanese by their German allies, especially Foreign Minister Joachim von Ribbentrop. At the time, Japanese officials were split over two alternatives, a "northern solution" (war with the Soviet Union) and a "southern solution" (war with Britain and the United States).[1]

From Tokyo, Richard Sorge reported on Ribbentrop's pleas and the Japanese reaction. Relying on reports from Hotsumi Ozaki, Sorge was able to keep Moscow informed as the southern-solution bloc gained the upper hand. On August 15 Sorge reported that the "excessive strain on the Japanese economy" precluded war any earlier than that winter. When he reported, at the end of September, that "[t]he Soviet Far East can be considered safe from Japanese attack," Moscow sent a message of thanks. In October, in response to Sorge's reporting, and possibly corroborating communications intelligence, Stalin began redeploying half the Far East Command to the western front.[2]

As the Japanese threat to his ideological homeland vanished, Sorge became eager to put his skills to use elsewhere. What was to be his final message to the GRU requested that he be recalled to Moscow or sent to Germany. But that message was never sent, for on October 18 he was arrested by the Japanese security police. Within days thirty-five members of his network were also apprehended.[3]

It would be another thirty months, after interrogation and occasional torture, before sentences were handed down. Two members of Sorge's network received life imprisonment. The Japanese were not so lenient with Sorge and Ozaki. On the morning of November 7, 1944, Sorge, forty-nine, and Ozaki, forty-three, were hung at Tokyo's Sugamo Prison.[4]

If Sorge had avoided detection and had been sent to Germany, he would not have been the only Soviet spy there. He would have joined Arvid Harnack, Harro Schulze-Boysen, and their networks. Both had been active in communist and other left-wing circles in Germany in the 1930s. In 1930, Harnack, an economics lecturer at Giessen University, began to organize groups of communists and left-wing sympathizers. Boysen had been arrested in April 1933 and tortured by the SS for his political activities, including his association with *Der Gegner*, a leftist publication. He spent three months in a "unofficial" concentration camp outside Berlin. Still, in 1934, Boysen, making use of family connections, was hired by the Air Ministry's News Department. In January 1941 he was appointed to the liaison staff of the Luftwaffe Chiefs of Staff.[5]

Harnack was recruited by the NKVD in August 1935 and assigned the code name BALT (later changed to CORSICAN). In early 1941 Harnack introduced Boysen, who he had recruited as a member of his network, to Soviet intelligence officer "Alexander Erdberg." Shortly afterwards, the NKVD would suggest to Boysen, code-named SENIOR, that he become head of his own espionage ring.[6]

Although Harnack's and Boysen's most valuable sources were probably in the Luftwaffe, the Air Ministry, the War Ministry, and the armed services high commands, they also had sources in the Foreign Office, Propaganda Ministry, Office for Racial Policy, German Office for the Protection of Workers, and the Berlin city government. Included in their network was Alfred Traxl of the Inspectorate of Signal Troops, Wolfgang Havemann of the Naval Signal School, and Colonel Erwin Gertz of the Air Ministry.[7]

Information provided by Boysen and Harnack was transmitted by radio to Moscow. Those transmissions also led to the destruction of the networks. During 1941, German monitoring stations detected 500 transmissions from clandestine transmitters, making it apparent that a major espionage network was operating. On July 30 the network began to unravel when the Geheime Feld Polizei (Secret Field Police) arrested radio opera-tor Johnann Wenzel, code-named HERMANN. A German report noted:

> From the many radiograms intercepted . . . which could be deciphered by the method ultimately revealed by WENZEL after a searching interrogation by the Gestapo, valuable clues were obtained regarding a Soviet information service existing in Berlin. In this way the arrest of this group, headed by . . . Harro SCHULZE-BOYSEN and . . . Arvid HARNACK . . . was made possible.[8]

The Gestapo arrested Schulze-Boysen and Harnack on August 30 and September 3, 1942, respectively, after a warning from Horst Heilman of the OKH Cipher Section had failed to reach Schulze-Boysen in time. By the day of their execution, December 22, 1942, more than eighty mem-bers of their espionage networks had also been apprehended.[9]

According to a Nazi Security Service/Security Police (SD/SIPO) study, the Schulze-Boysen network's most valuable intelligence fell in nine areas:

1. the strength of the German Air Force at the beginning of the war with the Soviet Union
2. the monthly production of the German aviation industry in the period June–July 1941
3. the fuel situation in Germany
4. plans for the intended German attack on Maikop (Caucasus)
5. the location of German headquarters
6. serial production of aircraft in the occupied areas
7. the production and storage of material for chemical warfare in Germany
8. the capture of a Russian codebook near Petsamo
9. the losses of German parachutists on Crete.[10]

The term "Rote Kappelle" (Red Orchestra) in the SD/SIPO report re-ferred to a loosely coordinated NKVD-GRU network in western and cen-tral Europe, which included the Schulze-Boysen and Harnack rings. The Red Orchestra designation was due to the German Reich's Main Security Office (RSHA).* To the RSHA, the orchestra's radio operators were "pia-nists," their transmitters "pianos," and their supervisors "conductors."[11]

The most prominent of the conductors was Leopold Trepper, known within the network as the "grand chef." In the spring of 1939, only months before war was to break out, he was sent to Brussels, posing as a Canadian industrialist, with the mission of establishing a secure com-mercial cover for an espionage network in France and the Low Coun-tries.[12]

In Brussels, Trepper established the Foreign Excellent Raincoat Com-pany, an export firm with branch offices in major European port areas.

---

* The RSHA had been formed in 1939 to unify secret police, criminal police, and party intelligence organizations.

After the fall of Belgium in May 1940 and the seizure of his company by the Germans, he moved his headquarters to Paris and established new cover firms: Simex in Paris and Simexco in Brussel. Both firms sold black market goods to the Germans and prospered as a result.[13]

Trepper directed seven distinct GRU networks in France, each with its own chief. The networks steadily gathered military and industrial secrets in German-occupied Europe, including information on troop locations and deployments, industrial production, the availability of raw materials, new German tank designs, and airplane production.[14]

Like Sorge, Trepper was able to gather much valuable information directly, through his contacts with high German circles. Under the pretense of being a successful German businessman he threw dinner parties at which he gathered information on the morale and attitudes of senior German officers, army troop movements on the western front, and operational plans for the eastern front.[15]

In addition, the contacts between Simex and its best customer, the Todt Organization, which was to construct Hitler's "Atlantic Wall," provided full details on German military fortifications and the deployment of German troops. As a bonus, those contacts supplied some of Trepper's agents with passes that permitted them unrestricted movement almost anywhere in German-occupied territory.[16]

At the same time Trepper maintained liaison with the French Communist party, which provided him, thanks to the reports from railwaymen, with valuable tactical intelligence on German troop movements, logistics, and bottlenecks. He also was able to tap into reports from immigrant workers on industrial production, while his man in Vichy was able to determine the German order of battle in France.[17]

In December 1941 Trepper's Brussels transmitter was rolled up by German security forces. The Red Orchestra Commando, a task force including representatives of the Gestapo, Abwehr, and Nazi Security Service, was formed in early 1942 at Hitler's personal order. Pianist after pianist was apprehended, and on December 5, 1942, Trepper himself was captured in Paris, at a dental office. After agreeing to collaborate with the Germans he began transmitting misinformation, possibly laced with warnings, back to Moscow. In September 1943 he escaped, and he remained in hiding until the conclusion of the war.[18]

There was one component of the Red Orchestra outside the reach of German internal security forces—the Rote Drei (Red Three) in Switzerland. Headed by Alexander Rado, code-named DORA, the Rote Drei's formation can be traced back to Rado's arrival in Geneva in 1936 to begin activities on behalf of Soviet intelligence. By April 1942 the basic structure of the Rado organization had been established, with Rado as group leader and three subgroup leaders, Rachel Dübendorfer (code-named SISSY), Georges Blun (LONG), and Otto Puenter (PAKBO).[19]

Of the three it was Dübendorfer and one of her agents who made the biggest contribution to the GRU's World War II efforts. Beginning in the summer of 1942, Dübendorfer began receiving the reports, via a cut-out (intermediary), of Rudolf Roessler—a German political refugee who had arrived in Lucerne in 1933 and started a small publishing company the following year.[20]

Roessler's publishing company was viewed by the Büro Ha, an unofficial Swiss intelligence agency, as an ideal cover for intelligence activities. Thus, the Büro recruited Roessler in the summer of 1939. Probably through his work for Swiss intelligence, whose military intelligence service operated a network in Germany code-named VIKING, Roessler had access to reports from four high-level German sources. He proceeded to pass to SISSY the reports from those sources, code-named WERTHER, TEDDY, ANNA, and OLGA.[21]

A subsequent study by the CIA concluded that the four sources were most probably Major General Hans Oster, the Abwehr chief of staff; Hans Bernd Gisevius, another Abwehr officer who served as the German vice-consul in Zurich; Carl Goerdeler, the civilian leader of the conservative opposition to Hitler; and Colonel Fritz Boetzel, commanding officer of the Southeast Army Group's intelligence evaluation office in Athens.[22]

While the Rote Drei never had to contend with German internal security forces, their work was hindered by Swiss security authorities. In mid-October 1943 Rado and his wife went into hiding to elude the Swiss police. In May and June 1944 Roessler, his cut-out Christian Schneider, and Dübendorfer were all arrested.[23]

Venlo and Aftermath

Although the Soviet Union had some of its most important networks decimated long before its war with Germany concluded, those networks were in place at the beginning of the war and provided much valuable intelligence during the war's first years. Britain was not so fortunate, for it was shortly after Britain's declaration of war that SIS suffered a catastrophic loss.

The SIS resident at the Hague, Major Richard Stevens, and Captain Sigismund Payne Best, the Hague resident of the Z-Organization,* were tricked by agents of the Sicherheitsdienst into believing that a high-ranking anti-Nazi Wehrmacht general wished to hold secret talks in London. The SD double agents held out the prospect of a military coup and Hitler's arrest. Instead, the two SIS officers found themselves being kidnapped at the German–Dutch frontier, near the town of Venlo, on November 9, 1939.[24]

While the direct result of the incident was the virtual closure of the

---

*The Z-Organization had been established in 1935 as a parallel intelligence network to SIS because it was felt that SIS heads of station were easily identifiable through the well-known use of British Passport Control Offices for cover. Stevens did not learn of the organization's existence or Best's role in it until September 4, 1939. The Z-Organization apparently made only a marginal contribution to the British intelligence effort.

Hague station the damage did not stop there. Under duress, Best and Stevens described in great detail the internal workings of SIS—which, at the very least, served to confirm information the Abwehr may have obtained from another SIS officer.[25]

The Venlo Incident further shook the SIS, which had withdrawn all its personnel from Prague, Warsaw, Bucharest, and Berlin once war had begun. In addition, the Wehrmacht's May 1940 Blitzkrieg forced closure of the stations in Paris and Brussels. The merging of the Z-Organization into SIS contributed little. The remaining SIS stations on the continent—Stockholm, Lisbon, and Berne—produced little of value.[26]

SIS was able to tap into the information produced by what were initially Polish intelligence networks. In the wake of the German invasion the Poles went into exile in France. When German troops entered France, they moved on to London. But Polish military intelligence had maintained its radio links with its remaining networks in Poland and elsewhere in Europe, including France.[27]

Among the the most prominent of the networks was INTERALLIE, based in Paris. The network's guiding hand was Colonel Wincenty Zarembski, the Paris representative of Polish Military Intelligence, who had operated from the Polish embassy. Zarembski had remained in France after the evacuation of the Polish General Staff to aid the hundreds of Poles who needed to escape to Spain. In Toulouse he discovered two Poles who had been Foreign Ministry wireless operators and convinced them to build a primitive transmitter.[28]

By late summer 1940 contact had been established with the Polish embassy in Madrid. A schedule for regular contact with the Polish director of military intelligence-in-exile in London was arranged. Zambreski succeeded in recruiting several Polish officers in Paris and other parts of occupied France. As military officers they had a good understanding of the information needed by the intelligence analysts in London. The most important of those officers was Captain Roman Garby-Czerniawski, code-named VALENTIN.[29]

Czerniawski's first radio message was received on January 1, 1941, and informed his listeners that his group would be known as INTERALLIE. VALENTIN divided the occupied territory into fourteen districts, each with its own couriers and chief agents. He took the intelligence provided from the districts, collated it, and transmitted it to London. That intelligence was based on the observations of roughly 120 agents situated near French channel ports, Luftwaffe airfields, and industrial centers. By the summer of 1941 an additional three transmitters were being employed.[30]

But by the summer of 1941 INTERALLIE had little time left. Czerniawski was betrayed by a subagent, along with twenty-one of the subagent's associates. Early on the morning of November 17 he was arrested while in lay in his Paris bed. In addition to seizing VALENTIN, the Abwehr also obtained a number of documents. With the aid of Mathilde

Carre, another member of the INTERALLIE network, it was able to identify and arrest the entire network in a mere three days.[31]

Carre's collaboration with the Abwehr was disastrous for INTER-ALLIE and SIS. She knew the locations of the four INTERALLIE wireless stations, their transmitting schedules, codes, and the hidden security checks placed in the texts of messages. Thus Abwehr personnel were able to deceive the London operators and obtain valuable information about SIS activities. As a precaution, Carre subsequently reported VALENTIN's arrest and declared that she would be running the network in the future.[32]

Finally, in late 1941 or early 1942 SIS began to suspect that all was not well with INTERALLIE. Those suspicions were confirmed in February, but SIS continued to accept messages in an attempt to turn the ploy back on the Abwehr as well as keep its agents alive. Eventually INTERALLIE's communications dried up, presumably because the Germans realized that the game was over.[33]

SIS's principal circuit in Vichy, designated ALLIANCE, suffered several early setbacks—the betrayal of a member who fell into the hands of the Abwehr and the loss of four of the six transmitters—but survived until September 1943. Ultimately it grew to include 3,000 active contributors, distributed across France, who reported a wide variety of intelligence. Initially the information concerned the location of Luftwaffe decoy airfields and activities at German submarine bases. Later, ALLIANCE's reporting included vital information about German rocketry. That information came at a high price—the apprehension and execution of about 500 ALLIANCE agents.[34]

; A SIS network of particular value after June 6, 1944, was AMICOL, which had been established after the collapse of INTERALLIE. Run by a Jesuist priest based in Bordeaux, it provided SIS with reports from more than 1,000 agents. One circuit, JADE/AMICOL, had contacts with railwaymen throughout the French national rail system and could report on German troop movements. In the aftermath of the Allied landings AMICOL transmitted several hundred reports, with the main transmitter, hidden in the attic of a convent, remaining undetected throughout the liberation of Paris.[35]

As might be expected, networks like those SIS operated in France and other countries were not duplicated in Germany. There was no resistance movement comparable to that in the occupied countries, no indigenous networks of Polish officers, and the communists owed their allegiance elsewhere. However, that didn't preclude some solitary sources of information.

One of those sources was Paul Rosbaud, who had been just a few months shy of forty-three years old when German troops marched into Poland. During World War I he had served in the Kaiser's army and his treatment by the British while their prisoner of war, had made a lasting and favorable impression on him. After the war Rosbaud studied chemistry and after graduation accepted a position with the giant Metallgesellschaft A.G. in Frankfurt. From there he joined a Berlin-based weekly metallurgy magazine, *Metallwirtschaft*. Officially a scientific adviser to the journal, he traveled throughout Europe to meet scientists and discuss their work. Eventually he left *Metallwirtschaft* to become a scientific adviser to the Springer Verlag publishing house.[36]

In the early 1930s Rosbaud came to know Francis Edward Foley, Berlin station chief for SIS. Once Hitler came to power Rosbaud began providing Foley with items of information, some of significance. That assistance temporarily ended with the creation of the GESTAPO, the suspension of civil rights, and Foley's public role in aiding refugees.[37]

The relationship between Rosbaud, code-named GRIFFIN, and SIS was reestablished before or shortly after the beginning of the new war. Thus he was able to report on Wernher von Braun's three-day conference, Der Tag der Weisheit (The Day of Wisdom), of September 28–30, 1939, which focused on what became the German rocket program. During that year Rosbaud also provided a list of German scientists interested in heavy water.[38]

At the end of 1939 Rosbaud once again stopped reporting, but he was reactivated in the fall of 1941. He resumed operations by helping to prepare a report on what was to be called the V-2 rocket, including a rough description of its cigar shape and a statement of its approximate dimensions. In the summer of 1943 he confirmed reports from two reliable sources suggesting that the German atomic energy program would fail to produce an atomic bomb, to the great relief of SIS and the British leadership.[39]

According to R. V. Jones, the SIS's director of scientific intelligence, Rosbaud's reports on the German atomic bomb program were particularly valuable. According to Jones, Rosbaud "helped us correctly to conclude that work in Germany towards the release of nuclear energy at no time reached beyond the research stage; his information thus calmed fears that might otherwise have beset us."[40]

Penetrating the Reich

In 1941 President Franklin Roosevelt established the first central intelligence agency of the United States, the Office of the Coordinator of Information. The man chosen to head the new office, which became the Office of Strategic Services (OSS) in June 1942, was William J. Donovan. The fifty-eight-year-old, stocky, gray haired, millionaire Wall Street lawyer hardly seemed to fit his nickname, "Wild Bill." Nor did other facts about him—he was a Hoover Republican and an Irish Catholic. But he had been known as Wild Bill since his youth. Donovan would proceed to build an intelligence empire that engaged in sophisticated research and analysis, special operations (from propaganda to sabotage), and traditional spying.[41]

One of the most important OSS officers operated from Switzerland. In early November 1942 Allen Dulles traveled from Vichy to Berne, the Swiss capital, on one of the last trains to cross the border before it was closed by German officers in response to the Allied landings in North Africa. He carried a suitcase containing two suits and a million-dollar letter of credit, and on November 8 he assumed the official position of Special Legal Assistant to the American Minister, Leland Harrison.[42]

With his grey hair, neatly trimmed mustache, and wire-rimmed glasses, Dulles looked more like a high-powered lawyer than an intelligence officer. But Dulles had come to Berne not to provide legal assistance but to recruit spies—just as he had during World War I. He took a fancy apartment in a medieval section of Berne, placed a sign on his door that read "Allen W. Dulles, Special Assistant to the American Minister," leaked word of his arrival to the local press, and waited for informants to get in touch.[43]

Early informants provided information that didn't stand up when checked against communications intelligence. But on August 19, 1943, Fritz Kolbe, a middle-aged and baldish German courier, visited Dulles. What Kolbe showed Dulles interested him immensely: a collection of 183 "flimsy" copies of what seemed to be original German Foreign Office telegrams. Kolbe told Dulles he would be back with more telegrams as soon as possible, then disappeared.[44]

Kolbe was given the alias "George Wood" by Dulles, who then waited for Kolbe to return. A little over six weeks later, on October 7, 1943, Kolbe reappeared with 96 telegrams totaling over 200 pages. Over the next sixteen months Kolbe visited Dulles on three more occasions, delivering more than 1,600 classified documents, mostly cables from German military attachés in twenty countries.[45]

Mixed in with the excitement in Washington and London intelligence circles was a sizable dose of suspicion. The most prominent skeptic was the anti-American Claude Dansey, former head of the Z-Organization and assistant chief of SIS. Dansey had opposed an OSS–SIS alliance in Europe and was fiercely proprietary about intelligence operations in Switzerland, having played a key role in organizing SIS's network in that country.[46]

But Donovan was confident enough to present some of the material, code-named BOSTON, to President Roosevelt. The information led the OSS to assemble, at the beginning of 1944, a portrait of the "gradually weakening fabric of the whole Nazi regime." Dulles radioed Donovan on April 12, 1944, that documents Kolbe brought him at the beginning of the month presented a "picture of imminent doom and final downfall."[47]

In June 1944 Donovan wrote President Truman:

> Over a period of 18 months OSS received over 1,600 true readings of secret and top secret German diplomatic correspondence between the Foreign Office and German diplomatic missions in 20 countries. Among the correspondence were reports from the German military and air attachés in Japan and the Far East, data on the structure of the German secret service in Spain,

Sweden and Switzerland, and significant items regarding German espionage activities in England and in the British Embassy in Istanbul.[48]

Others sources provided information on German scientists who might be involved in atomic research and advanced weapons programs. In the spring of 1943, even before Kolbe had arrived, Hans Bernd Gisevius, one of Rudolf Roessler's suspected sources, passed on information concerning the V-1 and V-2 programs and the location of the rocket research program headquarters at Peenemünde.[49]*

Dulles also received valuable intelligence from his eight French networks, which consisted of hundreds of agents. Those networks made it possible for the OSS to identify and locate all important German military units in France. Among Dulles's French sources was an official in the Paris office of the National Railroad Trust. Starting in September 1943, and continuing through the winter, he delivered a series of reports on troop movements in France, reports which permitted the OSS to plot the direction and magnitude of those movements. For nearly a year prior to the conclusion of the war he provided intelligence on rail conditions, rail traffic, and bomb and sabotage damage.[50]

As plans progressed for the Allied invasion of Europe, special arrangements were made for intelligence collection to support the Allied troops. Churchill and Roosevelt had decided at their August 1943 Quebec meeting to proceed with the liberation of France in 1944. Their reaffirmation of Allied invasion plans was followed by a long series of meetings between the OSS London chief, David Bruce, and C., Sir Stewart Menzies. Bruce pressed the case for an equal OSS voice in European espionage operations, and Menzies responded with an offer of equal partnership.[51]

As a result Operation SUSSEX was born; this would involve the dispatch of fifty OSS-controlled teams of two men each into northern France prior to the D-Day landings. But it soon became clear that these agents would have to be provided by General de Gaulle's Bureau Central de Renseignements et d'Action (Central Bureau for Intelligence and Action), headed by the thirty-two-year-old André Dewavrin. Described as a "cool, steely eyed and efficient," Dewavrin was a former military professor at St. Cyr, the French equivalent of West Point, who went by the alias Colonel Passy.[52]

Finally, on April 9, 1944, after delays caused by squabbling between de Gaulle and another exile leader, General Henri Giraud, the first OSS-controlled SUSSEX agents parachuted into France. Armed not only with automatic pistols but with concealed hacksaws for emergency escapes and "L" suicide pills, they began transmitting critical intelligence to London only weeks before the Allied landings, reporting on German troop movements and identifying targets for Allied bombers.[53]

Toward the end of the war, in addition to spying on Germany from

---

* V was used for *Vergeltung*, retaliation.

Swiss soil, the OSS also sought to provide intelligence for the advancing Allied forces by penetrating the Reich with its own agents. Directing the penetration effort was the future Director of Central Intelligence William Casey, at the time a wealthy thirty-two-year-old New York tax attorney. Casey coordinated the effort to send Polish, Belgian, and French agents to Germany's major crossroad cities.[54]

Of the thirty-four OSS teams parachuted into Germany only four could be considered successful. Part of their success was due to their use of the Joan–Eleanor communications system, which allowed them to radio their intelligence to aircraft flying overhead and equipped with the necessary recording equipment. Among the successful teams were PICKAXE, HAMMER, and CHAUFFEUR.[55]

PICKAXE operated in Landshut, near Munich, and was able to transmit nine messages to Joan–Eleanor aircraft. Those messages contained information on rail traffic in Landshut, road traffic, precise location of a communications center, and troop deployments. CHAUFFEUR parachuted to Regensberg on March 31, equipped with both Joan–Eleanor and wireless equipment. Aided by the manager and employees of a dairy which employed Belgian and French POWs, CHAUFFEUR gathered significant intelligence concerning defenses, troop movements, and target locations.[56]

HAMMER was the only team to operate in Berlin. Parachuting blind on March 2, 1945, the two HAMMER agents, who were Czech Communists, walked to a nearby town and took a train to Berlin. Along with the brother-in-law and sister of one agent as well as two other contacts, they patroled Berlin. They talked to soldiers and visited military areas and industrial plants, gathering whatever intelligence they could. However, they were able to transmit only one report via Joan–Eleanor.[57]

The Allied Target

Throughout the war, as the secret intelligence services of the Allied powers spied on their Axis enemies, one of the Allied powers was devoting a considerable effort to spying on its main allies. The Soviet NKVD and GRU were doing the spying, while Britain and the United States were the targets.

In Britain the recruits of the 1930s began to pay significant dividends in the 1940s. Four of the Magnificent Five, starting with Guy Burgess, managed to penetrate the British intelligence establishment. The flamboyant Burgess joined Section D, the SIS sabotage and black propaganda unit, in 1939.* Burgess produced German-language records that mixed propaganda with music, to be broadcast to Germany on or before the outbreak of war.[58]

---

* Black propaganda operations were unacknowledged operations, which often purported to be conducted by groups operating within enemy territory.

Burgess's greatest achievement, at least for the NKVD, was the assistance he rendered to Kim Philby in his quest to join SIS. Philby, after his stint as a *Times* war correspondent, had unsuccessfully attempted to join the British codebreakers at the Government Code and Cypher School. But thanks to Burgess's help, Philby found himself in Section D.[59]

Section D must have been viewed by Philby's Soviet masters as a foothold, since little of interest could be reported from that corner of the secret service. Soon the foothold was gone, as Section D was absorbed, in the summer of 1940, by the new Special Operations Executive. Burgess soon found himself out of the British secret world entirely when SOE fired him for irreverence. Philby was appointed an instructor at the SOE's training school in Hampshire.[60]

Following the Nazi attack on the Soviet Union, Philby, probably with NKVD encouragement, attempted to find an assignment that would be more useful to the Soviet Union. It did not take long before he had a job in the Iberian subsection of SIS Section V (Counterintelligence), which was attracted by his reporting experience in the Spanish Civil War.[61]*

One prominent historian, Hugh Trevor-Roper, who was involved in the secret intelligence world at the time, was "astonished" that Philby was cleared for secret intelligence work, for he was aware of Philby's communist background, but in September 1941 Philby began work in Section V. While the section was located away from the main SIS headquarters, it was located next door to the SIS Registry. Philby soon became friends with the chief archivist, so that in addition to access to work-related files on Spain and Portugal he gained access to a wide range of information. He was thus able to pass on to his Soviet controller two "sourcebooks" on SIS operations against Soviet targets. Philby was also instructed to search for information concerning British plans to conclude a separate peace with Germany and turn the anti-Nazi war into an anti-Soviet war.[62]

During 1942–43 Philby's area of responsibility was expanded by the head of Section V, Felix Cowgill, to include North Africa and Italy. That promotion was followed by another when Cowgill made Philby his deputy "in all intelligence matters." Philby was to repay Cowgill in an unusual way in 1944. Early that year SIS decided to reestablish Section IX, the old anti-Soviet section, "to study past records of Soviet and communist activity." Cowgill, who had served as head of the prewar Section IX, was the obvious choice to head the section. When, in late 1944, it became known inside SIS that C wanted to expand the section's mandate, Philby

---

* Philby's transfer to SOE left two Soviet agents in SOE, James Klugman and Ormond Uren. Klugman joined the Yugoslav section of SOE–Cairo in February 1942 and remained undetected and employed by SOE throughout the war. Uren, a junior officer in the SOE Hungarian section, was less fortunate. In April 1943 MI5 discovered that Uren was passing classified information to the national organizer of the Communist party of Great Britain. Christopher Andrew and Oleg Gordievsky, *KGB: The Inside Story* (New York: Harper Collins, 1990), pp. 295–96.

was instructed by Moscow Center, through his controller, to "do everything, but *everything*" to ensure that he became head of Section IX. Philby managed to undermine Cowgill and become section head.[63]

Even before Philby had worked his way into SIS, Anthony Blunt had managed to become part of MI5, joining in the summer of 1940. During his first year in the security service Blunt provided his Soviet controller with a steadily increasing flow of material. Blunt provided valuable information on MI5 itself—its internal structure, key officials, and agents. Of most immediate value was the large volume of intelligence on the German order of battle and operations he was able to deliver. Such military intelligence was acquired not through MI5 but through Leo Long, a former student of Blunt's and a member of MI14 which evaluated the strength and organization of the German army.[64]

The fourth member of the magnificent five to penetrate the British intelligence world was John Cairncross. For about a year, starting in the summer of 1942, Cairncross served as the NKVD's man in the Government Code and Cypher School, where his primary responsibility was to analyze intercepted Luftwaffe signals.[65]

Cairncross's most valuable contribution to the Soviet Union probably came toward the end of his stay at GC&CS, just before the summer 1943 Battle of Kursk, which turned out to be the last great German offensive on the eastern front. On April 30, 1943, based on intercepts of ENIGMA traffic, Britain sent Moscow a warning of an imminent German thrust against the Kursk salient, along with German intelligence evaluations of Soviet forces in the area. Cairncross provided far more than a warning derived from intercepts. He provided the intercepts themselves, along with the unit identifications that were routinely deleted from the sanitized COMINT provided by Britain.[66]

The most valuable intercepts were those that identified the disposition of Luftwaffe squadrons before the battle. Based on their fear that the German offensive might begin as early as May 10, the Soviets launched a preemptive air raid on May 6, targeted against seventeen German airfields chosen with the aid of Cairncross's information. As a result numerous German aircraft were destroyed on the ground in the initial raids as well as the raids that followed on May 7 and 8. The three-day air operation was considered the Soviet air force's greatest World War II campaign. Its 1,400 sorties resulted in the destruction of over 500 German aircraft, at the cost of 122 Soviet planes.[67]

Before joining GC&CS, Cairncross may have also provided the first intelligence on the U.S. and British atomic bomb programs, the MANHATTAN PROJECT and TUBE ALLOYS. In October 1940, while Cairncross was serving as private secretary to Lord Hankey, chairman of the British Scientific Advisory Committee a lengthy discussion of the U.S. and British programs took place before the committee. Hankey also served on the TUBE ALLOYS Consultative Commission in the fall of 1941, when Cairncross was still working for him.[68]

There is no doubt that Donald Maclean provided intelligence on the British program in the fall of 1941. On September 25, 1941, based on information provided by Maclean, the NKVD resident in London informed Moscow about the session of the TUBE ALLOYS committee, that British scientists were confident that a uranium bomb could be produced in two years, and that the bomb was a top British priority.[69]

The intelligence from Cairncross and Maclean was followed by a letter that a young Soviet physicist and Air Force lieutenant, G. N. Flerov, wrote to Stalin. Flerov had examined American and British scientific journals and noted a rather dramatic decrease in the number of articles on nuclear fission. His conclusion, which proved correct, was that nuclear research had been moved under the cover of military secrecy and that the United States was attempting to build an atomic bomb. Flerov wrote the Soviet dictator about his findings and added that "It is essential not to lose any time in building the uranium bomb."[70]

Flerov's impact is unclear, but the Soviets began building their own bomb while gathering whatever intelligence they could on the U.S. and British efforts. The first, and possibly most important, Soviet atomic spy was Klaus Fuchs, a nuclear scientist who had emigrated to England from Germany in 1933. In the spring of 1941 Fuchs was approached by Birmingham University professor of mathematical physics Rudolf Peierls, another German refugee scientist, about the possibility of participating in "war work" of "a special nature" at Birmingham.[71]

Fuchs received a security clearance for the special work, despite British knowledge of his membership in the German Communist party (KPD) and his continued statement of communist views while in Britain, for the need for qualified scientists overrode security concerns. Later in 1941, when German troops appeared to be on the verge of marching into Moscow, Fuchs offered to become a Soviet spy. Through a leader of the KPD underground in Britain Fuchs was put in touch with a GRU officer and became a key member of the GRU's wartime apparatus, providing information on the progress of the U.S. and British A-bomb programs.[72]

In 1943 Fuchs had the opportunity to provide his GRU controllers with detailed intelligence on the American program. That opportunity resulted from President Franklin Roosevelt's decision to "renew, in an inclusive manner, the full exchange of information with the British Government, regarding Tube Alloys." Roosevelt's decision led to the secret Agreement Relating to Atomic Energy, which Churchill and Roosevelt signed on August 19, 1943. The provisions of the agreement included "full and effective interchange of information and ideas" on bomb construction.[73]

In December 1943, as part of the implementation of that agreement, Fuchs left England as part of the British Tube Alloys delegation to visit its American counterpart. He also left Britain with directions on how to make contact with his American controller, an American citizen of Russian parentage, Harry Gold, code-named RAYMOND. Fuchs was not aware that Gold worked for the NKGB, that the GRU had been forced to turn him over to the NKGB.[74]

Not long after he arrived, in early 1944, Fuchs was able to pass along significant data on the Oak Ridge, Tennessee, uranium production plant, although he knew it only as Site X. In mid-July he delivered copies of manuscripts he had drafted while working on the project; these included information on the now-identified Oak Ridge, Tennessee, and its equipment, which included a computer for nuclear physics calculations.[75]

The next month Fuchs moved right to the heart of the U.S. atomic program when he was assigned to the Theoretical Physics Division at Los Alamos, New Mexico, where he had wide access—for the British scientists at Los Alamos were allowed access to several different components of the project, often giving them a better overview than their more compartmentalized American colleagues.[76]

In February 1945 Fuchs, while visiting his sister in Cambridge, Massachusetts, was able to provide Gold with a substantial amount of written information on the A-bomb project, including a report, several pages in length, which summarized the issues involved in constructing an atomic device. The report discussed the possibility of premature detonation of plutonium through spontaneous fission, the use of high explosives in the detonation process, the advantages of the implosion method over the gun method, the critical mass of plutonium as compared to uranium-235, and the production of the plutonium at the Hanford, Washington, reactor.[77]

Back at Los Alamos, Fuchs continued his espionage activities. In early June, a month before the test at Alamogordo, Fuchs drove to Sante Fe to meet Gold. There he handed RAYMOND documents which contained a sketch of the bomb and its components, information on the size of the bomb, descriptions of the core and initiator, and information concerning the intention to employ the bomb against Japan.[78]

Fuchs was not the only Soviet agent Gold serviced at Los Alamos. A few days before Fuchs had arrived, David Greenglass, a twenty-two-year-old communist GI, reported for work as a machinist. In August 1944 he was assigned to the E-5 implosion section. Subsequently he worked for the X-1 and X-4 sections, which were responsible for producing the high-explosive lenses used in the plutonium bomb. He was thus able to confirm Fuchs's information on the design and assembly of the bomb.[79]

In January 1945, a month before Fuchs's trip to visit his sister, Greenglass went home to New York on leave. His brother-in-law Julius Rosenberg was a long-time avowed Communist party member who had dropped out of the party in late 1943 to become an agent of the NKGB, reporting to Anatoly Yatskov (who used the cover name Anatoly Yakovlev). Rosenberg quizzed his brother-in-law on operations at Los Alamos. Greenglass then wrote out a number of notes and sketches, including several sketches of a high-explosive lens mold that he was familiar with. While the sketches may have been less than technically perfect and concerned only one of many working models, they still had significant value. At the very least, they indicated that Los Alamos scientists were dedicated to perfecting a high-explosive lens—an arrangement of shaped charges used to create an implosion shock wave—which implied that the gun-type bomb design had been abandoned. Rosenberg proceeded to arrange with Greenglass an identification signal so that a courier, Harry Gold, could identify himself at Los Alamos. The information Gold received from Greenglass—several pages of notes and sketches of the high-explosive lens mold—was assessed by Gold's case officer as being "extremely excellent and extremely valuable."[80]

Greenglass was neither the only nor necessarily the most valuable American at Los Alamos spying for the Soviet Union. Between September 1941 and July 1942, a physicist, who would be code-named PERSEUS, told an acquaintance that he had been invited to join the bomb project and offered to provide information. The acquaintance, Morris Cohen, who reportedly knew PERSEUS from the Spanish civil war, was also a Soviet agent, and he promptly passed the information to Moscow along with a recommendation to recruit the physicist.[81]

It was not a hard sell, as the physicist apparently believed that the United States intended to use the bomb against the Soviet Union, not Nazi Germany. At a meeting in Albuquerque PERSEUS provided Lona Cohen (Morris's wife) information about the construction and testing of the plutonium bomb that was tested at Alamogordo on July 16, 1945. Unlike Klaus Fuchs and David Greenglass, PERSEUS, who was alive as of October 1992, left Los Alamos undetected and has remained undetected.[82]

By at least March 1943 the contribution of the Soviet atomic spies was considered significant by Igor Kurchatov, the father of the Soviet A-bomb. At that time, he informed his Kremlin superiors that the information received from intelligence agents on aspects of the U.S. A-bomb program, such as isotope separation and nuclear combustion, would allow Soviet physicists to resolve all problems connected with the splitting of the atom "much earlier than thought possible by our scientists." Kurchatov also wrote that "[t]he material is of tremendous, inestimable importance for our State and our science. Now we have important guidelines for subsequent research which enabled us to bypass many laborious phases involved in tackling the uranium problem and reveal new scientific and technical ways of solving it."[83]

Double-Crossed

Just as the Allied intelligence services had their successes, so did the Germans. But the legacy of German World War II human intelligence operations was largely one of defeat and disaster. In particular, it was Admiral Canaris's Abwehr which found itself being neutralized or deceived on numerous occasions.

One of the Abwehr's spies in the United States was William G. Sebold, code-named TRAMP, a naturalized American who had been born in Germany and had served as a corporal in a machine-gun unit in the Kaiser's army. Blackmailed into espionage by the GESTAPO during a visit to Germany, he was given the assignment of serving as radio and microfilm channel for Major Nikolaus Ritter, head of the Abwehr Hamburg post's air intelligence section.[84]

The agents reporting through Sebold included Everett Minster Roeder, a draftsman at the Sperry plant on Long Island and probably the Abwehr's biggest producer of technical information in the United States; an Austrian artist's model, Lily Stein, who recruited other agents and served as a cut-out; Frederick Joubert Duquesne, a middle-aged German publicist; and Hermann Lang, a Norden Corporation inspector who had help steal the company's bombsight several years earlier.[85]

Sebold proved so proficient as a reporting channel that other officers at the Hamburg post obtained permission from Ritter for TRAMP to relay messages from their agents. As a result, Sebold became the communications channel for Paul Fehse, a cook who reported on ships movements; Carl Reuper, a naturalized American who was employed by Westinghouse Electric Company in Newark as an inspector; and Eduard Carl Heine, who received valuable intelligence for the price of a postage stamp. Reuper photographed plans of defense equipment while Heine wrote letters to manufacturers such as Consolidated Aircraft Corporation, getting in return reports such as "Development of Diesel Engines."[86]

Unfortunately for the Abwehr, while Sebold was serving Germany as a spy he was also serving the United States as a counterspy. Even before he had returned from Germany Sebold had contacted the American consul in Cologne and agreed to work with the FBI to uncover German intelligence operations in the United States. Shortly after arriving in the United States he turned over to the FBI four rolls of microfilm, which constituted the Abwehr's collection instructions for the four Abwehr agents for whom Sebold was to serve as a radio contact. As a result, the FBI discovered the details of the Abwehr's interest in possible provision to Britain and France of directional guidance for bombers, new developments in antiaircraft guns, developments in the aircraft industry, antifog devices, and developments with respect to gas masks.[87]

Throughout Sebold's service as an Abwehr communications channel all the messages to Hamburg were screened by the FBI for dangerous information. In addition, TRAMP's meetings with German agents had been filmed through a one-way mirror. On June 29–30, 1941, the FBI brought the farce to an end with the arrest of Sebold's German spy contacts.[88]

While not every German spy in the United States was apprehended before being able to report useful information, successful spies were the exception. Altogether ninety-five men and women were convicted of espionage on behalf of Germany during the years 1937–45.[89]

But as uninspiring as the Abwehr's performance was in the United

States, it hit rock bottom in Great Britain. The Abwehr's undoing started with Arthur Owens, an electrical engineer who had emigrated to Canada at an early age but returned to Britain in the mid-1930s. His job, with a company that held a number of Admiralty contracts, frequently took him to Germany and he would often return with technical information that he passed to the Admiralty.[90]

In 1936, at his request, Owens became an informant for SIS. That he was also working for the Abwehr soon came to SIS attention, and in December 1936 Owens confessed his double life. Rather than take legal action against him he was permitted to continue his role as Abwehr agent—while continuing to provide information to SIS or the Special Branch on his German contacts and the information they wanted.[91]

In January 1939 Owens received from the Abwehr, and was permitted by SIS to keep, a radio transmitter. The transmitter proved defective but shortly after Britain entered the war it was proposed that it should be used to establish contact with Hamburg (the Abwehr post running Owens) under the supervision of MI5. That contact quickly resulted in a meeting between Owens, now code-named SNOW, and Major Ritter. Ritter's instructions led to the discovery of a pair of German brothers, first recruited in 1938, who were serving as German spies. One of the brothers, who had little enthusiasm for serving the Reich, became MI5's CHARLIE.[92]

Those meetings with Ritter represented the first opening of a black hole into which all Abwehr agents in Britain would be drawn. From the fall of France in 1940, which effectively cut off communications between Britain and the Continent, to the return of British armies to France in 1944, MI5 controlled the German intelligence network in Britain.[93]

For the better part of the war the mechanism for turning the Abwehr into a liability was the Twenty (XX) Committee, established on January 2, 1941, and consisting of representatives from the intelligence services and other concerned departments. Chairing the XX Committee, which met a total 226 times, was MI5's representative, J. C. Masterman. Born in 1891, Masterman had been caught in Berlin at the outbreak of the first world war and spent the war as a "guest" of the German government. Aside from his teaching duties as a professor at Oxford University before the war, Masterman was a cricketer, hockey player, and writer of novels.[94]

Over the course of the war MI5, which ran the double agents under XX Committee direction, had 120 double agents on its rolls. Agents parachuting into Britain were either quickly apprehended because of their mistakes (and sometimes executed), turned themselves in, or were betrayed by the widening net of double agents controlled by MI5. Some of those double agents were allowed to maintain contact with the Abwehr, others operated under strict MI5 observation. Over time it became clear that the double agents could be employed for more than uncovering information about the enemy's espionage apparatus and personalities, its codes and ciphers, neutralizing enemy espionage operations, or even inferring the enemy's intentions from the requests for information. If handled with sufficient sophistication, the double agents could be used to deceive the Germans about Allied capabilities and intentions.

Possibly the most important double agent, who would play a key role in deceiving the Germans about Allied intentions in June 1944, was Juan Pujol, code-named GARBO. GARBO arrived in Britain in April 1942, having worked as a free-lance double agent in Lisbon for some time, after having failed to interest SIS in his services. He had volunteered his services to the Germans with the intent of betraying them. Masterman later recalled that GARBO "came to us therefore a fully fledged double agent with all his growing pains over—we had only to operate and develop the system which he had already built up."[95]

In early January 1944 the Abwehr asked GARBO to find out whatever he could about forthcoming Allied operations. GARBO's efforts would be conducted under the master plan of the London Controlling Section, which was in overall charge of deception operations. The basic objectives of the plan were to make the Germans believe the attack would come later than it actually would, that it would come in the east (Pas de Calais, or Straits of Dover) rather than in the west (Normandy), and that when the attack did come in Normandy it was only a prelude of the eventual attack in the east.[96]

To encourage such erroneous conclusions the Allied deception plan involved the establishment of a real Twenty-First Army Group and a notional First United States Army Group (FUSAG), which in turn consisted of the real U.S. Third Army and the fictional British Fourth Army. The location of those real and notional forces in the east and southeast would create the impression that the main thrust of the invasion would be in the east. Further, if the notional forces were reported to have remained in Britain after the initial assault that would help sell the idea that the main assault was yet to come.[97]

To explain the sources of the false information he was to pass the Abwehr GARBO began to deploy a notional network of subagents to report on the imaginary Allied forces. Initial attempts to cause the Abwehr to doubt whether there would be an invasion failed. But the reports of GARBO, his subagents, and other double agents did convince the Abwehr and the intelligence analysts at Foreign Armies West that the main thrust of the invasion would come at the Pas de Calais. An agent code-named TATE provided the Abwehr with all the plans for moving FUSAG troops by rail to their embarkation ports, reinforcing the notion that the Pas de Calais was the main target. Agent TREASURE reported the virtual total absence of troop movements in the southwest, opposite Normandy. Agent TRICYCLE, Dusko Popov, arrived in Lisbon with enough misinformation to choke his German employers, which it did.[98]

The reports of GARBO were of great value, not only before the invasion but during its crucial first days. In an attempt to further enhance his credibility with the Abwehr GARBO was allowed to transmit to Germany on the night of June 5–6, after the airborne troops had landed, but before the troops coming by sea had arrived. However, as he received no answer the operators may have been asleep.[99]

On June 9, GARBO reported, after an imaginary conference with his imaginary agents, on the order of battle in Britain. GARBO claimed that seventy-five divisions existed as of D-Day (compared to the actual fifty), that no FUSAG formation was taking part in the attack (which was certainly true), and that the Normandy landings were only part of a diversionary attack that would be followed by the main assault on the Pas de Calais.[100]

GARBO's warning went to, among others, Colonel Friedrich-Adolf Krummacher, chief of intelligence on Hitler's military staff, to whom it confirmed the conclusions that he (and Hitler) had already reached. The warning from GARBO led Hitler to cancel plans to employ Fifteenth Army tank and infantry units as reinforcements for his forces at Normandy.[101]

In addition, Hitler ordered infantry reinforcements to the Pas de Calais. As a result, a month after D-Day two of the Fifteenth Army's three tank divisions remained in the Calais area, while an additional three infantry divisions had been added to the nineteen that had been present on June 6.[102]

The deputy chief of the London Controlling Section, Sir Ronald Wingate, recalled the moments on June 10 when it became clear, from communications intercepts, that Hitler had issued and then canceled the transfer of troops to Normandy:

> It was a frightful movement—there were those big red blobs on the war maps, moving towards Normandy all the time. . . . Then . . . [w]e looked at the [intelligence]—there it was: Hitler had cancelled [his orders]. . . . The P.M. came in with Stewart Menzies and the P.M. said this was the crowning achievement of the long and glorious history of the British Secret Service—or something like that.[103]

The Soviet Union also contributed to the Abwehr's poor performance. After the launching of Operation BARBAROSSA, some of the followers of a White Russian general who had found asylum in Germany, Anton Turkul, made contact with the Germans and offered to provide intelligence by radio. The offer was accepted and the Abwehr was given the task of establishing the radio links. One radio, code-named MAX, was supposedly located in the area of the Kremlin.[104]

MAX's reports flooded in and were disseminated, in succession, to Abwehr headquarters, Foreign Armies East and Foreign Air Forces East, and army groups and air fleets. Messages arrived on an almost daily basis, many reporting on troop movements. But MAX was a creature of the NKGB.[105]

Among MAX's deceptions was one connected to Operation BAGRATION, which the Soviets began planning in April 1944. The actual operation was to be directed against Army Group Center. The deception plan was to indicate otherwise: that the offensive would be directed from the southern Ukraine to recapture the Balkans.[106]

On April 27, 1944, MAX reported that Stalin and his generals approved a plan under which the the Soviet First, Second, and Third Ukrainian fronts would be launched against the Balkans from the Soviet left flank south of Army Group North Ukraine. His report also claimed that the attacking Soviet forces would be partitioned into independent operational groups, each with specific political and military objectives.[107]

Once again MAX's information was taken seriously by the Foreign Armies East and incorporated into its June 13, 1944, enemy situation report, which predicted that the Soviet summer offensive would not be directed at Army Group Center. Thus Operation BAGRATION achieved strategic surprise and demolished Army Group Center.[108]

9

The Wrecking Crews

Whereas spying was commonplace, whether nations were at peace or at war, certain other covert activities were severely restricted in peacetime. Once war began, however, the political and moral restraints that inhibited sabotage and assassination were removed. Thus when the Czech military intelligence service approached the British Special Operations Executive in 1941 for assistance in carrying out an assassination no questions were raised, not even about who the target might be.[1]

In both the European and Asian theaters of war special operations would aid Allied forces, sometimes significantly, in their military operations. Like other forms of clandestine activity the precise impact of activities such as sabotage and assassination in shortening the war or saving lives would be difficult to quantify. However, unlike activities such as COMINT, aerial reconnaissance, and espionage, some special operations would make life in the short term even worse for some of those living under Axis rule. For others it would mean the end of life.

Set Europe Ablaze

On May 19, 1940, eight and half months after Nazi troops stormed into Poland, the British chiefs of staff considered a report with the uninformative title "British Strategy in a Certain Eventuality." The eventuality that could not be mentioned in the title was a French surrender.[2]

The strategy laid out in the report did not include a large land campaign against the Wehrmacht. Rather, the report envisioned a German defeat as the consequence of "economic pressure, air attack on economic targets in Germany and on German morale, and the creation of widespread revolt in her conquered territories."[3]

Eight days later, the chiefs of staff submitted a memorandum which contained the judgment that "stimulating the seeds of revolt within the conquered territories [was] of the very highest importance." The War Cabinet ratified the decision to establish an organization for subversive warfare. On July 22, the Special Operations Executive (SOE) was established.* SOE, whose very existence was secret, was to operate under the control of the Ministry of Economic Warfare—to the great distress of "C," who argued it was necessary that all undercover operations be under his control. SOE absorbed SIS's special operations unit, Section D, the sabotage section of the War Office, MI (R), and the Foreign Office Department of Propaganda.[4]

Winston Churchill's instructions to SOE were emphatic—"set Europe ablaze." A more detailed vision came in the form of a September 4, 1940, chiefs of staff paper on future strategy. The paper's emphasis was similar to the May report, again stressing the avoidance of any confrontation with the German army while attempting to subvert German control of the conquered territories through economic warfare, bombing, and subversive operations. The paper noted three ways that subversion would play "a valuable contributory factor towards the defeat of Germany": by forcing the Germans to increase their occupation forces, tying down forces that would otherwise be available for combat, and undermining the German economy through the sabotage of key industrial facilities and communications systems. In addition, a general revolt at the time of major operations of British forces could help bring about German defeat.[5]

The September paper was followed by a chiefs of staff directive to SOE. The November 25, 1940, directive stated that SOE's overall objective was "to prepare the way for the final stage of the war when, by coordinated and organized revolts in the occupied countries and by popular rising against the Nazi party inside Germany, direct and decisive military operations against Germany herself may be possible."[6]

SOE's first director, designated CD, was Sir Frank Nelson, Conservative M.P., former Indian Army officer, and former SIS officer in Basel. Though nearly sixty, Nelson could still put in sixteen-hour workdays. After beginning as head of the Eastern European Section, Major-General Colin Gubbins became director of operations, designated M, in the fall of 1940. Gubbins, who would eventually become SOE director, was a Sandhurst graduate, who had been sent to Warsaw in September 1939 to head the MI(R) mission there.[7]

Early SOE Operations

SOE's most important early operations were those in France, conducted by a number of SOE sections—including F Section (unilateral SOE

---

* By the time the SOE was disbanded on June 30, 1946 it had trained and equipped over 9,000 agents and placed them into enemy territory with differing levels of success. SOE representatives operated in France, Holland, Denmark, Norway, Germany, Yugoslavia, Greece, the Middle East, and the Far East. In many cases it operated in conjunction with the intelligence and special services of governments in exile.

operations) and RF Section (operations run in concert with the Free French).[8]

Initial attempts to get even one operational agent into France failed. It was not until March 1941 that the first operation, a joint Free French—SOE operation code-named SAVANNAH, was attempted. Its objective was the assassination of special German air crews whose planes dropped flares to designate British targets for bombing raids. However, when the team finally arrived in France, after delays due to disputes over the means of transportation, they discovered that the Germans had so tightened their security arrangements that the mission was impossible.[9]

F Section's first success was George Begue, who parachuted in on May 5–6, 1941. His signal that he had arrived without incident was followed by the arrival of more SOE agents, who became the basis for AUTOGIRO, F Section's first circuit.[10]

Among the more successful missions of 1941 was JOSEPHINE B, whose three members arrived on May 11–12, 1941. On June 6–7, 1941, they detonated sufficient explosives to totally destroy six of the Pessac power station's eight transformers, putting the station out of service for a year. A dozen of the power station's guards were put out of commission permanently by the Wehrmacht, which court-martialed and executed them for negligence.[11]

The next month, on July 5, 1941, RF Section dropped a two-man team with the inauspicious code name TORTURE. Their mission, to sabotage a German airfield at Carpiquet, near Caen, went uncompleted because the wireless operator was betrayed soon after landing by a local farmer. His partner abandoned the mission and eventually arrived in Toulouse, where he initiated a circuit designated FABULOUS.[12]

SOE's French operations in 1941 produced little of immediate value. According to one SOE agent:

> The casualty rate was extremely high. Almost all the agents sent to France in 1941 had been caught. I myself had managed to escape only thanks to an extraordinary series of events. I still had not been involved in any direct action. The equipment and communications supplied for our early operations had proved sadly inadequate.[13]

F Section's failures in 1941 led to the appointment of a new section head in September 1941. The new head, Colonel Maurice Buckmaster, had joined SOE in March 1941 and would stay for the duration. The former Eton College student had served in Paris as a reporter for *Le Matin* and subsequently joined the business world. In 1938 he joined the reserves and took an SIS course with the rank of captain. The following year he served in the British Expeditionary Force and was one of the last to escape from Dunkirk.[14]

Buckmaster had arrived in time to see the AUTOGIRO circuit collapse in 1942, leading to the arrest of fifteen members. But SOE also had its successes. On May 5–6 three men parachuted into Cher province with the assignment of destroying the radio transmitter towers at Allouis. The towers, which the Germans had been using to jam BBC broadcasts, were eliminated on May 9, without any losses to the SOE team.[15]

In September Sidney Jones arrived in France by sailboat, with the task of establishing a small circuit based in Marseilles. The group, designated INVENTOR, was to specialize in the sabotage of railways and harbor installations. And when the Wehrmacht marched into the southern half of France in November, the saboteurs set fire to fifty wagons bringing food to troops in Marseilles.[16]

While SOE's record in France in 1942 was mixed, its record in Holland was one of total failure. SOE's initial attempt to insert an agent into Holland, in August 1941, failed when an enemy patrol spotted the motorboat that was bringing him to the beach. Two agents were then parachuted in on September 6–7. Betrayal forced both to flee and attempt to return to England.[17]

In October SOE parachuted in Huub Lauwers and Thys Taconis to search for the missing pair. However, their radio was so faulty that they could not contact London until January 3, 1942. The radio's defects actually gave them a few more months of freedom, for German direction-finding isolated the address Lauwers was transmitting from and he was arrested on March 6. Three days later Taconis also became a German prisoner.[18]

SOE's failure to establish a successful network was to be a minor problem when compared to the consequences of Lauwers's capture. Lauwers was persuaded to transmit back to London under German control. When he did so, on March 21, he was certain that SOE would spot the omission of his security check. SOE noted the omission but concluded he was not operating under duress. It not only acknowledged his signal but informed him that another agent, Arnold Baatsen, would be arriving on March 27–28.[19]

Baatsen's arrival marked the beginning of Operation NORTH POLE, directed by Hermann J. Giskes of the Abwehr and J. Schreieder of the Sicherheitsdienst and followed on a daily basis by Canaris, Himmler, and Hitler. Each day Giskes and Schreieder communicated by teletype, which precluded interception, to Canaris, who relayed the information to Himmler and Hitler.[20]

With the Abwehr and SD in control of the only radio connection with London they began a deception operation which netted them SOE and Dutch agent after agent. Within two weeks another seven agents arrived. Before long all were either dead or in German custody and the Germans were in control of a second radio.[21] As an immediate result, another two agents and radio sets were parachuted straight into German hands. Three more agents and two radio sets arrived in June and July, giving the Germans six transmitters under their control.[22]

Then, in late June George Jambroes, a senior figure in the Dutch government-in-exile, his radio operator, and their radio were added to the German collection. The radio was used to report alleged low morale and security in the Orde Dienst resistance movement. In early September four more agents were welcomed by a German reception committee, giving the Abwehr and SD yet another transmitter.[23]

SOE continued to operate without a clue as to what Giskes and Schreieder were up to. Thirteen more agents fell into German hands in October and November. By December 1942 forty-three British agents had been captured by the Germans. More important, fourteen different transmitters were controlled by the Abwehr and SD.[24] The deception continued into 1943, with thirteen agents arriving between January and April. However, the German policy of keeping all their captives in the same place led to a leak, which reached the British embassy in Berne in June 1943. Finally, SOE received word that eight agents parachuted into Holland on March 1–2 were being held by the Germans.[25]

Incredibly, the head of the Dutch Section ignored the warning and proceeded to send another three agents and an eighteenth radio link to the Germans in May. The operation began to unravel only when two of the three new arrivals escaped, reaching Berne in November.[26]

Berne's SIS station chief Count Frederick Vanden Heuvel soon telegraphed London:

> During their interrogations it became clear that the Germans were completely aware of the whole organization with its codes and passwords. For a long time the Germans have been transmitting to England pretending to be its agents. They guess that at least 130 men have been arrested in this way so that the whole organization is in German hands.[27]

When it became clear that SOE had finally accepted that they had been deceived so massively, Giskes decided to send a last message, on All Fool's Day 1944, in the clear:

> . . . YOU ARE TRYING TO MAKE BUSINESS IN THE NETHERLANDS WITHOUT OUR ASSISTANCE STOP WE THINK THIS RATHER UNFAIR IN VIEW OUR LONG AND SUCCESSFUL COOPERATION AS YOUR SOLE AGENT STOP BUT NEVER MIND WHENEVER YOU WILL COME TO PAY A VISIT TO THE CONTINENT YOU MAY BE ASSURED THAT YOU WILL BE RECEIVED WITH SAME CARE AND RESULT AS ALL THOSE YOU SENT US BEFORE STOP SO LONG.[28]

Heavy Water

Fortunately for SOE, its operations in other Scandinavian countries were more successful. Of those nations, Norway was the most important. In 1942 and 1943 SOE launched a series of attacks on the Orkla pyrite mines in northern Norway. The pyrites from the Orkla mines were being used by the Germans to manufacture sulfuric acid, a key chemical for many industrial processes.[29]

The first of the operations, code-named REDSHANK, began on April 17, 1942, and had as its objective the destruction of the generators and transformers of the Bardhaug converter station, an essential component of the Lokken power grid that served the mine and the electric railway which transported the ore to Thamshaven for shipment. The SOE wrecking crew sent to carry out the mission had no problem in overpowering the small security guard. The result was an explosion that collapsed the walls, blew the roof off, and started a fire that, with the help of incendiary devices, burned for hours. The mines as well as the Orkla Metal Company, which relied on the mines for raw material for the manufacture of sulfur, were brought to a halt.[30]

Other operations against the Orkla mines included FEATHER I and FEATHER II. FEATHER I resulted in an October 31, 1943, attack that put out of commission five of the fourteen locomotives of the Lokken–Thamshaven railway, which was the only means of transporting the ore. FEATHER II was undertaken in May 1944 because production and export of pyrites had been partially restored. Three Norwegian saboteurs stopped the sole surviving heavy locomotive, removed the crew, and completely wrecked the engine.[31]

In September 1943 SOE launched a series of eight operations collectively code-named VESTIGE, which involved limpeting shipping on the Norwegian coast. The operations got off to a good start: VESTIGE I resulted in the destruction of the 2,700-ton *Hertmut,* a modern refrigerated vessel. But of the final seven VESTIGE operations, only VESTIGE III proved successful. Six pairs of limpet mines planted on the 7,000-ton coal ship *Jantze Fritzen* detonated prematurely but severely damaged the ship.[32]

Certainly the operations with the most strategic significance undertaken by SOE in Norway were those aimed at neutralizing the heavy-water production facilities that the Germans were counting on to produce what they believed to be a necessary component for developing atomic weapons. Intelligence obtained in March 1942 led the SIS director of scientific intelligence, R. V. Jones, to recommend action be taken to knock out the Norsk-Hydro facility at Vemork, the main source for heavy water.[33]

Responsibility for the operation, designated FRESHMAN, which reached its climax in November 1942, was first given to the Directorate of Combined Operations, with the SOE playing a support role—arranging for air transport, getting the saboteurs to Vemork, and providing communications. Unfortunately, one aircraft and the two gliders used in the operation crashed 100 miles from Vemork. The survivors were captured and shot on Hitler's personal order, despite their being in uniform.[34]

Opertion FRESHMAN was succeeded by GUNNERSIDE, which called

for four saboteurs to connect with the four-man SWALLOW team that had been parachuted into Norway in October 1942 to support the FRESH-MAN team. GUNNERSIDE arrived safely on February 16–17, 1943. On February 27–28 two of the saboteurs slipped into the Norsk Hydro plant, placed their explosive charges, lit the fuses, and departed.[35]

Although the resulting explosion caused the physical damage predicted and led to the loss of about a ton of heavy water, it did not put the Vemork facility out of commission for long. At the time of the explosion it had been producing 5 kilograms (11 pounds) of heavy water a day; after Germany rebuilt and enlarged the plant to a level unforeseen by the British, production rose dramatically, resulting in 200 kilograms being produced in June 1943—an average of 6.6 kilograms per day and the highest recorded during the war.[36]

It took a bombing attack by the U.S. Army Air Force to finally halt heavy-water production at Vemork. But that did not end the heavy-water threat since substantial stocks remained. When it was reported that they were to be transferred to Germany the War Cabinet called on SOE to ensure that the transfer was never completed.[37]

Paul Rosbaud was able to inform SIS that the heavy water would first travel by railroad from Vemork and Rjukan eastward to Lake Tinnsjo, where a ferry would then transport it another railway line, which would then take it to a port on the Skagerrak. It was decided that the best chance of halting the transfer was by trying to destroy the ferry. At 10:45 A.M. on Sunday, February 20, 1944, the explosive charges planted the night before on the *Hydro* exploded, putting the entire stock of Norwegian heavy water at the bottom of the lake, along with at least eighteen passengers and crew.[38]

ANTHROPOID

If any World War II covert operation raised the question of the moral responsibility for the costs imposed on already oppressed people it was a Czech-run, SOE-assisted operation that culminated on May 27, 1942. On that day SS-Obergruppenführer Reinhard Heydrich, head of the Reich's Main Security Office (RSHA) and Reichsprotektor of Czechoslovakia, was being driven from his country mansion to Prague. As head of the RSHA Heydrich commanded the dreaded GESTAPO, the SD-Inland (the party's internal intelligence service), the SD-Ausland (the party's foreign intelligence service), and the KRIPO (Criminal Police). His appointment as Reichsprotektor, on September 27, 1941, had signaled a crackdown in response to the untraceable sabotage that had reduced Czech industrial output by 30 percent.[39]

Heydrich was a devoted Nazi, who, unlike much of the leadership, was tall, blond, and athletic—the ideal Aryan. In addition, he was willing to kill in the name of Germany and racial purity, and his appointment as Reichsprotektor was followed by a proclamation of martial law and a new wave of executions and arrests. Before the end of November 1941 4,000–5,000 Czechs had been detained.[40]

The head of the Czech government in exile, Eduard Beneš, found himself confronted not only with the terror being inflicted by Heydrich on his homeland, but with demands from the British and Soviet governments for the Czech resistance to make a greater contribution to the war against Hitler.[41] His solution was to sanction a dramatic act to be carried out by Czechoslovak personnel, under the supervision of the director of Czech military intelligence, Frantisek Moravec. After some consideration Heydrich was chosen as the target. SOE was not initially informed of the target but agreed to assist, designating the mission ANTHROPOID.[42]

As the Reichsprotektor's chauffeur, approaching a sharp bend on the city's outskirts, slowed the Mercedes, Jan Kubis and Josef Gabcik stepped into the road. At the crucial moment Gabcik's Sten gun jammed. Heydrich was well aware that an attempt had been made to kill him. But rather than have his driver speed away from the area, Heydrich ordered him to stop and lept from the car, planning to shoot it out with his attackers. But a grenade thrown by Kubis, while not immediately killing the Reichsprotektor, resulted in sufficient damage to his spleen to cause his death on June 4.[43]

Gabcik and Kubis survived Heydrich by two weeks. On June 18, after a member of another SOE circuit betrayed them, Gabcik and Kubis were cornered, along with five others, in a church. Rather than let themselves be taken by the GESTAPO each ended his life with a bullet to the head.[44]

What made ANTHROPOID a controversial operation was not the question of the morality of killing Heydrich. Rather, it was that ANTHROPOID provided a dramatic example of the dilemma of special operations in wartime—the tradeoff between the gains from such an operation and the consequences to the local populace.

Even before Heydrich's assassins were tracked down reprisals had begun. During the night of June 9–10 GESTAPO and Wehrmacht units herded the 195 women and 95 children of Lidice into trucks and carted them away. Only 8 of the children were considered suitable for "Germanization," and the vast majority vanished. The village's the 199 males aged fifteen and over were rounded up and shot. The houses were torched, the burned-out walls dynamited, the sites bulldozed and ploughed under.[45]

The death of the assassins did nothing to curb the thirst of Hitler and other German leaders for revenge, for they worried that a wave of assassinations could follow unless "energetic and ruthless measures were taken." On June 23 the GESTAPO razed the hamlet of Lezaky, and a week later 115 individuals were executed. Between May 28 and September 1, a total of 3,188 Czechs were arrested and 1,357 condemned to death.[46]

In the wake of the reprisals many wondered if the ANTHROPOID mission was wise. Indeed, some in the Czech resistance had opposed the operation for fear of reprisals. In addition to the suffering it caused innocent Czechs, the mission did not galvanize the Czech people as hoped, but reduced the potential size of the Czech resistance and guaranteed that the SOE's Czech section would have only a marginal role in liberating the country from Nazi rule.[47]

D-Day Operations

At the beginning of 1943 the situation in France was not particularly good for SOE. Only six circuits had survived from 1942. Among the surviving circuits was PIMENTO, a group of railway workers, and WHEEL-WRIGHT, which consisted of twenty SOE-trained agents covering a huge territory in the southwest. The six circuits served as the foundation for another dozen networks established during 1943.[48]

One of the most successful circuits operating in 1943 was STOCK-BROKER, in the Belfort-Montbéliard-Besançon area along the Swiss border in eastern France. The network's saboteurs destroyed transformers at the Peugeot works at Montébeliard, the Leroy Foundries at Ste. Suzanne, and the Usines Winmer at Seloncourt. They also wrecked locomotive turntables and engines and derailed trains carrying German troops and equipment; and they blew up the Usines Maillard in Doubs province, the Koechlin works at Belfort, the telephone exchange at Dijon, the hangars containing German army supplies at the airfield near Vesoul, loading cranes at the Montébeliard and Nevers, and a steel railway bridge over the Haute-Saône canal.[49]

Nineteen forty-three also saw a significant increase of the role of the OSS in special operations in France. Initially, the OSS role had been restricted to supplying arms and other material as well as a small number of agents to work under French and British orders.* In 1943 the OSS escalated its air drops of both supplies and agents. The Americans dropped 20,000 tons of food, weapons, and ammunition to the resistance. In September, the OSS and SOE jointly dropped 5,750 containers of arms and continued to drop at least 5,000 containers a month until the following June.[50]

But as the year progressed the question became how SOE, OSS, and BCRA should prepare for D-Day. One option was to focus on building up existing circuits in urban areas while conducting small-scale sabotage when requested. Alternatively, they could further develop links with the *maquisards* (guerrillas) who operated in the countryside—hoping they would materialize at the right time and tie down the Germans far from the battlefield. The first alternative would continue SOE's covert role while the second would move SOE operations into the paramilitary area.

---

*In 1942, with the OSS just getting into special operations, the OSS and SOE divided the world into areas of responsibility, which left SOE responsible for most of Europe, particularly France. The arrangement also assigned SOE responsibility for India. The OSS was to be responsible for China, Burma, North Africa, Finland, and, in time, Bulgaria, Romania, and the northern part of Norway.

The first alternative, which would involve the destruction of power facilities as well as the mining of bridges and roads, would have a high nuisance value, but it would be unlikely to make any significant contribution to an Allied victory.[51]

Eventually the idea for JEDBURGH emerged: dozens of uniformed three-man teams would be infiltrated into enemy-held territory once the invasion began. Some JEDBURGH teams would gather intelligence while others would link up with the *maquisards* along with larger Special Air Service and OSS Operational Group units.[52]

The first JEDBURGH team to arrive in France, called HUGH, departed from Harrington Air Base on June 5–6 to the Chateauroux area. Eventually there would be 92 JEDBURGH teams in France. The 276 JEDBURGHs included 83 Americans, 90 British, and 103 French. Each team worked with groups of 30 to 50 resistance fighters. The JEDBURGH teams, equipped with jeeps, bazookas, and heavy machines dropped from Allied planes, quickly became a major factor in upending German defense plans.[53]

The American who landed as part of JEDBURGH team BRUCE was William Colby, code-named BERKSHIRE. The future director of central intelligence was twenty-four years old and a major in the U.S. Army Parachute Field Artillery. BRUCE's mission was to establish contact with a *maquis* network, designated JEAN-MARIE, that operated in central France. BRUCE would arrange for weapons and supplies to be parachuted to it and coordinate its activities—which included blowing up bridges, ambushing patrols, sabotaging communications lines, obstructing roads and rail lines, and attacking depots—with the requirements of Patton's Third Army.[54]

In June and July 1944, eight American OSS/SO officers and six radio operators parachuted behind enemy lines as part of nine JEDBURGH teams, most of which entered Brittany. Those teams armed and organized more than 20,000 men, who cut and recut railroad tracks, derailed trains, and destroyed engines to paralyze all rail traffic throughout the area. They ambushed German troop and supply movements on the roads. As a result a major part of the German forces in Brittany had to be diverted to combating the *maquis*.[55]

August and September saw an additional 69 American JEDBURGHs parachute into France. Like their predecessors, they focused on organizing attacks on railways, roads, and bridges and on cutting electric power and telephone and telegraph lines—all of which hampered German commanders in moving troops, receiving supplies, and communicating with each other. Thus the Paris–Beauvais–Dieppe railroad was cut ten times during the last two weeks in July.[56]

OSS Operational Groups (OGs) which were much larger than JEDBURGH teams, also arrived between June and September. Some of them operated alone while others directed resistance groups in operations where large numbers of American behind-the-line agents were considered vital. The achievements of the OGs included the cutting of 11 power lines and communications cables, the destruction of 32 bridges on key railway lines and highways in the Rhône valley, the mining of 17 roads, and the destruction of 2 trains, 3 locomotives, and 33 vehicles. In addition, the OG's killed 461 Germans, wounded 467, and received the surrender of more than 10,000 prisoners.[57]

In addition to the JEDBURGHs there were forty traditional SOE circuits operating on D-Day. Unfortunately, the only succesful circuits were not in the most desirable location—Normandy. The destruction of two networks, PROSPER and SCIENTIST, resulted in only a few arms caches available in north and northwestern France. In addition, two key circuits, ARCHDEACON and MUSICIAN, had been under Sicherheitsdienst control. As a result, eighteen SOE agents were lost.[58]

Some circuits did make valuable contributions. PIMENTO, which spread across the south of France from Toulouse, paralyzed a significant portion of mainline railroad traffic after D-Day. The network placed explosives on dozens of locomotives and on rolling stock, effectively closing down most of the railway yards and switching points in their area and bringing the entire Rhône valley rail network to a halt. Any train departing Marseilles for Lyons after June 5 would inevitably be derailed at least once during its trip. Meanwhile, WHEELWRIGHT proved effective at isolating the Toulin-based Wehrmacht Army Group G by cutting its power and telephone lines.[59]

It is probably impossible to precisely assess the contribution made by Allied special operations to the success of D-Day. However, the extent of railway sabotage, designed to prevent German reinforcements from reaching the beachhead during the first forty-eight hours of the invasion, was significant. At least 940 sabotage actions were conducted on the night of June 5–6, producing at least 486 cuts. And the sabotage did not end there. Throughout the campaign railway lines continued to be blown, trains derailed, and locomotives neutralized, with the result that the elite 2nd SS Das Reich Panzer Division took seventeen days to reach Normandy from Toulouse. It should have taken no more than three days. Along with the FORTITUDE deception campaign, which helped reaffirm the German High Command's belief that the Normandy landings were a diversion, the bridge-blowing and railway-cutting operations played a significant role in guaranteeing Allied success.[60]

Sabotage operations also helped the Allies by forcing the Germans to employ radio communications, which could be intercepted and deciphered by the British. In addition to attacking power cables, pylons, and bridges, Allied special operations also placed a great emphasis on the destruction of telephone lines. Thus the Wehrmacht's five signal battalions in France all received unprecedented attention during and immediately after D-Day. The Wehrmacht unit at Orléans was subject to attacks by three circuits, HERMIT, SHIPWRIGHT, and WRESTLER. As a result, by the time the unit was evacuated to Germany it had failed to restore any of its major telephone circuits.[61]

And Allied special operations in France and elsewhere continued to plague the Germans as Allied forces drove toward Germany. In Denmark, from August through September 1944, more than 300 acts of sabotage were conducted against the railways, resulting in the delay of eight German divisions on their way to the western front. The departure of the 416th Light Infantry Division, which was planned for October 6, was delayed until the 12th as a result of the cutting of lines, destruction of bridges, and the mining of embankments. When the 233rd Reserve Panzer Division and 166th Infantry Division tried to move out of Denmark in a single week in February 1945 they found saboteurs to be a major obstacle. At the end of the week more than half the forty-four trains to be employed were delayed as a result of sabotage, with six derailed.[62]

10

Aerial Spies

The Allied and Axis spies on the ground were only one part of the espionage networks dedicated to uncovering the enemy's secrets. In addition, the photographic reconnaissance capabilities developed during the 1930s became invaluable assets to the belligerents throughout the war.

The outbreak of war removed any peacetime inhibitions concerning aerial reconnaissance activities. Nations would no longer feel it necessary to disguise their reconnaissance squadrons with cryptic names. More important, it meant that diplomatic considerations no longer constrained the scope of reconnaissance operations.

Aerial photography would prove valuable in the expected ways—allowing potential targets to be identified and troop movements to be monitored. But new uses would also be discovered.

From Identification to Estimation

As war became more and more likely in the summer of 1939 Sidney Cotton's business trips to Germany increased, with Cotton taking a slightly different route between London and Berlin on each occasion. On each flight Cotton and his cameras saw new concentrations of fighters and bombers at the airfields below his flight path.[1]

Once Germany had invaded Poland Cotton's trips to Germany ended. In anticipation of a declaration of war the Admiralty appealed to SIS and Fred Winterbotham to provide intelligence on the ships in the German port of Wilhelmshaven. By flying a small Beechcraft inside the Dutch frontier the British were able to photograph the ships, which looked like gray pencils in the photographs. But enlargement allowed the experts at the Admiralty to identify individual units.[2]

Once war was declared military reconnaissance aircraft were free to join in—and less than an hour after the declaration a Bomber Command

Blenheim took off from Wyton Air Base on Britain's first official photographic reconnaissance mission. Once again the target was Wilhelmshaven, in preparation for a planned raid.[3]

The declaration of war also meant that it was no longer necessary to operate a civilian photographic reconnaissance unit. On September 22, 1939, Sidney Cotton's days as an SIS aerial spy came to an end, and he joined the RAF to start a secret unit.[4]

Cotton's first objective was to replace the Blenheims, which had already demonstrated their vulnerability to German antiaircraft fire, with the fastest fighter in the world, the RAF's Supermarine Spitfire. Its speed and altitude would allow it to overfly targets of interest and return safely. Although initially unsuccessful, Cotton soon persuaded Air Vice Marshal Sir Hugh Dowding, commander-in-chief of Fighter Command, to lend him two Spitfires.[5]

With his prize in hand Cotton proceeded to arrange a test of the plane's capability as a reconnaissance aircraft. An airfield near Lille, at Seclin, was chosen as the launch site and one of the Spitfires, N-3071, was brought over by two of Cotton's men. Every possible safeguard was adopted to maintain the secrecy of the activities of the detachment, which was given the title Special Survey Flight.* N-3071 had its own private hangar, which was kept locked, and the pilots of the British Expeditionary Force at Seclin could only guess at the plane's mission.[6]

Finally, on November 18 the moment of truth arrived. At 1 P.M., with Maurice Longbottom at the controls, the plane took off and headed for the German border and Aachen. In one sense the sortie was unsuccessful, for Longbottom did not reach his targets. But in a more important sense it was a stunning success. Longbottom was able to take several runs of high-quality photographs from 33,000 feet over Eupen and the country just west of the frontier. Never before had good photographs been taken at high altitude under wartime conditions by a camera mounted in a Spitfire. Taking photographs unchallenged during wartime was no longer a dream.[7]

The missions that followed would contribute not only to the military campaign against the Axis but to further developments in the fields of photographic reconnaissance and interpretation. In February 1940, the Admiralty was demanding photography of Wilhelmshaven, to determine if the *Tirpitz* had left dry dock, as sources had reported. Blenheim reconnaissance aircraft had been unable to provide the answer. But one of the four Spitfires possessed by the Photographic Development Unit had been fitted with an additional tank, allowing it to reach Wilhelmshaven. On February 10, both Wilhelmshaven and Emden were photographed from 30,000 feet by the Type B Spitfire. When the longer-range Type C Spitfire

---

* The headquarters at that time was called the Heston Flight, for its location. In November 1939 it would become Number 2 Camouflage Unit. In mid-January 1940 the name was changed to Photographic Development Unit, while in July 1940 it was renamed the Photographic Reconnaissance Unit, or PRU.

became available in April, Kiel could be added to the list of reconnaissance targets.[8]

The photographs of Emden and Wilhelmshaven provided the opportunity to try out the Swiss "Wild" machine for measuring the objects in reconnaissance photographs. It soon became apparent that a vast amount of information could be extracted about the ships in Spitfire photographs. Within forty-eight hours it was possible to produce plans of the Emden port and of the naval base at Wilhelmshaven, with all the ships depicted to scale.[9]

The next month photographic reconnaissance was able to contribute to planning for a bombing campaign to be directed against the Ruhr. A second Spitfire had been fitted with an additional tank and on March 2 took off from Heston for a mission over the Ruhr. The high-altitude, high-quality photographs that were brought back were used to produce a "mosaic." Overlapping prints were pieced together by photointerpreters and rephotographed, allowing for a wide area but detailed view. When Cotton unveiled the mosaic in front of Air Chief Marshal Sir Edgar Ludlow-Hewitt, Bomber Command commander-in-chief, Hewitt showed amazed delight.[10]

In the summer of 1940, after the early June retreat from Dunkirk, aerial reconnaissance took on even greater importance as the British watched for signs of an impending invasion. Photographic reconnaissance had been singled out in May by the Joint Intelligence Committee as the best means Britain had of avoiding a surprise attack. But before the British could devote complete attention to the Germans they had some questions to settle among themselves. The Admiralty demanded that the reconnaissance effort be completely devoted to monitoring enemy ports. Bomber Command objected on the grounds that bombing German targets was part of an anti-invasion strategy and this required reconnaissance support. Finally, it was decided to turn the PRU over to Coastal Command, whose prime responsibility was to watch invasion ports. In addition, it was decided to expand the reconnaissance effort, establishing forward bases in Scotland and Cornwall, to bring a large part of the enemy coastline within range.[11]

Initially the PRU pilots were photographing Dutch ports and the Channel coast and finding little. There were no sinister groupings of ships to suggest an imminent invasion. But a steady watch was required, so when cloud cover prevented high-altitude flights low-level missions were conducted.[12]

Although photographic reconnaissance produced no signs of an invasion force in July it did allow the British to monitor the buildup of German defenses along the French coast, knowledge of which would be vital in planning the Allies' return. New photographs of Cap Gris-Nez showed a network of newly trodden paths and the start of three pits, each pit twice as large as a house. The newly uncovered earth appeared as a harsh photographic white against the undisturbed grays of the natural landscape and had the look of new military construction. Less than a month later the first huge twelve-inch guns were in position. Other photographs showed the shadows of posts and newly turned earth at their bases, indicating the presence of telephone lines and the location of local headquarters.[13]

Photography also showed the tracks of numerous heavy vehicles converging on the Forêt de Guines, five miles inland from Calais, leaving no doubt as to where ammunition and stores for the invasion were being hidden. Fighter bases at the Pas de Calais and bomber bases also made attractive reconnaissance targets.[14]

Meanwhile, aerial reconnaissance began to show signs that German plans for the invasion of England were advancing. The landing craft, essential to any invasion, were being rapidly prepared in the Low Countries shipyards. Photointerpreter Michael Spender discovered five 130-foot barges with modified bows at Rotterdam, apparently for the landing of tanks and troops. By mid-August the photointerpreters could report that the invasion fleet lay ready at Antwerp, Rotterdam, and Amsterdam.[15]

At the end of August photoreconnaissance showed that the fleet was moving: 56 barges had departed from Amsterdam, and 100 had departed Antwerp. Late on August 31 eighteen of the missing barges were spotted at Ostend. Over the next seven days aerial photographs showed the barges gathering; by September 7 there were 270 assembled in Ostend harbor.[16]

Photographic missions over Boulogne, Flushing, Calais, and Dunkirk showed the Germans moving into position to strike—so much so that the country was warned of "imminent invasion" on September 7. Over the next ten days the number of barges increased steadily at the ports closest to Britain and were joined by packs of E-boats and other small craft. The Spitfires returned photographs of the supply bases and Channel ports and showed gatherings of merchant vessels waiting to move forward. Other photos showed convoys of barges moving down the coast, in such tidy formations that it was evident that the German navy was in charge.[17]

The climax came ten days after the warning of imminent invasion, on September 17. There were over 1,700 barges distributed between Calais, Dunkirk, Le Havre, Boulogne, Ostend, and Antwerp. In a secret session of Parliament that night Prime Minister Churchill told Parliament that "[a]t any moment a major assault may be launched upon this island . . . upwards of 1,700 self-propelled barges and more than two hundred seagoing ships, some very large ships, are already gathered at the many invasion ports in German occupation."[18]

For the next few days, while the ships gathered at the invasion ports, the German and British air forces fought the Battle of Britain. But the Luftwaffe's failure to gain air supremacy had led Hitler on October 12 to "postpone" the invasion (Operation SEA LION) until spring. British photointerpreters soon saw signs that the threat was over. They first saw signs of a decrease in activity. And then the photographs showed signs that the invasion fleet was beginning to disperse and the ports were returning to normal operations.[19]

Photographic reconnaissance was also instrumental in revealing severe deficiencies in the British air offensive against German targets. Britain had resorted to night bombing by April 1940 because German air defenses made daylight pinpoint raids too hazardous to attempt. Night attacks focused on single towns or industrial areas rather than special installations. In June 1941 the air staff decided that Bomber Command should concentrate, when moonlight was available, on attacking rail centers and other transportation targets. At other times, approximately 75 percent of the nights, it should continue attacks on major cities with the twin objectives of causing economic damage and reducing civilian morale.[20]

At first photographic reconnaissance of the areas being attacked was limited. That and the small scale of the reconnaissance photographs contributed, until the end of 1940, to a tendency to credit air crew reports and occasional reports from Germany which claimed major damage over the photographic evidence that showed little damage.[21]

But a major raid against Mannheim on December 16, 1940, produced disturbing results. Air crews reported that most bombs had fallen on the intended target area, with the center of the city being left in flames. On a second run, during daylight on December 21, the Spitfire photographs showed that there had been significant damage, but it was widely scattered, with much of it outside the target area. Similarly, at the end of December photographic reconnaissance of attacks on two oil plants at Gelsenkirchen showed that neither facility had suffered significant damage.[22]

In April 1941 a detailed study of wide-area daylight photographs of later raids established that the estimate of 300 yards in good conditions for night bombing accuracy was unrealistic; 1,000 yards was the correct figure, although 600 yards might be attainable under optimal conditions.[23]

Soon after the offensive resumed in June 1941 it became evident, through improved damage-assessment methods, that British bombers lacked both adequate accuracy in target location and satisfactory bomb-aiming equipment to produce the results that had been anticipated from area bombing. Only one in four of the bombers attacking German targets that claimed to have dropped their bombs within five miles of their targets had done so. In the industrial Ruhr the ratio was far worse—seven in one hundred.[24]

It was clear that unless the situation could be improved there would not be much point in continuing night bombing missions. As a result it became a high-priority task to develop new navigational aids—GEE, OBOE, and H2S—which permitted far more accurate night bombing.[25]

The value of that aerial reconnaissance–inspired effort would become evident in the Battle of the Ruhr bombing offensive, which began on March 5, 1943, with a raid on Essen. The bombing raid was the first to rely on OBOE and other new navigational aids to guide 442 aircraft to their targets. The campaign continued to July 25 and included 15,504 sorties, which dropped 42,349 tons of bombs. Day and night photoreconnaissance showed a significant increase in the accuracy of bombing, which was associated mainly with the effectiveness of OBOE.[26]

In early 1941 photointerpreter David Brachi extended the value of the images returned by the Spitfires and Blenheims. By early that year the covers of German shipyards had accumulated. Brachi was able to learn, step by step, the methods and pace of each shipyard. He would assign a code number to every new submarine as soon as its keel was laid and then monitor its progress in each subsequent photograph. The first report he prepared based on this study of successive aerial photographs set a precedent for the remainder of the war, for the report didn't simply inform the reader of what could be *seen* in the photographs, but it *estimated* future U-boat production.[27]

From his examination of the photographs Brachi knew that the 500-ton U-boats were usually off the slips after eight months. Since fitting out the boats required another two to three months he could add a submarine to his production estimate for eleven months ahead as soon as he saw a new keel laid down. Even German camouflage did not prevent such estimates, for the extent of camouflage was precisely related to the stage of construction.[28]

The estimate Brachi produced was a shocker—a doubled production of U-boats in four months, ten in March, twenty in July. As result, a new Admiralty estimate of U-boat production was produced, relying almost completely on Brachi's data. Once completed it was submitted immediately to Admiral John Godfrey, Director of Naval Intelligence. The next day the subject was raised at at meeting of the chiefs of staff, after which the production estimate went to Churchill. It was very shortly after this, on March 6, 1941, that Churchill's Battle of the Atlantic directive called for Britain to "take the offensive against the U-boat . . . wherever we can and whenever we can. The U-boat at sea must be hunted, the U-boat in the building yard or in dock must be bombed."[29]

Aerial reconnaissance was also crucial to the landings on Normandy in June 1944. From 1942 Spitfires and Mustangs repeatedly photographed a thirty-mile-wide strip of the European coast, from Holland to the Spanish frontier. The missions served two purposes—to apprise Allied planners of the status of the defenses they would have to overcome and to identify targets for Allied bombing missions.[30]

As D-Day approached low-oblique photographs showed the configuration of the terrain, beach obstacles and defenses, approach routes for landing craft, and inland routes from the beaches. As Allied troops advanced toward Berlin aerial reconnaissance continued to provide valuable intelligence, as in the crossing of the Rhine. Aerial photographs allowed a target array to be set up for Allied artillery, including a large number of the German flak batteries in position to attack the airplanes and gliders of the airborne troops.[31]

In the week before the crossing regular tactical reconnaissance missions were conducted at low altitudes to obtain oblique photography of both banks of the river. At dawn on March 23 photographs were taken of the section of the battle area of greatest interest to the airborne troops. After the photos were printed and interpreted and reports were prepared they were flown to Britain for the briefing of the airborne troops that evening, at which each platoon commander was provided with an overhead photograph of his target that was no more than twenty-four hours old.[32]

Rowehl's Squadron

With the beginning of the world war Theodor Rowehl's Squadron for Special Purposes expanded to three squadrons, each with 12 planes. Euphemisms no longer being necessary, it changed its name to the more forthright Reconnaissance Group of the Commander-in-Chief of the Air Force.* At its peak in 1941 the group would consist of between 200 and 300 men and about 50 planes. In addition to the He-111 there were Dornier Do-214 and Junker Ju-86 and Ju-88. Subsequently the Do-217, Henschel Hs-130, and the Heinkel He-410 all joined the reconnaissance fleet. A plane such as the Do-215 carried three cameras, one to shoot verticals and one each to shoot obliques to the left and right. The angles for the oblique shots could be either 30 or 60 degrees, depending on whether the objective was to increase precision (using overlapping coverage) or increase the amount of coverage. To help ensure that the plane and its pictures returned, all of Rowehl's aircraft carried a special oxygen-nitrogen mixture to be pumped into the engines—improving performance between 25,000 and 35,000 feet and allowing the planes to elude British fighters.[33]

The Luftwaffe had also, by the beginning of the war, established a formidable reconnaissance establishment. The three reconnaissance squadrons it operated in 1930 had grown to fifty-three with 602 airplanes. Thirty squadrons and 342 planes handled short-range missions while the remainder conducted long-range missions. Among the Luftwaffe long-range aircraft were the Do-17F and Ju-88. The 17F was an adaptation of a medium-range bomber that carried a pilot, an observer-cameraman, and a radioman-gunner. Its major limitation was its ceiling—18,000 feet. As a result the Ju-88D, a modified bomber with a 26,000-foot ceiling, was used against Russian targets.[34]

Early in the war, as German troops rolled over one opponent after another, the squadron and Luftwaffe reconnaissance units provided crucial intelligence. The blitzkrieg of Poland was aided by the photographs of Polish brigades, antitank barriers, and field fortifications provided to

* Rowehl resigned in December 1943, by which time the Germans had less need for strategic reconnaissance, inasmuch as they were on the defensive. The name of the group was also changed, to Bomber Wing 200, and it began performing many nonreconnaissance missions.

ground commanders. Shortly after Hitler decided to attack Norway in 1940 the High Command of the Armed Forces (Oberkommando der Wehrmacht, OKW) realized that it possessed no up-to-date maps of that country. Only a few hours were allowed to prepare a plan of attack and the general responsible for developing the plan was forced to rely on a Baedeker "to find out what Norway was like . . . what all the harbors were." To remedy the situation Rowehl's squadron began flying reconnaissance missions to fill the gap. Soon there were new photographs of the ports at which Wehrmacht troops might arrive and of many of the coastal batteries and airfields that were intended to protect the port areas. Included in the reconnaissance missions was one to determine if the British had occupied the northern port of Narvik. The results of the effort were valuable, but not without their limitations. The aerial photographs and their interpretation resulted in the overestimation of some coastal batteries, the underestimation of others, and the complete miss of yet others.[35]

The April 1941 invasion of Yugoslavia was also aided by a squadron of Rowehl's aerial spies based in southeastern Austria. Since Germany had not yet declared war on Yugoslavia, the pilots wore civilian clothes and the planes carried civilian markings. In the ten days leading up to the invasion the unit was particularly active, with the results of the their operations going to a photo unit in Göring's special train.[36]

But the major effort in early 1941 was reconnaissance over the Soviet Union. Rowehl had established a fourth squadron for this express purpose in January, a few weeks after Hitler issued the directive for Operation BARBAROSSA. The new squadron sent planes on both short and deep penetration missions from a variety of locations—from Cracow in Poland, from Bucharest and Plovdiv in Romania, from Kirkenes on the Norwegian coast. The deepest penetrations reached the Black Sea, some 750 miles away. The photographs acquired from such missions showed industrial targets as well as the newest Soviet field fortifications. The flights continued of course once Barbarossa began. Thus on June 26 one reconnaissance plane photographed the airfields surrounding Moscow. The Soviet fighters and antiaircraft fire that attempted to end the mission were unsuccessful, as both were unable to reach the height of the Ju-88.[37]

Air Razvedka

The Soviet 1936 *Field Service Regulations* designated aerial reconnaissance (*razvedka*) "as the principal means of the commander for obtaining strategic data . . . and the principal means for obtaining tactical information." But while German planes were busy overflying the Soviet Union in the latter half of 1941 searching out new targets for the advancing Nazi forces, Soviet aerial reconnaissance was virtually nonexistent. The German attack in June had ravaged the Soviet air forces and made it impossible for the Soviets to rely in any significant way on aerial reconnaissance to monitor the movements of the invaders.[38]

Before the German attack there were ten reconnaissance regiments subordinate to the military districts. By the end of July 1941 there were hardly any reconnaissance aircraft left. While all remaining aircraft became responsible for performing reconnaissance missions, with 10–13 percent dedicated solely to reconnaissance, few qualified as legitimate reconnaissance planes. Further, many reconnaissance missions were visual missions, with photographic capabilities being very limited in 1941. It was not until November 1941 that the first photographic reconnaissance unit was formed, equipped with Pe-2 aircraft. In 1942 the Soviets acquired some Spitfires left behind by the RAF after operating them from northern Russia against targets in Norway.[39]

In January 1942 German forces were isolated in a pocket in the Demiansk region, with the German Sixteenth Army establishing a strong defense grounded on extensive dug-in fortifications. For the first time the Soviets relied on aerial photography to determine the German defensive alignment, with the Sixth Air Army employing photographic reconnaissance to survey German positions. The photographs were used to produce 1:25,000 and 1:50,000 scale maps and analyzed by front cartographers. The photographic plots' accuracy varied from 80 to 100 percent for firing points, trenches, and pillboxes; 75 percent for artillery fire positions; and 30–50 percent for individual guns, mortars, and antiaircraft gun positions. A Soviet after-action report concluded that "[a]erial photography is a most effective means of revealing the actual outline of enemy defenses. The results of deciphering, assisted by ground reconnaissance, provide in the final analysis, exhaustive information about the enemy's defense."[40]

But visual reconnaissance was to remain the prevalent form of aerial reconnaissance for a substantial period of time. Even by the fall of 1942 only 25 percent of the flights involved photographic missions, partially due to weather conditions.[41]

In the summer of that year the German forces swept eastward to Voronezh on the Don River, followed by a thrust to the southeast toward the Don's great bend. Initial resistance by the Red Army was followed by the launching of a series of counteroffensives in the Voronezh region along the upper part of the Don as well as in its great bend. At the same time German forces drove eastward toward Stalingrad and southeast toward the Caucasus Mountains.[42]

In October the Soviet High Command (STAVKA) decided to begin a deliberate defense of Stalingrad and to lay the groundwork for a strategic counteroffensive along the approaches to the Caucasus Mountains. The STAVKA believed that the destruction of the German armies in the Stalingrad area would stop the German advance into the Caucasus, permit the Soviets to recapture the valuable Don and Kuban regions, and perhaps expedite the emancipation of the pivotal Donets Basin.[43]

During the preparations for the Middle Don phase of the counteroffensive (December 16–28) two air armies were assigned the responsibility "to conduct *razvedka* in the interest of the forthcoming operation, photograph the enemy defensive sector on the right bank of the Don, and

uncover the beginning and direction of transport of his operational reserves to the front." However, poor weather prevented aerial reconnaissance activities prior to December 8. From December 8 to December 15,
the Soviets flew 212 reconnaissance missions. The missions "fully uncovered the enemy's defense system and photographed the main defensive belt on the right bank of the Don and Chir Rivers in the sector from
Rossosh' to Nizhne-Chirskaia," to a depth of seven to nine miles. Additionally, aerial photographs were taken of enemy concentrations and airfields in Kantemirovka, Chertkovo, Millerovo, Tatsinkaia, and Mo-
rozovsk.[44]

Aerial reconnaissance provided two other important items of information—the Germans had few reserves opposite Soviet main attack axes
and they occupied none of the prepared defenses in the operational depth
of their rear area. According to an official Soviet account, "the quality of
air *razvedka* was very good, and ground commanders disposed of exhaustive data upon which to base their decisions in penetrating the enemy
defensive sector." The reconnaissance missions against Millerovo, Tatsinkaia, and Chemyshkovsky provided intelligence which aided Soviet
aircraft in their destruction of 120 German aircraft in attacks on those
bases, which in turn helped the Soviets achieve air superiority in the
initial phase of the counteroffensive.[45]

But the success at Stalingrad did not mean an end to German victories.
After three months of almost constant fighting, ending with Soviet de-
feats in February and March 1943, a pause set in on the eastern front.
During that time Hitler and his planners examined ways for the
Wehrmacht to expand upon its March victories and regain the strategic
initiative in the east. They soon set their sights on the Kursk bulge.
According to a postwar German account:

> The Kursk salient seemed particularly favorable for such an attack. A simul-
> taneous German offensive from north and south would trap powerful Rus-
> sian forces. It was also to be hoped that the operational reserves the enemy
> would throw into the fray could be smashed. Moreover, the liquidation of
> this salient would greatly shorten the front.[46]

The operation was code-named ZITADELLE (CITADEL).[47]

By May the STAVKA, through an intense intelligence collection campaign which included aerial reconnaissance, had trustworthy information
on the movement of German troops and ammunition toward the Orel,
Kromy, Bryarnsk, Kharkov, Krasnograd, and Poltava sectors. In the Orel
and Kromy areas aerial reconnaissance operations had identified more
than 900 tanks and had pinpointed 16 airfields in the same regions.[48]

As preparations for battle continued, the air reconnaissance units of
the armies attempted to obtain coverage of their entire sector of responsibility. However, between 70 and 80 percent of the reconnaissance
flights covered only the principal approaches into the defensive areas.

Night flights focused on rail lines and major highways the Germans used in moving their forces.[49]

Meanwhile, the General Staff and Red Army air force relied on special reconnaissance units to conduct strategic reconnaissance up to 280 miles into German-held territory and detect and monitor movements of German strategic reserve forces. Prior to the Kursk operation this meant monitoring German formations moving from the west or bordering army group sectors into the area.[50]

During the period leading up to Kursk repeated reconnaissance flights photographed roads, forests, population centers, airfields, and enemy defensive positions. Front-based photointerpreters analyzed the photos to determine changes in the terrain configuration and enemy deployments. In May and June photographs were used to place enemy defenses on a map to be used by attacking Red Army forces.[51]

The results of such photographic missions allowed Marshal of Aviation A. A. Novikov to report to the STAVKA on May 14, 1943:

> Aerial photographic reconnaissance by the 4th Reconnaissance Air Regiment by the end of 14 May 1943 in the region of Orel, Kromy established over 900 enemy tanks and up to 1,500 motor vehicles.
>
> The tanks are located 5–10 km behind the *front* line at the following points. 150 tanks and vehicles 2 km to the west of Kurakino Station (50 km to the southeast of Orel); 200 tanks and 100 vehicles to the south of Krasnaia Ivanovka (8 km to the west of Kurakino Station); 200 tanks and motor vehicles in the forest to the north of Sobakino (23 km to the southwest of Kurakino Station); 220 tanks and vehicles in a grove to the south of Staroe Gorokhovo; 90 tanks and 30 vehicles near Rogovka (50 km to the south of Orel).
>
> In the villages adjacent to Zmievka Station (35 km to the southeast of Orel), a significant number of motor vehicles and 50–60 tanks were noted. At Zmievka Station, 12 trains have unloaded with motor vehicles and freight; the station is covered by the fire of three antiaircraft artillery batteries.
>
> The tanks located outside the population points and woods have been partially dug in and camouflaged. Moreover, systematic air observation over the last three days at the 16 airfields in the Orel region has noted more than 580 enemy aircraft. I conclude that the enemy with the tanks and motorized units has taken a jump-off position and has created an air grouping in the Orel sector for assisting the ground forces.[52]

After Kursk Soviet forces launched a general offensive across the expanse of the eastern front from west of Moscow to the Black Sea. The offensive, which continued into 1944, was aided by both a strategic deception plan (*maskirovka*) and a variety of Soviet intelligence activities, including aerial reconnaissance.

The value of aerial intelligence was emphasized in the 1944 *Field Service Regulations*, as follows: "Aerial photo *razvedka*, which permits studying reconnoitered objectives with great reliability and completeness, is of greatest value." The regulation revised the distance from the front that consituted strategic and tactical reconnaissance to 500 kilometers (310 miles) for strategic reconnaissance and 100 kilometers (62 miles) for tactical.[53]

There were also greater resources available to carry out reconnaissance missions. Between January 1 and July 1, 1944, the number of reconnaissance aircraft available to the First Ukrainian Army rose from thirty to fifty-two. By the end of the year the figure would rise to ninety-three. By 1944 reconnaissance missions represented 25 to 30 percent of aircraft sorties, on some occasions reaching almost 50 percent.[54]

By August 1944 the forces of the German Army Group North Ukraine were straining to hold Soviet forces along the Vistula. In addition, Soviet forces attacked the weakened German Army Group South Ukraine, which was attempting to hold Romania. In only two weeks the Soviets destroyed the German force and drove deep into the Balkans, taking Romania and Bulgaria while threatening the German southern flank in Hungary.[55]

In late October, as Soviet forces on the main strategic direction, along the Vistula and Narev rivers, moved deeper into Poland the Soviet High Command began planning for the 1944–45 winter offensive. In preparation for the offensive the Soviets conducted air reconnaissance missions, employing units directly under the supervision of the High Command for strategic reconnaissance and units subordinate to the two front armies for tactical reconnaissance.[56]

Characteristically poor weather conditions prior to the offensive, along with heavy German flak, made tactical photography difficult. Despite the limitations Soviet reconnaissance aircraft photographed German tactical defenses three times prior to the attack. In the vicinity of the Magnushev and Pulavy bridgeheads in eastern Poland, German trenches and strongpoints were photographed four times, with mosaics of German defenses in those sectors stretching fifteen to twenty-five miles to the west. Such missions allowed detection of an additional six antitank barriers standing twelve to twenty-five miles from north to south and a series of intermediate positions and defense lines. Aerial reconnaissance also led to the detection of decoy defenses and artillery positions. Other photographic reconnaissance missions returned data on communications lines, key road junctions, and German airfields.[57]

Photographic reconnaissance also proved its value after the operation began on January 12. On January 16, after the weather cleared, reconnaissance operations included the entire front. Opposite Magnushev and Pulavy, reconnaissance "determined the direction of withdrawal of German forces and the location of friendly forward detachments and main force formations." The next day photographic reconnaissance missions confirmed the destruction of bridges at Seradz, Vyshorrud, and Kutno as well as the annihilation of eight railroad trains.[58]

On the same day, aerial reconnaissance detected an even more important fact—the arrival of significant German reserves. According to one Soviet account:

> Air *razvedka* determined that tanks were unloading in the Lodz region. This was tank corps "Grossdeutschland" transferred from Prussia. The commander of the 16th Air Army assigned the 241st Bomber Division the mission of launching air strikes. Operating in eight groups, the crews in three passes destroyed the railroad railbed at the arrival and departure switches and almost fully knocked out the rail center. Bombing from various directions and various heights disorganized the German air defense. Tankers soon secured Lodz, seized 400 rail cars with military equipment and cargo and 28 repaired engines. Because of the blows of aviation and *front* mobile forces, tanks corps "Grossdeutschland" suffered considerable losses and was forced to withdraw, having failed to advance into battle.[59]

Bodyline

In December 1942 the SIS received a report from a Danish chemical engineer who had been traveling on company business. He reported a conversation he had heard in Berlin: a professor at the Berlin Technische Hochschule and an engineer discussed a five-ton rocket with a maximum range of 120 miles and a capability to damage a 6-square-mile area. A second report followed on January 1.[60]

Those reports, a large number of reports from SIS sources that were to follow, information obtained overtly and surreptitiously from prisoners of war, and COMINT would prove significant as British intelligence and defense officials tried to piece together the facts concerning the alleged rockets. Photographic reconnaissance would also play a crucial role in establishing the validity of SIS reports, identifying production and launch sites, and assessing damage from bombing runs on those sites.

In early January 1943 the Photographic Reconnaissance Unit was asked to photograph Peenemünde, an area which had last been covered in May 1942. On January 19, two days after an SIS source claimed that a factory had been established there to produce rockets, the PRU overflew the area. The photographs from that mission, as well as one on March 1, revealed construction activity, including many large buildings and a power house. That information alone did not confirm or contradict the SIS reports.[61]

Prime Minister Churchill was informed on April 15, by a vice-chiefs of staff memo, of the reports concerning long-range rockets, and he was encouraged to appoint Duncan Sandys, Joint Parliamentary Secretary to the Ministry of Supply, to conduct an investigation. The prime minister agreed, and Sandys was instructed first to determine if the intelligence which pointed to the development of long-range rockets was reliable, and, if it was, to explore how precise intelligence about the rocket and any launching apparatus could be acquired and develop a program of countermeasures. The investigation was given the code name BODYLINE.[62]

A May 17, 1943, interim report from Sandys was heavily based on the results of several additional photoreconnaissance missions and the Central Interpretation Unit's analysis of the resulting photographs. On April 29 Sandys's was briefed on the CIU's findings. His briefer, armed with the reconnaissance photographs, pointed to a large power station near Peenemünde and the power lines that radiated from it throughout the experimental station. He explained that the huge new workshops among the trees indicated plans for large-scale production of some kind. But the key item were the enormous "earthworks" in the woods, with towerlike structures and three circular emplacements. Sandys was then shown enlargements of the earthworks and his briefer explained why he believed the towers might be test stands for launching missiles while the other features might indicate the testing of explosives.[63]

Sandys's report reflected his briefing. He concluded that the Germans had been engaged in long-range rocket development for some time and that "such scant evidence as exists suggests that it may be far advanced."[64] The report obviously mandated that SIS, GC&CS, and PRU all employ their special capabilities to collect further information on all aspects of any such program. Photographic reconnaissance missions in May showed trucks carrying unidentifiable cylindrical objects measuring thirty-eight feet by eight feet. But it was a June 12 mission that brought confirmation of the rocket hypothesis. In one of the photos R. V. Jones, the Air Ministry's Assistant Director of Intelligence (Science), noticed that a railway truck carried what might be a "whiteish cylinder about 35 feet long and 5 or so feet in diameter, with a bluntish nose and fins at the other end." Photographs from a June 23 mission showing two rockets lying horizontally on trucks confirmed and augmented Jones's assessment. Such rockets, first designated A-4, would become far better known as the V-2.[65]

In addition to monitoring the Peenemünde area PRU was covering northern France, looking for possible launch sites from which the rockets could be fired toward England. In early July a human source reported secret weapon activity at Watten, near Calais. Photographic missions showed that work on a railway to the site, necessary to transport rockets, was nearly complete and huge trenches were being dug.[66]

Two bombing raids followed. Peenemünde was attacked first, on August 17–18. Originally Bomber Command had planned to focus on the facilities for development and testing of the rockets. But Sandys convinced them that their primary targets should be the homes of the scientists and engineers associated with the program. As a result some key personnel died that night, including Dr. Thiel, who was responsible for rocket jet design. That the attack had also severely damaged the buildings was indicated by the results of a photographic reconnaissance mission on the 19th. Less clear was the extent to which the program was delayed, with postwar estimates varying from four weeks to six months.[67]

Ten days later, on August 27, U.S. bombers attacked Watten. The attack came just as a huge quantity of concrete was hardening. Photos from a damage assessment mission showed significant damage but less than complete destruction. The follow-up bombing attack on September 7 reduced the site to "a desolate heap."[68]

While the BODYLINE investigation was focused on the V-2 program, indications of another advanced weapon started to arrive. SIS reports from the end of July increasingly referred to a pilotless aircraft. These reports became all the more convincing because of decrypts of September 7 ENIGMA messages that referred to the Flakzielgrat (flak target apparatus) 76, which would become the V-1. In a September 25 report R. V. Jones argued that evidence that the V-2 would operate reliably did not preclude the Germans from pursuing a pilotless aircraft.[69]

Some time after Jones's report, probably toward the end of October, SIS sources reported on six sites in northern France, each consisting of a strip of concrete and a line of posts that were aligned with London. Reconnaissance missions had already identified construction in the Pas de Calais area and a November 3 mission produced confirmation of the SIS reports. By the end of the month the CIU had located eighty-two sites in northern France. The photographs showed that each site had three long, narrow buildings, each with a slightly curving end similar to a ski lying on its side, as well as a flat platform. On an extension of the platform was a series of studs, possibly where a ramp would be placed. Meanwhile, SIS provided a drawing which showed a 150-foot-long ramp with a 15 degree inclination.[70]

The CIU's analysis had led the Joint Intelligence committee's CROSS-BOW subcommittee* to conclude, on December 4, that "evidence is accumulating that the ski sites are designed to launch pilotless aircraft." Indeed, by early December Britain's intelligence analysts were able to determine the size of the V-1, via analysis of reconnaissance photographs taken over Peenemünde. Speed, range, and accuracy were estimated on the basis of decryption of plot reports from Baltic test stations.[71]

What photoreconnaissance could not provide, and others sources did not, was intelligence on the V-1 production rate and when Germany would begin its offensive. In light of what could be an imminent threat, a bombing campaign against the suspected launch sites began in December. By the first week in March, photoreconnaissance showed that fifty-four of the ninety-six launch sites that had been identified† had suffered major damage and nine were being repaired, while there was no evidence of repair work at thirty-one.[72]

Photographic reconnaissance would continue to locate and monitor production and launch sites for the V-1 and V-2 as well as allow damage assessment of bombing raids on those sites. However, no intelligence

---

* The code word BODYLINE had been changed to CROSSBOW on November 15.

† At the time it was thought there might be 120 launch sites. In fact, the 96 identified constituted the total set.

source, even when used to direct bombing raids, was able to eliminate the threat from the V-weapons. V-1 attacks on London began on June 13, 1944, one week after the Allied landings in Normandy. V-2 attacks began on September 8.

But the identification of the threats allowed time for British investigation of how to minimize the damage from at least one of the incoming terror weapons. The six-month interval between warning and V-1 attack allowed identification of fighter techniques to destroy the flying bombs. Although those techniques were apparently not fully in place on June 13, the fighters performed well even during the initial weeks of the bombardment. The interval had also allowed time to prepare for the use of anti-aircraft guns against the incoming rockets, although an initial misunderstanding resulted in bringing down some of the bombs on central London.[73]

Another countermeasure was the use, noted in Chapter 8, of Britain's double agents to mislead the Abwehr about the location of incoming V-1. Based on the assumption that Germany would be flying photoreconnaissance missions over the targeted areas, it would not be feasible to have the agents misrepresent *where* the bombs landed. However, since the bombs generally tended to fall short of central London, having the double agents provide correct points of impact for bombs that tended to have a longer than normal range coupled with *times* of impact for bombs that fell short would lead the Germans to further shorten the range of the V-1s, resulting in less damage to central London.[74]

According to one estimate the scheme reduced fatalities and serious injuries by one-third, or 2,750 fewer killed and 8,000 fewer seriously injured. However, a key assumption that produced the scheme turned out to be faulty, while data that could have led to its undoing were simply ignored by the Germans. There had been no German photographic reconnaissance from January 10, 1941, to September 10, 1944, due to British Fighter Command. In addition, some V-1s had been equipped with radio transmitters, which correctly indicated the time between launch and impact. Those results of course contradicted the reports of the double agents. But the Germans had so much faith in the British-controlled agents that they concluded that the fault must lie in the radiotransmitters.[75]

11

Black Magic

The value of communications intelligence was demonstrated in World War I and the years between the wars. But past triumphs did not guarantee future success, particularly in a security-conscious wartime environment. Nations that had suffered reverses through the codebreaking activities of their enemies may have learned the necessity of communications security. Further, code and cipher technology had increased dramatically. In addition, military technology and strategy had advanced since the end of World War I, and military forces would move more rapidly than they had in the past. The value of solutions to codes and ciphers would be significantly reduced unless they were produced quickly enough to guide the decisions of military leaders.

But COMINT, especially that derived from codebreaking, would prove of enormous importance for some of the participants in the new war. The reading of enemy messages would provide intelligence as good as or better than that which could have been obtained by a spy inside an enemy's military headquarters. And COMINT would also be a channel through which other nations could be deceived at crucial times.

Codebreakers

At the beginning of the war all the major combatants had in place codebreaking establishments, all of which would experience explosive growth during the course of the war. The United States began the war with the Army's Signal Intelligence Service and Navy's OP-20-G sharing responsibility for military and diplomatic COMINT. In July and August 1942 SIS was renamed successively the Signal Intelligence Service, Signal Security Division, Signal Security Branch, and then Signal Security Service. In July 1943 it would become the Signal Security Agency, a name it retained throughout the war.[1] But the title changes would not affect its mission, and by the end of the war it had ten thousand employees, a far cry from the seven it had in 1929.

In 1942, to upgrade the analysis of the COMINT the Special Branch of the Army's Military Intelligence Service was established. Heading the new organization was Colonel Carter W. Clarke, a Signal Corps officer. His deputy chief was Alfred McCormack, a prominent New York lawyer.[2]

As in the United States, Japanese military and diplomatic COMINT operations were divided between army and navy organizations. At the beginning of the war army COMINT operations were the responsibility of the 18th Section of the General Staff, retitled the Central Special Intelligence Bureau in 1943; this agency supervised all the signals intelligence (SIGINT) units assigned to area armies and air armies. Naval signals intelligence collection was directed by the Special Service Section of the Naval General Staff and carried out by the staff's Fourth (Communications) Department. The headquarters organization was divided into three sections (General Affairs, Communications Security, and Codebreaking Research), while interception activities were conducted by communications units stationed at various Japanese bases.[3]

Although war would ultimately lead to a consolidation of its human intelligence operations, Germany continued to operate the seven COMINT units it had before war began—as many COMINT units as the United States, Italy, Japan, and Britain combined. On the civilian side there was Pers Z of the Foreign Office, the Forschungstelle (Research Post) of the Postal Ministry, and Göring's Forschungsamt (Research Office).[4]

Four military organizations collected communications intelligence: the army's Main Post for Communications Reconnaissance, the navy's B-Dienst, the air force's Radio Reconnaissance Battalion 350, and the High Command of the Armed Forces' Cipher Branch. The Cipher Branch, with 3,000 employees at its peak, was the military COMINT organization that undertook the widest range of operations, attacking both military and diplomatic communications.[5]

In Britain, the Government Code and Cypher School at Bletchley Park, also known as War Station X and Room 47 Foreign Office, managed the entire COMINT effort. Work at GC&CS took place in a group of huts— single-story wooden buildings of assorted shapes and sizes. Hut 6 cryptanalyzed German army and air force ENIGMA traffic while Hut 3 produced intelligence reports based on Hut 6's solutions. Solving naval ENIGMA messages was the responsibility of Hut 8, while Hut 4 produced intelligence based on Hut 8's successes.[6]

Many key individuals were Room 40 veterans, including Nigel de Grey and Dilly Knox. Room 40's Alastair Denniston was in charge of GC&CS until illness hospitalized him in 1941. He was replaced by Commander Edward Travis.[7]

Alan Turing's eccentricity was surpassed only by his genius. He kept his coffee mug chained to a radiator to prevent theft, and converted his life savings into silver ingots and buried them in Bletchley Woods (and could not find them after the war was over). Among his intellectual feats was a paper entitled "On Computable Numbers" which extended the work of Czech mathematician Kurt Gödel. Gödel had proven, in 1931, that all complex mathematical and logical systems were, to some extent, incomplete. In "On Computable Numbers," published in 1936, Turing envisioned a machine that could move an infinitely long tape marked into squares to the right or left and could read and change or read and leave unaltered the 0 or 1 that appeared in each square. He demonstrated that while such a machine could compute anything that could be calculated it could not determine whether potentially solvable problems could be solved. It would become clear later that the hypothetical machine in his paper was the idealization of general-purpose computers.[8]

World War II also saw the birth of cryptographic units in Canada and Australia, units which would aid the Allied war effort and become significant partners in a postwar COMINT alliance. In June 1941 Canada established the Examination Unit of the National Research Council. Following up on a suggestion by General Joseph Mauborgne, head of the U.S. Army Signal Corps, the Canadians recruited none other than Herbert Yardley to head their new organization.[9]

The Examination Unit's staff grew to twenty-five within months, and by the end of 1941 they were involved in intercepting and decoding the simple traffic between German Abwehr controllers in Hamburg and their agents in Latin America. At the same time they were decoding messages to and from the Vichy delegation in Ottawa, which was suspected of covert propaganda operations in Quebec.[10]

But neither the American SIS or Bletchley Park considered Yardley remotely acceptable, because of the massive security breach that his 1931 memoirs, *The American Black Chamber*, represented. In January 1942, to the great relief of the Canadians, he left quietly after being dismissed. Yardley's departure and the arrival of a British director, Oliver Strachey, opened the way to closer cooperation with, and to some extent direction by, GC&CS—which included Britain providing keys to the Vichy codes.[11]

The war also led Australia to reenter the cryptographic world.* In January 1940 the Australia General Staff established a small cryptographic unit consisting of four academics from Sydney University who had volunteered to study foreign codes should such skills be needed in the future. In 1941 the unit became part of a Special Intelligence Bureau, which was able to break one of the codes used by the Japanese mission in Australia.[12]

---

*During World War I the Austrialian Naval Board set up its own version of Room 40. See Patrick Beesly, *Room 40: British Naval Intelligence 1914–1918* (New York: Harcourt, Brace and Jovanovich, 1982), p. 74.

Breaking ENIGMA

Solving the code and cipher systems of one's enemies would be a far more difficult task in World War II than it was in the previous war, due to the more complex process by which plaintext was transformed into letters and numbers.

The German military ENIGMA machine used in World War II originated even before the end of the previous world war, when, in April 1918, a thirty-nine-year-old electrical engineer, Arthur Scherbius, applied for a patent for a new type of cipher machine. Scherbius's ENIGMA would be adopted by the German navy in 1926, the army in 1928, and the air force in 1935. From their adoption through 1939 and then throughout the war repeated refinements would make solving the machine's messages progressively more difficult.[13]

ENIGMA machines looked like typewriters, with a twenty-six-letter keyboard and the letters arranged in the same manner as a standard German typewriter. Behind each keyboard was a "lampboard," which consisted of twenty-six small circular windows, arranged in the same pattern as the keyboard. Pushing a letter on the keyboard would send an electrical impulse through wired codewheels to illuminate a letter on the lampboard, but not the same letter entered on the keyboard. In translating a plaintext message into an enciphered message, each letter of the original message was typed into the keyboard and the resulting letter recorded. The resulting text would then be transmitted via Morse signals.[14]

What made ENIGMA so difficult to decipher was the process by which a letter in an original message was transformed into a letter for the transmitted message. This process involved, for the army and air force ENIGMA, among other things, three rotors in each machine (chosen from a set of five), each with twenty-six settings, and a plugboard which connected keyboard letters to lampboard letters. The result was that the first time the L key was pressed a B might light up. But because the rotors turned, further entries of L on the keyboard, however, would produce not B but other letters.[15]

Exactly how an original message would be transformed would depended on which 3 of the 5 possible rotors were chosen and the order in which they were placed in the machine. When the 60 rotor orders were combined with the 17,576 possible ring settings for each wheel order (26^3) and over 150 billion (150^{12}) possible plugboard connections, the possible number of daily keys came to approximately 159 trillion (159^{18}). An operator with a similar ENIGMA machine that was set up in the same manner as that of the sender could recover the original message by simply typing the received message into the machine. For those without information on the the choice of rotors, wheel orders, and plugboard connections the task was clearly considerably more difficult.[16] Indeed, the Germans thought it impossible.

The first successful attack on ENIGMA came many years before World

War II, by Marian Rejewski, Jerzy Rozycki, and Henryk Zygalski of
the German Cipher Section of the Polish Cipher Bureau. Their attack
on ENIGMA had been initially aided by Hans-Thilo Schmidt of the
Reichswehr Cipher Center. In 1931 Schmidt, who wanted money to help
in his continuous pursuit of women, contacted the French SR and offered
documents on ENIGMA's construction, instructions on its use, and
keys.[17]

The French proved unable to translate ENIGMA messages using the
documents from their new agent, designated HE, and passed the information on to the Polish codebreakers. By January 1938 Rejewski and his
colleagues were able to decipher about 75 percent of ENIGMA traffic,
largely on the basis of their own theoretical work. Producing solutions
was facilitated by their invention of the *bomby*, a computerlike machine.[18]

However, further refinements in ENIGMA in 1938 and early 1939, and
Schmidt's transfer, made the work of Rejewski's colleagues considerably
more difficult. The Poles therefore decided to open discussion with two
other nations, who had greater resources. Participants in the initial meetings, held on January 9 and 10, 1939, included GC&CS head Alastair
Denniston, Captain Gustave Bertrand, head of the SR espionage section
which specialized in cryptologic documents, the head of the Polish Cipher Bureau and the chiefs of its German Cipher Section, and two other
Britons.[19]

At another meeting in July the Polish codebreakers showed the *bomby*
and demonstrated how it worked, and how they had often been able to
determine the ENIGMA key in under two hours. The Poles also told
Denniston that they had prepared two Enigma duplicates, one for the
British and one for the French.[20]

The Polish *bomby* was the predecessor to the *bombes* developed at
Bletchley, largely due to the work of Alan Turing. The bombes were

> bronze-colored cabinets about eight feet tall and seven feet wide. The front
> housed rows of coloured circular drums, each about five inches in diameter
> and three inches deep. Inside each was a mass of wire brushes. . . . The
> letters of the alphabet were painted round the outside of each drum. The
> back of the machine [was] a mass of dangling plugs on rows of letters and
> numbers.[21]

Instrumental in producing solutions to ENIGMA messages were
cribs—possible plaintext versions of the enciphered message. Cribs might
come from solution of simpler systems, captured documents, radio chatter, or a good guess as to what a message might concern. A particular form
of crib was the "kiss," which occurred when two messages with virtually
the same content were sent, one in ENIGMA and one in a simpler system.
Turing dramatically advanced the ability to test for cribs. He me-
chanically matched a possible word or phrase to a portion of the inter-

cepted message and tested if there was a rotor position that permitted such an encipherment.

On May 22, 1940, the German air force ENIGMA became the first version of ENIGMA to be regularly decrypted by Bletchley Park. Stuart Milner-Barry, an international chess champion who had arrived at GC&CS just three months earlier, recalled: "What a moment it was! It was pure black magic."[22] That black magic would soon be put to good use.

Battle of Britain

In June 1940 British forces were evacuated from Dunkirk while the French Republic fell. In the United States, President Franklin Roosevelt was about to run for an unprecedented third term in office, pledging not to involve the United States in another European war was vital to his chances for reelection. It appeared that unless Britain reached some sort of accommodation with Hitler, she would be the German dictator's next target and would have to face the Nazi onslaught alone.

German strategy was based on the premise that before an invasion could be launched the Luftwaffe would have to neutralize the RAF by destroying its airfields and the aircraft that sought to challenge the attackers. Reich Marshal Hermann Göing had at his disposal three Luftflotten (air fleets), stationed in France, Belgium, Holland, Germany, Denmark, and Norway, with 1,580 bombers, 1,090 fighters, and 210 reconnaissance aircraft.[23]

Stopping the Luftwaffe was the responsiblity of Air Chief Marshal Sir Hugh Dowding, commander-in-chief of the RAF Fighter Command. Dowding could rely on a variety of assets: seven antiaircraft divisions, a balloon command, an observation corps, and twenty-nine secret radar stations spread across the southern coast of England. But when it came to numbers of aircraft the advantage was clearly with Göring, for the RAF possessed 900 fighters, only 675 of which could be expected to be available on a given day.[24]

Dowding did have one other asset available—the GC&CS's ability to read Luftwaffe communications traffic. While the basic German strategy came as no surprise to British leaders, decrypted ENIGMA material— code-named ULTRA—was able to offer more. Thus the Air Intelligence Directorate reported on June 28 that "the opening of the offensive on this country must be anticipated from 1 July onwards."[25]

Beyond telling Dowding when to expect the offensive, months of ULTRA had provided him with detailed information on Luftwaffe organization, order of battle, and equipment. By the beginning of July it had led to a significant reduction of Air Intelligence's estimate of the Luftwaffe's first-line strength from more than 5,000 aircraft (including 2,500 bombers) with reserves of 7,000 to 2,000 (including 1,500–1,700 bombers) and 1,000 respectively. Air Intelligence now also estimated that 1,250 rather 2,500 bombers would be available during the first week of full-scale operations, which would result in 1,800 rather 4,800 tons of bombs being dropped.[26]

In addition, ENIGMA decrypts provided, before the end of June, intelligence on Luftwaffe targets. Thus Dowding would begin the battle with a repository of information on the enemy's chain of command, the numbers and deployments of forces, and the characteristics of the weapons they would be employing. The Air Staff, knowing the new estimates were based on ENIGMA traffic, would "view the situation much more confidently than . . . a month ago."[27]

The preparatory phase of the Battle of Britain began on July 10, with the Luftwaffe embarking on a program of daylight attacks on ports, coastal convoys, and aircraft factories—all part of an attempt to wear down the RAF's fighter defenses in the southeastern section of the country.[28]

In the days and weeks following, reports based on decrypts, generally of low-grade Luftwaffe ciphers, concerned German air force intentions and tactics. One report warned that "German aircraft have instructions to carry out on 12.7.40 harassing attacks in target area Map 3 on aeroplane factories. Ship movements are also to be attacked." On July 15 one intercept revealed that "day attacks on England are only to be made when weather conditions offer sufficient cover against fighter attack." The following day it was reported that "[t]he German Air Force have given orders that for special reasons the balloon barrages at Bristol and Southampton must be attacked and destroyed whenever the opportunity presents itself."[29]

Throughout the battle ULTRA related to the Luftwaffe's organization and order of battle provided continuing help to Dowding, partially by providing context for the interpretation of decrypts of low-level Luftwaffe codes. In addition, interception of the transmissions of the German MF Safety Service, which controlled the take-off, approach, and landing of German aircraft, provided early warning of aircraft departures for operations, while direction-finding located the airfields. That information was of very limited value until September, by which time analysts had made substantial progress in integrating MF intercepts with other intercept data. As a result, it was possible to identify most bomber units shortly after the start of each operation and provide useful information about the forthcoming operation.[30]

But COMINT by no means allowed Dowding unrestricted insight to German plans and capabilities. Communications between Berlin and the Luftwaffe units operating against Britain, including those concerning strategic decisions, were carried by land lines. And without interception there could be no decryption.[31]

On August 15 the Luftwaffe combined diversionary attacks to the north with the main attack against southern England. The Luftwaffe conducted 1,786 sorties, and lost 75 aircraft—as compared to 34 for the RAF. The result was a German defeat that is generally considered as the battle's turning point, leading to Hitler's September 17 decision to postpone the invasion. However, according to the official history of British intelligence in World War II, "there is no evidence . . . that Fighter Command got advance warning of the [Luftwaffe's] intention either from Enigma or from the [Luftwaffe's] low-grade transmissions; brief forewarning of the two attacks was received, it seems, only from radar."[32]

In the end, COMINT, both in its high-grade and low-grade varieties, was far from the most important factor in the British victory. The skill and dedication of the RAF's pilots was clearly the foremost factor, while the availability of radar was also of great significance. But the British started out the battle at a disadvantage in aircraft. Under such circumstances, whatever information could be provided about the enemy's organization, tactics, and forthcoming operations helped preserve British forces and deplete those of the Luftwaffe.

Midway and the Assassination of Admiral Yamamoto

The surprise attack on Pearl Harbor was only the first in a series of Japanese successes. In the months that followed almost all the Imperial Government's initial objectives were achieved, ahead of schedule. Control was established over the areas of southeast Asia and the southwest Pacific that produced oil, rubber, tin, and bauxite. Japanese forces occupied key strategic points essential to the defense of those areas. Their defensive perimeter ran from the Kurile Islands southeastward through Wake, Guam, the Gilbert and Marshall islands. It ran westward along the northern coast of New Guinea, through Borneo, Java, and Sumatra up the Malaya Peninsula and then westward again from Indochina, across Siam and Burma, to the Indian border. The remaining immediate objective was complete control over the Philippines, which seemed imminent since the Allies' final refuge there, Corregidor, was about to fall.[33]

But some Japanese officials, including Admiral Isoruku Yamamoto, the commander-in-chief of the combined fleet and the chief architect of the the Pearl Harbor attack, understood that Japanese success in the war required more than a series of quick victories. It required the virtual destruction of the U.S. Pacific Fleet, particularly its aircraft carriers. In a long war the vastly superior industrial base of the United States would make Japanese victory virtually impossible. Since the Pearl Harbor attack did not result in the destruction of U.S. aircraft carriers, Japan would have to move quickly to eliminate them. Yamamoto selected Midway Island as the site of destruction in the belief that the United States would feel obliged to defend it with whatever forces were available—for Japanese control over Midway would extend Japan's defense perimeter another 2,000 miles eastward into the Pacific.[34]

The Battle of Midway, as Yamamoto saw it, would be the largest ambush in history. Japanese submarines would patrol between Hawaii and Midway, first reporting on the sortie of what was left of the U.S. Pacific

Fleet from Pearl Harbor and then joining in the battle. The Japanese navy would send approximately 200 ships and 700 aircraft. After the First Carrier Striking Force softened up Midway it would be seized by the Occupation Force. When the U.S. fleet raced to Midway's defense Japanese submarines would warn Yamamoto of their arrival, and his Main Body would then enter the battle. Elements of the Northern Force would close the trap, and thanks to their overwhelming superiority, the Japanese would finish the job started on December 7.[35]

But Yamamoto's vision would never be realized, in large part due to the U.S. codebreaker's new ability to break into the Japanese navy code that the United States designated JN25b. That ability would permit the U.S. Navy to deplete Yamamoto's forces at the Battle of the Coral Sea, and spring its own ambush at Midway.[36]

A message intercepted on March 25 allowed U.S. codebreakers to determine that a Japanese offensive was to be launched against Port Moresby and Tulagi. Communications intelligence proceeded to track the daily movement of planes, ships, equipment, and personnel to Rabaul, New Guinea, in preparation for movement into the Coral Sea.[37]

While the American codebreakers could not provide detailed information on the Japanese operational command, they provided Admiral Chester Nimitz, commander of the Pacific Fleet, with an estimate of the number of carriers, battleships, heavy cruisers, destroyers, and submarines the Japanese would employ. It was sufficient to allow Nimitz to issue CINCPAC Operation Plan 23-42, on April 29, committing the carriers *Lexington* and *Yorktown* to the Coral Sea. The ensuing battle began on May 7. While the United States lost more tonnage—including the *Lexington*—Japan suffered its first strategic losses of the war. Not only was the carrier *Shoho* lost, but the carrier *Shokaku* was heavily damaged and lost about 30 percent of her flying crews, while the carrier *Zuikaku* lost about 40 percent of her flying crews. All three carriers were therefore unavailable for the Battle of Midway, reducing Yamamoto's air forces by one-third.[38]

Prior to May 11 U.S. codebreakers knew that another Japanese campaign was to follow the Coral Sea operation. They surmised that it might begin between May 20 and June 20, but they did not know the objective, the precise date or time it would begin, or the precise composition of the enemy forces.[39] If the United States had had access to a message Yamamoto received on May 5 approving his plans for the Midway operation, the question would have been settled. But that message was hand-delivered so there was not even an enciphered text for U.S. codebreakers to try to unravel.[40]

On May 13, however, two Japanese messages were intercepted that provided the first clues to Yamamoto's intentions. One involved a request by a Japanese ship that eight charts be sent to Saipan and held there until the ship arrived. Seven identified charts covered the Hawaiian Islands.[41]

The second message was particularly important:

The following is the schedule of the Goshu Maru—Put ashore at Imieji all the freight on board and load air hose equipment and munitions of the Imieji (seaplane unit) and proceed to Saipan by Soneka. Inform me later of your contemplated movements with Occupation Force.

The Third Air will load its base equipment and ground crews and advance to AF ground crews. Parts and munitions will be loaded on the Goshu Maru as soon as that vessel arrives.[42]

Both Captain Edwin T. Layton, the Pacific Fleet's chief intelligence officer, and Joseph J. Rochefort, head of the codebreaking Combat Intelligence Unit (subsequently the Fleet Radio Unit, Pacific) in Hawaii, believed AF was the designator for Midway, in part because those coordinates had been used in intercepted messages from two scout planes in the vicinity of Midway. They had already determined that several designators that began with "A" represented locations in the general vicinity of Hawaii, so Midway would be consistent with their previous findings. It was also a logical target for the Japanese navy, perhaps the best other than Oahu, being a strategic outpost with excellent seaplane facilities and harbor.[43]

Their conclusion was accepted by Nimitz, who had been persuaded to rely on Rochefort by the CIU's performance in the Coral Sea. But Rochefort's assessment was not convincing to the head of OP-20-G, Commander John R. Redman, who believed that the Japanese were headed for Johnston Island.[44]

Rochefort and Layton approached Nimitz with a plan to provide proof that the AF designator represented Midway. A message would be sent via the untapped undersea telegraph cable between Hawaii and Midway to the commanding officer of the Midway Naval Base instructing him to

send a plain language message to Com 14 (Commandant 14th Naval District) stating in effect, that the distillation plant had suffered a serious casualty and that fresh water was urgently needed—to which Com 14 would reply, (also in plain language), that water barges would be sent, under tow, soonest.[45]

If the plan worked as intended, Japan would intercept the message and then disseminate the information in the Daily Intelligence Reports, which the United States regularly read. Nimitz approved the plan and the instructions were sent to the Midway commander on May 19. The Japanese fell into the trap.[46] The intercept unit in Melbourne (which had been relocated from Corregidor) provided a translation of an intercepted Japanese message: "The AF air unit sent following radio message to to commandant 14th Naval district. . . . At present time we have only enough water for two weeks. Please supply us immediately."[47]

Intercepted messages also provided up-to-date information on the forces that the Navy could expect to face. A message intercepted on May 18 established that the carriers *Kaga, Akagi, Soryu, Hiryu, Zuikaku,* and

Junyo would all be part of the coming campaign. Messages intercepted on May 19–20 identified additional forces and narrowed the possible dates. Messages on the 20th indicated that the intended occupation force would leave Saipan on the 27th. That, given estimated sailing times, led to the conclusion that the attack would be launched around June 1.[48]

By May 20, thanks to the decoded Japanese messages, Nimitz knew the targets, that the Japanese were going to employ massive force, and that the attack would come after June 1. From the 20th to the 24th decoded messages continued to update Nimitz's picture of Japanese intentions and forces. New departure dates indicated that the Midway Occupation Force and the Striking Force would arrive near Midway about June 4, with the occupation to begin two days later.[49]

On May 25 the decode of the final operations order to all Japanese commanders confirmed that the attack would begin on June 4. Three days later the Japanese navy changed from the JN25b to JN25c code, shutting off the flow of COMINT.[50] But by then Nimitz

> knew the targets; the dates; the debarkation points of the Japanese forces; he knew of the plan to station a submarine cordon between Hawaii and Midway; and he knew about the planned seaplane reconnaissance of Oahu, which never took place because he prevented their refueling at French Frigate Shoals.[51]

The U.S. Navy's success at Midway was also due in part to the exploitation of the Japanese COMINT effort as a channel for deception. Yamamoto had expected that U.S. carriers would not be dispatched to Midway until after he had launched his attack, and he did not establish submarine surveillance patrols to warn of arriving U.S. ships until June 3, by which time the ships were at Midway. To encourage such a belief the United States began a radio deception operation on May 25 to create the illusion of a U.S. carrier force in the southwestern Pacific.[52]

Thus when Japanese forces began to attack Midway they found they had fallen into a trap. In the ensuing battle Japan lost four aircraft carriers, the *Akagi*, the *Kaga*, the *Soryu*, and the *Hiryu*; the United States lost the carrier *Yorktown*.[53]

Midway highlighted the ways in which COMINT could contribute to the U.S. war effort. Nimitz observed that "Midway was essentially a victory of intelligence. In attempting surprise, the Japanese were themselves surprised. General George C. Marshall, Army chief of staff, stated that, as a result of cryptanalysis the U.S. was "able to concentrate our limited forces to meet their naval advance on Midway when otherwise we almost certainly would have been some 3,000 miles out of place."[54]

At the same time, Midway illustrated the fragility of intelligence derived from codebreaking. Had the Japanese replaced the JN25b cipher with the JN25c in early May, as they had planned, the crucial intelligence that guided Nimitz would have been unavailable as U.S. codebreakers struggled to solve the new cipher system.

Yamamoto had scored a significant, if not decisive victory at Pearl Harbor despite the efforts of U.S. codebreakers. At Midway he was defeated thanks, in significant part, to those efforts. On a third occasion the codebreakers' efforts would cost him his life.

On April 13, 1943, in preparation for a new offensive, Yamamoto decided to inspect forward naval bases off the southern tip of Bougainville, in the Solomons. That afternoon various base commanders received an encoded and enciphered message:

> On 18 April commander in chief Combined Fleet will inspect Ballale, Shortland, and Buin as follows: 1. Depart Rabaul 0600 in medium attack plane escorted by six fighters, arrive Ballale 0800. Depart at once in subchaser to arrive Shortland 0840. Depart Shortland 0945 in subchaser to arrive Ballale 1030. Depart Ballale by plane to arrive Buin at 1100. Lunch at Buin. Depart Buin 1400 by plane to arrive Rabaul 1540.[55]

The message was intercepted by U.S. COMINT stations and relayed to three special processing units known as Negat (OP-20-G), FRUPAC (Fleet Radio Unit Pacific at Pearl Harbor), and FRUMEL (Fleet Radio Unit, Melbourne). A special radio circuit allowed the units to exchange information instantly.[56]

The units noted with interest the variety of addressees. A first cut at decryption produced a Japanese text with a large number of blanks and geographic designators. But further work among the three processing units yielded Yamamoto's itinerary. That raised the question that Nimitz posed to Layton: "do we try to get him?" Layton responded: "You know, Admiral Nimitz, it would be just as if they shot you down. There is no one to replace him."[57]

When Yamamoto's plane, escorted by nine Zeros, approached Kahilin near Buin on the morning of April 18, eighteen P-38 Lightnings were waiting. After brief combat with the Zeros, four P-38s broke off, heading for the planes carrying Yamamoto and his chief of staff. A burst of twenty-millimeter cannonfire from the plane of Captain Thomas G. Lamphier hit Yamamoto's plane, which crashed, in flames, into the jungle, killing all on board. Admiral Mineichi Koga, Yamamoto's successor, acknowledged that "[t]here was only one Yamamoto, and no one is able to replace him . . . His loss is an insupportable blow to us."[58]

Zitadelle

Communications intelligence played a modest role in the Soviet defeat of the German counteroffensive at Kursk, which began on July 4 and 5, 1943. Such COMINT came from two basic sources—from Britain, ostensibly disguised as intelligence from a "reliable" or "well-placed" source, and from the Soviets' own efforts. The British attempt to disguise their COMINT product as coming from a human source failed because Magnificent

Five member John Cairncross was responsible for editing ULTRA intercepts pertaining to Luftwaffe deployments prior to ZITADELLE, and he dutifully passed the intelligence along to his Soviet controller in London.[59]

Among the Luftwaffe ciphers that the Bletchley Park codebreakers were able to read was one they code-named HEDGEHOG. From February 21, 1943, when it was first solved, through June 1943, Britain could read the communications of Army Group South's supporting air forces.[60]

Although it is no by means certain, the Soviets may have also surmised that the ostensible human intelligence the British were passing on concerning German army plans was the product of codebreaking. Obtaining that intelligence was a substantially more difficult task than cracking HEDGEHOG, an ENIGMA-based system. The Wehrmacht's non-Morse teleprinter transmissions, which generally relayed the most valuable operational information, employed the more sophisticated GEHEIM-SCHREIBER (Secret Writer) system (code-named FISH by the British). The FISH links included SQUID, which connected OKH and Army Group South.[61]

The British, by virtue of their ability to read German air force ENIGMA traffic, concluded on the basis of mid-March decrypts that a German objective was the elimination of the Kursk salient. By-mid April Bletchley Park was able, again through decrypted Luftwaffe signals, to monitor the buildup of air power in the region. On April 25 decrypted SQUID traffic yielded the Army Group South's assessment of Soviet deployments, and confirmed the conclusion that the German objective was the Kursk salient. On April 30 the British delivered the intelligence extracted from the April 25 decrypt, along with a warning of an upcoming German attack on Kursk, to the Soviets.[62]

Such warnings conflicted with the intelligence the GRU* was receiving from its Swiss network, which reported that ZITADELLE would commence in mid-June. But then U.S. and British decrypts in May and June—which indicated Japanese pressure for the Germans to refrain from any further offensives in 1943, inadequate Luftwaffe deployments to support a ground offensive, and transfer of Luftwaffe units out of Russia—seemed to call into question the likelihood of any German offensive in the coming months. Thus the Joint Intelligence Committee concluded on June 23 that several factors, including Axis reverses in North Africa and strategic bombing of Germany by the United States and Britain, precluded any German offensive in the immediate future. That conclusion was consistent with SIS and diplomatic reports suggesting that Hitler had postponed the next, decisive, offensive in Russia until the spring of 1944.[63]

Churchill's own analysis was more accurate. In a letter to Stalin drafted on June 13, he observed: "Our information about German inten-

---

* The RU became the GRU (Chief Intelligence Directurate) in 1942, with the formation of the Commissariat of Defense.

tions is conflicting. On the balance I think Hitler will attack you again, probably in the Kursk Salient."[64]

The Soviets, of course, were not simply relying on the intelligence provided by their British allies. Soviet acquisition of an ENIGMA machine, as well as various cipher parts and documents, may have helped their codebreakers break briefly into Germany army ciphers. On September 18, 1942, the signals officer of the XXX Corps (Army Group North) warned of the "well-organized Russian radio intelligence" effort, which was capable of reading "every one of our messages." In January 1943 the OKH Signals Division knew "with certainty" that in specific cases the Russians had decrypted some ENIGMA messages and instituted changes in equipment and procedures to enhance cipher security.[65]

The extent to which those changes protected German messages relating to ZITADELLE remains unclear. But the April 8 message to Stalin from Marshal G. K. Zhukov, the deputy supreme commander, contained an assessment of the forthcoming German summer offensive that was accurate and complete. The message forecast a German attempt to eliminate the Kursk salient, employing a pincer movement against its north and south faces; at the same time, an attack on its western face would seek to isolate the two Soviet army groups in the salient from each other.[66]

Soviet interception of unencrypted messages along with direction-finding allowed identification, prior to the offensive, of the headquarters and units of the II SS Panzer Corps, 6th Panzer, and 11th Panzer divisions. Likewise, Soviet SIGINT efforts located the 7th Panzer Division, XIII Corps, and Second Army headquarters.[67]

Germany found COMINT valuable both in the months leading up to the attack and once the battle was joined. Tactical COMINT proved of significant value on the battlefield—although it was not valuable enough to prevent a German defeat.

On April 18 intercepts of Soviet radio traffic revealed that the Second Air Army had shifted headquarters to Novy Oskol; the Germans could then infer the location of the headquarters of the Voronezh Front, to which the Second Air Army was attached for support. Within a month, German SIGINT detected the arrival of the Soviet 3rd Tank Corps in the Central Front sector. Certainty about the complete Soviet order of battle eluded the Germans, however, for Soviet communications security significantly improved during June. As a result Foreign Armies East cautioned that unidentified enemy units could have moved into the Kursk salient.[68]

In the period immediately after July 4 German signals intelligence operations provided a unbroken flow of data on Soviet deployments and movements, in spite of ever more effective Soviet radio security. During the first three days of combat the Ninth Army's XXIII Corps intercept units collected 695 Soviet messages. With 500 of those messages transmitted unencrypted and 86 percent of the encrypted messages solved, the German intelligence analysts had 668 messages to sift through for data.[69]

For the next eight days the German SIGINT contribution was less impressive—360 unencrypted messages, 363 encrypted messages, and a solution rate of 81 percent—although it yielded 654 messages for analysts to examine. But when the Soviets began their counteroffensive on July 12 German intercept operations became a crucial factor in operations. In August, when the Fourth Panzer Army fell back on Kharkov, German eavesdropping on Soviet signals yielded the most reliable information on the positions of retreating German units. The XIII Corps in the Orel salient considered COMINT to be decisive in ascertaining the concentration of Soviet forces and their objectives in time to take countermeasures.[70]

But that intelligence was not enough to ensure victory. The July 12 counteroffensive turned into one of the war's largest tank battles. The next day, with the outcome still to be determined, Hitler called off the offensive and ordered a number of divisions transferred to western Europe.[71]

BRUSA

Hitler's December 11, 1941, declaration of war on the United States made the United States a British ally in the European and Middle Eastern theaters. It would not be long before U.S. and British troops were fighting together in North Africa. But despite their common heritage and common cause, a comprehensive COMINT alliance would follow only after tough negotiations and over the opposition of key officials within each intelligence establishment.

Even prior to U.S. entry into the war there was contact between U.S. and British cryptanalysts. On September 5, 1940, British Army intelligence chief Major General Kenneth Strong inquired from London if the U.S. Army would agree to a full exchange with Britain of German, Italian, and Japanese code and cryptographic information. Although the Navy was unwilling to exchange more than intercepts, the Army responded favorably to Strong's inquiry, although not to the idea of a continuous exchange of intercepts.[72]

A still secret December 1940 agreement between the two countries, clearly limited in nature, followed. And for ten weeks in early 1941 four U.S. military officers (two Army, and two Navy), including Abraham Sinkov and Leo Rosen of SIS, visited GC&CS. The SIS contingent did not include William Friedman, who had suffered a nervous breakdown, apparently due to overwork, shortly after January 1. In addition to showing them several intercept stations their hosts also informed them that "[t]here have been times when operations orders of the high commands have been read in time for British forces to take advantage of them."[73]

They were also told that on several occasions the objectives of German

bombers had been established in time to have planes waiting to intercept them, allowing the RAF to shoot down a large number of the
attackers—once shooting down fourteen planes without a single bomb
being dropped.[74]

In return the visiting Americans provided information about the Japanese cipher machines, including an actual machine, technical information as well as material on Italian commercial codes, and possibly the
keys to the Japanese navy's merchantship code. This apparently led the
British, who reported that their crytographic unit in Singapore was getting good results but was limited by a lack of translators of Japanese, to
suggest cooperation with regard to Far Eastern COMINT. The British
offered to turn over the results if the United States would supply the
translators.[75]

In June 1941 the United States and Britain would agree that intelligence concerning Japan would be exchanged between Singapore and the
U.S. military authorities in the Philippines and between Singapore and
the U.S. Pacific Fleet. While the exchange apparently included information on the JN25 cipher, it did not cover cryptanalytic methods.[76]

But the Americans gave far more than they received during their visit,
possibly because SIS chief Stewart Menzies opposed broader intelligence
sharing. They were told of the Bletchley organization, provided information about Italian codes, and given a sample of the latest direction-finding
equipment. But, although Sinkov and Rosen believed at the time that "no
doors were closed to us," they were not shown a bombe, nor were they
even told of its existence.[77]

A major step toward broader cooperation occurred on August 10, 1941,
when a "senior representative" of GC&CS arrived in North America to
meet with U.S. and Canadian cryptanalytic authorities. The senior representative was Alistair Denniston, who spent August 10–23 in the United
States and the following two weeks in Canada. Although no formal arrangements resulted in the United States, the personal relationships established, including that between Denniston and Friedman, facilitated
cooperation.[78]

Full cooperation was still almost two years away. A small step toward
fuller cooperation took place in March 1942, with a special United States–
United Kingdom–Canada wireless conference in Washington, initiated by
the British. The conference established an integrated structure for intercept and direction-finding operations and concluded that all such operations should be directed from four centers in Canada, England and the
United States.[79]

But sharing direction-finding responsibilities was still a long way from
sharing cryptanalytic secrets. In mid-September 1942 a naval agreement
began to take shape—due largely to the British codebreakers' renewed
frustration with the German naval ENIGMA cipher and their failure to
live up to their promise to deliver a bombe to the U.S. Navy codebreakers
as they had promised in June.[80]

By August Bletchley's senior staff apparently reached the conclusion that solving the naval ENIGMA would reguire a massive attack, which would, in turn, require the acquisition of a large number of high-speed bombe machines that could cope with its complexities. The United States had the technical capability to produce the bombes needed.[81]

A visit to Washington by John Tiltman, a senior GC&CS official, was followed by the late September visit of Edward Travis, Bletchley Park's new director, by which time the U.S. Navy had already approved a plan to manufacture a high-speed bombe. Travis wished to conclude an agreement on cipher security and cryptanalysis. While he would have preferred an arrangement which kept all EMIGMA-breaking efforts at GC&CS, the bombe contract undercut his position. To make the deal more palatable to the British, the United States agreed to provide the Admiralty with some intelligence "from Japanese communications." And on October 2 Travis signed the first major British–American COMINT agreement.[82]

The agreement was a limited one, focusing only on naval matters in the Atlantic, but it did require Britain to provide the United States with raw naval ULTRA material on an almost daily basis. The agreement also called for a pooling of the U.S. and British bombe capacity, with the U.S. Navy undertaking to limit bombe production to a 100 machines. The British would remain responsible for the basic cryptanalytic attack on German naval ciphers, but once a break-in took place Bletchley and OP-20-G would divide responsibilities for solving the daily settings.[83]

The naval COMINT agreement did not immediately open the door for an agreement between GC&CS and the U.S. Army. As of early 1943, Bletchley Park was opposed to providing the U.S. Army with raw ENIGMA intercepts, which the U.S. wanted to permit independent evaluation, or information concerning bombes.[84]

General Marshall was informed that GC&CS would be prepared to share cryptanalytic secrets with the American army in Britain, but not in the United States. If the U.S. Army would establish a contingent at Bletchley Park, the British were "prepared to show [them] everything." But the British were adamant that no raw German army or Luftwaffe ENIGMA traffic would be sent to Washington.[85]

The U.S. Signal Intelligence Service, however, continued to press for access to such traffic in the United States, partly out of concern that Bletchley Park might be destroyed in a bombing raid. On February 23 it made a formal request that it receive raw ENIGMA, just as OP-20-G did. To bolster its claim the British were informed that the Signal Corps was far along in developing its own bombe equipment, which would give SIS a good chance of breaking into various ENIGMA ciphers.[86]

The prospect of the U.S. Army conducting its own uncoordinated bombe operations, with a bombe the British were told "bore no external nor internal resemblance to the British bombes . . . and . . . was capable of solving several other types of cryptographic traffic problems," concerned the British.[87]

Negotiations continued through March and April 1943. U.S. Army officials decided to send a special high-level delegation to England. Examination of operations in England might suggest ways acceptable to the British to satisfy the U.S. requirement for German ENIGMA data. William Friedman as well as Colonel Alfred McCormack and Colonel Telford Taylor of Special Branch arrived in London on April 25.[88]

In the meantime negotiations were under way in Washington between Commander Travis and Colonel Carter Clarke. That mission would be a step toward achieving an agreement but not before some difficult moments, characterized by a National Security Agency historian as "G-2 and the British authorities walking around and eyeing each other like two mongrels who had just met."[89]

On May 17, 1943, the agreement commonly referred to as the BRUSA agreement was reached between G-2 and the London Signal Intelligence Board.[90] The actual—and peculiar—title of the document is:

Agreement between the British Code and Cipher School and U.S. War Department concerning cooperation in matters relating to:

U.S.	British
Special Intelligence A	Special Intelligence
Special Intelligence B	Y Intelligence
TA Intelligence	Y Inference.[91]

The agreement did not upset Bletchley Park's monopoly on the decryption of ENIGMA traffic, while providing the U.S. Army with the results of that decryption. The agreement provided for the complete exchange of decrypts of Axis military, air force, and Abwehr/secret service cipher traffic. It also specified that the United States would "assume as a main responsibility the reading of Japanese Military and Air codes and ciphers" while the British "will assume as a main responsibility the reading of German and Italian Military and Air codes and ciphers."[92]

Both nations also agreed to special security regulations concerning intelligence obtained from cryptanalysis of high- and low-grade enemy codes and ciphers and to distribute such intelligence to the minimum number of people necessary. The agreement noted that

the preservation of secrecy in regard to either category [high- or low-grade ciphers] is a matter of great concern to both countries and if the highest degree of security is to be maintained, it is essential that the same methods should be pursued by both countries at every level and in every area concerned, since a leakage at one point would jeopardize intelligence from these sources not in one area only but in all theaters of war and for all services.[93]

The Battle of the Atlantic

The Wehrmacht's blitzkriegs through France and the Soviet Union and the Luftwaffe's bombing raids on Britain were the most visible signs of the Nazi menace. But Winston Churchill understood that neutralizing the U-boat threat to Atlantic shipping was imperative if Britain was to survive the war. For the ships that traveled from the United States to Britain carried food and other vital supplies, without which the nation could not function, much less fight. Churchill would write:

> The Battle of the Atlantic was the dominating factor all throughout the war. Never for one moment could we forget that everything happening everywhere, on land, at sea, or in the air, depended ultimately on its outcome . . . [D]ominating all our power to carry on the war, or even keep ourselves alive, lay our mastery of the ocean routes and the free approach and entry to our ports.[94]

During first two years of the war Britain was losing the crucial battle, as U-boats sent millions of tons of vital cargo to the ocean floor and sank more ships than Britain and the United States were building. By the end of April 1941 Britain had lost over 3 million tons of shipping to the U-boats. In March meat rations had been reduced for the fourth time. In April cheese rationing was introduced. Many other commodities had long been restricted, and some were becoming virtually unavailable.[95]

Among the reasons for the U-boats' success was Wilhelm Tranow's B-Dienst. By March 1940 it had achieved the first breaks into the British Merchant Navy Code, which had been introduced in January 1940. After May 1940, when cryptographic materials were first captured from British merchant ships, the B-Dienst's ability to read British shipping messages grew.[96]

The B-Dienst also had considerable success against British naval ciphers used to transmit operational information. By April 1940 it was quickly reading between 30 and 50 percent of the messages sent in British Naval Cypher No. 1. On August 20, 1940, No. 2 (code-named MÜNCHEN [MUNICH] by the Germans) replaced No. 1, and B-Dienst had more difficulty until a change in encoding procedure made its job much easier.[97]

The success of the German codebreakers was not matched initially by the Hut 8 codebreakers. Reading U-boat communications, which were transmitted using the Heimisch, or Home Waters, code (code-named HYDRA by the Germans, DOLPHIN by Bletchley Park), would provide knowledge, at least, of the general location of the U-boats.[98] But the naval ENIGMA machine was a much more difficult opponent than the Luftwaffe machine. Thus the most potentially valuable result of an engagement with the Kriegsmarine was the recovery of cryptographic equipment and documents.

In June 1940, a naval ENIGMA and copy of the regulations for its use was recovered from the U-13. But even that equipment, along with previously unknown rotors, two of which were captured from U-33 that February, did not allow a regular, or even frequent, flow of decrypts. The naval

ENIGMA key system did not possess the vulnerabilities that had allowed the codebreakers of Hut 6 to break into the Luftwaffe ENIGMA.[99]

With no apparent way of analyzing the machine, the British began to explore the possibility of capturing keys. The first proposal apparently came from Ian Fleming, the future creator of James Bond, who was serving as personal assistant to Director of Naval Intelligence John Godfrey. Admiral Norman Denning, a postwar Director of Naval Intelligence, recalled: "A lot of Ian's ideas were just plain crazy. . . . But a lot of his farfetched ideas had just that glimmer of possibility in them that made you think twice before you threw them in the wastepaper basket." One less than crazy idea was his September 1940 plan, code-named Operation RUTHLESS, which envisioned a fake crash in the English Channel, a call for help, and a German ship coming to the rescue. The unfortunate German crew was to be killed, and their ship towed back to a British port with all its cryptographic material. Although the plan was approved, the British could not find a suitable German ship and the operation was never attempted.[100]

While nothing came of Fleming's specific plan, the basic idea would prove to be the key to success. An indication of the value of such operations came as a result of the late February 1941 British raid on the Lofoten Islands, which lie just off the Norwegian coast. The raid had a number of objectives, including the destruction of herring- and cod-oil factories. Any documents that could be recovered would be a bonus.[101]

And there was a substantial bonus for Hut 8, when Lieutenant Sir Marshall George Clitheroe Warmington, of the *Somali*, shot the lock off a wooden box he discovered on board the German ship *Krebs*, which had been damaged during the raid. In addition to the rotors that were in the box, which Hut 8 already had, there was a variety of documents, including the ENIGMA key tables for February.[102]

The contents of the box were delivered to Godfrey, who passed them on to Bletchley Park and Alan Turing on March 12. The impact was dramatic. That day ten solved messages were transmitted, via teletype, to the Navy's Operational Intelligence Center (OIC). The following day the number of solutions climbed to thirty-four. For the next week the number of daily solutions remained the same or greater, with Hut 8 deciphering much of the Home Waters February traffic. The knowledge gained from deciphering the February traffic also allowed the codebreakers to unravel, between April 22 and May 26, all the naval ENIGMA traffic for April and subsequently, with delays of about a week, much of the May traffic.[103]

But the improvement in Hut 8's productivity still left much to be desired, as indicated by the failure to break *any* April traffic before April 22. On April 30 Bletchley Park sent eleven general and seven U-boat messages to the OIC, none of which was less than twelve days old. The OIC's Submarine Tracking Room had to rely far more than they preferred on direction-finding, which could tell them where a U-boat was at a given moment but not where Admiral Karl Dönitz, head of the submarine fleet, was sending them.[104]

Without a steady supply of up-to-date ENIGMA traffic, the Submarine Tracking Room could only guess the routes that convoys should take to avoid the U-boat wolf packs. The result was mounting losses of ships and their cargoes. Then Harry Hinsley, who was one of the primary analysts of Hut 8's output, came up with an idea, or followed up on Fleming's.[105]

Among the decrypts that came across Hinsley's desk, thanks to the documents taken from the *Krebs*, were those from German weather ships, which included messages from the ships and acknowledgments that they were received. On each of those ships was an ENIGMA machine, its associated manuals, indicators book, and key lists. The lists gave the ENIGMA settings that were to be used each day of the month throughout the German navy. Some ships carried the key lists for two or three months, depending on the duration and timing of their cruise. At the time Hinsley did not know whether this was the German practice, but it seemed highly probable to him. If he was correct there was an obvious way to assist Hut 8 in solving the naval ENIGMA.[106]

On May 7, the weather ship *München* became the first victim of Hinsley's idea. Under escort, she headed for a British port; cryptographic material had been transferred to the destroyer *Nestor*, which would arrive at Scapa, in the Orkneys, on May 10. Two days later, near Iceland, U-110 was forced to surface by the Royal Navy's Escort Group 3. The group's commander, Joe Baker-Cresswell, who remembered the story of the *Magdeburg*, made sure to retrieve whatever cryptographic materials he could.[107]

Together the materials from the *München* and U-110, which included cipher machines, the short-signal book, the weather codebook, and a naval grid chart, had a dramatic impact. On May 21 the average time between interception of a message and transmission of its decrypted version to the OIC was eleven days. This figure dropped, for unexplained reasons, to thirty-four hours on May 28, but for the following three days there were no solutions at all. Starting on June 1, when the seized keys came into force, interception-to-teleprint time dropped markedly. Only four hours and forty minutes elapsed between the intercept of a German message at 12:18 A.M. and the arrival of its translation at the OIC.[108]

The *München* seizure represented a demonstration of feasibility rather than a final solution. For once the keys it carried expired, it would be necessary to acquire a new set. The British hoped the Germans would continue to assume that the disappearing ships had been sunk along with their cryptographic materials. In a June 19 memo Hinsley nominated the next target—the *Lauenberg*. Its resulting seizure provided the keys for July. With the knowledge these solutions provided, DOLPHIN was read virtually without interruption from August 1 and with little delay, until the end of the war.[109]

Yet the the British cryptographic victories had no immediate impact on the Battle of the Atlantic. There was little difference in the extent of losses between May (a slow solution month) and June (a fast solution month) as well as between July (fast) and August (slow). Losses in July and August did decline by over two-thirds from those in May and June, but clearly not because of Hut 8. In the later two months, more escorts were available to accompany convoys across the Atlantic, ships were moving at faster speeds, and air cover was increased. In addition, numerous U-boats had been transferred from the Atlantic to attack shipping headed for the Soviet Union. The U-boats that replaced them had less experienced crews.[110]

But the potential seemed great, and there was certainly no reason not to continue. However, after seven months of reading the naval ENIGMA traffic there was a major setback. On October 5 a separate key net, code-named TRITON by the Germans, was created for Atlantic U-boat command communications. On February 1, 1942, introduction of a four-rotor ENIGMA machine for the TRITON net, replacing the three-rotor model, caused a blackout to fall on Hut 8. For the remainder of the year Hut 8 solved only three days of TRITON keys.[111]

To make matters worse, by February the B-Dienst had broken into British Naval Cypher No. 3, which they code-named FRANKFURT. Introduced in June 1941 for use by the British, Canadian, and American navies, by December the B-Dienst was able to read up to 80 percent of its signals, although perhaps only 10 percent could be read in time for the decrypts to be operationally useful.[112]

A variety of intelligence sources, including aerial reconnaissance, mitigated the effect to some extent, as did a useful store of knowledge that had been built up about U-boat operations—including items such as speed and endurance. In addition, the vulnerable Home Waters and Mediterranean ENIGMA ciphers, which were solved at a rate of 14,000 per month, produced intelligence on the construction of new U-boats, their preparation and crew training, and their departures. The German decision to launch Operation DRUMBEAT, which targeted shipping off the east coast of the United States, also reduced the danger to Atlantic convoys.[113]

But the impact of the blackout was still significant, particularly after the United States adopted convoys in response to DRUMBEAT and the U-boats returned in full force to the Atlantic after June. North Atlantic sinkings came to approximately 600,000 in the second half of 1941, when Hut 8 was reading the U-boat traffic. In the last half of 1942 some 2 million tons of fuel, food, ammunition, and other supplies were lost.[114]

Before 1942 was over new documents would arrive at Bletchley Park—the Short Signal Book and Short Weather Cipher, which were recovered from U-559 in November, arrived at Hut 8 on November 24. Two days earlier the OIC had pressed Bletchley Park to give "a little more attention" to the four-rotor ENIGMA code-named SHARK by GC&CS; the OIC observed that "the war can be lost unless BP do help." On December

13 the breakthrough came as a result of the decryption of the three-rotor ENIGMA weather messages transmitted by shore weather stations. Weather reports were transmitted from U-boats in four rotor ENIGMA to the weather stations, which retransmitted them in its three-rotor ENIGMA.[115]

The cryptanalysts discovered that on any day the four-letter indicators (which determined the rotor settings) for regular U-boat messages were identical to the three-letter indicators for weather messages except with an extra letter. As a result, it was only necessary to check twenty-six possibilities for the fourth letter (i.e., check the fourth rotor in twenty-six positions) once the daily weather cipher indicators had been determined. Before the 13th was over, the first solution of the four-rotor ENIGMA U-boat key began to emerge.[116]

Hut 8 was again able to provide crucial intelligence concerning U-boat plans. Except for two periods, totaling 17 days in January and February, early 1943 saw Hut 8 producing solutions in time for them to be of operational value—rarely longer than in seventy-two hours and often in less than twenty-four. Even the introduction of a new weather codebook did not stop Hut 8. For the 112-day period from March 10 to June 30, the cryptanalysts recovered the SHARK keys for 90 days.[117]

The breakthrough had an immediate impact. The sinkings of January and February were half those of November and December. But it was not sufficient that things merely were not as bad as they had been before the breakthrough. For the number of U-boats in the Atlantic and Arctic was increasing throughout the spring—from 92 in January to 111 in April. And the number of Allied ships sunk increased at an alarming rate—from 29 in January to 50 in February to 95 in March. In a single March battle 45 U-boats managed to send dozens of ships to the bottom.[118]

But May saw the culmination of a major success with Convoy SC 127, whose route had been reconfigured in response to decrypts produced by Hut 8 and OP-20-G. The fifty-seven-ship convoy was carrying a large selection of items needed by Britain, from grain to tanks. Every last ship arrived at its destination on May 1 and 2, the convoy having completely eluded the U-boats.[119]

Such success would become more common, aided by Hut 8's discovery that the B-Dienst had broken into Naval Cipher No. 3; this discovery led to a new cipher, which the B-Dienst did not penetrate, starting on June 10, 1943. Churchill would tell the House of Commons on September 21, 1943, that during the previous three months not a single merchant ship had been lost to enemy action in the North Atlantic. Cheers followed.[120]

While ULTRA deserves a substantial share of the credit for neutralizing the U-boat threat, it deserves only part of the credit. That Britain did not lose a single ship in the quarter of a year prior to Churchill's announcement was most directly the result of Dönitz's withdrawal of his U-boats from the North Atlantic on May 24. That decision was based on Dönitz's recognition that "[i]n the Atlantic in May the sinking of 10,000 tons was paid for with the loss of one U-boat, while not very long before that time one boat was lost for the sinking of about 100,000 tons." Calling such losses "unbearable," he ordered the seventeen U-boats that were operating on the North Atlantic convoy routes to move to "less-endangered" areas to the south—eliminating their ability to threaten the crucial convoys that would not only sustain Britain but allow the Allies to make their long-promised return visit to Europe.[121]

ULTRA made its contribution to that decision. The evasive routing that it permitted, along with the increased cipher security that followed the discovery that Naval Cipher No. 3 was compromised, helped make possible the "unbearable" losses that resulted in Dönitz's decision. But a number of other factors also made significant contributions, including the greater number of escorts, increased air cover, sonar and aircraft radar. It is impossible to precisely sort out their exact contribution.

In the larger context of the war it is again impossible to be precise about ULTRA's role in Germany's defeat through its contribution to winning the Battle of the Atlantic. Harry Hinsley, who wrote the official British history of World War II intelligence, estimated that it shortened the war by two years. It might be more accurate to say that ULTRA helped shorten the war by three months—the interval between the actual end of the war in Europe and the time the United States would have been able to drop an atomic bomb on Hamburg or Berlin—and might have shortened the war by as much as two years had the U.S. atomic bomb program been unsuccessful.[122]

12

Knowing the Enemy

World War II intelligence operations produced a flood of information—from spies, communications intercepts, aerial photos, prisoner and deserter interrogations, and a wide range of open sources (including radio broadcasts, books, newspapers, and magazines). Much of that information, including data on potential targets and enemy military intentions and capabilities, was produced in direct support of military operations. But the wide variety of sources employed and the huge volume of information produced was also the result of the insatiable appetite of each nation's intelligence apparatus for information about all facets of enemy and enemy-controlled societies.

The desire for such information reflected that World War II, to an even a greater extent than World War I, was a war in which the outcome was dependent on far more than the forces in being at the beginning of the war or the military skills of those forces. Producing or importing the food and supplies needed for the civilian population, maintaining the allegiance of the population, and industrial production, particularly that supporting military operations, were all vital parts of the war effort. It was crucial to identify—in addition to military vulnerabilities—economic, political, or social weak spots that might be exploited to impede the enemy war effort.

Foreign Armies East

It is not surprising that Nazi Germany, with the largest and most fractured intelligence community, also had the greatest number of organizations involved in analysis. Included were three organizations whose primary function was to produce economic intelligence: the War Economy Branch of the War Economy and Armaments Department (after 1942, the Foreign Bureau of the Field Economy Department), Bureau III (Foreign Economies) of the Economics Ministry, and the Foreign Statistics Branch of the Reich Statistical Department. Military intelligence producers included the Foreign Air Forces (Fifth) Branch of the Luftwaffe General Staff, the Foreign Navies Branch of the Naval War Command, the Foreign Armies West (Third) Branch of the Army General Staff, the OKW Operations Staff Ic, and the OKW's Foreign Information Division.[1]

In addition, there was Foreign Armies East (Fremde Heere Ost, FHO). The FHO would not only have an impact on German strategy during World War II but would become the basis for Germany's primary postwar intelligence service. With Hitler's rise to power, the renunciation of Versailles, and the increase in the size of the German army, Foreign Armies dropped its cover designation as T3. It also expanded—to cope with the increased flow of intelligence from attachés, radio intelligence, and Abwehr agents. Most of its information still came, however, from open sources, particularly the daily and military press. The officer responsible for Great Britain and the Commonwealth would receive, among other publications, the *Daily Telegraph*, the *United Services Review*, the *Journal of the Royal United Services Institution*, and the *Royal Engineers Journal*.[2]

On November 10, 1938, Franz Halder, the new chief of the General Staff, split Foreign Armies into Foreign Armies East and Foreign Armies West. The latter organization remained the Third Branch of the General Staff, while Foreign Armies East became the Twelfth Branch.[3]

At the outbreak of the war FHO was headed by Lieutenant Colonel Eberhard Kinzel, who had served in T3 in 1933 before becoming military attaché to Poland. Although Kinzel's organization issued the official handbook that grossly underestimated Soviet military strength prior to Operation BARBAROSSA, he survived in his position for almost a year. However, as 1941 drew to a close Hitler and Halder had become sufficiently concerned about the quality of the FHO's intelligence to conclude that Kinzel should go.[4]

Halder soon told Lieutenant Colonel Reinhard Gehlen that he was to be the new head of the FHO. The pereptually frowning Gehlen was the son and grandson of career officers. He had joined the army as an enlisted man in 1920, and after attending infantry and artillery schools he was commissioned as a second lieutenant on December 1, 1923.[5]

Over the next ten years he was promoted to lieutenant (in 1928), served in the Third Prussian Artillery Regiment, and was assigned a prize place in the cavalry school. In 1933 his character and ability were judged to be outstanding enough (by those judging such things at the time) to result in his selection to attend the Armed Forces Academy.[6]

Gehlen graduated with distinction in 1935, establishing himself as one of the most industrious students at a special seminar on the Soviet Union. While some students pursued women in the evening Gehlen, according to fellow officers, "kept piles of books about Russia in his room and used to go to bed at night with a heavy volume of the statistical yearbook on the Soviet Union."[7]

Gehlen was assigned, on October 6, 1936, to the Army General Staff's Operations Department, where he reported to the future Field Marshal Fritz Erich von Manstein. For the next two years he assisted von Manstein in preparing a number of operational plans, including those for the annexation of Czechoslovakia. After an assignment to an artillery regiment, he became, in March 1939, one of the planners for the attack on Poland.[8]

Between the beginning of the war, by which time he held the rank of major, and his assignment as chief of FHO he served in a succession of posts: from intelligence officer to the 213th Infantry Division, to the OKW Fortifications Department, then back the Operations Department, as General Halder's aide-de-camp, and yet another stint in the Operations Department as Eastern Group chief.[9]

On April 1, 1942, Gehlen celebrated his fortieth birthday and third day as head of FHO.* Gehlen's FHO was elevated by Halder so that it reported directly to the chief of the General Staff. Under Gehlen the FHO was authorized to produce its own analysis concerning major operational issues, including planned German offensives, expected Soviet attacks, and probable Soviet military capabilities and intentions.[10]

Once in control Gehlen moved quickly. On his first day he assembled every member of the FHO—from group heads down to orderlies—and made it clear that there would be a dramatic difference under the Gehlen regime. He told the group that he expected total devotion to the job, unceasing effort, and, most of all, strict secrecy.[11]

Gehlen soon concluded that not only were new attitudes and procedures necessary, but that new personnel would also be required. One after another section heads and desk officers were replaced. Only junior personnel or officers who had recently joined the FHO, and were not part of the old culture, were allowed to remain. In addition to replacing personnel, Gehlen expanded the size of FHO, doubling the number of officers (from twenty-four to fifty) and increasing total personnel to several hundred.[12]

Among those who survived the Gehlen purge was Captain Gerhard Wessel, who had recently joined FHO. Beginning in May 1942 Gehlen, Wessel, and Major Danko Herre began the restructuring. Wessel was placed in charge of Group I (Research Group), which was responsible for producing daily situation reports on the strength, locations, and equipment of Soviet forces. Herre directed the activities of Group II, which evaluated intelligence reports and prepared general studies on the Soviet Union.[13†]

New personnel flowed into Group I, which was organized into six desks, four of which corresponded to the three German army groups (North, Center, South, A) on the eastern front. (Two additional desks

* Gehlen would become a full colonel in December 1942.

† Left untouched, initially, were the four less important groups: III, Balkans and the Middle East; IV, Scandinavia; V, Printing and Drawing; and VI, Administration.

dealt with partisan warfare and air reconnaissance.) Each desk, consisting of a desk officer, an assistant, and an aide, was responsible for monitoring the daily status of the enemy on its army group's front. Their reports were required to indicate the location of enemy units, their strength, the history of their formation, equipment, and composition of personnel. Each change in the strength of a Russian unit was recorded on an "alteration slip."[14]

All Group I's desks were required to produce, on a daily basis, a situation report on the Soviet formations facing their group. In addition, they were responsible for preparing drafts of the "Brief Estimate of the Enemy Situation" to be finalized by Wessel and given to Gehlen to take with him to the chief of the General Staff's 10 P.M. situation conference (and then incorporated in the chief's reports to Hitler at later situation conferences). Enemy situation maps (scale 1 : 1,000,000), indicating changes in enemy forces, the results of aerial reconnaissance, and any regroupings of enemy forces, were also the responsibility of the Group I desks.[15]

Group II (Overall Military Situation/Russia) investigated the underlying conditions that determined the daily situation. Desk IIa studied the primary elements, particularly Soviet manpower potential, using the 1939 census as its primary data base. A May 1942 estimate concluded that the Soviets could create sixty new rifle divisions, if there were no draft of eighteen-year-olds, who were needed on the farms.* Beyond manpower, IIa studied all aspects of the Soviet economy; lists, grouped by geographical areas, were maintained for each branch of industry showing production figures. Group IIb, relying on captured letters, POW interrogations, and newspapers, investigated the secondary factors, including morale, food, the political situation, and education.[16]

Group IIc monitored the enemy order of battle, entering new details about enemy units on one of its 30,000 troop identification slips. Each slip showed the date the unit was reported, its location, the source of information, and its reliability. To the extent known, the slips also showed each unit's strength, armament, losses, national composition, field post number, commanders, and history. Each day the desk would produce a "Survey of Soviet Russian Formations," supplemented by 1 : 1,000,000 and 1 : 300,000 maps. The survey listed the number of various enemy formations in front of each German army group in three areas—at the front, in front reserve, and in deep reserve.[17]

Group IIc also maintained the "Units Card Index" and a "Special Card Index," which represented the sum of FHO knowledge about Red Army commanders, establishments, organization, training schools, or field post numbers. Personnel files provided details on Soviet generals and all officers from divisional commander and above.[18]

In addition, IIc produced other indices and reports, with varying fre-

---

* As it turned out, some eighteen-year olds were drafted, resulting in the creation of sixty-four rifle divisions.

quency: comparisons of German and Soviet forces (on a daily basis); surveys of fronts, armies, and corps (on a thrice-monthly basis); a list of all enemy formations; a survey of Red Army formations that had appeared since the beginning of the war; a survey of Red Army units that had been destroyed or dissolved since the war began, and a monthly report on the status of Soviet armor.[19]

Section IIz, responsible for the interrogation of Soviet prisoners-of-war and the evaluation of captured documents, grew to such an extent that it became Group III, with the old Group III being renumbered. One section of the new group, IIIb, studied Soviet military manuscripts. Group IIIb liaison officers, stationed at the Abwehr's Warsaw center for captured material, and with army group intelligence sections, expedited the FHO's acquisition of Red Army manuscripts and examined all papers for data on the partisans as well the organization, equipment, and training of the Red Army.[20]

Group IIIc served as a repository for Soviet Defense Ministry orders or instructions while IIId collected leaflets as well as newspapers and letters captured from the Red Army postal service. Documents of special importance were translated by IIIf, while IIIg collected regulations and Soviet books in a library. Soviet radio was monitored around the clock by IIIh. A periodical report entitled "Intelligence Service East—Detailed Information" was produced by IIIe. The report informed its recipients of new Russian tactics and weapons.[21]

In a move that would have postwar implications, Gehlen sought not only to improve the quality of analysis done by FHO, but to give the FHO its own collection capability. This was done by coopting the Abwehr's field espionage organization directed against the Soviet Union. The head of the organization, Major Hermann Baun, felt that his organization's operations were being hampered by the establishment and identical location of Abwehr field organizations for sabotage and counterintelligence.[22]

As a result, in the summer of 1942 Baun moved his WALLI I organization from Suleyovek to the Ukrainian town of Vinnitsa. As the unit's affiliation with the FHO became closer, Gehlen became more persistent about the need for the improvement and expansion of WALLI I's product. As a result, Baun recruited new agents, accelerated and improved the training of agents headed for the Soviet Union, and increased the supply of technical equipment.[23]

Turning WALLI I into an adjunct of the FHO was not Gehlen's only attempt to increase the intelligence available to the FHO at any given time. Troops were ordered to report every ten days on the number and location of enemy guns facing them. Gehlen also requested data on the arrests of Soviet agents behind German lines, information which would reveal areas of Soviet interest. Army group intelligence staffs were provided with FHO intelligence requirements to aid them in prisoner-of-war interrogations.[24]

The data collected and forwarded to FHO's various components produced a mountain of reports on all aspects of the Soviet life—since everything had an impact on the ability of the Soviets to resist the German onslaught. Reports and studies included "The Urals as an Economic and Industrial Area," "Steel Production," "Armaments Industry," "Survey of the Higher Military Commanders of the Red Army," "Electrical Power," "Stalin's Career and Daily Routine," "Ice Break-Up in Russia," and "Agriculture and Collective Farms."[25]

But the primary purpose of Gehlen's organization was to support German military operations with up-to-date, accurate information on Soviet military capabilites and intentions. And with respect to Soviet intentions there were some significant failures.

On May 1, 1942, the FHO issued "Evaluation of the Total Enemy Situation and Its Possibilities of Development," which concluded that it was not possible to detect indications of a "large-scale operation with far-ranging objectives." The FHO reasoned that with the arrival of new German forces, the Red Army only appeared to hold the initiative, and its actions in any given area could not be sufficiently successful to force the Germans to divert forces from the planned offensive in the Ukraine. Rather, the FHO believed Soviet intentions to be defensive, noting that "[f]orces sufficient for a large-scale offensive are lacking."[26]

But eleven days later the Red Army launched a massive counteroffensive against Kharkov—an attack which compelled the Wehrmacht into an extensive realignment and delayed the start of the German summer offensive until June 28. While the FHO correctly predicted the direction of the Red Army's attack, they had predicted a minor local operation, not a full-scale counteroffensive.[27]

The FHO also miscalculated with respect to the Soviet counteroffensive in defense of Stalingrad, Operation URANUS. In August 1942 Gehlen foresaw that possibility in "Thoughts Regarding the Further Development of the Enemy Situation in the Autumn and Winter." That assessment noted three operational possibilities: the recapture of Stalingrad; an assault against the Sixth Army's deep flank with Rostov as the objective, to cut off the Caucasus; or attacks against the particularly weak positions at the bridgeheads of Serafimovitch and Korotoyak.[28]

But over the next several months intelligence derived from captured documents, prisoners of war, communications intelligence, and Abwehr spies convinced Gehlen that the main Red Army winter offensive would be directed against Army Group Center. In November German tactical COMINT produced hard evidence of new, massive Soviet troop concentrations behind the Don front. On November 12 the FHO concluded on the basis of the new information that the near future might bring an attack against the Third Romanian Army, with the objective of cutting the road to Stalingrad, threatening German forces stationed to the east, and compelling a withdrawal of the German forces in and around Stalingrad.[29]

The FHO also concluded that available Soviet forces were insufficient to conduct "far-reaching operations," although the FHO noted that a weaker offensive might be directed at Army Group B after the muddy season ended. On November 6 Gehlen issued "Estimate of the Enemy Situation in the Front of Army Group Center," which concluded that the forthcoming Red Army offensive would be directed at Army Group Center. The estimate stated that it was *evident* that Red Army preparations for action in the south were not sufficiently advanced to mandate a conclusion that the near future would see a large operation in the south simultaneous with the predicted offensive against Army Group Center.[30]

On December 10 Gehlen and the FHO issued "Possible Indications for a Beginning Russian Shift of Main Effort from the Middle Front Section of the Don Front." The study maintained that Red Army troop deployments from the beginning of November allowed the conclusion that the enemy was planning a decisive operation against Army Group Center, combined with a limited operation on the Don front.[31]

Operation URANUS opened on November 19 and achieved complete surprise. By November 23 the Red Army had encircled the Sixth Army of Field Marshal Friedrich Paulus. It was not until December 9 that Gehlen and the FHO modified their view that the main Soviet offensive would be targeted at Army Group Center and admitted that the Soviets might have shifted the main focus of their forces away toward the southern sector of the front.[32] That it was possible, in this case, to determine Soviet intentions from the data available was indicated by the intelligence staff of Army Group B, which accurately predicted the Soviet main thrust using the same intelligence available to FHO.[33]

The culmination of the FHO's most serious failure occurred in June 1944, with the Red Army's decisive attack on Army Group Center. On March 30, 1944, Gehlen's organization produced a comprehensive estimate of the enemy situation, in which he specified several assumptions about Soviet intentions, which influenced subsequent FHO estimates of the expected Red Army summer offensive. It was assumed that the offensive would be directed against Army Groups A and South. It was argued that Soviet successes on the southern wing of the eastern front threatened to open the way for a Red Army advance into the Balkans and General Government (German-occupied Poland) by destroying the German front between the lower Dnestr and the Pripyat marshes. Since the Soviet High Command was well aware of these possibilities, they would undoubtedly order Red Army forces deep into the General Government between the Carpathian Mountains and the Pripyat region before the construction and fortification of a continuous German defensive front.[34]

On June 13 the FHO issued its "Comprehensive Estimate of the Overall Enemy Situation before the German East Front and Presumed Enemy Intentions." The assessment predicted that the Soviet summer offensive would be launched between June 15 and 20, and it claimed that all available intelligence supported the FHO's earlier conclusion that the main thrust would be delivered against Army Group North Ukraine.[35]

But on June 22, 1944, the Soviets initiated Operation BAGRATION, which resulted in the destruction of Army Group Center. The operation involved four complete Russian field armies, one tank army, and a massive logistical effort requiring 75,000 railroad carloads of troops, equipment, and supplies—directed against Army Group Center, exactly where the FHO said they would not attack.[36]

R&A

Near the end of July 1941, Archibald MacLeish, the Librarian of Congress, took part in an all-day session with representatives of the American Council of Learned Societies, the Social Science Research Council, the National Archives, and leading scholars from several universities. That session was not another gathering of academics and intellectuals to present papers on some obscure topic. The purpose was to help select a group of advisers to assist the newly established Office of the Coordinator of Information (COI) in directing its research and analysis effort.[37]

Not long afterwards James Phinney Baxter, president of Williams College and an authority on American diplomatic and military history, was named to head a COI Research and Analysis (R&A) Branch. Baxter asked an old friend, William L. Langer of Harvard, to assist him by managing a group of research scholars to exploit published materials at the Library of Congress. When Baxter resigned in September 1942, Langer took his place for the war's duration.[38]

Langer had risen from South Boston and the rigorous Boston Latin School to the Coolidge Chair in Diplomatic History at Harvard. Believing that history could be useful to society, he had designed a number of projects as proof—texts, encyclopedias, atlases, and a series of semipopular volumes.[39]

Along with Langer, the individuals who initially worked in the Research and Analysis Branch were Ivy League academics, the largest number coming from Harvard and Yale. Included in this group was Sherman Kent, who after the war would become head of the CIA's Office of National Estimates.[40]

Although the entire branch never exceeded 1,000, Langer's staff produced an immense volume of work. That work covered a wide range of subjects for a diverse set of purposes. R&A studies assisted national policymakers and OSS decision makers. There were also in-depth studies of enemy, occupied, and allied nations. The map division provided the Secret Intelligence and Special Operations branches with detailed maps for combat missions as well as large survey maps for policymakers. By the end of the war R&A had produced over 3,000 formal research studies and 3,000 original maps.[41]

Producing those reports depended not only on information from spies, aerial reconnaissance, communications intelligence, and prisoner-of-war interrogation, but on open sources, collected by OSS's Interdepartmental Committee for the Acquisition of Foreign Publications. In six months during 1943 the committee's publications section processed over 30,000 issues of original newspapers and periodicals and over 66,000 issues on microfilm. In one week 45,000 pages of foreign publications arrived.[42]

The subjects of R&A studies covered a vast number of economic, political, sociological, and military subjects: the status of rail traffic on the Russian front and in Japan, the attitudes of the Roman Catholic church in Hungary, Charles de Gaulle's political ideas, the looting and damaging of art works, the Indian Communist party, trade routes in the Congo basin, Japan's electric power industry, and the relation of tin acquisitions to airplane production in Japan.[43]

The content of those reports reflected the varied disciplines of the R&A scholars. Historians sought precedents from World War I and its aftermath, economists examined the possible consequences of a "hard peace." Anthropologists studied Japanese films while psychologists listened to Goebbels's speeches for signs of upcoming military operations.[44]

Reports on the political and social conditions in Germany and Japan sought to inform decision makers of the possible impact of military action on morale, the implications of changes in government, and the likely impact of subjecting particular targets to bombing attacks. One report examined nine aspects of National Socialist Germany: its government, Nazi control of the economy and businessmen, labor, the fate of traditional culture, natural science, religion, education, spiritual coordination and the war machine.[45]

Another explored, in three pages, "German Morale after Tunisia." The report noted that some observers believed the German defeats at Stalingrad and in Tunisia had weakened German morale so dramatically that "collapse is conceivable." The report cautioned that such an analysis was based on predicting the morale of the populace in a totalitarian state as if it was a democratic state. Morale, the report argued, was an insignificant factor in the German situation and would continue to be so until "military defeat smashes the elaborate system deployed by Nazism to control morale."[46]

"Possible Political Changes in Nazi Germany in the Near Future" indicates the difficulty in trying to "read tea leaves" in the midst of war with a totalitarian enemy. Reacting to a reported establishment of a triumvirate of Reich Marshal Göring, Field Marshal Wilhelm Keitel, and Admiral Dönitz, R&A analysts wrongly concluded that it implied "the subordination of the Nazi Party to the military." They also concluded that "it implies that Hitler recedes for the time being into the background and that the Nazi Party is transferred into an organ of this triumvirate."[47]

Toward the end of August, "Changes in the Reich Government" examined the impact of state and party positions held by Himmler, following his assumption of the role of minister of the interior. The report listed the nine state and party position helds by Himmler and examined Himmler's impact on Germany's eastern policy, changes in the Reich Labor Service, and changes in Prussia.[48]

In July 1944 R&A briefly explored the implications of the July 20 attempt on Hilter's life, concluding that "[a]lthough German defeatism will be increased by the effort of the military to oust the Nazi government, it is unlikely that an opposition can again manifest itself before the German armies are decisively crushed."[49]

The type of in-depth reference work often produced by R&A is illustrated by "South Germany." In 21 chapters running over 1,500 pages, it examined political and social organization, the press, public welfare programs, economic controls, public finance and banking, labor, agriculture, food, industries and mineral resources, fuels, transportation, electric power, gas, water, and telecommunications.[50]

Japanese social and political relations were also addressed by R&A on a number of occasions. And it is clear that most such reports had absolutely no impact on U.S. military strategy or the successful conclusion of the war in the Pacific.

A March 19, 1942, two-part report examined social relations in Japan. First, social relations as revealed by the national social structure were examined. The phenomenon of group rule as well as the relationship among political, economic, and religious frameworks and social structure were explored. Second, the various types of control (civil, military, religious, family) were surveyed. The study observed that "to deal effectively with Japan either directly or indirectly, some understanding of its social structure and forms of control is essential. A characteristic of the government is group rule and rotating responsibility, all acts of the central government being carried on in the name of the Emperor."[51]

Other studies on Japanese society and politics included "Japanese Labor: The Labor Union Movement," "Japanese Films: A Phase of Psychological Warfare," and "Japan's Cliques: The 'Batsu.'" The labor study examined the degree of unionization and government attitudes and actions concerning unions, as well as the history and characteristics of the labor movement, the decline of unions, and propaganda and Japanese labor. The report observed that "Japanese labor, constituting as it does one-fourth of the gainfully employed population of Japan, represents an important group, which if profitably appealed to, might significantly influence the policies or composition of the Japanese Government in the future."[52]

The study of Japanese films assessed the utility of the films as propaganda vehicles and their propaganda content. One part of the study examined the basic themes of the films, another explored their attitudes toward life, love, fatherland and emperor, war, death, and religion; a third part evaluated the technical proficiency of the films.[53]

The study of the "batsu"—a small group of persons who served as advisers to the emperor and were viewed suspiciously by the average

Japanese—suggested they would make a profitable propaganda target "when and if Japan suffers military reverses," since the "Japanese people have had no share in their selection and have, on the other hand, a background of distrust which may be played upon."[54]

The variety of R&A reporting, as well as the extraordinary methods used to produce data and draw conclusions, is well illustrated by R&A's effort in the wake of the German invasion of the Soviet Union. In their initial drive the Wehrmacht seized a network of ten major rail links, which were their means of supplying food, weapons, and other material to approximately 200 divisions. The Germans' basic requirement was to deliver enough material to keep their troops adequately supplied. Their ability to do so was heavily influenced by the capabilities of the railroads they had seized.[55]

From the very incomplete data available, R&A economists sought to determine the capacities of the Soviet rail system as well as the supply requirements of the invading armies. If successful, they would be able to predict the earliest dates at which the German spring offensive could resume.[56]

During early 1942, as the surviving German forces on the eastern front endured bitter cold, the R&A Economics Division ventured out into the much milder Washington winter to gather data on a wide range of intra- and extrasystemic factors. Local railway officials were asked to provide technical information on the efficiency of locomotives at subzero temperatures and the conversion of Soviet track to standard European gauge. They also explored the daily forage requirements of the horses used by the German infantry and calculated volume and weight of rations shipped to the German troops.[57]

Starting with U.S. Army ordnance requirements, the R&A economists projected the daily tonnage of ammunition consumed at seven different levels of combat by infantry, Panzer, and motorized divisions. They averaged meteorological data over a period of years, combined the results with hard information that had been obtained for a particular eighteen-day period of the war, and used that combination to develop a statistical model of meteorological conditions.[58]

Once they had quantified all possible pivotal factors in the German supply situation (at minimal and maximal levels), they attempted to correlate the raw tonnage of supplies deduced to have been depleted by 200 divisions in 167 days over a 1,500-mile front with the capacity of the road and rail network under conditions of intense fighting. As a result of this combination of data collection, extrapolation, and analysis R&A concluded that alleged German difficulties of supply were not more than localized disruptions and of less importance in halting the German advance than the resistance of the Red Army. Relying on very little solid information they deduced that the German rail system, when supplemented by motor vehicles, had proved able to deliver 16,650,000 tons of supplies required during the previous 5^1/$_2$ months of 1942—although the system was sometimes strained to its breaking point and disruptions sometimes delayed or limited the extent of operations.[59]

The economists also estimated that 35,000 additional freight cars were required to support every 200-kilometer advance into Soviet territory, and that the Germans could divert those cars from the civilian economies of the Axis-occupied nations without an immediate loss of German war production.[60]

The authors also observed that rail facilities had proven barely adequate during the first six months of the invasion, and that minimal success resulted from the vast stores of material accumulated in advance of the invasion. Since these stocks had been significantly dissipated during the campaign, and although they could not predict the relative condition of the Soviet armies, they concluded that it was almost inevitable that the Germans would be much weaker when the Russian winter ended.[61]

Industrial Intelligence

Of all the combatants none was more cognizant than Great Britain of the role that industrial capacity, and thus industrial intelligence, would play in modern war. That recognition had led the cabinet to approve, in 1929, the creation of the Industrial Research (Intelligence from 1931) in Foreign Countries subcommittee of the Committee of Imperial Defence.[62]

The subcommittee's functions, however, were limited to industrial intelligence policy. To actually produce such intelligence an Industrial Intelligence Centre (IIC) was established in March 1931, with Major Desmond Morton as its chief and only staff member. Morton had been on loan from the Secret Intelligence Service to the subcommittee, where he was involved in a study of industrial conditions in the Soviet Union. From 1931 to 1935, when it was attached to the Department of Overseas Trade, the IIC was funded through the SIS. The IIC would expand over the course of the decade, attaining a staff of twenty-five by September 1938. It would also shift its primary focus from the Soviet Union to Nazi Germany.[63]

While the IIC benefited from the reporting of diplomats, armed service intelligence organizations, attachés, and the SIS, most of its information came from open sources. One former IIC member estimated that well over 80 percent of the IIC's information came from reference works, newspapers, industrial journals and newsletters, yearbooks, League of Nations publications, and similar material. Thus information might come from *The Efficiency Standard of Living in Japan, The Mineral Industry of the British Empire and Foreign Countries,* or the *Petroleum Press Service* newsletter.[64]

The primary product of the IIC during the 1930s was the "General Survey of Material Resources and Industry in Their Bearing upon National War Potential," a different survey being produced for each country of interest. Between August 1935 and September 1936 surveys were produced for Japan, Germany, the Soviet Union, China, Italy, and the Netherlands East Indies. Another thirty-three surveys were produced between September 1936 and January 1938.[65]

Also among the IIC's most important products in this era were a variety of memoranda concerning subjects such as Japan's salt imports, Italian manufacture of synthetic silk, French purchase of titanium tetrachloride, the Belgian aircraft industry, Polish weapons supplies in wartime, and the American aircraft industry.[66]

Reports on German industry produced between 1933 and 1939 included "Germany: Imports from Scandinavian Countries in the Case of War," "Economic Warfare against Germany: Notes on the Probable Situation in 1939," "Germany: Supply of Copper in War," and "Germany: Pig Iron Imports."[67]

During the 1930s

> the Centre's activities acted as a constant reminder to the official grand strategists that the resources required for modern warfare had to be reckoned as much by petrol dumps, railway yards and chemical refineries as by tanks, aircraft and destroyers . . . [and that] it was certainly no more important to know the number of Panzer divisions in Germany than it was to realize that the German industrial complex in the Ruhr was likely to need over seven million tons of imported iron ore in the first year of the war and that the bulk of this vital import came from Sweden through the port of Rotterdam.[68]

Following the outbreak of war the IIC and associated committees were abolished, with their functions being transferred to the newly established Ministry of Economic Warfare (MEW), which had an Intelligence Branch of its own. That branch's organization had been planned between February and July 1939 by Desmond Morton, who became its head when the MEW opened for business that September. MEW defined the Intelligence Branch's purpose as keeping

> under constant observation the enemy's economic potential for war with the object of assisting other branches of intelligence in detecting in advance his possible intentions, in estimating his strength and weaknesses and in selecting points vulnerable to attack by any weapon that we should command—blockade, pre-emption, submarine warfare, air attack, political and psychological propaganda.[69]

The branch's original six sections were reorganized into two departments in November. Blockade Intelligence (which would be renamed the General Branch) was responsible for aiding the daily activities of the ministry, and particularly providing intelligence in support of the contraband control system. The Economic Warfare Intelligence Department succeeded the IIC in providing intelligence to the military services and other government agencies. After the fall of France it would become the

Enemy and Occupied Territories Department, and then in April 1941 the Enemy Branch.[70]

A key player in the production of industrial intelligence, the Enemy Branch was not alone. The service intelligence branches all had an interest and responsibility in producing industrial intelligence relevant to their missions, while the Joint Intelligence Committee (JIC) represented the final authority.

With the advent of war overt sources decreased in relative importance in assessing the German economy, with COMINT and photographic reconnaissance being, according to the JIC, "the most valuable." Even access to such powerful sources did not make estimation an easy task. At the end of 1941 the Enemy Branch was overestimating the rate at which the German stock of raw materials was declining, but it did not consider the situation to be critical, despite the heavy requirements of the fighting on the eastern front. However, in March the JIC forecast that the renewed fighting in the Soviet Union would leave the Third Reich with its stock of raw materials exhausted and industrial potential reduced. After the United States suggested that the British were overemphasizing the impact of raw materials, the JIC revised the estimate to suggest that any deterioration would be "gradual." By the end of 1942 the Enemy Branch was still underestimating the German inventory of raw materials, but it did not suggest that the Germans were at a critical point.[71]

As early as December 1941 the MEW judged the labor situation to be a growing problem for the Nazi regime. The Enemy Branch estimated that during 1941, despite the quintupling of the armed forces to 10 million men, the German work force had grown by 1.75 million to 2 million—due to population growth, the additional employment of women, and the "acquisition" of foreign workers. At the same time, it wrote that if the number of workers was "weighted according to the estimated capacity of each group," the German labor force was effectively 1 million fewer at the conclusion of 1941 than it had been a year earlier.[72]

That judgment, as well as the conclusion that the effective civilian labor force had declined by 12 percent or more since the end of 1938, led MEW to conclude in December 1941 that Germany had siphoned an excess number of individuals from the industrial and agricultural work forces. As a result, it would have to release men from the armed forces during the winter to ensure that Germany would not begin the 1942 campaign with substantially less equipment than it relied on in 1941.[73]

In June 1942 the Enemy Branch accepted that its forecast had been wrong, that there had been no factory leave during 1941–42 for the armed forces. Increased employment of women, use of foreign workers, and exploitation of POWs had allowed Germany to begin 1942 with the same number of workers it had at the beginning of 1941. It argued, however, that the civilian labor force was less efficient than previously.[74]

Food was another, and easier subject for the Enemy Branch in 1941–42. The decline in production and consumption during the first six months of

1942 was clear to the branch. In June it estimated that the average German diet was under 2,000 calories, while that of the heavy worker was substantially less than 3,000 calories. The estimate explained the decline by a less than satisfactory 1941 harvest and a shortfall in imports. It also reported that little could be expected from southeastern Europe or the Ukraine in the year ahead. The branch concluded that Germany was almost totally dependent on her own production, while facing shortages of labor, machinery, and fertilizers.[75]

At the end of the year the MEW's intelligence arm accurately reported that there had been a substantial increase in food consumption, resulting in a rise in calorie intake for heavy workers from 2,500 to 3,000 per person. The Enemy Branch's reporting thus indicated that Germany had substantially recovered from the food crisis that had been developing earlier in the year.[76]

Throughout the war a subject of major concern to MEW and the Enemy Branch was the German oil supply. In July 1941 it was estimated that if the current level of fighting continued, oil consumption in enemy and enemy-occupied territories would surpass new supplies by 250,000 tons each month. After eight months Germany's 2,000,000 tons of freely available oil would be exhausted and the Reich would be unable to maintain the level of fighting unless some of the 2,850,000 tons of oil in transit or distribution could be drawn upon. In August the estimate of the monthly excess was increased to 375,000 tons, resulting in MEW's observation that "it does appear highly probable that a prolongation of the Russian campaign for even a few months will, through its effect on oil, begin to affect Germany's war potential or her strategic mobility, or both."[77]

German forces, as it turned out, were not seriously affected in 1941 by a lack of oil, and the General Staff did not use oil supply difficulties as an excuse for military defeats. But both British intelligence and German officials realized that 1942 would be a different story. Based on MEW's analysis, the JIC confidently predicted in March 1942 that the main thrust of Hitler's summer offensive would be directed at the Soviet oilfields in the south. Hitler's Directive No. 41, produced in the spring, called for the summer offensive to be directed south, and included the seizure of Soviet oil fields among its objectives.[78]

It would not always be possible to establish such links between the oil situation and German strategy. Thus, "[b]etween December 1942 and mid-1943 the German oil situation was indeed critical but the authorities could not assess the effects on German strategy."[79]*

---

* It has been argued that a misunderstanding of the role of petroleum in the German economy led to a less than optimal choice of strategic bombing targets in Germany. See Alfred C. Mierzejewski, "Intelligence and the Strategic Bombing of Germany: The Combined Strategic Targets Committee," *International Journal of Intelligence and Counterintelligence* 3, no. 1 (1989): 83–104.

The Cold War Era and Beyond

13

New Adversaries

Even before World War II was concluded signs of division began to appear among the Allies. At the February 1945 Yalta conference the Allies discussed their differing visions for a postwar Polish government. At the July 1945 Potsdam conference the United States resisted Soviet pressure to recognize the Soviet-installed governments of Romania, Hungary, and Bulgaria.[1]

Those disagreements would be followed by even more serious disputes during the remainder of the decade—over whether the Soviet Union would withdraw its troops from Iran (1946), over events in Turkey and Greece (1947 and 1948), and, most dramatically, over Berlin (1948). Then in 1950 U.S. and British forces were employed to resist North Korea's invasion of South Korea, while Stalin supported North Korea and China with weapons and words. The allies of World War II had become adversaries and potential enemies.

Reorganization

The end of the war and the change in international alignments affected the intelligence activities of both East and West. Britain abolished the Special Operations Executive (transferring parts of the organization and some personnel to SIS), the Ministry of Economic Warfare, and the Political Warfare Executive. Britain did maintain SIS, the Security Service, and the military service intelligence agencies as well as the Joint Intelligence Committee. In 1946 it established a Joint Intelligence Bureau to coordinate defense intelligence.

The United States dismantled the Office of Strategic Services. Donovan's plan for establishing a postwar central intelligence agency represented a threat to both the military intelligence agencies and J. Edgar Hoover, who hoped to see his bureau's World War II Latin American–

oriented Special Intelligence Service given a worldwide mandate. Leaks to newspapers hostile to the Roosevelt–Truman administration resulted in stories in labeling the proposed new agency as a "Super Gestapo" that would "spy on the world and home folks."[2]

On September 20, 1945, President Harry Truman signed Executive Order 9621, "Termination of the Office of Strategic Services and Disposition of Its Functions," which abolished the OSS effective with the "opening of business October 1, 1945." The same order transferred the Research and Analysis and Presentation branches to the State Department, where they were consolidated into an Interim Research and Intelligence Service. The remainder of the OSS was transferred to the War Department, where it became the Strategic Services Unit. At the same time, Truman instructed Secretary of State James Byrnes to set up a new organization to coordinate foreign intelligence.[3]

The Byrnes effort resulted in Truman's signing a January 22, 1946, directive establishing a National Intelligence Authority (NIA), a Director of Central Intelligence (DCI), and a Central Intelligence Group (CIG). The directive made the DCI, through the CIG, responsible for "the correlation and evaluation of intelligence relating to the national security." The CIG also received vaguely worded authorization to engage in foreign espionage activities.[4]

In 1947, as part of the general consideration of the national security apparatus necessary for the post–World War II era, the CIG gave way to the Central Intelligence Agency. According to the National Security Act of 1947 the CIA's principal function was to be the correlation and evaluation of intelligence collected by other departments (i.e., the military). However, other provisions of the act authorized it to perform services of "common concern" as well as "other functions and duties related to intelligence affecting the national security as the National Security Council may from time to time direct." The later provision, identical to a provision in the Truman directive establishing the CIG, also permitted the new agency to engage in foreign espionage. The legislation also explicitly prohibited the CIA from exercising any domestic police powers.[5]

The creation of the CIA helped bring about a dramatic, albeit temporary, restructuring of the Soviet intelligence apparatus. Reports from the MGB* resident and Soviet ambassador in Washington on the National Security Act were closely followed by Stalin and the Politburo. The Soviet dictator, who interpreted the establishment of the Defense Department, National Security Council, and CIA as preparations for war, ordered that all available material about the act be translated.[6]

The MGB reports from Washington were used as the basis for a proposal by Foreign Minister V. M. Molotov to bring foreign intelligence operations under his control. He argued that a unified civilian and foreign

---

* In 1946 all people's commissariats (NKs) became ministries(Ms). Hence the NKGB became the MGB.

military intelligence structure would give the United States a distinct advantage over a divided Soviet system. Thus it was necessary to combine MGB and GRU foreign intelligence operations in one organization.[7]

Molotov's proposal had the additional benefit, from Stalin's perspective, of loosening the grip on the security apparatus of Lavrenti Beria, whose protégé headed the MGB. Thus in the fall of 1947 the Komitet Informatsyia (KI, Committee of Information) was established. Although formally under the Council of Ministers, it was headed by Molotov, giving the Foreign Ministry much greater influence on foreign intelligence activities than in the past. One aspect of that increased influence was that Soviet ambassadors were given authority over Soviet intelligence operations in their country.[8]

To some the arrangement may have looked good on paper, but it did not work in practice. According to one Soviet defector there was "incredible confusion. The residents, the professional intelligence officers, resorted to incredible subterfuges to avoid informing their ambassadors about their work, since the diplomats had only amateurish knowledge of intelligence work and its methods."[9]

The beginning of the end came in mid-1948 when the GRU elements of the KI were transferred back to the Ministry of Defense, apparently as a result of orders from Defense Minister Nikolay Bulganin, who insisted that the armed forces recover direct control over its intelligence elements. The resumption of military control was undoubtedly facilitated by the fact that GRU personnel had been segregated into all-GRU units within each KI component.[10]

In December 1948 two former MGB elements, the Soviet Colony and Émigré departments, responsible for monitoring Soviet diplomats and staff abroad and émigrés, were returned to the MGB. Thus the KI consisted only of what had been the foreign intelligence elements of the MGB. Around December 1951 the remaining MGB personnel were returned to that organization.[11]

The Soviet Target

In the spring and summer of 1948 the CIA's Office of Special Operations was assigned its initial mission against the Soviet target: "to collect secret intelligence on the Soviet Union itself, its military intentions, atomic weapons and advanced missiles; on Soviet actions in Eastern Europe, North Korea and North Vietnam; on Moscow's connections with foreign communist parties and groups fighting for national liberation." The demands placed on the CIA by the Pentagon were immense. During one briefing an Army colonel pounded the table and demanded "an agent with a radio on every goddamn airfield between Berlin and the Urals."[12]

Operations began in late 1949 with the airdropping of agents into the Soviet Union, part of the infiltration operation code-named REDSOX. For the next five years agents were sent into the Soviet Union by land, sea, and air from a variety of locations—Scandinavia, West Germany, Greece, Turkey, Iran, and Japan. According to Harry Rositzke, a member of the CIA's Soviet Russia Division at the time, the agents "covered intelligence targets from the Murmansk area to Sakhalin, mostly on the margins of the Soviet landmass, some deep within." But those operations would never amount to much in the five years before they were terminated. The losses were high, the expenditures substantial, and the results minimal.[13]

But the CIA was far from the only U.S. intelligence organization gathering information about the Soviet Union. The military services, most particularly the Air Force, operated a variety of human and technical programs designed to penetrate the Soviet curtain of secrecy.

Military attachés, especially in Stalinist Russia, were of little use in collecting information concerning activities at military bases, production sites, or atomic energy facilities far from Moscow. Occasionally they could collect some very useful information within the Moscow area—particularly since the Soviet leadership would bring some of their latest military hardware to Moscow for the yearly May Day and Revolution Day parades as well as for Soviet Air Day shows.

In a November 1948 letter, Colonel H. M. McCoy, the chief of the Air Material Command's intelligence department, informed the Air Force chief of staff that

> [a]n estimated 95% of the qualitative intelligence on Russian aircraft, and usually first knowledge of the existence of new types of aircraft becomes known to our Air Attache during the 1 May Air Show and the earlier practice flights. Based on the past two years' experience from six to nine months elapse until other confirming and qualitative data on these new aircraft comes thru other sources.[14]

To collect the information, U.S. military attachés used the most sophisticated photographic and electronic equipment that they could carry, overtly or covertly, in the vicinity of the parade. Included were a binocular camera and a variety of tripod arrangements with zoom lenses and telescopic sights capable of still photography and motion-picture photography.[15]

Such equipment was employed by Major Edison K. Walters, the acting air attaché, when he attended the Soviet Air Day Show on July 17, 1947, and shot thirty photographs, primarily of YAK-15 fighters. Held at Tushino Airdrome in Moscow, the show included 348 military aircraft. Walters reported on the twenty-one events that constituted the three-part show, including a mock battle between nine TU-2s and four fighters as well as his observation that Stalin "appeared to be in excellent health and had a suntan."[16]

That the reporting of military attachés at public events constituted such a significant component of intelligence gathering in 1948 is a good indication of the limited nature of the U.S. collection effort at that time.

But during the course of 1948 and subsequent years the military intelligence services would dramatically expand their use of technical collection systems, particularly ground stations and aircraft, to gather intelligence about the new adversary.

On April 5, 1948, Stuart Symington, Secretary of the Air Force, sent a short note to General Carl Spaatz, Air Force Chief of Staff:

> A pretty queer looking map was sent me along with a memorandum I was sending Secretary Marshall on what we know is across from the Bering Straits. I asked that the map be looked into, found it was wrong in some places, and attach it. In addition, however, I also found that there are no pictures of any kind of these airfields. Isn't there some way we could take pictures?[17]

What was across from the Bering Straits was Chukotski Peninsula. What particularly concerned Air Force officials was the possible existence of airfields, for Soviet aircraft based at such airfields could, according to Air Force intelligence, "reach the largest number of strategic installations in North America with least effort and greatest effect," as well as carry out tactical operations against U.S. forces in Alaska.[18]

At approximately the time that Secretary Symington was expressing his concern about the apparent lack of photographs,* several intelligence sources indicated unusual activity in the northern, northeastern, and eastern areas of Siberia—including the construction of airfields, launching sites, and military bases. Such information required confirmation by photographic reconnaissance.[19]

With that requirement and Symington's note in mind, the Air Force Directorate of Intelligence recommended that aircraft fitted with long-focal-length cameras be assigned to conduct oblique photography missions against the Chukotski Peninsula and, ultimately, other targets.[20] What was being proposed was a program of peripheral reconnaissance; U.S. planes would fly outside Soviet territory but by using oblique photographic techniques would be able to photograph installations inside Soviet territory.

Discussions between the Air Force, State Department, and Joint Chiefs of Staff concerning the minimum distance outside Soviet borders the planes would be required to fly to satisfy the dictates of prudence and international law concluded in August 1948. As result planes from the Seventy-second Photo Reconnaissance Squadron began flying missions— apparently code-named LEOPARD—against a variety of locations on the Chukotski Peninsula. The oblique photography of the Uelin, Lavrentiya,

---

* In fact, photographs of certain coastal portions of the Chukotski Peninsula had been taken on December 22, 1947, from a U.S. aircraft involved in electronic reconnaissance activities. The primary object of the mission was collection of signals from Soviet radar installations. Photography was a secondary mission, to be attempted only if weather conditions were opportune. Due to the short focal length of the cameras, no significant intelligence resulted.

Mys Chaplina, and Provideniya areas of the peninsula revealed "very little activity in those areas at the time of the missions, and no visible bases at these particular sites from which any long range bombing attack could be launched." At the same time it was noted, in a comment that presaged the overflight programs of the 1950s, that "there well might be elaborate inland bases on which no information is available or which no photo coverage exists."[21]

By October 1949, in addition to the LEOPARD missions, other sets of missions with code names such as RICKRACK, STONEWORK, and OVERCALLS had been flown and had produced over 1,800 photographs. The STONEWORK missions, conducted prior to November 1948, focused on the Kurile Islands—a series of islands extending 700 miles from northern Japan to southern Kamchatka—and Kamchatka. OVERCALLS missions began on October 30, 1948, and continued through July 27, 1949, focusing on twenty-eight targets ranging from the Kuriles up Kamchatka, around the Chukotski Peninsula, and along the East Siberian Sea.[22]

The OVERCALLS missions revealed no indication of a reported bomber and fighter base in the Provideniya Bukhta area but revealed the existence of airfields at Velkel, Anadyr, and Lavrentiya as well as several well-dispersed storage and barracks areas in the vicinity of Provideniya. The missions also showed the growth of activities at Provideniya, Petropavlovsk, and Anadyr as well as the utilization of Petropavlovsk and the Tarinski Bay Naval Base as submarine bases.[23]

The United States was also was also heavily involved in electronic reconaissance flights, popularly known as ferret flights. As with photographic reconnaissance, the Alaskan Air Command was heavily involved in the secret flights. As of July 1948 the AAC had two B-29 aircraft which were equipped for ferret missions. The AAC-managed flights collected information on radar emissions and the electronic emissions of guided missiles or pilotless aircraft. The first priority for radar sites was to establish their location, the second to determine the radar's function—early warning, aircraft control, gun-laying antiaircraft, or active countermeasures. After identifying the location of an electronic emission related to a guided missile or pilotless aircraft, the next subject of concern was whether the signal was for ground-to-air control, air-to-air control, or some other purpose. Additionally, a communications intercept program was conducted on an experimental basis and each aircraft had one position allocated to the COMINT function.[24]

The intercepted signals permitted analysts to determine whether the radar was used for early warning purposes, ground-controlled interception, or gun-laying purposes. The pulse width of the signals would provide an indication of the radar's minimum range and equipment design, while the other characteristics would be important "to the Research and Development personnel who use the characteristic information in designing equipment to counter the emission."[25]

Officially, the AAC flights were to remain forty, and later twenty, miles offshore in conducting missions. However, a major purpose of the program was to get the Soviets to turn on the entire set of radars that would be used in wartime—and provide the United States with a complete order of battle. In some instances planes would penetrate briefly into Soviet airspace to get the Soviet air defense radars to begin full-scale operation.

On other occasions flights actually penetrated deep into Soviet territory. At the time Richard Meyer was a first lieutenant and a copilot assigned to the 46th Reconnaissance Squadron at Ladd Field, Fairbanks, Alaska. Meyer recalls that in the "summer of 1948 we were given a new project requiring an all-volunteer crew to fly a highly modified, stripped down B-29 on special missions. The aft compartment of the aircraft was jammed with electronic receivers and consoles for about five to eight operators. These operators had not been part of the squadron before; they were temporary for these special missions only." The first mission departed from Ladd Field on August 5, leaving Alaskan air space near Point Barrow, then flying deep into Siberia and exiting into the Sea of Japan. After nineteen hours, forty-five minutes the plane landed at Yokota Air Base, near Tokyo. Further missions into the Soviet Union were conducted on August 8, September 1, and September 6. The August 8 mission reversed the flight path—going from Yokota Air Base to Ladd Field in seventeen hours, forty-five minutes. The third mission consumed a little under twenty hours from Ladd to Yokota, with the fourth and final flight returning the plane to Ladd in exactly seventeen hours.[26]

Great Britain may have also been flying electronic intelligence missions directed at the Soviet Union at this time. In September 1948 a Lancaster and a Lincoln aircraft, each fitted with a camera and modified as a SIGINT prototype, journeyed to Habbaniya, Iraq. From that location several eight-hour SIGINT sorties were flown, which could have easily involved a flight path along the Soviet border. In December 1949 more aircraft flew to Iraq to conduct SIGINT sorties.[27]

A third component of the early U.S. airborne reconnaissance program involved the monitoring of Soviet atomic weapons testing and production. Eventually a variety of means were employed to monitor above- and below-ground nuclear explosions. But initially the Air Force's Long-Range Detection Program—known first as Project CENTERING and later as Project COTTONSEED—relied almost exclusively on airborne collection. Since the object of the CENTERING/COTTONSEED missions was to collect air samples exiting the Soviet land mass it was not necessary for those missions to approach or enter Soviet territory, as was the case with photographic and electronic reconnaissance missions. Consequently, the risk of being shot down by Soviet fighters was considerably smaller.[28]

As was the case with the other elements of the airborne reconnaissance effort, the atomic monitoring effort relied on modified bombers such as the B-29. The B-29s would have a large, boxlike can installed on top of the aircraft. The cans were filter holders, and filters about the size of photographic plates (approximately eight by ten inches) were installed in the holders.[29]

Some of the modified B-29 aircraft flew routes along the Turkish border and over the Mediterranean; others flew missions from Japan to Alaska. From the beginning of the program to September 3, 1949, the radiation count on a filter exceeded fifty counts per minute 111 times. Any count greater than fifty resulted in an Atomic Detection System Alert. All 111 alerts had been determined to be the result of natural occurrences—volcanic explosions, earthquakes, or normal fluctuations in background radioactivity.[30]

Alert No. 112 was different. On September 3 a WB-29 weather reconnaissance plane flew a routine mission from Japan to Alaska. At an altitude of 18,000 feet, a filter paper exposed for three hours registered 85 counts per minute. The second filter paper was checked and found to show 153 counts per minute. As a result, other planes were dispatched and picked up even higher readings. A filter paper exposed at an altitude of 10,000 feet on a weather flight from Guam to Japan produced a measurement of more than 1,000 counts per minute.[31]

The data collected by the flights led a study panel to conclude that the data "are consistent with the view that the origin of the fission products was the explosion of an atomic bomb whose nuclear composition was similar to the Alamogordo bomb and that the explosion occurred between the 26th and 29th of August at some point between the east 35th meridian and 170th meridian over the Asiatic land mass."[32]*

The implications of the Soviet bomb were significant. The Joint Chief of Staff's Joint Intelligence Committee revised upward its estimate of the Soviet atomic bomb stockpile. It was projected that the Soviets would possess 10–20 bombs by mid-1950, 25–45 by mid-1951, 45–90 by mid-1952, 70–135 by mid-1953, and 120–200 by mid-1954.[33]

The UKUSA Agreement

Along with its aerial reconnaissance program the United States began establishing new ground SIGINT stations to focus on the Soviet Union. The Air Force Security Service's 3rd Radio Squadron Mobile was reactivated on November 12, 1949. The squadron consisted of nine officers, fifty-eight airmen, and three detachments. Detachment A, at Davis AFB, Adak, in the Aleutian Islands, operated twelve rhombic antennas to receive signals over moderate to long distances.[34]†

That network would expand dramatically over the course of the next several decades. But it would be necessary, given the vastness of the

---

* It was later determined that the blast took place at Semipalatinsk on August 29.

† A rhombic antenna consists of a wire several feet off the ground and attached to posts in the shape of a diamond. Each side is approximately ten feet long, and at one end the wire is connected to a coaxial cable that runs underground to a centrally located operations building.

Soviet target, for the United States to rely on its allies to augment its own SIGINT effort. The foundation for that cooperation had been laid during World War II with the BRUSA and Naval SIGINT agreements. In September 1945 President Truman indicated his approval of U.S. SIGINT operations in peacetime and collaboration "in the field of communications intelligence between the United States Army and Navy and the British." That decision also envisaged a continuation of cooperation with Canada, Australia, and New Zealand.[35]

Similar conclusions were being reached in London, Ottawa, Melbourne, and Wellington. In Ottawa, at a meeting on December 31, 1944, Norman Robertson and other officials of the External Affairs department met with the chief of the General Staff, General Charles Foulkes, and National Research Council Chief C. J. Mackenzie, and decided to continue Canadian SIGINT operations.[36]

The primary reason was a political one. As Foulkes explained:

> The position of Canada in respect of defence and peacetime economy, on the one hand, as a member of the British Commonwealth and, on the other, as an essential economic and military partner of the United States is a paramount political factor. This position . . . indicates the need for Canada sharing the fruits of the intelligence activities of the two other Powers in keeping Canada in their confidence . . . if a pooling of intelligence is in the best interests of Canada, it will be enhanced by Canada's making a contribution to the pool.[37]

In London, the chiefs of staff met on November 21, 1945, to discuss SIGINT cooperation. They concluded that Britain would offer the United States an arrangement of "100% cooperation" in the production of SIGINT. However, they also agreed that "less than 100% cooperation would not be worth having."[38]

But the desire for cooperation did not prevent a prolonged round of negotiations. The negotiations began in Washington during fall 1945, with Government Communications Headquarters director Sir Edward Travis and Harry Hinsley representing the United Kingdom and a joint OP-20-G and Army Signal Security Agency team representing the United States. Differences immediately arose over the British desire to speak for Canada, with Canadian consent, in the negotiations. The American negotiators were adamantly opposed to such an arrangement, strongly favoring full "bilateral agreements with the Canadians on all intelligence matters." The rationale was laid out in a December 1945 memo prepared for the director of the Military Intelligence Service, which noted that due to "Canada's strategic position with respect to the United States and Russia, it is believed that all consideration of U.S. intelligence relations with that nation should be made independently."[39]

A similar problem arose with regard to Australia and New Zealand: the British claimed the right to act as their spokesman and the Americans pointed to wartime bilateral arrangements with those countries and insisted they should be full and independent parties to the negotiations. One British draft agreement after another was rejected or drastically altered by the U.S. representatives. The negotiations continued for well over a year.[40]

In addition to conflict over the role of Canada, Australia, and New Zealand, there was also a fundamental disagreement over whether SIGINT concerning all countries should be included in the final sharing arrangement. During the first stages of the negotiations the United States insisted that some intelligence concerning China would not be shared. By late 1946 intelligence on the Philippines and Latin America were also to be excluded.[41]

Finally in 1948 the five nations agreed to the U.K.–U.S.A. Security Agreement, commonly known as the UKUSA Agreement, as the basis for SIGINT cooperation. The agreement specified divided responsibility for SIGINT collection among the five participating nations. The United States and the United Kingdom were designated as first parties, and the remainder as second parties. Canada was assigned the responsibility for covering the northern Soviet Union and part of Europe, Britain for portions of Europe (including the Soviet Union) and Africa, Australia and New Zealand focused on communications in their geographical area, and the United States was responsible for the remainder.[42]

VENONA

It was not long after the UKUSA agreement was signed that American and British codebreakers were able to jointly exploit Soviet communications that had been intercepted in 1944 and 1945. The ability to break into those communications was one of several postwar events that resulted in significant setbacks to Soviet intelligence operations.

On September 5, 1945, Igor Gouzenko, a GRU code clerk at the Soviet embassy in Ottawa, stuffed more than 100 documents under his shirt—including pages from the diary of the GRU resident. Gouzenko succeeded in defecting and obtaining protection from Canadian authorities, although not easily.[43]

When the police began translating Gouzenko's documents and interviewing him they discovered a major Soviet espionage effort in Canada—an effort which penetrated the Department of External Affairs cipher room, the Royal Canadian Air Force intelligence department, Parliament, the National Research Council, the Department of Munitions and Supply, and, in the person of Allan Nunn May, Canada's atomic research laboratories. The Soviets had acquired engineering blueprints of weapons, as well as samples of enriched uranium-235.[44]

Gouzenko's documents and debriefings also revealed intelligence on Soviet cipher systems, evidence of espionage by Alger Hiss and U.S. Treasury official Harry Dexter White, and the existence of a Soviet spy in British intelligence code-named ELLI.[45]

In November 1945 Elizabeth Terrill Bentley, who had served as courier for major Soviet espionage rings, began to tell the FBI about those rings—which included employees of the OSS, War Department, War Production Board, Foreign Economic Administration, and the Treasury, Agriculture, and Commerce departments. Her information led the FBI to seriously investigate charges made in 1939 by Whittaker Chambers concerning Soviet intelligence penetration of the U.S. government. While none of the agents named by Bentley and Chambers were prosecuted for espionage, they all ceased to be of significant value to the Soviet Union. Among those forced out of sensitive positions was Alger Hiss, who had left the State Department in 1946 to become president of the Carnegie Endowment for International Peace. The Chambers testimony was only the last nail in the coffin for Hiss. In addition to Chambers's claims, there was information provided by the French years earlier, probably based on testimony from GRU defector Walter Krivitsky, concerning the espionage activities of Alger and Donald Hiss. In addition, Gouzenko reported that he had heard in Moscow of a Soviet agent in the State Department who had been very close to former Secretary of State Edward Stettinius and was still in position to report on important issues.[46]

The information provided by Gouzenko and Bentley did not threaten the activities of Cairncross, Burgess, Maclean, and Philby, who continued their espionage activities on behalf of the Soviet Union. Cairncross moved from SIS to the Treasury after the war, providing intelligence at monthly intervals to his case officer, Boris Krotov. The only major loss was Anthony Blunt, who left MI5 due to the exhaustion and stress of his double life.[47]

It was almost three years after Bentley's defection when the beginning of the end for Burgess, Maclean, and Philby arrived—in the person of the tall and gangly Meredith Gardner, a brilliant cryptanalyst for the U.S. Army Security Agency (ASA). Gardner spoke six or seven languages and was one of the rare Western scholars who read Sanskrit. Before World War II he had taught languages at a southwestern university. From there he joined Friedman's Signal Intelligence Service, after which he taught himself Japanese in three months, to the astonishment of his fellow cryptanalysts. During the war he had specialized in breaking Japanese codes and ciphers. After the war his focus shifted to the communications of the new enemy.[48]

On October 29, 1948, Gardner made his first break into NKGB communications that had been intercepted, but never analyzed, during 1944 and 1945. That he was able to do so was the result of several factors, beginning with the OSS's 1944 acquisition of 1,500 pages of an NKVD/NKGB codebook recovered by the Finns. The book listed 999 five-digit code groups, with each group representing a different letter, word, or phrase. Ordered by President Roosevelt to return the codebook to Moscow, OSS director William J. Donovan complied, but not before making a copy of the original. By itself, the codebook would be of little use to Gardner or any other

Western cryptanalyst because of the nature of the NKVD/NKGB enciphering process, which began with the replacement of each word (or on occasion a letter) by a five-digit number group from the codebook. Then the code clerk in each NKGB residency would add to each group another five-digit number drawn from a series of randomly generated numbers on a "one-time pad," the only copy of which was held at NKGB headquarters in Moscow. If, as required by Center regulations, the pad was used only once, the encoded message was virtually unbreakable. But during the last year of the war the vast quantity of communications being transmitted from the United States and Britain resulted in the Center sending out the same pad more than once. In addition, the FBI acquired some plaintext versions of NKGB ciphered telegrams from New York to Moscow in 1944. And Igor Gouzenko was also able to provide information on NKGB and GRU cipher procedures. Finally, the continued U.S. interception of Soviet traffic to and from the United States during the war (in contrast to Britain's cessation of such collection during the war) provided the vast majority of the messages the cryptanalysts had to work with.[49]

Even with the lapses in Soviet communications security, solving the messages was a laborious process, and over the next five years only 1 percent of the 200,000 available trade, diplomatic, and intelligence messages were solved.* But those messages, code-named VENONA in the United States and BRIDE in the United Kingdom, contained valuable clues to Soviet espionage activities—in some cases providing conclusive evidence of treason, in others providing clues to be followed up by the FBI and MI5.[50]

But before the cryptanalysts, counterintelligence authorities, and circumstances ended the espionage careers of Burgess, Maclean, and Philby, they were able to provide their Soviet masters with valuable intelligence. While Philby's career has been the most scrutinized, in fact and fiction, Maclean was clearly the most potentially valuable of the three. For although Philby could and did provide valuable information on what British, and for a time U.S. intelligence services were doing vis-à-vis the Soviet Union, Maclean could provide information on Western foreign policy and military initiatives and capabilities.

In May 1944 Maclean arrived in Washington as Second Secretary of the British embassy. In October he was promoted to First Secretary, a position he occupied until September 1, 1948. From Washington, Maclean went to Cairo, where he served until October 1950 when he returned to London to head the Foreign Office's American Department.[51]

His positions in Washington and London, and the specific functions he performed, allowed him to pass his Soviet controllers a wealth of top-secret information. In September 1946 he received from the British military attaché a thick top-secret report, *Latest Developments of the Ameri-*

---

* Because Soviet NKGB codes were changed in 1945 subsequent intercepted traffic could not be decoded using the recovered codebook.

can Army. The report included a chart detailing the month-by-month fluctuations of Army and Air Force strength at every base, in the United States and overseas—as well as information on the sizes, types, and capabilities of every piece of equipment used by U.S. infantry divisions.[52]

From February 1947 to September 1948 Maclean served as Britain's Washington representative on atomic energy issues. As British Secretary of the Combined Policy Committee (CPC) and representative to the Combined Development Trust (CDT), he attended a top-secret three-day meeting in November 1947 to discuss what atomic energy and weapons information could be declassified.[53]

Although the McMahon Act of 1946 had prohibited the exchange of new atomic information with any foreign nation, it did not cover either the information discussed at the declassification meeting or the acquisition of raw materials related to production of nuclear weapons. Maclean's presence at CPC meetings gave him access to high-level policy discussions concerning atomic energy and its military uses. His presence at CDT meetings, which he never failed to attend between March 1947 and his departure from Washington, allowed him to report on Western attempts to acquire the uranium necessary to construct atomic weapons. The CDT directed a highly secret program to buy up the world's deposits of uranium, which the United States, Britain, and the Soviet Union did not have on their own territory, but the Belgian Congo did.[54]

Only two days after Maclean attended his first CPC meeting, the State Department was informed by the U.S. embassy in Brussels that Foreign Minister Paul-Henri Spaak of Belgium had been asked by a Communist party senator "if a secret treaty between U.S. and Belgium concerning uranium existed." Further questions, accusations, and inflamed emotions followed. And after five weeks, on March 11, the Belgian government fell.[55]

Maclean also had a pass that permitted him to visit the Atomic Energy Commission without an escort, a privilege that was not extended to members of the cabinet and Congress or FBI director J. Edgar Hoover. Between the summer of 1947 and September 1948 Maclean used his pass twelve times, sometimes at night.[56]

Burgess undoubtedly also provided information on allied operations in Korea, for from 1948 to the summer of 1950 he served in the Foreign Office Far Eastern Department. In 1949 he was fully briefed on the situation in Korea and saw a variety of intelligence and military reports from General Douglas MacArthur's headquarters in Tokyo, the War Office, and the Joint Intelligence Committee.[57]

Burgess's next assignment was with the Washington embassy, where he joined the 37-year-old Philby, who had arrived in September 1949 as the new SIS/MI5 liaison to the U.S. intelligence community. Although all military SIGINT was transmitted through the British Joint Services Mission, Philby was intimately involved in the exchange of VENONA–BRIDE material.[58]

But while Philby looked on—literally—the VENONA traffic began to yield some of its secrets. Gardner would later recall how Philby would stand over his shoulder, smoking a pipe, and watch him work on the intercepted messages. In January 1949, just three months after Maclean's departure from Washington, the British government was officially notified that further work on the VENONA traffic indicated that information had been transmitted to the Soviets in 1944 and 1945 from a source in the British embassy in Washington. ASA had uncovered two Churchill-to-Truman messages, with their Foreign Office serial numbers included, among the intercepted traffic. They quickly identified the spy's code name—HOMER. Soon after Philby was indoctrinated into VENONA, he realized that HOMER was Maclean.[59]

In August 1949 FBI special agent Robert Lamphere delivered more bad news to Britain's leaders. He informed them that someone, "probably a British scientist, had been giving information about the atom bomb to the Russians." Previously he had discovered in the decrypted Soviet traffic verbatim sections of a scientific report written from Los Alamos. When he located the original of the report in the Atomic Energy Commission's files he discovered that its author was Klaus Fuchs.[60]

The decrypts also showed that the source of the report had a sister who attended an American university, as did Fuchs. By the time he was identified Fuchs's usefulness was dramatically less than it had been at Los Alamos. With Fuchs now working in the British nuclear program, and the 1946 Atomic Energy Act severely limiting the nuclear data that the United States could provide Britain, he no longer represented a means of discovering what the Americans were doing. But his unmasking as a spy, and his confession in January 1950, led to the identification of several other atomic spies. On May 26 Fuchs identified a picture of Harry Gold as RAYMOND, his American controller. Gold proceeded to provide information, which when combined in February 1950 with intelligence from a newly deciphered 1944 cable, implicated David Greenglass in atomic espionage. (Greenglass had been demobilized and left Los Alamos in June 1946.) Greenglass's June 1950 confession implicated his sister and brother-in-law, Ethel and Julius Rosenberg. Julius was arrested the next month, Ethel in August.[61] Greenglass claimed that his brother-in-law had boasted to him of operating a Soviet espionage ring that had provided, in addition to atomic secrets, a wide variety of other scientific and technical intelligence, including studies of an atomic plane and space satellites.[62]

Meanwhile the search for HOMER continued. At the end of 1950 the list of suspects numbered thirty-five. By early March 1951 the Foreign Office had narrowed the search to a short list of four. By early April there were only two candidates—Paul Gore-Booth and Donald Maclean. Naturally, Philby suggested that Gore-Booth was the mole.[63]

But in mid-April the final piece of the puzzle was provided by VENONA. A decoded message revealed that for a period of time in 1944 HOMER contacted his NKGB controller twice a week in New York, traveling from Washington under the cover of visiting his pregnant wife—a pattern of activity that fitted Maclean perfectly and no one else at all.[64]

Even though there was no doubt on the part of MI5 that Maclean and HOMER were the same person, it was impossible to arrest him on the basis of the intercepts. Since there was no thought of revealing the VENONA project in court, the United States and Britain being unaware at the time that both British (Philby) and American (William Wiesband of the Armed Forces Security Agency) sources had told the Soviets of the project, it would be necessary to gather other evidence. It was hoped that surveillance and interrogation of Maclean would be sufficient.[65]

The delay allowed Philby to act and Maclean to escape. Philby decided to employ Burgess, who was about to be sent home in disgrace after yet another series of indiscretions, to warn Maclean. Shortly after landing in Britain on May 7 Burgess informed the MGB's Yuri Modin. Philby also provided additional information which pointed to May 28 as the day MI5 would begin to interrogate Maclean.[66]

On the 24th boat tickets to France were purchased. On the evening of Friday May 25, Burgess drove up to Maclean's large house just as he was preparing to sit down to a birthday dinner. To Mrs. Maclean's consternation Burgess insisted that Maclean leave with him. Once in France MGB officers provided them with false papers, which took them first to Vienna and then to Moscow.[67]

The escape terminated not only their espionage careers but those of Cairncross and Philby. Unsigned notes, describing confidential Whitehall discussions, found in Burgess's flat were identified as being written by Cairncross. After an interrogation during which he denied being a spy but admitted passing confidential information to the Soviets, Cairncross resigned from the Treasury.[68]

Philby immediately came under suspicion in London and Washington because of his long-standing relationship with Burgess and because Burgess had resided in his house while serving at the embassy. On June 13 CIA counterintelligence chief William Harvey submitted a memo to DCI Walter Bedell Smith arguing that "Kim Philby was a Soviet agent." That memo was followed by a letter from Smith to "C," Sir Stewart Menzies, informing the SIS chief that Philby was no longer welcome in the United States.[69]

Philby departed Washington on June 12, 1951. Many SIS officers and all MI5 officials involved in the case soon became convinced that Philby had been a long-term Soviet agent. In a meeting with Dick Goldsmith White of MI5 Philby was unable to explain who had paid for his travels in Europe between 1934 and 1936. Additional investigation yielded nine more reasons for suspecting Philby. These covered his personal relationships, his handling of the Volkov affair,* and the jumps in Soviet intelligence com-

---

* In 1945 an NKGB officer serving in Istanbul, Constantine Volkov, contacted the British embassy there and indicated that he wanted to defect for a price. The information he offered

munications traffic between London and Moscow after he received briefings about Volkov and VENONA.[70]

Philby, whose career in SIS had survived the attempts of two Soviet defectors to unmask him, was not to escape a third time. At the end of July Philby was informed by C that he would have to resign and that in lieu of a pension he would receive a £4,000 settlement. In December 1951 he was summoned to a judicial inquiry at MI5. According to an MI5 officer of the era: "There was not a single officer who sat through the proceedings who came away not totally convinced of Philby's guilt."[71]

VENONA also led to the conclusive exposure of two Soviet sources in Australia. The NKGB's two most important agents in the External Affairs department were compromised by decrypts of messages from the Soviet embassy in Canberra to Moscow. The messages were intercepted at Coonawarra, a joint Anglo-Australian facility just south of Darwin, and solved by GCHQ analysts in Britain. Among the decoded traffic was a British report entitled "Security in the Western Mediterranean and Eastern Atlantic," which had been provided to the Australian External Affairs Post-Hostilities Department.[72]

That report was only one of many received in Australia from Britain on the subject of postwar policy. Other material concerned postwar defense plans, atomic policy, armistice planning, East European policy, relations with France, Middle East policy, and base sites. Since the Australian External Affairs Department did not practice the rigid compartmentation that existed in the Foreign Office, a single source in Canberra could have access to a wider range of material than someone in a comparable position in London.[73]

Jim Hill, code-named TOURIST in the VENONA traffic, was the first Soviet agent identified in External Affairs. Hill's role was revealed by a decrypt which gave the serial number of one of the diplomatic telegrams Hill had provided to the Soviets. Additional decrypts identified the other agent in External Affairs as the Oxford-educated communist diplomat Ian Milner, code-named BUR, who had moved from External Affairs for a position with the United Nations. From New York he apparently provided information, which the Soviets considered valuable, on the Austra-

---

included the identity of five Soviet spies in the British intelligence and security services, including a British counterintelligence official. As chief of SIS counterintelligence Philby was given the matter to handle, although it would have seemed advisable to handle such a case outside of MI5 and SIS counterintelligence channels. Philby quickly informed his Soviet controller. By delaying his trip to Istanbul he ensured that he would not arrive until after the NKGB had an opportunity to act. An unconcious Volkov was returned to the Soviet Union on a stretcher, under the pretense that he was ill. The identity of the British counterintelligence official Volkov would have named is generally presumed to be Philby. For a dissenting view see George A. Carver, Jr., "A Fresh Look at the Cambridge Comintern," *International Journal of Intelligence and Counterintelligence* 5, no. 1 (1991): 109–22.

lian delegation to the United Nations. On the basis of the decrypts Hill was called back to Australia in July 1950; after interrogation there he was transferred to a job that eliminated his access to classified information. Milner, on the other hand, decided to escape the closing net by heading east to Czechoslovakia.[74]

14

New Players

The years after World War II were notable not only for the beginning of the Cold War: as nations devastated or defeated in war were rebuilt, new nations and alliances appeared. Those changes resulted in the emergence of new intelligence services, including those that would be of major significance in the international intelligence arena. Some would operate on the front lines of the Cold War; others would play significant roles in the formulation and implementation of their nations' foreign and defense policies.

Reconstruction

In Europe new intelligence services emerged in both victorious and defeated nations. The new French central intelligence service was a successor to the Direction Générale des Études et Recherches (DGER), which had been established in 1943 as the Direction Générale des Services Spéciaux (DGSS), with the merger of the Gaullist Bureau Central de Renseignement et d'Action (BCRA) and the Service de Renseignement (SR) of the Algeria-based General Giraud. The BCRA was headed by André Dewavrin, whose nom de guerre was Colonel Passy, and gathered intelligence on the German forces in France as well as directing and aiding resistance groups.[1]

With the end of the war more than a name change was required. During the war the DGSS's main focus, naturally enough, was the activities of German forces in France, although it did operate several networks in the Balkans and Middle East as well as monitoring the activities of certain French refugees in the United States.[2]

However, change was delayed by bureaucratic inertia and a French penchant for internal spying. A January 1945 memorandum issued to the DGER's top officials directed the organization to concentrate on three domestic targets: the internal situation in the country and public opinion, political parties, and resistance movements. The DGER proceeded to open mail, tap telephones, and build up a force of 10,000 to conduct surveillance.[3]

Its internal activities did not go unnoticed, particularly by the strong French Communist party, which charged that the secret service had launched a series of covert operations to weaken it. The resulting outcry produced several changes in the DGER. Dewavrin reorganized the service, ridding the agency of its most unprincipled members and reducing the size of its bloated departments. It was also renamed, becoming the Service de Documentation Extérieur et de Contre-Espionage (SDECE; Service for External Documentation and Counterespionage). Its founding decree specified that the organization was "meant to seek, outside national boundaries, all information and documents which might inform the government" and that it was to "carry no power on French territory, but operate only in foreign countries. Any counter-intelligence operation in France will rest with a special division of the Department of the Interior."[4]

As the end of World War II approached, Reinhard Gehlen, chief of Foreign Armies East, looked to the future and saw the victorious Soviets as a threat to the West. And he had something to offer—a detailed set of files on the Soviet Union and WALLI I's agent network. On April 5, 1945, just four days before he would be fired by Hitler for his pessimistic reports, Gehlen ordered duplicates of the FHO's card index, reports, aerial photographs, estimates, and other files placed in fifty steel cases and stored in various locations.[5]

The FHO's top leadership (Gehlen, Wessel, and Baun) agreed to offer their organization's services to Britain or the United States. They also agreed it would be necessary for them and other key FHO members to disperse and stay in hiding for a while to avoid being seized immediately by any of the invading armies. When passions had cooled somewhat it was hoped that the British or Americans would be willing to use their talents. But an offer to the British, conveyed by Baun, elicited no response.[6]

Wessel went to Bavaria, taking most of the steel cases. Gehlen was able to find refuge, along with other FHO officers and staff, within twenty miles of Wessel. While Gehlen was able to avoid initial discovery by the Allied forces he did not completely control the timing of his capture. Believing he and the other FHO members to be members of the SS, a local shepherd informed the Americans.[7]

As a result, Gehlen found himself on his way to Miesbach, where a U.S. Army Counter-intelligence Corps (CIC) detachment under Captain Marian E. Porter was located. Porter's reaction was not what Gehlen had hoped for. To Gehlen's announcement—"I am head of the Section 'Foreign Armies East' in General Army headquarters"—Porter simply replied—"You were, General." Gehlen's claim that "I have information to give of the highest importance to your government" also left the CIC officer unimpressed. "So have they all," he responded, and shipped him off to a prisoner-of-war camp in Salzburg. But when top army officials in Germany heard that the Russians were interested in the whereabouts of the general and the content of his files they became intensely interested, and locating Gehlen became a top priority.[8]

In July Gehlen was discovered in a special POW camp in Oberursel, near Frankfurt, and Brigadier General Edwin Luther Sibert, the senior American intelligence officer for General Omar Bradley's Twelfth Army Group, was informed. At a quickly arranged meeting Gehlen explained the operations of Foreign Armies East and predicted that its Soviet target would be the cause of more trouble. Gehlen told Sibert that Stalin would not permit Polish, Czechoslovakian, Bulgarian, or Romanian independence, would seek to control Finland from Moscow, and would attempt to reestablish Germany as a communist state. The strength of Soviet armed forces, Gehlen concluded, would allow Stalin to risk war in order to seize West Germany.[9]

Gehlen also claimed he could back up his conclusions with the material FHO had collected, with the help of former FHO staff members. He merely needed to reacquire the hidden documents and assemble the necessary staff from the POW camps where they resided. Gehlen also offered the prospect of reviving the WALLI I network in the Soviet Union.[10]

Sibert was sufficiently impressed to accept Gehlen's offer. The files were recovered, staff members assembled, and Gehlen permitted to form the "Gehlen staff cell"—first in the Historical Research Section, and then in the Seventh Army's Intelligence Center in Wiesbaden. Their primary work was a history and analysis of German intelligence operations directed at the Soviet Union. They also produced reports on Soviet tank production, the locations, strength, and composition of Soviet divisions, and the morale of the Red Army and the Soviet population.[11]

Sibert, convinced of Gehlen's value, began looking for approval from the War Department to establish a Gehlen-run intelligence service targeted on the Soviet Union. After talking to Walter Bedell Smith, Eisenhower's chief of staff (and a future DCI), they alerted the War Department to their discovery.[12]

There was sufficient War Department interest so that in August 1945 Gehlen found himself, along with five aides, on his way to Washington. After arriving in early September, Gehlen met with Brigadier-General John R. Magruder, head of the Strategic Services Unit, and Major-General George V. Strong, head of Army Intelligence. But neither made an immediate offer to fund Gehlen.[13]

It was not until February 1946, with Gehlen still residing in the United States, that the Army's reluctance to approve his proposal faded. That month Soviet forces had occupied northern Iran, an act of aggression in the view of both the American public and leadership. Gehlen's warnings about Soviet intentions took on even greater plausibility.[14]

In July Gehlen began his journey back to Germany to establish an intelligence organization under American supervision, near Oberursel. His project was to be conducted only on a limited and experimental basis. And when he arrived he had to deflect a challenge from Baun, who, in Gehlen's absence, had convinced Sibert to permit him to reestablish WALLI I independent from Gehlen's authority.[15]

With Baun's challenge deflected Gehlen's organization began operations, scoring a major coup with Operation BOHEMIA in the summer of 1948—when a shakeup in Soviet-dominated Czechoslovakia permitted Gehlen's agents to successfully entice the head of Czech intelligence's West German operations to defect, bringing with him a mass of files. The result was the decimation of Czech espionage operations in western Germany.[16]

But Gehlen's group was living a perilous existence. Many in Army intelligence (G-2), for political and security reasons, objected to American support. As a result, G-2 tried to interest the Central Intelligence Group in taking control of, and providing the money for, Gehlen's unit. After considering the matter the CIG declined.[17]

In September 1948, however, the CIA and the Army agreed to conduct a joint study before making a final decision about Gehlen and his staff. The bulk of the work was done by the CIA's James Critchfield, who, after a two-month study, transmitted a 2,000-word message to CIA headquarters. Critchfield stressed that the Gehlen organization was already firmly established, with 4,000 employees, and not amenable to being carved up and distributed to different U.S. interests. There were only two options, Critchfield informed the CIA: eliminate the organization or control it.[18]

Controlling it was preferable, Critchfield argued. Eventually a sovereign Germany would emerge, with its own intelligence service, and the United States would be better off taking part in shaping its direction and controlling it for as long as possible.[19]

Critchfield also recommended a more elaborate study of the organization, to find out more about its operations and value. In response the CIA assigned him responsibility for supervising the unit and gave him two years to conduct a thorough investigation. At the same time, negotiations began between Critchfield and Gehlen. After numerous long sessions it was agreed that the CIA would determine the intelligence requirements that governed the organization's operations. In addition, a CIA officer would be assigned to each department head and the CIA would receive all the reports and evaluations produced.[20]

There was one point of intense disagreement: Gehlen initially refused to give the names of the organization's field agents. He did relent to the extent of providing the names of the top-ranking 150 members of his organization. But through financial pressure, personal contacts, and discussions about specific projects the United States was able to uncover much more about those working for Gehlen.[21]

On May 13 the negotiations concluded with an English-language settlement, followed by a German-language version ten days later. With the beginning of the 1950 fiscal year on July 1, 1949, the CIA assumed control of the "Gehlen Organization," also known as "The Org."[22]

Operations in the early years included several penetrations of the East German government. The Org obtained copies of government decrees and minutes from various ministries, letters from the Soviet High Command, and directives from the East German Politbüro. In 1948 it recruited Hermann Kastner, the vice president of the German Democratic Republic, who reported on the Central Committee of the Liberal Democratic party, the presidency of the People's Congress, the National Council of the National Front, and the cabinet. Kastner also described his conversations with Soviet politicians, diplomats, and generals.[23]

In Czechoslovakia, the Org placed an agent in the Skoda arms factory. It also recruited a typist in the Ministry of Commerce, who provided information on trade between Czechoslovakia and East Germany, and a technical draftsman, who handed over plans for an important component of a guidance mechanism used in weapons and missiles.[24]

While Gehlen conducted his operations at U.S. direction, he sustained his ultimate objective—leading the intelligence service of the new German state. On May 21, 1952 Gehlen provided Chancellor Konrad Adenauer with a memo on the establishment of a federal intelligence service, the core of which would be the Gehlen Organization. Undoubtedly with the Nazi-era experience of intelligence fragmentation in mind as well as a desire to become German intelligence czar, Gehlen proposed that the future intelligence service should be responsible for all German political, military, and economic intelligence operations, as well as foreign counterintelligence operations.[25]*

Markus Wolf

During the years that Reinhard Gehlen was first convincing the United States that he had something of value to offer and then directing the operations of his Org, another German was on his way to becoming a major figure in the world of international espionage. Markus Johannes Wolf was the son of a socialist playwright and doctor. Raised in Stuttgart, Wolf left Hitler's Third Reich for the Soviet Union with his family in 1934. From 1934 to 1937 he studied Russian at the Karl Liebknecht School in Moscow, then attended a Comintern college in Kushnarenkovo, and finally entered the Moscow high school for aircraft construction in 1942.[26]

In 1945, at the age of twenty-two, Wolf returned to Germany. His assignments apparently included agitation and propaganda, and he played

---

* Gehlen envisaged a transfer to German control on April 1, 1953, but it was not to occur until 1956, following West German acceptance into NATO in 1955. The new organization was called the Bundesnachrichtendienst (Federal Intelligence Service).

a major role in establishing Berlin radio. In addition to becoming its controller, with Soviet backing, he broadcast reports on the Nuremberg war crime trials, using the name Mark F. Wolf At the same time he broadcast political commentaries under the name Michael F. Storm.[27]

Wolf went on to become a foreign affairs specialist, traveling to Poland and Czechoslovakia in 1948. After returning to Berlin he went on to Moscow as first counselor of the East German mission.[28] But Wolf's destiny was to become head of East German foreign intelligence operations. The process began with the August 16, 1947, establishment of the fifth department of the Criminal Police, K-5, the first East German secret police organization. On February 20, 1950, K-5 became the Ministerium für Staatssicherheit (MfS; Ministry for State Security).[29]

While the ministry established a West Department to penetrate West Berlin and West Germany in 1951 another institution, the Institut für Wirtschaftswissenschaftliche Forschung (IWF; Institute for Economic Research), was also charged with foreign intelligence operations. After eighteen months in Moscow Wolf returned to East Germany to become operational head of IWF. The IWF suffered a major setback when West German counterintelligence penetrated one of its camouflaged offices, an ostensibly private East–West trading firm located in Hamburg, resulting in the arrest of thirty-six members by the spring of 1953. The IWF was soon dissolved, and a new foreign intelligence organization formed under the auspices of the Ministry of the Interior, which temporarily replaced the MfS.[30]

Wolf was named to head the new department, initially known as Main Department XV.* The creation of the new department represented not only a reorganization, but an increased emphasis on foreign intelligence operations, particularly those directed against the Federal Republic.[31]

Wolf was selected as operational head of the IWF thanks to General Alexandr Semenovich Panyushkin, the head of the Soviet MGB's First Chief Directorate. In 1950 Panyushkin directed several major inventories of the East German personnel to find an individual to direct East German foreign intelligence operations. None of the dozen or more names forwarded to MGB chief Ivan Serov and the Ministry's Executive Council proved acceptable.[32]

Panyushkin continued the search and eventually discovered Wolf, who impressed him as a young, aggressive, intelligent German communist. He was well-suited to intelligence work, with an intuitive grasp of operational concepts and essential details. He was also respected by his peers in East German intelligence and received Panyushkin's strong recommendation. Serov believed that Wolf's alertness and youth would allow him to energize the East German service.[33]

---

* In 1956 Main Department XV became the Hauptverwaltung Aufklärung (HVA; Main Department for Intelligence) of the Ministry for State Security. A year earlier the Ministry of State Security had been reestablished, taking control of internal security, secret police, and foreign intelligence functions.

Once in charge, Wolf recruited carefully. After a prolonged visit to various MGB training centers he established a more demanding training program for Main Department XV officers. He also arranged to have senior MGB officers serve as final judges on his graduating agents. With the East German service on firm ground it was given the mission of spying on its Western counterpart and NATO.[34] Over the years it would serve as part of an extended Soviet intelligence network that also included the Polish, Czechoslovakian, Bulgarian, and Hungarian intelligence services. But Wolf would become the best known of the communist spymasters.*

Isser Harel and the Mossad

During the early morning of June 30, 1948, six weeks after Israel became a state and in the midst of war with its Arab neighbors, a group of Israeli political, military, and intelligence officials gathered in Tel Aviv. The topic of discussion was the complete restructuring of the Israeli intelligence community. Chairing the meeting was Isser Beeri, known as "Isser the Big" because of his height. Among the other attendees was Isser Harel, known as "Isser the Little" for his diminutive stature.[35]

Beeri was head of Israel's National Information Service, which had a history far lengthier than that of the six-week-old Israeli state, for it could trace its origins back to the 1929 Zionist Congress at Zurich. As a result of that congress the Jewish Agency for Palestine was formed and later created the Haganah, a Zionist underground resistance force operating in British-ruled Palestine. To provide intelligence for the agency the Sherut Yediot, or Information Service, was established.[36]

In 1940, to deal with the increased intelligence demands of World War II, the Sherut Yediot became the Sherut ha'Yediot ha'Artzit (National Information Service), known as the SHAI. Among those benefiting from the SHAI's activities was the British Special Operations Executive. SHAI officers interrogated newly arrived refugees from Czechoslovakia, Poland, Germany, Belgium, France, and the Netherlands. In response to SOE guidance SHAI officers collected a vast array of documentary material—maps, documents, and picture postcards.[37]

From the fall of Nazi Germany until 1948 the SHAI's primary objectives included promoting the establishment of an independent Israeli state; infiltrating British mandate offices in order to inform the Jewish and Zionist leadership of British attitudes and proposed actions; collecting political intelligence that could be used in Zionist propaganda; penetrating Arab and anti-Zionist factions in Palestine and abroad; and providing security for the arms-smuggling and illegal immigration programs of the Haganah.[38]

The SHAI had considerable success against the British mandate target.

---

* But as John Le Carre told one interviewer, Wolf was *not* the model for the Karla of the George Smiley novels.

SHAI agents penetrated customs, police, and the postal services, and offices dealing with transport. As a consequence Arab guerrilla forces had far more of their arms seized than the Haganah did, since SHAI agents were able to tell the Haganah what the police knew about Haganah arms-smuggling activities.[39]

In early 1948 the SHAI obtained a document revealing an arms deal between Czechoslovakia and Syria that would have resulted in Syrian acquisition of 10,000 rifles and 10,000,000 rounds of ammunition—which would have equaled the Israeli arsenal. Israeli leaders ordered the ship transporting the arms sunk. Although the orders were successfully carried out, the ship's cargo was recovered. By August 19 it had been loaded on another ship and was headed to Syria. But the SHAI's intelligence coup was hardly futile—four Israeli agents managed to hijack the ship, not only denying the equipment to Syria but acquiring it for Israel.[40]

The SHAI's successes did not prevent its extinction. The June 30 meeting was not held to make decisions so much as to hear Beeri convey Prime Minister David Ben-Gurion's decision on restructuring the intelligence services. The most momentous decision was that the SHAI was to be dismantled, with its functions being distributed among three new agencies. The General Staff's Sherut ha'Modi'in (Intelligence Service) was to be responsible for battle intelligence, field intelligence and counterintelligence, censorship, and communications intelligence. The existing General Staff Intelligence Department was soon absorbed by the new Intelligence Service.[41]

Beeri also informed the gathering that a secret intelligence service, the misleadingly named Political Department (ha'Mahlaka ha'Medinit), would be established within the Foreign Ministry. The new service would be charged with collecting political, military, and economic intelligence outside Israeli borders. It would be directed by Boris Guriel, who had served in the British army during World War II and had survived capture by the Nazis.[42]

Ben-Gurion also directed that an internal security service be established. The Sherut ha'Bitachon ha'Klali (General Security Service) was also referred to by its acronym, SHABAK, and as Shin Bet, for its initials in Hebrew. Named to head the new service was Isser Harel, who in his role as Tel Aviv station chief directed surveillance operations against right-wing movements such as the Irgun Zvai Le'umi, which refused to accept the authority of Ben-Gurion and the Haganah.[43]

Harel was born in 1912 in Russia. His father was a famous rabbinical scholar; his mother was the youngest daughter of rich vinegar manufacturer. But after the Bolsheviks seized power, they also seized the family business, without compensation. By the time he was sixteen Harel was a committed Zionist. Believing it was necessary to learn to farm, he left school before his final exams to spend a year with other young Zionists on a collective farm in Riga.[44]

In January 1930 he left Russia for life on a kibbutz near Tel Aviv. In the summer of 1944 he took over the Jewish (or Internal) Department and turned it into the SHAI's most efficient department. That experience had made him the logical choice to head the Shin Bet.[45]

But the structure established in late June 1948 would last only a few years. The Israeli Defense Forces (IDF), having found the Political Department unable or unwilling to satisfy its intelligence requirements, established its own offices in Paris and other European capitals in 1950. An apparent compromise was engineered by Reuven Shiloah, the Adviser on Special Duties to the Foreign Minister and Chairman of the Coordinating Committee on the Intelligence Services. The exclusive franchise for foreign intelligence collection operations would remain with the Political Department but IDF intelligence officers would be assigned to the Political Department for the duration of their foreign duty. But that did not prevent the IDF from continuing to run independent agents.[46]

A more drastic change would take the place in 1951. The Political Department's overseas officers were accused of being more interested in using their overseas assignments to pursue extravagant lifestyles than in collecting intelligence. Once again Reuven Shiloah was asked to investigate.[47]

After obtaining Ben-Gurion's agreement to his proposed solution, Shiloah summoned the heads of the various intelligence services. He informed the trio that foreign intelligence should be consolidated in one organization—that Israel needed an organization like the U.S. Central Intelligence Agency, which he had been introduced to during a 1950 visit to Washington. But he could not agree to the IDF suggestion that such an organization be located in the IDF. He also announced that the Political Department was to be abolished and replaced by a new organization reporting to the prime minister.[48]

On March 2, 1951, Prime Minister Ben-Gurion issued a directive establishing the Mossad ha'Merkazi LeTeum (Central Institute for Coordination), subsequently renamed the Mossad Letafkidim Meouychadim (Central Institute for Intelligence and Security).* Directly subordinate to the prime minister's office, the Mossad was assigned no active role in covert operations, only espionage. It could only approve or reject covert operations proposed by military intelligence, which was responsible for selecting the targets, planning the operation, and implementation.[49]

Appointed to head the Mossad was intelligence adviser Shiloah. But in September 1952 Shiloah's tenure as Mossad chief ended after a disastrous operation in Iraq. From several candidates Ben-Gurion chose Shin Bet head Harel to become the new Mossad head.[50]

At the time Harel assumed command of the Mossad it consisted of little more than three small rooms, a staff of about a dozen, and a secre-

---

*In 1963 the Mossad was given its present name, Ha-Mossad le Modiin ule-Tafkidim Meyuhadim (Institute for Intelligence and Special Tasks).

tary to the director—who was on the verge of a nervous breakdown. Harel promptly informed Ben-Gurion that abolishing the Mossad would be better than continuing its present style of operation. Ben-Gurion immediately increased the budget by a factor of ten.[51]

Kang's Legacy

A year after Israel attained its independence Chiang Kai-shek's Nationalist regime was driven from the Chinese mainland by the Chinese Communists. The new Chinese government included a number of intelligence and security units. As with Israel, the initial intelligence organizations of the new government could trace their origins to the days when the rulers governed a movement, not a nation.

By the early 1930s a Political Security Bureau had been established in Jiangxi (Kiangsi). Officially a government office, it was, in reality, Mao Tse-tung's power base in Jiangxi.[52] Another organization had emerged in 1927, when Chiang Kai-shek's Koumintang (KMT) launched a massive and successful assault against the Chinese Communist party (CCP) cadres. That success only whetted the KMT's appetite. In an attempt to further decimate the CCP the KMT established a Investigation Section. To counter the new Nationalist secret service Chou En-lai, as chief of the party's Military Commission, formed a Special Work Committee. While its initial functions were to organize safe meeting places and eliminate Communist turncoats, it soon grew into a full-scale intelligence and security service. In April 1928 it established a special unit, the Intelligence Cell, to infiltrate hostile security services.[53]

But the Special Work Committee could not prevent the arrest and defection of a key CCP official in 1931. That event was followed by arrests and executions of CCP personnel. Chou En-lai, who still headed the military commission, appointed a group of senior cadres to direct the party's intelligence and security activities and correct whatever deficiencies existed. Chou chaired the committee and appointed four additional members, including a cadre who would come to be known as Kang Sheng.[54]

The son of rich landowners, Kang was among the most sophisticated of the Chinese communists, but his origins did not prevent his developing a close relationship with the peasant-born Mao. It was in Shanghai, in 1924, that Kang became a committed communist activist. In the years that followed he was involved in some of the milestones of the CCP's early years—protests against the British and Japanese in 1925, urban revolts in 1926 and 1927, and the KMT's devastating purge of communists in April 1927.[55]

Not long after creating the new intelligence service, Chou En-lai felt an increasing danger of arrest. In August 1931 he headed for the rural Communist camp in the mountains of Jiangxi. Before leaving Chou appointed

Kang Sheng as head of the entire Communist intelligence and security apparatus, a post he held for the next two years.[56]

In 1933 Kang began a four-year stay in Moscow to complete his political education. During that time he had frequent and close contacts with the NKVD. His Moscow sojourn concluded after the outbreak of all-out war between China and Japan in July–August 1937.[57]

In the latter half of 1938, as a result of the Sixth Central Committee Plenum, the CCP's central units were reorganized. The Political Security Bureau was abolished as a distinct organization and its functions, along with those of the Special Work Committee, were assigned to a newly formed Social Affairs Department (SAD). The SAD operated under the direction of the Politburo, with Kang Sheng as its director, and was assigned both internal and external functions: surveillance of Communist party, government, and military organizations as well as espionage operations. Kang was also appointed head of the Intelligence Department of the Military Affairs Commission.[58]

SAD's power increased in 1941 with the beginning of an all-out intelligence campaign directed against the Japanese while maintaining the previous high level of operations directed against the KMT. An August 1, 1941, Central Committee "Decision on Investigation and Research" called for movement away from overreliance on the subjective evaluation of enemy intentions and toward greater emphasis on objective investigation. The decision called for stepping up investigation and research into the history, environment, and events within and outside the country; it mandated that the Central Committee set up a research organization to gather and study information about the international and domestic political, economic, and cultural situation and social relations in "enemy, friendly and our own territories."[59]

The SAD and Intelligence Department were not the only intelligence units; a variety of other party and military units were engaged in intelligence and security activities. A "Meteorological Bureau" performed communications intelligence operations. The CCP's Political Department had two divisions: the Anti-Subversion Division, responsible for eliminating enemy agents, traitors, and undercover elements, and the Division for Work on Enemy and Puppet Armed Forces, which handled prisoners of war and ran agitprop and sabotage operations within the enemy's military.[60]

The Sixth Central Committee Plenum also resulted in the creation of a United Front Work Department within party organizations at all levels. These departments were responsible for penetrating the KMT and the Japanese in order to conduct espionage and subversive operations. A Liaison Bureau was also established, with the ostensible purpose of conducting liaison with the KMT concerning their "common" war against Japan. Its real function was to provide cover for CCP intelligence collection directed at the KMT.[61]

With the communist conquest of the mainland in 1949, the CCP had to establish a full-fledged governmental structure, including intelligence units. By October 1949 an Intelligence Administration had been established under the Government Affairs Council.* That same month the Ministry of Public Security (MPS) was created to handle countersubversion, counterintelligence, surveillance of Chinese people returned from overseas and those who were politically suspect, monitoring of internal travel, protection of economic and military installations, border patrol, and management of "labor reform" camps. It was also assigned the task of intelligence operations within Macao, Hong Kong, and Taiwan.[62]

The Military Affairs Commission's military intelligence department became the Intelligence Department of the People's Liberation Army (PLA) General Staff, while the Meteorological Bureau became the PLA's COMINT service. At the same time, the Social Affairs Department continued as a strictly CCP organization and the most important of the intelligence services. Kang Sheng, however, did not continue as head of the SAD. In fact, he had been removed as head of both the Social Affairs and Military Intelligence departments in 1945, following complaints from senior cadres. Although no longer officially charged with intelligence and security responsibilities, he would exercise significant influence on Chinese intelligence operations in the 1950s and beyond.[63]

Over the next several years the Chinese intelligence community underwent further change. The first Central Committee meeting to examine the intelligence and security system took place in May 1951. Among the results was the continuation of the SAD as the nation's premier foreign and domestic intelligence service.† In addition, two new CCP intelligence organizations were established. A central United Front Work Department was established, charged with maintaining links with Chinese citizens overseas who could be used, when needed, for covert operations. Also created was an International Liaison Department to maintain relations with out-of-power communist and revolutionary groups and to fund, train, and supply arms to some of those groups.[64]

---

* In 1952 the Intelligence Administration would be officially abolished. However, it continued to operate as a secret organization until it was actually disestablished several years later.

† In 1962 the SAD would be divided into two units: the (Central) Investigation Department and the Administrative and Legal Work Department, with the former responsible for intelligence and security work.

15

Secret Wars

World War II had seen a wide variety of special operations conducted by both Allied and Axis powers—including black propaganda, paramilitary operations, and assassinations. Nations would develop their own terminology and euphemisms for such activities. United States officials would talk in terms of "covert action," "special activities," and, in extreme cases, "executive action." In Britain one euphemism was "secret political action." In the Soviet Union there were "active measures" and "wet affairs."

However they might be referred to, such techniques would continue to be employed in the postwar era to achieve foreign policy objectives. Not only the superpowers but a variety of other nations would employ such techniques. Some operations would advance a nation's interest, others would prove to be failures, and still others would backfire in dramatic and embarrassing fashion.

Special Procedures

When the U.S. National Security Council (NSC) convened for the first time on December 19, 1947, the battle for Europe was already under way, and it was feared that Italy and France were both vulnerable to the appeal of their Communist parties. With Secretary of State George Marshall refusing to let the State Department conduct covert activities, the council turned to the CIA. Under the provisions of NSC directive 4/A, the CIA was authorized to undertake a broad range of covert activities to prevent a Communist party victory in the upcoming Italian elections. DCI Admiral Roscoe Hillenkoeter assigned the task to the CIA's Office of Special Operations, which established a Special Procedures Group (SPG) on December 22.[1]*

---

* Hillenkoeter asked CIA general counsel Lawrence Houston if the National Security Act authorized the CIA to engage in such activities. Houston replied that the CIA's fifth function according to the National Security Act, which would often be cited as an authorization for covert operations, was clearly intended only as an authorization for espionage. Hillenkoeter proceeded anyway.

The SPG's activities were part of an overall American effort which included the provision of food, a letter-writing campaign by Italian-Americans, speeches by congressional and business leaders, and the threat from President Truman to withhold aid to any Italian government that included communists. The SPG's covert activities, funded by $10 millions, included the provision of funds to centrist Italian political parties, black propaganda, and disinformation. Forged documents and letters ostensibly originating from the Communist party were circulated. SPG-funded publications focused on the Red Army's brutality during its occupation of Germany, as well as the impact of communist rule in Poland and Czechoslovakia. In the election the Christian Democrats gained an overall majority of forty seats.[2]

The SPG was also successful around the same time in supporting moderate labor groups in France. In the light of such successes, and the continued Cold War, it was not surprising that the NSC authorized the creation of a permanent covert action organization. On June 18, 1948, on the recommendation of State Department policy planning chief George Kennan, NSC 4/A was superseded by NSC 10/2.[3]

The top-secret three-page directive began by noting "the vicious covert activities of the USSR, its satellite countries and Communist groups to discredit and defeat the aims and activities of the United States and other Western powers." It went on to establish, within the CIA, an Office of Special Projects to conduct covert operations—which, according to the directive, included

> propaganda, economic warfare; preventive direct action, including sabotage, anti-sabotage, demolition and evacuation measures; and subversion against hostile states, including assistance to underground resistance movements, guerrillas and refugee liberation groups, and support of indigenous anti-communist elements in threatened countries of the free world.[4]

The Office of Special Projects was soon renamed the Office of Policy Coordination (OPC). While the OPC's operations were directly under the supervision of the DCI, he had little authority in determining its activities. The OPC's activities were the responsiblity of the office's director, who was nominated by the Secretary of State. Policy guidance came from the Secretary of State and Secretary of Defense.[5]*

Moving over from his position as deputy assistant secretary of state for occupied areas to serve as OPC director was Frank Gardiner Wisner. A thirty-nine-year-old Mississippian, Wisner had placed third in his class at the University of Virginia Law School and had practiced with an eminent Wall Street law firm. After joining naval intelligence during the war, he was transferred to the OSS and served in Africa, Turkey, Romania, France, and Germany.[6]

* This peculiar situation would continue until 1952 when the OPC and CIA Office of Special Operations were merged, becoming the CIA Directorate of Plans.

Resistance

With Wisner in charge OPC pursued a variety of covert operations. One of Wisner's favorite programs, black propaganda, would lead to the establishment of Radio Free Europe and Radio Liberty. A more deadly aspect of early OPC operations was the paramilitary operations and support for the resistance groups that had emerged in eastern Europe and the Soviet Union. Those operations had an ulterior motive—in 1949 NSC-50, "Central Intelligence Agency and National Organization for Intelligence," had emphasized the value of establishing relations with anti-Soviet resistance groups as means of gathering intelligence.[7]

Among the areas of OPC involvement were the Baltic states and the Ukraine. OPC was not alone, for Baltic operations would be conducted in conjunction with the Gehlen Organization and Britain's Secret Intelligence Service. The Gehlen Organization recruited, on behalf of the OPC, from the 20,000 Latvian, Lithuanian, and Estonian émigrés who were living in Germany at the time. The Org would screen and evaluate the possible recruits and make recommendations to the OPC concerning suitability.[8]

The British role stemmed from the location of their occupation zone in Germany, which included the Baltic coast. Early on, SIS came up with the idea of infiltrating agents from the sea. In contrast to air-drop operations, which were noisy and likely to attract Soviet attention, boat landings could be done in silence, and thus in secret. The OPC agreed to fund the boat operations, the Gehlen Organization was instructed to form a special boat unit, and the British agreed to direct its activities.[9]

One of the earliest landings took place on September 30, 1951, along the coast of Latvia. But by that time the partisans' war with the Red Army was really over. The last recorded battle in Latvia took place in February 1950. The Estonian partisan forces had been reduced to isolated bands, while only about 5,000 Lithuanian partisans remained. In addition to the hostility of the Red Army, the partisans felt, with justification, that the primary focus of the Americans and British was intelligence, not guerrilla warfare. The Organization provided just a few crates of pistols and submachine guns in response to Estonian requests. The Lithuanian partisan army disbanded in 1952.[10]

Agent infiltration continued until 1956 and exacted a heavy toll. Civilian casualties in Lithuania, Estonia, and Latvia have been estimated at 75,000. Lithuanian partisans claimed to have killed 80,000 Soviet soldiers and between 4,000 and 12,000 Communist officials and collaborators (the Soviets admitted to losses of only 20,000).[11]

The situation in the Ukraine was similar to that in the Baltic. On September 5, 1949, two OPC agents parachuted into the Ukraine, after a flight from Germany across central Europe. Two days earlier the commander of the insurgent Ukrainian forces, which had been estimated as between 50,000 and 200,000 in 1947, had ordered the deactivation of the army and its conversion into an underground resistance group. Those forces, operating out of forests and mountains, had raided military and militia posts and distributed anti-Soviet propaganda.[12]

Once again the overall effort would involve the OPC (and the CIA Directorate of Plans after 1952), the SIS, and the Gehlen Organization, although the OPC and SIS had different preferences in Ukrainian resistance organizations. Both OPC and Gehlen's Org screened and trained up to 5,000 émigrés for the program. The British took the lead in infiltration, although the OPC and CIA were also involved. British infiltration flights went through Cyprus; CIA flights passed through Greece and western Germany.[13]

In 1951, the SIS dropped three groups of agents, six agents to a group, into the Ukraine, the foothills of the Carpathians, and southern Poland. All eighteen were never heard from again. A CIA four-man team infiltrated along the Baltic coast but was not productive. Three missions involving five agents dispatched to the Ukraine and Moldavia also failed.[14]

The failure was not surprising. The initial postwar bureaucratic confusion in the Soviet Union caused by the war was largely eliminated by the early 1950s. The population was closely monitored and informers of the secret police were numerous. Once again, by the time the agent groups began to arrive the resistance forces had been mortally wounded. Remnants of the resistance groups held out until 1953, when regiment-sized security troops carried out a final battle employing air and artillery support.[15]

Also supporting resistance groups in eastern Europe and the Soviet Union was the French SDECE. From 1949 to 1954, almost 100 operatives were parachuted into into Czechoslovakia, Yugoslavia, Romania, Byelorussia, and Lithuania. A special SDECE unit, Matériels d'Informations Normalisees pur les Opérations Spéciales (MINOS) was created to carry out the infiltrations.[16]

MINOS recruited and trained suitable immigrants from the Eastern bloc, teaching them close combat, sabotage techniques, and parachuting. Little more is known about the unit, but it was apparently no more successful than the OPC-SIS operations.[17]

WIN

The largest paramilitary effort in the Soviet bloc, and the most disastrous, had the Polish regime as its target. Poland lay directly across the Red Army's line of advance for Soviet troops moving into western Europe, and it was there that the best chance for stopping such an advance lay. Just as one reason for dealing with resistance groups elsewhere in the Soviet bloc was to have a capability to attack the Soviets behind the lines in case of war, so it was in Poland.

In the early 1950s, a golden opportunity appeared to arrive. Western intelligence services had believed that in 1947 the Soviets had succeeded in wiping out Polish resistance groups operating in Poland, including the Freedom and Independence Movement (WIN). But a Pole arrived in London and contacted General Wladyslaw Anders. WIN, he told the exiled general, still existed. Funds and equipment from the West might revive it. Anders passed the message on to the SIS, and soon the OPC-CIA and SIS were heavily involved in trying to establish WIN as part of a resistance network that could harass the Red Army in time of war.[18]

Although Anders refused to provide details as to who made up WIN, both the OPC and the SIS proceeded to airdrop money, arms, ammunition, and radios to WIN groups throughout Poland. Contact between WIN Inside (in Poland) and WIN Outside (in London) was maintained by letters from those in Poland, occasional meetings, and a courier. The reports Wisner, SIS, and WIN Outside received in 1951 claimed that as a result of their support, WIN was well on its way to becoming a force that would be able to impede any Soviet advance into western Europe. By 1952 WIN was asking for greater support, even requesting an American general to help organize the group. It claimed 500 active and 20,000 partially active members, as well as 100,000 sympathizers who would be prepared to fight in the event of war.[19]

What Wisner, SIS, and the London WIN group did not realize was that WIN Inside was nothing more than a sequel to the TRUST operation. By mid-1947 the Polish Security Forces (UB) had thoroughly penetrated WIN, and even turned some of its leaders. The UB was able to monitor WIN American personnel, plans, and operations. As a former CIA operations officer noted, "Every agent, dollar, and radio dispatched into Poland ended up in UB hands." Finally, the charade was ended on December 27, 1951, when Polish radio broadcast full details of the operation, providing the Soviets with a major propaganda victory.[20]

AJAX

On August 24, 1953, the Shah of Iran offered a toast to CIA officer Kermit "Kim" Roosevelt. Roosevelt, a grandson of Theodore Roosevelt and a former OSS officer, was the chief of the CIA Plans Directorate Near East and Africa Division. The shah told Roosevelt: "I owe my throne to God, my people, my army—and you."[21]

Of the four individuals or groups named by the shah, Roosevelt's role was one of the more important. The events culminating in the shah's toast began with the 1951 nationalization of the Anglo-Iranian Oil Company (AIOC) by the Iranian Majlis (parliament), under the direction of Prime Minister Mohammad Mossadegh.

With its property in Iranian hands the AIOC sought relief from the British government, who turned to the SIS. The SIS, in turn, approached the CIA, first in 1951 and again in November 1952. The AIOC's loss of property did not concern the U.S. government or the CIA. President Truman signed an NSC directive on June 27, 1951, stating that U.S. policy should make "clear both our recognition of the rights of sovereign states to control their natural resources and the importance we attach to international contractual relationships." The United States preferred a negotiated solution to Britain's use of force.[22]

At the same time, the NSC document noted that "the loss of Iran to the free world is a distinct possibility through an internal communist uprising, possibly growing out of the present indigenous fanaticism or through communist capture of the nationalist movement." As Roosevelt wrote in his memoirs, "The British motivation was simply to recover the AIOC oil concession. We were not concerned with that but with the obvious threat of Russian takeover."[23]

On June 25, 1953, Roosevelt arrived for a meeting in the office of Secretary of State John Foster Dulles. He carried a twenty-two-page paper he had drafted, a revision of a more detailed SIS paper, which outlined objectives of a covert action operation directed against Mossadegh. Designated Operation AJAX, the plan was approved and Roosevelt, with British agreement, was placed in charge.[24]

Roosevelt traveled to Iran in late July, entered with false identification papers, and assured the shah that Eisenhower and Churchill would be behind him if he tried to dismiss Mossadegh. Although Roosevelt had only four or five CIA agents at his disposal, he was able to rely on a more extensive network of SIS assets as well as the SIS communications link through Cyprus to communicate with Washington.[25]

The key to AJAX's success would be whether Roosevelt succeeded in getting the 200,000-man Iranian army to back the shah against Mossadegh. Mossadegh had already assumed the position of defense minister, and, in spring 1953, tried to replace the shah as commander-in-chief.[26]

The ensuing struggle for control of the army and the 50,000-man police force aided Roosevelt. The Majlis refused to approve Mossadegh's request for expanded powers, and he retaliated by dissolving the Majlis on July 19. On August 8 Mossadegh opened trade talks with the Soviet Union, which resulted in AJAX receiving final approval from Eisenhower. In addition, it was clear that Mossadegh was rigging the referendum that was in progess on his dissolution of the Majlis. Mossadegh's actions, along with a new conversation with Roosevelt, also led the shah to act. He departed, with the Queen, for the town of Ramsar on the Caspian Sea, but he sent a subordinate with decrees firing Mossadegh and appointing General Fazollah Zahedi in his place.[27]

However, the subordinate was arrested while attempting to present the dismissal decree to Mossadegh. Following a Teheran Radio broadcast on August 16 announcing an attempted coup by foreign elements, nationalist supporters of Mossadegh, as well as Tudeh (Communist) party members, took to the streets. They were counteracted by up to 6,000 pro-shah rioters armed with clubs, knives, and an occasional pistol. Many of the rioters were funded by the $100,000 in CIA money given two Iranian SIS agents; others were sent into the streets by the Ayatollah Kashani under urging from the SIS agents. Full-scale rioting followed on August 18 and 19. On the 19th pro-shah army tank units attacked Mossadegh's residence. With his allies in control the shah returned from Italy, where he had fled after the rioting began, and was paraded in triumph through the streets of Teheran. Meanwhile, Mossadegh, who had originally escaped, surrendered on August 21.[28]

The Lavon Affair

About a year after Mossadegh's ouster, a covert operation targeted on the United States and Britain was about to be launched. In this instance, the architect was not the Soviet enemy, but Israel. The operation, code-named SUSANNAH, had its origins in 1951 when the head of military intelligence, Benjamin Gibli, decided that Israel should create a fifth column inside Egypt to destroy civil and military installations in time of war. To lay the groundwork for such a network he sent Shlomoh Hillel to Egypt, with a mission to uncover potential agents among the most talented young Jews of Egypt.[29]

Joining Hillel in the summer of 1951 was Avraham Dar, an officer in Unit 131, the special operations unit of military intelligence. The papers Dar carried with him indicated he was John Darling, a Gibraltar-born sales representative of a British electronics company. Dar was able to recruit two prominent Jews—Moshe Marzouk of Cairo and Shmuel Azar of Alexandria—to head networks in their areas.[30]

In August 1951 Dar, who had replaced Hillel as the chief agent of Israeli military intelligence in Egypt, departed. He left behind the Cairo and Alexandria cells, each with an Israeli officer in command and with a radio transmitter to contact Tel Aviv.[31]

In 1954 Israeli leaders had become alarmed over the course of events in Egypt. King Farouk had been overthrown by Gamal Abdel Nasser, who crystallized nationalist sentiment. One result of that sentiment was the demand that Britain and France turn over their ownership and control of the Suez Canal. Israel feared that if Nasser's world stature continued to rise, Britain and France would be forced to comply. And in 1954 it appeared that Prime Minister Winston Churchill was indeed preparing to turn the canal over to Nasser.[32]

The Suez Canal in Egyptian hands was unacceptable to the Israeli leaders. One possible course of action was to discredit Nasser and the Egyptian nation, making it seem to be unalterably hostile to the West. In 1954 Avri El-Ad was ordered to take command of the Egyptian network. El-Ad was an Austrian Jew who had, upon arriving in Palestine, hebraized his name to El-Ad. His legend was, of course, quite different. To Egyptians he was Paul Frank, a wealthy West German businessman and former SS officer. To give this cover the maximum chance of success El-Ad had not only traveled to Germany to procure an authentic West German passport, but he had submitted to excruciatingly painful surgery to reverse his circumcision so that if captured he could not immediately be identified as a Jew.[33]

On July 2, 1954, El-Ad and his agents in Egypt began operations. The first target was the Alexandria post office in the El-Ramel district. It was hoped that the bombing of a series of mailboxes would be blamed on the extermist Moslem Brotherhood. Two of Shmuel Azar's subordinates, Victor Levy and Philip Nathanson, walked into the facility and slid a home-made bomb down a narrow mail chute. However, when the bomb exploded a few minutes later, it did little damage. In addition, the Nasser regime's censors prevented any press reporting on the incident.[34]

The next strike was more successful. On July 10 the network received coded instructions via Israeli state radio. Four days later incendiary devices were planted in the U.S. Information Service libraries in Cairo and Alexandria. More important than the extent of the damage that resulted were the reports of the Middle East News Agency on the apparent new wave of terrorism that had gripped Egypt.[35]

The next attacks were planned for July 23, Revolution Day. The Cairo team was to plant explosive devices in the Rivoli Theater and in the check-in room at the main railway station. Their homemade devices were duds, and little, if any, damage resulted. The Alexandria team was not so lucky. While Levy and Nathanson waited in line at their next target, Alexandria's Rio Cinema, the explosive device in Nathanson's pocket ignited in a burst of smoke and flame. When a policeman who came to his aid discovered the remains of an explosive device in his pocket Nathanson was placed under arrest, as was Levy.[36]

Within days the Egyptian security service had extracted enough information to arrest Marzouk, Azar, and all their subordinates. Only El-Ad managed to escape, fleeing to Europe.* Naturally, the prime minister and other high-level officials denied authorizing the operation. Defense Minister Pinchas Lavon was forced to resign, although Lavon denied having given his approval. The issue of who was the highest ranking official to give the order would reemerge over the years—along with accusations of deceit and forgery.[37]

Front Groups

From June 22 to June 29, 1955, the World Assembly for Peace took place in Helsinki. According to its sponsors, 1,841 persons from 68 countries attended. The assembly ended with a "Helsinki Appeal" that demanded a

---

*El-Ad's ability to escape placed him under a cloud of suspicion. That cloud darkened when he was detected meeting with Egyptian military intelligence officers in Vienna. In Bonn, Shin Bet agents saw him pass sensitive intelligence documents to an officer from the Egyptian military attaché office. In 1959, following one of the most secretive trials in Israeli history, El-Ad was convicted on security violations. He died at age sixty-seven in July 1993 in self-imposed exile in Los Angeles.

united front of peace movements, German unification outside NATO, and an end to a "policy of strength, military blocs and the arms race."[38]

The World Assembly was the creation of the World Peace Council (WPC), one of many front groups established and directed by the KGB and the International Department of the U.S.S.R. Communist party's (CPSU) Central Committee. The WPC had been founded in 1949 as the World Committee of Partisans for Peace. In 1950, the same year it was expelled from France for "fifth column activities," it adopted the name World Peace Council and moved to Prague, where it operated until 1954. In 1957 it relocated to Vienna, where it would remain until its 1968 move to Helsinki.[39]

By 1955 the WPC was one of several Soviet front groups. The World Federation of Trade Unions, headquartered in Austria, had been formed jointly by the American Congress of Industrial Organizations, the British Trade Union Congress, and the Soviet All-Union Central Council of Trade Unions. But by 1949 all noncommunist Western trade unions had left due to the pro-Soviet policies of the federation. The federation sought to consolidate trade unions throughout the world under Soviet control, to support strikes in noncommunist countries, and to serve as a major Soviet propaganda outlet.[40]

Other front groups in existence by 1955 were the Women's International Democratic Federation (WIDF), International Organization of Journalists (IOJ), International Association of Democratic Lawyers (IADL), Christian Peace Conference (CPC), International Federation of Resistance Fighters (FIR), World Federation of Scientific Workers (WFSW), World Federation of Democratic Youth (WFDY), World Congress of Doctors (WCD), and the International Radio and TV Organization (OIRT).[41]

Representatives from many of these groups attended a January WPC meeting in Vienna, which concluded with a "Vienna Appeal" designed to spread ban-the-bomb pledges and the collection of still more signatures. Subsequent to the World Assembly of Peace, the World Federation of Democratic Youth held its Fifth International Festival of Youth and Students in Warsaw. During 1955 other front groups focused on prohibitions of atomic weapons, disarmament, and opposition to German rearmament. The World Congress of Doctors held an International Medical Conference on Radioactivity, in Japan. It concluded, not surprisingly, that "explosions of atomic and hydrogen bombs should not be allowed to be repeated and that the use of atomic energy should be limited to peaceful and constructive purposes."[42]

Wet Affairs

It is not surprising that individuals who had no problem in terrorizing an entire population and killing tens of thousands would consider assassination an expedient means of eliminating individuals considered troublesome. The first Soviet assassination organization was the NKVD's Directorate of Special Tasks, established in December 1936. Over the next eighteen years it changed organizational forms and names on several occasions. With the creation of the KGB in 1954, the "wet affairs" organization was redesignated as the Thirteenth Department of the First Chief Directorate. Under Nikita Khrushchev's rule the collective leadership would examine proposals for significant Department 13 operations.[43]

Just as émigré organizations and leaders had been of great concern to the Cheka, émigré organizations and leaders were of concern to the MGB and KGB in the 1950s. The MGB attempted to assassinate the leader of the People's Labor League (NTS), Georgiy S. Okolovich, in February 1954. The NTS was considered particularly troublesome because of its efforts to recruit Soviet soldiers stationed in East Germany. The attempt failed when the MGB officer who was responsible for directing the assassination, Captain Nikolay Khokhlov, defected.[44]*

Khokhlov's defection gave Western intelligence services a look at the exotic assassination devices that MGB technicians had developed. Of the three weapons he brought with him, two were built into cigarette cases, while the other superficially resembled an ordinary small automatic pistol. One of the unusual features of all the devices was that they were virtually noiseless.[45]

The pistol, which was about four inches long and four inches tall, weighed about twenty-three ounces when loaded. Three different types of bullets—lead, steel, and poisoned—were included in each clip. The lead bullet was designed to disable the target, after which the steel bullet could be used to kill. The poisoned bullet was designed to be used at very close range.[46]

Less obvious instruments of death were the two king-size leather cigarette cases. The cases' hinged top would fall back, revealing what appeared to be the tips of cigarettes, which served to hide the firing mechanism underneath. One of the weapons contained two .32-caliber barrels, while the other had four. The weapons could be fired by pressure on bars opposite each barrel, allowing any combination of barrels to be fired.[47]

Different weapons were used to kill Lev Rebet and Stefan Bandera. On October 10, 1957, Rebet, a Ukrainian nationalist émigré, was climbing the circular staircase to his office, while a KGB officer was walking down the stairs. The two met about halfway between two floors. The KGB officer fired a spray of prussic acid, from a seven-inch-long noiseless "pistol," into Rebet's face. The inhaled gas had the same effect as sniffing glue—the severe contraction of blood vessels caused Rebet's heart to simply stop. He lurched silently forward and fell on the staircase. Initially it was believed that he died from a heart attack.[48]

---

*In 1957 the Soviets tried to assassinate Khokhlov, who was poisoned with radioactive thallium, which caused hideous brown stripes, dark splotches, and black-and-blue swellings on his face and body. In addition, a sticky secretion oozed from his eyelids and blood seeped through his pores. Only a major effort by U.S. army doctors saved his life.

In April 1959 Rebet's assassin, Bogdan Stashinsky, was called to Moscow and assigned the task of eliminating Stefan Bandera, director of the Organization of Ukrainian Nationalist Revolutionaries. In October 1959 Stashinsky, seeing Bandera pull into his driveway, let himself into Bandera's apartment building and waited. As Bandera tried to remove the key from the front door's lock with his left hand, while holding several packages in his right, Stashinsky moved toward the front door and fired the poison gun into Bandera's face. Bandera lurched back and to the side. Although there was some suspicion of potassium cyanide poisoning, there was insufficent evidence to prove it.[49]

In early 1959 Stashinsky had a personal audience with KGB chairman Aleksandr Shelepin. Shelepin read a Presidium decree of November 6, 1959, awarding Stashinsky the Order of the Red Banner for executing an "important government commission."[50]

But the award did not stop Stashinsky from regretting his actions. At the urging of his wife he turned himself in to American authorities in West Berlin. Only then did they know why and how Rebet and Bandera died. Stashinsky's trial in October 1962 became a worldwide sensation and propaganda disaster for the Soviet Union.[51]

The Soviets were by no means alone in resorting to assassination to eliminate troublesome enemies. One day in November 1958 in West Germany, Ait Ahcene, a representative of the Algerian Front de Libération National (FLN), who were fighting to expel France, headed for the autobahn that would take him to Bonn. After he had driven about two miles a Mercedes pulled in front of his car, forcing Ahcene to slow down. A second Mercedes drew up beside Ahcene, and a machine gun was fired at the Peugot, sending it out of control. Ahcene's car swerved badly, turned over, and came to rest in a ditch alongside the road. A few months later he died in a Tunisian hospital.[52]

Ahcene was one of several victims of a French assassination campaign, directed by the SDECE and the Directorate for Territorial Surveillance (DST). To obscure the French government's role in the operation, a fictional "Red Hand" organization was created to claim credit for the assassinations. Actually running the Red Hand organization was a brain trust drawn from the DST and three SDECE branches—Research, Service 7, and the Action Service. After an officer was selected and given a target, he would formulate a plan and present it to the brain trust. If the brain trust approved, they would pass it on the president of the Parliament, who would ratify it.[53]

In 1959 George Puchert, an arms dealer who had been doing business with the Algerian nationalists, became another Red Hand victim. An explosive device, placed under the hood of his car, blew up the entire front of his vehicle a few seconds after he began driving. Puchert was killed instantly. Inside the car, investigators discovered the imprint of a red hand.[54]

In addition to arms traffickers and FLN representatives, prominent supporters of the rebels were also eliminated. George Laperche, a leftist intellectual, who had made several contacts with the nationalists, was one of those. One day a package apparently containing books arrived in the mail. When Laperche opened the package an enormous explosion followed. He died several hours later.[55]

16

Superpower Espionage

On March 4, 1953, Joseph Stalin's life and reign as Soviet dictator came to an end. But Stalin's death did not end the Cold War. Throughout the 1950s the superpowers continued to bolster their military forces and engage in a multitude of diplomatic offensives to support their positions.

Less visibly, the superpowers continued their espionage war. The United States would not only continue its peripheral reconnaissance operations, but it would begin to establish a network of SIGINT stations around the Soviet Union. The United States would also explore various methods for conducting reconnaissance over Soviet territory. The Soviets, with no close allies located near the United States, lacked the options of setting up ground stations or staging reconnaissance flights from bases near the United States. Thus, at least with respect to events in the United States, the Soviet Union had to depend heavily on human sources.

Attachés, Travelers, and Agents

The United States also continued its human intelligence efforts. Attachés continued to monitor visually, and with whatever sensor equipment they could surreptitiously bring along, air shows and parades. They also took photographs during authorized visits to Soviet airfields. On July 30, 1953, the air attaché, along with the Canadian and British air attachés, observed an aircraft similar to the U.S. B-47 at Ramenskoye, just outside Moscow. The photographs taken by the U.S. attaché showed the aircraft to be one and a half times larger than the main Soviet bomber, the TU-4, with a tail section and fuselage very similar to those of the B-47.[1]

Attachés were able, on occcasion, to gather intelligence about facilities to which they had not been invited. On March 3, 1953, Major George Van Laethan drove along the Kiev highway on the way to Vnukovo Airport, equipped with a vest-pocket radar detector to intercept radar emanations.

The signals were then recorded on a wire recorder. Just thirteen miles south of the highway, Major Van Laethan's detector picked up the signals from a new temporary AAA (antiaircraft artillery) position that was in the process of being installed.[2]

Beginning in 1953, the United States attempted to make better use of official travel in the Soviet Union. In January the U.S. Intelligence Advisory Committee approved the Travel Folder Program for the Soviet Bloc: "a coordinated U.S.–U.K. program for improving the collection of intelligence through official travel within the Soviet bloc countries." Travel folders were prepared that specified the need for different types of intelligence—industrial, military, and scientific facilities—and were keyed to travel routes between major Soviet cities. The CIA would collate the requirements from various Washington agencies and transmit them to Moscow, where the "Moscow coordinator" (the U.S. Naval Attaché) would make the travel folders available to other attachés and embassy staff members.[3]

A second program, run by the CIA and code-named REDSKIN, involved nonofficial travelers from the United States as well as European and third-world nations. The travelers included tourists, business executives, journalists, scientists, academics, athletes, chess players, and church leaders recruited to gather information during their trips through the Soviet Union. The information they were asked to gather was obtainable without breaking the law; they were not required to penetrate secret installations or recruit Soviet citizens. Rather, the REDSKIN program sought to take advantage of ordinary travel itineraries to gather intelligence about facilities in main metropolitan areas and along the main transportation routes.[4]

A major effort was involved in providing the tasking for the travelers. Technical requirements concerning atomic energy, aircraft production, and missile installations had to be translated into simple requirements for visual information from trains, planes, or roads that could be performed by an individual with no particular technical background. A traveler might be asked to identify the color of the smoke being emitted by a specific factory chimney or the color of a sand pile outside a specific plant.[5]

The information provided by the REDSKIN program helped close many information gaps concerning the Soviet Union. At the beginning of the program "analysts in Washington were ignorant across the whole range of Soviet industrial production—facilities, output, technology, bottlenecks." The travelers who purchased Soviet typewriters, who noted the serial numbers of the Soviet-made boxcars and civilian airplanes, and who photographed and examined products of Soviet technology on display at trade fairs allowed analysts to deduce annual production figures, the availability of machine tools, and the alloys employed in production.[6]

In addition to employing attachés and travelers, the CIA did achieve a full-fledged penetration of the Soviet military establishment in the person of Lieutenant Colonel Peter Popov. In 1953, in Vienna, Popov dropped a note into an American diplomat's car:

> I am a Russian officer attachéd to the Soviet Group of Forces Headquarters in Baden bei Wien. If you are interested in buying a copy of the new table of organization for a Soviet armored division, meet me on the corner of Dorotheergasse and Stallaburgasse at 8:30 P.M., November 12. If you are not there I will return at the same time on November 13. The price is 3,000 Austrian schillings.

After an initial meeting Popov, now code-named ATTIC, was introduced to his case officer, George Kisvalter. Kisvalter, who had joined the CIA's Soviet Russia Division in 1952, had lived in St. Petersburg before the revolution and spoke fluent Russian, French, German, and Italian.[7]

Popov identified himself as a graduate of the Military Diplomatic Academy assigned to the GRU's intelligence cell in Vienna, and as a case officer working against Yugoslavian targets. His information was not restricted to GRU personnel and operations but also included valuable intelligence on Soviet military doctrine and weapons, such as the 1951 Soviet army field regulations, which Popov and Kisvalter spent an entire meeting photocopying.[8]

In July 1954 Popov returned to the Soviet Union for home leave. There he acquired information concerning Soviet nuclear submarines and guided missiles, which he provided to Kisvalter upon his return to Vienna. In 1955, without warning, Popov was transferred to the illegals support section of the GRU Operational Group in East Berlin. In that capacity he processed illegal agents passing through East Berlin on their way to their foreign assignments. Popov continued to report in person to Kisvalter, crossing into the Western sector from the East. His reports extended beyond information of interest to counterintelligence authorities and encompassed a wide range of military information—including sensitive details concerning Soviet missiles and their guidance systems. He also picked up information from the reserve officers' courses he attended on a regular basis as well as from conversations with high-ranking officers stationed with the Group of Soviet Forces Germany.[9]

Ground Stations

The early years of Popov's relationship with the CIA was also a time when the CIA and the Air Force were involved in a variety of technical collection projects. Among the major developments of the 1950s was the creation of a series of ground stations on the Soviet periphery that intercepted Soviet communications and radar signals.

One of the earliest U.S. sites in Europe was established in May 1952 at Kirknewton, Scotland, a small farm village approximately thirteen miles southwest of Edinburgh. Over the next year different antenna systems were tried and their performance evaluated. By June 1953 the interim antenna field consisted of five antennas, all of which would eventually be dismantled and replaced by eleven rhombic antennas.[10]

By the end of 1953 the United States Air Force Security Service's (US-AFSS) 37th Radio Squadron Mobile, otherwise known as USA-55, consisted of 17 officers and 463 airmen.* Initially USA-55 focused solely on intercepting voice and Morse messages. Its targets included military and commercial naval traffic along the Kola Peninsula, near Murmansk. A higher priority was the interception of communications concerning the construction of new Soviet radar systems and Soviet air movements.[11]

Over the next several years USA-55 broadened its range of interception operations. By 1955 it was monitoring the new Soviet radars that were coming on line to replace those the Soviets had obtained from the United States and Britain under Lend-Lease. It was also conducting fax intercept operations, intercepting pictures and information transmitted on Soviet domestic news lines to outlying areas. In addition, Kirknewton was heavily involved in the interception of multiplex radioteletype signals; to facilitate this, an all-Cyrillic-character teletype machine was employed.[12]

Another early SIGINT station was established in Britain at Chicksands Priory, the site of World War II intercept operations, in 1952. The USAFSS 10th Radio Squadron Mobile was installed there, but this time the target was the Soviet air force—specifically, the voice communications of Soviet pilots with each other and with ground controllers.[13]

One U.S. ally whose territory offered an almost ideal location for monitoring the Soviet Union was Turkey. On October 2, 1951, the U.S. Air Forces Europe (USAFE) first proposed the establishment of signals intelligence stations in Turkey. Ten days later, air force headquarters in Washington gave USAFE permission to further examine the possibility. Fourteen months later, on January 13, 1953, a Department of Defense Site Survey Team headed by Colonel Arthur C. Cox of the USAFSS arrived in Ankara "to locate a site conducive to the creation of Radio Squadron Mobile in Turkey."[14]

By the mid-1950s the USAFE effort, code-named Project PENN, had resulted in the establishment of USAFSS sites at Karamursel, on the southeast shore of the Sea of Marmara, Sinop, and Samsun, on the Black Sea coast. Information from Karamursel could provide the first data on new Soviet naval systems and tactics, since the Black Sea was the Soviet training ground where new equipment and operational doctrine were tested. In addition to monitoring naval activity, Karamursel also monitored test launches associated with the early Soviet missile program.[15]

---

* Over the years the size of the Kirknewton contingent decreased to 300 and its mission shifted. Its major targets became commercial non–radio links between major European cities. The station was also partly responsible for the security of the Washington–Moscow "hot line" as the cable passed through Kirknewton en route to Moscow. On August 1, 1966, USA-55 was closed.

Sinop (or, more accurately, Diogenes Station) also began operating in the mid-1950s. Sinop is a fishing port and farm center with a population of just over 18,000 people. The station was established two miles west of the town and is a 300-acre facility on a bleak 700-foot hill at the end of the peninsula. The base monitored high- and very-high-frequency transmissions of Soviet air and naval activity in the Black Sea area and Soviet missile testing activities.[16]

By mid-1955 long-range radar had begun operating at Samsun, almost at the same time that Soviet ICBM testing commenced at Kapustin Yar. With its initial range of 1,000 miles, the AN/FPS-17 radar could detect and track the intermediate-range missiles fired to the southeast toward the Afghan border and intercontinental-range missiles fired eastward to the Pacific Ocean in the area around Vladivostok in Siberia. The data provided by the radar about the Soviet IRBM program was fairly complete and included the missiles' speed, altitude, track, and approximate range. The collection operation also allowed the United States to detect the shift from the irregular pattern of experimental test firings to the regular five-month pattern, which indicated a switch to production.[17]

Detection of tests of the longer range multistage ICBM along the 70-degree track toward the Pacific began in late 1956. A variety of shots were recorded, including stage-separation tests, maximum altitude attempts, and finally long-range firings impacting about 1,000 miles from the launch site. Tests that began in the summer of 1957 extended beyond the 1,000-mile range of the AN/FPS-17 and included eight tests during June, July, and August along the Siberian track. As a result, the radar was modified to increase its range to 3,000 miles at extreme altitudes.[18]

Patrolling the Periphery

While U.S. attachés and travelers explored whatever parts of the Soviet Union they could, and as ground stations in friendly territory listened, a variety of aircraft continued conducting photographic and electronic reconnaissance missions while flying near or, on occasion, over Soviet borders.

In 1951, following reports of an extensive underground installation or missile-launching site on the southern tip of Karafuto—an island that had been Japanese territory but was controlled by the Soviet Union as a result of World War II—the Far Eastern Air Forces (FEAF) conducted a peripheral mission to photograph the area. That and further missions failed to support the reports but did indicate a 40 percent increase in aircraft between January and April 1951.[19]

When the aerial photographic reconnaissance program was in its earliest stages, the idea of overflying Soviet territory was rejected because the risks were considered to be too great. By 1951, however, overflights of portions of Soviet-controlled islands had begun. On October 9, 1951, an RB-45 took off from Yokota Air Base at 10:30 A.M. Designated Project 51, the aircraft's mission was to conduct reconnaissance over the southern end of Sakhalin Island. At an altitude of 18,000 feet, employing both regular and radar cameras, all the targets were photographed. Neither flak nor Soviet fighters were encountered, and the aircraft returned to Yokota by the preplanned route and landed at 2:40 P.M.[20]

By mid-1954 the Air Force had apparently conducted at least two over-flights of the Murmansk-Kola inlet, with radar scope photography having been obtained on the initial mission and standard visual photography on the second. In addition, there were apparently at least four flights over Siberia, including coverage of Wrangel Island and Vol.[21]

At the same time as the United States was continuing peripheral and overhead photographic reconnaissance flights, it was also continuing electronic reconnaissance (ferret) missions. Between May and July 1950 several bases for ferret planes were established in Great Britain. The 72nd Strategic Reconnaissance Squadron, with its RB-50s, arrived at Burtoon-wood after initially having been set up in Sculthorpe, Norfolk. A detachment of the 91st Strategic Reconnaissance Squadron, with RB-45 Tornados, arrived at Manston Air Base in Kent, while an RB-29 squadron was temporarily stationed at Lakenheath. In addition, Brize Norton served as a base for RB-36 reconnaissance bombers on detachment from the United States.[22]

Among the planes penetrating into Soviet territory were those flying from Brize Norton. Such flights were scheduled when it was believed that there had been a significant change in the Soviet air order of battle. When a penetration was planned the Kirknewton ground station would be informed in advance to ensure that the full complement of personnel and equipment were on duty at the appropriate times. Such penetrations, in addition to collecting intelligence on radar systems, allowed the United States to determine if new Soviet aircraft weapons were used and how effective they might be. In part this was accomplished by Kirknewton's eavesdropping on the chatter between Soviet pilots trying to intercept the ferret plane.[23]

One of the major products of the European missions conducted under the direction of the U.S. Air Forces Europe was the the frequent publication of the *USAFE Radar Order of Battle: European Soviet and Satellite Areas*. The document would provide a sketch of each type of radar system and information on its function, the type of installation, frequencies, performance, and accuracy as well as the distribution of radars in the western Soviet Union.

Flying uninvited into or even near Soviet territory was a risky business. More than 100 U.S. airmen flew what would turn out to be one-way reconnaissance missions. Twelve of those may have been taken prisoner after their planes were shot down, according to Russian President Boris Yeltsin.[24] On October 7, 1952, an RB-29 took off from Hokkaido Island in the vicinity of Nemura, just south of the Soviet-controlled Kurile Islands, and disappeared after tracking indicated that the craft "merged" with two

Soviet fighters. The aircraft and crew of eight were lost. Japanese eyewitnesses indicated that the RB-29 crashed on the Soviet side of the international demarcation line. According to the Soviet account two Soviet planes approached the B-29 and instructed it to follow them to a Soviet airstrip. When the U.S. plane opened fire the Soviet aircraft shot it down. The remains of the plane's navigator, Captain John Dunham, were recovered in 1994.[25]

On July 29, 1953, an RB-50 was attacked by Soviet MiGs. This time the attack took place over the Sea of Japan, about 70 nautical miles southeast of Vladivostok, and was successful. In keeping with the cover story for such flights, a Department of State press release stated that the plane was "on a routine navigational training mission over the Sea of Japan [when it] was attacked by Soviet MiG-15 aircraft." The press release went on to report that at the time of attack the aircraft was flying at 20,000 feet and was "well over international waters approximately 40 statute miles southeast of the nearest Soviet territory at Cape Povortny."[26]

Only one crewman, copilot Captain John E. Roche, was rescued, approximately eleven hours after he was sighted in the water by a rescue plane. In that interval the badly injured pilot, Stanley Keith O'Kelley, slipped beneath the surface. As many as seven crewmen may have survived, only to be captured by the Soviets and never returned to the United States. According to the State Department press release an American rescue plane "dropped a lifeboat to a group of four survivors . . . at 5:50 P.M. July 29. These four survivors were seen making their way to the lifeboat. A second group of three survivors was sighted approximately one half mile east of the spot where the lifeboat was dropped." According to a former Soviet intelligence officer, Gavril Korotkov, six of the crew wound up in the hands of Soviet counter-intelligence. Since none would work for their captors they were sent to Gadhala prison in Siberia.[27]

In the years 1952–55 there were at least seven incidents, with over thirty crewmen dead or missing as a result. On June 29, 1958, after a three-year hiatus that followed an attack on a Navy reconnaissance plane on June 22, 1955, Soviet fighters attacked a C-118 transport plane that had gone off course, into the southern Soviet Union. The plane crash landed, the crew destroyed the plane on the ground, and after nine days of interrogation the crew was returned. Over the next two years there would be at least six incidents involving Air Force or Navy reconnaissance planes, resulting in at least six deaths and eleven disappearances.[28]

The Tunnel

On April 21, 1956, Soviet action terminated Operation GOLD—eleven months and eleven days after it began. Planning for the project began in 1953. According to the CIA's official history of the operation, "exploratory discussions were held in Washington to plan the mounting of an attack on Soviet landlines in East Germany with special emphasis to be placed on the Berlin area." Included in the discussions were representatives from the British SIS, who along with CIA had tapped into Soviet land line communications in Vienna in 1951.[29]

After months of study the CIA-SIS team drew up a plan for a tunnel approximately 500 yards long, extending into East Berlin to tap into the land lines from Soviet air force headquarters at Karlshorst to Berlin. The project had to be completed secretly under the feet of Soviet troops and East German guards. Earth had to carted away unseen, while the entrance to the tunnel had to be small enough to avoid attracting attention from the East. It would also be necessary to construct the tunnel in such a way that there was a minimum of noise involved and no manifestation of the tunnel on the surface. Ventilation, both for the benefit of the personnel and electronic equipment, was also required. Air conditioning also had to be installed, so that the ground above the tunnel would not heat up.[30]

William Harvey, who had helped get Kim Philby booted from the United States, was given the overall command. The CIA and SIS agreed on a division of labor. The CIA would "(1) procure a site . . . and drive a tunnel to a point beneath the target cables . . . (2) be responsible for the recording of all signals produced . . . [and] (3) process in Washington all of the telegraphic material received from the project." The SIS would "(1) drive a vertical shaft from the tunnel's end to the targets; (2) effect the cable taps and deliver a usable signal to the head of the tunnel for recording; and (3) provide for a center . . . to process the voice recordings from the site."[31]

The tunneling took nearly seven months. Inspection of candidate sites narrowed the options to two, with the final selection being based on the availability of land and the availability of "complete collateral intelligence on the area." On February 25, 1955, the tunnel was completed. The three land line cables that were tapped into each carried one telegraph and four telephone lines. The intercepted communications were recorded on 600 tape recorders in the warehouse; 1,200 hours and 800 reels of tape were consumed each day. In Washington fifty CIA employees fluent in German and Russian listened to the tapes to extract intelligence.[32]

But on April 21, 1956, the tunnel was discovered. The CIA's official history concluded: "Analysis of all available evidence—traffic passing on the target cables, conversations recorded from a microphone installed in the tap chamber, and vital observations from the site—indicates that the Soviet discovery of [the tunnel] was purely fortuitous."[33]

But Soviet discovery was not purely fortuitous. The SIS personnel working on the tunnel were segregated from the SIS personnel from the Berlin station. But there were three members of the Berlin station who were aware of Operation GOLD, and one of those three was George Blake, who had been recruited by the Soviet civilian intelligence service several years earlier. The Soviets had stage-managed their discovery of the tunnel so that it appeared accidental.[34]

Despite Soviet knowledge, the operation at a minimum apparently provided valuable order-of-battle information, allowing the United States to determine "which Russian troops were where," according to the deputy chief of the processing section.[35] It is not clear how much disinformation was deliberately passed on the lines. But the sheer volume of communications that passed through the tapped lines would have made it impossible for the Soviets to engage in a widespread disinformation effort.

In addition, there was one important fact of which neither George Blake nor the Soviets were aware. A CIA Office of Communications officer, Carl Nelson, had several years earlier made an important discovery—that the echoes of plaintext versions of electrically enciphered messages traveled along the same wire as the enciphered messages. These "artifacts" or "transients" eliminated the requirement to decipher such messages. In the absence of the knowledge of this discovery the Soviets would have felt secure in sending enciphered messages on the lines, believing that although the CIA and SIS might be picking up the enciphered messages they would not be able to unravel them. They were wrong.[36]

From AQUATONE to IDEALIST

Whatever the value of the "take" from the Berlin tunnel, it certainly paled in significance to the intelligence produced by an operation that began less than three months after the tunnel was closed. In one sense, Project AQUATONE was a product of Soviet construction of a missile testing center at Kapustin Yar on the Volga. Late in 1954, a number of apparent telemetry signals from Soviet missile launches had been intercepted from the vicinity of the Kapustin Yar area. Certain characteristics of the signals revealed a similarity to the telemetry system designed by German scientists for the Soviets. Further intercepts obtained by Army Security Agency personnel in Turkey conclusively established that the signals were indeed telemetry.[37]

Obtaining photographs of the center became a top priority for the CIA. General Nathan Twining, Air Force Chief of Staff, said that it could not be done. The agency then turned to the British, who flew a Canberra from Germany to the Volga and into Iran—obtaining "some fair pictures." But one such fate-tempting mission was enough for the British, whose plane arrived in Iran full of bullet holes. The CIA appealed to Twining to have the Air Force develop a plane that could fly high enough so that it could fly over Soviet radar. However, the Air Force required that every plane be an all-purpose plane with some fighter capability, some maneuverability, and so on. Clearly, the CIA would have to do it itself.[38]

After a November 24, 1954, meeting with the secretaries of state and defense, DCI Allen Dulles, and several military officers, President Eisenhower approved a program to build thirty special high-performance aircraft. The CIA's Directorate of Plans was placed in charge of the project, and a special Development Project Staff was established. Richard

Bissell, a special assistant to Dulles, was given responsibility for running the program.[39]

Bissell had been one of the primary managers of the Allied shipping effort during World War II. After the war he worked on the Marshall Plan and has received credit for "selling" the program to Congress. That was followed by a brief term in the Truman White House. In 1954 he joined the CIA as Dulles's special assistant.[40]

To actually lead the design effort, the CIA turned to Clarence L. "Kelly" Johnson of Lockheed, who had established himself as a brilliant and fast designer. He had already designed the P-38 fighter-bomber and the F-104 Starfighter, and he had already proposed development of a spy plane.[41]

In December 1954 Johnson began work, with a goal of August 1955 for the first flight. On August 4, 1955, the first plane was flown from a secret CIA facility at Groom Lake in Nevada. On August 8 it made its first official flight. It was given the unclassified designation U-2 for Utility-2 to hide, at least on paper, its reconnaissance role.[42] It also bore the classified code name IDEALIST.

The U-2 was a single-seater, with a wingspan of 80 feet and a length of 50 feet. It could cruise at 460 miles per hour and photograph 120-mile-wide swaths while flying at about 68,000 feet. Its ability to fly at such a high altitude was believed to make it invulnerable to Soviet air-defense missiles and fighters.[43]

The U-2s were tested for speed, altitude, range, and photographic capability. The latter was demonstrated to President Eisenhower when he was presented with U-2 photographs of San Diego, as well as one of his favorite golf courses. Of great importance were the radar avoidance tests. U.S. radar operators were warned that strange planes would be flying over U.S. territory. Despite the advance notice the U-2 flights either went unseen or were imperfectly tracked. Those tests, according to Eisenhower, "gave us confidence that, in the then existing state of radar efficiency and the inability of fighter planes to operate at altitudes above some fifty thousand feet, U-2 reconnaissance could be undertaken with reasonable safety."[44]

By the first half of 1956 the CIA had begun deploying U-2s to overseas bases. The first two U-2s were sent to Lakenheath, England, where Detachment A was to operate under the cover of the notional 1st Weather Reconnaissance Squadron, Provisional (WSRP-1). However, following an espionage fiasco later that year, the Crabbe affair, the British government decided that it preferred the flights not to originate from British soil. Detachment A/WRSP-1 was moved to Wiesbaden, West Germany.[45] A second detachment, Detachment B/WRSP-2, was established at Incrilik Air Base near Adana, Turkey. Subsequently, it would absorb Detachment A and comprise as many as seven pilots and five aircraft.[46]

While the CIA was preparing to begin the overflight program, the civilian-run National Advisory Committee on Aeronautics (NACA) was providing a cover story for the operation. In the spring of 1956 NACA announced the development of a new airplane (the U-2) for use in high-altitude meteorological studies. The planes would be used, according to the committee, to collect data on weather conditions in the vicinity of the Baltic Sea.[47]

The first operational U-2 overflight, over eastern Europe, took place on June 20, 1956. Later in the month Bissell received Eisenhower's authorization to begin flights over the Soviet Union, if favorable weather conditions occurred within the following ten days. After that Bissell would have to ask again. Three days later, after being informed that conditions over central Russia were good, Bissell sent a signal to Wiesbaden authorizing the first flight.[48]

On July 4, Article 347 (as the specific aircraft was known), piloted by Harvey Stockman, took off from Wiesbaden. Stockman flew over East Berlin, across northern Poland and into Byelorussia as far as Minsk. At that point he turned the aircraft left and headed for Leningrad. The mission was completed without incident, but not without being detected by the Soviets. MiG fighters had been scrambled and sent after the U-2, but they were unable to reach it. After Leningrad Stockman headed back down the Baltic coast of Estonia, Latvia, and Lithuania and returned to base.[49]

Four more missions followed in short order, two on July 5 and two on July 9. On July 5 one flight left Wiesbaden, passed through Polish airspace, traveled east to Kiev, turned north toward Minsk, eventually overflew Moscow, and returned over Leningrad and the Soviet Baltic states. Once again, Soviet MiGs tried but failed to intercept the intruder.[50]

The five missions produced a large quantity of data of interest to intelligence analysts. Photographs showed the heavily defended areas of Moscow and Leningrad as well as the industrial activity around those cities, and they delineated atomic plants, launching pads, and aircraft caches. They also revealed that Soviet ICBM activity was accelerating.[51]

In addition, the missions revealed that the feared Soviet jet bomber threat, represented by the MYA-4 Bison and the TU-95 Bear, was relatively small. The initial flights had overflown most of the identified bomber bases as well as the production factory near Moscow. Their findings contradicted the just issued National Intelligence Estimate, which estimated 65 long-range Bisons and Bears in service, 470 for mid-1958, and 800 (500 Bison and 300 Bear) by mid-1960. The U-2 data when combined with an analysis of the Soviet industrial base and doubts about the efficiency of the Bison's power plant led the CIA to infer that their previous conclusions, based on attaché observation at the 1955 air show, were wrong.[52]

The missions escaped Soviet territory unscathed, yet they did not, as noted, escape undetected. On July 11 the Soviets protested the intrusions to the State Department. The note specified, for the first two missions, the route flown, the depth into Soviet territory the plane penetrated, and the time spent overflying Soviet air space. According to the Soviet note the July 4 route was Minsk, Vilnias, Kaunas, and Kaliningrad; the depth was 320 kilometers; and the time was one hour, thirty-two minutes. One of the July 5 routes was given as Brest, Pinsk, Baranovichi, Kaunas, and Kaliningrad. The note concluded that the "violation of the air frontiers of the Soviet Union by American aircraft cannot be interpreted as other than intentional and conducted for the purposes of reconnaissance."[53]

By the time the note was delivered the Soviets knew the speed, altitude, and range of the U-2 but not the capabilities of the camera systems. Most important, they did not know how to prevent the plane from flying over their territory. Their air-defense missiles were optimized for 60,000 feet, after which they began to run out of control in the thinner air. While the CIA believed the missiles had a potential to reach 70,000–80,000 feet, it never happened.[54]

But Soviet political protests were effective. As a result of the diplomatic note of July 11 no flights were undertaken for several months. The program resumed in late 1956, and in 1957 Detachment C/WRSP-3 opened at Atsugi, Japan. Additional operating locations were set up in Pakistan, at Lahore and Peshawar. Planes flying from the Pakistani bases searched for atomic energy installations along the Trans-Siberian Railway, locating and photographing a large radar near the terminal site for missile launchings from Kapustin Yar and overflying missile test activities at Tyuratam, where the SS-3, SS-4 IRBMs, and SS-6 ICBMs were being tested.[55]

The very existence of the Tyuratam facility was discovered by a U-2 pilot. Richard Bissell recalled that the pilot

used his authorization to deflect from his course. He was flying over Turkistan, and off in the distance he saw something that looked quite interesting and turned out to be the Tyuratam launch site—and unlike almost every other target we went after, not even the existence of that had been suspected . . . and he came back with the most beautiful photographs of this place, and within about five days the photo-interpreters had built a cardboard model of the whole Tyuratam site—roads, railway sidings, feeder roads, everything.[56]

The U-2 was also used extensively for overflights of other areas of the world (China, the Middle East, Indonesia) as well as peripheral reconnaissance missions which included photography, electronic intelligence, and nuclear monitoring. Francis Gary Powers recalled that

I flew my first electronic surveillance mission along the borders outside Russia, the specialized equipment monitoring and recording Soviet radar and radio frequencies. . . . We usually flew from Turkey eastward along the southern border of the Soviet Union . . . as far as Pakistan, and back.[57]

Often such missions involved monitoring missile launches, launches the United States apparently knew about several days in advance— probably because the prolonged countdown was being detected at Turkish ground stations. The U-2s flying peripheral missions during these events were armed with highly sophisticated interception equipment. One unit came on automatically the moment the launch frequency was used and intercepted all signals sent out to control the rocket.[58]*

Nuclear debris collection was a second major aspect of the peripheral U-2 program. In 1958, a U-2 was sent to Bodø to collect debris from nuclear tests being conducted on the Arctic islands of Novaya Zemlya and Franz Josef Land. The Atsugi detachment was also heavily involved in such collection, since wind patterns and upper atmospheric currents transported debris from the Semipalatinsk test site in the direction of Japan.[59]

Several of the U-2 missions were flown by Royal Air Force pilots. Most of those missions involved flights over the Middle East or along Soviet borders to monitor missile and space launch sites. However, on two occasions between January 1959 and May 1, 1960, the RAF pilots overflew Soviet territory, breaking fundamental rules. Flight Lieutenant John Mac-Arthur flew around the target twice while Squadron Leader Robert Robinson continued a mission despite leaving a contrail—actions which were prohibited to CIA pilots.[60]

The peripheral missions constituted the bulk of the flights. There were fewer than twenty overflight missions between July 1956 and March 1958. The frequency of overflight missions began to decline further in 1958 as high officials, particularly the president, grew more anxious about the possibility and consequences of an incident.[†] The intelligence community had assumed from the beginning it would take the Soviets about two years to develop effective countermeasures.[61]

The usual routine following the completion of an overflight called for immediate processing overseas for high-priority targets. The film was then sent on to the CIA's photographic interpretation center where a meeting would be held in the auditorium. On the screen would be a map of the Soviet Union, with a squiggle showing the route flown by the U-2, along with a blowup of particular areas. CIA officials would brief the interpreters on what to look for.[62]

REDSKIN and ATTIC

The wealth of data produced by U-2 operations did not make human intelligence operations irrelevant. Legal travelers continued to provide

---

* Only one overflight mission was devoted to electronic intelligence-gathering. The U-2's size did not allow it to carry both photographic and electronic intercept equipment.

† In addition, the Strategic Air Command grounded all its U-2s on July 10, 1958, after two fatal crashes in twenty-four hours.

valuable information concerning Soviet strategic bombers and submarines, nuclear propulsion systems, manned space programs, and bacteriological warfare capabilities. In fact, much of the collection requirements were based on the products of U-2 reporting.[63]

Tourists flying on civil nonjet aircraft managed to produce "small-format" aerial photos of the SA-2 surface-to-air missiles that had been detected earlier by U-2 overflights. Further, they discovered previously unknown SA-2 locations. Altogether, they photographed more than twelve SAM missile tests. More important, travelers "provided an extraordinary amount of information on high-priority targets. They supplied thousands of photographs of facilities for the production of ICBMs, and of the sites at which ICBMs had been deployed."[64]

Travelers also provided a substantial amount of information concerning the early stages of the Soviet antiballistic missile program to go with the information provided by the German technicians who returned from the Soviet Union, where they had been forcibly transported after World War II to work in the program, and from clandestine sources. The information concerned construction of a new test range at Sary Shagan in the south-central Soviet Union, an institute involved in a 1956 antimissile test, and activity in and around several ABM sites in the Leningrad area.[65]*

Travelers also described one of the first Soviet nuclear submarines, a missile-launching destroyer, and scores of missile-support facilities and direction-finding antennas. Their reports on aircraft markings doubled the estimate of the production of one type of aircraft.[66]

While the REDSKIN program continued through the 1950s, ATTIC did not. In December 1958 Popov was transferred back to Moscow, where he found the KGB waiting. After interrogation he was allowed to resume contacts with the CIA in Moscow and pass on disinformation. The charade continued until October 16, 1959, when Popov and his Moscow case officer, Russell Langelle, were arrested by the KGB while exchanging a note on the Moscow bus.[67]

Popov was subsequently executed. The U.S. gain from his sacrifice was large. Popov provided information on specification of Soviet weapons including tanks; tables of equipment for Soviet tank, mechanized, and rifle divisions; and descriptions of Soviet army tactics in the utilization of atomic weapons—which might have reduced U.S. defense R&D expenditures by as much as a half billion dollars.[68]

The Committee

Stalin's death on March 5, 1953, set in motion a struggle for succession that would take several years to fully resolve. One of those who had his

---

* What the United States believed about the Soviet missile program in 1954, from the full range of intelligence sources, can be found in NIE 11-6-54, *Soviet Capabilities and Probable Programs in the Guided Missile Field*, October 1954.

sights set on supreme power was Lavrenti Beria, former secret police chief and, at the time of Stalin's death, a member of the Politburo. On March 15 Beria completed the merger of the MGB into the Ministry of Internal Affairs (MVD) and took command of the enlarged ministry. He also replaced many experienced officials with those whose prime virtue was their loyalty to him.[69]

Beria's obvious attempts to replace Stalin alarmed his Politburo colleagues, including Khrushchev, Molotov, Malenkov—who had their own ambitions. Before the end of June Beria found himself under arrest. The MVD underwent a purge, albeit a relatively bloodless one. Following a secret trial, Beria and six of his closest associates were executed.[70]

In order to eliminate the threat from the concentration of such power in one ministry, internal affairs and state security responsibilities were again divided into two ministries. To handle state security functions the Committee of State Security (Komitet Gosudarstvennoy Bezopasnosti, KGB) was established on March 14, 1954. It was assigned responsibility for foreign intelligence, counterintelligence, and countersubversion, while the MVD retained control of the internal troops, border troops, and prison camps.[71]

The turmoil among the Soviet leadership and the changes in the Soviet security establishment did not prevent the achievement of some impressive human intelligence successes during the decade. Those successes were particularly important because of the Soviet Union's limited ability to employ technical collection systems against targets in the United States.

Some of those successes involved penetration of Western intelligence services, penetrations that would have poisonous effects years after they were uncovered. But for those in Moscow's foreign and defense establishment, knowledge of Western intelligence operations was of less value than was knowledge if the affairs of Western foreign ministries and defense establishments.

In 1955 the KGB used photographs taken at a homosexual party in Moscow to blackmail a clerk in the office of the British naval attaché, John Vassall, into serving as an agent. When he returned to London Vassall was first assigned to the Naval Intelligence Division, followed by assignments to the office of the Civil Lord of the Admiralty, and the Admiralty Military Branch. Over a period of four years Vassall turned over thousands of highly classified documents on British and NATO naval policy and weapons development.[72]

Another Englishman, Harry Houghton, was recruited in 1951 by the Polish UB while serving at the British embassy in Warsaw. When he returned to England and began work at the Underwater Weapons Establishment at Portland, Dorset, where he had access to top-secret documents on antisubmarine warfare and nuclear submarines, he was taken over by the KGB.[73]

George Pacques, who had been recruited by the NKGB in 1944, went on to serve, after the war, as chef de cabinet and adviser to several French ministers. Late in 1958 Pacques began to specialize in defense affairs, and for the next four years he had constant access to classified documents at whatever institution he was affiliated with, which included the French general staff, Institut des Hautes Études de la Défense Nationale, and NATO headquarters. Among the documents he provided the KGB was the complete NATO defense plan for western Europe.[74]

A bilingual Canadian economist, Hugh Hambleton, was also among the KGB's agents in NATO. The MGB had begun cultivating Hambleton in 1951, and the KGB began gleaning the benefits in 1957. Four the next four years he provided a flood of NATO documents, from military plans to economic forecasts at his bimonthly meetings with his Soviet controller.[75]

The KGB also benefited from the activities of Markus Wolf's HVA. By 1958, according to an HVA defector, there were 2,000–3,000 penetration agents in place in West Germany. Wolf had already adopted the strategy of targeting lonely, usually middle-aged female government employees with access to classified information. Irmgard Roemer was one of the many targets who succumbed. A forty-four-year-old secretary in the Bonn Foreign Office, responsible for handling communications with embassies abroad, she provided carbon copies to her HVA lover.[76]

Throughout this time Stig Wennerstrom, who had been recruited in 1948, was spying for the GRU. In April 1952 he arrived in Washington to assume his new position as Swedish air attaché. He was instructed by Moscow to focus on providing whatever information he could on the most recent developments in bombers, fighters, guided missiles, bombsights, radar, high-frequency radio, and advanced photoreconnaissance equipment.[77]

When his Washington tour of duty ended in June 1957, Wennerstrom returned to Sweden where, in October 1957, he became head of the Air Section of the Defense Ministry's Command Office. The Soviets asked him to provide any information about Swedish departures from its position of neutrality, about the visits of American military-aviation experts to Sweden, and U.S. provision of military equipment, including any nuclear weapons.[78]

Wennerstrom had access to a wide range of documents on the Swedish military modernization program—a program that included a network of secret airfields, massive underground submarine and destroyer pens blasted out of rock cliffs along the east coast, a radar network, and an air force with supersonic jet fighters.[79]

Initially, according to Wennerstrom, the information he provided mainly concerned U.S. military aircraft and their navigational equipment. He also reported on movements of American military personnel to Stockholm from the Pentagon and from the headquarters of the U.S. Air Forces Europe in Wiesbaden. Subsequently, the focus of his reporting shifted to American equipment employed by the Swedish armed forces. He was particularly successful in providing information on U.S. guided missile systems, including the air-to-air Sidewinder and ground-to-air Hawk and the HM-55 Bomarc.[80]

17

Spies and Moles

On August 19, 1960, the United States achieved the first successful recovery of a reconnaissance satellite payload. Although space reconnaissance would revolutionize intelligence, it would not lead to an abandonment of traditional spying. Seven days earlier, one of the most valuable spies in history, a well-connected colonel in the GRU, would make his first approach to Westerners, in what would become a prolonged attempt to become an agent of the United States or Britain. Meanwhile, a U.S. military officer was already passing a variety of sensitive documents to the GRU.

An officer in the Polish UB who had been sending classified information to the West for two years would soon defect. His defection would lead to the arrest of two moles—one in the British Secret Intelligence Service, another in the West German BND (Bundesnachrichtendienst—Federal Intelligence Service). The identification of those moles would help fuel a molehunt that would have a dramatic impact on the CIA, MI5, and SDECE for the next decade.

Superpower espionage and counterespionage would not be the only intelligence activities that would have a significant impact on the world during the 1960s. In the early 1960s two Israelis were being prepared for missions that would provide exceedingly valuable data to the Israeli intelligence community, data that would have its most dramatic impact during June 1967.

SNIPER and Two Moles

In early 1958 the CIA station chief in Bern, Switzerland, received the first in a series of fourteen letters. Each was signed Heckenschütze (Sniper), and appeared to be from a Soviet-bloc intelligence officer. In December 1960, SNIPER (or BEVISION, as the CIA designated him) defected, arriving in West Berlin and identifying himself as Michal Goleniewski, an officer in the Polish UB.[1]

In addition to providing information that revealed a Soviet penetration of the British Underwater Weapons Establishment, Goleniewksi also provided information that led the British and Germans to conclude that their own foreign intelligence services had been penetrated. In the case of SIS, Goleniewski's information helped end the betrayal of George Blake, after almost eight years. At his 1962 trial Blake would be sentenced to forty-two years in prison, purportedly one year for every British officer or agent who died because of his activities.[2]*

The second mole unearthed by SNIPER's information was Heinz Felfe, chief of the BND's Department IIIF–Counterespionage. Felfe had been born in 1918 and served as an officer in the Nazi's SS Security Service. In 1946, after being imprisoned in Canada for his SS activities, he was released, probably because he had offered his services to British intelligence and they had accepted. In addition to serving as an informer on activities at the University of Bonn, Felfe worked as an interrogator at a refugee camp until 1951.[3]

That year he was able to join the Gehlen Organization, thanks to Hans Clemens, a former SS colleague. Clemens was not only a member of the Gehlen Organization, but a Soviet agent. Felfe soon became the second Soviet penetration of the future BND.[4]

Felfe joined the counterespionage department of the organization's Karlsruhe office. His intelligence, knowledge, and abilities soon led to a promotion to Pullach headquarters. Once there, his high-quality work attracted Gehlen's approving notice. Gehlen's positive view of Felfe would help prolong his tenure as a key Soviet penetration.[5]

When Soviet intelligence officer Peter Deriabin defected in 1954, he told the CIA of two Soviet agents in the BND, code-named PETER and PAUL. Deriabin, however, could provide no solid leads to their identity. But then, in December 1955, a captured Gehlen agent was tried, in public, in East Germany. Clare Petty, a CIA counterintellligence officer, examined the information that came out of the trial and concluded that it could have originated only with a high-level source in the Gehlen Organization. An investigation produced two suspects, including Felfe.[6]

But Felfe's performance reinforced Gehlen's initial impression, leading him to ignore warnings from the CIA and his own Org. Felfe, after all, had identified one highly placed KGB agent and produced apparently valuable intelligence on East German and Soviet intelligence operations.[7]

That productivity meant little compared to the harm he was able to do. According to his own account, Felfe provided the KGB and its predecessors approximately 15,000 photographs and 20 microtape recording spools. He provided lists of Gehlen Organization agents, cover addresses

* With KGB help, Blake would escape from prison in 1966. He has lived in Moscow ever since. In 1990 he published his memoirs, *No Other Choice* (New York: Simon & Schuster).

of informants, internal reports on current operations, and monthly counterespionage reports. Felfe admitted to betraying ninety-four agents.[8]

Two items of information provided by SNIPER revitalized the CIA case against Felfe. One of his early letters informed the Americans that the UB was receiving BND reports, passed on from the KGB. That made it likely that PETER or PAUL was still operating—or both were. Subsequently, Goleniewski reported a conversation with General Oleg Gribanov, chief of the KGB's Second Chief (Counterintelligence) Directorate. According to SNIPER, Gribanov had bragged that of the six BND officers who traveled to the United States on a CIA orientation tour in 1956, one of whom was Felfe, two were Soviet agents.[9]

Felfe again became a prime suspect and Operation UJDROWSY, as the CIA called its new investigation of Felfe, began. It was not long before the investigation turned up a lifestyle well beyond the means of a employee of the BND—a ten-room chalet in Bavaria, private school for his son, a comfortable apartment in Munich, and an impressive wardrobe. Felfe was arrested on November 6, 1961. Both he and Clemens received lengthy sentences.[10]

Penkovskiy

On April 20, 1961, a man was ushered into a suite of rooms at the Mount Royal Hotel, London. Waiting there were four intelligence officers, two from the Central Intelligence Agency and two from the British Secret Intelligence Service.

Their guest, Oleg Vladimirovich Penkovskiy, was born on April 23, 1919, in the Caucasian town of Ordzhonikidze. In 1937 he entered the Second Kiev Artillery School as well as joining the Komsomol (Young Communists). After graduating in 1939 he saw his first combat duty, initially as commander of an artillery unit in the Ukraine and then in the Soviet–Finnish war. During 1939–40 Penkovskiy was wounded in action and decorated four times. During the remainder of the war he divided his service between Moscow and the First Ukrainian Front.[11]

After the war ended Penkovskiy attented the Frunze Military Academy (1945–48) and then the GRU's Military Diplomatic Academy (1949–53). He made full colonel in 1950 and married the daughter of a top general, who was the chief of the Political Directorate of the Moscow Military District.[12] Graduation from the MDA was followed by assignments with the GRU's Fourth (Near Eastern) Directorate and as assistant military attaché (senior assistant to the GRU resident) in Ankara. Turkey proved to be his last foreign assignment, for he was recalled in November 1956 as a result of a dispute with his superior. As Penkovskiy was preparing to become the GRU resident in India, the KGB discovered that his father had been a White Army officer who may have survived the civil war—a flaw in his heritage that cost him the India assignment.[13]

Instead, Penkovskiy remained in Moscow and watched his career stall.

In June 1960 there was reason for optimism. He was assigned as a member of the Selection Board for the MDA and then designated head of the incoming class for 1960–63. A top instructor's position normally meant promotion to major-general. But the KGB intervened and in August he was told that the job was not to be his.[14]

On August 12, 1960, the first of Penkovskiy's attempts to indicate that he had important information to provide the West was unsuccessful, as were several more. The various American, Canadian, and British visitors to Moscow who he approached, as well as the U.S. embassy there, feared a KGB provocation. But after consultations in Washington between an SIS representative, Howard Shergold, and Richard Helms, CIA Deputy Director for Plans, it was agreed that the two spy services would run Penkovskiy jointly.[15]

Initial contact was made through Greville Wynne, a representative of British electrical, steel, and machine-making companies, whose business often took him to Moscow. Wynne had been recruited in November 1960 by SIS to make contact with the Soviet State Committee for the Coordination of Scientific Research Work, which served as a cover for KGB and GRU scientific and technical collection operations. That month Penkovskiy was assigned to the committee.[16]

On December 8, 1960, Wynne went to Moscow's Shermeteyevo Airport with Penkovskiy and other committee members to greet arriving British delegates. In the process of waiting with Penkovskiy for a long-delayed flight to arrive, Wynne began to establish a personal relationship, culminating in an April 6 attempt by Penkovskiy to pass a package to Wynne. Two weeks later the GRU colonel arrived in London as head of a Soviet "trade" delegation whose mission was to acquire advanced Western technologies in a variety of areas, including steel, radar, communications, and concrete processing. Waiting for him in a suite of rooms on the floor above those of the Soviet delegation were Joe Bulik and George Kisevalter of the CIA and Howard Shergold and Michael Stokes of the SIS.[17]

Even before he entered the suite Penkovskiy had already provided extremely valuable intelligence. Shortly after arriving at Heathrow, he passed Wynne a package of classified Soviet material. Included were seventy-eight pages of secret and top-secret material, most of which Penkovskiy had copied by hand. The majority of the documents concerned missiles, including four photocopies of plans for construction sites of missile-launching installations. There was also information on the little known V-75 antiaircraft missile, designated SA-2 GUIDELINE by NATO. Penkovskiy also provided manuals on several medium-range and intermediate-range missiles and their ground equipment, the SS-1, SS-4, SS-5, and SS-6.[18]

The debriefing sessions, which ran from April 20 to Penkovskiy's return to Moscow on May 6, also produced valuable information. Examining copies of photos taken at the 1960 May Day parade, Penkovskiy was able to identify tactical surface-to-surface missiles for troops in the field, the SA-2 antiaircraft missile, and the SS-1 MRBM. In addition, he reported on Soviet nuclear testing activities.[19]

Penkovskiy also told his audience of the locations of over twenty strategic targets in the Moscow area, including the command posts of the PVO (Air Defense Forces) and the Moscow Defense Zone and several General Staff directorates. Such targets, he said, "must all be blown up by atomic prepositioned bombs, rather than by means of aircraft bombs or rockets which may or may not hit the vital targets."[20] He went on to observe that

> [a] small group of saboteurs equipped with such weapons should plant them governed by a time mechanism in the locations from which all these headquarters can be destroyed. Irrespective of what other attacks will be made at H-Hour, these essential headquarters must be destroyed by planted bombs. All military district headquarters must be destroyed.[21]

Penkovskiy returned to Moscow armed with enough CIA- and SIS-provided brochures on British steel technology to make it seem that he had spent his time gathering intelligence rather than disclosing it. The brochures, along with his introduction (under CIA-SIS direction) of a British steel expert to a London-based GRU officer, greatly pleased the committee and the GRU.[22]

Back in Moscow Penkovskiy resumed his collection efforts. On May 27, when Wynne returned to Moscow, Penkovskiy handed him a package of approximately twenty exposed rolls of film and other materials. On July 2 he passed two typewritten pages and seven containers of undeveloped film, hidden in a candy box, to Janet Chisholm. "Accidental" meetings with Chisholm, the wife of an SIS officer at the embassy, would become a frequent channel for passing information while in Moscow. The typewritten pages contained a significant statement by Marshal Sergei Varenstov, the commanding officer of missiles and ground artillery for the Soviet ground forces, on Berlin, as well as details of Soviet missile brigades in Germany. Information on Berlin was of particular value because the United States had to deal with Khrushchev's threats to conclude a separate peace treaty with East Germany.[23]

In addition to the Berlin-related material Penkovskiy had also delivered information concerning Soviet intelligence strategies and personnel. Among the documents on the film were a thirty-six-page top-secret document on "Personnel Communications in Agent Intelligence," which provided new details on GRU operating methods; the sixty-eight-page top-secret "Matters Concerning Agent Communications and the Control of Agents"; and a forty-three-page work plan for Penkovskiy's committee for the third quarter of 1961. Penkovskiy also provided a list of sixty students of the Military-Diplomatic Academy, all on track to become GRU officers.[24]

The CIA's "Evaluation of the Counterintelligence Product," prepared after the receipt of the July 2 material, summarized Penkovskiy's contributions with respect to Soviet intelligence organization and operations. According to that analysis, he had delivered unique information concerning the Soviet intelligence structure, new information on a staff component responsible for sabotage, subversion, and assassination in support of military operations, the identities of more than 300 Soviet intelligence officers and over a dozen agents active in the West, and evidence concerning Soviet intelligence training and procedures for agent communications.[25]

Trips to London and Paris followed on July 18 and September 20 respectively. On the evening of July 18 Penkovskiy again met CIA-SIS debriefers, the first of thirteen meetings during his three-week London stay. By the end of his visit he had been debriefed thirty times.[26]

Penkovskiy, who had been code-named HERO by the CIA, arrived in Paris to attend the Soviet Trade Fair, a visit approved by GRU chief General Ivan Serov. On the ride in from the airport Penkovskiy handed Wynne a package containing eleven rolls of undeveloped film.[27] In addition to the information on those rolls Penkovskiy had much to report to the CIA-SIS team. He told them that the R-12 (SS-4) "is already adopted and is being serially produced. Its range is 2500 kilometers. The R-14 (SS-5) is being prepared for serial production. It has a range of 4500 kilometers [2,800 miles]. Both ranges I have given are for the rockets carrying atomic warheads."[28]

Penkovskiy's material would be distributed to the appropriate individuals in the U.S. and British intelligence communities through two special compartments, intended to protect the information and obscure the fact that it was coming from a single source. The CIA designated all of Penkovskiy's documentary material IRONBARK, while the product of his oral reports was code-named CHICKADEE. The British used RUPEE and ARNICA.[29]

The commitment to obscuring the fact that a single source was responsible for IRONBARK and CHICKADEE material was extreme. Because some of what Penkovskiy told his audience in London was substantially different from what U.S. intelligence had believed, DCI Allen Dulles had asked analyst Raymond Garthoff to evaluate CHICKADEE material along with some other Penkovskiy material. When Garthoff asked the head of the Soviet Russia Division, David Murphy, whether CHICKADEE and IRONBARK materials came from the same source he was told that they did not.[30]*

Penkovskiy's trip to Paris would be his last journey to the West. The three sets of sessions in London and Paris had totaled approximately 140

* Garthoff recalls that the deception affected his conclusions with regard to the CHICKADEE material. Had he known the same source had provided the IRONBARK material, he would have given more credence to some, although not all, of the CHICKADEE material. Interview with Raymond Garthoff, August 18, 1993, Washington, D.C.

hours and produced about 1,200 pages of transcripts. Penkovskiy also had provided 111 exposed rolls of film, 99 percent of which was legible. His reporting, written and oral, resulted in an estimated 10,000 pages of intelligence reports.[31]

Back in Moscow, Penkovskiy continued to meet with Janet Chisholm, who had been code-named ANNE. However, after a January 19, 1962, meeting with ANNE he noticed a car making a U-turn on a one-way street. That, along with the two men in dark overcoats in the backseat of the car, led Penkovskiy to conclude that he or ANNE was under KGB surveillance. As a result, he resorted to the use of dead drops—places where documents could be hidden until picked up by the CIA. To minimize the chance of detection no dead drop was used more than once, and there was only a single drop and pickup operation each month.[32]*

Renewed KGB interest in Penkovskiy's father caused further problems. In a March 5 letter he informed the CIA and SIS that a planned trip to Italy had been postponed and a trip to Geneva had been canceled. He was hoping to travel to the United States in April, but he noted that "at the present it's going badly because KGB counterintelligence are rummaging around concerning my father." By that time the KGB may have been more interested in the son's activities. Trips to Brazil and Cyprus in May and July were blocked by the KGB.[33]

Despite his concerns and intensified KGB surveillance Penkovskiy continued to place material in dead drops. On September 5 he attended an American embassy reception and passed some material. September 6 would be the last time he was seen by Western representatives before his arrest. On October 12 Penkovskiy was arrested—apparently detected as a result of routine surveillance of Janet Chisholm.† Her husband's SIS role was known to the KGB, thanks to George Blake, who had served in Berlin with him. Wynne was arrested in Hungary on November 2. The Soviets never learned the extent of Penkovskiy's activities, but what they knew resulted in a death sentence. At his May 1963 trial his position in the GRU went unmentioned. Not only would it have meant publicly admitting the GRU role in the work of the State Committee for the Coordination of Scientific Research Work, but it would have meant acknowledging the existence of the GRU. Penkovskiy was executed on May 16. Wynne received an eight-year sentence and was traded for Konon Molody in April 1964.[34]

A top-secret summary, titled "Penkovskiy's Positive Production," pre-

---

* Penkovskiy had other means of communications, including seemingly innocent tourist postcards. He used one to call off further direct contacts after January 12.

† Numerous theories have been advanced to explain the KGB's detection of Penkovskiy. At least two Soviet spies in the U.S. intelligence community may have had access to some of Penkovskiy's production. Jack Dunlap (NSA) had a number of Penkovskiy's less sensitive documents, attributed only to "a reliable source." In addition, William Whalen (see below) may have had access to some documents. Information about such documents could have allowed the Soviets to narrow the range of suspects.

pared by the CIA's Soviet Division, summed up Penkovskiy's contributions. His disclosure that the SA-2 became operational at 4,000 feet allowed the Strategic Air Command to develop new attack tactics to fly below that altitude. He also provided a copy of the *Soviet Forces Field Service Regulations* and the 1962 draft revisions, which provided unique information on the projected effects of nuclear weapons in the battlefield, as well as the operational procedures for the protection of troops.[35]

The CIA study also credited Penkovskiy with providing complete technical specifications of all Soviet tactical surface-to-surface ballistic missiles and free rockets, along with unique information on their ground support equipment. The Penkovskiy material included an article by Defense Minister Rodion Malinovsky, regarded by the CIA to be "the best single document on Soviet armored fighting vehicles ever received by the Department of the Army." The forty-three-page, single-spaced article contained specifications of the Soviet T-55 and T-62 tanks and had a major impact on the design of the American M-60 battle tank.[36]

Penkovskiy provided that and all the other articles that appeared in the "Special Collection" of the key Soviet military journal *Voyennaya Mysl* (Military Thought). While the CIA was aware of the existence of a confidential version of the journal and had acquired numerous issues, it was Penkovskiy who revealed to them that there was a top-secret version. The first issue, published in 1960, contained "The Theory of Military Art Needs Review," "Some Problems of Modern Operations," "New Developments in Operational Art and Tactics," "The Suitability of Modern Means and Methods of Conducting Operations," "Intelligence at the Level of Modern Missions," and "Questions of the Control of Missile Units in an Offensive Operation."[37]

He also provided several other defense publications, including three ("Artillery Information Collection," "Information Collection of Missile Units and Artillery," and "Information Bulletin of Missile Troops") that were issued only to "special list" personnel. The "Information Collection of Missile Units and Artillery" included graphs and formulas for the warheads connected with chemical and nuclear weapons, which informed the reader of the optimum height of burst for chemical warheads, the varying areas of contamination to be expected in different wind conditions, and the resulting casualties that would be suffered by enemy troops.[38]

Penkovskiy's counterintelligence production was also phenomenal. He identified hundreds of KGB and GRU officers, including all members of his class at the Military-Diplomatic Academy and GRU station members in Ceylon, India, Egypt, Paris, and London.[39]

Whalen

Soviet intelligence recruits during the early 1960s included a retired American lieutenant colonel, William Henry Whalen. Whalen had joined the army in October 1940. After spending World War II in the United States, Whalen was assigned to the European theater three days after the German surrender. By early 1948 he was back in the United States to take up his new assignment with the army's Office of the Assistant Chief of Staff, Intelligence (OACSI), where he was assigned to the Executive Office. From December 10, 1951, to February 1952 he served as a plans and policy officer with the Army Security Agency.[40]

Intelligence assignments continued. In early February 1952 Whalen began an orientation tour in preparation for his assignment to Detachment M, OACSI, which was responsible for the security of signals intelligence information provided by ASA to army units. On May 29, 1952, he was assigned to serve as a Detachment M representative in Tokyo. From mid-July 1957 to early July 1959 he was assistant chief, U.S. Army Foreign Liaison Office, OACSI. His next assignment was with the Joint Chiefs of Staff's Joint Intelligence Objectives Agency (JIOA), where he served first as deputy chief, and then, from July 2, 1959, to July 5, 1960 as chief.[41]

The JIOA was responsible for several projects, the most prominent of which was Project PAPERCLIP, which involved the recruiting of Nazi scientists to work in the U.S. space, missile, and aircraft programs. But it was his service in the Foreign Liaison Office that provided the GRU with an opportunity to enlist his aid. The office's functions included liaison with the military attachés of foreign nations in Washington, including those of the Soviet Union.[42]

According to Whalen, in March 1959 he met with Colonel Sergei A. Edemski, then the acting Soviet military attaché in Washington and Whalen agreed to trade classified documents for cash. He provided Edemski with three classified U.S. Army manuals. He continued to provide Edemski with documents, meeting him once a month in shopping center parking lots in Alexandria, Virginia.[43]

With Edemski's departure in early 1960, Whalen was turned over to another Soviet intelligence officer, Mikhail A. Shumaev, who also served as First Secretary of the Soviet embassy. However, on July 4, 1960, Whalen had his first heart attack, never returned to active duty, and officially retired in February 1961. That did not stop him from wandering the halls of the Pentagon until early 1963, trying to pick up information for his Soviet clients through conversations with JIOA acquaintances.[44]

But Whalen's efforts after his retirement did not satisfy Shumaev, who frequently admonished him for inadequate production. Whalen's attempts, under instructions from Shumaev, to find an accomplice or obtain employment in the Defense Department failed. Finally, during an early 1963 meeting Whalen informed Shumaev that he was unable to provide more information and suggested that they end their relationship. The Soviets persisted, but with no effect.[45]

Even with Whalen's lack of production in 1962 and 1963, his overall effort was impressive. In his meetings with Edemski and Shumaev he provided oral information he obtained from a variety of sources, including information from military associates and reading material related to his JIOA duties.[46]

Whalen was knowledgeable about three Joint Chiefs of Staff (JCS) plans for the employment of nuclear weapons throughout the world in event of war. The plans specified exact targets to be destroyed, the units responsible for destroying them, and the types of nuclear weapons to be used. He was able to pass on information concerning troop movements, the reorganization of U.S. Army combat units, including combat units equipped with Honest John nuclear rockets, and defense plans for West Germany and France.[47]

He also provided seventeen classified manuals and bulletins concerning Army nuclear field and air defense artillery. The manuals included *Air Defense Artillery Missile Battalion NIKE-HERCULES, Field Artillery Missile Batallion, HONEST JOHN Rocket, Self-Propelled, Staff Officers Field Manual: Atomic Weapons Employment,* and *HAWK Data Book.* An Army technical assessment concluded that the intelligence derived from the manuals would allow the Soviets to counter the systems by tactical and electronic means.[48]

Those seventeen manuals were the tip of the iceberg, as Whalen had access to approximately 3,500 documents within the JCS organization. Despite that, the Army's Deputy Chief of Staff, Operations concluded that Whalen had "seriously, but not critically, degraded the capability of the US and its Allies to successfully wage general or limited war." Whalen's activities would cause a loss of effectiveness and result in greater casualties.[49]

Whalen ended his espionage career before being detected, but he did not escape for long. FBI agent Donald Gruentzel, conducting a damage assessment of the activities of Stig Wennerstrom, who was arrested in 1963, encountered Whalen's name. At the same time the FBI learned that there was a Soviet agent in the Pentagon.[50]

Evidence presented to a grand jury on July 12, 1966, led to Whalen's indictment. As part of a deal with the prosecution, the retired lieutenant colonel was not indicted for espionage. Instead, he was charged with being an agent of the Soviet Union and conspiring to gather or deliver defense information pertaining to "atomic weaponry, missiles, military plans for the defense of Europe, estimates of comparative military capabilities, military intelligence reports and analyses, information concerning the retaliation plans by the U.S. Strategic Air Command and information pertaining to troop movements."[51]

Whalen's trial was conducted under a gag order prohibiting the press from publishing any information from Whalen's confession, even though it had been made in open court. No media account mentioned his connection with PAPERCLIP. Although his connection with the JIOA was mentioned in court, no one reported the agency's mission. The Army press release concerning his background ended in 1955, and described Whalen only as an officer in the JIOA.[52] Whalen received a fifteen-year sentence.[53]

Cohen and Lotz

In January 1962 Kamal Amin Ta'abet arrived in Damascus. Ta'abet was born in Beirut to Syrian parents, who, in 1948, moved the family to Argentina, where they opened a textile business. Ta'abet himself had become a successful businessman, but he found that Argentina was no substitute for Syria. So he returned to his homeland to stay. At least that was his story.[54]

Syrian counterintelligence authorities would not learn for several years that Ta'abet was actually a Jew, Eliahu Ben Shaul Cohen, and that what they thought they knew of his background was a carefully constructed fabrication. Cohen had actually been born in Alexandria in 1928. In 1949 his parents and three brothers moved to Israel, while Eli remained behind to help coordinate Jewish activities.[55]

During the summer of 1955 he was secretly brought to Israel to undergo training to become a member of Unit 131 of AMAN (the IF Intelligence Branch), which operated in Egypt. However, after returning to Egypt he found himself under surveillance by the Mukhabarat, Egypt's secret police. During the initial phase of Israeli participation in the 1956 Suez War, he was detained by Egyptian security forces. In February 1957 he arrived in Israel, after having been expelled with the other remaining Jews in Alexandria.[56]

Once in Israel, Cohen settled into civilian life, becoming an accountant. In 1960 he was approached by a representative of AMAN, who wished him to rejoin their ranks. Cohen resisted their persistent attempts, until he was suddenly fired from his job, when he turned to AMAN for employment. Initially he was to be sent back into Egypt, but the AMAN had second thoughts when they realized that the Egyptians kept detailed dossiers of their population, and Cohen was already known to them.[57]

Cohen's Syrian background made him an obvious choice to become a deep-cover illegal in that country, which had become the most radical of the Arab states. Its politics, geographic proximity, and large arsenal made it a major concern to Israeli leaders. But Cohen could not simply arrive in Syria. No cover would hold up under such circumstances. Thus, on February 3, 1961, he left Israel on an El-Al flight to to Zurich. There he switched identities, and Kamal Amin Ta'abet boarded a flight for Santiago, Chile. By deplaning at a transit stop in Buenos Aires, Ta'abet got into Argentina without documentation.[58]

For almost a year Cohen built up his cover as a successful businessman and Syrian patriot. He attended Arab social and cultural meetings as well as Arab nightclubs. In addition to professing his patriotism, he became a well-known supporter of the local Arab newspaper and its editor, and he established friendly relations with the Syrian diplomats and military attachés working out of the embassy. In particular, he became friends with the new Syrian military attaché to Argentina, Colonel Amin el-Hafaz, who had been exiled from Damascus because his fanatical Ba'athist party leanings worried even the radical Syrian leaders.[59]

Cohen developed contacts at the lavish Syrian embassy dinner parties he attended, where he trumpeted his love of Syria and claimed that he wished to visit his homeland and invest large sums of money in its economy. When he announced his plans to make his first visit to Syria his influential friends were glad to supply him with letters of introduction, addresses, and promises of support for his Syrian endeavors.[60]

Of course, Cohen did not announce that before arriving in Syria he would be making a secret stop in Israel. Cohen arrived in Syria on the liner *Astoria*, which he had boarded in Genoa on January 1, 1962. Days after arriving, he renounced his Argentine home and vowed never to leave Syria.[61]

Less than two months later, on February 25, the communications duty officer at AMAN headquarters in Tel Aviv received Cohen's first transmission. Longer reports would be written in secret ink and smuggled out to a European contact in hidden compartments in the furniture he exported.[62]

Throughout his tenure Cohen would have a lot to report. His contacts would include the head of the radio and press section of the Propaganda Ministry and the nephew of the army's chief of staff. Friends in the Syrian air force would frequently command Cohen to visit them at their offices or at air bases. At Syrian air bases Cohen could talk to the pilots, ask about their planned tactics in the event of war with Israel, and even receive technical briefings on the Syrian MiG and Sukhoi aircraft and their armaments. He was thus able to supply AMAN with a list of all pilots in the Syrian air force.[63]

In September 1962, after a visit to Israel, he returned to Syria via Europe. A friend proceeded to take him on a guided tour of Syria's Golan Heights fortifications. Cohen visited each fortification and observed the positioning of every gun, trench, machine-gun nest, and tank trap. The exact value of Cohen's information in such areas may be questioned, since ground and aerial reconnaissance may have been able to provide much of the data concerning weapons locations. But certainly Cohen's in-person report and information he would have picked up in talking to Syrian officers at the location would have been of value to the AMAN.[64]

Cohen was also able to provide high-grade political intelligence on the bitter infighting between the Nasserites and Ba'athists. The quality of his political intelligence went up even further after March 1963, when a coup left the Ba'ath party, and some of his closest friends, in control of Syria. Included was General Amin el-Hafaz, former military attaché in Buenos Aires and the new Syrian strongman.[65]

In 1964 Cohen provided Israel with detailed plans of the entire fortification system defending the key town of Kuneitra. Another report concerned the arrival of more than 200 Soviet T-54 tanks. He later provided copies of the entire set of Soviet-devised plans on how Syria would attempt to cut off the northern segment of Israel in the event of a surprise attack.[66]

While Cohen was on good terms with many high-ranking Syrians, there was one who was suspicious. Unfortunately for Cohen that official was Colonel Ahmad Suedani, the chief of the Syrian army's intelligence branch. During November 1964, on a trip back to Israel, Cohen indicated that he felt uncomfortable in Suedani's presence.[67]

Cohen did not improve his chances of survival by his casual manner of communication. Between March 15 and August 29, 1964, he transmitted about 100 radio messages, each about nine minutes long. When he arrived back from Israel in late 1964 he resumed broadcasts immediately, which could have allowed a Syrian counterintelligence officer to link the resumption of broadcasts to his return. In addition, he continued his practice of frequent lengthy transmissions, prompting nearby foreign embassies to complain to the Syrians of interference with their own radio transmissions. Between December 2 and January 18, 1965, he sent 31 messages to the Mossad, all at 8:30 in the morning.[68]*

But on January 18, 1965, Cohen's espionage career came to an abrupt end, when a squad of Syrian intelligence officers and commandos, led by Colonel Suedani, burst into Cohen's apartment. With the help of the GRU and Cohen's repeated lengthy broadcasts, they had located the source of the illicit transmissions. Tried and found guilty of espionage, Cohen was publicly hanged in Damascus in May 1965.[69]

During the same period that Eli Cohen was operating as a deep-cover illegal in Syria, Ze'ev Gur-Aryeh was performing the identical mission in Egypt. Gur-Aryeh was also having enormous success, becoming a part of the elite in Egyptian society and passing valuable intelligence back to Israel.

Gur-Aryeh was "masquerading" as a German businessman named Wolfgang Lotz. In fact, Wolfgang Lotz was Gur-Aryeh's original name, having been born to a Jewish mother and Austrian gentile father in Germany in 1921. In 1933, after his parents' divorce, and with Hitler in power, mother and son arrived in Palestine and Wolfgang's name was changed.[70]

During World War II he served with the British army. In the 1948 war he was commissioned as a lieutenant and placed in command of an infantry platoon consisting of new immigrants. Then, in 1959 Gur-Aryeh was recruited by Unit 131.[71] Transformed back into Wolfgang Lotz, he returned to Germany to establish a cover story. He was to be the wealthy owner of a horse-breeding ranch and riding academy, who had

---

* In 1964 the Mossad took over responsibility for Cohen, as a result of assuming control of the AMAN's Unit 188 (the successor to Unit 131).

been a loyal soldier in Hitler's Wehrmacht, and subsequently emigrated to Egypt.[72]

Lotz arrived in Egypt in December 1960 and fit comfortably into the country's prosperous German colony. He encouraged rumors that he actually had served, not in the Wehrmacht, but in the SS. Such rumors helped him gain access to the secretive group of Nazis living in Egypt. More important, Wolfgang Lotz became a confidant of important members of the Egyptian government and military. In addition to posing as a successful businessman he played the role of extravagant host, staging lavish parties and flashing large sums of money. His free-spending ways, which led to his being dubbed "the champagne spy," made him a favorite among high-ranking Egyptian officers who congregated at his home. His friends included Colonel Abedel Rahman, the deputy chief of military intelligence; General Favad Osman, chief of security for Egypt's rocket sites; and assorted admirals and generals.[73]

His lavish entertaining paid off. He was able to radio to Israel detailed information on Egyptian troops and their armor. Intelligence on air force developments, designations, and dispositions was also acquired. Lotz was also able to provide an encyclopedic and highly accurate order of battle for the Egyptian military.[74]

Lotz was also able to obtain a complete list of German scientists living in Cairo, their addresses, the location of their families in Germany and Austria, and their role in the Egyptian rocket and weapons programs. He also provided a microfilm of the blueprints of the electronic control systems for Egyptian missiles.[75]

In addition to pure intelligence collection Lotz was involved in covert action operations. In 1964 he began to mail threatening letters to the German scientists in Egypt who were involved in Egyptian weapons programs. A CIA study suggests that Lotz may have also been used in "executive action" operations.[76]

This flood of information continued for nearly five years. Periodically, Lotz would travel to Europe for debriefings. However, as with Cohen, he relied heavily on radio to transmit his intelligence. And like Cohen, his carelessness led to his downfall. On February 22, 1965, a little over a month after Cohen was captured in Damascus, the Lotz family returned to their Cairo home and found six heavily armed representatives of the Egyptian security service. The Egyptians, with the help of the GRU, had tracked and located Lotz's transmissions.[77]

Aware that Lotz was a spy, the Egyptians believed him to be a German who had been duped into working for Israel. Despite undergoing brutal interrogaton and sensory deprivation, he maintained his cover. After a month-long show trial that began in late July 1965, and despite being charged with ten offenses that carried the death penalty, Lotz was sentenced to life imprisonment. But in 1968 he returned to Israel, along with the captured Operation SUSANNAH agents, as part of a postwar prisoner swap. He died in 1993.[78]

The Great Molehunt

SNIPER's defection in late 1960, along with the arrests of Blake and Felfe, set the stage for what would become an obsession among some in the CIA and the British Security Service (MI5). The Blake and Felfe cases indicated that the KGB was still capable of penetrating the intelligence services of major Western powers. To some in the CIA it would become an article of faith that the CIA *must* be penetrated, just as some in MI5 concluded that British intelligence was still penetrated at the highest levels. Before it was over the molehunt would also touch the French SDECE and the Canadian security service.*

While the Blake and Felfe cases laid the groundwork, it was Anatoliy Golitsyn and James Jesus Angleton who were the key catalysts. On December 15, 1961, Golitsyn rang the bell of the CIA's station chief in Finland and asked for asylum. The CIA was already aware of Golitsyn, having rejected him as a candidate for recruitment because of his seeming adamant support of the Soviet leadership.[79]

Golitsyn, like Penkovskiy, had reached a dead-end in his career. In 1945, at age nineteen, he began attending an artillery school for officers in Odessa, then transferred to a military counterintelligence course. After graduation he joined the MGB, spending three years with a section responsible for the security of Soviet citizens abroad. That assignment was followed by further studies, three months in the anti–U.S. counterintelligence branch, two years in Vienna, where he first monitored the activities of Soviet émigrés and then operated against British intelligence, and more studies. His assignment to Finland was preceded by a tour in the NATO Section of the First Chief Directorate's Information Department. But his grandiose plans to restructure the KGB fell on deaf ears.[80]

Golitsyn, given the code name AELADLE, became the first Soviet defector in two years. When he arrived in Washington one question that the CIA wanted answered was: Did the KGB have a mole in the CIA or other intelligence agency? The CIA official responsible for protecting the agency from such moles was James Jesus Angleton. Angleton was forty-four years old at the time, having been born in Boise, Idaho, on December 9, 1917. His father, James Hugh Angleton, had served under General John H. "Black Jack" Pershing in Mexico, chasing Pancho Villa. In 1933 he took the family to Italy, having purchased the local National Cash Register franchise.[81]

Angleton's success allowed the family to occupy a palazzo in Milan. James Jesus attended a British preparatory school, Malvern College, and returned to Italy for the summers. Malvern was followed in 1937 by Yale, where he helped establish an influential poetry journal, *Furioso*. Graduation in 1941 was followed by service in the infantry, where the OSS found

---

* The Canadian aspect of the molehunt is discussed in Chapter 24.

and recruited him that same year. In London he received his introduction to counterintelligence as a member of the OSS's X-2 section.[82]

Angleton rose quickly through the OSS and, after the Normandy invasion, was sent to Rome. By war's end he had become the counterintelligence chief for Italy and one his first postwar tasks was to help the Italians rebuild their intelligence capability. In 1947 he joined the CIA, and the following year he was involved in the CIA's attempt to influence the Italian elections.[83]

In early 1951 Angleton became the first head of the Special Operations Group, which handled liaison with the young Israeli intelligence services. It would be a position he would hold for over twenty years. But his primary function during his last twenty-one years in the CIA began in late 1954, as a result of the report of the Doolittle Commission, established by DCI Allen Dulles in 1954 to review CIA clandestine operations, which recommended "the intensification of the CIA's counterintelligence efforts to prevent or detect and eliminate penetrations of CIA."[84]

Dulles appointed Angleton to head the newly created Counterintelligence Staff. To consider the possibility that the CIA had been penetrated by the KGB, Angleton quickly established the Special Investigation Group. The SIG became a small, very elite unit. In 1962 it was staffed by eight trusted and uncommunicative officers.[85]

Angleton, though, did not initially have responsibility for debriefing Golitsyn. That was the task of the Soviet Russia Division, headed by David Murphy. And there were significant limits to what Golitsyn could tell Murphy. His job in the NATO Section had been writing a digest of intelligence on NATO, based on the reports from the KGB's foreign sources. Although he saw their reporting, he was not told their identity. As a result, he could only offer clues, which when combined with information from other defectors, or information developed in a investigation, might pinpoint the Soviet spies. His clues aided the unmasking of Admiralty spy John Vassall; John Watkins, a former Canadian diplomat; and Canadian professor Hugh Hambleton, who had worked in NATO.[86]

Golitsyn also suggested that the SDECE had been penetrated by a ring of KGB agents. That suggestion led to a letter from President Kennedy to President de Gaulle, delivered by courier in the spring of 1962, informing him that according to a Soviet defector the French government, including its secret services, had been penetrated by the KGB. De Gaulle ordered General Jean-Louis du Temple de Rougemont, director of the General Staff's intelligence division, to go to Washington to talk to the defector.[87]

Rougemont was sufficiently impressed by his discussions with Golitsyn that in May 1962 a joint DST-SDECE team arrived in Washington to conduct a more detailed debriefing. From the French, Golitsyn received another code name: MARTEL. From Golitsyn the French heard some stunning accusations. In addition to alleging that an influential Frenchman working at NATO was passing documents to the KGB and that the

KGB had infiltrated de Gaulle's entourage, he also claimed that the SDECE had been seriously penetrated by the KGB. The penetration allegedly consisted of a ring of twelve agents, informally code-named SAPPHIRE. The SAPPHIRE agents, Golitsyn reported, allowed General Sakharovsky, head of the KGB's First Chief Directorate, to brag in 1959 that he was in possession of all the SDECE's reorganization plans. MARTEL also informed his debriefers that the Soviets were aware of plans to establish, at de Gaulle's request, a special SDECE section for scientific intelligence, targeted at the United States.[88]*

Golitsyn's relations with the CIA's Soviet Russia Division began to deteriorate within a few months of his arrival. Indications that he could be difficult began appearing before he had even arrived in Washington, when he complained about the lack of a special CIA plane to fly him to the United States. He began to exhibit indications of paranoia and an inflated view of his importance, demanding to see President Kennedy, as well as $15 million to organize the overthrow of the Soviet government.[89]

Complaints about Golitsyn grew, and in the absence of any further hard information, the Soviet Russia Division was only too willing, in late 1962, to turn him over to Angleton and his Counterintelligence Staff—an action that made sense because the defector had begun to claim that not only the CIA but the British, French, and Norwegian intelligence services were also penetrated, and Angleton's staff was responsible for liaison with those services.[90]

During this time, with his status with the CIA on shaky ground, Golitsyn reconsidered a long-standing offer from MI5 to travel to Britain. He had already been visited twice by Arthur Martin, a senior MI5 official, during 1962. Martin, an aggressive counterintelligence officer and friend of Angleton's, indicated that Golitsyn would certainly be welcome if he chose to visit. With Philby not forgotten, and the Blake case fresh in his mind, Martin's fear was of yet more moles.[91]

---

* Golitsyn's charges did have an impact within the French government and on U.S.–French relations. Outside the SDECE the suspects included Jacques Focart, de Gaulle's personal adviser on intelligence and security matters, Louis Joxe, who held a position similar to vice premier, and diplomat George Gorse, who had served on missions to the Soviet Union. Investigations produced no evidence that any of them was a Soviet agent.

Within the SDECE Golitsyn's accusations touched several high officials, including deputy head Colonel Léonard Hounau and counterintelligence chief Colonel René Delseny. The consequence was a November 1963 visit from the SDECE's Colonel Lannurien, who carried a letter of complaint from the SDECE to DCI John McCone. De Lannurien himself later became a suspect.

The dissatisfaction with Golitsyn's accusations, along with the relationship between the CIA and the SDECE station chief in Washington, Philip de Thiraud de Vosjoli, led to a break in French–U.S. intelligence relations in 1964. For the next three years the United States was denied access to French communications intelligence.

According to Faligot and Krop, de Lanurrien arrived in November to interrogate MARTEL. After he returned and spoke to SDECE chief General Paul Jacquier, Hounau was dismissed as a result of Golitsyn's accusations. Roger Faligot and Pascal Krop, *La Piscine: The French Secret Service since 1944* (New York: Basil Blackwell, 1989). pp. 210–29.

During his short stay Golitsyn, code-named KAGO by the British, met with Martin, MI5's chief scientist Peter Wright, and SIS officer Stephen de Mowbray. The interaction between the four produced charges concerning Soviet moles in Britain and what Golitsyn called the "Strategic Deception Plot." Martin was already suspicious of MI5's deputy director Graham Mitchell. When Golitsyn told his hosts that, after the Philby affair, he had heard talk of a "Ring of Five" in the KGB, they concluded that the fifth spy was Mitchell. (The other four were clearly Philby, Blunt, Burgess, and Maclean.) Thus Mitchell, who they code-named PETERS, was the first target.[92]

Golitsyn, based on a conversation he had at KGB headquarters and MI5's suspicion's concerning the death of Labour party leader Hugh Gaitskell, concluded that Gaitskell had been assassinated by the KGB to clear the way for Harold Wilson. As with many of Golitsyn's charges, it was based far more heavily on extrapolation and deduction than solid information. But it was enough, despite its logical flaws, for Martin to open an investigation designated OATSHEAF.[93]*

In addition, Golitsyn, possibly with encouragement from his hosts, explicated on the existence of the Strategic Deception Plot. In 1958 the KGB had elevated the importance of disinformation and established a Department D in the KGB's First Chief Directorate. The East European satellite services dutifully followed suit. Golitsyn reported that the Soviets had a master plan to manipulate the West into believing that some form of détente might be possible. In addition, Golitsyn suggested that the apparently growing Chinese–Soviet split was nothing but a fake to deceive the West, as was the Albanian–Soviet split.[94]

Golitsyn's stay in Britain was cut short due to a garbled press leak concerning his presence. Although his stay produced 153 investigative leads (known as "serials"), the then head of SIS, Sir Dick Goldsmith White, called it a "rotten harvest." He found Golitsyn full of ideas and theories but possessing few facts. Even Angleton concluded in the fall of 1963 that Martin had no case against Mitchell. It was a view shared by the FBI.[95]†

Once back in the United States Golitsyn fully spelled out his theories and claims to Angleton, who bought them all—the Strategic Deception

---

* Golitsyn and Martin ignored the fact that at the time of Gaitskell's death his likely successor was the very anticommunist George Brown. A similar charge made by Golitsyn was that the Israeli foreign minister at the time, Golda Meir, was a KGB agent. His conclusion stemmed from his impression that an Israeli VIP visiting the Soviet Union in 1957 was a KGB agent, and Golda Meir was the only Israeli VIP to visit during that time.

† Martin and Wright responded by simply shifting targets. Their new candidate was Sir Roger Henry Hollis, director of MI5, who they code-named DRAT. The investigation was conducted by the FLUENCY Committee, with Martin as chairman. A five-year effort by the committee produced no convincing evidence against Hollis. However, the "Hollis was a spy" thesis has produced numerous books and much controversy. No subsequent Soviet defector has given credence to the charge. Defector Oleg Gordievsky has specifically stated that neither Hollis nor Mitchell was a mole.

Plan, Gaitskell and Wilson, and the mole in the CIA. There was little Angleton could do about the first two, but the primary mission of the Counterintelligence Staff was to prevent and detect penetration of the agency.* Thus Angleton, with the help of Golitsyn, began a molehunt that would have serious negative consequences for the CIA for at least a decade.

In November 1964 the molehunt, officially designated HONETOL, began. What followed was the investigation of at least forty senior CIA officers. At least fourteen became official suspects and were examined closely.[96]

From November 1964 to April 1965 the molehunt was directed by a joint CIA-FBI committee, whose CIA members, including Angleton, were drawn from the Counterintelligence Staff and the Office of Security. In that period the committee investigated fourteen main CIA suspects, an effort which cost hundreds of thousands of dollars. CIA officer Leonard McCoy observed: "At the height of HONETOL the FBI seemed to be following more suspect CIA officers in the United States than they were following KGB agents."[97]

Golitsyn had offered five items of information about the mole: the suspect's name began with a K, it possibly ended with a -ski, he had worked in Germany, he was of Slavic descent, and his KGB code name was SASHA. That was sufficient to ruin the careers of numerous CIA officers. One was Peter Karlow, who had worked in Berlin and whose original family name was Klibanksi. Despite the failure of the CIA and FBI to find any information against him, Karlow was forced to resign in September 1963, after twenty-two years of government service.[98]

It was not long before Golitsyn and the molehunt began to have a negative impact on the CIA's collection activities. In 1964 Soviet Russia Division chief David Murphy cautioned overseas stations to "back away, take it easy, and be careful" of all Soviet contacts. William E. Colby, CIA director from 1973 to 1976, recalled that "Soviet operations came to a dead halt." Rather than running the expected thirty or more sources inside the Soviet Union, the division had only five sources.[99]

Angleton's suspicions of other Soviet defectors, all of whom Golitsyn proclaimed to be fakes designed to distract the CIA from his revelations, led to underutilization of their information, or worse. NICK NACK was a GRU officer who occasionally contacted the FBI while on temporary assignment in New York. NICK NACK's first contact was in the early 1960s (the second would be around 1972). Angleton dismissed NICK NACK (dubbed MORINE by the CIA) as a provocation and refused to distribute his information to foreign intelligence services. Fortunately, the FBI passed his information on to the British, who subsequently ar-

---

* Angleton did journey to Britain in 1964 after Harold Wilson became Prime Minister. He told his friends in MI5 that he had new and secret information confirming their suspicions. However, they would have to agree not to pass the information on. Since convincing evidence would require drastic action, the MI5 officers did not agree.

rested Frank Brossard, an engineer in the Air Ministry, and Dr. Giuseppe Martelli of the Atomic Energy Authority.[100]

Yuri Ivanovich Nosenko suffered a worse fate than simply being ignored. An eleven-year veteran of the KGB when he defected in Geneva in 1964, Nosenko had worked in naval intelligence, analyzing both open-source information and intercepts of U.S. military communications. During his KGB career he alternated between the Second Chief Directorate's First Department, which monitored American embassy employees and journalists in the Soviet Union, and the Seventh Department, which had been created in 1955 to recruit agents from Western tourists visiting the Soviet Union. He was the first senior officer from the Second Chief Directorate to defect.[101]

In 1962, when Nosenko first contacted the CIA in Geneva, he provided information on Soviet surveillance directed at the U.S. embassy in Geneva, Soviet security operations at their Geneva embassy, candidates for recruitment among Soviet personnel in Geneva, KGB operations directed against the U.S. embassy in Moscow, the KGB's 1952 recruitment of a code clerk in the U.S. embassy in Moscow, and the location of fifty-two microphones planted in the Moscow embassy. He also provided information that led to the arrests of John Vassall and U.S. Army sergeant Robert Lee Johnson.[102]

Nosenko planned to disclose new information when he defected in 1964. That information concerned an alternate Politburo member he felt might be susceptible to sexual blackmail, a U.S. Army major who had spied for the Soviets in Berlin and Washington, and an official at NATO headquarters who had given the KGB top-secret cryptographic material.[103]

But Nosenko, dubbed AEFOXTROT by the CIA, ran afoul of Golitsyn, who labeled him a false defector, one more attempt by the KGB to discredit him. Even before his arrival in Washington, Angleton, his CIA contact in Geneva, David Murphy, and DCI John McCone had all been persuaded that Nosenko was a KGB plant.[104]

His position was further weakened by lies he told the CIA to gain their acceptance as an agent, and then to force their hand in accepting his defection.* In addition, he claimed to have seen Lee Harvey Oswald's KGB file, and he asserted that not only did the KGB have no role in President Kennedy's assassination, but it had never debriefed Oswald. This struck Angleton and others as rather odd, given Oswald's service at a Japanese base for the top-secret U-2 missions.[105]

In two other cases, Nosenko offered far less sinister explanations of

---

* It was standard CIA policy to encourage potential defectors to remain in place, which would be advantageous in two regards: the CIA would continue to have access to information from their source, and the Soviets would not take countermeasures to reduce damage from the information in U.S. hands. Nosenko invented an ominous recall telegram to make it appear that he had no choice but defection. See Gordon Brook-Shepherd, *The Storm Birds: Soviet Post-War Defectors* (London: Weidenfeld & Nicolson, 1988), p. 185.

certain events than Golitsyn. He suggested that a 1957 visit to the United States by the KGB's V. M. Kovshuk involved contacting a low-level source, code-named ANDREY, not the highly placed mole Golitsyn claimed such a visit implied. And rather than Peter Popov having been betrayed by a CIA mole, Nosenko claimed that it was routine surveillance of an American diplomat.[106]

As a result of suspicions about his bona fides, Nosenko spent from August 14, 1965, to October 27, 1967, in solitary confinement at a tiny cement house at the CIA's training facility at Camp Peary, Virginia (formally known as the Armed Forces Experimental Training Center). During that period he was subject to hostile interrogation and numerous prolonged lie detector tests, some of which were rigged to indicate he was lying.[107]*

Nosenko's status changed only after internal studies raised questions about the handling of his case and observed that Nosenko had provided an enormous amount of useful information. On October 28, 1967, primary responsibility for Nosenko was transferred from the Soviet Russia Division to the Office of Security. In October 1968 Director of Central Intelligence Richard Helms agreed to begin the process of releasing Nosenko. In March 1969 he became a CIA consultant at $16,500 a year. In April he was released from all security restrictions. No subsequent Soviet defector cast doubt on Nosenko being a true defector. Those who had specific information backed his legitimacy.[108]

---

* The prime mover in the decision to imprison Nosenko and subject him to hostile interrogation was David Murphy, with Angleton's consent. See Samuel Halpern and Hayden Peake, "Did Angleton Jail Nosenko?" *International Journal of Intelligence and Counterintelligence* 3, no. 4 (1989): 451–64.

18

Technological Espionage

In early 1960 Allen Dulles and Richard Bissell requested the resumption of what had become a somewhat dormant U-2 program. There had been no deep overflights of Soviet territory since the September 1959 Camp David meeting between Eisenhower and Khrushchev. With a summit meeting scheduled for May, a concerned Eisenhower offered a prescient comment on February 8. He noted that "he [had] one tremendous asset in a summit meeting . . . his reputation for honesty. If one of these aircraft were lost when we were engaged in apparently sincere deliberations, it would be put on display in Moscow and ruin the President's effectiveness."[1]

Dulles and Bissell wanted to obtain photographs of ICBM launch sites in the northern Urals and westward near the White Sea, as well as bomber bases, factories, and other installations. Eisenhower approved a mission, and the resulting April 9 overflight produced photography indicating that the Soviet ICBM program was progressing at a much faster rate than anticipated. Unfortunately, the quality of the photographs was less than desired, so Dulles and Bissell requested approval for another mission. The main target would be the ICBM facility at Plesetsk, where the April 9 flight found evidence of an operational ICBM facility.[2]

The mission, Dulles and Bissell argued, would be far above average in importance. A delay until after the summit would risk losing the opportunity to photograph the missiles, which might be camouflaged by then. In addition, climatic conditions limited the months when a productive mission could be flown to April through July. If the mission were postponed until July and the weather was poor, there would be no opportunity to photograph the Plesetsk site until the following April. Dulles and Bissell's arguments proved convincing to Eisenhower; on April 25 he authorized another mission. Eisenhower's military aide, General Andrew Goodpaster, informed Bissell that one additional mission could be flown prior to May 1, but none after May 1.[3]

Goodpaster's instruction, probably inadvertently, left open the possibility of flying on May 1. On that day Francis Gary Powers took off from Peshawar on a flight that was scheduled to conclude at Bodø, Norway. The flight would take him over the heart of the Soviet Union—over the Tyuratam Cosmodrome to monitor any space-launching activity that might have been scheduled to coincide with the May Day celebration; an industrial complex at Sverdlovsk; the primary target at Plesetsk; and finally on to Archangel and Murmansk to collect information on activities at the long-range bomber, submarine, and other military bases in the area.[4]

Powers never made it to Norway. At five o'clock on the morning of May 1, Nikita Khrushchev received a call from Minister of Defense Rodion Malinovsky, who informed him that a U-2 had entered Soviet air space and was headed toward Sverdlovsk. Khrushchev ordered the plane be brought down by any means necessary. And somewhere over Sverdlovsk, Powers's plane was brought down. Believing Powers dead, the United States invoked the U-2's cover as a weather research plane, claiming it had simply strayed off course. When Khrushchev produced not only the plane's cameras, but its pilot—alive and well—Eisenhower admitted the U-2's mission and accepted personal responsibility. Eisenhower's statements forced Khrushchev's hand, and the Soviet leader canceled the summit.[5]

The incident resulted in cancellation not only of the summit, but of overflights of Soviet territory. While the CIA initially "suspended" operations over the Soviet Union for seven months and adopted a wait-and-see attitude concerning possible future overflights, there was no great expectation that another U-2 would ever be permitted to overfly the Soviet Union.[6]*

But the United States would soon have another means of peering into the Soviet interior—photoreconnaissance satellites. Those initial satellites marked the beginning of a decade-long expansion, by both the United States and the Soviet Union, of their technological capabilities for spying on each other and the rest of the world. It would be a decade during which each side's "technical collection systems" would not be lacking in targets, as each superpower dramatically expanded its nuclear arsenal, as China joined the nuclear club, as the United States and the Soviet Union nearly came to blows over Cuba, as Israel and the Arabs engaged in another war, and as the Soviets invaded Czechoslovakia and fought with the Chinese.

---

* The end of overflights did not by any means result in the end of the U-2 program. Over the the next thirty-plus years U-2s would be employed in both peripheral and overflight reconnaissance missions against targets in Asia, the Middle East, Central America, and the Caribbean, and for disaster relief purposes in the United States. In 1960 U-2 targets outside the Soviet Union included the Israeli nuclear facility at Dimona and the French nuclear test site in the Sahara. Seymour Hersh, *The Samson Option: Israel's Nuclear Arsenal and American Foreign Policy* (New York: Random House, 1991), p. 63.

CORONA

Just over three months after the shootdown of Powers's U-2 another United States reconnaissance program produced its first images of the Soviet interior. The program's origins could be traced back to 1946 and the work of a U.S. Air Force think tank based in Santa Monica, California.

On May 2, 1946, the RAND Corporation published a *Preliminary Design for an Experimental World Circling Spacecraft*. The 324-page study concluded that it was possible, with minor advances in the technology of the time, to develop a launch vehicle to place a spacecraft in orbit, although the payload would be limited to less than 2,000 pounds.[7]

Another RAND report on the subject of satellites followed on February 1, 1947. *Reference Papers Relating to a Satellite Study* contained two papers on the potential uses of satellite reconnaissance. James Lipp, head of the RAND satellite project, examined the feasibility of using electro-optical systems to conduct reconnaissance and transmit their images using television-type technology.[8]

Further RAND work on the subject of satellite reconnaissance continued into the early 1950s. But those studies ran up against Air Force skepticism concerning the feasibility and value of the images that could be produced. That skepticism did not preclude further study, and on March 1, 1954, RAND published its two-volume Project FEEDBACK report on the feasibility and value of satellite reconnaissance.[9]

The Project FEEDBACK report did not produce an immediate rush to authorize development of a satellite reconnaissance vehicle. But on November 27, 1954, the Western Development Division (WDD) of the Air Research and Development Command issued Systems Requirement No. 5, "System Requirement for an Advanced Reconnaissance System."[10]

The idea was given an important additional impetus on February 14, 1955, when President Eisenhower was presented with the report of the Technological Capabilities Panel, which he had established to investigate how advanced technology could be applied to defense and intelligence activities. The TCP's report, *Meeting the Challenge from Surprise Attack*, stated:

> We must find ways to increase the number of hard facts upon which our intelligence estimates are based, to provide better strategic warning, to minimize surprise in the kind of attack, and to reduce the danger of gross overestimation or gross underestimation of the threat. To this end, we recommend the adoption of a vigorous program for the extensive use, in many intelligence procedures, of the most advanced knowledge in science and technology.

Among the report's recommendations was the development of a satellite reconnaissance system.[11]

A month later, on March 16, 1955, the Air Force issued General Operational Requirement No. 80, officially establishing a requirement for an advanced reconnaissance satellite. While RAND continued to study reconnaissance satellite concepts, including electro-optical and film recovery, interested contractors developed their proposals. And on October 12, 1956, the Air Force awarded a contract to the Lockheed Corporation to develop Weapon Systen 117L (WS-117L), the Advanced Reconnaissance System.[12]

WS-117L would, in fact, come to comprise three projects, which would subsequently be separated. The MIDAS (Missile Defense Alarm System) would be devoted to developing a spacecraft with infrared sensors that could detect Soviet missile launches. The DISCOVERER project would focus on the development of a recoverable space capsule. The core of WS-117L was Project SENTRY (subsequently SAMOS), the aim of which was to develop a reconnaissance satellite that would radio its images back to earth. The images would be recorded on film, the film would be electronically scanned, and the images would be turned into a series of electronic signals, which could then be transmitted to a suitable ground station. Back on earth, those electronic signals could be reassembled into a picture.[13]

On February 7, 1958, concerned about problems that had arisen in the SAMOS program, President Eisenhower authorized a second satellite reconnaissance program, based on DISCOVERER. The new project, given the code name CORONA, would be run by the CIA and Richard Bissell. The objective of CORONA would be to develop a satellite that recorded its images on film and returned the film to earth for analysis.[14]

A little less than a year later, on January 21, 1959, the first CORONA test vehicle was ready for launch. In the intervening year Bissell's CIA technicians had worked on developing a reliable and adequate camera system, as well as a reliable system for recovering the film capsule when it had been ejected from the spacecraft. But there was no camera system or capsule on board, the first priority being to determine that the rocket could place a spacecraft in the proper orbit.

The launch planned for January 21 had to be canceled due to an accident that damaged the rocket's first stage. It was five weeks later, on February 28, that *Discoverer 1* was placed into a 114- by 697-mile orbit. But subsequent attempts to eject and recover a capsule met with failure after failure—encompassing eleven launches and eighteen months.[15]

On August 10, 1960, three months and nine days after the last U-2 overflight of the Soviet Union, *Discoverer 13* went into orbit. The next day it ejected a capsule. Although the primary method of recovery (by an airplane equipped with a special device to snag the capsule's parachute) failed, the backup method (recovery from the ocean) was successful.[16]

Discoverer 13 did not contain camera equipment, so there was no film inside the capsule. But *Discoverer 14*, orbited on August 18, would carry a camera system into space, making it the first operational CORONA mission. After some difficulty, the satellite obtained an orbit of 113 by 502 miles, with an 80-degree inclination, which allowed it to overfly all of the

Soviet Union. As it began to pass over Soviet territory, its camera began to operate as programmed. Its first photos were of the Mys-Schmidta Air Base in the Soviet Far East, about 400 miles from Nome, Alaska.[17]

After the film capsule was recovered the next day, in the air, it was shipped back to Washington to be studied by the interpreters at the CIA's Photographic Interpretation Center. As was the case with U-2 missions, CIA representatives briefed the interpreters on the targets of interest. There was a dramatic flair to the CORONA/*Discoverer 14* briefing. After the photointerpreters filled the auditorium, PIC director Arthur Lundahl announced that it was "something new and great we've got here." Jack Gardner, who was Lundahl's deputy, opened a curtain that showed a map of the Soviet Union. Instead of a single squiggly line across the map, there were six or seven vertical stripes emanating from the poles and moving diagonally across the Soviet Union. The interpreters knew that those stripes represented the portions of the Soviet Union that had passed under *Discoverer 14*'s camera and their immediate reaction was to cheer. After being briefed on what to look for, especially for missile sites at Plesetsk, they began work on OAK-8001, the first photointerpretation report based on satellite photography. The photos were dark and of poor quality, with a resolution in the area of 50 to 100 feet. But to Andrew Goodpaster they were "like the dog that walks on its hind legs, remarkable that it happens at all."[18]

The remainder of 1960 saw continued launchings of CORONA, the approval on August 25 of plans to establish a special secret office (the National Reconnaissance Office) to provide centralized management to the aerospace reconnaissance program, and the first attempt at a SAMOS launch. The CORONA launches (*Discoverers 15–19*) apparently added little intelligence to that returned by *Discoverer 14*. The launch of *Samos 1* failed, with the satellite never reaching orbit. On January 31, 1961, *Samos 2* went into orbit, but it produced no more of value than *Samos 1*. In fact, the subsequent SAMOS launches failed to produce any useful photography, and the program was terminated after five to ten launches, in 1962 or 1963.[19]

But while SAMOS made no contribution to the intelligence community's knowledge of events in the Soviet Union, CORONA did. From mid-June 1961 (with a launch on June 16) through the end of the year, good photographs were recovered from several satellites. A CORONA mission that began on August 30 provided enough detail to confirm Plesetsk as the first Soviet ICBM site and to establish what such a site looked like. The photographs showed the SS-6 ICBM in a launching site identical to the configuration that existed at Tyuratam.[20]

The Missile Gap Disappears

The impact of the CORONA photography was devastating. For several years the National Intelligence Estimates (NIEs) had predicted quite sizable Soviet ICBM deployments by the early 1960s, deployments that threatened the security of the United States. The belief that there was an imminent missile gap in the Soviet favor had become an issue in the 1960 presidential campaign, with candidate John Kennedy using the gap as a prime example of Republican weakness with respect to defense.

Several years before the campaign, by the time "Main Trends in Soviet Capabilities and Policies 1957–1962" was published in November 1957, the Soviets had already tested an ICBM and it was believed that they might have about ten prototype ICBMs for use in 1959 or even earlier, depending on accuracy and reliability requirements.[21]

A little over a year later, in NIE 11-4-58 of December 23, 1958, the intelligence community stated its belief that the Soviets intended to acquire a sizable ICBM operational capability at the earliest practicable date. The NIE also pointed out the absence of sufficient evidence to judge conclusively the magnitude and pace of the Soviet program to produce and deploy ICBMs. However, based on indirect evidence, including production capacity and capacity to construct launch facilities, to establish logistic lines, and to train operational units, the intelligence community believed the Soviets "could achieve an operational capability with 500 ICBMs about three years after the first operational date [1959]."[22]

Over the next several years that judgment was revised downward, in the absence of intelligence to sustain its earlier high estimates of the pace of Soviet ICBM deployments. The 1959 NIE estimated that the Soviets might have 140 to 200 ICBMs on launchers by mid-1961 and, speculatively, 250 to 350 by mid-1962 and 350 to 450 by mid-1963. Though smaller than earlier estimates, they were consistent with an effective Soviet missile attack that would destroy the vulnerable strategic bomber bases of the Strategic Air Command, particularly since it was believed that improvements in the accuracy and reliability of Soviet ICBMs had sharply reduced the number required to effectively attack the U.S. target system.[23]

The December 1960 NIE "Main Trends in Soviet Capabilities and Forces 1960-1965," reflected different views by various intelligence organizations. As might be expected, the Air Force took the most pessimistic view, predicting 200 ICBMs by mid-1961, some 450 by mid-1962, and 700 by mid-1963; the CIA predicted 150, 270, and 400 for the same periods. At the low end were the Air Force's military rivals. The Army and Navy jointly predicted deployments of 50, 125, and 200.[24]

Between the December 1960 NIE and that issued on January 10, 1962, the Kennedy administration had taken office, pledging to eliminate the missile gap that candidate Kennedy had loudly and persistently claimed existed. Among the first things Robert McNamara did after being sworn in as Secretary of Defense on January 20, 1961, was to go with his Deputy Secretary, Roswell Gilpatric, a former Air Force secretary, to the Air Force intelligence office at the Pentagon.[25]

McNamara wanted to see if the Soviets had truly attained strategic superiority, and its extent, so that he could plan measures to close the gap. He and Gilpatric spent many hours, over a period of three weeks,

examining the CORONA photos. The images failed to support the estimates of Air Force intelligence. The Soviet ICBM, the SS-6, was huge,
heavy, and cumbersome. It required an extensive support and security
apparatus and would have to be moved about on railroad tracks or extremely heavy roads. CORONA missions were producing photographs all
along and around the railroad tracks and major highways of the Soviet
Union, showing no missiles.[26]

McNamara's conclusions were made public at a February news conference, which McNamara believed would be an off-the-record affair. The
first question concerned whether there was a missile gap. His response,
that "there were no signs of a Soviet crash effort to build ICBM's" and that
no missile gap existed, set off a stampede of reporters to the phones.
McNamara remembers that "all hell broke loose" and "you couldn't hold
the door locked."[27]

McNamara's statement didn't completely reassure the intelligence
community, which was concerned that Soviet ICBMs might be located in
areas not photographed or that had been camouflaged. NIE 11-8-61 of June
1961 argued that the Soviets might have 50 to 100 operational ICBM
launchers and, therefore, the ability to bring all SAC operational air bases
under attack with their force. In any case, the estimate concluded that the
Soviets would have 100 to 200 operational launchers within the next year
and would almost certainly be able to attack then.[28]

But by September 1961 new intelligence had a dramatic impact on
intelligence community estimates. One item was a top secret report,
"The Soviet ICBM Program," which was based on information from Penkovskiy. The report had been distributed on May 16, 1961, but apparently
too late to have an impact on the June NIE. In the interval there was far
more time to reflect on its implications. It stated that, according to Penkovskiy, Khrushchev's statements regarding substantial Soviet ICBM
tests, production, and deployment represented a bluff. The study further
recounted Penkovskiy's view that while the Soviets had the capability of
firing one or two test ICBMs, they did not even have hundreds of test
missiles, but only tens.[29]

Based on Penkovskiy's reporting, Ed Proctor, chief of the Directorate of
Intelligence's ad hoc guided missile task force, proposed revised estimates
of the number of ICBMs the Soviets might have in the 1961 to 1965
period. Proctor estimated that the Soviets then had 25 or fewer ICBMs,
would have between 25 and 50 in mid-1962, and would have between 75
and 150 and in mid-1963.[30]

The second, and more conclusive, source was CORONA photography
from July. As a result, NIE 11-8/1-61 of September 21 estimated only 10 to
25 deployed Soviet ICBMs, with no significant increase likely in the
forthcoming months. The expected number of Soviet ICBMs by mid-
1963 was 75 to 125. The Soviets had apparently chosen to deploy only a
small number of first-generation ICBMs and to concentrate their efforts
on a smaller second-generation system for deployment, probably in
1962.[31]

ZENIT

With the launch of *Sputnik I* in 1957 the Soviet Union had scored the first victory in what would be a three-decade space race. But in the crucial area of photographic reconnaissance satellites, it was the United States that jumped ahead, even if its success was not trumpeted. It was an advantage the United States never relinquished, always remaining ahead in crucial areas of reconnaissance satellite technology.

Although the Soviets had less of a need for such a system, they were not far behind. An article in the December 1961 issue of *ONI Review* observed:

> The USSR has a distinct intelligence advantage over the United States in that it is permitted to collect overtly by conventional means much of the intelligence required prior to commencement of hostilities. However, because of a general distrust of the West, and because of the threat posed to the security of the Soviet Union by the Western long-range nuclear strike capability, the Soviets can be expected to develop photoreconnaissance satellites in the 1961–65 time period.[32]

The first successful Soviet photographic reconnaissance satellite, developed under the production code name ZENIT, followed only a few months later, when *Cosmos 4* was launched on April 26, 1962. In its 185- by 205-mile orbit, with a 65-degree inclination, the satellite could view targets throughout the United States.[33]

There were differences in the programs, however. Soviet satellites operated in higher orbits and at lower inclinations than those of the United States, the latter difference being due to the different latitudes which encompassed the two rivals. The higher orbits of the Soviet satellites reduced the atmospheric drag and allowed them to stay in orbit longer, although such orbits limited the detail available in the photographs. In addition, while the United States satellites returned only a film capsule, which was returned to earth over the Pacific Ocean, the entire Soviet satellite was returned to a site within Soviet territory. Thus it was the entire *Cosmos 4* that returned to earth three days after its launch.[34]

Four further photoreconnaissance satellites were orbited in 1962, the final one (*Cosmos 12*) on December 22.* After *Cosmos 12*, the Soviet program was dormant until March 21 of the following year. It was not a matter of problems in the program, but the reality of the Soviet winter. A small error in retroburn timing could mean an error of several hundred miles in the location of the module when it returned to earth. Instead of landing on the flat plains of Kazakhstan, the capsule would land deep in a snow-covered forest.[35]

The March 21 satellite remained in orbit eight days. The next month marked the first time the Soviets placed two photographic reconnaissance

---

* The COSMOS designation did not necessarily signify a reconnaissance satellite. The designation was used for almost all Soviet satellites.

satellites, *Cosmos 15* and *16*, in orbit in the same month. *Cosmos 16* became the first Soviet reconnaissance satellite with a double-digit life-time, ten days.[36]

In November, the Soviet Union launched the first of a series of second-generation reconnaissance satellites. The satellite probably carried a bigger film supply and higher-resolution optics. It was recovered after six days. The record for 1963 was a total of seven successful launches.[37]

Expanding the Net

The success of the United States in developing and orbiting photographic reconnaissance satellites was only the first step in the 1960s effort to develop and deploy an increasingly sophisticated and extensive network of technical sensors to monitor developments across the planet. By the end of 1963 there were at least two important additions to the U.S. space reconnaissance effort. The United States had established a constellation of ELINT (electronic intelligence) satellites in 300-mile circular orbits that monitored Soviet, Chinese, and other air defense and ICBM warning radars. Such information was crucial in preparing to neutralize (through electronic countermeasures) or destroy those radars in the event of war.[38]

In July 1963 the U.S. "close-look" photographic reconnaissance satellite program, code-named GAMBIT, became operational, with the launch of spacecraft carrying the KH-7 camera system.* Whereas the CORONA satellites provided pictures of broad areas, the purpose of the GAMBIT program was to provide detailed pictures of much smaller targets. To do this, KH-7 satellites operated at lower altitudes than the CORONA's. Two of the four KH-7 satellites launched in 1963 dipped to as low as seventy-six and eighty-seven miles above the earth. Although technical problems would prevent the first photography from being obtained before 1964, when that photography was returned it would have a resolution of eighteen inches.[39]

In August a new version of CORONA was launched, with the KH-4A camera system. The camera systems on CORONA had progressed dramatically since the first launches provided photos with resolutions of 50–100 feet. The KH-4A system could provide images with 10-foot resolution.[40]

---

*In 1962 the United States created an elaborate structure for the classification for intelligence produced by certain types of intelligence collection systems and for information about those systems. The code names for satellite and certain aerial reconnaissance programs (e.g., CORONA, GAMBIT) were part of the BYEMAN system. The optical systems used on photoreconnaissance satellites were designated KEYHOLE (KH), followed by a number. The CORONA camera system then being used was designated the KH-4, because three previous camera systems had been used on CORONA satellites. The KH-5 and KH-6 designations were assigned to the optical systems associated with two short-lived special-purpose programs, ARGON and LANYARD. The GAMBIT camera system was the seventh system, not counting the SAMOS system (which was ignored), employed in the photographic satellite effort.

The value of satellite photography was addressed at a December 5, 1963, CIA briefing to the National Security Council on Soviet military strength. The CIA told the council that "by far ou[r] best source [of intelligence] is reconnaissance satellite photography." Satellite photography, the CIA explained, gave the United States "solid coverage of all the large cities, all but one of the key submarine bases, all of the heavy bomber bases, and [deleted] percent of the rail network of the USSR." With respect to Soviet ICBM complexes, the CIA believed that it had "identified all of them."[41]

Once the GAMBIT program became fully operational in 1964 the GAMBIT and CORONA programs worked in tandem. A CORONA mission, during which film would be returned at two intervals, would produce a broad view of portions of the Soviet Union, eastern Europe, or China. Based, in part, on the examination of the CORONA photographs, targets would be selected for the GAMBIT/KH-7 mission that would inevitably follow the end of a CORONA mission.

On July 29, 1966, a *Titan 3B–Agena D* blasted off from Vandenberg Air Force Base with a new camera system, the KH-8, for the GAMBIT program. Eleven days after that launch a new camera system for the CORONA program, the KH-4B, was launched into space. The KH-4B offered improved resolution over its predecessor: objects with any dimensions of five feet or more could be spotted by the new camera system.[42]

After four years of operation, the KH-4A and KH-7 programs were terminated in 1967, with the KH-4B and KH-8 becoming the sole photographic satellites. The KH-4A program concluded on March 30, 1967, with its forty-sixth successful launch in fifty-one launchings. The mean lifetime was 23.6 days. The KH-7 program concluded with the successful launch of June 4, 1967. Thirty-six of thirty-eight KH-7 launches had successfully placed the close-look satellite in orbit. The mean lifetime was 5.5 days.

The expanded U.S. use of technology for intelligence collection could also be seen in the atmosphere, on the ground, on the sea, and even under the sea. The loss of a U-2 was not a surprise to Allen Dulles and Richard Bissell. They knew that eventually the Soviets would develop countermeasures to the slow-moving U-2. With that eventuality in mind, Bissell, in 1957, had begun thinking of developing a successor to the U-2.[43]

In November 1958 a panel of experts informed Bissell that it appeared feasible to build an aircraft that could fly at a speed and altitude that would make radar tracking very difficult. Bissell and Dulles approached Eisenhower and requested and received funding for the preparation of proposals by contractors (Lockheed and Convair) for development of a high-speed, high-altitude reconnaissance plane.[44]

On August 20, 1959, the Lockheed and Convair proposals were presented a joint Defense Department–Air Force–CIA panel. The proposals were identical with respect to speed (Mach 3.2) and first flight (22 months from contract award), but the Lockheed proposal promised more range

(4,120 vs. 4,000 nautical miles total, and 3,800 vs. 3,400 nautical miles at altitude). Lockheed's Advanced Development Project Office and Kelly Johnson won. The program to develop a new reconnaissance plane was code-named OXCART.[45]

On April 26, 1962, the first OXCART, or A-12 (as Lockheed called it), was taken on an unannounced and unofficial maiden flight. Four days later the A-12 officially lifted off from the runway at the CIA's secret Groom Lake facility in Nevada. It was a modest flight, climbing to 30,000 feet and reaching a speed of 340 knots—a far cry from its future performance.[46]

The CIA's success with OXCART did not go unnoticed by the Air Force. In late 1962 the CIA's main competitor for reconnaissance dollars ordered a fleet of modified A-12s. Among the modifications would be addition of a second seat for the Reconnaissance System Operator (RSO) who would accompany the pilot. Upon being turned over to the Air Force the aircraft would be renamed SR-71.[47]

About two years later, on December 22, 1964, the first SR-71A flight took place at Palmdale, California. By this time the SR-71A's existence had been made public by President Lyndon Johnson, seeking to convince the electorate of his commitment to defense. The plane was 107 feet long, with a wingspan of 55.6 feet, and a fuselage 64 inches in diameter. What the plane looked like to an observer depended on the vantage point, since to "look at a three-view drawing of the SR-71 is to see three totally different aircraft—one like an arrow, another like a flying saucer, and a third like an enormous bat."[48]

It was not until late 1965, after all the problems demonstrated in test flights had been solved, that the CIA's A-12s were declared operational at design specifications. Those single-seaters were capable of flying at Mach 3.6 (2,400 miles per hour), at an altitude of 92,500 feet.[49]

However, it was another eighteen months before an OXCART would actually embark on an operational mission. In May 1967 there was substantial apprehension that surface-to-surface missiles might be introduced into North Vietnam, as well as concern over U.S. ability to detect such a deployment. As result, on May 16, President Johnson approved a proposal for an OXCART mission.[50]

That mission and the others over North Vietnam that followed were code-named BLACK SHIELD. The first mission, lasting three hours and thirty-nine minutes, followed one flight line over North Vietnam and one over the Demilitarized Zone. The cruise legs were flown at Mach 3.1. Of 190 known SAM sites, 70 were photographed, along with 9 other priority targets.[51]

Seven BLACK SHIELD missions followed between May 31 and August 1967. By mid-July it was concluded that there were no surface-to-surface missiles in North Vietnam. Another fifteen missions were flown between August 16 and December 31, 1967. On October 28 a North Vietnamese SAM site fired a single, unsuccesful missile at an OXCART. It represented the first of more than 1,000 missiles that would be unsuccessfully fired at the OXCART/SR-71A over the next thirty years.[52]

But the CIA's A-12/OXCART program would be shot down—by the U.S. Air Force. The United States could not afford two supersonic spy plane programs. When the political fighting ended the Air Force emerged the winner. Early in March 1968 SR-71s, designated SENIOR CROWN by the Air Force, began to arrive at Kadena Air Base, Japan, to take over the BLACK SHIELD mission. On May 21 President Johnson confirmed Secretary of Defense Clark Clifford's decision, made five days earlier, to terminate the A-12/OXCART.[53]

While the A-12/SR-71A was, with the exception of satellites, the most dramatic use of technology for intelligence purposes, it was by no means the only aerial reconnaissance system of importance introduced during the 1960s. The first RC-135, a RC-135B, entered the SAC inventory in December 1965—beginning the replacement of thirty obsolescent RB-47Hs and ERB-47Hs that were then "performing the ELINT portion of the Global Peacetime Airborne Reconnaissance Program."[54]

Over the next thirty years numerous modifications of the RC-135 would be made, with configurations changing to take account of technological advances and changing missions. The primary function of almost all RC-135s would be electronic intelligence–specific targets would include radar systems and the telemetry from missile tests, particularly Soviet radar systems and missile tests.[55]

While KEYHOLE satellites were circling the earth, and OXCARTs and RC-135s were patrolling the skies, the United States was also busy expanding its network of listening posts on land. In 1964 Chicksands, along with a similar installation at San Vito dei Normanni, in Italy, received AN/FLR-9 "Elephant Cage" antennas. The AN/FLR-9 consists of three arrays, each made up of a ring of antenna elements around a circular reflecting screen. In the middle of the triple array is a central building, which contains the electronic equipment for forming the directional beams for monitoring and direction-finding. The entire system is about 900 feet in diameter. Eventually AN/FLR-9s would be located at additional sites in England, Germany, Turkey, Japan, Alaska, the continental United States, and the Philippines.[56]

On August 1, 1966, the National Security Agency took over control of the Menwith Hill station in the United Kingdom, dispossessing the Army Security Agency, which had run the facility since its inception in 1960. Soon after the takeover giant dish-shaped antennas began going up, some accompanied by golfball-like radomes on concrete pedestals.[57]

NSA's takeover marked a reorientiation of Menwith Hill's focus, with increased attention to be given to the collection of strategic intelligence against diplomatic and economic targets. Areas targeted by Menwith Hill included Europe (western and eastern) and the Soviet Union east of the Urals. Additionally, Menwith Hill would serve as a key facility in intercepting Soviet satellite communications.[58]

Turkey continued to host important ground stations in the 1960s, including those at Sinop, Samsun, and Diyarbakir. But the most important U.S. ground stations, at least for monitoring the Soviet missile tests from Tyuratam, were those established in Iran by the mid-1960s. Whereas the Turkish bases would pick up a missile after it had climbed over 250 miles, the Iranian sites could pick up the missiles after 60 miles. Thus the Iranian sites could intercept telemetry from the last moments of the firing of the missile's first stage, whereas the Turkish sites could intercept the telemetry from the last moments of the firing of the missile's second stage. The difference was not inconsequential, for it translated into a greater degree of confidence in the resulting estimates of missile dimensions and throw weight.[59]

Altogether, the United States maintained seven intelligence sites in Iran, probably including a facility for monitoring the seismic signals from Soviet nuclear tests at Semipalatinsk. Two sites were near the western shore of the Caspian Sea, two near Klarabad in the middle of the Caspian's southern shore, two in the northeast, and one at Behshahr. The two major Iranian posts operated by the CIA, known as Tacksman I and Tacksman II, were at Kabkan, forty miles east of Meshed in northeastern Iran, and at Behshahr, on the southeastern corner of the Caspian Sea.[60]

In the 1960s, before the revolutionary changes that shook that region took place, the United States also maintained SIGINT sites in Morocco (Sid Yahia), Libya (Wheelus Air Base), and Kagnew in Ethiopia. The Kagnew site was considered particularly valuable because of the peculiar "ducting" phenomenon, which resulted in communications from the Soviet Union being accessible to Kagnew's antennas. Kagnew was also an example of the hidden impact of intelligence requirements. A Senate subcommittee investigating overseas commitments of the United States, chaired by Stuart Symington, disclosed in 1970 that the Kagnew facility had been obtained from the regime of Haile Selassie in exchange for hundred of millions of dollars in economic and military assistance. Meanwhile, Sid Yahia targeted communications in the Middle East and Africa.[61]

The ducting phenomenon that made Kagnew so valuable was not the strangest phenomenon that the United States attempted to exploit in the 1960s for SIGINT collection. That distinction undoubtedly goes to the "moonbounce" phenomenon. To capitalize on the fact that signals emanating from an area on earth would bounce off the moon and could then be detectable at other locations the United States established Project FLOWER GARDEN in the early 1960s. The objective was to collect intelligence on Soviet radars, using large passive antennas to gather the signals after they bounced off the moon. Among the specific targets, by June 30, 1962, were suspected radars in the Sary Shagan and Kamchatka impact areas. Systems used to receive the signals included the Jodrell Bank Observatory's 250-foot antenna, a 143-foot antenna in Scotland, and a site on the Chesapeake Bay. Successful moonbounce signals were apparently received from TALL KING radars.[62]

Probably the least exotic component of the 1960s U.S. technical collection network were the slow, lumbering ships that were operated by NSA and the Navy to collect communications and signals intelligence. The idea was to emulate the Soviet practice of deploying spy trawlers along the coast of its intelligence targets. NSA official Frank Raven recalled that what was wanted was a ship that "could mosey along a coast relatively slowly, take its time, and spend time at sea."[63]

Two types of spy ships, with the cover designation AGER (Auxiliary General–Environmental Research) and AGTR (Auxiliary General–Technical Research) would be deployed during the 1960s. Their patrols would allow them to monitor the Soviet naval base at Vladivostok, China, North Korea, Cuba, and an assortment of South American, North African, and Middle Eastern countries.[64]

Such missions could prove hazardous, as the crew of the USS *Liberty* discovered when their ship was bombed by Israeli planes during the Six-Day War. On January 8, 1969, the USS *Pueblo* (AGER-2) departed Yokosuka. The *Pueblo*'s mission was to "sample the electronic environment of east coast North Korea [to] determine the nature and extent of naval activity off North Korean ports." On January 23, 1968, fifteen days after departing Yokosuka, one crewman of the *Pueblo* was dead and the rest were in North Korean custody. It was a year before they were to be freed. By that time the AGER-AGTR program had been discontinued.[65]

The year before NSA and the Navy initiated the AGER program, a far more secretive program was approved by President Eisenhower. It was potentially the naval program most likely to cause a serious incident with the Soviet Union. Initially code-named HOLYSTONE, it involved the use of specially equipped attack submarines to collect electronic, communications, and photographic intelligence (the latter through periscope photography). The program's primary target was the Soviet Union, but at times Vietnam and China were targets of the operation.[66]

The missions, which usually lasted about ninety days, were especially dangerous. Not only did the submarines patrol near Soviet ports, but some missions took place inside Soviet naval ports. Not surprisingly, there were some close calls. In 1963 the USS *Swordfish* was covertly monitoring a Soviet naval exercise in the northwestern Pacific, when local military radio traffic experienced a dramatic increase. A Soviet vessel had detected light glinting off the periscope and electronic-intercept antennas of the *Swordfish*, which were a foot or two above the water. With the Soviets chasing, the *Swordfish* dived for cover, and, according to a former crew member, several Soviet ships "spent the better part of two days dropping depth charges here and there" as they chased it off Kamchatka Peninsula.[67]

That chase actually proved to be an intelligence windfall for U.S. naval intelligence analysts. Between the *Swordfish* and a U.S. spy plane flying overhead, the United States was able to record virtually all the radio chatter emanating from the Soviet search vessels. The consequence, according to one crewman, was that "[w]e got to know exactly what the

Soviets' capabilities were" for attempting to trap and destroy the latest U.S. nuclear submarines.[68]

An even closer call occurred in mid-November 1969, involving the SSN-637 Sturgeon-class submarine, the *Gato*, which was monitoring a Soviet sub in transit from the White Sea to the Barents Sea. An error in estimating the speed of the Soviet submarine resulted in a collision between the two vessels, with the Soviet submarine hitting the *Gato* at a ninety-degree angle. The *Gato* was struck in the heavy plating that served as the protective shield around the vessel's nuclear reactor and sustained no serious damage. The *Gato*'s weapons officer immediately took steps to prepare for a confrontation—running down two decks and preparing for orders to arm the SUBROC nuclear torpedo and three smaller nuclear-tipped torpedoes.[69]

Fortunately, the captain of the Soviet submarine appeared to believe it had struck a sea mount or similar underwater object, and the sub surfaced moments later. Subsequently, Soviet ships and planes searched the area. Meanwhile, the *Gato* sailed for two days to reach an area in the Atlantic where it could break radio silence.[70]

While no submarine in the HOLYSTONE program was lost during a mission, one was lost returning from a mission. Part of the secrecy surrounding the USS *Scorpion*, which sank near the Azores with ninety-nine crew members on May 22, 1968, is undoubtedly due to the fact that it was on its way back to Norfolk, Virginia, after having completed a HOLYSTONE mission.[71]

Extending the Net, Soviet Style

While the United States was strengthening its technological capabilities of watching the Soviets, their allies, and other areas of the world, the Soviet Union was expanding its technical collection apparatus. Beginning in 1964 its photographic reconnaissance satellite program began a period of explosive growth. Twelve photoreconnaissance satellites were launched in 1964, nine of the first-generation and three of the high-resolution second-generation models. The final satellite, and its film, never made it back to earth. A retrorocket failure left it marooned in orbit. The Soviets had, however, prepared for such an event; Western space-tracking radars subsequently detected that *Cosmos 50* been blown into ninety-eight fragments.[72]

Over the next three years the number of reconnaissance launches steadily increased. There were seventeen in 1965 (including ten high-resolution satellites), twenty-one in 1966, and twenty-two in 1967.[73]

A 1967 National Intelligence Estimate concluded that the Soviet space reconnaissance program had four major objectives: (1) to allow precise targeting of U.S nuclear forces, especially ICBM sites, and monitoring of the sites' status and deployments, (2) to map areas of general military interest, particularly those bordering the Soviet Union, (3) to monitor the development and testing of new military systems in the United States and Communist China, and (4) to monitor large-scale military and naval activity.[74]

The NIE reported that the low-resolution satellite weighed 10,400 pounds, had a resolution of 10 to 30 feet, and probably also collected ELINT. The higher resolution system was judged to weigh 12,000 pounds and achieve a resolution of 5 to 10 feet.[75]

On March 21, 1968, the first third-generation Soviet photoreconnaissance satellite, a low-resolution model, was launched. In late October the first high-resolution third-generation spacecraft went into orbit. By the end of the year twenty-nine photoreconnaissance spacecraft had been placed in orbit. The same year marked the deployment of a fully operational ELINT satellite constellation, with launches in February (*Cosmos 200*), August (*Cosmos 236*), and October (*Cosmos 250*).[76]

Throughout the 1960s the Soviets continued to expand their fleet of intelligence collection ships, known to the U.S. Navy as AGIs, for Auxiliary–General Intelligence. The initial AGIs were converted Okean-class fishing boats, built in East Germany beginning in 1959. While the equipment carried by such vessels could vary from mission to mission, a typical AGI might carry direction-finding equipment, high-frequency antennas, rod and dipole antennas, and multiple radar receivers.[77]

By 1960 AGI operations had begun. The *Vega* patrolled off the coast of Virginia in April 1960 and entered Long Island Sound to monitor the USS *George Washington*'s launch of a dummy Polaris missile. Similar ships conducted missions off Newfoundland (near the Canadian early warning radar system) and in the Mediterranean during the fall of 1960. In 1961 surveillance of the Polaris base at Charleston, South Carolina, began. Similar surveillance operations were established off U.S. SSBN bases at Rota, Spain, and Apra Harbor, Guam, in 1964 and Holy Loch, Scotland, in 1965 as well as the English Channel, the Turkish and Danish straits, Norway, Alaska, Gibraltar, southern France, Hawaii, and both U.S. coasts.[78]

The extensive Soviet use of such ships was partially a matter of necessity. The Soviets did not have, at the time, a series of allies ringing the United States, on whose territory ground stations could be established. But there was also a certain advantage to relying on AGIs. Whereas even the most advantageously situated of the U.S. ground stations was no closer than several hundred miles from Soviet launch facilities, AGIs could get as close as the three-mile limit allowed. As a result, intercept operators would be in a much better position to capture telemetry and ground communications.[79]

A Valuable Ally

While the United States and the Soviet Union were expanding their technical collection networks, their allies were doing the same, often at the urging and with the financial assistance of the superpowers. The United States, in particular, benefited from the efforts of Canada.

By 1966 Canada's Communication Branch of the National Research Council was operating at least nine SIGINT stations, including stations involved in ocean surveillance operations. Stations at Inuvik, Churchill, and Frobisher Bay were apparently targeted primarily on the Soviet Union, with a particular interest in Soviet air forces and air defense forces. Larry Clark, who worked at the Churchill station (which was closed in 1968), recalled that he first monitored Soviet commercial communication networks and moved on to monitoring Soviet aircraft flights.[80]

The Canadian Forces Station at Alert evidently had the northern Soviet Union as its primary target, although China and other countries' communications may have also been intercepted from that site. In 1974, Alert would be described as "[t]he Defence Department's major electronic eavesdropping post in Canada. Day and night . . . Canadian military personnel intercept and record radio transmissions from the Soviet Union, China, and other countries."[81]

The intercepts from Alert were transmitted to another station, at Leitrim, just a few miles south of Ottawa, where some analysis of the intercepts may have been conducted. The Alert intercepts were also relayed to NSA. The Leitrim facility also intercepted diplomatic communications, which would then be sent on to NSA or GCHQ for cryptanalysis.[82]

19

Crisis Intelligence

The 1960s saw some of the century's most productive spies as well as major advances in aerospace reconnaissance systems. But neither the designers of new reconnaissance systems, nor spies like Penkovskiy, Cohen, and Lotz could know exactly how their activities might influence history.

Before the decade concluded the United States and the Soviet Union would approach the brink of nuclear conflict over Cuba, the Arabs and Israelis would fight a war with long-lasting implications, and Soviet actions would make clear their willingness to resort to extreme measures to safeguard their eastern European empire. Each case would serve to illustrate the utility and limitations of intelligence in the 1960s—and help spur some of the advances of the 1970s.

The Missile Crisis

At about 9 P.M. on October 15, 1962, Ray Cline, the CIA's Deputy Director for Intelligence, placed a call to McGeorge Bundy, President Kennedy's special assistant for national security affairs. Because they were speaking over a nonsecure telephone line, Cline was circumspect in telling Bundy that "[t]hose things we've been worrying about in Cuba are there."[1]

Bundy knew exactly what Cline was talking about. The "things" were Soviet offensive missiles deployed ninety miles from American territory. Cline's call followed the discovery, by photointerpreters from the National Photographic Interpretation Center, of medium-range missiles. The images had been produced by a U-2 overflight on October 14. Bundy told Cline that he wanted to see the photography as soon as possible, and Cline promised he would have the material ready early the next morning.[2]

President Kennedy was not to learn of the new developments until the next morning. Since the president had just returned from a strenuous campaign trip, and since there was nothing he could do that evening, Bundy decided to let him get the rest he would need. It was not until 8:30 on the morning of October 16 that Bundy arrived at the president's bedroom to deliver the sobering news.[3]

As Cline's call indicated, the news had not come as a complete shock, although it did contradict the best estimates of the intelligence community, which had been monitoring the military buildup in Cuba and trying to determine its exact character. The difference to the United States between a buildup of defensive weapons and the deployment of offensive missiles or bombers was a dramatic one. Soviet merchant ships were photographed several times on their way to Cuba. U-2s, while no longer flying over the Soviet Union, overflew Cuba at least once a month. The resulting imagery showed plenty of signs of a military buildup, including airfields under construction, tanks, and self-propelled guns at the Managua military camp, and a large concentration of Soviet artillery pieces outside Havana. But there were no signs of offensive weapons.[4]

On July 11, 1961, the U.S. Intelligence Board had approved the publication of "The Military Buildup in Cuba," which observed that while "[t]he Soviet Bloc continues to extend considerable military assistance to Cuba in the form of military equipment, training, and technicians and advisers . . . [t]here is no evidence that any nuclear weapons or guided missiles are now in Cuba."[5]

Many human sources, mostly Cuban exiles, were asserting the presence of offensive missiles. By January 1962 there were over 200 such reports.[6] But the Cuban exiles clearly had an ulterior motive, as they hoped for U.S. intervention to unseat Castro. And report after report did not hold up when checked out by the CIA. R. Jack Smith, head of the CIA's Office of Current Intelligence at the time, noted:

> The eye-witness reports of huge missiles moving down Cuban roads at night were not decisive because they were the reports of untrained observers, often peeking out of the edge of window blinds, who could not tell the difference between a shrouded 35-foot-long defensive weapon and an offensive one. To a layman, the Soviet SA-2 looks big enough to destroy half the eastern seaboard of the United States.[7]

By mid-February there were also reports of large groups of Soviet personnel being seen across the island. Such reports disturbed Director of Central Intelligence John McCone. McCone had assumed the director's position on November 29, 1961, replacing Allen Dulles, who had been forced to resign as a consequence of the Bay of Pigs fiasco. The fifty-nine-year-old McCone was a hard-line conservative Republican. Although most of his adult life had been spent in private business, he had served as Undersecretary of the Air Force in 1950 and 1951 and as chairman of the Atomic Energy Commission from 1958 to 1960.[8]

McCone, who was naturally suspicious of the Soviets and Cubans, ordered that the number of monthly U-2 overflights be increased from one to two. The missions were flown in the early morning hours of clear days, before the appearance of rain clouds. Each mission could photograph almost all of Cuba.[9]

In addition to increased overflights, the NSA and its military service components also began to increase SIGINT collection operations targeted on Cuba. In June a C-130 Airborne Communications Reconnaissance Platform was transferred from Europe to the United States to conduct SIGINT operations, designated QUICK FOX, against Cuban-Soviet targets. During July, additional aircraft and ships patrolled the skies and seas near Cuba, intercepting signals and taking photographs.[10]

Over the summer and into the fall, there would be clear signs of increasing Soviet activity, including dramatic increases in the number of Soviet cargo and passenger ships arriving during July and August. The passenger ships were also reported to be bringing a different type of Soviet—young, trim, physically fit, and disciplined, which suggested they might be combat troops. There were also reports that some ships were unloaded at night under tight security. But none of the reports unequivocally established the presence of offensive missiles. It was also considered possible that the Soviets were in the process of establishing COMINT/ELINT or electronic warfare sites, targeted on Cape Canaveral.[11]

Despite the lack of hard evidence, McCone began to focus on the possibility that the Soviets were in the process of deploying offensive missiles in Cuba, specifically medium-range ballistic missiles (MRBMs) and intermediate-range ballistic missiles (IRBMs). MRBMs, with a range of about 1,100 nautical miles, would be able to reach as far north as Philadelphia and as far west as Oklahoma City. IRBMs could reach all U.S. targets except some in the Pacific Northwest. In an August 21 meeting with Secretary of Defense McNamara and several other high officials, McCone stated: "If I were Khrushchev, I would put MRBMs in Cuba and I would aim several at Washington and New York and then I would say, 'Mr. President, how would you like looking down the barrels of a shotgun for a while? Now let's talk about Berlin. Later, we'll bargain about your overseas bases.'" However, in the absence of evidence his audience was not convinced. That did not discourage McCone from raising the subject with President Kennedy on August 22. The next day, at a meeting with Kennedy, Rusk, McNamara, Bundy, and others, McCone again indicated the deployment of an extensive SAM network made little sense unless they were there to help conceal the presence of MRBMs by preventing U.S. reconnaissance. That same day Kennedy issued National Security Action Memorandum 181, ordering a variety of studies, including "an analysis . . . of the probable military, political and psychological impact on the establishment in Cuba of either surface-to-air missiles or surface-to-surface missiles which could reach the U.S."[12]

By the time of that meeting the CIA had received refugee reports concerning the presence of missiles in Cuba with shapes and sizes resembling the SA-2 GUIDELINE, which had brought down Francis Gary Powers. A U-2 mission on August 29 brought back conclusive evidence of surface-to-air missile sites in Cuba. The CIA concluded, in a September 6 report, that eight SAM sites were being constructed on a crash basis, making it possible that some could be operational within two weeks.[13]

By the time of the August 29 mission, the DCI was on a month-long European honeymoon, but he was briefed on the results of the mission. He sarcastically observed: "They're not putting them [the SA-2 sites] in to protect the cane cutters. They're putting them in to blind our reconnaissance eye."[14]

The SAM discovery and McCone's views, which were repeated in several cables, led to stepped-up reconnaissance, employing specially equipped B-47s and Navy Constellations, along with U-2s carrying photographic and electronic intelligence equipment. A September 5 U-2 mission covered all the portions of Cuba that had been obscured by cloud cover on August 29, discovering three new SAM sites. It was clear that an island-wide defense network was being established.[15]

But neither mission turned up evidence of offensive missiles. Getting approval for another overflight mission proved difficult, apparently due to resistance from McGeorge Bundy and Dean Rusk. In light of an inadvertent U-2 incursion into Sakhalin airspace on September 7 and the shoot-down of Chinese Nationalist U-2 over China, Rusk was fearful of an escalation in tensions following another incident.[16]

Thus the most up-to-date photographic intelligence available to the Office of National Estimates, faced with the president's request for a Special National Intelligence Estimate on the buildup, was that from the August 29 and September 5 missions. Combining that intelligence with communications and human intelligence, the ONE produced, on September 19, "The Military Buildup in Cuba." The estimate offered reassurance, stating that "we believe that the military buildup which began in July does not reflect a radically new Soviet policy toward Cuba, either in terms of military commitments or of the essentially defensive character of the military buildup in Cuba."[17]

This key conclusion was based on some crucial premises. One was that the Soviets realized that any attempt to turn Cuba into an offensive base in order to protect the Castro regime might provoke a U.S. military response. In addition, it was observed that establishment of medium- or intermediate-range missiles "would be incompatible with Soviet practice to date," in which such weapons were never placed on the territory of their eastern European satellite states.[18]

The estimate failed to convince McCone. He would later observe that

[t]he majority opinion in the intelligence community, as well as State and Defense, was that this would be so out of character with the Soviets that they would not do so. They had never placed an offensive missile in any

satellite area. I pointed out that Cuba was the only piece of real estate that they had indirect control of where a missile could reach Washington or New York and not reach Moscow. So the situation was somewhat different.[19]

While the analysts at the ONE were telling the president that, despite the temptation, the Soviets were unlikely to install offensive missiles in Cuba, the Soviets were in the process of doing just that. Large-hatched ships, such as the *Poltava* and *Omsk,* unloaded their cargoes of launchers, missiles, and support equipment at Mariel. Other ships arrived in early October to unload additional missiles, which were then moved under tight security, at night, to remote sites in the interior of Cuba.[20]

Continued limitations on U-2 operations reduced the chances of detecting the missiles once they arrived at their final destinations. The planes were to fly no closer than twenty-five miles from the Cuban coast, putting them just out of reach of the SA-2s. A September 17 mission, hampered by weather conditions, failed to produce any usable photography. Attempts to use RB-47s and specially modified B-52s proved unsuccessful. While some human-source reporting alleging the presence of MRBMs appeared more credible than previous reports, the HUMINT track record was so poor that the reports were not considered conclusive. Former CIA official Victor Marchetti observes that "when you read 5,000 stinking reports . . . it's hard to put a lot of reliance on one."[21]

McCone, via long-distance phone calls to his deputy, Marshall Carter, lobbied for resumption of U-2 overflights. After he returned to Washington, he continued his campaign at a meeting with Rusk, McNamara, Bundy, and others, on October 3. The DCI pointed out that there had been no U-2 coverage of central or western Cuba since September 5. Hence it was impossible to state definitively whether there were missiles in Cuba.[22]

The following day, at a meeting attended by McCone, Carter, and senior officials from Defense, State, and the JCS, the National Reconnaissance Office (NRO) and JCS Joint Reconnaissance Center were directed to present to an October 9 Special Group* meeting alternative plans for overflights, including the use of U-2s to cover the Cuban interior. The use of additional aerial reconnaissance systems was also to be considered.[23]

The urgency was reinforced by the increasingly credible HUMINT which reached the CIA in late September. Of particular significance were two reports. In Havana, a source reported seeing a missile about sixty-five to seventy feet long. He quickly identified a picture of an SS-4 MRBM from a group of photographs of Soviet missiles. The second reported a convoy moving toward the San Cristobal area on September 17.[24]

The October 9 NRO-JRC presentation, which came two days after a peripheral U-2 mission had uncovered four additional SAM sites, was followed by President Kennedy's approval, on October 10, of a U-2 flight

---

* The Special Group was reponsible for reviewing U.S. covert action and sensitive reconnaissance operations.

over western Cuba. But it was not until the 14th, when favorable flying weather appeared, that a U-2, equipped with a high-resolution general-coverage camera designed to provide detailed information over an extremely large area, was able to cover the target area.[25]

The next day photointerpreters at NPIC detected military vehicles and tents. They expected that they would next see preparations for construction of an SA-2 site or cruise missile launchers. Instead, the photos showed six canvas-covered objects more than sixty feet long.[26] Examination of the "black books" on various Soviet missile systems led to the conclusion that they were SS-4 SANDALs, which were seventy-four feet long. After Arthur Lundahl, head of the NPIC, was informed he told Cline of his interpreters' conclusions and, in response to questioning from Cline, indicated that the missiles didn't appear to be ready to fire.[27]*

Approximately three and a half hours after Bundy informed the president of the photointerpreters' finding, Kennedy and what became the Executive Committee (EXCOM) of the National Security Council met for the first time. Among those present was Lundahl, who answered the President's "Are you sure these are Soviet MRBMs?" by saying that he was "as sure of this as a photointerpreter can be sure of anything."[28] Kennedy and his advisers were faced with determining how the United States should respond. That issue would be resolved, at least temporarily, by President Kennedy's decision, announced to the public on the evening of October 22, to initiate a naval quarantine of Cuba.

During the crisis the U.S. intelligence community had three basic tasks: monitoring developments at the identified missile sites, discovering any other sites in existence, and monitoring other events of importance in Cuba; monitoring Soviet ship movements on the high seas; and determining if there were any signs in the Soviet Union of a heightened state of military alert that might indicate an impending attack.

At the October 16 meeting the president directed that the frequency of U-2 missions be increased. The next day six U-2 missions were flown. Those missions provided the photointerpreters at NPIC with proof that the Soviets were building at least six MRBM sites and SS-5 IRBM sites in Cuba. The eighty-two-foot long SS-5 was considered to carry a five-megaton warhead.[29]

Meanwhile, NSA and its military components launched a massive SIGINT effort. RB-47H ELINT aircraft, flying from MacDill Air Force Base, Florida, averaged three missions a day—recording all signals from Cuban surveillance radars and radars at surface-to-air missile sites. Also listening in were six RC-121 Super Constellation aircraft, which carried

---

* Photointerpreters would subsequently discover, prior to late morning on October 16, an additional and more fully developed site at San Diego de los Banos, near the first site. The interpreters were also suspicious of a "unidentified installation" a little over four miles from San Cristobal. The October 14 photography also showed that IL-28 bombers were being uncrated at San Julian airfield. Dino Brugioni, *Eyeball to Eyeball: The Inside Story of the Cuban Missile Crisis* (New York: Random House, 1991), pp. 214–15.

about half a ton of sophisticated eavesdropping equipment. In addition to patrolling the skies outside Cuba, the NSA was also watching and listening to events from the sea. The USS *Oxford* monitored Soviet ships as they moved into and out of Havana harbor and eavesdropped on Soviet communications.[30]

To gather more information on developments in the Soviet Union, the CIA and NRO attempted to place a new CORONA spacecraft into orbit. The spacecraft had been sitting on a booster at Vandenberg Air Force Base for a considerable time, part of a plan that had been developed to have such a satellite always available for use in a crisis. However, the launch failed.[31]

The collection efforts targeted on Cuba, along with the information Oleg Penkovskiy provided on Soviet missiles, allowed the CIA to prepare a detailed memorandum on October 19 concerning the Cuban SS-4 and SS-5 sites. The memorandum provided information on the SS-4's range (1,020 nautical miles), accuracy (1–1.5 mile Circular Error Probable), warhead weight (3,000 pounds), and yield (from 25 kilotons to 2 megatons). The document also noted the number of salvos the launcher could fire (three), the refire time (five hours), and the number of missiles per launcher (two). It also specified that two of the sites were already operational and that the SS-5 sites would become operational during December.[32]

The manual provided by Penkovskiy showed the "footprint," or deployment pattern, of the SS-4s, which had been confirmed by KH-4 images of SS-4 facilities in the Soviet Union. The Penkovskiy material was even more critical in providing information on refire rates as well as means of assessing changes in the status of the sites.[33]

The information on the refire rate was of great value during an EXCOM debate over the proposal to launch an air strike against the missile sites. The committee wanted to tell the president how long it would take for the second launch of the missiles if the proposed air strike did not fully destroy the launch sites.[34]

That and related material helped push the president's decision toward quarantine and away from immediate military action. Richard Helms, deputy director for plans at the time, recalled:

> We looked at power and fuel lines, launching booms and all the other details which were in the manual. The assessment gave President Kennedy three extra days. The big issue of the moment was whether to send in the Air Force to take out the missile bases. . . . With the aid of the material Penkovskiy delivered we were able to tell the President "this is what we've got here and it will take them X days to be ready to fire. . . . I don't know of any single instance where intelligence was more immediately valuable than at this time."[35]

The same day that the CIA provided the memo on the SS-4 and SS-5 sites the U.S. Intelligence Board approved Special National Intelligence

Estimate (SNIE) 11-18-62, "Soviet Reactions to Certain US Courses of Action on Cuba," which had been commissioned by the president. That was followed the next day by SNIE 11-19-62, "Major Consequences of Certain US Courses of Action on Cuba."

The estimators noted that "any blockade situation would place the Soviets under no immediate pressure to choose a response with force." Rather, they could rely on a variety of political actions, including threatening retaliation in Berlin. While they observed that the likelihood of a Soviet military response to a U.S. use of force would be greater than if the United States resorted to blockade, they also offered the surprising conclusion that

> there would probably be a difference between Soviet reaction to all-out invasion and Soviet reaction to more limited US use of force against selected objectives in Cuba. We believe that the Soviets would be somewhat less likely to retaliate with military force in areas outside Cuba in response to speedy, effective invasion than in response to more limited forms of military action against Cuba.[36]

Between the October 19 estimate and the President Kennedy's October 22 announcement of the quarantine, intelligence collection, of course, continued at a fever pitch. U-2 flights indicated that another two MRBM sites had become operational, for a total of four, and that another two would reach that stage by the end of the week. Photos also showed at least thirty-five IL-28 BEAGLE bombers being assembled at San Julian. Imagery, and probably ELINT, also indicated that twenty-two of the twenty-four SA-2 sites in Cuba were operational. Nuclear storage bunkers had also been identified in the imagery, although no nuclear warheads had been identified.[37]

President Kennedy's speech did not affect U.S. missile crisis intelligence activities, at least in terms of its basic targets—Cuba, the high seas, and the Soviet Union. But there were new elements to be considered. Would the Soviets, now confronted by worldwide knowledge of their activity and the U.S. quarantine, continue, halt, or disassemble the missile sites? Would Soviet ships on the high seas turn around or try to run the quarantine? Would Khrushchev and other Soviet leaders order Soviet nuclear and other forces to a higher stage of alert? Over the next six days the U.S. intelligence community sought to answer those questions. The indications produced were mixed or unclear. Late in the evening of October 23, the NSA reported that the product of its direction-finding operations (actually run by the Naval Security Group Command) indicated that at least five Soviet missile-carrying ships bound for Cuba had changed course and were probably on their way back to the Soviet Union. Although the Navy could not verify the information until daylight hours, the CIA watch officer was sufficiently convinced to wake DCI McCone with the news. Later the next day it was determined that sixteen of eighteen Soviet ships, some with large hatches, had either turned back or come to a halt.[38]

As for events in the Soviet Union, the CIA had reported on October 23: "We have not detected any unusual activity or alerting of Soviet forces during the first few hours after the President's speech." On October 25 the Watch Committee did report that Soviet armed forces were increasing their state of readiness. The next day the committee observed that while the Soviets had completed measures for an alert, there were no signs of significant deployments.[39] Such judgments were undoubtedly heavily based on U.S. monitoring of Soviet military communications channels.

On October 23–24 NSA monitoring of Cuba also revealed the presence of two new scrambled communications links, although not the exact locations. Although it could not be determined if the discovered links were established to support the missile sites, a postcrisis study noted that they "would have met the requirements of the deployed offensive missile units in Cuba for a communications system which is both very secure and capable of handling large volumes of traffic."[40]

The photographs of developments in Cuba, however, gave the president and his advisers reason for concern. Photography showed some work on the additional missile sites progressing quickly—even faster than previously. By October 27 the imagery indicated that all six MRBM sites were operational, with a total of twenty-four positions and the potential to fire forty-eight missiles in two salvos. In addition, the overhead images also indicated that the two IRBM sites would become operational in December. Finally, photography taken on October 25 showed that two Il-28 BEAGLE bombers had already been assembled, that three more were in the assembly process, and that the crates for another twenty bombers were at San Julian airfield.[41]

Then, on October 28 the CIA's Foreign Broadcast Information Service informed the White House that "Moscow Domestic Service in Russian at 1404 GMT [Greenwich mean time] on 28 October, broadcast a message from Khrushchev to President Kennedy stating the USSR had decided to dismantle Soviet missiles in Cuba and return them to the Soviet Union 28 October."[42]

It was not until the afternoon of November 1 that the NPIC's interpreters, scrutinizing the most recent overhead photography, saw the signs that the Soviets were following their words with action. The photographs showed that missiles had been removed and launch stands had been crated at a number of sites. Other signs were the removal of missile-ready tents, the bulldozing of some launch pads, the removal of camouflage netting, and the formation of convoys of trucks to transport the dismantled equipment. Similar signs could be seen at the IRBM sites. However, construction of the nuclear storage areas and assembly of bombers at San Julian airfield continued.[43]

Throughout November, the U.S. intelligence community continued to monitor the missile sites, nuclear storage areas, airfields, port areas, and

Soviet ships on the high seas. What both U-2 and low-altitude photographs eventually showed was the appearance of missiles and missile equipment at Mariel and their shipment back to the Soviet Union. On November 25 signs that the Il-28 bombers at San Julian were being disassembled first appeared in the photography. Photography of Soviet ships allowed the Office of Naval Intelligence to publish, in December, a table listing ships, the Cuban ports they departed from, and the number of missile transporters, erectors, launch stands, and other equipment each was carrying. Just as the ships returning the missiles were photographed on the high seas, so were those carrying the bombers back. To make sure the United States had unequivocal evidence, the Soviets partially removed the tops of Il-28 shipping crates so that the fuselages inside could be seen inside.[44]

Surveillance of Cuba would not end, of course, with the end of the missile crisis, particularly since the United States could never be absolutely certain that every missile and bomber that had arrived in Cuba had been returned to the Soviet Union.* Thus the November 30, 1962, "Guidelines for the Planning of Cuban Overflights," stated:

The United States Government has a high priority need for the following:
  a. Continuing evidence on the removal of offensive weapons systems from Cuba.
  b. Evidence of any reintroduction of offensive weapons systems into Cuba.
  c. Evidence of the concealment of offensive weapons systems in Cuba.[45]

The Six-Day War

On the morning June 5, 1967, Israel launched a devastating air strike on Egyptian airfields, an attack timed to coincide with the end of the Egyptian air force's early morning alert. The Israeli action came after weeks of increasing tension and the Israeli cabinet's judgment that Egypt was preparing for war.

Only a few months earlier the idea of Egyptian leader Gamal Abdel Nasser choosing war was dismissed by the AMAN, as it had been for years before. During the mid-1960s AMAN believed that Egypt would not be prepared for war any earlier than 1969. In an October 1964 assessment

---

* It was not until after the crisis that the United States knew for sure that the Soviets had actually delivered thirty-six nuclear warheads for the missiles to Cuba. Overhead photography at the time showed that vans that had been seen at the missile sites were the first things that arrived at Mariel for shipment to the Soviet Union. Subsequent satellite photography showed those vans at SS-4 sites, leading to the conclusion that they contained nuclear warheads. It was discovered only after Soviet revelations many years later that six Frog short-range tactical missiles equipped with nuclear warheads had also been deployed, and the Soviet forces had authority to employ them against an invasion force. Dino Brugioni, *Eyeball to Eyeball: The Inside Story of the Cuban Missile Crisis* (New York: Random House, 1991), pp. 538–48.

AMAN concluded that an Arab attack on Israel was not likely prior to 1968–70. Ezer Weizman, head of the Israeli General Staff from 1966, wrote that "[n]o one predicted a full-scale war before 1969." The AMAN analysis was focused on the condition of the Egyptian economy, the state of its armed forces (which had not fully incorporated newly received Soviet weapons systems), and the deployment of Egyptian troops in Yemen to support the republican forces in a civil war.[46]

The AMAN's underlying premise was that Egypt would not start a war as long as its forces were significantly inferior to Israel's. AMAN considered this to be the case in 1967, as it had been earlier in the 1960s. In early May AMAN explicitly stated that there was "no chance" that war would break out in the coming year.[47]

Heading AMAN during this critical period was Aharon Yariv, who had been born in Moscow in 1920, emigrated to Palestine in 1935, and joined the Haganah in 1939. To Yariv's and Israel's surprise, on May 14 and 15 lead units of two Egyptian divisions began moving across the Suez Canal and establishing positions in the Sinai Peninsula. On May 16 Nasser demanded the the United Nations Emergency Force (UNEF) be withdrawn from the Israel–Egyptian border. At a General Staff meeting in Tel Aviv on the 17th, Yariv expressed the view that Egypt's actions were designed to deter an Israeli attack on Syria, a view based largely on the defensive nature of the Egyptian deployment in the Sinai. AMAN believed that Nasser would order his army and tanks to withdraw after a show of force. What AMAN did not know at the time was that the Soviet Union was giving both Egypt and Syria false information about Israeli Defense Forces (IDF) troop movements and U.S. plans.[48]

But on May 18, news of U Thant's capitulation to Nasser's demands led to a change in the AMAN's assessment of the situation. The withdrawal of U.N. forces would "give the Egyptian [deployment] an offensive—and not only defensive character," AMAN concluded. AMAN further concluded that the Egyptians were probably surprised by U Thant's quick acceptance of their demands, but could not, for reasons of face, pull back from the brink.[49]

At a General Staff meeting on May 19 Yariv argued that Nasser's intentions were not inevitably aggressive; as long as the Egyptians had not reached full strategic cooperation with the other Arab states and their main forces were divided between the two banks of the Suez Canal they would hold back.[50]

But the intelligence flowing into AMAN indicated a deteriorating situation. Reports indicated that Egypt had ordered three of the brigades that had been stationed in Yemen to return home. Then, on May 20, Egyptian forces seized control of Sharm el Sheikh, at the peninsula's southern tip, giving them control of the Gulf of Aqaba, Israel's commercial link to Africa and Asia. The next day Nasser ordered a general mobilization of the Egyptian army. AMAN concluded that the Egyptian entry into the Sinai had been intended as a limited action, but Nasser had been carried along by his actions into a situation with dramatic political, if not military, objectives.[51]

On May 22, AMAN again incorrectly assessed the next Egyptian move. It noted the possibility that Egypt might close the Straits of Tiran, thus closing the Gulf of Aqaba, but concluded that such action was unlikely. At midnight Nasser announced the closure of the straits to Israeli shipping, and an Egyptian batallion was parachuted into Sharm el Sheikh.[52]

The closure of the straits, which Israel had always considered a casus belli, led Yariv to tell a May 23 General Staff meeting, attended by Prime Minister Levi Eshkol, that "[t]he post-Suez period is over. It is not merely a question of freedom of navigation. If Israel does not respond to the closure of the straits . . . the Arab states will interpret Israel's weakness as an excellent opportunity to assail her security and her very existence."[53]

On May 30 Jordan's King Hussein arrived in Cairo, to the surprise of AMAN. Hussein and Nasser proceeded to sign a mutual defense treaty, which was followed by Arab predictions of Israel's imminent extinction. At a June 2 cabinet meeting Yariv provided extensive information about Arab military deployments and morale, and he stated AMAN's conclusion that Israel would win any war. On June 4 the Israeli cabinet, meeting in Jerusalem, voted for war. Intelligence that Egypt had transferred commando units to Jordan, which implied the imminence of cross-border sabotage attacks as part of an Egyptian first strike, led Eshkol to advocate war.[54]

The next day it was Egypt's turn to be surprised: the timing and, in some cases, the direction of the air assault came as huge shocks to Egypt. While Israeli intelligence estimators had not performed well in the period leading up to the war, Israeli intelligence collection proved to be of immense value in planning the air strike and the military campaign that followed.

The Israeli air force's intelligence department had monitored the activity at Egyptian air bases, allowing the air force's operations planners to devise a plan that succeeded in dramatic fashion. The planners knew that Egyptian air bases had been on dawn alert for weeks—with expanded interceptor patrols constantly in the air between 4:00 or 5:00 and 7:00 A.M., in anticipation of an Israeli attack. They also knew that after the alert ended the pilots returned to base and headed off, along with the ground control teams, to breakfast. During this time technicians manning SAM radars would be fatigued, while fighters would be moved to outdoor maintenance areas. Air force chief Motti Hod explained to IDF chief of staff Yitzhak Rabin on June 4 that

[f]or the past two weeks, we have been keeping watch on the precise movements of the Egyptian air force. . . . At first light they take off on patrol, staying up for about an hour. Then they return to base and go off for breakfast. Between seven and eight, everything is dead, and 7:45 in the morning is the ideal timing for us.[55]

The Israeli pilots struck at 7:45, destroying 304 of Egypt's 419 aircraft.

Over the next six days Israeli forces racked up devastating victories on three fronts. By noon on June 5, Egypt had lost 309 of its 340 serviceable aircraft, including all of the TU-16 bombers that could be used against cities. Three IDF armored corps broke into Egyptian territory, took the Gaza Strip, and penetrated to the heart of the Sinai.[56]

To the east, Israeli forces took on the Jordanian army. In response to the Jordanian strafing of a small Israeli airfield, Brigadier General Hod struck back. The Israeli air force caught thirty Jordanian planes on the ground, delivering a crippling blow. Nor did the Israeli ground forces find the Jordanian army a difficult adversary, rolling through the West Bank in a matter of days.[57]

Syria had also struck Israel on the opening day of the war. Syrian planes had bombed an oil refinery, Israeli positions at the Sea of Galilee, and an air base. Israel responded with an air strike that destroyed fifty-seven Syrian planes, all but eliminating the Syrian air force. Ground combat, however, did not begin until after the Egyptian and Jordanian campaigns were virtually completed. On June 9, Minister of Defense Moshe Dayan instructed the IDF to seize the Golan Heights, from which Syria had been conducting artillery attacks in peacetime. During the first day of fighting, four breaches were made in the Syrian line. At dawn the next day Israeli pressure increased; by noon Kuneitra, on the Golan Heights, had fallen into IDF hands and the road to Damascus was open.[58]

While the key factor in Israel's victory was the skill of the Israeli Defense Forces, that skill had been supplemented by human, photographic, and signals intelligence. A major in the Egyptian signals corps, known as "Suleiman" or "Captain X," had been recruited in Cairo several years earlier. Over the course of the war Suleiman reported detailed information on Egyptian troop strength, movements, battle plans, and morale. During the chaotic first three or four days of battle, he provided AMAN with precise battlefield damage assessment reports on the consequences of the Israeli air force's surprise attack and the ground forces' rapid march through the Egyptian defenses in the Sinai desert. He, however, did not live to see the end of the war, being killed in an IDF bombing raid.[59]

Another reputed spy was Ali al-Atfi, the masseur to both Nasser and his aide, Anwar Sadat. In the view of many Egyptian security officials, he relayed detailed intelligence reports to his Israeli handlers on Egypt's upcoming political and military actions. Atfi was allegedly recruited by the AMAN while on vacation in Holland.*

Prior to 1967, photographic coverage of targets in the Sinai and Egypt presented a problem. Israeli leaders feared such missions would create or exacerbate military tension, lead to unfavorable responses from the West, and possibly result in war. During May 1967 the cabinet vetoed IDF

---

* Atfi died in Cairo's Central Prison in 1990, after serving eleven years of a fifteen-year sentence for espionage.

proposals to step up aerial reconnaissance missions. But in the final days prior to the June 5 air strike, the cabinet approved repeated short- and long-range reconnaissance missions to acquire up-to-date intelligence on Arab military deployments.[60]

The Israeli wartime COMINT effort was also notably successful. On June 6, at about 2 P.M., a general order from Nasser to his forces was intercepted. Nasser ordered his forces in Sinai to retreat to the Suez Canal, following the breakthroughs by Israeli divisions on the northern and southern Sinai axis earlier that day. That intelligence permitted the IDF General Staff to order the opening of the June 9 offensive against Syria in the southern Golan Heights.[61]

Israel's COMINT effort not only permitted an advance view of Egyptian intentions, but it also permitted Israel to influence Egyptian actions. Before the war AMAN had broken the Egyptian army code. Once the war began the AMAN was able to neutralize Egyptian commanders and units by issuing false orders. An AMAN radio operator played the role of a senior Egyptian army officer and directed a lost tank batallion through the Sinai. The operator guided the batallion away from advancing Israeli forces, and, after the cease-fire, toward a POW depot. A MiG pilot was ordered to release his bombs over the sea. Since the Israelis were able to provide him details about his wife and children, he concluded the orders were authentic and abandoned the bombs and the plane over the sea.[62]

End of the Prague Spring

A June 13, 1968, special memorandum by the CIA's Board of National Estimates observed: "The related crises in internal Czechoslovak politics and in Soviet–Czechoslovak relations seem to have eased—at home, into a delicate and perhaps temporary domestic equilibrium and, abroad, into an uneasy truce with Moscow." It also noted that "if quiescence has been restored to the relationship, it is by no means assured indefinitely." The memo's final paragraph noted that

> there is a good chance that relations between Prague and Moscow will again become very tense. The Soviet leaders, or at least most of them, wish to avoid drastic and costly military action. Nevertheless, should Dubcek's control threaten to collapse, or should the Czech's regime's policies become, in Moscow's view "counterrevolutionary," the Soviets might once again use their troops to menace the Czech frontier.[63]

On August 20, 1968, Soviet and Warsaw Pact troops stormed into Czechoslovakia and ended the "socialism with a human face" experiment that marked Alexander Dubcek's regime. The invasion had its origins in late 1967 when Soviet leaders acquiesced in the Czech Communist party's removal of hard-liner Antonin Novotny as first secretary and his replacement by Dubcek.[64]

Dubcek's ascent to power unleashed reformist sentiment within the party and Czech society. The new Czech leader's reform program was incorporated into the Action Program of April 1968, which called for greater intraparty democracy, more autonomy for other political parties and parliament, restoring basic civil rights like freedom of assembly, vigorously continuing political rehabilitation, and economic reforms. Dubcek also permitted the establishment of several new political clubs and abolished censorship.[65]

Such developments alarmed the aging oligarchs who ran the Soviet Union and other Warsaw Pact countries. The poison of liberalization, they feared, might spread to their countries. Walter Ulbricht, the East German Communist party leader, and Pyotr Shelest, Soviet Politburo member and Ukrainian party boss, were particularly concerned. Such a dramatic shift in domestic policy was also seen as a serious threat to the unity of the Warsaw Pact. In light of internal liberalization, the Czech commitment to following the Soviet line in foreign policy and being a loyal member of the Warsaw Pact was considered questionable.[66]

But there was still a leap to be made between fears and a decision to invade, because of potential international repercussions and possible Czech resistance to such an invasion. The decision would be made by the Soviet Politburo, largely by five key members—General Secretary Leonid Brezhnev, Prime Minister Kosygin, President Nikolai Podgorny, chief ideologist Mikhail Suslov, and Shelest. Initially, the inner circle was divided and uncertain as to the proper course of action. Kosygin and, surprisingly, the hard-line Suslov both urged caution. Shelest was a strong, and probably the earliest, advocate of armed intervention. Brezhnev had no firm position.[67]

As a result the information flowing into the Politburo from the KGB and GRU may have had an impact on the ultimate decision. And there are indications that the information available to the decision makers was far from objective. In the aftermath of Dubcek's ascension to power, the regular operations of the KGB and GRU networks in Czechoslovakia were reduced, with the dismissal of 80 to 100 KGB agents who were serving with the Czech Ministry of the Interior. GRU collaborators in the Czech military were also dismissed.[68]

In the absence of those sources, the Soviet leadership and intelligence services relied on the alarming reports coming from the East German and Polish leaders, Walter Ulbricht and Wladislaw Gomulka, which undoubtedly had more weight than they might otherwise. In addition, the Czech antireformist coalition provided pessimistic reports.[69]

With many of the usual channels of information closed the Soviet leadership decided to suspend the rule prohibiting KGB espionage activities in the East European satellite countries. General Kotov, the chief KGB adviser in Prague, obtained copies of the personnel files of all State Security officers from State Security's director. The Deputy Minister of the Interior, Viliam Salgovic, was recruited by the KGB. Another KGB recruit in the Interior Ministry made it possible for the KGB to eavesdrop on telephone conversations in the ministry. The KGB also placed listening devices in the homes of reformist leaders. Much of the intelligence obtained was used after the invasion to arrest State Security officers and others loyal to the reformist regime.[70]

The KGB also ordered thirty illegals operating in the West to travel to Czechoslovakia posing as tourists. Its leadership believed that the Czech counterrevolutionaries would be more honest concerning their subversive schemes when talking to individuals they believed to be from the West than in conversations with East Europeans. Meanwhile, the KGB's Eighth Directorate decrypted large volumes of Czechoslovak diplomatic communications.[71]

The reports coming from the various groups of human sources, and the heads of the KGB and GRU, stressed the dangerous course of events in Czechoslovakia. Alarming reports arrived in the form of the KGB's estimate of the outcome of the Czechoslovak Party Congress and a memorandum from two key antireformists, A. Indra and D. Kolder, appears to have reached the Central Committee on August 13–15 and was passed on to the Politburo as high-priority material. Such reports were undoubtedly exploited by those favoring military intervention to bolster their case.[72] Specifically, KGB estimates of the composition of the delegations to the Fourteenth Extraordinary Party Congress, as well as the reports provided by key hard-line Czech communists, supported the arguments of Soviet interventionists that the congress would result in the defeat of the Soviet sympathizers in Czechoslovakia.[73]

At the same time, KGB headquarters dismissed any intelligence that contradicted the conspiracy theories, such as that forwarded by thirty-four-year-old Oleg Danilovich Kalugin from Washington, where he was head of political intelligence. Kalugin claims that he acquired "absolutely reliable documents" establishing that neither the CIA nor any other U.S. agency was behind political events in Czechoslovakia. Rather, Kalugin told Moscow Center that the Prague Spring had surprised Washington. According to Kalugin, on returning to Moscow he discovered that the KGB had ordered that "my messages should not be shown to anyone, and destroyed."[74]

Instead, readers of KGB reports were told of the strength of the Czechoslovak party and of substantial working-class support for the replacement of Dubcek and the reformers. KGB chairman Yuri Andropov warned of a large-scale Western plot to undercut Communist party control of Czechoslovak security.[75]

In addition to reporting information, or misinformation, the KGB also fabricated the majority of the "evidence" of Western conspiracies against Czechoslovakian socialism used to justify the invasion. The KGB illegals ordered into Czechoslovakia were instructed to put up posters and slogans calling for the end of communism and Czechoslovak withdrawal from the Warsaw Pact. In addition, the KGB orchestrated the planting and discovery of arms caches, which *Pravda* reported as evidence of plans for an armed uprising by Sudeten revanchists.[76]

While the KGB monitored events in Czechoslovakia, the CIA and other U.S. and Western intelligence agencies tried to monitor developments and estimate the likely Soviet course of action. The CIA's Foreign Broadcast Information Service carefully monitored Czechoslovakian and Soviet media. Diplomats and CIA officers stationed in Moscow, Prague, and other East European capitals also reported what they could find out. Western SIGINT agencies, particularly the NSA, the GCHQ, and the BND monitored the airwaves for signs of troops movements.

There was little human intelligence from the Soviet side but, according to a former intelligence community analyst, East Europe was a "sieve." What East European sources reported was the Soviet concern with events in Czechoslovakia, in particular a July letter from the Soviet leadership to the Polish Communist party indicating the Soviets were concerned about the developing situation and determined to deal with it. But none of the reporting explicitly pinpointed an invasion. And human-source reporting in the weeks prior to the invasion had been "so slow to arrive that it proved of little value to current intelligence publications."[77]

KEYHOLE satellites photographed Czechoslovakia and surrounding territory. Signs of an impending invasion that might show up in satellite photography were increased activities at airfields, troop departures, extensive logistic activities, and, most dramatically, the massing of troops near the Czech border. A KH-8 launched on August 6 performed poorly and was deorbited after nine days, so the CIA was forced to rely solely on the KH-4B area surveillance satellite launched on August 7. A film package returned before August 21 proved reassuring because it showed no indications of Soviet preparations for an invasion.[78]

When the second and last of the CORONA buckets was recovered and analyzed, it clearly showed Soviet preparations—including massing troops—for an invasion. Although the imagery proved quite valuable for those studying the Soviet mobilization process, it was of no warning value, for by the time that second bucket was recovered the invasion was over. Thus the Czech invasion became the second major military event in two years to highlight the limitations of satellite photography that was considerably less than instantaneous.[79]

A report of the House Select Committee on Intelligence indicated that revelatory communications intelligence had not arrived in Washington until after Czech radio had announced the invasion. The intelligence the House committee referred to may have included intercepts obtained from sites, possibly West German sites, on the border. According to one former intelligence official these intercepts included a "see you in Prague" message from a radio operator of a Soviet infantry division to an artillery unit.[80]

The gaps in U.S. technical collection resulted in the U.S. intelligence community losing track, during the first two weeks of August, of a Soviet combat formation that had moved into northern Poland. DCI Richard Helms would subsequently assure the President's Foreign Intelligence Advisory Board that U.S. performance would have been better "if West Germany had been the target rather than Czechoslovakia."[81]

While it is clear that knowledge of such a planned attack against West Germany would have been of enormous importance in attempting to forestall such an attack or neutralize it, it is less clear whether strategic warning of a Soviet invasion would have been of significant value to the United States. A warning to the Soviets against such a move probably would have gone unheeded. Moreover, the Czechs may have been no more inclined to fight if they had advance warning than they were when it became clear that an invasion was in progress.

But even without the conclusive information that human, communications, or photographic intelligence might have provided, some believe that Czechoslovkia still represented an intelligence analysis failure by the U.S. intelligence community. Within the intelligence community there was a distinct minority in *every* agency that believed that the Soviet Union would resort to military force to unseat the Czech reformers. A variety of factors persuaded the minority that an invasion was coming, including the scale of the buildup, the extent of Soviet efforts to get troops into Czechoslovakia, the nature of the "exercises," and the infiltration of military and intelligence personnel.[82]

But official intelligence community estimates never concluded that there was better than a fifty–fifty chance of a Soviet invasion. Cynthia Grabo, an analyst who served on the interagency Watch Committee, and who was in the minority, concluded that the failure was an example of a chronic U.S. intelligence community tendency to err on the side of under-warning. Beyond a failure to understand the specifics cited here, she also concluded that the failure was due to

- a widespread belief that the Soviet Union had "matured" since the suppression of the Hungarian revolt in 1956, and would not do such a thing again,
- a failure to perceive how seriously the Soviet leaders viewed the situation in Czechoslovakia,
- a prevalent view that the value of detente to the Soviet leadership would deter Soviet leaders from military action,
- a variety of errors in making use of the intelligence data available.[83]

20

The Technical
Revolution Continues

While the 1960s were notable for direct U.S–Soviet confrontations over Berlin and Cuba, the 1970s would see an attempt to regulate the arms race between the two superpowers. During that same decade simmering conflicts in the Middle East and southwest Asia would explode into wars—wars which involved major client states of the superpowers. The decade would also be notable for major advances in space imagery and COMINT capabilities and the use of those capabilities to support arms control, crisis monitoring, and the fighting of wars.

RHYOLITE

Lloyd K. Lauderdale was one of thousands with advanced degrees working for the CIA in the 1960s. Lauderdale would move on to work for a government contractor, but not before he made a dramatic contribution to U.S. intelligence collection capabilities. Science fiction writer Arthur C. Clarke first proposed that spacecraft in geosynchronous orbit would be ideal communications relays. Lauderdale first suggested that satellites in such orbits could be used for signals intelligence collection.

The speed of a satellite in geosynchronous orbit, 22,300 miles above the earth, matches the speed of the earth's rotation. The satellite essentially hovers above a single point on earth. Although such a satellite would be useless for photographic purposes, it would be invaluable for intercepting the telemetry signals from missile tests, including ABM tests. Telemetry signals radioed back from the missile to the test center provide information on numerous missile characteristics and capabilities, including throw weight, number of warheads, and warhead accuracy. Signals from the Sary Shagan test site, which was heavily involved in ABM testing, were particularly difficult to intercept because the facility is located in the central Soviet Union.

A geosynchronous orbit guarantees that the satellite would be on duty at all times. Between 1972 and 1975, the Soviets conducted a total of 181 research and development missile tests, with flight times of twenty-five to thirty minutes. Thus at most there were ninety-one hours of missile telemetry associated with those launches to be monitored for those four years. Another 211 launches to test operational systems were also conducted. A satellite that operated in low-earth orbit would often be over the Southern Hemisphere, North America, or western Europe, and not in position to intercept the telemetry signals during a test.[1]

Albert Wheelon, the CIA's deputy director for science and technology, was, according to one former CIA officer, "the most ascerbic son-of-a-bitch I ever met." But Wheelon was also a brilliant visionary and he fully supported Lauderdale's concept. Others did not. The National Security Agency believed that millimeter wave-length and microwave signals could not be intercepted from anywhere outside a relatively short and narrow area. But Lauderdale and the CIA's Office of SIGINT Operations undertook to develop a geosynchronous telemetry intelligence satellite, in conjunction with defense contractor TRW. The effort, code-named Project RHYOLITE, produced a series of satellites capable of intercepting signals across the VHF, UHF, and microwave frequency bands.[2]

The first RHYOLITE satellite was boosted into orbit by an Atlas-Agenda D rocket, apparently launched on June 18, 1970, from Cape Canaveral, and probably stationed over Borneo to receive telemetry signals from liquid-fueled ICBMs launched from Tyuratam in a northeasterly direction toward the Kamchatka Peninsula impact zone. The second launch, on December 4, 1971, failed to attain orbit due to a booster malfunction, and thus it was not until March 6, 1973, that a second RHYOLITE made it into orbit. That spacecraft replaced the first RHYOLITE over Borneo, with the initial satellite being moved to a position over the Horn of Africa.[3]

Telemetry intelligence, while initially RHYOLITE's primary function, was not its sole function. A satellite in RHYOLITE's orbit was also ideal for intercepting communications. While a low-earth orbiting satellite would be continually passing in and out of the range of conversations, a geosynchronous satellite would always be on station. And RHYOLITE, somewhat to the surprise of the CIA, proved quite capable of intercepting communications across the VHF, UHF, and microwave frequency bands. In his study of Christopher Boyce and Andrew Daulton Lee, Robert Lindsey wrote that the satellites' antennas "could monitor Communist microwave radio and long-distance telephone traffic over much of the European landmass, eavesdropping on a Soviet comissar in Moscow talking to his mistress in Yalta, or on a general talking to his lieutenants across the great continent." When Richard Nixon and Henry Kissinger became aware of RHYOLITE's COMINT capability, they ordered more extensive use of the satellite for eavesdropping purposes.[4]

Controlling the satellites and receiving the signals intercepted was a ground station located in central Australia, officially titled the Joint Defense Space Research Facility, code-named MERINO, and commonly known as Pine Gap. The latter designation resulted from its location, about twelve miles southwest of Alice Springs in a valley called the Pine Gap. The central Australian location had an important advantage that other sites that had been considered, such as Guam, did not have. Because of the distance between the Australian coast and central Australia Soviet AGIs would be unable to eavesdrop on the facility.[5]

Big Bird Arrives

In 1969 Ronald Inlow, the chairman of the U.S. Intelligence Board's Committee on Imagery Requirements and Exploitation (COMIREX), was sent to talk to James Schlesinger, then the assistant director of the Bureau of the Budget. Inlow's mission was to save another of Albert Wheelon's projects—which the press would eventually dub "Big Bird"—from the budget ax. Inlow successfully convinced Schlesinger that the satellite program was necessary to support U.S. arms control policy.[6]

And on June 15, 1971, a Titan 3D rocket, with 3 million pounds of thrust, carried a 30,000-pound cylinder, 40 feet long and 10 feet diameter, into an elliptical 114- by 186-mile orbit, with a 96.4-degree inclination.* The cylinder was a photographic reconnaissance satellite, the first launch in a program code-named HEXAGON. Its inclination ensured that it would cover the entire earth from pole to pole in a sun-synchronous orbit—that each daylight pass over an area was made at an identical angle to the sun, avoiding differences in pictures from different angles. On the days that a particular area was overflown it would be overflown twice, once in daylight and once in darkness.[7]

The satellite's optical system, designated KH-9, consisted of two cameras with 60-inch lenses, which could operate individually or obtain overlapping photos of a target. The overlapping photos could then be used with a stereoscope to extract additional information about the target's dimensions. The cameras were able to produce images covering a much wider area than the KH-4B, but with a resolution of 2 feet, almost as good as the 18-inch resolution of the KH-7. Whereas the KH-4B camera system has a swath width of 40 by 180 miles, the KH-9 system was twice that, 80 by 360, resulting in a fourfold increase in the territory that could be covered by a single photo. And while the KH-4B returned two film capsules, the KH-9 returned four.[8]

A third camera system would be carried on five HEXAGON missions. This twelve-inch mapping camera would have its film fed into a fifth capsule and be returned at the end of the mission. A secondary experi-

---

*The size of the satellite would allow it to host a variety of other projects. Thus the new generation of surveillance satellite would often carry antennae to collect signals intelligence and to relay messages from U.S. agents in the Soviet Union and elsewhere.

mental system was used to transmit pictures by radio signals—essentially the same system that had failed when it operated on SAMOS. The results were no better this time and the system was eventually jettisoned.[9]

The KH-9 represented a major advance in U.S. reconnaissance capabilities. The greater film capacity meant longer lifetimes and that film could be returned as frequently as with the KH-4B in normal circumstances. The first KH-9s would return film capsules every three or four days; in emergencies, a complete reel could be returned without drastic damage to the overall mission. Most important, the tremendous swath width of the KH-9 meant that true wide-area searches could be conducted to locate new missile fields, test ranges, and nuclear facilities. This translated not only into more comprehensive military intelligence but more confidence in U.S. ability to monitor arms limitation agreements, as Inlow had told Schlesinger.[10]

The first KH-9 mission would last fifty-two days, a fraction of the lifetime of later missions. Another would not be launched until January 20, 1972. During that interval the United States would continue to operate both the KH-4B area surveillance and KH-8 close-look systems, with KH-8 missions following KH-4B missions to allow more detail to be obtained concerning new targets spotted in KH-4B photos.

The final KH-4B mission began on May 25, 1972. The next day at 11:00 P.M., as the final KH-4B was circling the earth, at Spasso House in the Kremlin, Leonid Brezhnev and Richard Nixon signed what would become widely known as the SALT I and ABM treaties. The Strategic Arms Limitation Treaty set limits on the number of launchers each side could maintain—1,710 for the United States (1,054 ICBM and 656 SLBM), and 2,358 for the Soviet Union (1,618 ICBM and 740 SLBM). No more more than 313 ICBMs could be heavy missiles such as the SS-9.[11]

Without CORONA and its successors there would have been no possibility of reaching agreements such as those signed at Spasso House. The treaties contained no provisions for on-site inspection. Rather, "national technical means of verification" were to be used, a term which most emphatically included CORONA, GAMBIT, HEXAGON, RHYOLITE, the ferret satellites, and their Soviet counterparts.

The Yom Kippur War

The Egyptian attack across the Suez Canal on October 6, 1973, initiated the Yom Kippur War, a conflict with high stakes not only for Israel, Egypt, and Syria, but for the United States and the Soviet Union. It was a war in which the participants and the superpower observers used whatever intelligence collection capability they had to determine what was happening on the battlefield.

That Egypt had significant initial success may have been due in part to extensive aerial reconnaissance missions over Israel that began in the spring of 1971. In early March, four Soviet An-22 (Antonov-22) transport planes arrived at the Cairo-West Air Base. Their top-secret cargo was four MiG-25 Foxbat reconnaissance aircraft, designated the X-500, capable of Mach 3.2 at 73,000 feet. The specially configured MiG-25s had five camera ports for high-resolution photography.[12]

The Soviets went to extraordinary lengths to protect the planes. Soviet-manned SAM batteries defended the bases along with, according to some sources, units of the Soviet Spetznaz (Special Forces). Soviet pilots flew the planes on missions over virtually all of Israel. While the Israelis often scrambled F-4 Phantoms to intercept the unwanted visitors, all their attempts to intercept the planes were unsuccessful.[13]

The Soviet pilots would fly their MiGs parallel to the Israeli coast, allowing precision photography of every square mile of Israel. The information was passed on to the Egyptian Military Intelligence Department, which used it for target selection and deployment scenarios. The bulk of the missions were flown over the Golan Heights, producing high-resolution photographs of Israeli antitank defenses, which were passed on to the Syrians, and the Sinai Desert, which resulted in the identification of top-secret Israeli defensive positions in the strategic Mitla Pass.[14]

When war did come Israel received a valuable payoff from the SIGINT activities conducted by the AMAN's eavesdropping organization, Unit 8200. Even before the war began SIGINT stations at Umm Hushiba, Mt. Hermon, and the Jordan Valley had operated continuously to monitor military developments.[15]

One of the first payoffs came on October 7, when a communications intercept made it clear that King Hussein would not throw the Jordanian armed forces into the war. Just as Soviet COMINT, along with Richard Sorge's information, had permitted Stalin to shift troops from the Soviet Far East to confront the Wehrmacht, so Israeli COMINT allowed the Israeli Defense Forces to relocate tanks from the Jordanian front to deal with Syria and Egypt.[16]

A week later intercepted Egyptian communications gave AMAN an indication that the Egyptian high command was being deceived by commanders in the field. Up to October 14 intercepted Egyptian communications indicated that the high command was receiving accurate and tempered reports from the field. However, on October 14 Egyptian field officers reported great victories and territorial gains that existed only in their imaginations. Without knowledge of the true situation the high command was unable to exercise effective control, and unable to prevent further Israeli victories.[17]

Just a few days later, on October 16–17, Israeli COMINT tracked Egypt's 25th Armored Brigade as it traveled from the Egyptian Third Army enclave toward the crossing zone. The early warning permitted General Ariel Sharon's division to set a trap, which resulted in almost complete destruction of the brigade.[18]

Israeli photographic reconnaissance also contributed to the ultimate Israeli victory. The war's first day saw virtually all Israeli photoreconnaissance aircraft over the battlefield, in an attempt to provide a comprehensive picture of enemy deployments. Included were not only the sophisticated multisensor RF-4E Phantom, which could fly at Mach 2.17, but the jet-powered Teledyne-Ryan 147 and Chukar remotely piloted vehicles (RPVs).[19]

During the course of the war both the superpowers followed events closely, with the Soviets at one point threatening unilateral intervention and the United States increasing the alert status of its military forces. Aside from reports by their allies, both employed their own independent collection capabilities to determine what was happening on the battlefield.

Soviet photographic reconnaissance satellites were less sophisticated than those of the United States, with shorter lifetimes and poorer resolutions. At the time the Soviets were operating three varieties of their third-generation photographic satellites—low, medium, and high resolution—with lifetimes of fourteen to twenty-eight days. But with the limitations also came a certain flexibility: the satellites could be launched in response to a particular crisis, maneuvered without fear of drastically shortening their lifetimes, and returned to earth after short periods of time without putting a significant dent in Soviet satellite reconnaissance capabilities. Thus in situations such as the Yom Kippur War the GRU did not hestitate to launch satellite after satellite, maneuver the satellites to maximize their time over the battlefield, and bring satellites back early, in order to closely monitor the battlefield. In a period of three and a half weeks the Soviets launched seven photographic reconnaissance satellites, almost four times the rate during the rest of the year.[20]

On October 6, with *Cosmos 596* already in orbit, the high-resolution *Cosmos 597* was placed into orbit. Within two days the new spy satellite was overflying the battlefield daily, and *Cosmos 596* was returned to earth, six to eight days ahead of schedule. Similarly, *Cosmos 597* was ordered back to earth after only six days, with *Cosmos 598* already in orbit and ready to continue the monitoring operation.[21]

The pattern continued with the unusually short missions of *Cosmos 598* (October 10–16) and its successor, *Cosmos 600* (October 16–23). *Cosmos 599* and then *Cosmos 602* and *Cosmos 603* also monitored developments. The last two satellites were maneuvered to maximize coverage of the western Sinai, where the Egyptian army was in imminent peril from the Israelis. A launch on November 10 was followed the next day by an agreement to end the hostilities, which was followed by four additional launches over the next forty days—apparently to monitor compliance with the agreement.[22]

The United States also attempted to monitor events on the battlefield. U.S. and British SIGINT stations in Italy (San Vito), Cyprus, and Turkey (Sinop) may all have focused on the Middle East war. In addition, on October 12, 1973, an SR-71 departed Griffis Air Force Base, New York, on Operation GIANT REACH. Operating over the eastern Mediterranean, the SR-71 was able to collect data from the southern and northern fronts. That mission, along with another aircraft mission on October 25, was of little help because, according to the House Select Committee on Intelligence, they "straddled the most critical phase of the war."[23]

Nor did the United States get much help from its film-return photographic reconnaissance satellites. A KH-9, which had been launched on July 13, completed its mission a week after the war's beginning. A KH-8, launched on September 27, was in orbit during the entire war. But by the time their photographs were in the hands of the analysts, they represented only history. One CIA analyst recalled that "we had wonderful coverage but we didn't get the pictures until the war was over." As a result he had a portfolio of photos of the situation that had existed right after the war began, but "a portfolio no one wanted to see."[24]

This lack of timely intelligence represented to the House Select Committee a serious threat to the United States. Because the CIA and the Defense Intelligence Agency (DIA) relied on overly optimistic battle reports, "the U.S. clashed with the better informed Soviets on the latter's strong reaction to Israeli cease-fire violations. Soviet threats to intervene militarily were met with a worldwide U.S. troop alert. Poor intelligence had brought America to the brink of war."[25]

Lourdes

In early 1974 the Soviet GRU completed installing the first of several large satellite antennas at Los Paliacios, Cuba. Those antennas represented an addition to a SIGINT complex first established by the Soviets in the mid-1960s, and known as Lourdes for the location of the buildings that contained the monitoring, processing, and analysis equipment.[26]

When the facility was first established, its primary targets were U.S. high-frequency communications, particularly U.S. Navy fleet communications. The installation of the satellite antennas in early 1974 came just three months before the first Hughes-Western Union WESTAR satellite (launched on April 13, 1974) became operational, and marked the first use of Lourdes to intercept satellite communications. In December 1977 it was reported that additional antennas for communications satellite (COMSAT) monitoring had recently become operational.[27]

The satellite communications intercept function would become Lourdes's primary function over the years. In 1979 a satellite photo of the GRU area at Lourdes showed further evidence of that mission—the first of what became known as the LOW EAR Collector, a sixteen-foot dish used to intercept satellite communications. That year the facility was described as consisting of "vast antenna farms, big dish satellite receiver terminals and multi-channel high-speed microwave relay systems."[28]

The Space Reconnaissance Club Grows

On December 2, 1975, China recovered a capsule ejected from its *China 4* spacecraft, which had been launched less than a week earlier, on November 26. With that launch China became the third nation to conduct photographic reconnaissance from space.

China 4 weighed approximately 5,940 pounds, coming as close as 110 miles to the earth and moving as far away as 289 miles. With its inclination of 63 degrees, the spacecraft's cameras could view all but the very northern Soviet Union, Canada, and Scandinavia. Only five days after the capsule recovery, *China 5* was launched into a similar orbit, presumably with the same mission.[29]

China also became the third nation to conduct electronic intelligence operations from space, with the launch of *China 6* on August 30, 1976. The 600-pound satellite would stay in orbit until November 25, 1978, collecting the emissions of Soviet, Vietnamese, and other radar systems.[30]

Through the remainder of the decade China would make sparing use of space reconnaissance—with only two further photographic satellite launches (on December 7, 1976, and January 26, 1978) and no electronic intelligence satellite launches. But those launches did allow China, particularly the PLA's Military Intelligence Department, to overfly and photograph Soviet and Vietnamese territory with impunity.

Quantum Leap

Two days after China recovered the *China 4* film capsule, the United States placed another KH-9 into orbit. In the fifteen years since the beginning of the U.S. space reconnaissance program, approximately 200 photo-reconnaissance satellites had been orbited. The lifetime of area surveillance missions had increased from less than a month to five months for the most recent KH-9s. The lifetime of close-look missions had grown from a few days for the first KH-7 missions to over 50 days for the mid-1970s KH-8 missions. And while there were fewer than 50 days in 1961 when the United States had at least one operational photographic reconnaissance satellite in orbit, in 1975 there were 332 such days.

In addition, the quality of the product had improved dramatically. As noted earlier, the area covered in a single KH-9 image far surpassed that in a KH-4B photo. There were also marked improvements in resolution. The KH-9's two-foot resolution was almost the equivalent of that of the earlier KH-7 close-look system. In addition, in 1969 the Air Force had been able to make significant improvements in the resolution of the KH-7's successor, the KH-8.[31]

But there were still gaps in the U.S. program. In the fifty-one days between May 17 and July 8, 1976, no U.S. imagery satellites were in orbit. A lot could happen in fifty-one days—troops could be mobilized and deployed, aircraft redeployed, nations invaded. In addition, as the U.S. intelligence community was reminded by crisis after crisis—Cuba in 1962, the Six-Day War in 1967, Czechoslovakia in 1968, and the Yom Kippur War in 1973—satellite photos that were insufficiently timely had little value.

A satellite that would solve both problems was propelled into a polar orbit on a Titan 3D booster, launched from Vandenberg Air Force Base on the morning of December 19, 1976. Seemingly, yet another KH-9 had been placed into orbit. Although it was first assumed to be a KH-9 by Western observers and a SIGINT satellite by the Soviets, the payload was the first launch of a new type of reconnaissance spacecraft. The new satellite was known by three designations: the KH-11, for its optical system; KENNAN, for the program code name; and 5501, to designate the specific type of satellite (55) and mission number (01).[32]

The KH-11 represented a personal triumph for Leslie Dirks, the CIA's Deputy Director for Science and Technology, and for his predecessor Carl Duckett. Dirks had come to the CIA after obtaining a B.S. at the Massachusetts Institute of Technology in 1958 and a research degree from Oxford University in 1960. In 1962 Dirks and colleagues in the CIA's science and technology directorate began pondering whether the United States could launch a reconnaissance satellite that could be kept secret not only from the American public but from the Soviet Union as well. If the Soviets did not know that such a satellite was in orbit, they would take no steps to hide weapons or activities as it passed overhead. Dirks and his colleagues quickly concluded that a secret satellite in low-earth orbit was not feasible, for the Soviet space detection and tracking network would detect the launch and orbit of the satellite. On the other hand placing the satellite in a higher parking orbit and bringing it back to low-earth orbit when needed, even if it fooled the Soviets, had a major flaw. As the film sat in space unused it would begin to degrade, and by the time the secret satellite received the call the entire film supply might be worthless.[33]

The alternative to film brought Dirks and his colleagues back full circle to the concept of a television-type imagery return system. Whether or not such a satellite could be kept secret from Soviet space watchers, it could send back timely data. While the technology was no more at hand in 1962 than it was in 1952, Dirks realized that it might be at hand in 1972. For the next ten years he kept the project alive, looking for advances in technology that would permit such a system, seeking support for research into relevant areas.[34]

By 1969 the Cuban missile crisis, Six-Day War, and Soviet invasion of Czechoslovakia had demonstrated the potential value of a real-time system. COMIREX undertook to study the matter systematically, examining each of those events. The study explored how the intelligence community, the president, and other high-level officials could make use of such data in a crisis. It focused on what information could have been obtained in each situation, how it might have changed perceptions of the crisis, and the utility of such information.[35]

The study's conclusions were sufficiently positive for both the CIA and Air Force Office of Special Projects to present proposals for a real-time system. Eventually, after bureaucratic battles and end-runs by scientific advisers, the CIA's proposal was accepted as the basis for the real-time satellite. The product of that effort, the KH-11 that was launched on December 19, 1976, was about 64 feet long, was 10 feet in diameter, and weighed about 30,000 pounds.[36]

The key to the KH-11 being able to produce imagery in real time was the charged-couple device, or CCD, which had not been invented with any reconnaissance application in mind. The CCD originated at Bell Labs in the late 1960s when William S. Boyle and George E. Smith sought to invent a new type of memory circuit. It rapidly became apparent to them that the tiny chip of semiconducting silicon they unveiled in 1970 had other applications, including imaging (because silicon responds to visible light). CCDs would become widespread in hundreds of civilian and military programs, including medical imaging, plasma physics, ground astronomy, the Galileo spacecraft, the Hubble space telescope, and home video cameras.[37]

A KH-11's optical system scans its target in long, narrow strips and focuses the light onto an array of charged-couple devices with several thousand elements. The light falling on each CCD during a short, fixed period of time is then transformed into a proportional amount of electric charge. In turn, the electric charge is read off and fed into an amplifier, which converts the current into a whole number between 0 and 256 that represents a shade of color ranging from pure black to pure white. Thus each picture is transmitted as a string of numbers, one from each picture element, or pixel.[38]

In addition to the CCDs a crucial element of the KH-11 optical system was a mirror, which reflected the light from the target area onto a secondary mirror, which then refocused it on the CCDs. Without a good mirror in front of them, even the best CCDs would produce poor photographs. But the ninety-two-inch-wide mirror on the first KH-11 was very good.[39]

After collecting the visible light and transforming it into an electrical charge, 5501 would then transmit the data to one of two Satellite Data System (SDS) spacecraft* for relay to the KH-11 ground station at Fort Belvoir, Virginia, about twenty miles south of Washington. Surprisingly, no attempt was made to encrypt the KH-11 signals received at Fort Belvoir, on the grounds that use of a dish sufficiently large to intercept the signals would easily be detected.[40]

As a result of its electronic method of transmitting data the first KH-11 would remain in orbit for 770 days, when it would be replaced by 5502. There was one serious initial limitation on the new system. While it could transmit its data instantaneously, it could do so for only two to four hours a day. The power required to transmit its data to an SDS satellite

---

* The first two SDS spacecraft were placed in orbit in June and August 1976. The SDS orbit would take the craft as close as 250 miles to the earth when it passed over the Southern Hemisphere and as far away as 24,000 miles when it passed over the Northern Hemisphere, making it ideal as a relay for the KH-11 imagery when the satellite was transmitting over the Soviet Union. An SDS satellite would take eight to nine hours to pass over Soviet territory, leaving it available to receive and transmit KH-11 imagery for long stretches of time.

was so great that it drained power far faster than it could be replaced by the satellite's solar panels. It would therefore be several years before it would be possible to consider terminating the KH-8 and KH-9 programs.[41]

Verification Politics

The potential impact of technical collection on international events was particularly evident on June 18, 1979, when Jimmy Carter and Leonid Brezhnev signed SALT II. Far more complicated than SALT I, SALT II provided for equal ceilings on the number of strategic nuclear delivery vehicles (2,400, to be further reduced to 2,250 by the end of 1981), the total number of MIRVs (multiple independently targetable reentry vehicles) and heavy bombers with long-range cruise missiles, the number of MIRVed ballistic missiles (1,200), and the number of MIRVed ICBM launchers (820). It also imposed limits on the number of warheads specific missiles could carry and bans on the construction of additional fixed ICBM launchers and on increases in the number of fixed heavy ICBM launchers.

But some members of the U.S. Senate, which would have to ratify the treaty, were concerned over the issue of verification, a concern which was heightened by several events. The compromise of information concerning RHYOLITE (which had been renamed AQUACADE), due to Christopher Boyce and Andrew Daulton Lee, alarmed some senators.

In an attempt to compensate for any loss in AQUACADE's value, the Carter administration decided to modify the focus of another satellite program, code-named CHALET. CHALET spacecraft had been designed in the early 1970s to serve as the U.S. intelligence community's primary means of collecting UHF communications intelligence from space. The primary targets of CHALET were the facilities associated with the Soviet missile program—missile sites; research, development, test, and evaluation sites; defense ministries; and defense industries.[42]

Unlike RHYOLITE, the CHALET program had no telemetry interception role when first conceived. Consequently, the first CHALET satellite, launched on June 10, 1978, had a pure COMINT mission. However, the second spacecraft was modified before its October 1, 1979, launch to allow the interception of the same type of signals that were accessible to AQUACADE.[43]

To help convince the public of the ability of the United States to verify the SALT II agreement, someone in the Carter administration leaked word of CHALET's modification to *New York Times* reporter Richard Burt. His front-page story would not only result in a new code name, VORTEX, being assigned to the program, but in some trouble for Burt when he was nominated by the Reagan administration for a position in the State Department.

Of course, in addition to space assets the United States had a variety of airborne and ground systems involved in monitoring Soviet strategic weapons programs, and thus providing some of the intelligence required for arms control verification. Among the most prominent ground systems was one located on a rocky plateau in southeastern Turkey.

Detecting and tracking Soviet missiles was the primary function of two radars at Pirinclik Air Base, a satellite operation of Diyarbakir Air Station—an AN/FPS-17 detection radar and an AN/FPS-79 tracking radar. The antennas of the two radars, which could detect an object 1 meter in diameter up to 5,000 miles away, were fixed permanently toward the northeast, with the Soviet border 180 miles away. The electronic beams of the radars operated through a natural "duct" in the mountain around the plateau, picking up Soviet missile and space launches as they rose above the horizon.[44]

After the detection radar indicated that a missile or space launch had taken place, the AN/FPS-79 would swing "its white round face in a noiseless arc in the same direction, ready to track the missiles along their course." In addition to detecting and tracking launches from Tyuratam and Kapustin Yar via radar, the presence of VHF and UHF antennas at Pirinclik allowed the interception of communications associated with missile and space launches.[45]

From late July 1975 to November 3, 1978, the Turkish government shut the station down, along with all other U.S. intelligence facilities in Turkey. This was the Turkish government's response to a congressional embargo on arms sales to Turkey—the U.S. government's response to Turkey's actions in Cyprus. During that time, U.S. housekeeping personnel rotated one radar dish to prevent roller bearing damage while the Turks locked up a key piece of radar equipment to make sure the radar was inoperative.[46]

That the the Turkish sites were subject to the vagaries of the U.S.–Turkish–Greek–Cypriot relations might have been less disturbing had the United States not lost the even more significant network of ground stations in Iran in early 1979. This loss included the two major Iranian posts, Tacksman I and Tacksman II, at Kabkan and Behshahr. The Kabkan facility itself was in stark contrast to the surrounding area—a remote mountainous locale inhabited by nomads. However, it was not the local environment that interested the CIA, but rather the fact that Kabkan was only 650 miles south of the Tyuratam space center and ICBM test facility.[47]

The Behshahr facility consisted, by 1978, of four major units: a command center built into a hilltop, a radar antenna inside a thirty-foot-high dome, a radio monitoring device atop a steel tower, and a relay station pointed upward for communication with U.S. satellites. The radio monitoring device had four eight-foot-long arms studded with quill-like protrusions. The arms almost joined at the front and pointed toward the Caspian

Sea. By the beginning of 1979 one hundred U.S. technicians operated the equipment.[48]

The loss of the stations was damaging in two ways. The sites had unique capabilities. They were capable of direct line-of-sight monitoring of the Soviet test site at Tyuratam; whereas the Turkish bases would pick up the missile after it had climbed above 250 miles, the Iranian sites could pick it up after 60 miles. As a result the Iranian sites could pick up telemetry from the last moments of the second stage, which translated into a greater degree of confidence concerning missile dimensions and throw weight. In addition, the Iranian site enjoyed a better duct for listening to ground and air communications.[49]

A worst-case view was given by one official in 1979:

> Kabkan is not replaceable. No tricks are going to overcome that in the short run, and the short run could be three or four years. It is going to affect our capability on verification. I don't think people realize how important that base was, not just for SALT, but generally for keeping up with the Soviet missile program. It provided basic information on Soviet missile testing and development. You're talking about a pretty big loss. It's serious.[50]

Coming after the public exposure of the RHYOLITE compromise, the loss further increased concern about U.S. ability to verify SALT II. Thus the Secretary of State at the time, Cyrus Vance, has written:

> The loss of the collection stations in Iran . . . was a serious setback, both in the sense of temporarily impairing our ability to check Soviet compliance with certain SALT limitations and in its impact on key senators, such as John Glenn, who had become the Senate's leading expert on monitoring.[51]

The Chinese Target

By the end of the 1970s the technical collection networks of the superpowers and their allies had expanded dramatically from 1960. Two of America's most important intelligence allies—Australia and Britain—were operating a variety of ground stations for signals interception.

Included were three sites targeted on China. The first site established was a joint British Government Communications Headquarters (GCHQ)-Australian Defense Signals Directorate (DSD) facility at Little Sai Wan on Hong Kong, with a contingent of 140 Australians. Until the mid-1970s the Hong Kong facility was targeted almost exclusively on China, but with the establishment of a Soviet naval base at Cam Ranh Bay it became heavily involved in monitoring Soviet naval traffic along East Asia.[52]

In 1976 the intercept effort was expanded with construction of a huge new complex at Tai Mo Shan in Hong Kong's New Territories. The aerial farm at the new facility was even larger than the one at Little Sai Wan. The following year the GCHQ and the British Royal Air Force built the

Stanley Fort Satellite Station, code-named Project KITTIWAKE. That same year the Australian government approved DSD's participation in the operation. The mission of the satellite station was to eavesdrop on Chinese satellite communictions and intercept telemetry from Chinese nuclear weapon, missile, and satellite test activities.[53]

21

Penetrations, Sunken Subs, and Sudden Death

The 1970s saw no crises as serious as the Cuban missile crisis, no agent as valuable as Oleg Penkovskiy, no single technical advance quite so dramatic as the initial use of space for intelligence purposes. But the decade was marked by a number of notable events in the history of intelligence and a number of instances in which intelligence successes or failures helped shape world events.

Each superpower and its allies would achieve notable penetrations of the other's national security establishments, including their intelligence services. The United States would continue its highly profitable program of seeking to acquire Soviet weaponry. And the United States, the Soviet Union, and Israel would all demonstrate their willingness to resort to extreme forms of covert action to protect what they perceived to be their national interests.

Penetrations

The United States was able, once again, to penetrate the GRU, in the person of Colonel Anatoli Nikolaevich Filatov, who approached the CIA in the mid-1970s while stationed in Algiers. In the fourteen months before being transferred back to GRU headquarters, he provided the United States with a variety of Soviet intelligence and military secrets. After his transfer back to Moscow, Filatov continued to provide information for another year, at which time he was detected filling a dead drop.[1]*

The CIA was also able to penetrate the Soviet Foreign Ministry. Aleksandr Dmitrevich Ogorodnik, code-named TRIGON, became an agent in 1974, while serving as second secretary of the Soviet embassy in Bogotá,

---

* The inevitable death sentence was commuted to fifteen years' imprisonment in exchange for U.S. release of two KGB agents who had been arrested for espionage and had no diplomatic immunity. As of 1990 Filatov was an inmate at the Perm 58 labor camp.

Colombia. In 1975 he returned to Moscow and a position in the ministry's Global Affairs Department. Among the information flowing into the department were KGB intelligence reports and the year-end comprehensive report of each Soviet ambassador. Ogorodnik's espionage career appears to have ended by the spring of 1977, and certainly by July 15, 1977, when his case officer, Martha Peterson, was arrested at a dead drop.[2]*

West Germany's BND also came up with some valuable recruits, including East German Rear Admiral Winfried Baumann-Zakrowski. From the mid-1970s until 1985, the BND was receiving military and scientific secrets from a prominent Soviet journalist, Ilya M. Suslov. Suslov, an editor for the Novosti Press Agency and the former host of a television program on space exploration, was accused of having cajoled "well-known people who had done much for Soviet science" into providing him with secret information in exchange for promises of publicity, and then passing the information to the BND.[3]

The KGB and GRU were also busy, with high-ranking agents on several continents. In Iran, the Soviets had Major General Ahmad Mogharebi on their payroll. Mogharebi had first provided intelligence to the Soviets in the early 1950s and, from 1967 until his 1977 arrest, he served as Deputy Chief of Staff for Plans of the Iranian supreme commander's staff and as a KGB agent. Another KGB agent, an illegal, operated undetected in the United States from 1962 to 1974, collecting scientific and technical intelligence.[4]

Among the GRU's agents was Brigadier General Jean Louis Jeanmiare, the retired commander of the Swiss Air Protection Service, who had been recruited after his 1961 retirement. In the years between his recruitment and arrest in 1976, he probably provided the Soviets with information on Swiss aircraft capabilities, air defense plans, and early warning systems. In Japan, from 1975 to December 1979, retired Japanese Major General Yukihisa Miyanaga was, according to a CIA study, a "highly productive GRU source," who recruited two of his former subordinates who were still serving with Japanese military intelligence. Meanwhile, in South Africa Dieter Felix Gehrhardt, who would become the commandant of the Simonstown Naval Station, had been spying for the the GRU since 1964.[5]

In three other cases the KGB and GRU were able to penetrate into the heart of the U.S. and British technical collection program.

Prime, Boyce, and Kampiles

In early January 1968, while passing through a Soviet checkpoint in Berlin, Corporal Geoffrey Arthur Prime passed a note to a Soviet officer requesting that he be contacted by Soviet intelligence. At that time Prime

---

* According to various accounts Ogorodnik managed to commit suicide before serious interrogation began.

was assigned to the British SIGINT station at RAF Gatow, an assignment that was scheduled to end in August.[6]

With the concurrence of his Soviet controllers Prime applied for, and received, a job processing Russian-language intercepts at the Government Communications Headquarters. Before beginning work in late September, Prime spent a week at the Soviet compound in East Berlin, where he was trained in radio transmission, cipher communications, photography with a Minox camera, and other elements of the trade. Before returning to Britain he was given the code name ROWLANDS, a set of one-time pads, and secret writing materials.[7]

For the next six and a half years Prime served with the the GCHQ's London Processing Group (LPG), subsequently the Joint Technical Language Service (JTLS), which transcribed foreign-language conversations. The LPG's location in London, away from GCHQ in Cheltenham, and the nature of its work limited Prime's value to the Soviets. After his initial reports, which revealed the communications channels being monitored and the scrambler phones that had been penetrated, the Soviets only needed information as to new targets or channels.[8]

Prime's value was further compromised by his loss of his one-time pads, which the Soviets did not replace until 1974. But what he had to communicate was only of marginal value. It would not be until 1975 that he would become a full-fledged agent again. In March 1976 he moved from JTLS to GCHQ itself, where he was assigned to the Special SIGINT (J) Division of the Directorate of SIGINT Operations and Requirements, whose target was the Soviet Union. On November 1 he became a section head and regularly attended meetings where discussions concerning GCHQ's most sensitive operations were held.[9]

But his career at GCHQ was to be short-lived. By the summer of 1977 he was feeling the pressure of his double life. And the conviction of two young Americans for betraying satellite secrets to the KGB reminded him of the likely consequences if he was caught. At first Prime decided to defect, but he couldn't bring himself to take that irrevocable act. Instead, on September 20, 1977, he resigned.[10]

During his time at Cheltenham Prime made at least one trip to Vienna with film of documents he had photographed. When he left GCHQ he still had fifteen rolls of Minox film, with about 500 pictures of top-secret documents taken between the time of his resignation and his most recent trip to Vienna. In April 1980, in response to a KGB request, he would again fly to Vienna to deliver his take.[11]*

The two Americans whose conviction had so alarmed Prime were Christopher Boyce and Andrew Daulton Lee. In April 1975 Lee had walked through the front door of the Soviet embassy in Mexico City and

---

* Prime's espionage may never have come to Western attention had it not been for his sexual assaults on young girls. In 1982 his attacks on young girls attracted police attention, and his wife turned him in. In October 1982 he was sentenced to thirty-eight years in prison—thirty-five for espionage, three for sexual assault.

handed a typewritten note to the first official he encountered: "Enclosed is a computer card from the National Security Agency crypto system. . . . If you want to do business, please advise the courier."[12]

Lee, who was more familiar with peddling marijuana than crypto cards, was acting as an intermediary for his boyhood friend, Christopher Boyce. Despite being a twenty-two-year-old college dropout, and working at a $140-a-week job, Boyce had access to secrets about some of the most advanced U.S. satellite reconnaissance programs. For Boyce worked in the Black Vault of TRW, a bank-style vault with a three-number combination and an inside door with a key lock. Inside the vault, he monitored the secret communications traffic relating to various CIA-TRW satellite projects.[13]

Those projects included RHYOLITE, described in a briefing to Boyce as a "multipurpose covert electronic surveillance system." Boyce also was briefed on ARGUS, the planned follow-on system to RHYOLITE, and PYRAMIDER, described by CIA Deputy Director for Science and Technology Leslie C. Dirks as "a system to provide a means for communicating with CIA agents, foreign agents, emplaced sensors and provide backup communications for overseas facilities." Agents would communicate with the satellite using a portable transceiver.[14]

Boyce compromised them all. He would claim that his actions were his way of retaliating against the U.S. government for a host of sins, including the war in Vietnam; domestic hypocrisy; events in Chile; and what he claimed was U.S. deception of Australia, host of the RHYOLITE Eastern Hemisphere ground station, concerning the ARGUS program. He had a wealth of material to choose from, with fifty to sixty messages a day passing through his hands, messages which were kept on file for a year.[15]

Within a year after beginning work in the Black Vault Boyce, using Lee as a courier, began providing the Soviets with roll after roll of film full of photos of upcoming key cards and messages concerning the CIA-TRW satellite reconnaissance programs. All together, Lee would make seven trips to meet with KGB officers. On March 15, 1976, he arrived in Vienna and delivered ten rolls of film, containing a month of ciphers; RHYOLITE communications traffic between TRW, the CIA, and the RHYOLITE ground station in Australia, and a thick technical report on the proposed ARGUS system.[16]

In early October 1976 Boyce, for the first time, joined Lee in Mexico City. Once there it became apparent that, as much as the KGB may have valued the intelligence Boyce was providing on U.S. satellites, they thought he could be more useful elsewhere. The KGB would be willing, Boyce was told, to provide $40,000 to pay for college and graduate school. Boyce would become a Soviet or Chinese specialist and find a job with the State Department or CIA. Before the month was out Boyce had applied for admission to the University of California at Riverside.[17]

But the KGB's plan to turn Boyce into a mole was torpedoed by Lee's impulsive behavior. Such behavior led his handler, Boris, on one occasion, to pack him in a car and toss him out onto the road. But the lesson did not have a permanent effect. On January 6, 1977, eager to get money to purchase drugs from a Mexican supplier, Lee tried to get Boris's attention by throwing a Spanish–American dictionary, on which he had marked "KGB," onto the embassy grounds. Fearing that Lee was a terrorist and his dictionary was a bomb, the Mexican police immediately arrested Lee and discovered a sealed envelope with microfilm strips inside. The strips contained 450 frames concerning the PYRAMIDER project, which had been started in February 1973, and shelved.[18]

Within a few months Boyce and Lee were being tried separately. There was no mention at the trial of RHYOLITE or ARGUS, since the very existence of U.S. SIGINT satellites was (and still is) classified. The focus of their trial was their disclosure of PYRAMIDER. On July 18 Lee, who served as Boyce's courier, received life imprisonment. On September 12, Boyce, who had been granted the clearances and had the responsibility for protecting the information, received forty years.[19]

The third Soviet penetration of Western technical collection operations occurred in 1978 when William Kampiles, a former CIA employee who had been frustrated in his attempts to move from the CIA Operations Center, which monitored incoming intelligence, to the Directorate of Operations, sold the GRU a copy of the *KH-11 Technical Manual.*

Kampiles, a 1976 Indiana University graduate, started work at the CIA in March 1977, as one of about sixty-five watch analysts in the seventh-floor CIA Operations Center. Despite the secrecy oaths, code words, and access to highly sensitive intelligence, Kampiles found the work tedious. Instead of using the fluent Greek he had learned from his parents to work for the CIA overseas, his life in the CIA was a drab procession of twelve-hour shifts in a single room.[20]

His requests for a transfer to the Directorate of Operations were undermined by his record, which was not sufficiently impressive to stimulate interest there. Continued requests were matched by deteriorating performance. In November 1977, after only eight months in the CIA, and after receiving a formal letter indicating dissatisfaction with his performance, he resigned.[21]

Before departing for good, Kampiles pilfered copy 155 of the KH-11 manual and took it with him, minus the classification markings he cut off, on a February 1978 trip to Greece. On February 22 or 23 he went to the Soviet embassy and told "an older, balding, fat Soviet official" he could provide information on a long-term basis.[22]

When Kampiles returned a day or so later he was greeted by Major Michael Zavali, a military attaché and officer in the GRU. At that meeting, Kampiles provided Zavali with two or three pages of the KH-11 manual—its table of contents, summary, and an artist's conception of what the satellite looked like. On March 2 Kampiles requested $10,000 for the remainder of the manual but settled for $3,000.[23]

Zavali expressed interest in obtaining additional documents from Kampiles and instructed him to give priority to information on U.S. military capabilities, military installations, and CIA personnel abroad rather than on what the U.S. knew of Soviet military capabilities.[24]

Kampiles's career as a GRU agent was sabotaged shortly after his return by his own actions. He told a CIA friend that he had been in Athens and conned the Soviets, receiving $3,000. Kampiles's statement set off a chain of events that resulted in his admitting to the FBI, who knew that the Soviets never paid money without receiving information, that he had sold the KH-11 manual.[25]

The manual, according to Leslie Dirks, described "the characteristics of the system, its limitations, and its capabilities" and described the "process of photography employed by the KH-11 system and illustrates the quality of the photos and the process used in passing the product along to the users of the system." It also detailed the "responsiveness and timeliness in the delivery of the 'product.'" Page 8 of the sixty-four-page manual described the satellite's "limitations in geographic coverage."[26]

Possession of the manual would, said Dirks, "put the Soviet Union in a position to avoid coverage from this system. For example, by rolling . . . new aircraft under test into hangars when the system passes overhead, thereby preventing photographs of the new airplanes." In addition, knowledge of the quality of the photographs could enable the Soviets to devise effective camouflage.[27]

The acquisition of the manual was a particularly valuable coup for the Soviets, who had completely misunderstood the mission of the first two KH-11s, launched in December 1976 and February 1978. The Soviets had interpreted press reports concerning U.S. development of a real-time photographic reconnaissance satellite to be launched in the 1976–77 time period as referring to a modified version of the KH-9, which was launched with a different type booster into a lower orbit. The KH-11 launches were believed by the Soviets to be connected with the U.S. SIGINT satellite program. As a result they had taken no precautions in hiding military activities and weapons systems from the satellite's optical system when it passed overhead.[28]

China's Mole

Larry Wu-Tai Chin began his employment with the U.S. government in 1943 with the U.S. Army Liaison Mission in China. In 1948 he worked as an interpreter in the American consulate in Shanghai and two years later took a job as a secretary-interpreter at the American embassy in Hong Kong. During the Korean War Chin interviewed Chinese prisoners captured by U.S. and Korean troops.[29]

In 1952 he began monitoring Chinese radio broadcasts for the agency's Foreign Broadcast Information Service (FBIS) Okinawa unit. In 1961 he moved to Santa Rosa, California, where he continued to work for FBIS. From 1970 until his retirement in 1981, Chin worked as an analyst in the

FBIS office in northern Virginia and also served as the FBIS document control officer.[30]

Chin's career as a spy may have begun in the early 1940s, when he apparently received espionage training while still a college student. In 1952 Chin was paid $2,000 by Chinese intelligence agents for having located Chinese POWs in Korea. He also provided Chinese agents with information on the intelligence being sought from Chinese prisoners by U.S. and Korean intelligence officers. In 1967 he allegedly began regular meetings with his People's Republic controllers in Hong Kong. Between 1976 and 1982, Chin met four times with a courier for Chinese intelligence, "Mr. Lee," at a shopping mall near Toronto International Airport. Speaking in Cantonese, Chin handed over undeveloped film of classified documents from FBIS.[31]

The information Chin provided led the PRC to pay him several hundred thousand dollars over a thirty-year career. Although the FBIS is best known for its translation of the public broadcasts of foreign nations (and less known for its translations of the broadcasts of clandestine and black radios), the service's analysts also use classified intelligence reports to help assess the significance of foreign broadcasts. Further, Chin's skill as an interpreter and his long tenure gave him acess to a great deal of highly classified data. Thus Chin "was more than a guy . . . listening to People's Republic of China broadcasts and translating People's Daily." According to testimony given at his indictment Chin "reviewed, translated and analyzed classified documents from covert and overt human and technical collection sources which went into the West's assessment of Chinese strategic, military, economic, scientific and technical capabilities and intentions," and in 1979 passed on such an assessment to "Mr. Lee."[32]

Wolf's Master Spy

By the 1970s Markus Wolf was firmly established as chief of the Main Department for Intelligence (HVA) of the Ministry for State Security (MfS) and as the premier espionage chief in the Soviet satellite countries. From 1970 to 1974 he achieved his greatest coup, with the penetration of the office of the West German Chancellor Willy Brandt.

That penetration had its origins in 1956 when an HVA agent, posing as a political émigré, arrived in West Germany. Guenter Guillaume and his wife, Christel, settled in Frankfurt, and in 1957 he began his political career, joining the Social Democratic Party. He became a party functionary, devoted considerable effort to the SDP cause, gained the trust of his superiors, and was promoted. His professed political views were somewhat to the right of center. In the 1960s the nature of his work gave him access to little strategic intelligence. However, in 1970 he was recommended for a position in the Bundeskanzeleramt, the Office of the Federal

Chancellor. His superiors praised his "diligence and devotion," "reliability," and "unbounded trustworthiness."[33]

Before being appointed Guillaume had to overcome the opposition of General Gerhard Wessel, Reinhard Gehlen's successor as head of the BND. In a letter to Horst Ehmke, head of the chancellor's office, Wessel voiced certain suspicions concerning Guillaume. But Ehmke was determined to appoint Guillaume, accepting his word that he was not a spy.[34]

Guillaume became Brandt's personal assistant and confidant, his primary responsibility being liaison between the chancellor's office and SDP headquarters, allowing him to provide the HVA with biographical details on the SDP leadership. In addition, he accompanied Brandt on his travels and gained detailed knowledge on his private life, including his preference for young women.[35]

But his position in the chancellor's office and his relationship to Brandt gave him access to far more than inside political information. From Brandt's trusted assistant, the HVA—and the KGB—received copies of nineteen secret and confidential telex messages concerning the substance of a secret NATO conference, German Foreign Ministry discussions with Richard Nixon and Henry Kissinger, Western positions on the Berlin four-power agreement, and two Nixon letters on U.S. relations with Europe. He was also able to inform the HVA of the attempts of West German counter-intelligence (BfV—Bundesamt für Verfassungsschutz—Federal Office for Protection of the Constitution) to prevent penetration of the SPD. During Brandt's 1973 Norway vacation, Guillaume had access to the chancellor's classified communications traffic. Unquestionably, this was only a fraction of the material Guillaume delivered.[36]

The intelligence received from Guillaume was particularly valuable during the negotiation of treaties with the Federal Republic. Advance knowledge of West German negotiating strategies allowed the East German regime to obtain maximum benefits with a minimum of concessions.[37]

In the spring of 1973 suspicions about Guillaume were heightened, when the BfV concluded that previously intercepted coded MfS messages, sent to GEORGE and CHR in 1956 and 1957, were most likely intended for Guillaume and his wife. In May 1973 the minister of the interior informed Brandt of the new concern, but neither took action. In his memoirs Brandt would observe that "I had not taken the suspicion seriously, and—not for the first time—found I had overestimated my knowledge of human nature."[38]

Guillaume's dual life finally came to an end on April 24, 1974, when he was arrested in his Bad Godesberg apartment. Brandt was forced to resign, and a parliamentary investigation of the West German security services followed. In 1981 Guillaume was released from prison as part of a spy exchange. He returned to East Germany, was promoted to colonel, and was awarded an honorary doctorate in law. Wolf would later comment that "the original idea was not to get Guillaume attached to Brandt, this happened by sheer accident and we thought it would be stupid not make the most of what seemed such good fortune."[39]

Project JENNIFER

On April 11, 1968, while on a routine patrol that had taken it about 750 miles northwest of Hawaii, a Soviet Golf-class submarine surfaced to recharge its batteries. Instead, the submarine exploded and sank in waters three miles deep. Going down with the submarine was its crew of seventy, three nuclear-tipped missiles, and cipher material.[40]

What was a tragedy for the Soviet navy was an unprecedented opportunity for the U.S. intelligence community. The Soviets, knowing only the general area where it had disappeared but not what happened to the submarine, began surveillance of all possible disaster sites, listening for radio transmissions and sending out their own. While the Soviet navy proved unable to locate the ship, the U.S. Navy did. A set of ocean-bottom hydrophones, part of the Navy's Sound Surveillance System (SOSUS), allowed Navy analysts to locate the submarine to within a ten-square-mile area. A Navy research ship, the *Mizar*, was sent to the area to determine the submarine's precise location.[41]

The idea of mounting an effort to recover the Soviet submarine originated with Carl Duckett, the CIA's Deputy Director for Science and Technology. At first, DCI Richard Helms thought the idea preposterous. "You must be crazy," was his response. The United States had certainly devoted extensive effort over the years to acquiring Soviet weapons systems of varying sorts, including MiG aircraft. But recovery of a submarine represented a quantum leap. However, after further consideration Helms approved Duckett's suggestion.[42]

The advantages to be gained by salvaging the submarine and its contents were considered obvious by intelligence officials. On board the submarine would be an array of coding and decoding devices. It was also believed that the submarine was armed with three nuclear missiles—either the 350-mile-range SS-N-4 SNARK or the 700-mile-range SS-N-5 SERB—and some nuclear-tipped torpedoes. In addition, documents concerning Soviet nuclear targeting policy might be on board.[43]

Examination of the warheads would provide the United States with an insight into the state of Soviet nuclear technology—particularly the reliability, accuracy, and detonation mechanisms of the missiles. Recovery would also give naval analysts their first chance to examine Soviet torpedoes. Examining the homing devices incorporated into the design of the torpedo would aid those responsible for designing countermeasures. The steel used in the hulls could be subjected to metallurgical analysis to determine the depth to which Soviet subs could dive.[44]

At the time a prize of great value was considered to be the cipher machines and Soviet code manuals that might be stored in watertight safes. (Subsequently, some intelligence experts played down the value on the grounds that the Soviet code machines, like U.S. machines, are constructed to permit the operator to reset circuits and insert new coding and encoding discs at random.)[45]

With approval from the White House, the CIA proceeded to contact Howard Hughes, whose organization had a passion for secrecy. Additionally, the new president of Hughes Aircraft was Albert "Bud" Wheelon, who only a few years before served as the CIA's Deputy Director for Science and Technology. Hence Hughes and the CIA began work on Project AZORIAN.[46]

Hughes, along with its subcontractors, produced the *Glomar Explorer*—36,000 tons, 618 feet in length, and 115.5 feet in the beam—to serve as a floating, highly stable platform. Amidships a high derrick would pass piping directly through the "moon pool" in the ship's hull, which could be opened or closed. The moon pool was a 200-foot-long, 65-foot-wide pool into which an object could be lifted from the sea. A companion to the ship was a huge submersible barge, the *HMB-1*, roughly the size of a football field, which would be covered by an oval roof. The barge would carry the gigantic retrieval claws that would grapple for the submarine and raise it. The roof would prevent Soviet reconnaissance satellites from photographing the cargo.[47]

On November 4, 1972, the *Glomar Explorer* was launched, ostensibly to mine the ocean floor for precious metals such as titanium, manganese, uranium, copper, and nickel. Of its 170-man crew, picked by the CIA, 40 men made up the mining staff and knew of the ship's secret mission. After its test run the ship returned to Los Angeles, rendezvoused with the *HMB-1* and, on June 20, 1974, headed out to sea on the recovery mission. At that point Project AZORIAN became Project JENNIFER.[48]

By the middle of July the submarine site was reached and the *Glomar Explorer* proceeded with its work, with the guidance of a computer and bottom-placed transducer so that the barge would stray no more than 50 feet from the mother ship. Pipe from the ship was attached to giant grappling claws, which resembled a series of six interconnected ice tongs hanging from a long platform. The ship's crew then began to feed length after length of pipe through the hole. By the time the claw reached the Soviet submarine 16,000 feet below, the pipe itself weighed more than 4,000 pounds. Claw operators used television cameras equipped with strobe lights to see what they were doing.[49]

According to accounts given by U.S. officials, as the claw began to encircle the sub, two or three prongs became entangled in the seabed. The claws were pulled through the seabed to encircle the submarine, but in the process some of the prongs were bent out of shape and thus were unable to support the submarine fully. At 5,000 feet the rear two-thirds of the submarine, which included the conning tower, three missiles, and the vessel's code room, broke off and sank back to the seabed. The front third was raised into the moon pool. Among the items recovered were two nuclear torpedoes and the bodies of six Soviet seamen, including the submarine's nuclear weapons officer. The journal he had kept of his training and assignments was also recovered, and it provided detailed information on Soviet naval nuclear systems operation and procedures. The *Glomar* returned on August 12, 1974.[50]*

It was also discovered that the subs used wooden two-by-fours in the building of some compartments—an extremely crude method—and the exterior welding of the hull was uneven and pitted, with the hull itself not being of constant thickness. Hatch covers and valves proved to have been crudely constructed in comparison to those on U.S. submarines. Two torpedoes recovered were determined to be powered by electric motors, while another two were steam-powered, which indicated that the submarine's firing tubes were not interchangeable. Several books and journals were recovered, some of whose pages could be deciphered after chemical treatment. Apparently included was a partial description of Soviet ciphers in effect in 1968.[51]

The six Soviet seamen were buried at sea in a nighttime ceremony on September 4, 1974. Before the vault carrying their bodies was lowered into the ocean the U.S. and Soviet national anthems were played. In a short address that followed, the speaker noted that "the fact that our nations have had disagreements doesn't lessen in any way our respect for [the seamen]," and that "as long as nations are suspicious of each other . . . brave men will die as these men have died in the service of their country." The fifteen-minute ceremony was filmed by the CIA and, in 1992, a tape of the ceremony was given to President Yeltsin by DCI Robert Gates.[52]

Plans to salvage the remainder of the submarine, designated Project MATADOR, were canceled after public disclosure of the initial recovery attempt. But throughout the 1970s the United States was able to acquire access to a variety of other Soviet weaponry. Operation SAND DOLLAR involved the recovery of Soviet missile test warheads that splashed down in the Pacific Broad Ocean Area at the conclusion of long-range ICBM tests. In 1976, MiG-25 pilot Viktor Belenko defected from the Soviet Union with his plane, landing in Japan. Before being returned to the Soviet Union, after insistent Soviet demands, the entire plane was disassembled at Hyakuri Air Base and examined by members of the Air Force Foreign Technology Division. The engines, radar, computer, electronic countermeasures, automatic pilot, and communications equipment were

* A June 1993 a report issued by a panel of experts under the office of Russian president Boris Yeltsin claimed that the United States had recovered two warheads. The level of radiation the panel suggested was removed from the sub would be consistent with that contained by two nuclear torpedoes. The panel's claim was said to be made on the basis of Russian information, not Western press accounts—perhaps indicating that the Soviet navy had used mini-subs to investigate the wreckage subsequent to U.S. press reports of the recovery operation. William J. Broad, "Russia Says U.S. Got Sub's Atom Arms," *New York Times*, June 20, 1993, p. 4; "CIA Raising USSR Sub Raises Questions," *FBIS-SOV-92-145*, July 28, 1992, pp. 15–16.

placed on blocks and stands for mechanical, metallurgical, and photographic analysis.[53]

Examination of the plane, as well as debriefing of the pilot, sharply altered Western understanding of the plane and its missions. Among the discoveries was a radar more powerful than any previously installed in any interceptor or fighter, and the use of vacuum tubes rather than transistors. Vacuum tubes, although a more primitive technology than transistors, are resistant to the electromagnetic pulse (EMP) created by nuclear detonations.[54]

Hit Teams

The 1970s would be marked not only by silent espionage penetrations, secret recoveries, and technological advances, but by some visible and noisy operations. A prime example is Israel's use of bombs and bullets to retaliate for terrorist attacks, particularly an attack that attracted attention throughout the world.

On September 5, 1972, in Munich, seven members of the Black September organization, a secret branch of the Palestine Liberation Organization (PLO), seized eleven Israeli athletes in the Olympic Village. They then demanded that Israel free 234 of their colleagues from prison in exchange for the athletes who remained alive after the kidnapping (one athlete and one coach were killed in the kidnapping operation).[55]

German authorities agreed to the terrorists' demand that a plane be provided to transport them and their hostages to Cairo, although the intention was to have German sharpshooters "take out" the kidnapper's at the airport. As Zvi Zamir, the chief of the Mossad, watched, the Germans botched the operation. While some of the Black September terrorists were hit by the first wave of shots, several were able to kill the handcuffed hostages as they sat in the helicopters that had brought them to the airport.[56]

To consider retaliation for Munich Israel set up a special committee, designated Committee X, chaired by Prime Minister Golda Meir and Defense Minister Moshe Dayan. The committee decided to eliminate any Black September terrorists involved, directly or indirectly, in the massacre. The Mossad established a set of hit squads, directed by Mike Harrari, the Mossad's forty-six-year-old operations chief, who had served as a radio operator with the Mossad LeAlyia Bet in Rome after World War II. After completing IDF service in 1950, he joined the Shin Bet. After his switch to the Mossad, he became an agent-runner in Europe in the 1960s and deputy head of operations before the end of the decade. In 1970 he became chief of operations.[57]

The first victim of the hit squads was Wael Abu Zwaiter, the head of Black September operations in Italy, who had been involved in the May 1992 massacre at Israel's Lod airport as well as a Black September attempt on an El-Al plane in August 1971. On October 16, 1972, a Mossad operative shot twelve bullets into Zwaiter outside his house as he returned home from an evening with a friend. On December 8, Mahimun Hamchari, the number two Black September official in France, was blown to bits in his Paris apartment by an explosive charge placed in his telephone. The explosives were detonated when Hamchari answered a phone call and acknowledged that he was speaking. A few weeks later, Hussein al-Shir, the resident Black September agent in Cyprus and the PLO's contact with the KGB in Cyprus was killed by explosives placed under his bed.[58]

April 1973 saw Israeli hit teams strike at several targets. Black September's Basil al-Kubaisi, who periodically traveled to Europe to arrange for the purchase and delivery of arms, was assassinated in Paris. More significant was Operation Spring of Youth. A combined Mossad–General Staff Reconnaissance Unit force landed on the beach at Beirut just after midnight on April 9. Ninety minutes later they broke into an apartment on the Rue Verdun and proceeded to kill Muhammad Najjar Abu and Kamal Adwin, two senior figures in Black September, and Kamal Nasser, the PLO's chief spokesman.[59]

Next was Mohammad Boudia, the head of the Black September organization in France and liaison to several European terrorist groups. On the night of June 27, 1973, Boudia left his car across the street from the apartment of a female friend. The next morning a bomb behind the seat was triggered as he took his place behind the wheel.[60]

Boudia's elimination left the primary target, Ali Hassan Salameh—the "Red Prince." In addition to being Black September's operations chief, Salameh also headed Force 17, which was responsible for protecting Yasir Arafat. In addition, Salameh served as the PLO's liaison to the CIA.[61]

In early 1973 the Mossad obtained information that Salameh would be operating out of a temporary base in Norway while he established a Black September network that would cover Scandinavia. The Mossad concluded, possibly on the basis of information from a Black September courier who had been intimated into becoming a Mossad agent, that an Arab waiter in the town of Lillehammer, Ahmed Bouchiki, was Salameh. On his way back to his apartment one July evening, Bouchiki was confronted by two members of the Israeli assassination squad, who shot him dead.[62]

Unfortunately for all involved, Bouchiki was truly Bouchiki. While the Mossad's information that Salameh was in Norway was correct, he was not where they believed him to be. Although neither of the assassins was apprehended, several members of the support team were, resulting in jail terms for them and extremely embarrassing publicity for Israel.

In early 1979 the Mossad finally caught up with Salameh in Beirut, his home base. A Volkswagen packed with explosives was parked on a street Salameh rode through. As his car passed the Volkswagen, the explosives were detonated by a Mossad operative, killing Salameh, the two bodyguards riding with him, and four persons in the vicinity.[63]

Make the Economy Scream

Many observers would point to Chile as one of the CIA's great covert action successes prior to 1970. In 1964 the CIA spent $2.6 million in support of Chile's Christian Democratic Party and its presidential candidate, Eduardo Frei. Exactly how that money affected the outcome of the race, which Frei won with 56 percent of the vote, may be impossible to say. But the CIA was certainly pleased with the results.[64]

This was not the first time that the CIA had sought to ensure a favorable outcome to a Chilean presidential election. In 1958 it had also supported the Christian Democrats. In both cases the opposition feared by the CIA was the Socialist Party and its candidate, Salvador Allende Gossens, whose platform included land reform, nationalization of major industries (especially copper), redistribution of income, and close relations with socialist and communist countries. As the 1970 election approached Allende was again running, arguing that Frei's moderate measures had failed to produce a fairer society. Aware that Allende would be running, the White House had been considering means of stopping Allende since December 1969. In March 1970 the 40 Committee, responsible for approving covert operations, approved the first anti-Allende propaganda campaign. Two months later, the committee approved an additional $300,000 for anti-Allende electioneering.[65]

The 1970 election featured three major candidates: Allende, a Christian Democratic candidate (Frei was forbidden by the constitution from running for a second consecutive term), and a conservative candidate. Despite a variety of CIA media and propaganda operations to undermine Allende, as well as support for the Christian Democratic candidate, Allende emerged from the September 4 election as the plurality winner, with 36 percent of the vote. Since Allende failed to obtain an absolute majority, the final choice had to be determined by a joint vote of the 50 senators and 100 members of the Chamber of Deputies. However, this gave the United States little hope, since the congress traditionally confirmed the plurality winner as president.[66]*

In the wake of Allende's plurality victory, and highly likely election by the Chilean congress, the Nixon administration began to consider various means of blocking his accession to power. Although the United States, according to the CIA, "had no vital interests within Chile," Nixon was concerned about what would happen to the substantial holdings of com-

---

* The automatic election tradition clearly flew in the face of the intent of the law's framers, since if they had wanted automatic approval of the plurality winner there would have been no point in requiring the congress to select the president under such circumstances. The law recognized a basic problem in plurality voting systems when there were more than two candidates—a candidate could be the plurality winner yet be the *last* choice of a *majority* of voters. That is, if there are three candidates (A, B, C) and 100 voters and 40 prefer A to B to C, 30 prefer B to C to A, and 30 prefer C to B to A, then A would be a plurality winner despite being the last choice of 60 percent of the voters.

panies such as ITT and Anaconda Copper under an Allende regime. On September 15, 1970, Nixon informed DCI Richard Helms that an Allende regime was unacceptable to the United States and instructed the CIA to play a role in organizing a military coup to prevent Allende from ever taking office.[67]

Helms's handwritten notes from September 15 meeting read:

One in 10 chance perhaps, but save Chile!
worth spending
not concerned risks involved
no involvement of Embassy
$10,000,000 available, more if necessary
full-time job—best men we have
game plan
make the economy scream
48 hours for plan of action.[68]

In accord with Nixon's orders a Chilean Task Force was assembled and began operations on September 18. Four CIA officers were inserted into Chile, and the U.S. military attaché in Santiago, Paul Wimert, was placed under operational direction of the CIA station chief. The campaign proceeded on two tracks. Under Track I (which was approved by the 40 Committee), the CIA employed a variety of covert political, economic, and propaganda tactics to manipulate the political scene. Track I included $250,000, which was never spent, to help convince Chilean legislators to break with tradition and select a candidate other than Allende. Other funds were spent on a propaganda campaign to convince three key elements in Chile—Frei, the Chilean political elite, and the Chilean military—of the need to prevent Allende from assuming office. The campaign included subsidization of radio programs, political advertisements, and political rallies of an anti-Allende group, placement of articles in newspapers, and the financing of a small newspaper. The campaign also included the direct mailing of foreign news articles to President Frei, his wife, selected military leaders, and the Chilean domestic press.[69]

In addition, in accord with Nixon's instructions to "make the economy scream," efforts were made to create financial and political panic to produce a military coup. Multinational corporations were approached to take such actions as as cutting off aid to Chile, stopping the shipments of spare parts, and causing runs on financial institutions.[70]

Track II involved direct efforts to produce a military coup—efforts that were kept secret from not only the State Department, but from the 40 Committee itself. The CIA proceeded to make twenty-one contacts in two weeks with key Chilean military personnel to assure them that the United States would support a coup d'état. Among those contacted were General Roberto Viaux, who had led a minor insurrection in 1969, ostensibly over military pay, and General Camilio Valenzuela, the commander of the Santiago garrison, who was supported by moderate conservatives on active duty in the army and navy. However, a major obstacle was the commander-in-chief of the army, General Rene Schneider, who strongly supported the constitutional process. It was clear to coup supporters that he would have to be, at the very least, abducted.[71]

At an October 15 meeting at the White House National Security Adviser Kissinger told Thomas Karamessines, the CIA's deputy director for operations, that the CIA was to keep "the pressure on every Allende weak point in sight—now, after the 24th, after 3rd November [inauguration day], and into the future until such time as new marching orders are given." The next day CIA headquarters cabled the Santiago station: "It is firm and continuing policy that Allende be overthrown by a coup. . . . We are to continue to generate maximum pressure utilizing every appropriate resource."[72]

On October 17 a Chilean army officer and navy officer met with the army attaché assigned to the CIA and requested eight to ten tear gas grenades, three .45-caliber submachine guns, and 500 rounds of ammunition. The CIA suspected that the weapons might be used to kidnap Schneider, but since the officers were not member of the Viaux group, which the CIA expected to do the kidnapping, it was not certain. The weapons were sent to Chile on October 19 and handed over to the Chilean officers early on October 22. Meanwhile, General Valenzuela informed the CIA that he and several other officers were ready to mount a coup, beginning with the abduction of General Schneider.[73]

When Valenzuela's October 19 attempt to kidnap Schneider failed, the CIA, believing the plotters would fail, apparently tried to discourage them, severing contact. But the CIA's action did not discourage Viaux's group from attempting to kidnap Schneider. It was shortly after 8 o'clock on the morning of October 22 when they stopped Schneider's car and mortally wounded him, either in response to Schneider drawing his handgun or because his assassination was part of Viaux's plan.[74]

Schneider's death served to rally the army behind the constitution, as predicted by the CIA station chief in Chile. Allende was elected president by the Chilean congress on October 24, 1970. The CIA was instructed to "stay alert and to do what we could to contribute to the objectives and purposes of Track II." The CIA spent an additional $1.5 million in support of the opposition newspaper *El Mercurio*. Financial support was given to labor unions and trade associations with the intention of encouraging economic and political disorder. Even assassination was considered. The economy-crippling truckers' strikes of 1972 and 1973, which halted virtually all transportation in Chile for months at a time, and which led up to General Augusto Pinochet's coup of 1973, may well have been financed by the CIA.[75]

Pinochet's coup, on September 11, 1973, settled the Allende problem permanently. The Chilean president died during the assault on the presidential palace—whether by a self-inflicted wound or at the hands of Pinochet's troops is not clear. Allende was far from the only Chilean to die as a result of the Pinochet coup; estimates range from 5,000 to 25,000. And three years later the Pinochet regime engaged in some covert action of its own, in Washington, D.C. On September 21, 1976, agents of the Chilean intelligence and secret police agency, DINA, killed former Allende defense minister Orlando Letelier with a car bomb, killing his American passenger as well.[76]

The Afghan Coup

Just as the United States attempted to rid itself in 1973 of a leader it considered a threat to its interests, the Soviet Union attempted in 1979 to do the same in Afghanistan. Only after attempts to eliminate that leader failed did the Soviets turn to military intervention. Then the KGB and GRU played a major role in paving the way for the invading forces.

The origins of the problem could be found in the April 1978 communist coup that overthrew the republican regime of Mohammad Daoud, killing Daoud and his family in the process. The coup produced an immediate contest for power between Barbak Karmal, leader of the Parcham faction of the Afghan Communist party, and Noor Mohammed Taraki, head of the rival Khalq faction. While the KGB preferred Karmal, who had been on their payroll for many years, Taraki had the support of Brezhnev and emerged victorious. Karmal sought sanctuary in Czechoslovakia.[77]

But Brezhnev's support did not prevent Taraki from being murdered, in September 1979, by his deputy prime minister Hafizullah Amin. Publicly, Moscow accepted Amin's coup, congratulated him on his "election," and expressed "the conviction that in the future too the fraternal relations between the Soviet Union and revolutionary Afghanistan will continue to develop on the basis of [their] treaty of friendship, good neighborliness and cooperation." Privately, the Soviets despised the new Afghan leader.[78]

Nor was the KGB optimistic about Amin's chance of survival. The Kabul residency reported bitter opposition to Amin from Islamic leaders, threatened Afghan army mutiny, and imminent economic collapse.[79] The Soviet Politburo discussed and agreed that Amin should be removed from both his office and the planet. Carrying out such "wet affairs" was the responsibility of Department 8 of Directorate S (Illegals) of the KGB's First Chief (Foreign) Directorate. Lieutenant Colonel Mikhail Talebov, an Azerbaijani who had spent several years in Kabul and could pass as a native, was selected to carry out the Politburo's wishes. In late autumn 1979 he arrived in Kabul carrying poison provided by Department 8. He was soon employed, with the help of KGB assets, in the presidential palace as a chef. But Amin assumed that the Soviets would try to remove him and proceeded to appoint relatives to all key posts and surround himself with a large contingent of bodyguards. And according to Vladimir Kuzichkin, a defector who had served in Directorate S, "Amin was as careful as any of the Borgias. He kept switching his food and drink as if he expected to be poisoned."[80]

Since Amin would not go quietly, and reports began to arrive from Kabul indicating that he was planning to expel all Soviet advisers, the Politburo considered its options. At a special meeting on December 12, 1979, a more extensive response was decided upon.[81]

Even before that meeting elite KGB units had been infiltrated into Afghanistan, ostensibly to guard the Soviet embassy. On Christmas night, 1979, the Soviets began a massive airlift to Kabul International Airport, while additional Soviet troops entered the country by road. Two days later a Soviet armored column moved out of the airport toward the presidential palace, which was defended by 300 fanatically loyal guardsmen and 3,000 regular soldiers. Leading was an assault group of the specially trained KGB Alpha Squad commandos, dressed in Afghan uniforms, and headed by Colonel Boyarinov, commandant of Department 8 special operations training school at Balashika.[82]

Boyarinov, who ordered that no witnesses in the palace were to survive to report on what happened, led the assault. Amin and his mistress were located on the top floor and eliminated. Before the assault concluded about a dozen of Soviet soldiers were killed, including Boyarinov—who was mistaken for a member of the palace guard and gunned down by his own troops.[83]

With Amin eliminated and the Soviets in control, Barbak Karmal was brought back from Czechoslovakia to head the new regime. Karmal, of course, welcomed the Soviet troops that began to flow into the country in an attempt to neutralize the forces opposing communist rule.

22

Elusive Truths

Advances in intelligence technology in the 1960s and 1970s further revolutionized the nature of intelligence. The United States and the Soviet Union, superpowers in intelligence as well as military matters, were able to look deep into each other's territory on a daily basis. Over the course of any year thousands of images of the adversary's military facilities would pass across the desks of analysts from the Central Intelligence Agency, Defense Intelligence Agency, KGB, and GRU. Those same analysts would also read the product of their country's vast eavesdropping operations.

Smaller powers, even though lacking satellite capabilities, had also developed impressive capabilities to produce imagery and communications intelligence in support of political and military leaders. Some, particularly the closest U.S. allies, also received some satellite intelligence as part of intelligence liaison relationships.

But the ability to collect a vast volume of data was not a guarantee of fully understanding the capabilities, actions, or intentions of other nations. Such truths would often prove elusive. The data produced by both technical and human intelligence collection were often incomplete or contradictory, requiring interpretation by analysts, who, at times, filtered the data through the prism of their own beliefs. At other times, the analysts had to contend not only with their own prejudices, but with political pressures from national leaders.

Concept and Consequences

During a brief ceremony in October 1972, Lieutenant General David Elazar, IDF chief of staff, named Major General Eliyahu "Eli" Zeira director of AMAN. Born in Haifa in 1928, Zeira joined the underground PAL-MACH youth organization at the age of eighteen, and followed that with service in the HAGANAH. During the 1948 war he quickly rose from squad leader to company commander, and three years later he became one of the first IDF officers to attend a comprehensive commander's course at Fort Benning, Georgia.[1]

Immediately after his return to Israel Zeira became director of strategic planning in the General Staff Branch, a choice assignment for an officer in his early twenties. For the next twenty-five years Zeira proceeded to climb the IDF ladder. Prior to October 1972 he had served as commander of operations in the General Staff, deputy AMAN commander, and military attaché in Washington.[2]

By the time Zeira took command of AMAN, Anwar Sadat had been president of Egypt just over two years, since Gamal Abdel Nasser's death in September 1970. Not long after assuming power Sadat began to threaten a new war with Israel. In early 1971 he proclaimed that year to be "the year of decision." But the year passed without action. The next year was also filled with proclamations of imminent war. In addition, there were twenty instances, in 1972, of Egypt "mobilizing" for war, conducting large-scale maneuvers close to the Suez Canal, and instituting civil defense measures, such as shutting down Cairo airport and sounding air raid sirens. But Sadat's calls for a holy war became routine, while no action followed the Egyptian mobilization measures. Thus while Israel initially increased its front-line forces, mobilized reserve units, and readied the national economy for war, it soon stopped what were extremely costly, and apparently pointless, responses.[3]

The Egyptian failure to follow threatening gestures with decisive action was perfectly consistent with a concept that had developed within AMAN during the late 1960s and early 1970s. The concept, which stated that the Arabs lacked the intention as well as the capability of attacking Israel in both the short and medium term, was based on three intermediate conclusions. First, it was believed that Israel's overwhelming victory in 1967 and its continued control of the occupied territories, which added territorial depth, gave the nation an unrivaled military advantage—fully appreciated by the Arabs. Egypt would not, it was believed, attack unless it could strike deep into Israel and destroy Israel's major military airfield. In addition, Syria was believed to be unwilling, on its own, to chance war with Israel.[4]

The institutional view Zeira inherited in October 1972 had been "confirmed" by the events of that past June—when Sadat expelled nearly 30,000 Soviet military advisers from Egypt in a move to assert Egyptian independence. That action convinced AMAN that Sadat was not serious about war with Israel.[5]

But Sadat had moved quickly to prevent the expulsion from completely wrecking his relations with Moscow and to ensure the continued arms supplies and intelligence support necessary to conduct a war. The initial shipment of SCUD B SS-1 surface-to-surface missiles reached the port of Alexandria in the spring of 1973. When fired from parts of Egypt and Syria, the missiles, although of poor accuracy, had sufficient range

(170 miles), to reach major Israeli cities. Sadat's belief that the missiles would deter Israel from launching strikes deep into Egypt proved to be the determining factor in his decision to go to war.[6]

In April the Mossad and AMAN obtained strong indications of war preparations in Egypt and Syria, including a report from a high-level human source. Several sources indicated that Sadat had chosen May 15 for the initiation of an assault across the canal, employing five divisions. At an April 15 meeting of the General Staff Zeira maintained that there was only a slim chance of war, a view challenged by Mossad chief Zvi Zamir, who contended that there was no assurance that Egypt would not attack. Certainly, he argued, Egypt's preparations—including the presence of antiaircraft missiles to protect canal-crossing divisions, the deployment of sufficient bridging equipment, and the deployment of an effective antiaircraft system for the protection of the Nile valley—were disturbing, and there was a reasonable probability that war would occur. Similarly, the IDF chief of staff was skeptical of Zeira's analysis and ordered some defensive responses.[7]

Even had Sadat not expelled the Soviet advisers the "concept" would have undoubtedly led AMAN to dismiss the prospect of war that spring. In fact, Sadat intended to go to war in May 1973, when the tides for crossing the canal were ideal and Israel would be busy celebrating its twenty-fifth anniversary. Only Soviet pressure and the promise of further arms deliveries led him to postpone the assault until October.[8]

To AMAN, unaware of the actual reason for the lack of action, the postponement was a validation of the concept. Further, AMAN believed that the Egyptian and Syrian troop mobilizations and maneuvers that month were designed to heighten concern over the Arab-Israeli conflict prior to the July U.S.–U.S.S.R. summit, with the expectation that the result would be pressure on Israel to be more accommodating.[9]

Not surprisingly, when Egypt and Syria resumed their threatening troop movements in August and September, AMAN again interpreted those movements as mere posturing. Dismissed as bravado were Syria's massive and unprecedented troop deployments along the cease-fire lines, as well as the deployment of a dense antiaircraft missile network opposite Israel's Golan defenses. AMAN interpreteted the action as a defensive move to protect the corridors to Damascus against Israeli air attacks.[10]

A September 13 air battle involving Israeli air force (IAF) aircraft on a reconnaissance mission over Syria was further evidence, in Zeira's eyes, that war was a slim possibility. The IAF had again demonstrated its decisive air superiority. Only if Syrian armored and antiaircraft capabilities improved would they contemplate a renewed war of attrition, but such improvement was not expected until late 1975. Zeira reiterated his judgment at a meeting of Foreign Ministry executives on September 21.[11]

Egypt's activities during August and September included earth-moving operations near the canal, building new access roads, and training troops to breach the earth ramparts that sloped down to the water. On September

24 and 25 AMAN detected indications of new Egyptian troop movements—from their Nile bases toward the Suez Canal. Additional reports
indicated that boats were being moved to canalside positions, leaves were
being canceled, and rank-advancement exams for Eygptian officers were
rescheduled from October to November. Before the month ended AMAN
would also report that Egyptian reserve units had been mobilized.[12]

But AMAN's Research Department concluded on September 26 that
there would be no war, since Syria would not go to war without Egypt and
Egypt had no intention of going to war. When the Egyptian army began its
Tahir 41 exercises on October 1, 1973, AMAN circulated a fact sheet to
the IDF Southern Command concerning the maneuvers that would be
taking place near the canal. The exercise objective was listed as "complete capture of Sinai."[13]

As part of Tahir 41 hundreds of thousands of front-line Egyptian troops
arrived near the canal, along with bridging equipment, armored formations, and SAM batteries. To help convey the message that nothing more
than an exercise was involved, both Egyptian and Syrian forces broadcast
deceptive communications in which reservists were demobilized, leaves
ordered, and units scheduled for routine training far from the canal. Intercepted messages indicated that leaves would be renewed on October 8,
the day after the scheduled end of the exercises. Additionally, some officers had been permitted to go on pilgrimage to Mecca.[14]

But on the very day that Tahir 41 began, one of AMAN's human
sources reported that the exercise was simply a ploy to prevent Israel from
taking defensive measures, and that it would be abruptly transformed
into an Egyptian attempt to recapture a significant part of the Sinai. The
Egyptians hoped to then induce the United States and the Soviet Union to
pressure Israel to withdraw from the occupied territories. The order for
Operation Badr, issued on September 30, informed its readers that a prearranged code word would be used to convert the exercise into a real attack.[15]

But neither the nature of Tahir 41 nor the reporting of AMAN's own
agents altered Zeira's perception. The AMAN chief refused to consider
war as a possibility, believing that the Egyptian movements were consistent with large-scale exercises. He attributed Egyptian alerts in northern
and central sectors of the canal area to Egyptian fears that Israel would use
the exercise as a pretext for military action. In addition, Zeira argued that
there would be no Arab attack since the Soviets, the sole arms supplier to
both Egypt and Syria, were opposed to war. Compounding his rigid out-
look, Zeira refused to authorize additional photoreconnaissance missions
over Egypt and Syria. Thus, despite all the activity, Zeira concluded that
"[t]he situation is completely normal and will not develop into a war and
there is no intention of turning it into war."[16]

The views of Zeira and AMAN, and the resulting IDF inaction, were
questioned by several high-level officials outside of AMAN. IDF Deputy
Chief of Staff Major General Yisrael Tal did not see the evidence as indi-

cating a low probability of war. The Northern Command's Major General Yitzhak Hofi (later to become chief of the Mossad) was disturbed by Syrian troop concentrations and the failure to strengthen the Golan Heights defenses. And Zvi Zamir also dissented from AMAN's reassuring conclusion, believing war to be highly probable.[17]

But with one exception, neither Zeira nor senior AMAN officers were willing to entertain alternative interpretations of the available intelligence, even when those interpretations came from within AMAN's ranks. On October 1 twenty-year-old novice intelligence officer Binyamin Siman-Tov, assigned to the Southern Command and stationed along the front lines, produced a report entitled "Movement in the Egyptian Army—Possibility of a Resumption of Hostilities." The report, labeled "Top Secret—EXTREMELY URGENT," claimed that the Tahir 41 exercise was really the prelude to an offensive operation. However, it failed to convince the chief AMAN officer in the Southern Command, Lieutenant Colonel David Gedaliah, who ignored it. A second report by Siman-Tov, "Situation Report on the Egyptian Army: 13/9/73–2/10/73," suffered the same fate at Gedaliah's hands.[18]

Possibly Siman-Tov's lack of stature contributed to Gedaliah's dismissal of his conclusions. Yet an AMAN brigadier general had no more success: on October 2 Brigadier General Yoel Ben-Porat, chief of the AMAN Collection Department, urged the AMAN director to begin mobilizing key personnel in the reserves, or overseas, but Zeira refused to act of out of "panic."[19]

The next day the head of AMAN's Research Department, Brigadier General Aryeh Shalev, acknowledged and dismissed a "worrying report from a reliable source from 30 September saying that on 1 October . . . Egypt was about to attack Sinai, and the Syrians would act simultaneously on the Golan." War was still, according to Shalev, "not . . . likely . . . a low probability." On October 4, after the Soviet Union began evacuating its citizens from Egypt and Syria, Ben-Porat again called for, and Zeira again refused, a limited mobilization. Zeira did, however, accuse Ben-Porat of insolence.[20]

Supporting Zeira's view was Lieutenant Colonel Yona Bendman, the director of the Egypt Division of the AMAN Research Department. On October 4 he wrote:

> Notwithstanding the existence of military strength on the Canal front which appears to be ready for action, to the best of our knowledge there has been no significant change in Egyptian evaluation of their military potential versus [the IDF]. Therefore the probability of an Egyptian attack is unlikely.[21]

It would not be until the early morning of October 6, Yom Kippur, that Zeira would be convinced, on the basis of a report from the same Mossad source who had warned of an Egyptian attack in May, that Egypt and Syria were about to attack. Israel's failure to be prepared for the Egyptian-Syrian attack led to temporarily significant Arab military gains and a longer lasting gain in Arab morale, brought Israel to the brink of employing nuclear weapons, led to a decline in Israeli morale, and resulted in the needless death of numerous Israeli soldiers.[22]

The Agranat Commission, charged with assessing responsibility for the debacle, concluded:

> In the days preceding the Yom Kippur War, AMAN (Research) had plenty of warning intelligence, provided by the Collection Department of AMAN itself and by other collecting agenices of the state. AMAN (Research) and the director of AMAN did not correctly evaluate the warning provided by these pieces of intelligence, because of their doctrinaire adherence to the "kontzepziya" and because of their readiness to explain away . . . the enemy [moves] along the front lines . . . as a defensive deployment in Syria and multi-arms in Egypt, similar to exercises that had taken place in the past.[23]*

Team A versus Team B

On November 5, 1976, two groups of intelligence analysts confronted each other across a long table at the CIA's headquarters in Langley, Virginia. The CIA contingent, led by CIA veteran Howard Stoertz, but consisting of young and inexperienced analysts, was designated Team A. The second group, Team B, consisted of much older men, from outside the government, who had been commissioned to produce a competitive national intelligence estimate on Soviet strategic forces and objectives.[24]

The meeting on November 5 was, in at least one sense, the climax of numerous battles over questions of Soviet strategic capability and intentions.[†] In 1969 the CIA and Pentagon agreed that one version of a new Soviet ICBM, the SS-9 SCARP, carried three warheads. However, they hotly debated the capacity of the missile, its accuracy, and whether the

---

*Zeira, Shalev, and Bendman were all relieved of their positions, in accord with the Agranat Commission's recommendations. For a critique of the commission's approach and its conclusions, see Janice Gross Stein, "'Intelligence' and 'Stupidity' Reconsidered: Estimation and Decision in Israel, 1973," *Journal of Strategic Studies* 3, no. 2 (1980): 147–77.

†The meeting was a product of concerns expressed by the President's Foreign Intelligence Advisory Board. The board had noted a series of articles published in *Foreign Policy* magazine by Albert Wohlstetter, a well-known strategic analyst, which accused the intelligence community of consistently underestimating the number of missiles the Soviets would have in their arsenal at specific points in the future. The board suggested having an outside team of experts produce a competitive NIE on Soviet strategic forces. In June 1976 DCI George Bush authorized such an exercise. There would be three B teams, which would examine Soviet air defenses, missile accuracies, and strategic objectives. It was the third team that confronted CIA analysts at Langley. Strobe Talbott, *The Master of the Game* (New York: Knopf, 1988), p. 146; Daniel Callaghan, *Dangerous Capabilities: Paul Nitze and the Cold War* (New York: Harper Collins, 1990), p. 378; the Wohlstetter articles and critiques of the articles can be found in the Summer 1974, Fall 1974, Summer 1975, and Fall 1975 issues of *Foreign Policy*.

warheads were independently targetable—a capability that could allow a medium-size ICBM force to threaten a larger force.[25]

Toward the end of the Johnson administration, a National Intelligence Estimate concluded, without any dissents, that the SS-9 was not MIR-Ved.* The estimate did note that the SS-9 might be able to dispense its three warheads in a manner that would allow them to potentially damage or destroy several Minuteman sites. In 1969 the Nixon administration, and most particularly Secretary of Defense Melvin Laird, argued that the triangular footprint of the SS-9 made it "functionally equivalent to a MIRVed missile," and that the Soviets might be attempting to develop a capability to destroy a sizable portion of the U.S. ICBM force in a first strike. Laird's position, which was supported by the Defense Intelligence Agency and the Air Force, was fundamental to the administration's case for the Sentinel antiballistic missile system, designed to protect ICBM forces.[26] John Huizenga, then deputy director of the CIA's Office of National Estimates, believed "the game was being played because the Soviet MIRV was necessary as a threat to justify the Safeguard system. There's no doubt that the White House was determined that there should be an intelligence finding that the Soviets were engaged in MIRV testing."[27]

The battle between the CIA and the Nixon administration over the SS-9 dragged on for several months; it included Laird's declassifying intelligence briefings on the SS-9 as well as the president's public statement that the SS-9 was MIRVed. A "Memorandum to Holders," a short addendum to the NIE prepared the previous October, was drafted in August, and most of the agencies agreed with the CIA's conclusion that

> the Soviets recognize the enormous difficulties of any attempt to achieve strategic superiority of such order as to significantly alter the strategic balance. Consequently, we consider it highly unlikely that they will attempt within the period of this estimate to achieve a first strike capability. . . . For one thing, the Soviets would almost certainly conclude that the cost of such an undertaking along with all their other military commitments would be prohibitive. More important, they almost certainly would consider it impossible to develop and deploy the combination of offensive and defensive forces necessary to counter successfully the various elements of U.S. strategic attack forces. Finally, even if such a project were economically and technically feasible the Soviets would almost certainly calculate that the U.S. would detect and match or overmatch their efforts.[28]

---

* U.S. National Intelligence Estimates, along with a variety of other national intelligence products, are issued under the imprimatur of the Director of Central Intelligence, *with the approval of the National Foreign Intelligence Board* (known as the U.S. Intelligence Board from 1958 to 1976). Thus the estimates are coordinated among the several U.S. intelligence agencies, including the CIA, DIA, NSA, State Department's Bureau of Intelligence and Research, military service intelligence chiefs, and several other civilian intelligence units. When an agency disagrees with a particular conclusion it may express its view in a dissenting "footnote."

The paragraph remained in the text of the memorandum throughout the review process and was to be part of the final estimate that would be placed before the U.S. Intelligence Board. Before its submission an assistant to Secretary Laird asked DCI Richard Helms to delete the paragraph since "it contradicted the public position of the Secretary." Laird himself raised the subject with Helms, arguing that the paragraph went beyond intelligence into the policy area, subverting the president's policy. Finally Helms succumbed to the pressure and ordered the offending paragraph deleted. However, Thomas L. Hughes, director of the State Department's Bureau of Intelligence and Research, reinserted the deleted paragraph as a dissenting footnote.[29]

The question of a missile's MIRV capability was only one of a multitude of questions that U.S. intelligence analysts tried to answer about each type of Soviet missile. An October 15, 1975, report on the SS-19 ICBM, produced by the Air Force Foreign Technology Division and published under the auspices of the Defense Intelligence Agency, covered the full range of missile system characteristics, including range and payload performance, payload options, accuracy, reliability, retargeting, effectiveness, vulnerability, employment, guidance and reentry error, and MIRV footprint.[30]

The data used to produce the assessments in the report included imagery, telemetry and communications intercepts, and radar-tracking measurements. But the conclusions produced did not simply fall out from the data collected. Complex methodology and basic assumptions had to be applied to the raw data to produce the assessments found in the October 15 report. As a result, in the 1970s and beyond, intelligence analysts in the varying branches of the U.S. intelligence community, particularly the CIA, DIA, and Air Force intelligence, would often differ concerning the characteristics, and thus the threat presented by, Soviet strategic weapons systems.

Whether the Soviets intended to use their missiles in a preemptive first strike or as a means of intimidation was even more difficult to answer on the basis of such data. But such issues, along with the question of weapons systems capabilities, were examined by the two teams in their respective reports, which were completed in December 1976.

Heading Team B was Richard Pipes, a intensely anti-Soviet professor of Russian history at Harvard University. Pipes's team comprised a collection of hard-liners—Professor William van Cleave, retired ambassador Foy Kohler, RAND analyst Thomas Wolfe, former DIA director Daniel Graham, and former Air Force Chief of Staff John Vogt. Their advisory panel included Paul Nitze, who believed that Soviet intentions grew with capabilities—that the Soviets would be willing to exploit any strategic superiority they had, in some instances to the brink of war, in the belief that if nuclear war resulted, they would come out "ahead." In a similar vein, Daniel Graham had told the readers of *Reader's Digest* that "[t]he

Soviets have not built up their forces, as we have, merely to deter a nuclear war. They . . . see an enormous persuasive power accruing to a nation which can face the prospect of nuclear war with confidence in its survival."[31]

Such views were reflected in Team B's report on Soviet strategic objectives. Team B agreed that "all the evidence points to an undeviating Soviet commitment to what is euphemistically called 'the worldwide triumph of socialism' but in fact connotes Soviet global hegemony."[32]

Team B's dark view of Soviet goals was matched by a pessimistic view of the prospects for the West:

> *Within the ten year period of the National Estimate the Soviets may well expect to achieve a degree of military superiority which would permit a dramatically more aggressive pursuit of their hegemonial [sic] objectives,* including direct military challenges to Western vital interests, in the belief that such superior military force can pressure the West to acquiesce or, if not, can be used to win a military contest at any level.[33]

Undoubtedly, there was a mutually reinforcing relationship between Team B's views of Soviet strategic activities and their view of strategic objectives. Pipes and his colleagues expressed concern with regard to ICBM and SLBM programs, civil defense, military hardening, mobile missiles, the Backfire bomber, and ABM. They concluded that the "extensive hardening program connected with Soviet command and control clearly demonstrates Soviet intent to achieve a true war fighting capability as opposed to acceptance of a mutual deterrence concept." Soviet civil defense efforts were also alarming, striking Team B as being "integrated with all other military programs to maximize Russia's capabilities to fight a nuclear war and emerge viable from it."[34]*

Not surprisingly, they viewed the Tu-22M Backfire bomber, which many believed was primarily intended for use against NATO and China, in the most threatening light, concluding that the plane "clearly possesses interncontinental capability which means that if deployed in significant numbers it would pose an incremental threat to the strategic balance."[35]

Team A's report, *Soviet Forces for Intercontinental Conflict Through the Mid-1980s,* based on the same data as Team B's, expressed the unanimous judgment of the U.S. intelligence community that "the Backfires will continue to be assigned to theater and naval missions." But with regard to several other conclusions there was considerable disagreement.

---

*Daniel Graham has said that the Soviet civil defense effort was particularly alarming to Team B members (Talbott, *Master of the Game,* p. 146). The alarm may have been compounded by a perception that there had been a dramatically increased emphasis on such activities. That perception may in turn have partially resulted from the dropping of COMINT coverage of such activities in the early 1970s and the resumption in the mid-1970s. Rather than seeing the effort develop over several years, Team B members were confronted with the changes at once.

Whereas the CIA, the Office of Naval Intelligence, and the State Department's Bureau of Intelligence and Research concluded that "it is correspondingly unlikely that they will be assigned to intercontinental missions," the DIA and several other intelligence organizations suggested that such a conclusion was unwarranted.[36]

Contributing to differing conclusions concerning Backfire were the differing estimates of Backfire characteristics and mission profiles. The CIA estimated that the Backfire's unrefueled range was between 3,500 and 4,150 nautical miles with a 10,000-pound payload. The uncertainty concerning range was due to the CIA's lack of information as to whether the Backfire was designed solely for subsonic performance (which would yield a higher range) or for both subsonic and supersonic flight. In contrast, the DIA and Air Force assistant chief of staff for intelligence estimated the plane's range at 5,400 nautical miles, based on the assumption that the plane would carry a 20,800-pound payload and was designed for subsonic high-altitude missions.[37]

There was also disagreement within the intelligence community over the Backfire's upgrade potential. While the CIA believed that some modifications to the plane—such as adding external fuel tanks or using weapons bay fuel tanks—would be relatively easy, it also believed that other improvements in the Backfire's performance would be needed to compensate for any resultant significant increase in weight from carrying large quantities of fuel. The Air Force assistant chief of staff for intelligence, however, believed that the Backfire as it was then constituted could carry additional fuel without further improvements.[38]

The National Intelligence Estimate also offered some contrasting conclusions concerning Soviet objectives and intentions, although some of those contrasting conclusions were in the form of State Department dissents to the main estimate. The main estimate observed that "the continuing persistence and vigor of Soviet programs give rise to the question of whether the Soviet leaders now hold as an operative, practical objective the achievement of clear strategic superiority over the US during the period of this Estimate."[39]*

Concerning Team B's most significant fear that the Soviets would exploit strategic superiority for geopolitical gain, the State Department INR director Harold Saunders observed that "it [is] unlikely that the Soviet leaders anticipate any improvement in the USSR's strategic situation via-à-vis the US over the next 10 years which would substantially influence their behavior—and especially their inclination for risk-taking—during periods of crisis or confrontation with the West."[40]

---

* There have been contrasting reports as to the extent to which the content of the NIE was influenced by the November 5 meeting, which apparently resulted in Team B's rout of their much younger CIA opponents. The view that it resulted in a 180-degree reversal is disputed in U.S. Congress, Senate Select Committee on Intelligence, *The National Intelligence Estimate A-B Team Episode Concerning Soviet Strategic Capability and Objectives* (Washington, D.C.: U.S. Government Printing Office, 1978), p. 2.

With respect to the civil defense effort the INR director was also less anxious than Team B, the DIA, and the military service intelligence organizations. He wrote:

> The Department of State believes that the Soviet civil defense program is seen by the Soviet leadership primarily as a prudent hedge against the possibility of attack by a nuclear-armed adversary. Moreover, the Department of State believes that these Soviet civil defense efforts will not materially increase Soviet willingness to risk a nuclear exchange and will not undermine the deterrent value of US strategic attack forces.[41]

While differing conclusions concerning weapons systems characteristics, civil defense programs, and upgradeability of weapons systems could at least be debated by reference to the evidence, differing views concerning the Soviet willingness to risk nuclear war or what constituted a worthwhile victory in such a war were far harder to debate in any meaningful way. For those views were the product of fundamental beliefs about the values of the Soviet leadership—views that had developed, for senior officials and the members of Team B, over decades.[42] Members of Team B could see Soviet attempts to develop a war-fighting capability and minimize damage as being motivated by the goal of Soviet world hegemony. Others, such as the director of INR, questioned whether the Soviet leaders, as morally reprehensible as they might be, could ever conclude that the benefits of a "victory" in a nuclear war could outweigh the enormous costs involved.

"Well into the 1980s"

On January 16, 1979, Mohammed Reza Pahlavi, the Shah of Iran, in the wake of increasing protests and riots, climbed aboard a 707 aircraft and fled the country he had ruled so autocratically for twenty-five years. The American intelligence community was taken by surprise, despite the fact that the shah and his regime were subject to frequent study. In February 1976 the CIA's Office of Political Research produced an eighty-three-page study on *Elites and the Distribution of Power in Iran*. The study focused on the shah and key people in his family and court, the bureaucracy, parliament, the army, the religious community, and the industrial elite.[43]

The study noted that "the Moslem clergy in Iran are among some of the Shah's fiercest critics," with the bulk of the clergy subscribing to the view that the shah, supported by the United States and Israel, was attempting to establish a totally secular society and destroy Islam. It is also noted that Ayatollah Ruhollah Khomeini, "who for a decade has been carrying on his campaign against the Shah from exile in Iraq," gave his blessing to the violence-prone "People's Warriors" organization. The study concluded, however, that unless they were to succeed in assassinating the shah, "the terrorists do not threaten the stability of the regime."[44]

In August 1977 a sixty-page CIA study more directly addressed the question of the stability of the shah's regime. *Iran in the 1980s* considered Iran's human resources, techniques for feeding the population, education and training, the economy, the society, military affairs, politics, and foreign affairs.[45] The study was produced under several basic assumptions; including "The Shah will be a participant in Iranian life well into the 1980s" and "There will be no radical change in Iranian political behavior in the near future." Not surprisingly, the CIA predicted "evolution not revolution."[46] An update of the study, produced in October, converted assumptions into conclusions. The nine-page update declared: "The Shah seems to have no health or political problems at present that will prevent him from being the dominant figure in Iran into and possibly throughout the 1980s."[47]

Almost a year later the CIA still saw no looming threat, declaring in a twenty-three-page Assessment, "Iran after the Shah," that "Iran is not in a revolutionary or even a 'prerevolutionary' situation." A mid-August DIA Intelligence Appraisal noted the renewal of religiously motivated civil disturbances but, while suggesting the high probability of further disturbances, concluded that "[t]here is no threat to the stability of the Shah's rule."[48]

Even four days before the shah's departure, a CIA intelligence memorandum focused on the radicals in the Iranian opposition movement, noting the protests under way but giving no hint that the shah's fall was imminent. The report observed that the "opposition to the Shah of Iran has never been a cohesive movement. It is a collection of widely disparate groups with differing ideologies and rival leaders."[49]

That U.S. intelligence reporting and analysis concerning Iran was deficient had been noted before the shah's escape. National security adviser Zbigniew Brzezinski had found the comments provided by DCI Stansfield Turner at a November 1978 meeting "inept and vague," which led him to induce President Jimmy Carter to send a note to Turner that he was "not satisfied with the quality of our political intelligence."[50]

But by the time the president wrote his note it was too late, at least too late to suddenly improve U.S. reporting on Iran. One major aspect of the problem was a long-standing agreement between the CIA and the shah's intelligence and secret police organization, SAVAK, under which the CIA would refrain from contacts with the opposition to the shah. Under the agreement information was to be provided by SAVAK. Since the United States was so concerned with the shah's value as a strategic political ally and the operation of the SIGINT stations targeted on Soviet missile test facilities, it was willing to comply.[51]

Turner, while noting the chancy nature of predicting revolutionary change, subsequently acknowledged that "the CIA could have done a better job of emphasizing the deep currents that were running against him. This should have been done over the previous three or four years. Only then would there have been any real chance of our getting the Shah to change his course."[52]

That failure was the result of not understanding the degree of dissatisfaction with the shah or the increasing lure of Islamic fundamentalism. As indicated above, it was not expected that the opposition groups would coalesce under Khomeini's leadership or that the fundamentalists would be sufficiently strong to remain in control when the opposition fractured after the shah's departure.[53]

The lack of contact with the opposition was partly responsible for the failures. But according to Turner another contributing factor was that "some of the CIA's key analysts were hung up on the durability of the Shah," which was the result of an erroneous premise:

> What we all saw in Iran in the autumn of 1978 was a Shah who, although beleaguered, still had control of a powerful army, police, and secret intelligence service, the SAVAK. Our assumption was that if the dissident movements began to get out of control, the Shah would simply step in with whatever amount of force was necessary to control. He never did that. Perhaps he was so out of touch with his own country that he did not appreciate how serious the situation was until corrective action would have caused too much bloodshed. Or perhaps he could not face difficult decisions because he knew he was dying. Whatever the explanation, our assumption that he would not hesitate to employ whatever force he needed was dead wrong.[54]

An anonymous article in the CIA's journal *Studies in Intelligence* suggested that inadequate information about the shah's condition may have significantly contributed to the analytic failure:

> As the troubles in Iran mounted, most Shah-watchers felt, as in the past, that he would "tough it out," that he would choose "the iron fist" option if he needed to, as he had in the past. But there was progressive concern over his moodiness and dispirited reactions, and the observation was shared widely that he was suffering from "a failure of will." . . . [I]t may well be that the different quality in the leadership he displayed during Iran's final crisis stemmed from his being able to give only part of his energy to fighting for Iran's life, since he was fighting for his own.
>
> Without overstating the case, it seems clear that had we known the Shah was suffering from cancer of the lymph nodes since 1973, our government's judgments as to his ability to deal with the revolutionary forces that swept through Iran would probably have been quite different. Serious doubts would likely have replaced the guarded optimism concerning the Shah's ability to weather the storm.[55]

23

A New Decade

The 1980s would mark the fourth decade during which the Cold War would serve as the central focus of U.S., Soviet, and European intelligence operations. Those operations would illustrate the continued importance of techncial collection, the tremendous potential of human intelligence, and the ways in which intelligence alliances could aid senior or junior partners.

The early years of the new decade would also see superpower intelligence operations conducted in a period of exceptional tension. The rhetoric of the new Reagan administration, the U.S., NATO, and Soviet military buildups, and Soviet paranoia would cause Soviet leaders to fear imminent U.S. military action. Meanwhile, the continued Soviet strategic buildup, events in Afghanistan, and the Soviet destruction of a civilian airliner in 1983 reaffirmed the new U.S. administration's long-held beliefs.

With a Little Help from Their Friends

In June 1980 twenty KGB experts arrived in Warsaw to examine and evaluate more than 100 pounds of classified documents delivered to the Polish Security Service, the SB, by James Durward Harper, a forty-six-year-old Silicon Valley electrical engineer. The documents, which Harper had acquired from his girlfriend, a defense contractor employee, concerned ballistic missile defense and Minuteman survivability. They included *Endoatmospheric Nonnuclear Kill Technology Requirements and Definition Study, Discrimination Decoy Performance Requirements, Minuteman Defense Study (Final Report),* and *Report of the Task Force on U.S. Ballistic Missile Defense.*[1]

Harper was paid $100,000 for his documents, almost certainly from the KGB's treasury. While the documents were of little value to the Polish government, they were of great interest to the Soviet Union, and Harper's case officers received a letter of commendation from KGB chairman Yuri Andropov.[2] The SB's operation of Harper illustrated the KGB's continued intimate relationship with the intelligence and security services of the communist regimes in East Germany, Czechoslovakia, Poland, Hungary, and Bulgaria.[*]

That relationship had changed over the years, however. In the early 1950s, according to a secret CIA study, "the KGB exercised almost total control over such services, and Soviet nationals often served in key positions in them." An agent such as Harper would simply have been "transferred" from the SB to the KGB. Beginning in the late 1950s the KGB became quite liberal in passing information of interest to the intelligence services of Poland, Czechoslovakia, Hungary, East Germany, and Bulgaria. By the mid-1970s those services operated with a greater degree of independence, with the liaison relationship becoming "much more the advisory mechanism the Soviets . . . always claimed it was."[3]

While operating with greater independence, the services still served as adjuncts to the KGB and GRU. In the United States, they not only added to the pool of personnel that could be used to conduct espionage operations, but they increased the territory that could be covered. Soviets officials were not permitted to travel to a wide variety of areas—including parts of Los Angeles County where numerous defense contractors were headquartered, Houston, and Silicon Valley. East European intelligence officers, posing as diplomats, faced no restrictions beyond those faced by American citizens.[4]

At the same time it was receiving documents from Harper, the SB was running another agent in southern California, whose reporting was also far more useful to the Soviet Union than Poland. Starting in 1979, William Bell, an engineer with Hughes Aircraft, delivered a variety of documents to Marian W. Zacharski, an SB officer posing as an executive of the Los Angeles–based Polish-American Machinery Corporation (POLAMCO). The documents provided secret information on the F-15 lookdown shootdown radar system, the quiet radar system for the B-1 and Stealth bomber, an all-weather radar system for tanks, an experimental radar system for the U.S. Navy, the Phoenix air-to-air missile, a shipborne surveillance radar, the Patriot surface-to-air missile, and a NATO air defense system. The documents provided by Bell may have saved the Soviet Union tens of millions of dollars and several years in developing a variety of military technologies.[5]

Bell was arrested in 1981 and sentenced to eight years in prison. Harper, however, continued his activities. In September 1980 he provided the SB with a listing of documents in the safe of his wife's employer. Upon

[*] The relationship between the Soviet and Yugoslav services was ruptured as a result of the Tito–Stalin rift of 1948. Relations with the Albanian services ended when Albania sided with China during the early days of the Sino–Soviet split. The Romanians ended their liaison relationship with the KGB in 1964.

receipt of the documents Harper was paid an additional $20,000. In February 1981 Harper delivered more documents to the SB, this time in Mexico City, and received $70,000. A subsequent meeting saw an exchange of eight documents for $50,000.[6]

But Harper became nervous about his activities and the possible consequences. An attempt to anonymously negotiate an immunity agreement with the CIA, through a lawyer, failed. Eventually Harper would be identified through information provided by a CIA penetration of the SB, leading to his arrest in October 1983.[7]

Only weeks before Harper's arrest an officer of another East European intelligence service was arrested for attempting to acquire classified documents, documents whose ultimate destination would have been Moscow. This time the intelligence service was the Bulgarian Durzhavna Sigurnost (DS; State Security). The unlucky DS officer was Penyu B. Kostadinov, an assistant counselor at the Bulgarian Commercial Office in New York, whose official duties involved the promotion of trade and the placement of Bulgarian scientists in university exchange programs.[8]

The FBI monitored Kostadinov as he paid money to an American graduate student who was cooperating with the bureau, provided him with a list of desired documents, and accepted a classified document from the American, "Report on Inspection of the Nevada Operations Office."[9]*

At the time of Kostadinov's arrest U.S. Army Sergeant Clyde Lee Conrad had been spying for two KGB allies—the Hungarian Interior Ministry's III Main Group Directorate, popularly known as the State Security Authority (Allavedelmi Hatosag, AVH) and the Czech Main Directorate of Intelligence (Hlavni Sprava Rozvedky, HSR)—for eight years. From November 1974 until August 1979, and then from November 1980 till his retirement in September 1985, Conrad served at the headquarters of the U.S. Army's Eighth Infantry Division, in Bad Kreuznach, Germany.[10]

Conrad, who began his espionage career in 1974, was the key figure in an espionage network that included agents in West Germany and Sweden and provided secret U.S. and NATO documents to the Czech and Hungarian services.[†] The network provided information on missile sites in West Germany, a secret oil pipeline in West Germany to resupply tanks, ammunition dumps, and "General Defense Plans" for the defense of Central Europe.[11]

Farewell

The French presidential elections of 1981 brought Socialist candidate François Mitterand to power. Mitterand, in turn, appointed Pierre

---

* The Nevada Operations Office is the Department of Energy organization responsible for managing nuclear testing activities.

† Conrad, who received over $1 million in payment for his espionage, was arrested in 1988 and in 1990 was sentenced to life imprisonment by a German court.

Marion, the former head of Air France and the director of North American affairs for SNIAS aerospace company, to head the SDECE. Marion's short tenure (he resigned in November 1982) was marked by significant changes as well as acrimony within the French intelligence service.[12]

Marion proceeded to alter the service's personnel and organization, removing fifty top officials suspected of being unsympathetic to the left. He also reorganized the service along more centralized lines, limiting the independence of its divisions and tightening up the command structure. He sought to improve the agency's capability to gather economic, financial, industrial, and scientific information. Additional emphasis was also put on counterterrorism and counterespionage. To emphasize the break with the past the SDECE was retitled the Direction Générale de la Sécurité Extérieure (DGSE; Directorate General of External Security).[13]

A decree of April 2, 1982, stated that the DGSE's mission was to "seek and exploit intelligence advantageous to the security of France, also to detect and disrupt, throughout the national territory, espionage activities directed against French interests in order to prevent the consequences."[14]

But changing the name of the organization proved far easier than changing the organization. Marion's management ideas were particularly unpopular at headquarters, and as many as 500 of the service's employees may have left. Some officers were reportedly irritated by his irascibility and unwillingness to delegate authority. DGSE's failure to predict the Israeli invasion of Lebanon as well as a wave of terrorist attacks in France, some of which appeared to have been planned abroad, further undercut Marion's standing.[15]

Apparently Marion's resignation was precipitated by his futile attempt to find out what France's counterespionage service, the Directorate for the Surveillance of the Territory (DST), was doing. The DST's reluctance to inform Marion of its activities may have been partly because it was in one important instance invading the DGSE's area of responsibility.

In 1981 a French businessman delivered to the DST a letter from "a Soviet friend" who suggested a meeting in Moscow. The friend was Vladimir Ippolitovich Vetrov, a fifty-three-year-old KGB officer. Vetrov and the French businessman had become friends during Vetrov's stay in Paris from 1965 to 1970. But according to Vetrov's letter, his high position in the KGB precluded any future foreign assignment.[16]

Vetrov was a senior officer in the First Chief Directorate's Directorate T, which was responsible for scientific and technical espionage—a mission which had grown in importance. In 1963 the FCD's Tenth Department had been upgraded to the directorate level. Known as the Scientific and Technical Directorate until 1968, it was then redesignated Directorate T. In 1970 a high-level governmental review of Directorate T resulted in a resolution passed by the Council of Ministers and the party's Central Committee calling for expansion of the directorate's operations and an improvement in the quality of work.[17]

DST accepted the offer and assigned Vetrov the code name FARE-

WELL. Beginning in 1981 FAREWELL, who was responsible for evaluating the material collected by Directorate T, provided the DST with more than 4,000 documents on Soviet scientific and technical espionage. The documents included Soviet plans to steal Western technological secrets and Soviet assessments of the value of its covert technology acquisition activities.[18]

FAREWELL provided a complete list of all organizations involved in scientific and technical intelligence, as well as detailed information about their structure and operations. These organizations included the Military-Industrial Commission (VPK), which assigned tasks to the five collection agencies: the GRU, Directorate T, the State Committee for Science and Technology (GKNT), a special unit of the Academy of Sciences, and the State Committee for External Economic Relations (GKES).[19]

Vetrov also provided several reports concerning the goals, successes, and results of the Soviet scientific and technical intelligence collection effort. One 128-page VPK document, detailing collection efforts in 1979, credited the collection agencies with having acquired 156 technical samples and 3,896 documents and Directorate T with completing 557 collection tasks of 2,148. Eighty-seven of the samples and 346 documents were "used in a practical way in research projects and in the development of new weapons systems and military materials, as well as in the improvement of weapons systems in current use." The document also claimed that the Soviet military aircraft industry saved about 48.6 million rubles (about $65 million).[20]

Two documents provided by FAREWELL reported on collection operations in 1980. A top-secret VPK document, dated June 19, 1981, reported that the VPK assigned 3,617 scientific and technical acquisition tasks in 1980, of which 1,085 were completed before the end of the year. The completed tasks benefited 3,396 Soviet research and development projects. While much of the information came from unclassified Western sources, 90 percent of the intelligence considered most useful was acquired through KGB and GRU clandestine collection operations.[21]

The KGB's summary of collection operations was apparently based on a different accounting system than that employed by the VPK. Directorate T reported that in 1980 it acquired 5,456 "samples" (machinery, components, and microcircuits), with 44 percent going to defense industries, 28 percent to civilian industries, and 28 percent to the KGB and other agencies.[22]

In addition to providing information on Soviet objectives and successes, FAREWELL also provided information crucial to neutralizing those efforts. That information included a list of 250 KGB "Line X" officers—those stationed at Soviet embassies with a mission to collect scientific and technical intelligence. The majority of Line X officers who would be expelled from France in 1983 were selected from the list handed over by FAREWELL.[23]

FAREWELL's documents also gave the West over 100 leads concerning the agents recruited by the Line X officers in ten Western nations, including the United States, West Germany, and France. The agents whose careers were shortened by FAREWELL's activities included Pierre Bourdiol, a French engineer who worked for the KGB from 1973 to 1983, and West German Manfred Rotsch, the head of the Planning Department of the Messerschmitt-Bolkow-Blohm (MBB) aircraft company. Bourdiol was able to deliver information on the Ariane rocket, while Rotsch delivered specifications of the Tornado fighter and several army missile systems. FAREWELL also helped end the double life of Dieter Felix Gehrhardt, the South African naval officer who provided information on a variety of antiaircraft missiles.[24]

Vetrov's documents also indicated that the KGB's East European allies played a significant role in the scientific and technical espionage campaign. In 1980 approximately half the intelligence provided by Directorate T came from East European services.[25]

The information from Vetrov was shared with the United States and other allied countries. President Mitterand informed President Reagan at a private meeting while the leaders were on their way to the July 1981 economic summit in Ottawa. Several weeks later, DST chief Marcel Chalet visited Vice President George Bush to discuss FAREWELL. Rotsch's arrest followed the DST warning to the German government of a high-level mole in MBB.[26]

FAREWELL's career as a Western agent was to be a short one, but not because of the efficiency of KGB security officials or due to the penetration of the DST, CIA, or other allied intelligence service. In February 1982 Vetrov and his mistress were in his car, in a Moscow park, when a man knocked on the car window. Perhaps fearing that his role as French agent had been discovered, Vetrov panicked, stabbing the man to death, and then attempted to kill his mistress. Foolishly, he returned to the park an hour later to find the police and his mistress, still alive, at the scene. In the late fall of 1982 Vetrov began a twelve-year prison term.[27]

Officials reading his mail noticed that he dropped hints about a big project he had been forced to abandon. When KGB officers confronted him during the winter of 1982–83 Vetrov quickly confessed to his espionage activities on behalf of France. Before 1983 was over Vetrov had been executed.[28]

Vetrov's career as a double agent ended in 1982, but his impact continued years afterward. The U.S. and Western campaign against Soviet scientific and technical intelligence activities, conducted both clandestinely and publicly, was fueled by the information FAREWELL provided.

Operation RYAN

The Soviet invasion of Afghanistan had ended all hopes that the SALT II would be ratified in 1980, and U.S.–Soviet relations deteriorated further that year with the U.S. boycott of the Moscow Olympic Games. But the last year of the Carter administration would quickly become a fond memory for many Soviet leaders when compared to the early years of the Reagan administration.

The fears of the Soviet leadership were evident in May 1981 at a major KGB conference in Moscow. In a secret address to the conference General Secretary Leonid Brezhnev denounced the policies of the new American administration, which, he charged, was preparing for nuclear war. As a result, the Politburo had concluded that the highest priority of Soviet foreign intelligence operations would be the collection of intelligence on the nuclear threat from the United States and NATO. KGB chairman Yuri Andropov then informed the audience that in response to the Poliburo's concern the KGB and GRU would, for the first time, work together in an operation code-named RYAN—Raketno Yadernoye Napdenie (Nuclear Missile Attack). While many of the American experts in the KGB's First Chief Directorate were skeptical of the need for Operation RYAN, it was an operation endorsed by Andropov and the chief of the FCD, Vladimir Kryuchkov.[29]

To monitor Western activities that might indicate a coming attack the Soviets could rely on their extensive technical and human collection networks. COSMOS satellites would make their daily passes over the United States and Europe, photographing missile fields, airfields, and other military installations of interest. Launch of the first KH-11-type real-time satellite was still eighteen months away, so there would be some delay between the act of photography and the time when analysts at the GRU's Space Intelligence Directorate would be able to analyze the images for threatening signs.[30]

But the Soviets also could rely on their extensive SIGINT networks. Their low-earth-orbit radar ferrets could detect any heightened radar activities in the United States and western Europe.[31] For communications intelligence, the Soviets could rely on a combination of ground stations, rooftop antennas on diplomatic and trade establishments, and AGIs patrolling critical naval facilities.

From outside the United States the Soviets could use their facility at Lourdes to monitor a variety of U.S. civilian and military communications links. Many of the more than 300 ground stations of varying sizes located in the Soviet Union and eastern Europe could be employed to monitor NATO activities in western Europe.[32]

Inside the United States the KGB and GRU employed ten different facilities to collect COMINT—three in Washington (the old and new embassy buildings and the military attaché building), four in New York (the Soviet residential complex in Riverdale, the Soviet mission to the United Nations, and two Soviet recreation facilities on Long Island), one at Pioneer Point, Maryland (a recreation complex), one in Chicago, and one in San Francisco (the consulate). Their embassy rooftop COMINT gear allowed the Soviets to intercept phone communications from government limousines as well as to and from the Pentagon, State Department, and CIA. The Glen Cove, Long Island, complex could "sweep signals from all of the Northeast corridor." The Pioneer Point facility was located in the main microwave transmissions corridor between Norfolk, Virginia, headquarters for the Atlantic Fleet, and the Tactical Air Command headquarters at Langley Air Force Base, Virginia.[33]

Diplomatic and other Soviet establishments in Europe used to collect COMINT included four in the United Kingdom, seven in West Germany, two in France, four in the Netherlands, two in Italy, and two in Norway, as well as others in Finland, Sweden, Denmark, Greece, and Turkey.[34] As they had for years, Soviet AGIs continued to monitor U.S. ballistic missile submarine bases at Guam; Holy Loch, Scotland; Rota, Spain; and Charleston, South Carolina.[35]

To direct the KGB's human intelligence operations in support of RYAN, instructions were sent out to the residents in all Western countries, Japan, and some third-world states. While some residencies were asked only to be on watch for obvious signs of an imminent crisis, such as the evacuation of the U.S. embassy, the residencies in NATO countries were required to closely monitor all political, military, and intelligence activities that might be associated with a Western attack. It was expected that residencies would make Operation RYAN their first priority in their "Work Plans for 1982," which they submitted to headquarters in December 1981. Further guidance from the KGB followed in January 1982, emphasizing the priority of detecting Western preparations for attack.[36]

Those in the field, such as the London residency, were less alarmist, but they were required to report information which, while not worrisome to them, further alarmed those who had initiated RYAN. Andropov's selection as general secretary in November 1982, following Brezhnev's death, ensured that RYAN would remain a high priority of Moscow Center. Early in 1983 some Soviet bloc intelligence services became involved in the operation. The London residency of the Czech HSR was instructed to collect military as well as political information bearing on RYAN.[37]

On February 2, 1983, KGB residencies received a new top-secret instruction, "Permanent Operational Assignment to Uncover NATO Preparations for a Nuclear Missile Attack on the USSR." Attachment 1 of that document consisted of two sections. Section 1, "Immediate Tasks of Residencies for Collecting Information and Organizing Their Work," had seven elements to it, including collecting data about places where government officials and members of their families are evacuated; identifying the location of specially equipped civil defense shelters or premises; determining the location of blood donor reception centers and the price of blood; and keeping under observation the most important government institutions, headquarters, and other installations.[38]*

---

* How a residency went about actually collecting such information at times reflected the resident's own view of the threat of Western attack. Thus the London resident delegated the responsibility for monitoring official cars and lighted windows during and after working

Only a month later Soviet officials received two doses of alarming news. But the news did not come from satellite photography, highly sensitive communications intercepts, or secret reports from KGB or GRU residencies. It was news they could see on American television or read about in the *New York Times*. On March 8, 1983, while addressing the National Association of Evangelicals, President Reagan denounced the Soviet Union as an "evil empire," "the focus of evil in the modern world." On March 23, in a nationwide television address, he discussed the Soviet threat and laid out his vision of a ballistic missile shield. Reagan's vision would lead to the Strategic Defense Initiative (SDI), popularly known as "Star Wars." To an already paranoid Soviet leadership, Star Wars seemed one more indication of hostile intent.[39]

The landslide victory of Margaret Thatcher in the June 9 British elections further alarmed the Soviets. Shortly after the election the KGB's London residency received a telegram from the Moscow Center which stressed the importance of RYAN, claiming that the Reagan administration was continuing to prepare for nuclear war. None of the Line PR (political intelligence) officers in the residency believed the center's claims and some were concerned that the transmission of intelligence in response to Operation RYAN requirements was creating a vicious cycle, in which intelligence concerning possible preparations only further validated the view that an attack was being prepared.[40]

In August the residencies in NATO countries received further instructions, signed by Kryuchkov, specifying Western intelligence activities that might signal an impending attack. The activities, essentially the same as those the KGB and GRU would undertake if the Soviet Union was planning an attack, included increased disinformation operations directed against the Soviet Union and its allies; secret infiltration into the Warsaw Pact of sabotage teams with nuclear, bacteriological, and chemical weapons; and increasing "repressive measures by the punitive authorities against progressive organizations and individuals."[41]

In the following months the level of anxiety would only rise. U.S.–Soviet relations would sink even lower in September, and Soviet alarm would reach its height in November.

Shootdown

On the night of August 31, 1983, the United States was expecting the Soviet Union to conduct a test of its SS-X-24 solid-fuel missile. The SS-X-24, which the U.S. intelligence community expected to carry multiple warheads with high accuracy, would be fired from the Plesetsk test

---

hours at key institutions, in addition to the daily habits of government officials and their families, to a single junior KGB officer, who did not have access to a car. Christopher Andrew and Oleg Gordievsky, *Instructions from the Centre: Top Secret Files on KGB Foreign Operations 1975–1985* (London: Hodder & Stoughton, 1991), p. 81.

site in the northwest Soviet Union on a course toward the Kuchi Impact Zone on Kamchatka.

To monitor the test the United States had launched one of two special Alaska-based RC-135 aircraft, designated COBRA BALL. Their missions, designated BURNING STAR, monitored the reentry phase of Soviet and Chinese ICBM, SLBM, and IRBM research and development tests. A CO-BRA BALL aircraft would fly at 29,000 feet and carry three sensor systems—the Advanced Telemetry System (ATS), which automatically searches a portion of the frequency band and makes a digital record of all signals present, and two camera systems.[42]

The Ballistic Framing Camera System carried by COBRA BALL images all the dummy warheads and decoys during reentry, while the Medium-Resolution Camera (MRC) System photographs the individual reentry vehicles. The MRC's imagery is employed to estimate reentry vehicle size, which can be used to estimate the yield of the warhead when it is actually packed with nuclear explosives. Because the United States was uncertain about the exact time the test would take place, the COBRA BALL, which could fly for up to ten hours unrefueled and eighteen with refueling, would fly figure eights in the vicinity of the expected impact zone, although well outside Soviet territory.[43]

COBRA BALL was not the only intelligence resource the United States was employing to monitor the expected missile test. The frigate *Badger*, carrying intercept equipment, was stationed in the Sea of Okhostsk. The AQUACADE and VORTEX SIGINT satellites were also undoubtedly ready to intercept telemetry signals associated with the missile test. In addition, two radar systems were probably on duty that night. The hundred-foot-high COBRA DANE phased-array radar, located on Shemya Island, Alaska, had been constructed primarily to monitor the last stages of just such missile tests. A ship, the USNS *Observation Island*, carried a radar designated COBRA JUDY, as well as SIGINT equipment, to monitor the very last moments of warhead flight prior to splashdown.[44]

The Soviets did not go ahead with the missile test that night. But even without expected missile tests, the United States and its ally Japan monitored events in the Soviet Far East. As of August 1983 the 1,000-man Chobetsu, Japan's signals intelligence agency, operated approximately ten listening posts from its territory—listening posts targeted on the Soviet Union, China, North Korea, and other countries as well as stretches of the Pacific. One of those listening posts was located on the island of Wakkanai, twenty-seven miles across the La Perouse Strait from Sakhalin. The post's regular target was the Soviet air force, including the conversations between pilots and ground control.[45]

The major U.S. SIGINT facility in Japan was (and still is) the one located at Misawa Air Base, where over 1,500 men and women from the entire group of U.S. military SIGINT units are assigned. Four miles north-west of Misawa is the AN/FLR-9 antenna system. The antenna system, located 400 miles south of Sakhalin Island, allowed the various military SIGINT units to eavesdrop on Soviet army activity, the Soviet operations in Afghanistan, Soviet naval operations in the Pacific, and Soviet air force operations in the Siberia.[46]

While much was secret about the Misawa facility's operations, its existence and general purpose were no secret to the Soviet Union, the Japanese, or interested Americans. The same could not be said about another U.S. SIGINT unit in Japan, designated Project CLEF. CLEF was located on Wakkanai, and its existence was known only to a select group of Japanese officials. The unit had begun operations in 1982, with the mission of monitoring Soviet General Staff and Air Defense Force frequencies to determine whether additional collection sites were necessary.[47]

While those SIGINT personnel waiting for a missile test heard nothing, the SIGINT stations that regularly monitored the Soviet Far East would pick up something far more explosive. During its flight the CO-BRA BALL aircraft had crossed paths with Korean Air Lines flight 007, on its way from Anchorage to Seoul with 240 passengers and 29 crew and attendants. But the plane was flying off course—sufficiently off course to take it over the militarily sensitive Kamchatka and result in the Soviets' scrambling fighters to pursue the intruder.* KAL 007 received a temporary reprieve when it escaped Kamchatkan air space before the fighters could reach it and resumed flying over international waters. But its course took it over Sakhalin Island and once again Soviet fighters, including an Su-15, were scrambled.[48]

While Soviet pilots were chasing KAL 007, thinking at least initially that it was an intruding RC-135, various U.S. SIGINT stations eavesdropped without understanding exactly what was happening. Air Force personnel assigned to the Electronic Security Command unit at Elmendorf Air Force Base in Alaska, home of an AN/FLR-9, listened as the Soviets announced an alert and began monitoring the intruder's flight path. Since COBRA BALL's patrol area was well to the southeast, it was concluded that the Soviets must be breaking in a new radar operator or simulating a U.S. intrusion in order to practice a new tracking technique.[49]

A Russian linguist assigned to Misawa, while scanning voice frequencies known to be associated with low-level Soviet Air Defense communications, also overheard the Soviet pilots. But as was the case at Elmendorf, the communications did not appear to portend any momentous events.[50]

The first sign that something significant was in progress came at 2:43

---

* The reason for the plane being off course is the subject of a multitude of articles and books— with explanations ranging from innocent error to a sinister intelligence operation by the United States. The plane's black boxes, released in January 1993 by Russian president Boris Yeltsin, indicate pilot error as the cause. See Murray Sayle, "Closing the File on Flight 007," *The New Yorker*, December 13, 1993, pp. 90–101.

A.M., when Misawa intercepted the snapping-on of a secure communications link, as a major Soviet radar site on Iturup Island filed an urgent message to military district headquarters at Khabarovsk, reporting an unidentified aircraft approaching Sakhalin. More signs of Soviet activity followed, as more secure communications links became active, and more Soviet interceptors were scrambled. But Misawa was too far away from Sakhalin to monitor the conversations between Soviet pilots and their ground controllers, so it could hear the pilots responses to orders but not the orders themselves.[51]

The Soviet interceptor activity ceased at 3:47 A.M. Tokyo time and the exercise seemed to come to a sudden end. What did not come to an end, however, was the communications between Sakhalin and Khabarovsk, which left the eavesdroppers on Misawa wondering what was happening. The answer was provided by Project CLEF, where an operator who "happened to be working on the right frequency at the right time" overheard the Soviet pilots as they chased KAL 007 over Sakhalin. The operator heard an Su-15 pilot shout "Zapustkal," which signified that a missile had been fired. After the Soviet operation concluded he replayed the tape and apparently also heard the phrase "The target is destroyed."[52]

It would still be several hours before the United States and Japan would understand the significance of those phrases. What followed the realization that a Soviet pilot had shot down KAL 007 and ended the lives of all 269 aboard was another use of COMINT for political purposes. What would normally be tightly held intelligence, signified by the above-top-secret Special Intelligence (SI) classification, would be laid out for the world. The first presentation of such evidence came at Secretary of State George Shultz's press conference at 10:45 A.M. on September 1, after, according to Shultz, a "heated internal debate over whether we could use such intelligence without dangerously compromising the means by which we got it."[53]

In his news conference Shultz provided several items clearly derived from COMINT. He informed his audience that the United States knew when KAL 007 had come to the attention of Soviet radar, that the Soviets had tracked the aircraft for approximately two and a half hours, that a pilot reported visual contact with the aircraft, and that the Soviet plane was in constant contact with its ground control. He also told the press when the Soviet pilot reported a sighting of the plane and of the pilot's report that he had fired a missile and that the target had been destroyed. He concluded by stating: "The United States acts with revulsion to this attack. Loss of life appears to be heavy. We can see no excuse for this appalling act."[54]

The use of COMINT in public forums did not end there. The United States pressed its indictment of the Soviet Union at the United Nations. Rather than relying on the Project CLEF tapes, the United States used the tapes produced by the Chobetsu unit on Wakkanai, a use opposed by some Japanese staff officers for fear of compromising Japan's COMINT capability. While that unit was manned only during the daytime and thus made no contribution while the Korean airliner was being chased, its tapes were of higher quality than those of the CLEF unit. An appreciative President Reagan wrote Prime Minister Yasuhiro Nakasone, telling him that the tapes made for an effective presentation.[55]

ABLE ARCHER

To the Reagan administration, the shootdown represented dramatic proof that everything the president had been saying about the Soviet regime was true. On September 5, 1983, President Reagan signed National Security Decision Directive 102, "U.S. Response to Soviet Destruction of KAL Airliner." The NSDD observed that "[t]his Soviet attack underscores once again the refusal of the USSR to abide by normal standards of civilized behavior and thus confirms the basis of our existing policy of realism and strength."[56]

The directive also informed its readers in the national security bureaucracy that the United States was not about to let the Soviets off the hook with some harsh words and an embarrassing day at the United Nations. NSDD-102 specified actions to be taken, including "a major public diplomatic effort to keep international and domestic attention focused on the Soviet action."[57]

To the Soviet leadership the U.S. reaction was another sign, in an already hostile environment, of the West's malevolent intent. The Soviets were worried about more than words, since they were also facing the first deployment of Pershing II IRBMs in West Germany on November 23. Under such conditions Operation RYAN was viewed as being of even more importance.[58]

Then, from November 2 to 11 NATO began a command post exercise, designated ABLE ARCHER, to practice command and communications used to authorize the employment of nuclear weapons in the event of war. Although no troop or nuclear weapons movements were involved, the exercise did entail the simulation of the orders to be given to launch nuclear weapons as well as the imaginary movement of troops through different alert levels.[59]

The United States and NATO regularly held such command post exercises, but ABLE ARCHER was more extensive than its predecessors, apparently involving a different message format in ordering the escalation from conventional to nuclear conflict. The Soviets and their Warsaw Pact allies, of course, employed their signals intelligence resources to monitor the exercise. In addition to detecting the change in communications procedures, the Soviets also detected that some bases observed radio silence, possibly a sign that U.S. forces had been placed on alert.[60]

As dictated by Operation RYAN, human intelligence resources were also employed to monitor the exercise. Observation of U.S. bases in Europe brought reports of a change in the patterns of officer movement. The

London KGB residency received from Moscow a list of individuals in Britain believed likely to be involved in discussions with U.S. representatives prior to a first strike, as well as a variety of key installations that should be watched. Included were important Ministry of Defence facilities, underground command bunkers for government officials, NATO offices, U.S. and British military airfields, nuclear submarine bases, communications and intelligence centers, and the prime minister's residence at 10 Downing Street.[61]

While the Soviets and their allies monitored ABLE ARCHER, the United States and its allies used *their* SIGINT resources to monitor the monitors. The United States and its allies discovered an extraordinarily abrupt rise in the volume and importance of Warsaw Pact communications. What they apparently did not discover at the time was that Moscow increased the alert status of about a dozen nuclear-capable Soviet fighter aircraft stationed in East Germany and Poland, apparently in response to the perceived threat from ABLE ARCHER.[62]

The first real inside information on the level of Soviet concern came several weeks after ABLE ARCHER's conclusion. KGB officer Oleg Gordievsky, who had been spying for SIS for over fifteen years, and stationed in London, reported that the Soviet leadership greatly feared that the United States was preparing to launch a first strike. This report caused President Reagan to remark, "it's something to think about." However, the U.S. intelligence community believed at the time, as expressed in two 1984 Special National Intelligence Estimates, that the war scare was intended to intimidate the West, and possibly affect the outcome of an internal Soviet power struggle.[63]

While the conclusion of ABLE ARCHER relieved some of the anxiety in the Kremlin, it did not lead to a reevaluation of Operation RYAN. Only twelve days after the exercise concluded, very real cruise and Pershing II missiles arrived in Britain and West Germany. In January 1984, FCD chief Kryuchkov reaffirmed the overwhelming importance of RYAN, warning that the risk of nuclear war had reached "dangerous proportions."[64]

The Moscow Center proceeded to add several new items to the London KGB residency's monitoring task: attempts to increase "anti-Soviet feeling," particularly in the armed forces and civil services, the movement of cruise missiles, and the deployment of noncombat units and civilian agencies likely to be placed on war footing if the "crisis" deepened. In addition, London's banks, post offices, and slaughterhouses were not to be ignored. The center believed that preserving the banking system was a high priority while, in the event of approaching war, the food industry would begin a mass slaughter of cattle and place the carcasses in cold storage.[65]

By the summer of 1984 the anxiety level concerning Western nuclear intentions had largely disappeared in the International Department of the Central Committee and the Foreign Ministry, the two most important foreign policy organs, undermining the priority attached to RYAN. But the fatal blows occurred when the two leading military alarmists disappeared from the scene during the second half of 1984. Chief of Staff Marshal Nikolai Ogarkov was dismissed in September, while Minister of Defense Dmitri Ustinov died in December.[66]

Neither the anxiety of the Soviet leadership nor the hostility of the Reagan administration toward the Soviet regime brought the world close to nuclear war during the fall of 1983. But the paranoia of the Soviet leadership inserted a bias in the Soviet intelligence effort that put the most sinister interpretation on every fact collected. Any objective appraisal of Western intentions became impossible. Fortunately, even the sequence of events in fall 1983—the shootdown of KAL 007, ABLE ARCHER, the deployment of Pershing II and cruise missiles—was not even remotely sufficient to push the world to the brink of war. But under other circumstances the bias could have had more serious effects.

24

The Year of the Spy

Between late November and early December, following a bizarre week in which three major spy arrests were made, the American media began referring to 1985 as the "year of the spy." The arrests followed several major spy cases earlier in the year. In September a former CIA employee suspected of having revealed CIA operations to the KGB had escaped an FBI dragnet. And in June there had been arrests associated with a naval spy ring, which reportedly did devastating damage to the U.S. Navy.

The year was made all the more unusual by the defection and redefection, in a matter of months, of a KGB official. He left behind clues that resulted in one of the November arrests and a controversy over whether there had indeed been a defection. Meanwhile, another KGB official's defection represented a clear triumph for the West.

Changing Sides

On September 12, 1985, the British government announced that Oleg Gordievsky, who only a few months before had been the KGB Resident-Designate for the London Residency, had requested political asylum in the United Kingdom.[1]

Born in 1938, the son of an NKVD official, Gordievsky entered the Moscow Institute of International Relations, a training ground for the KGB and diplomatic service, in 1956. The day before the Berlin Wall went up in August 1961 he was sent to the Soviet embassy in East Berlin for training. After returning to Moscow in 1962 he spent another year in training, followed by a three-year stint in Department S (Illegals) of the First Chief Directorate (FCD). In January 1966 he received his first foreign assignment, the embassy in Copenhagen, directing the KGB illegals network in Denmark. By the time Gordievsky headed back to Moscow in 1970, he was completely alienated from the Soviet system, partly as a result of the invasion of Czechoslovakia.[2]

Back at KGB headquarters from January 1970 to October 1972, Gordievsky obtained a transfer from administrative to political duties. His new assignment was the First Chief Directorate's Third Department, which directed KGB operations in Britain, Australia, New Zealand, and Scandinavia. The department's primary task was to rebuild the KGB establishment in Britain, after the September 1971 defection of Oleg Lyalin from the London residency. Lyalin, who had been recruited by the British Security Service six months before his defection, provided information on KGB plans for sabotage and assassination in the event of war. The British government followed his defection by expelling ninety KGB and GRU officers and telling fifteen who were on leave not to return. All that were left were the eight KGB and five GRU officers whose true roles Lyalin did not know.[3]

Gordievsky arrived back in London in the autumn of 1972, prepared to consider Western offers. The British Secret Intelligence Service made first contact and by the summer of 1974 he had agreed to serve as a double agent. For the next four years he provided the SIS and the Security Service with information on KGB operations in Britain. He also provided information leading to the arrest of two Soviet spies in Norway, one in Military Intelligence and another in the Foreign Ministry.[4]

In 1982, after four years at KGB headquarters at Yasenovo on the outskirts of Moscow, Gordievsky returned to London for his third and last tour as a KGB representative, as deputy to the resident. While in Britain he provided information which proved vital to the 1984 arrest of Arne Treholt, a Norwegian diplomat, for spying for the Soviet Union. In 1984 he told the British of the attempt of a middle-level Security Service officer, Michael Bettaney, to offer his services to the KGB. Gordievsky, who helped in preparations for Mikhail Gorbachev's first visit to Britain in December 1984, was thus able to provide the British with intelligence about the rising Politburo member, his wife, and personal aides.[5]

Bettaney's arrest was followed by the expulsion of the resident, making Gordievsky the acting director of all KGB operations in Britain. But in May 1985 he was called home, apparently to be prepared for formal appointment as resident. It soon became clear that he had fallen under suspicion. It would be another nine years before it became clear that information provided by CIA employee Aldrich Ames—who had first offered to spy for the KGB in April—led to Gordievsky's recall. However, he was able to inform SIS of his predicament, and SIS managed to smuggle him out of the Soviet Union.[6]

Gordievsky's defection was followed by Britain's expulsion of twenty-five Soviet intelligence officers. With Gordievsky safely in Britain, SIS passed on to the CIA Gordievsky's information about the Soviet reaction to Operation RYAN, including a fifty-page paper the defector had produced entitled "Soviet Perceptions of Nuclear Warfare." The paper concluded that the Soviet leadership was very much prone to believe its propaganda about "aggressive imperialist circles" and that the West had to be careful, lest its actions increase Soviet paranoia to a point that drove them over the brink.[7]

Six weeks before the November 1985 Geneva summit meeting between President Reagan and the new Soviet leader, Mikhail Gorbachev, DCI William J. Casey flew to London to meet secretly with Gordievsky. Casey's primary interest was Gordievksy's firsthand knowledge of the personalities, habits, idiosyncrasies, and operating sytles of Gorbachev, his wife, and senior aides.[8]

A Change of Heart

In the late afternoon of November 6, 1985, Vitaly Yurchenko boarded a special Aeroflot Ilyushin jet at Washington's Dulles International Airport for a flight to Moscow. Two days earlier Yurchenko, at a bizarre news conference at the Soviet Union's new Washington embassy, had claimed that the CIA had drugged, kidnapped, and incarcerated him in an attempt to force him to betray Soviet secrets.[9]

While sticking to this story may have helped save his life, Yurchenko knew that the facts were quite different. A little over three months earlier, on August 1, the forty-nine-year-old KGB officer had telephoned the CIA's Rome Station, located in the American embassy on the Via Veneto. At a quickly arranged meeting Yurchenko indicated his desire to defect.[10]

At that time Yurchenko had been a member of the KGB for twenty-five years, having transferred from the Soviet navy to the KGB's Third Directorate (Armed Forces Counterintelligence) in 1960. From 1961 to 1965 and from August 1967 to December 1968 he worked as an operations officer and the deputy chief in the KGB Special Department for the Black Sea Fleet. From December 1968 to May 1972 he was assigned to the KGB residency in Egypt as a Soviet adviser to the staff of the Egyptian navy in Alexandria. That assignment was followed by three years of service as deputy chief of the Third (Intelligence) Department of the Third Chief Directorate, whose responsibilities included the recruitment of foreigners using the resources of Soviet military counterintelligence as well as the insertion of agents into Western intelligence agencies.[11]

In August 1975 Yurchenko received his first overseas assignment, as security officer at the Soviet embassy in Washington. In that position he was operating under what had previously been known as the SK (Soviet Colony) Section of the First Chief Directorate's Directorate K (Counterintelligence); he was responsible for the security of Soviet establishments and citizens in Washington, for protecting classified information, and for handling foreign visitors. Yurchenko was also responsible for detecting misconduct or "unhealthy attitudes" or other indications of vulnerability of members of the Soviet delegation who might then be exploited by a hostile intelligence or security service.[12]

In September 1980 Yurchenko returned to Moscow and served until March 1985 as chief of the Fifth Department of Directorate K. His department investigated suspected espionage incidents involving KGB staff personnel, information leaks concerning the First Chief Directorate, and performed other security functions. From April to July 1985 he was deputy chief of the FCD's First Department, which exercised operational control over legal KGB residencies in the United States and Canada, provided operational guidance, issued intelligence requirements, reviewed cases, and handled the asssignment of staff personnel to conduct the directorate's operations abroad.[13]

When Yurchenko defected he was able to speak from experience in areas that directly interested the CIA and FBI. One area concerned the organizational structure and procedures of the First Department, as well as those of Directorate K. More important, there was the ever present question of whether the KGB had succeeded in penetrating the CIA or other government agencies. Although he was not aware of any ongoing penetration, Yurchenko could provide clues concerning two former intelligence community employees who had provided valuable information to the KGB.

Yurchenko knew the first as ROBERT and remembered that he had been fired from the CIA for drug and alcohol abuse and had sold information to the Soviets in Austria in the fall of 1984. The second was code-named MR. LONG and had been an employee of the National Security Agency. The man had called the Soviet embassy during Yurchenko's tenure as security officer, sometime between 1977 and 1979 Yurchenko believed, to arrange a meeting.* He spent three hours in the embassy, where he was given instructions on how to meet with a KGB representative in Vienna. Again, Yurchenko could not recall the former NSA employee's real name but did provide a physical description and the approximate location of his home, somewhere near Beltsville, Maryland.[14]

Yurchenko also disclosed the existence of a previously unknown KGB unit, Department R, the Special Reserve, of which there was no mention in the CIA's secret 1984 study *KGB and GRU*. The Special Reserve had been formed following the 1971 expulsion of 135 KGB and GRU officers from Great Britain and Belgium, to ensure that in the event of similar mass expulsions there would be an in-place contingent of embassy-based KGB officers. While engaging in no espionage activity, members of the Special Reserve sought to spot potential recruits, worked with front groups, and performed other diplomatic functions.[15]

The defector also helped settle a couple of long-standing controversies. One concerned Leslie James Bennett, formerly an official of the Royal Canadian Mounted Police (RCMP) Security Service. Bennett, who had served in British signals intelligence in World War II, had emigrated to Canada in 1954 and joined the RCMP. Eventually he became head of the Security Service section responsible for monitoring and neutralizing Soviet operations in Canada. When several operations failed, in ways that

---

*It would later be established that it was on January 15, 1980.

seemed to indicate the presence of a penetration, Bennett, who was an unpopular outsider, came under suspicion. Although there was no conclusive proof against him, Bennett would be hounded out of the RCMP in 1972 and emigrate to Australia. Yurchenko revealed that there was indeed a mole in the RCMP Security Service during part of Bennett's tenure—Gilles G. Brunet, whose father, Josaphat Brunet, had been the first director of the security service (1956–57).[16]

The second controversy involved Igor Orlov. Orlov had worked for the CIA in Germany and some in the intelligence community believed him to be a KGB agent code-named SASHA. Yurchenko confirmed that SASHA and Orlov were one and the same.[17]

Yurchenko also passed on corridor gossip concerning the fate of Nikolai Federovich Atramanov, a Soviet navy captain who had defected to Sweden in 1959. It was not long after his defection that he arrived in the United States, under the sponsorship of the Office of Naval Intelligence. In his debriefing he provided ONI with information on Soviet use of AGIs, Soviet nuclear strategy, and Soviet destroyer tactics against submarines. Subsequent to the debriefing, he was given a new name, Nicholas Shadrin, and a position as a translator in the Naval Scientific and Technical Intelligence Center. In 1966 Shadrin transfered to the Defense Intelligence Agency (DIA).[18]

That same year Shadrin was approached by a Soviet intelligence officer who tried to recruit him. Shadrin did not flatly refuse the offer, but he reported it to the FBI. Despite his initial reluctance, Shadrin was persuaded to become a double agent, pretending to accept the Soviet offer while feeding the KGB CIA-doctored disinformation. The CIA had been convinced that Shadrin's Soviet case officer was willing to work for the CIA, and that success in this case would lead to his promotion to chief of the KGB's First Department.[19]

After several years of contact with the KGB, Shadrin began making trips abroad to meet his controller. He never returned from a December 20, 1975, meeting in Vienna. Yurchenko reported that he heard that Shadrin had died accidentally as a result of a KGB kidnapping attempt, having been fatally chloroformed while struggling in the back seat of a sedan with Soviet agents who were trying to spirit him out of Austria.[20]

While providing his information to the CIA and FBI Yurchenko grew progressively more dissastisfied with his life as a guest of the CIA. The lack of Russian-speaking debriefers, the CIA's unwillingness to let him to go to a Russian-language bookstore, rejection by a former lover who he had hoped would leave her husband in Canada, and concern over the publicity attached to his defection (which he feared would translate into dire consequences for his wife and child in the Soviet Union) led him to consider what would seem to be an unthinkable option—redefection.[21]

On November 2 Yurchenko walked out of a Georgetown restaurant, leaving his CIA companion behind, and walked to the Soviet embassy's residential quarters, where he presumably told the same story that he told two days later to the press. His redefection, combined with his status—employed and at liberty—after his return, led some to speculate or conclude that his redefection had been planned from the beginning.[22] But the alleged benefits from such a ploy—knowledge of how the United States dealt with defectors, discouraging the CIA from accepting other defectors, and embarrassing the CIA—did not compare to the potential losses from the disclosure of information and the possibility that Yurchenko would never return. Further, any attempt to misdirect the CIA, FBI, or other agencies, would be dissipated as the result of his redefection. Finally, even if the KGB had no expectation that the agents Yurchenko burned would provide more information, it reduced the value of their information if the United States knew not only who had provided information to the KGB, but what specific information had been provided.

In early 1993 Director of Central Intelligence Robert Gates stated that the CIA had concluded that Yurchenko was a bona fide defector: "My view, and I think the view of virtually everybody in this building, is that Yurchenko was genuine. He provided too much specific information, including in the counterintelligence arena, that has been useful, for him, in my judgment to have been a plant."[23]

Undone

Although Yurchenko was gone by the end of November, his information had resulted in the November 24 arrest of Ronald Pelton, the former NSA employee Yurchenko had known as MR. LONG. Using the temporary defector's clues the NSA produced a data base of 900 suspects, which was then narrowed to 100. When tapes of telephone calls that might have been from MR. LONG were played for NSA officials one was emphatic that the voice was that of Ronald Pelton.[24]

Pelton, a fourteen-year veteran of NSA, had resigned his $24,500-a-year job with NSA's A Group in 1979, after declaring personal bankruptcy.* Over the next five years he met Soviet agents approximately nine times, often in Vienna, to provide classified information. While he had no classified documents to turn over, his memory was enough to earn him about $37,000 from his Soviet handlers.[25]

A key factor in reducing the list of suspects so drastically was Yurchenko's recollection that Pelton had provided information on a Navy–NSA project code-named IVY BELLS. Eliminating those without access to such information dramatically reduced the number of potential suspects.[26]

IVY BELLS was only one of five projects Pelton disclosed to the Soviets, projects that were simply labeled A, B, C, D, and E during his trial. The

---

* A Group of NSA's Directorate of Operations was responsible for intercept operations directed at the Soviet Union and the East bloc. Other regional groups at the time were B Group (Asian communist countries), and G Group (all other countries). Subsequent to the collapse of the Soviet Union the directorate was reorganized.

IVY BELLS operation had originally been a CIA-conceived offshoot of Project JENNIFER. After the cover was blown by press reports, the CIA abandoned the project, only to have it picked up by the Navy and NSA. A Navy-NSA team, operating from a submarine, had installed a large pod on a key Soviet military communications cable located on the seabed of the Sea of Okhotsk. The pod could be wrapped around the cable and could tap into it without actual direct contact with the wires in the cable, by a process known as induction. The pod's tape could record about four to six weeks of signals traffic on the cable's various channels. Should the Soviets raise the cable for inspection or maintenance, the pod would simply break away from the cable and fall to the ocean floor, leaving no evidence of a tap.[27]

Twice a year Navy frogmen, employing a minisub or underwater robot, would locate the pod and change the tapes. The tapes would then be sent to NSA for transcription and, if necessary, decoding. Since the Soviets believed the cable was impregnable they did not always use their most advanced cipher systems when communicating via the cable. In some cases communcations were sent in unenciphered form. The communications provided intelligence on Soviet military forces and plans for maneuvers. Particularly valuable were communications involving ballistic missile tests, the warheads of which often landed around the nearby Kamchatka Peninsula. That such information might be months old did not significantly decrease its value in assessing ballistic missile capabilities.[28]

Pelton pointed out to the Soviets where he remembered the tap to be. Although he was off by several hundred miles, the Soviets were able to locate the pod. Thus in 1981 U.S. overhead imagery showed a dozen Soviet ships gathered over the exact spot where the pod had been attached to the cable. When a U.S. submarine arrived to collect the tapes and install new ones, the pod was missing. A code-word report concluded that the operation had been compromised, but it was not until Yurchenko came along that the NSA was able to discover the cause of the compromise.[29]

The other projects Pelton compromised included an operation run from the U.S. embassy in Moscow, a joint U.S.–U.K. operation, an improved method of intercepting Soviet microwave transmissions,* and equipment used to relay intercepted communications to computers for immediate analysis. In addition, he divulged information contained in the sixty-page "Signal Parameters File," produced in 1978 and specifying what was known about each Soviet signal of interest to NSA.[30]

Pelton's arrest came only after he had admitted his activities to the FBI. Had he shut his mouth and called a lawyer he would likely have walked away, since there was no evidence other than the phone call that he had

---

* Possibly the CHALET/VORTEX signals intelligence satellite, the first of which had been launched in 1978.

any contact with the Soviets. There was certainly no physical evidence—no surveillance photographs or audio tapes of his passing information to the KGB. And Yurchenko could hardly have been expected to testify for the prosecution. However, Pelton did talk, and on June 5, 1986, he was convicted by a jury in Baltimore of espionage. He was subsequently sentenced to life imprisonment.

While MR. LONG resides in prison, ROBERT was never arrested, although the CIA was quickly able to establish his identity. The only logical candidate for ROBERT was Edward Lee Howard, who had been discharged in 1983 after a polygraph examination had turned up petty theft, continued drug use, and heavy drinking. Consistent with Yurchenko's information, Howard had visited Europe for eight days in September 1984. Prior to his polygraph Howard had been scheduled to join the CIA's Moscow station. In preparation he had been briefed on the intricate procedures used by the agency in Moscow, the code names of the agents, and other information that might help identify them.[31]

The information Howard provided to the KGB apparently led to the arrest and ultimately the execution of Adolf G. Tolkachev, an electronics expert at a Moscow aviation institute. Tolkachev was arrested on June 14, 1985, during a meeting with his CIA case officer, Paul M. Stombaugh, Jr. Tolkachev, who had begun providing information during the Carter administration, passed on data concerning Soviet research in aircraft technology, including stealth technology, electronic guidance, countermeasures, and radars.* Howard had been scheduled to take over the Tolkachev account.[32]

FBI agents confronted him at his home in Santa Fe, New Mexico, on September 19, hoping that he would confess. Two days later, with the help of his wife, also a former CIA officer, he eluded the FBI's surveillance, traveled to Tucson, Arizona, and flew on to Copenhagen and then Helsinki. Howard later claimed he spent the next eight to nine months traveling in Canada and Latin America under an assumed name. Finally, in June 1986 he walked into the Soviet embassy in Budapest and was soon on his way to Moscow.[33]

On November 22, 1985—two days before Ronald Pelton would be arrested, one day after another major spy arrest—the FBI ended the espionage career of Larry Wu-Tai Chin. Chin had continued his intelligence activities on behalf of China into the 1980s. In 1981 he met with the vice minister of the Chinese Ministry of Public Security in Hong Kong and Macao. In February 1982 Chin traveled to Beijing, where high government officials honored him with a banquet, told him he had been promoted to deputy bureau chief in the ministry and awarded him $50,000. As late as February 1985 he met Chinese officials in Hong Kong.[34]

Chin had been undone by Yu Shensan, the son of two prominent Chi-

---

*Tolkachev might have also provided information which led to the U.S. discovery of a phased-array warning radar at Krasnoyarsk/Abalakova, the location of which violated the ABM Treaty.

nese revolutionaries. Before his defection in 1986, Yu headed the Foreign Affairs Bureau of the Ministry of State Security. The ministry had been established in 1983 on the recommendation of the State Council in an attempt to better coordinate China's foreign intelligence operations and reduce leaks of internal government discussions. The new ministry took over the intelligence, counterintelligence, and security functions of the Ministry of Public Security, as well as the intelligence functions of the Investigation Department.[35]

Yu Shensan was able to provide the United States with extensive information about Chinese intelligence operations abroad, including the names of Chinese agents and suspected agents from other nations operating in China. He may have provided information concerning Chin's activities, possibly as early as 1982, the year the FBI first placed a wiretap on his phone.[36]

Chin's jury returned a guilty verdict on February 6, 1986. On the morning of February 21 Chin tied a garbage bag over his head. Discovered by a guard at 8:45 A.M., he was pronounced dead at 9:30 A.M.[37]

On May 20, six months before the late November flurry of arrests, the FBI had apprehended John A. Walker, Jr., at the time a Norfolk-based private detective. The arrest ended an espionage career that had begun in 1968 when Walker, then communications watch officer at the Atlantic Fleet submarine command in Norfolk, visited the Soviet embassy. Walker managed the message traffic for all U.S. submarines in the Atlantic, Arctic, and Mediterranean, and he had something to sell. That day it was a key list, for which the Soviets gave him between $1,000 and $2,000.[38]

Walker would become a major prize for the KGB, providing an enormous volume of cryptographic material over the next eight years. Using a special device provided by the Soviets he was able to transmit to them the wiring pattern of the KL-47 cryptographic machine. That information, along with the technical manuals Walker supplied, allowed the Soviets to construct their own machine, which would then be fed the key lists he provided.[39]

Walker's duty at Norfolk was followed by radio school at San Diego and stints on the USS *Enterprise* and the USS *Niagara Falls*. During his three years on the *Niagara Falls* Walker, as classified materials systems (CMS) custodian, had complete access to wide variety of crytographic machines on the ship—the KW-7, KWR-37, KG-14, KY-8, and KL-47—and provided the KGB with copies of nearly all the keys for the machines.[40]

After service on the *Niagara Falls* Walker returned to Norfolk, serving at Atlantic Fleet amphibious force headquarters and then Atlantic Fleet surface force headquarters until his August 1976 retirement. Retirement did not end his activities on behalf of the KGB. In 1975 he had already recruited his own agent, Senior Chief Radioman Jerry Whitworth, who began by providing Walker with the classified *Tactical Satellite Communications System AN/WSC-5* manual.[41]

Between 1975 and 1983 Whitworth would alternate between shore and sea duty, serving in succession at the Naval Communications Station Diego Garcia (1975–76), on the USS *Constellation* (1976–78), on the USS *Niagara Falls* (1978–79), at Naval Telecommunications Center, Alameda Naval Air Station, California (1979–82), and on the USS *Enterprise* (1982–83). In each case he had access to a wide range of cryptographic materials. While at the Alameda facility he earned a bonus from the KGB on several occasions for having supplied a complete month's key list.[42]

By the end of Whitworth's *Enterprise* tour John Walker had added two agents to his network, his brother Arthur, recruited around 1980, and his son Michael, recruited shortly after joining the Navy in December 1982. Although Michael did not have access to cryptographic documents as Whitworth did, he was able to provide documents of value to the KGB. His access to the burn bag of secret documents on the USS *Nimitz* allowed him, around November 1984, to provide his father with documents such as *Fleet Tactical Library Cover and Deception Manual*, *Air Strike Operations*, *Surface Strike Operations*, *Nuclear Tomahawk Land Attack Cruise Missile* (TALM-N), *Anti-Ship Missile Defense* (ASMD), and *Electronic Warfare Countermeasures*.[43]

Walker and his network of spies were uncovered because his former wife, who had long known of his espionage, finally informed the FBI of his activities. Walker's arrest was followed by those of his son, brother, and Jerry Whitworth. Walker and his brother would receive life sentences, his son 25 years. Whitworth, who Walker would testify against, would be the biggest loser of all, receiving a sentence of 365 years in prison and will be first eligible for parole when he is 107 years old. In addition, he was saddled with a fine of $410,000.[44]

By the 1980s Walker was being run by First Chief Directorate's Department 16, a "small and tightly compartmented unit of about 30 officers," which targeted Western communications personnel. As a result Yurchenko did not learn of the operation until after Walker's arrest, when he was briefed on the affair. He told his debriefers that the KGB considered the Walker–Whitworth operation as the greatest in its history, even surpassing the atomic spy operations of the 1940s. He also stated that the information had allowed the Soviets to decipher "more than a million" secret U.S. messages. In addition, one of the senior KGB officers who briefed Yurchenko claimed that in the event of war, the Soviet ability to read enciphered American messages would be "devastating" to the United States.[45]

Yurchenko's assessment was echoed by many government officials and Western analysts, who argued that the espionage activities of the Walkers and Whitworth may have helped the Soviets gain important insights into Navy tactics and capabilities, as well as having helped the Soviets develop a quieter class of ballistic missile submarine.[46]

But it is also true that some of those advantages would have decreased over time and would have made a tangible difference only in the event of a war between the United States and the Soviet Union. The advantage that the Soviet Union gained from being able to monitor U.S. naval movements through its reading of U.S. naval messages was progressively reduced after the Navy discovered the nature of Walker's activities.* In addition, the information they acquired about tactics and capabilities, from documents or their enhanced ability to monitor U.S. naval exercises, would also have been reduced over time as technology and tactics changed. Furthermore, the prospect of war was remote, meaning that much of the information would never have been used. Finally, in the event of war such information would have been strategically significant only if the war were a very limited naval war. If the United States and the Soviet Union had engaged in any significant nuclear exchange, the war at sea would have dimmed in importance.[47]

Israel's Master Spy

On November 21, 1985, the day before Larry Wu-Tai Chin was taken into custody by the FBI, Jonathan Jay Pollard was arrested outside the Israeli embassy in Washington, D.C. Pollard had already been questioned by the Naval Investigative Service and FBI about his possible involvement in espionage after his acquisition of documents unrelated to his work had been discovered. Along with his wife, who would be arrested two days later, he had made a mad dash in the hopes of finding refuge in what was technically Israeli territory. But despite Pollard's pleading he was turned away, into the hands of the waiting FBI.[48]

It soon emerged that the thirty-one-year-old Pollard could legitimately claim that he was one of the most productive spies, possibly the most productive spy, in Israel's history. Extravagant claims were nothing new to Pollard, but in the past there had been no substance to them. While a student at Stanford he told friends that he and his father had fled Czechoslovakia in 1968 when his father's role as a CIA operative was discovered. (His father was actually a professor and microbiologist at Notre Dame.) While at Stanford he had claimed to be a colonel in the Israeli army and a member of the Mossad, even sending himself a telegram addressed to Colonel Pollard. Other imaginary occurrences included the killing of an Arab while on guard duty at a kibbutz.[49]

His penchant for falsifying his past continued after college and included entering false employment and educational data on his application for government employment. But in September 1979 he began work as an analyst for the Navy Fleet Operational Intelligence Office, which was responsible for monitoring the movements of military and merchant ships around the world. In June 1984 he became a watch officer for the Anti-Terrorist Alert Center, Threat Analysis Division, Naval Investiga-

---

* It should also be noted that there were and are a large number of naval communications networks, each with their own keys. The Walker–Whitworth material did not allow the Soviets to read all of them.

tive Service, responsible for reviewing daily classified message traffic received by ATAC and passing along relevant messages to the analyst responsible for monitoring potential terrorist threats in a particular geographic area. In order to do the job he was granted a Special Intelligence–TALENT-KEYHOLE clearance, giving him access to information derived from satellite photographs and communications intercepts.[50]

Several months before his transfer to ATAC, in early 1984, Pollard was told by a family friend about a lecture given by Colonel Aviem Sella, a rising star in the Israeli air force, who had served as chief of operations from 1980 to 1983. Sella, who was working on a doctorate in computer sciences at New York University, had spoken about the Israeli operation to bomb Iraq's Osirak nuclear reactor in 1981, including how Israel tried to ensure that the United States and other countries would not be able to detect preparations for the attack.[51]

Pollard expressed interest in meeting with Sella, and on May 29, 1984, the two met at the Washington Hilton Hotel, a short distance from Pollard's apartment. Pollard expressed his willingness to supply Israel with classified information and described the type of documents he could provide. Sella asked Pollard to provide a sample when they next met.[52]

But before there would be another meeting Sella had to determine if the Israeli government was interested in running a spy in the U.S. intelligence community, an act which, if discovered, would be a major embarrassment and severely strain the key U.S–Israeli strategic relationship. Reportedly, when Sella returned to New York he discussed Pollard's proposal with Yossi Yagur, the science counselor at the Israeli consulate in New York and a represenative of the Defense Ministry's Office of Scientific Liaison (Lishka Lekishrey Mada, LAKAM).[53]

A more accurate title for LAKAM would have been the "Office of S&T Intelligence and Liaison." A 1977 CIA study of the Israeli intelligence community listed the principal targets of Israeli intelligence operations, including the "collection of scientific intelligence in the US and other developed countries." LAKAM, which had offices in New York, Boston, Washington, and Los Angeles, had been set up in 1960 to conduct such scientific intelligence operations by Shimon Peres, then deputy minister of defense. It had proved crucial in supporting Israel's nuclear development program and in 1968 acquired blueprints for France's Mirage jet fighter, plans which helped Israel develop its own Kfir fighter.[54]

Yagur informed LAKAM's head, Rafi Eitan, of developments and requested instructions. Eitan had joined the Mossad in 1951, rising to the position of deputy chief of operations before leaving in 1972. In 1960 he had participated in the operation to kidnap Adolf Eichmann. When Ariel Sharon became Minister of Defense in Menachem Begin's Likud government he requested that Eitan be appointed head of LAKAM. Upon receipt of Yagur's message Eitan flew to New York to meet with the scientific counselor and Sella. On June 18, Eitan told Yagur to have Sella set up a second meeting with Pollard.[55]

There was a common reason why Pollard offered to provide intelligence and Israeli officials accepted his offer. After participation in two intelligence exchange conferences with Israel, Pollard had concluded that Israel was being denied information important to its defense. At the same time Israeli defense and intelligence officials were far from completely satisfied with the intelligence exchange relationship.[56]

That relationship, if not perfect in Israeli eyes, was close and long-standing. Israel had provided the United States with Soviet equipment captured during its wars with Eygpt and Syria, studies of lessons learned from the wars, and communications intelligence. The United States had, in turn, provided Israel with valuable intelligence on several vital occasions. Communications intelligence obtained through the RHYOLITE satellite system was passed to Israel during the 1973 war. In 1976 satellite photos of Entebbe airport were given to the Israeli Defense Forces to aid their planning of the Israeli rescue mission. The United States regularly provided intelligence derived from satellite photography, and at times satellite photographs themselves.[57]

But there were limits, and those limits often chafed. Israeli requests in the 1970s for a film-return satellite had been turned down, as had later requests for a ground station to access KH-11 imagery. And some of the satellite photography Israel wanted access to was withheld. After Israel's attack on the Iraqi Osirak reactor Deputy DCI Bobby Ray Inman ordered that Israel should be provided only with photographs of targets within 250 miles of its borders. The United States also withheld, or provided in sanitized form, reports on weapons systems employed by Arab states, in order to protect the sources and methods employed to produce those reports.[58]*

Pollard brought to their second meeting, on July 7, a brown leather briefcase filled with highly classified documents, which he obtained by virtue of his clearance and could remove from ATAC by showing his courier card. The most impressive included a satellite photograph of the Osirak reactor, taken only hours after the 1981 Israeli air strike that Sella had commanded. Sella described the type of information, primarily technical, that Israel required. He also told Pollard that Israel did not require intelligence on terrorism and that he would receive $30,000 per year for ten years of service, in addition to monthly cash payments, which rose from $1,500 to $2,500.[59]

---

* There were at least two reasons why the United States would want to deny Israel access to reports revealing sources and methods. There could be no guarantee that the Israeli intelligence or defense community was not penetrated by a hostile intelligence service, including the KGB. Soviet penetration is not unprecedented. In 1962 "Israel Beer," who served as a principal aide to the army chief of staff and the official of AMAN, was revealed to be a Soviet agent who had adopted the identity of the real Beer, who had disappeared in 1938. In 1989 it was charged that a Soviet spy in the Israeli Defense Ministry had been identified. Richard Deacon, The Israeli Secret Service (New York: Taplinger, 1980), pp. 162–63; Stephen Green, "Damage Caused by 'Friendly Spies,'" Christian Science Monitor, May 22, 1989, pp. 18–19. In addition, some of the means employed in monitoring Arab nations, such as the VORTEX signals intelligence satellite, were also used to intercept Israeli communications.

LAKAM's chief was suitably impressed with Pollard's samples and in November Pollard and his wife traveled to Paris, at Eitan's direction, where Pollard met with Eitan, Sella, and Yagur. The meetings, which lasted several days, covered operational plans, tasking, and compensation. Yagur provided a detailed description of the weapons systems and other topics on which Pollard should focus. Yagur, too, indicated a lack of interest in documents relating to terrorism.[60]

Pollard's routine, from at least January 1985 until shortly before his arrest, was to deliver documents every Friday to the Washington apartment of Irit Erb, the secretary of the Israeli embassy's science counselor, for photocopying. On Sunday he would retrieve those documents that had to be returned to their classified repositories.[61]

What documents he delivered was based, at least in part, on the monthly "tasking" sessions he had with Joseph Yagur, who had replaced Sella as Pollard's case officer when Sella returned to Israel after completing his courses at NYU. Yagur apparently had obtained access to a catalog of DIA documents, which he used in formulating requests. Tasking also came from military intelligence officials, who often wanted the complete versions of the documents that the United States had provided in sanitized form, for example, a handbook on certain Soviet weapons systems that had various pages or photographs blacked out.[62]

During the summer of 1985 Pollard and his wife traveled to Israel at LAKAM's expense. They were entertained at a dinner held in Pollard's honor, attended by Sella, Yagur, and their wives. A few days later Pollard met with Rafi Eitan, who urged him to accelerate his efforts on Israel's behalf. At his meeting(s) with Eitan he may also have been asked to provide documents related to U.S. intelligence operations against Israel, U.S. knowledge of Israeli arms deals, and U.S. knowledge of Israeli intelligence operations in the United States.[63]

By the time Pollard was arrested he had delivered more than 1,000 classified documents, "the majority of which," according to a Justice Department memo, "were detailed analytical studies containing technical calculations, graphs and satellite photographs." The memo also observed that a "substantial number of [the] documents were hundreds of pages in length [and] more than 800 . . . were classified top secret." Those documents provided information on:

- PLO headquarters in Tunisia (including a description of all the buildings)

- The specific capabilities of the Tunisian and Libyan air defense systems

- Iraqi and Syrian chemical warfare production capabilities (included were detailed satellite pictures and maps showing the location of factories and storage facilities)

- Soviet arms shipments to Syria and other Arab states, including specifics on the SS-21 ground-to-ground and SA-5 antiaircraft missiles

- The naval forces, port facilities, and lines of communication of various Middle Eastern and North African countries

- The MiG-29 fighter

- U.S. assessment of Israeli military activities

- Pakistan's program to build an atomic bomb (including satellite photographs of its Kahuta nuclear facility).[64]

Israel's use of some of that information, in planning a bombing raid on the PLO headquarters in Tunis, illustrated why the United States did not wish to provide it in the first place. The data supplied on the Tunisian and Libyan air defense systems and on PLO headquarters, as well as intelligence obtained on naval movements in the region, helped the Israeli planes evade detection and complete their misssion.[65]

Pollard also provided information about U.S. military activities and intelligence capabilities. Included were "details about ship positions, aircraft stations, tactics and training operations," as well as documents which "reveal much about the way the United States collects information."[66]

Pollard's arrest proved, as might have been expected, a huge embarrassment for the Israeli government—although not as great as it would have been if Pollard had not initially refused to cooperate with prosecutors—giving Yagur, Erb, and Sella (who was in the country at the time) a chance to escape. Prime Minister Shimon Peres moved quickly to limit damage, issuing an apology and characterizing the operation as unauthorized. In addition, Eitan was dismissed from his positions as head of LAKAM and special adviser on terrorism, while the government announced that LAKAM was being disbanded. It also made no effort to help Pollard, who would be sentenced to life imprisonment.[67]

The Peres government's subsequent actions raised doubts about the sincerity of its apology. Rafi Eitan was appointed to head Israeli Chemicals, a large government-owned corporation, while Aviem Sella was promoted to brigadier general and commander of Israel's second largest air base, Tel Nof.* Nor was LAKAM really abolished. Rather its name was changed and it was made subordinate to the Foreign Ministry. And a U.S. investigating team found the Israelis less than fully cooperative.[68]

The committee appointed by the Israeli prime minister to investigate the Pollard affair charged that Eitan "did not consult with the relevant ministers on the recruitment and running of Pollard."[69] Similarly, a report issued by a subcommittee of the Knesset's Defense and Foreign Affairs Committee, headed by former Foreign Minister Abba Eban, stated that Eitan bore

---

* He would resign in March 1987, after the United States refused to permit officers to visit the base, to avoid becoming "a burden to either the country or the Israeli Defense Forces."

full and direct responsibility for the decision to recruit and run Pollard. He did not report this to his superiors, and thus received no approval therefor. He was duty-bound to have understood that an action such as this was liable to imperil important interests of Israel, and to damage the friendly relations between Israel and the United States.[70]

Both Eitan and Pollard disputed the rogue operation portrayal. According to Eitan, "All my actions, including Pollard, were done with the knowledge of those in charge." Pollard commented that "the type of collection guidance I received suggested a highly coordinated effort between the naval, army and air force's intelligence services."[71]

Remarks by Yitzhak Rabin, then defense minister, to an Israeli investigating commission imply that high-level officials, certainly Rabin, at least, had knowledge that LAKAM had a means of acquiring U.S. intelligence documents that the United States did not want Israel to have. Rabin told the commission that he assumed that Eitan might be getting the information from a source in Britain or other NATO nation that would have authorized access to some of the information denied Israel.[72]

In 1993 Prime Minister Yitzhak Rabin appealed to President Bill Clinton to shorten Pollard's sentence. Secretary of Defense Les Aspin expressed his opposition in a letter to the president, stressing three points: the requirement to maintain control over the disclosure of intelligence to foreign governments, the damage done by Pollard's disclosures, and Pollard's alleged inclusion of classified information in letters from prison. Clemency was denied.[73]

25

End of an Era

During the year of the spy there appeared to be no possibility that the Cold War would be over any time soon. The year began with the ossified Konstantin Chernenko still in power in the Kremlin, while Soviet forces engaged in a bloody conflict in Afghanistan. The Soviet Union continued its extensive human and technical intelligence operations as well as a variety of "active measures."

For the United States 1985 started well, with the launch of a new SIGINT satellite, but the year would be largely one of disaster for U.S. intelligence collection operations. In addition to the loss of human sources in the Soviet Union, the United States also suffered a major setback in its space reconnaissance program, which would severely limit coverage of the Soviet Union and other nations for several years to come. At the same time, CIA covert action operations in Afghanistan would make life difficult for the Soviet forces in that country. A key U.S. decision in 1986 would help drive the Soviet Union out of Afghanistan in 1988.

While the United States and the Soviet Union continued their confrontation, other nations, including France, would seek to protect what they considered their vital interests through intelligence collection and covert action—although the results were not always those intended.

Rainbow Warrior

At 11:38 P.M. on July 10, 1985, a bomb tore a 3½ by 10-foot hole in the engine room of the *Rainbow Warrior* as it lay docked at New Zealand's Auckland harbor. Soon a second bomb destroyed the ship's propulsion system. Those explosions prevented the *Rainbow Warrior*'s owner, Greenpeace, from using it to lead a flotilla of vessels to the vicinity of Moruroa atoll in the South Pacific, to protest French plans to conduct a series of underground nuclear tests.[1]

The attack, as the world would soon discover, was no accident; it was a covert operation carried out by officers of the French DGSE. That operation had its genesis in the concern of Admiral Henri Fages, head of the Centre d'Expérimentations Nucléaires on Moruroa, over possible Greenpeace action to disrupt the French testing program, which was to include tests of the sixty-kiloton warhead for the new Hades tactical missile and the French neutron bomb.[2]

While the head of the DGSE, Admiral Pierre Lacoste, agreed that the Greenpeace flotilla should not be allowed to reach Moruroa, he believed that the simplest solution was to tow the ship away if it entered French territorial waters. But Fages wanted to prevent the ship from ever getting that far and in a March 4 lunch with Defense Minister Charles Hernu, Lacoste's direct superior, argued that DGSE action was required. The result was a memo from Hernu to the DGSE ordering an increase in intelligence activities to "forecast and anticipate the actions of Greenpeace." The term *anticipate*, which in French can mean "forestall" or "prevent," was underlined twice.[3]

That memo set in motion an operation involving at least nine DGSE agents. Christine Cabon, who had previously infiltrated the PLO, was assigned to penetrate the far less fearsome Greenpeace organization in Auckland. Greenpeace had announced plans to keep the *Rainbow Warrior* stationed off the French test site for several weeks, and the DGSE wanted to know if that was likely: Was the ship sufficiently equipped for such a stay? How experienced was the crew? Cabon was able to report on the organization's activities, suggest ways to undermine those activities, and collect maps and other information to support the covert action phase of the operation, code-named SATANIC.[4]

SATANIC commenced on June 22, 1985, when an ostensibly Swiss married couple, Alain-Jacques and Sophie-Claire Turenge, arrived at Auckland airport and drove immediately to the Travel Lodge Hotel. Neither Swiss nor married to each other, the couple were really Major Alain Mafart and Captain Dominique Prieur, both of the DGSE. In previous assignments Prieur had infiltrated antinuclear groups in Europe and terorist movements in Africa. The next day Jean-Louis Dorman arrived in Auckland and checked in at the South Pacific Hotel, where he could see the *Rainbow Warrior* from his room. Dorman was really Colonel Louis Pierre Dillais, head of the French naval special warfare school.[5]

On June 25 at least three more DGSE officers arrived in New Zealand, on board their yacht, the *Ouvea*. Roland Verges was a senior sergeant-major and eleven-year veteran of the Frogman Training Center (CINC) in Aspretto, Corsica. Gerald Andries, a six-year DGSE veteran, and Jean Michael Barcelo were also based in Corsica. The fourth crew member was Xavier Maniguet, a doctor with an expertise in diving medicine, who may have been employed by the DGSE solely for the *Rainbow Warrior* mission.[6]

Verges and his fellow crew members had been assigned responsibility for transporting the bombs that would sink the Greenpeace ship as well as a Zodiac dinghy, black Yamaha outboard motor, and diving equipment. The bombs had been offloaded on the coast near Kaitaia before the *Ouvea* went through customs. Mafart and Prieur were to organize the getaway, while Dormand would supervise the operation.[7]

After stopping at Opua the *Ouvea*'s crew traveled to Whangarei; on July 6 they arranged, by telephone, a meeting with Mafart and Prieur. Another meeting followed a few days later near the village of Kaiwak. By the time the meetings ended Mafart and Prieur had possession of the Zodiac and the diving equipment.[8]

It appears that Mafart and Prieur then proceeded to pick up the explosives and deliver them, along with the Zodiac and the diving equipment, to the pair of frogmen who had been given the job of placing the explosives on the Greenpeace ship. The pair arrived in New Zealand on July 7, after a month of training for their sabotage mission. On July 8 the *Rainbow Warrior* returned to Auckland harbor. The following day another DGSE officer, François Verlet, arrived, with the assignment of inspecting the target prior to the final phase of the operation. At 9 P.M. on July 10, after attending a party on the ship, Verlet was able to make his report.[9]

At 9:30 the nightwatchmen at the Auckland marina noticed one or two persons, the evidence varies, landing from a Zodiac craft and heading for a Toyota van, which had been rented by Mafart and Prieur. Two hours later the first blast hit the ship. At the time twelve people were still on board, including Captain Peter Willox and expedition photographer Fernando Pereira. Both men quickly left the ship, but Pereira then made a fatal error in judgment, returning to the ship to retrieve his photographic gear. He had barely entered his cabin before the force of the second explosion turned the ship on its side and killed him instantly.[10]

The toll could have been much worse:

> Had the bombs gone off an hour later, when everybody on board had retired for the night, there could have been four deaths from the first explosion, five from the second. Had they detonated an hour earlier, the 14 people at the skipper's meeting would have been trapped in the fish hold. The entire leadership of the Greenpeace Peace Flotilla would have been eliminated.[11]

Pereira's death made it not only sabotage but murder. On July 11 the marina watchman provided a description of the Toyota van he had seen the night before. When Mafart and Prieur returned the van on the 12th, the clerk at the car rental agency tipped off the police, who apprehended the pair before they could leave New Zealand. Although the crew of the *Ouvea* was questioned by the police, they were let go in the absence of any evidence linking them to the bombing. The frogmen and Dillais kept low profiles until they were able to leave on July 26.[12]

Mafart and Prieur, of course, would not confirm any French role in the bombing. But accusations were naturally directed toward France and the DGSE. In an attempt to end such charges Prime Minister Mitterand appointed Bernard Tricot, a long-time Gaullist, to draw up a report within two weeks. On August 25, Tricot declared: "At the governmental level, no decision was taken to cause damage to the *Rainbow Warrior*."[13]

Tricot's report was subject to ridicule, and finally on September 17, the prestigious *Le Monde* reported that the "Rainbow Warrior was sunk by a . . . team of French military personnel." Three days later Defense Minister Hernu and DGSE head Lacoste resigned.[14]

Meanwhile, Mafart and Prieur remained in jail in New Zealand. Both would be sentenced to ten years in prison, but a $9 million U.N.-mediated settlement between the respective governments reduced their sentences to three years and allowed them to serve those years with their families on the Hao atoll in French Polynesia. The *New Zealand Herald*, the nation's largest circulation newspaper, reacted bitterly to the arrangement, stating that "the Rainbow Warrior aftermath now stands as a contemptible episode of New Zealand history."[15]

The deal with France proved not only that the New Zealand government could be bought but that it could also be swindled. The sentences were not due to expire until July 1989, but in late December 1987, Alain Mafart was evacuated from Hao due to an alleged stomach condition. A Royal New Zealand Air Force plane, which would have carried a doctor to examine Mafart, was denied landing rights at the atoll's French military airport. In the final days of the 1988 French election campaign, Prime Minister Jacques Chirac announced that Prieur was being returned to France, claiming that she was pregnant and authorized to leave under the agreement between France and New Zealand. Prime Minister David Lange of New Zealand responded that he had not given his approval as required in the agreement and that Prieur's return marked "a clear breach of France's obligations under international law." By the summer of 1989 Prieur had been promoted to major. In early 1994 an official French government Gazette announced that Mafart was to be promoted to lieutenant colonel.[16]

Secret Eyes and Ears

A second explosion took place in the Pacific in the summer of 1985, one which the DGSE could honestly claim was not its responsibility. On August 28, the U.S. National Reconnaissance Office (NRO) was prepared to launch a new KH-11 spacecraft to replace one that had been deorbited earlier in the month. But just minutes into the flight an engine failure left ground controllers with no choice but to activate the payload's self-destruct mechanism, sending its remains into the Pacific Ocean.

The Titan 34D was the launcher not only for the KH-11, but also for the KH-9, the only other U.S. satellite imaging program.* Until an investigation determined the cause of the failure and any necessary corrections were made, no further launches could be attempted.

---

* The KH-8 program was terminated in 1984.

NRO's year had begun more auspiciously, with the successful launch of the space shuttle orbiter *Discovery* on January 24 on the first secret mission in fifteen shuttle flights. Earlier that week, Brigadier General Richard F. Abel, the Air Force director of public affairs, warned reporters not to speculate on the payload and threatened that the Department of Defense was ready to launch an investigation in the event of any unwelcome stories.[17]

The warning did not stop the *Washington Post* from revealing that the secret payload was a new SIGINT spacecraft. The spacecraft had been developed under the code name MAGNUM, but that name had been changed to ORION by the time of launch. Most important to the U.S. intelligence community was that the shuttle's military astronauts were able to place the satellite in its proper geosynchronous orbit.[18]

That satellite, which weighed about 6,000 pounds, was apparently placed in orbit over Borneo. It was reported to have two huge parabolic antennas, one for intercepting communications and telemetry signals and the other for relaying the signals to the ground station at Pine Gap, Australia.[19]

ORION was the successor to the RHYOLITE/AQUACADE program, although the exact degree of improvement is not known outside of those involved in the ORION program. But whatever ORION's capabilities they did not mitigate the loss of the KH-11. As a result the United States would have to rely on a single KH-11 satellite, which had been launched in December 1984, until NRO was satisfied that the next launch would prove more successful. After studying the results of the investigation that followed the August failure, and making any adjustments that were considered necessary, the NRO and other relevant authorities were able to plan another launch for April 1986.

On April 18, a Titan 34D carrying a KH-9 sat on its launch pad at Vandenberg. At 10:45 A.M. the launch vehicle lifted off the pad from the Space Launch Complex 4. Within eight seconds, with the launch vehicle at 800 feet, there were signs of trouble. Trouble soon became disaster, as one of the solid rocket boosters ruptured, sending out a twelve-foot ball of fire and then totally exploding. Within a fraction of a second, the other solid rocket booster and the Titan core exploded because the initial explosion triggered the Titan's self-destruct system.[20]

Everything, including the KH-9 in the upper stage, was turned into an orange and black fireball that was described as "spectacular" by someone who saw it from eleven miles away. The disaster at Vandenberg was followed in short order by a disaster of far greater proportions in the Soviet Union—a disaster that the remaining KH-11 would be active in monitoring. On Saturday, April 26, a nuclear accident took place eighty miles from Kiev, at the Chernobyl nuclear power plant, in its reactor Unit 4. As the result of a series of safety violations—such as running the reactor without the emergency cooling system and removing too many control rods—a small part of the reactor went "prompt critical." The effect was the equivalent of a half ton of TNT exploding on the core. Four seconds later a second explosion blasted the 1,000-ton lid off the reactor, destroyed part of the building, and brought the 200-ton refueling crane crashing down on the core. This was fired by a "fireworks" display of glowing particles and fragments escaping from the units, setting off thirty fires in the building. In addition, the huge blocks of granite in the reactor core caught fire, spewing out plumes of highly radioactive fission products.[21]

The first solid indication that the United States received concerning the accident was from an official Soviet statement on Monday, April 28. There had been indications of unusual activity around Kiev on Sunday, probably from communications intelligence, but it was not clear what was happening. It was only the following day that the situation was clarified.[22]

Once alerted to the disaster, the intelligence community responded by turning its full set of resources on the Kiev area. WC-135 nuclear-monitoring aircraft were deployed to RAF Mildenhall to fly missions over Germany, Switzerland, Italy, and the Mediterranean. A VORTEX signals intelligence satellite sucked up all military and relevant civilian communications within several hundred miles of Chernobyl. The lone KH-11 was programmed to obtain photography as soon as possible. Its last visit had been almost two weeks before. The first opportunity for the KH-11 to provide imagery came on Monday afternoon. However, given its orbital path the photo had to be taken from a considerable distance and, even with computer enhancement, showed very little. Moreover, had it been closer to its target, the smoke that was hovering over the reactor area would have probably obscured the site. The following morning the distance was still too great to produce a good photo, but by evening the KH-11 had approached close enough to return the first good imagery of the accident site. The picture was reported to be "good and overhead."[23]

With the photos in hand analysts at the National Photographic Interpretation Center discovered that the roof of the reactor had been blown off and the walls were pushed out, "like a barn collapsing in a high wind," said one source. Inside what was left of the building, there was an incandescent mass of graphite. Some tendrils of smoke and the blackened roof of the adjoining building indicated that at some point the fire had been more active. The graphite settled down into a glowing mass while radioactive material from a pile that had contained 100 tons of uranium was still being vented through the open roof and into the atmosphere.[24]

The photos revealed activity in the surrounding areas, activity that was quite remarkable given the perilous situation at Chernobyl. The KH-11 photos showed a barge peacefully sailing down the Pripyat River and men playing soccer inside the plant fence, less than a mile from the burned-out reactor. The photos of the town of Pripyat showed that there had been no evacuation.[25]

To supplement such data, collected after the event was announced to the world, the intelligence community looked back through information collected by other forms of surveillance. Tapes from the Air Force's Defense Support Program launch-detection satellite responsible for monitoring the Soviet Union, recorded the day of the explosions, showed infrared images of a sudden flash in the vicinity of Kiev, apparently the explosion that shattered the reactor. Communications traffic from the day before the explosion indicated that emergency measures were being undertaken and that reports of those measures were sent to Moscow.[26]

Among those briefed was the House Permanent Select Committee on Intelligence. "We were shown satellite pictures of the reactor building from before and immediately after the explosion," committee member George D. Brown, Jr., of California, said after a closed-door hearing on Thursday, May 1. "They were dramatic, with the roof beams collapsed and debris scattered around the plant. No bodies were visible," he added.[27]

KH-11 photos taken on Thursday morning, May 2, showed no smoke at all, leading an interagency panel to believe that it was possible that the fire had been put out, as the Soviets contended the day before. Only the day before, the panel had predicted that the fire might burn for weeks. Some analysts said they detected shimmering over the reactor, suggesting that the graphite was still burning. It appeared that the Soviets were dumping dirt or sand on the fire from helicopters. One KH-11 photo showed a helicopter hovering directly in the plume of the radioactivity.[28]

The satellite photos provided data that allowed analysts to determine the validity of reports that Unit 3, adjacent to the damaged Unit 4, was affected by a meltdown or fire. Further satellite photos allowed a U.S. task force to come to the conclusion on May 3 that there was no problem with the other Chernobyl reactors. Lee M. Thomas, head of the task force, announced on the basis of the photos that "we see no problems with the other units."[29]

The KH-11 undoubtedly continued to monitor the cleanup, sending back pictures of the Mi-8 helicopters (which had lead shields on their floors). The helicopters flew hundreds of missions day after day, dropping sacks into the broken roof of the reactor from heights of more than 650 feet. They then sealed the roof shut with tons of lead pellets, which rolled into whatever cracks remained between the sand bags.[30]

While the United States was experiencing serious difficulties with its photoreconnaissance program the GRU was getting used to the benefits of real-time imagery. The second fifth-generation Soviet reconnaissance satellite, *Cosmos 1552*, was placed in orbit on May 14, 1984, and operated for a record 173 days, far longer than usual for Soviet imagery satellites. Unlike the previous generations, the fifth-generation satellites did not return film in a capsule or with part of the spacecraft. Instead, the new generation of Soviet spy satellites relied on electro-optical imaging, with their imagery being relayed via a geosynchronous relay satellite. No longer would the Soviet Union be forced to return satellites early in an attempt to monitor a crisis.[31]

Cosmos 1552 would be followed by fifth-generation launches in March 1985, February 1986, August 1986, and December 1986. In each case the resulting satellite would exceed *Cosmos 1552*'s lifetime, with *Cosmos 1810* (of December 26) spending 259 days in orbit.[32]

Nineteen eighty-five marked another significant milestone for the Soviet space reconnaissance program. A 1984 CIA study noted that "while the Soviets are heavily involved in the use of satellites to collect ELINT data, they seem less interested in COMINT collection via satellite."[33] That apparent lack of interest was reflected in the absence of geosynchronous COMINT satellites such as VORTEX or ORION.

But in 1985 the Soviet Union placed *Cosmos 1738*, its first geosynchronous SIGINT satellite, into orbit. Along with its successors, which included *Cosmos 1961* and *Cosmos 2054*, it orbited over the Western Hemisphere at fourteen degrees west longitude. Apparently, the Soviet signals intelligence complex at Lourdes, Cuba, serves as the ground control station, which ultimately relays the signals to the GRU.

Cosmos 1961 was described by Tass as carrying "experimental apparatus for relaying telegraph-telephone information operating in the centimeter waveband."[34] But beyond relaying the telephone and telegraph communications from the United States and Latin America, the satellites were probably employed to intercept telemetry data from tests conducted in the Caribbean of the Trident D-5 submarine-launched ballistic missile.

The Secret War for Afghanistan

While the Soviet military's space program was doing quite well in the mid-1980s, the Soviet military was less successful in its only actual conflict on earth. The situation would take a serious turn for the worse in 1986, in part due to the CIA's ostensibly covert operation in Afghanistan.

Soon after William J. Casey took over as Director of Central Intelligence in 1981 he met with the CIA's Deputy Director for Operations, John McMahon, and his staff to receive a briefing on Afghanistan. Casey listened as the briefers explained how, after the Soviet invasion, President Carter had approved furnishing weapons to the resistance movement, extending a preinvasion program that included the provision of medical supplies, communications equipment, and technical advice as to where arms could be acquired.[35] After the briefing was completed Casey told them:

> This is the kind of thing we should be doing—only more. I want to see one place on this globe, one spot where we can checkmate them and roll them back. We've got to make the Communists feel the heat. Otherwise we'll never get them to the negotiating table. Anyone can see what they're up

to. . . . They're surrounding the oil. They're putting themselves in a position to shut off sixty percent of the world's petroleum sources.[36]

In the ensuing years growing U.S. support for the mujahideen (which included six major political groups and 90,000–100,000 active insurgents) would play a key role in driving the Soviets from the country. By fall 1981 the United States was involved with China, Pakistan, Egypt, and Saudi Arabia in a covert aid program. Saudi Arabia provided money, Egypt assisted with training, China contributed weapons, and the United States supplied Kalishnikov rifles, antitank missiles, and other weapons from U.S. and Egyptian stocks. Copies of Soviet weapons were produced by CIA-controlled factories in Egypt and the United States. In addition, some weapons, such as SA-7 antiaircraft missiles, were upgraded.[37]

A key player in facilitating the delivery of arms was Pakistani president Mohammed Zia Ul-Haq, who committed his principal intelligence organization, the Inter-Services Intelligence Directorate (ISID). Weapons would arrive by air in Pakistan, aboard planes whose markings were constantly changed. Under agreement with Zia the arms were then placed under the jurisdiction of the ISID, which was responsible for overseeing their transfer by a Pakistani army unit, the National Logistics Cell, to mujahideen leaders. Among the arms were surface-to-air missiles, which shot down at least sixty Soviet helicopters in the first year.[38]

In December 1982 Ronald Reagan instructed the CIA to again increase the quality and quantity of weapons being sent to the resistance. For the first time, some heavier weapons, including bazookas, mortars, grenade launchers, mines, and recoilless rifles, were supplied; they were reported entering Afghanistan in increasing numbers by late January 1983. Also sighted were U.S.-supplied communications equipment, rangefinders for rocket launchers, silencers, and other equipment.[39]

Late in March 1983 Casey arrived in Islamabad to confer with Zia. Among the subjects discussed was the question of providing Stinger surface-to-air missiles to the guerrillas. Assistant Deputy Director of Operations Edward Juchniewicz observed that with a Stinger, "a nearsighted, illiterate Afghan could bring down a few million dollars' worth of Soviet aircraft." Zia agreed that the ISID would distribute the advance weapons if the U.S. would provide Pakistan with 100 of its own.[40]

A large increase in funding began in the fall of 1983 with a secret amendment to the defense appropriations bill, rechanneling $40 million of DOD money to the CIA for the Afghan operation. The amendment passed in large part because of a top-secret letter to the committee from John McMahon. Part of the money was for Oerlikon heavy antiaircraft cannons. Another $50 million for more supplies and weapons was reprogrammed in July 1984. But Stingers were not part of the package.[41]

By the 1985 fiscal year expenditures for support of the resistance reached $250 million per year. The money was used to purchase mainly Soviet-made arms and ammunition from countries such as China, Egypt, and Israel. After arms were delivered to Pakistani ports and airfields, the ISID would take control and deliver the weapons (or at least a portion of them) to the mujahideen leaders in Peshawar. In additon to weapons, U.S. dollars bought medical supplies, food, and clothing for an estimated 200,000–300,000 full- or part-time insurgents.[42]

In March 1985 Ronald Reagan signed National Security Decision Directive 166, which authorized increased military aid to the mujahideen and made it clear that the goal of the effort was to drive the Soviets from Afghanistan. The directive was, at least in part, a product of intelligence concerning changes in Soviet strategy and tactics. As a result of the new policy CIA and military officers supplied communications equipment and trained Pakistani instructors on how to use it. The Pakistanis, in turn, trained the mujahideen. The CIA also supplied delayed timing devices for tons of C-4 explosives, to be used for urban sabotage and guerrilla attacks, long-range sniper rifles, a targeting device for mortars, and wire-guided antitank missiles. In addition, the CIA provided satellite reconnaissance data of Soviet targets on the Afghan battlefield, plans for military operations based on the satellite data, and communications intelligence.[43]

Support was further increased in October 1985 when Congress secretly appropriated $470 million for fiscal year 1986. Part of the funding was used for ammunition and small weapons. More significantly, part of those millions went for the purchase of advanced Stinger missiles. The decision to provide Stingers was made, not without considerable debate, in March 1986. Some in the CIA had argued that the Stingers would be too easy to trace. But by summer the initial shipment of 150 was being distributed to some of the insurgents.[44]

On the first day of their use in Afghanistan, Stingers downed three Soviet helicopters. Several hundred additional aircraft succumbed to the Stingers in the following two years. The success of the initial shipment led to a more widespread program. By March 1987 more than 300 missiles had been delivered, with hundreds (maybe 600) more in the pipeline. In addition, the Stingers, including some of a more accurate later model, were being widely distributed among the resistance groups. When the program began in 1986 each four-man rebel unit, after a six- to eight-week course, was given just one launcher and one missile at a time. Before another missile was released the unit had to show that it still had the launcher. By mid-1987 more than one missile was handed out at a time.[45]

Estimates of the ratio of targets hit to missiles fired range from four to eight of ten. Whatever the case, the Stingers clearly had an effect beyond the simple destruction of Soviet planes: Soviet and Afghan warplanes were forced to drop bombs from an altitude of 10,000 feet rather than their previous 2,000 to 4,000 feet, greatly reducing their accuracy. An Army study concluded that the Stingers "changed the nature of combat" in the civil war and were the "war's decisive weapon."[46]

In the second half of 1987 the Reagan administration decided to provide the guerrillas with long-range 120-millimeter mortars and mine-clearing equipment to help them attack Soviet and Afghan military bases. The insurgents had been pressing for such weapons to permit more effective attacks on eight major Soviet airbases and approximately thirty smaller Soviet or Afghan garrisons with airstrips scattered around Afghanistan. The long-range mortars allowed attacks from a greater distance, while the mine-clearing equipment would allow insurgents to penetrate isolated bases.[47]

In 1987, at the suggestion of William Casey, mujahideen penetrated up to fifteen miles into Soviet territory. The attacks included one on an industrial site. Fear that the attacks would result in Soviet retaliation led the Pakistani prime minister to cancel the operation.[48]

In addition to supplying the resistance with weapons, the CIA also provided at least $2 billion in counterfeit Afghan currency. The counterfeit currency allowed the resistance to pay the exorbitant fees of mule drivers and truckers hauling supplies inside Afghanistan, in addition to providing funds for outright bribery.[49]

Six weeks before the Soviet Union was to begin its withdrawal on May 15, 1988, weapons were pouring into Afghanistan for the resistance fighters—TOW antitank missiles, 120-millimeter Spanish mortars, and advanced antitank cannons. Giant U.S. C-5A transports were being met by scores of trucks belonging to Pakistan's government-run trucking line. Despite the Soviet withdrawal the United States continued, at first, to supply the mujahideen. After initial resistance the Soviet Union accepted the U.S. position that the United States would reserve the right to continue aid to the resistance as long as the Soviets continued to aid the present Afghan government. The U.S. program effectively ended on January 1, 1992, in response to a fall 1991 U.S.–Soviet agreement to cut off all arms to the factions. By that time the alliance that had driven the Soviets from Afghanistan had fragmented.[50]

The Pakistani government received enormous benefits as a result of serving as a conduit for U.S. arms to the rebels. In addition to selling advanced weapons to the Pakistanis the Reagan administration turned a blind eye to Pakistan's ultimately successful attempt to develop an atomic bomb.[51] But the KGB and Afghan secret police imposed costs in the form of a terror campaign within Afghanistan.

In 1985, according to a Pakistani intelligence report, the KGB and its Afghan counterpart began "a high-intensity terrorist campaign" aimed at high-impact targets such as "urban population centers, transport and communications facilities . . . selected to cause maximum loss of property, to generate fear and create widespread panic."[52] The campaign was clearly intended to send a message to Zia—that support of those terrorizing Soviet soldiers in Afghanistan would result in terror in Pakistan. The bombings would also, the Soviets hoped, create tensions between the Afghan refugees in Pakistan and the Pakistani population.

Although the KGB planned the bombings, they were carried out by agents, often Pakistanis, operating under the direction of the Afghan Ministry of State Security, best known by its Afghan acronym, WAD.* WAD officers received six months of training in Moscow by the KGB. KGB officials operating from Soviet diplomatic and cultural missions in Karachi, Islamabad, and other locations, would serve as supervisors for the WAD officers and, according to a Pakistani intelligence report, control the distribution of funds for WAD operations in Pakistan.[53]

In October 1985 the control room of the Pakistani television network in Peshawar was bombed. Three additional bombs were set off in other parts of the city. WAD agents who were captured after the attack disclosed that they had instructions to harass and terrorize Western relief agency workers. The following January an attempt, apparently by WAD, to bomb a Peshawar movie house filled with 150 people was thwarted when the agent was arrested before he could complete his mission. By 1987 bombings were occurring at the rate of one every two weeks.[54]

Bombings were only one part of the terror campaign, which also included the assassination of resistance officials in Pakistan. On January 5, 1986, a resistance commander was gunned down from a passing car. In other cases attempts were made to blow up the house and officers of resistance leaders. In the fourteen months prior to that six prominent mujahideen commanders had been killed, although internal rivalries may have explained some of the murders.[55]

Another tactic was to provide weapons to dissident tribesmen living on the Pakistani border. The KGB and WAD provided Kalishnikov automatic rifles as well as rocket launchers and funds to tribesmen willing to attack mujahideen personnel and harass Pakistani civilians. In December 1985 the Pakistani internal affairs minister claimed that 300,000 rifles had been smuggled into the Khyber tribal area, along with rocket launchers and antiaircraft missiles.[56]

Then, in August 1988 a plane crash claimed the lives of Zia, the Chairman of the Joint Chiefs of Staff Committee, and the U.S. Ambassador. A number of the possible culprits were obvious—opponents in the Pakistani military, the Indian Research and Analysis Wing and, of course, WAD and the KGB.

---

*WAD is the acronym for Wazarat-e-Amniyat-e-Daulati. It was known as the Worker's Intelligence Establishment (KAM) when it was established in 1979. Subsequently, WAD became KHAD, Khidmat-Ittelaat-e-Dauli (Government Information Service). In 1985 KHAD became WAD. KHAD's first director, Najibullah, would become Afghanistan's last Marxist ruler.

26

*A New World
of Disorder*

By August 1990 the changes in Soviet foreign policy that resulted from the policies of Mikhail Gorbachev brought an end to the East–West conflict that had been a central factor in world affairs since 1945. Without those changes U.N. action following Iraq's invasion of Kuwait would have been impossible.

That invasion illustrated that the end of East–West conflict did not mean an end to conflict. Further, the Persian Gulf War and its aftermath, with numerous discoveries concerning the Iraqi nuclear weapons program, illustrated the need for extensive intelligence capabilities in the post–Cold War era.

Several months after that war ended hard-line forces in the Soviet Union, including the chairman of the KGB, attempted to displace Mikhail Gorbachev. Within weeks of their attempt they were in jail and the Soviet Union was living on borrowed time. The implications of the failed coup and the Soviet demise were dramatic for the KGB. While the GRU survived as the military intelligence agency of the new Russian state, the KGB was shattered—its functions divided into a number of agencies.

Throughout the former East bloc, the intelligence agencies of the communist regimes were replaced by new services, which perhaps would be more respectful of democratic ideals. The collapse of the East German regime meant an end to refuge for many of Markus Wolf's agents and the discovery of others. For Markus Wolf it would ultimately mean a trial for treason.

The end of the Cold War has focused attention on a nonviolent form of conflict—economic competition—and the role of intelligence in that struggle. Since high-tech economic competition occurs largely among the Western nations and the Pacific rim, economic espionage often involves targeting the business enterprises of an allied nation, using both human sources and communications intercepts.

In the post–Cold War era a prime purpose of the intelligence services of the United States, its West European allies, Russia, and a variety of other nations will be the monitoring of the sale and/or purchase of advanced weaponry or its components by Pakistan, India, Israel, North Korea, Iran, Iraq, and others.

This task may become easier thanks to improvements in U.S. and Russian space reconnaissance capabilities as well as the deployment of space reconnaissance systems by France, Germany, and Japan. The implications of the deployment of similar systems by nations such as Israel and India are ambiguous; space reconnaissance systems may provide reassurance or aid in planning an attack on an enemy.

The Gulf War

On July 16, 1990, Walter P. "Pat" Lang, the Defense Intelligence Officer for the Middle East and South Asia, carefully examined satellite photographs taken that morning. A day earlier there was nothing to be seen in southeastern Iraq except empty desert, but that day the story was different. Lang could see the beginning of an Iraqi brigade of Soviet-made T-72 tanks.[1]

The next day's photos were even more disturbing. They showed the entire Hammurabi Division of the Republican Guard—300 tanks and over 10,000 men—positioned near the Kuwaiti border along with another Republican Guard division. One day later a third division showed up in border photographs.[2]

The movement of those three divisions to the border was not consistent with the expectations of the U.S. intelligence community. The community had produced a National Intelligence Estimate in the fall of 1989 which concluded that while Saddam Hussein wished to dominate the gulf region the eight-year war with Iran had so drained Iraq's resources that Iraqi military action to achieve that objective was unlikely.[3]

There was a reassuring explanation, accepted by many intelligence analysts: the Iraqi dictator was simply using the troop movements to pressure Kuwait in their ongoing negotiations over oil. But that explanation became less believable to Lang as the end of the month approached. On July 30 Lang, in a memo prepared for the director of the Defense Intelligence Agency, reported that Iraqi movements did not make sense if the only objective was to intimidate Kuwait. He wrote that "I do not believe that he is bluffing. I have looked at his personality profile. He doesn't know how to bluff. It is not in his past pattern of behavior."[4]

The photographs Lang examined on the morning of August 1 led him to issue a warning message predicting an attack by that night or the next morning. A CIA assessment circulated that morning reached the same conclusion, which was born out when Iraqi forces stormed into Kuwait on the morning of August 2.[5]

The invasion would be followed by U.N. economic sanctions and an ultimatum: withdraw from Kuwait by January 15 or the United Nations would feel free to use military force to expel Iraqi forces from Kuwait. Actually carrying out such a threat would require intense diplomatic, military, and intelligence activity in the intervening months. A multinational force would have to be assembled, operations plans drawn up; and information collected about Iraqi defense systems, conventional offensive capabilities, command and control links, and nuclear, biological, and chemical weapons programs. In the interim forces would be deployed to Saudi Arabia, as part of Operation DESERT SHIELD, to deter any further action.

The primary means for collecting intelligence on Iraq and Kuwait, particularly in the period before military action began, were U.S. space reconnaissance systems, including the VORTEX and ORION signals intelligence satellites. Of particular importance would be the three varieties of imagery satellites that the United States had in operation. Three KH-11s were in orbit, although the oldest, launched in 1984, may have had a limited capability. Also in orbit was at least one Advanced KH-11 and one LACROSSE satellite. The Advanced KH-11, also known as the Improved CRYSTAL because the KH-11's code name had been changed to CRYSTAL in 1987, is identical to the KH-11 in one important respect: it relies on an electrooptical system to transmit its data in real time. Two features unique to the Advanced KH-11 are its infrared imaging capability and the Improved CRYSTAL Metric System (ICMS). The infrared imagery capability extends into the thermal infrared region and allows for some imagery to be produced at night, while the ICMS allows the imagery to be used more effectively for mapping purposes.[6]

The LACROSSE satellite, which had been launched in December 1988, was the culmination of a program first approved during George Bush's tenure as DCI, when it was code-named INDIGO. Rather than depending on reflected visible light or heat to produce imagery, LACROSSE relied on the radar pulses it generates and then receives back from its target. While the resulting imagery was not in the same class as that of the KH-11 or Advanced KH-11, with a resolution of between three and five feet, it did have one major advantage over other U.S. space imagery systems. Neither the KH-11 nor the Advanced KH-11 could produce imagery in the presence of significant cloud cover, which prevented light or heat from reaching the spacecraft sensors. Radar pulses, on the other hand, could easily penetrate cloud cover, allowing LACROSSE to send back images even on cloudy days.[7]

The United States also began to employ several other intelligence assets, which were either deployed to Saudi Arabia or were traditionally operated from territory close to Iraq. U-2 and TR-1 aircraft flew imagery and SIGINT missions lasting up to ten hours. RC-135 RIVET JOINT aircraft deployed to Riyadh monitored Iraqi communications. In addition, U.S. and British ground-based SIGINT collection sites in the vicinity—on Cyprus, and in Turkey, Italy, and Oman—were undoubtedly targeted on Iraq and Kuwait.[8]

The United States proceeded to use these assets, along with human intelligence, to update its data on the Iraqi military, economic, and political systems as a prelude to target selection and planning for the ground offensive. HUMINT was used to "nominate, target, and destroy key Iraqi command, control, communications, and other military targets." According to an Army assessments one of its sources "significantly contributed to the impact of the air campaign and thereby shortened the ground campaign."[9]

In the meantime, the Soviet Union, although militarily uninvolved, also monitored the situation in the Persian Gulf. Already in place was *Cosmos 2072*, a real-time spacecraft launched on April 13. Less than forty-eight hours after the invasion, at 10:45 P.M. Moscow time on August 3, *Cosmos 2089* was launched from Plesetsk into a 62-degree, 117- by 198-mile orbit, and proceeded to pass over the Middle East once a day during its 59-day mission. On October 16 *Cosmos 2102* was launched and subsequently dropped into a very low orbit to produce more detailed pictures of troop concentrations in the gulf area. Another real-time system, launched on December 21, would further enhance Soviet capability to follow events in the region.[10]

The devastating air campaign that began on January 15 was followed on February 22 by the "Hail Mary" ground campaign that would force the Iraqi troops out of Kuwait. U.S. intelligence collection was instrumental in identifying targets for air attack, which in turn weakened Iraq's overall military capability. Further, for U.S. and allied forces to bypass dug-in Iraqi forces in entering Kuwait it was imperative to know where they were, knowledge provided by overhead reconnaissance. U.S. success in the ground campaign was also influenced by Iraq's lack of a reconnaissance capability. It had no reconnaissance satellite, the one Mirage F-1 reconnaissance plane that the Iraqi air force attempted to fly was shot down, and even commercial satellite photography was denied to Iraq after August 2.

In addition to satellite systems, U-2s, and TR-1s, the United States employed a number of other aerial reconnaissance systems—RF-4C Phantoms, F-14s with tactical reconnaissance pods, P-3 Orion ocean surveillance aircraft (flown over land), and unmanned aerial vehicles. U.S. systems were supplemented by a variety of foreign aircraft, including six Royal Air Force Jaguar reconnaissance aircraft and a French C-160 GABRIEL signals intelligence aircraft.[11]

The U.S. intelligence system, aided by allied systems, produced a wealth of invaluable data during Operations DESERT SHIELD and DESERT STORM, but there were still numerous gaps, indicating the difficulty, even when equipped with a sizable constellation of space reconnaissance systems and aircraft, of providing the all the intelligence information desired by military commanders.

There were several areas where intelligence performance was less than fully satisfying to U.S. and allied military commanders—in providing a broad view of the battlefield, in locating the mobile Scuds, in providing bomb-damage assessment (BDA), and in providing intelligence (particularly imagery) in a timely manner.

Despite the fact that the United States had more imagery satellites in orbit than during any part of the Cold War, and they all could return imagery in real time, none of the satellites had the ability to provide the wide-area coverage similar to the defunct KH-9 satellites. With each satellite overhead for only a short period of time each day, commanders would only have access, at any one time, to glimpses of small portions of southern Iraq and Kuwait. The lack of broad coverage made it difficult to fix the table of organization of some Iraqi units, led to an overestimation of Iraqi troop numbers, and required that numerous reconnaissance systems be employed to cover the area that a single wide-area system could.[12]

The lack of a broad-area capability also made it difficult to locate the mobile Scuds used to terrorize Israel and Saudi Arabia. Scud launch tactics "eliminated photo-reconnaissance as a contributor. Scuds were launched at night by mobile groups that left hidden, underground sites for launch locations only as long as necessary to launch."[13]

The bomb-damage assessment problem could not be blamed on the lack of a broad-area search capability. Rather, the problem partly resulted from the difference in the way agencies in Washington and analysts in the field approached the problem. Intelligence agencies in Washington judged aircraft or tanks to be destroyed if destruction was clearly shown by satellite or aerial photography; U.S. Central Command analysts factored in pilot reports in assessing the impact of bombing raids. In addition, in many cases the small holes on the outside of a target, which meant serious internal damage, were not detectable even by high-resolution U.S. imagery satellites.[14]

The Fall of the KGB

On August 20, 1991, not long after the failure of the coup, a crowd of up to 20,000 Muscovites assembled around the statue of Felix E. Dzerzhinsky, demanding that "Iron Felix" be demolished. The crowd cheered wildly and chanted "Down with the KGB!" as two construction cranes raised the twelve-ton bronze monument from its pedestal in the center of a traffic circle outside KGB headquarters.[15]

Surprisingly, an element of the KGB played a key role in the defeat of the forces seeking to oust Mikhail Gorbachev. A day earlier the head of the Alpha Group of the KGB's Seventh Directorate had been ordered by KGB chairman Vladimir Kryuchkov to storm the Russian republic parliament building, arrest Boris Yeltsin, and bring him to a "special location" in the wooded suburb of Zavidovo. Major General Viktor Karpukhin proceeded to develop the necessary plans, and then decided that he would not carry them out. That decision, according to Yeltsin, forced the coup plotters to cancel their attack.[16]

Not surprisingly, given Kryuchkov's actions, drastic reform of the

KGB's leadership and structure was on Gorbachev's agenda after he returned to Moscow. Reform began within days, with reformer Vadim Bakatin becoming the new KGB chairman, and was followed by Gorbachev's appointment of a close aide, Yevgeny Maksimovich Primakov, to head the KGB's First Chief Directorate, which the Soviet president said should be established as a separate agency.[17]

The sixty-one-year-old Primakov had most recently served as Gorbachev's shuttle diplomat to Baghdad during the Persian Gulf crisis. Before that he had been a journalist for *Pravda*, possibly working with the KGB in the 1960s, and a specialist in Arab affairs. At a press conference two days after his appointment he described himself as a fan of British spy novelist John Le Carre.[18]

In addition to revealing his literary tastes Primakov summarized his views about what his service should be doing: preventing the return of the Cold War, stopping the proliferation of nuclear weapons, fighting international terrorism and narcotics trafficking, providing favorable conditions for economic and scientific development, and halting economic manipulation that would damage the Soviet economy.[19]

Primakov also announced that the last vestiges of Operation RYAN were being eliminated, revealing that he had halted what he described as a special monitoring program to warn against a U.S. nuclear attack. "Today, naturally, that tracking program, which involved huge material and human resources and so on, has been abolished," Primakov said.[20]

In October four new agencies were established out of the corpse of the KGB. The Committee for the Protection of USSR State Borders took over control of more than 300,000 border troops of the former KGB. The KGB's counterintelligence and counterterrorist functions were assigned to the new Inter-Republican Security Service (MSB), headed by Bakatin. The cryptographic and SIGINT missions that had been the responsibility of the the the KGB's Eighth Directorate and Department 16 of the First Chief Directorate were assigned to the USSR President's Committee for Government Communications. Primakov's First Chief Directorate became the Central Intelligence Service (TSSR).[21]

With the dissolution of the Soviet Union at the end of 1991, the two new foreign intelligence organizations were quickly converted into branches of Boris Yeltsin's Russian government. The government communications committee became the Federal Agency for Government Communications and Information (FAPSI). The Central Intelligence Service became the Russian Foreign Intelligence Service (Sluzhba Vnezhney Rasvedki, SVR), with Primakov continuing as head. A law passed in the summer of 1992 defining the SVR's mission as the collection of "political, economic, scientific/technical and ecological intelligence."[22]

In addition to restoring ties with some of the former Soviet bloc intelligence services, Primakov has sought new intelligence alliances with former adversary intelligence services. In August 1992 talks between Yeltsin and German intelligence officials, including the intelligence coordinator and head of the BND, produced an agreement for SVR–BND cooperation with respect to terrorism, narcotics, organized crime, proliferation, and money laundering. By October 1 both services had opened up liaison offices in their respective embassies.[23]

Later in the month Director of Central Intelligence Robert Gates arrived in Moscow for discussions with Primakov and other Russian intelligence and security officials. After Gates's visit a statement by the U.S. embassy mentioned drug trafficking, terrorism, and proliferation as possible targets of CIA–SVR cooperation.[24]*

In February 1993 Primakov visited Germany, where he followed up on the agreements that had been reached in August, met with the intelligence coordinator Bernd Schmidbauer, and visited the Pullach headquarters of the BND. Three months later the peripatetic SVR chief traveled to the United States to hold talks with new CIA director James Woolsey.[25]

The intelligence service least affected by the political turmoil of 1991 was the GRU, which simply followed the U.S.S.R.'s Ministry of Defense as it became the Ministry of Defense of the Commonwealth of Independent States and then the Russian Ministry of Defense. However, there were several changes in the top leadership of the GRU. At the time of the coup the GRU director was Colonel General Vladlen Mikhailovich Mikhailov, who had replaced General Petr Ivashutin in 1987, after a twenty-three-year reign by the former KGB official.[26]

In October Mikhailov was replaced by General Yevgeniy Timokhin. According to two Soviet GRU officers, writing in the December 17, 1991, issue of *Nezavisimaya Gazeta* under assumed names, such a change was long overdue. They wrote that Mikhailov was "a man lacking not just a specialized education but even the slightest idea of strategic military intelligence," who believes that the Ivory Coast is located in South East Asia, "confuses Ayatollah Khomeini with Mengistu Haile Mariam, and the latter with Emperor Haile Selassye."

---

* The new spirit of cooperation did not stop the SVR from continuing to run an agent within the CIA's Directorate of Operations, Aldrich Ames. Ames was finally arrested in 1994, after having provided information to the KGB and SVR for nearly a decade. When recruited in 1985 he was counterintelligence chief of the operations directorate's Soviet/Eastern European Division. Ames provided information that betrayed at least eleven CIA agents to the Soviets and led to the execution of at least four. The CIA sources compromised by Ames included General Dmitri Polyakov of the GRU (whose code name was GTACCORD), Oleg Gordievsky (GTTICKLE), a Soviet intelligence officer stationed in Moscow (GTCOWL), an East European security officer (GTMOTORBOAT), a lieutenant colonel in the GRU (GTMILLION), a KGB officer (GTFITNESS), as well as others who were code named GTBLIZZARD, GTGENTILE, GTPROLOGUE, GTPYRRHIC, and GTWEIGH. Polyakov, GTFITNESS, and GTMILLION were all executed. (Bill Miller and Walter Pincus, "Ames Pleads Guilty to Spying, Gets Life Term," *Washington Post*, April 29, 1994, pp. A1, A18; "Statement of Facts, United States of America v. Aldrich Hazen Ames," Criminal No. 94-64-A, United States Court for the Eastern District of Virginia, April 28, 1994, p. 10).

The Trial of Markus Wolf

Markus Wolf retired from the HVA in 1986 at age sixty-three, because, he claimed, he could no longer tolerate the corruption and abuse of privilege that was endemic to the East German regime. Of his own boss, Minister of State Security Erich Mielke, Wolf remarked that "It's hard to find a good word to say for him."[27]

Many might say the same of Wolf, who combined a devotion to Communist party doctrine with a fondness for a comfortable lifestyle. He had country homes in East Germany and the Soviet Union, drove a Volvo instead of a Trabant, had unlimited access to Western goods, and pursued women avidly.[28]

For whatever reason, by late 1989 Wolf openly advocated reform, appearing on television talk shows and in panel discussions, and he was a featured speaker at huge East Berlin rally on November 4. In an interview, the former HVA chief said: "We must turn our backs on the old doctrine. . . . People with different opinions but who were not enemies of the state got arrested and persecuted and this dangerous ideological perversion must stop."[29]

Wolf also acknowledged that "[e]veryone who had a high function in a socialist country in the last decades bears responsibility, if not in a legal then in a moral sense."[30] But being held morally responsible and legally responsible had two very different sets of consequences.

After the October 1990 reunification of Germany leading members of the East German regime, including Wolf, became potential targets for prosecution. In an attempt to avoid any unpleasant consequences of legal responsibility, Wolf and his wife got in their Volvo and traveled through Czechoslovakia to Austria and then on to Moscow. But any chance that Moscow could be a permanent place of refuge ended when the August 1991 coup attempt failed and Wolf's chief patron, KGB chairman Vladimir Kryuchkov, was arrested.[31]

After unsuccessfully seeking asylum from Austria and Sweden, Wolf returned to Germany the following month, was immediately arrested, but was freed on bail after ten days in jail. On September 24, 1992, he was charged with treason, espionage, and bribery. In May 1993 his trial began in a Düsseldorf courtroom, proceeding in the midst of a constitutional challenge as to whether Wolf, who had directed espionage activities against Germany under the auspices of a separate state, could legally be tried for treason.[32]

Among those appearing for the prosecution was Klaus Kinkel, German foreign minister and former head of the BND. Wolf's lawyers hoped he would say something to support their client's claim that all intelligence services were basically the same. The judge, however, would not allow such questions. Also testifying for the prosecution was none other than Guenter Guillaume, Wolf's star agent.[33]

When his trial ended on November 24, Wolf denounced the trial as a political farce and predicted he would be found guilty. And on December 6, 1993, he was pronounced guilty and sentenced to six years in prison, although Wolf appealed the sentence.[34]

The Crowded Heavens

Operation DESERT STORM demonstrated the immense requirements that could be placed on spy satellites in wartime. That lesson, along with continuing extensive peacetime intelligence requirements, guarantees that the United States will maintain an extensive space reconnaissance effort well into the next century. Similarly, Russia continues to operate an extensive space espionage network. At the same time, it is certain that there will be newcomers to the space reconnaissance club, with France leading the way.

In a May 6, 1991, address to the Institut des Hautes Études de la Defense Nationale in Paris, Defense Minister Louis Joxe repeatedly emphasized that allied victory in the Persian Gulf War was largely due to U.S. reconnaissance satellites, and he made it clear that continuing to rely on U.S. technology was not a satisfactory option for Europe. Joxe told his audience:

> Without allied intelligence we were nearly blind. Our extreme dependence on American sources of information . . . was flagrant, particularly in the initial phase. [It] was the United States that provided, when and how it wanted, the essential information necessary for the conduct of the conflict.[35]

Joxe went on to argue that no nation could seriously have worldwide ambitions without operating its own fleet of reconnaissance satellites: "Not to possess this capacity would affect the very status of the nation." He also noted that, aside from enhancing the status of a nation, "observation satellites get around the legal constraints imposed in overflights by aircraft and make possible global coverage."[36]

But France did not need the impetus of the Gulf War to launch a space reconnaissance program. In the early 1980s France had plans to develop a photographic reconnaissance satellite, designated SAMRO. Those plans were succeeded in the late 1980s by plans to develop the HELIOS photo-reconnaissance spacecraft (named after the all-seeing god of the sun), with Italy and Spain as junior partners.

HELIOS, which is expected to weigh about 5,500 pounds and have a resolution of about three feet, will store the images it collects on a magnetic tape recorder, waiting till it passes over Europe to transmit them to the ground. On the ground will be seven facilities, with ground stations being dispersed as far as possible in French, Spanish, and Italian territory to widen the area in which the spacecraft can send back their images.[37]

The first HELIOS (scheduled to be launched in 1995) will probably be followed by a second identical spacecraft in 1996. A third HELIOS, to be launched before 2000, will include sensors capable of detecting missile launches and nuclear explosions. Some of HELIOS's images will be provided to the Western European Union's photographic interpretation center at Torrejon, Spain, for verification of arms control treaties.[38]

Even before the first launch France began developing plans for a second-generation model, equipped with an infrared imager that will permit night photography. In addition, use of a data-relay satellite to be launched by the European Space Agency would permit HELIOS's data to be returned in real time.[39]

HELIOS is only one element of the ambitious French space reconnaissance program. Shortly after the turn of the century, around 2004, France is planning to launch the first OSIRIS satellite, which may be built with German cooperation. Like the U.S. LACROSSE system, OSIRIS will produce images through the use of radar.[40]

While France is the nation most committed to developing a space reconnaissance capability, several other nations may follow. On September 19, 1988, Israel launched a 300-pound satellite designated *Offeq 1* (*Horizon 1*) into an orbit consistent with that of a photoreconnaissance satellite. That was followed by the April 3, 1990, launch of *Offeq 2*. Both spacecraft were described as experimental, with Yu'val Neeman, head of the Israeli Space Agency, claiming that "*Offeq 2* has absolutely no surveillance or reconnaissance facilities."[41]

But Neeman also acknowledged that a reconnaissance satellite "might come later." And in March 1991 Defense Minister Moshe Arens told the Knesset that "I assume nobody should be surprised if, one of these days, we will launch a satellite with intelligence-gathering capability."[42]

As of early 1995 *Offeq 3*, with or without a reconnaissance capability, has yet to appear. Scheduled for 1995 is the launch of the geosynchronous Amos satellite, which might be the forerunner to a SIGINT satellite in the same orbit.[43]

Other nations that could join the space reconnaissance club include India and Japan. Since 1987 India has been launching earth resources remote-sensing satellites. Its polar launch vehicle is able to deploy reconnaissance satellites weighing 7,000 pounds into low-earth orbit. Deployment of such satellites would allow India to monitor events in Pakistan on a more regular basis and without the risk of aircraft overflights. It would also, of course, allow India to enhance its ability to target Pakistani facilities in the event of war.

Despite its technological prowess and four commercial observation satellite programs, which can also be used to produce military intelligence, Japan has been hesitant to deploy high-resolution military reconnaissance satellites. The impediment has been political. Domestically, the memory of extensive Japanese intelligence operations to support military aggression has made the satellite issue a sensitive one. And Japan's neighbors, as a result of past history, are also concerned about indications that Japan might be examining their territory in the kind of detail that spy satellites can provide.[44]

Pulling Japan toward developing such a spacecraft are concerns over North Korean nuclear activities and the security of shipments of high-grade plutonium from Europe to Japan. On January 17, 1994, Deputy Vice Defense Minister Noboru Hoshyuyama, said that "I would say it is desirable that the Defense Agency launch [military] satellites particularly in this age when satellite information has become [routine]." In August the Tokyo-based Defense Research Center proposed that Japan launch a constellation of three military reconnaissance satellites that could detect objects as small as five meters across.[45]

Economic Espionage

The collection of certain types of economic intelligence—including the makeup of a nation's economy, its vulnerabilities, and the natural resources within a nation's borders—has been an accepted function of intelligence agencies since at least World War I. The collection of intelligence concerning trade practices and negotiating positions in trade talks has also been commonplace. But industrial espionage—the stealing of corporate plans or technologies—is another matter, particularly when the means of espionage is planting or recruiting a source in a foreign company in contrast to relying on COMINT.

Although there is evidence that Japanese companies have engaged in industrial espionage against foreign companies, there is no evidence of direct Japanese government involvement in such activities. On the other hand, the French DGSE has conducted a coordinated and extensive campaign to steal industrial secrets, including those of U.S. companies. During his short tenure as DGSE chief Pierre Marion, according to his own testimony, established a twenty-agent branch to acquire the secret technologies and marketing plans of private companies. The branch was formed with President Mitterand's knowledge and, Marion said, "was not directed [only] against the United States, but was worldwide."[46]

During Marion's tenure the branch acquired inside information on competing bids, allowing France to win a billion-dollar contract to supply jet fighters to India. Stolen American technology allowed the French to build a computer, which was then named DGSE.[47]

Such activity has continued since Marion's departure. In the late 1980s DGSE attempted to infiltrate the European offices of IBM, Texas Instruments, and several other U.S. electronics companies. Among the beneficiaries of such DGSE operations was the struggling government-owned computer firm, Compagnie des Machines Bull.[48]

The extent of the French effort is indicated by a twenty-four-page 1991 DGSE memorandum, "DEST Collection Plan," listing industrial intelligence requirements and related targets in the United States. The targeted companies included Boeing, Ford Aerospace, General Dynamics, Lockheed, Hughes Aircraft, Pratt and Whitney, Rockwell International, and TRW—a "who's who" of American high-tech companies. The specific information targeted covered the activities of ongoing negotiations, marketing strategy, weapons sales to foreign countries, civilian technology (e.g., high-definition television), and a large number of military technologies (including military space launch vehicles, SDI technology, and aircraft programs).[49]

In addition to high-tech private companies two other types of organizations were targeted. Government organizations such as Los Alamos National Laboratory, the National Aeronautics and Space Administration, National Oceanographic and Atmospheric Administration, and the Commerce Department were also included. Also of interest to the DGSE were the activities of a considerable number of financial firms—their development strategies, European offices, accords with Japanese financial firms or banks, and the lawyers and consultants used for any operation.[50]

Aside from seeking to penetrate foreign companies the DGSE has employed a number of other methods to gather industrial intelligence. The communications of foreign firms, including IBM, are routinely intercepted. Ten to fifteen break-ins are conducted each day at large hotels in Paris to copy documents left in their rooms by visiting businessmen and diplomats.[51]

French industrial intelligence operations are among the most aggressive and best known, but other European nations are also involved in such operations, according to a former IBM security consultant. Included in this group are Britain, Germany, the Netherlands, and Belgium. Britain established a small group under the Joint Intelligence Committee to monitor commercial intelligence produced by GCHQ and SIS collection operations. The BND has reportedly been instructed to target research facilities and companies in Great Britain, the United States, Italy, and France.[52]

India also conducts extensive scientific and technical intelligence operations, particularly in the United States. Among its targets are computer technology, with India hoping to dominate the Third World market. The FBI expressed its displeasure to the deputy director of RAW in 1993, when it detained him moments before he was to board a plane to leave the United States, where he had spent five months traveling (under FBI surveillance) and visiting his agents.[53]

As noted earlier, the Soviet Union was heavily involved in scientific and technical intelligence collection, through Directorate T of the KGB's First Chief Directorate as well as the GRU. The end of the Cold War, while leading to a reduction in Soviet attention to U.S. and West European military affairs, has not led to any apparent reduction in technology acquisition operations. Indeed Russia's dire economic straits have only increased the urgency for high-tech intelligence.

Thus in his first press conference as foreign intelligence chief Yevgeniy

Primakov observed that the intelligence service "must provide favorable conditions for the development of the economy and scientific and technical progress in the country." In April 1992 DCI Robert Gates told a congressional committee that Russian scientific and technical intelligence collection operations were "just rolling forward" under Primakov. Nine months later, in January 1993, Gates reported that both the SVR and GRU were still engaged in aggressively collecting technological information.[54]

The Russian quest for scientific and technical information was a large factor in the June 1993 decision to considerably increase military aide to Fidel Castro's regime. That aid was undoubtedly the price the Russians were willing to pay to keep the Lourdes signals intelligence center, which was upgraded in 1990, in operation. As of 1989 there were at least seven satellite intercept antennas in operation at Lourdes. Even before that upgrading the satellite dishes at Lourdes could intercept data from more than 100 U.S. communications satellites, which relay communications within the United States and between the United States and Europe. Other communications satellites that can be monitored from Lourdes include those of Brazil, Mexico, Canada, the European Space Agency, and the European Telecommunications Satellite Organization.[55]

Thus far the United States has resisted the temptation to engage in purposeful industrial espionage for the benefit of American companies, but monitoring and neutralizing such activities by other nations has become a high priority of the CIA.

Proliferation

The last decade of the twentieth century has seen the end of the East–West conflict that threatened to culminate in destruction on a scale unprecedented in history. But as DCI James Woolsey said in early 1993, speaking from the American point of view, the threat of the dragon has been replaced by a jungle of poisonous snakes. None of those snakes has the resources to produce a nuclear arsenal remotely as large as that of the Soviet Union or Russia. But that is of little comfort to those nations that may be threatened by a snake's bomb. Nor is it comforting to think that many of the nations that are pursuing nuclear weapons are ruled by leaders who are, at best, technically rational. It is not difficult to imagine some of them venting their rage with a bomb smuggled into a city or carried atop an advanced missile they have developed.

Intelligence collection and covert operations have and will be used by nations seeking to secretly acquire a bomb. The Iraqi, Israeli, and Pakistani bomb projects were all helped along by the operations of their intelligence services—as was the Soviet project.[56]

For those nations seeking to limit or prevent proliferation intelligence will be a crucial factor. It will not compensate for ignoring a nation's attempts to acquire nuclear weapons—as the United States did with Pakistan for many years—or for lacking the will to confront nations attempting to develop nuclear weapons. It will not guarantee success, but it will increase the probability of success.

Attention to the proliferation problem is, of course, not simply a product of the end of the Cold War. The United States has been monitoring the North Korean nuclear program for approximately twenty years. In the 1970s satellite imagery alerted the United States to the existence of a research installation, roads, railroad tracks, power grids, housing, and storage areas. In 1980 a satellite returned imagery that indicated that a new reactor was going up at Yongbyon. Further photos showed a thirty-megawatt, graphite-moderated, gas-cooled machine that burned natural uranium. During 1988–89 further satellite imagery revealed a second large building that seemed perfectly suited for reprocessing plutonium.[57]

In the winter of 1991, as the Soviet Union was in the process of dissolving, U.S. imagery satellites detected North Korean workers digging trenches in frozen ground between Yongbyon's principal facility for reprocessing nuclear fuel and one of two facilities suspected of storing nuclear wastes. The conclusion drawn by the CIA was that the North Koreans were planning on burying the pipes between the two facilities and thus concealing their connection from International Atomic Energy Authority (IAEA) inspectors.[58]

Surveillance has, not surprisingly, continued into the post–Cold War era. U.S. imagery satellites detected trucks pulling up to the reprocessing plant, possibly to haul away equipment, prior to the arrival of IAEA inspectors in 1992. Similarly, U.S. imaging satellites monitoring Iraq have detected uranium-enrichment machinery being moved around on trucks or buried to evade detection by U.S. inspectors.[59]

Nor is the United States the only nation focusing substantial attention on the problem of proliferation. Among the concerns of the German BND and Federal Armed Forces Intelligence Office (FAFIO) has been Iran's nuclear program. In a September 1992 study FAFIO, based on information from the BND, observed that the "facilities that have been built so far and the equipment and materials procured are indispensable for producing nuclear weapons," and that the facts "cannot leave any doubt about Iran's intentions to produce nuclear weapons."[60]

Russian concern over the proliferation problem was demonstrated by the unprecedented public release, in 1993, of a seventy-seven-page SVR report, "Proliferation of Weapons of Mass Destruction." The seven sections of the report cover various aspects of nuclear, chemical, biological, and ballistic missile proliferation—including the threat to world stability, indicators of development or possession, and international mechanisms for preventing proliferation. The appendix examines the status of development of weapons of mass destruction in sixteen different countries, from Algeria to South Korea.[61]

The surprising discoveries after the Persian Gulf War concerning the extent of the Iraqi nuclear weapons program led some to question the adequacy of U.S. or other nations' intelligence services for monitoring proliferation. One observer noted: "In spite of the massive intelligence-gathering means at the disposition of several nations, including overhead reconnaissance and electronic intercepts, there seem to have been serious deficiencies in the general assessment of Iraq's nuclear program."[62]

However, there are reasons to be cautiously optimistic. The demise of the Soviet Union has made it possible for the United States to devote a greater share of intelligence analysis and collection (human and technical) to the problem. In addition, U.S. space reconnaissance capabilities are considerably more extensive today than they were in the 1986–88 period, when Iraq was undoubtedly building many of the facilities that were discovered after the Persian Gulf War. And, as indicated previously, the United States is not alone in assigning a high priority to intelligence collection on proliferation.

Also, since having *some* of the ingredients to construct a nuclear bomb or other weapons of mass destruction is not sufficient to produce such a weapon, it is not necessary for nations to be denied *every* ingredient but only enough to prevent a successful conclusion to such a project. Consequently, it is not necessary for intelligence to identify all the aspects of a nuclear program to permit effective counteraction. In 1992 the United States and Germany were able to take actions in an attempt to inhibit weapons programs about which they surely did not have complete knowledge. The United States was able to persuade China and Argentina to cancel planned transfers of key technology to Iran. That same year, research workers in several German research institutes received an "early warning report" from the BND, informing them that while the "Centre des Études et de Recherches Scientifiques, Damascus/Syria [is] active in the civilian sphere . . . the focus of its tasks is clearly the field of militarily relevant research and development."[63]

The Next Century

As long as there is conflict among governments or between governments and hostile groups intelligence services will be kept busy. Intelligence technologies—both collection and analytical—will become even more sophisticated. The CIA is already able to take imagery from its imagery satellites, such as the Advanced KH-11, and produce three-dimensional movies of foreign targets, whether cities or military installations. The U.S. National Reconnaissance Office is testing hyperspectral sensors, which can simultaneously capture images of objects using conventional cameras, heat-detecting infrared sensors, and radar and ultraviolet sensors. They would allow analysts to see an object's shape, density, temperature, movement, and chemical composition.[64]

At the same time humans will still be needed as spies—to provide documents, technical samples, and on-site reporting. They will also be needed as analysts to turn the images and signals produced by advanced sensors into judgments about motivations, capabilities, and intentions.

It can be argued that in the twentieth century intelligence played a crucial role in helping to defeat Hitler, played a significant role in preventing the Cold War from turning into a nuclear war, and kept the superpower arms race from getting totally out of hand. What impact it will have in the next century cannot now be determined. Intelligence in the hands of those who prefer to avoid war or have a legitimate need to defend themselves can help prevent wars or at least increase the probability that aggressors are defeated. In the hands of those interested in coercion and conquest it is another effective weapon of war.

Abbreviations Used in the Notes

ACSI   Office of the Assistant Chief of Staff for Intelligence

DDEL   Dwight D. Eisenhower Library

DDRS   Declassified Documents Reference System

FBIS   Foreign Broadcast Information Service

JPRS   Joint Publications Research Service

MRB   Military Reference Branch

MRR   Microform Reading Room

NARA   National Archives and Records Administration

RG   Record Group

Notes

1 A Shady Profession

1. J. M. Roberts, *The Penguin History of the World* (New York: Penguin, 1990), p. 657.

2. John Terraine, *White Heat: The New Warfare 1914–1918* (London: Leo Cooper, 1992), p. 7.

3. Thomas P. Hughes, *American Genesis: A Century of Invention and Technological Enthusiasm 1870–1970* (New York: Penguin, 1990), p. 15; Daniel R. Headrick, *The Invisible Weapon: Telecommunications and International Politics 1851–1945* (New York: Oxford University Press, 1991), p. 6.

4. Nigel West, *GCHQ: The Secret Wireless War 1900–86* (New York: St. Martin's Press 1986), p. 6.

5. W. J. Baker, *A History of THE MARCONI COMPANY* (New York: St. Martin's Press, 1971), p. 25.

6. Ibid., pp. 26, 28, 35.

7. Alfred Gollin, *No Longer an Island: Britain and the Wright Brothers 1902–1909* (Stanford, Calif.: Stanford University Press, 1984), p. 5.

8. Ibid., pp. 8–12.

9. Fred Howard, *Wilbur and Orville: A Biography of the Wright Brothers* (New York: Ballantine, 1988), p. 137.

10. Peter Gudgin, *Military Intelligence: The British Story* (London: Arms and Armour, 1989), p. 27; Thomas Fergusson, *British Military Intelligence 1870–1914: The Development of a Modern Intelligence Organization* (Frederick, Md.: University Publications of America, 1984), pp. 13n5, 26–27.

11. Fergusson, *British Military Intelligence*, pp. 11, 13n5.

12. Ibid., p. 212.

13. Henri Navarre, *Le Service de Renseignements 1871–1944* (Paris: Plon, 1978), p. 15.

14. Ibid., p. 16.

15. Ibid.; Christopher Andrew, "France and the German Menace," in Ernest May (ed.), *Knowing One's Enemies: Intelligence Assessment before the Two World Wars* (Princeton, N.J.: Princeton University Press, 1984), p. 135.

16. Heinz Hohne, *Canaris: Hitler's Master Spy* (New York: Doubleday, 1979), p. 143.

17. Wilhlem J. C. E. Stieber, *The Chancellor's Spy: The Revelations of the Chief of Bismarck's Secret Service* (New York: Grove Press, 1979), p. 97.

18. Hohne, *Canaris*, p. 143.

19. Ibid., p. 145.

20. Ibid., p. 143; David Kahn, *Hitler's Spies: German Military Intelligence in World War II* (New York: Macmillan, 1978), p. 32.

21. Kahn, *Hitler's Spies*, p. 32.

22. Peter Deriabin, *Watchdogs of Terror: Russian Bodyguards from the Tsars to the Commissars* (Frederick, Md.: University Publications of America, 1984), pp. 135–36.

23. William C. Fuller, Jr., "The Russian Empire," in May, *Knowing One's Enemies*, p. 104; M. Batyushin, "Cryptography during World War I: A Tsarist Russian's View," *Studies in Intelligence*, Summer 1977, p. 21.

24. Nathan Miller, *Spying for America* (New York: Paragon, 1989), pp. 159–60.

25. Ibid., p. 161.

26. Ibid., pp. 163–64.

27. Jeffrey Dorwart, *The Office of Naval Intelligence: The Birth of America's First Intelligence Agency 1865–1918* (Annapolis, Md.: Naval Institute Press, 1979), pp. 72–73, 78.

28. Fergusson, *British Military Intelligence*, pp. 202–3.

29. Ibid., pp. 203–4.

30. Christopher Andrew, *Secret Service: The Making of the British Intelligence Community* (London: Heinemann, 1985), p. 38; David French, "Spy Fever in Britain, 1900–1915," *Historical Journal* 21, no. 2 (1978): 355–70.

31. Andrew, *Secret Service*, pp. 48–49.

32. Ibid., pp. 49, 53.

33. Ibid., p. 53.

34. Ibid., p. 58.

35. Ibid., p. 50.

36. Ibid.; Nicholas F. Hiley, "The Failure of British Espionage against Germany, 1907–1914," *Historical Journal* 26, no. 4, (1983): 872, 876–78.

37. Andrew, *Secret Service*, pp. 50–51.

38. Robert K. Massie, *Dreadnought: Britain, Germany, and the Coming of the Great War* (New York: Random House, 1991), pp. 611–12.

39. F. H. Hinsley, E. E. Thomas, C. F. G. Ransom, and R. C. Knight, *British Intelligence in the Second World War*, vol. 1 (New York: Cambridge University Press, 1979), p. 16; Hiley, "The Failure of British Espionage," p. 876.

40. Hinsley et al., *British Intelligence*, p. 16; F. H. Hinsley and C. A. G. Simkins, *British Intelligence in the Second World War*, vol. 4 (London: HMSO Books, 1990), p. 4; Hiley, "The Failure of British Espionage," p. 878.

41. Andrew, *Secret Service*, p. 74; Nigel West, *MI6: British Secret Intelligence Service Operations 1909–1945* (London: Weidenfeld & Nicolson, 1983), p. 5.

42. Andrew, *Secret Service*, p. 74; West, *MI6*, p. 5.

43. Andrew, *Secret Service*, p. 75.

44. Philip Knightley, *The Second Oldest Profession: Spies and Spying in the Twentieth Century* (New York: W. W. Norton, 1986), p. 89.

45. Andrew, *Secret Service*, p. 78.

46. Ibid.

47. Ibid.; Hiley, "The Failure of British Espionage," p. 880.

48. Andrew, *Secret Service*, p. 79; Hiley, "The Failure of British Espionage," p. 888.

49. Andrew, *Secret Service*, p. 82.

50. Ibid., p. 83; Hiley, "The Failure of British Espionage," p. 881.

51. Andrew, *Secret Service*, p. 83.

52. Ibid.

53. Ibid., p. 84.

54. Ibid.

55. Holger H. Herwig, "Imperial Germany," in May, *Knowing One's Enemies*, p. 65; Kahn, *Hitler's Spies*, p. 32.

56. Kahn, *Hitler's Spies*, p. 32.

57. Ibid., p. 33.

58. Ibid., p. 34.

59. Andrew, *Secret Service*, p. 65.

60. Herwig, "Imperial Germany," pp. 64–65, 70.

61. Fuller, "The Russian Empire," pp. 106–7.

62. Ibid., p. 115; Harold C. Deutsch, "Sidelights on the Redl Case: Russian Intelligence on the Eve of the Great War," *Intelligence and National Security* 4, no. 4 (1989): 827–28.

63. Fuller, "The Russian Empire," p. 115; Ian D. Armour, "Colonel Redl: Fact and Fantasy," *Intelligence and National Security* 2, no. 1 (1987): 170.

64. Armour, "Colonel Redl: Fact and Fantasy," pp. 170, 180–81.

65. Yves Glyden, *The Contributions of the Cryptographic Bureaus in the World War* (Laguna Hills, Calif.: Aegean Park Press, 1978), p. 9; Andrew, "France and the German Menace," p. 129.

66. Glyden, *The Contributions of the Cryptographic Bureaus*, p. 10.

67. Ibid.

68. Ibid., p. 11.

69. Ibid.

70. Ibid., p. 15.

71. Ibid., pp. 20–21; Kahn, *The Codebreakers*, p. 614; Christopher Andrew and Keith Nelson, "Tsarist Codebreakers and British Codes," *Intelligence and National Security* 1, no. 1 (1986): 6–12.

72. Howard, *Orville and Wilbur*, p. 163.

73. Fergusson, *British Military Intelligence*, p. 173.

74. Ibid, p. 188.

75. Ibid., p. 187.

2   The Great War: Spies and Saboteurs

1. Robert K. Massie, *Dreadnought: Britain, Germany, and the Coming of the Great War* (New York: Random House, 1991), pp. 865–66; Jules Witcover, *Sabotage at Black Tom: Imperial Germany's Secret War in America, 1914–1917* (Chapel Hill, N.C.: Algonquin Books of Chapel Hill, 1989), pp. 33–34.

2. Witcover, *Sabotage*, p. 36.

3. Kenneth Strong, *Men of Intelligence: A Study of the Roles and Decisions of Chiefs of Intelligence from World War I to the Present Day* (London: Cassell, 1970), p. 8.

4. Massie, *Dreadnought*, pp. 877, 908; Witcover, *Sabotage*, p. 38.

5. Ulrich Trumpener, "War Premeditated? German Intelligence Operations in July 1914," *Central European History*, March 1976, p. 64.

6. Ibid., pp. 64–65.

7. Ibid., p. 66.

8. Ibid., pp. 66–67.

9. Ibid., p. 67.

10. Ibid., p. 68.

11. Ibid.

12. Ibid., pp. 68–69; David Kahn, *Hitler's Spies: German Military Intelligence in World War II* (New York: Macmillan, 1978), p. 36.

13. Trumpener, "War Premeditated?" p. 69.

14. Ibid., p. 70.

15. Ibid.

16. Ibid., p. 78.

17. Ibid., pp. 78–79.

18. Ibid., pp. 80–81.

19. Ibid., p. 83.

20. Nigel West, *MI6: British Secret Intelligence Service Operations 1909–1945* (London: Weidenfeld & Nicolson, 1983), p. 9.

21. Ibid., pp. 10, 11.

22. Office of the Chief of Staff, U.S. War Department, "On the Intelligence System Necessary in Case U.S. Troops Are Ordered to the Continent," April 15, 1917, War College Division Correspondence, RG 165, MRB, NARA, pp. 13–19; Michael Occleshaw, *Armour against Fate: British Military Intelligence in the First World War* (London: Columbus, 1989), p. 191.

23. West, *MI6*, p. 12.

24. Occleshaw, *Armour*, p. 187; Leon C. Messenger, "The White Lady Intelligence Network," *Studies in Intelligence*, Summer 1988.

25. Ibid., p. 188.

26. Ibid.

27. Ibid., p. 187.

28. Henri Navarre, *Le Service de Renseignements 1871–1914* (Paris: Plon, 1978), pp. 18–19.

29. Ibid., p. 20; Richard Deacon, *The French Secret Service* (London: Grafton, 1990), p. 93.

30. Robert B. Asprey, *The German High Command at War: Hindenburg and Ludendorff Conduct War War I* (New York: Morrow, 1991), pp. 218–20; Deacon, *French Secret Service*, p. 93.

31. Deacon, *French Secret Service*, p. 93.

32. Ibid., p. 94; Navarre, *Le Service*, p. 21.; Asprey, *German High Command*, pp. 222–23.

33. Navarre, *Le Service*, p. 21.

34. Ibid.

35. J. F. N. Bradley, "The Russian Secret Service in the First World War," *Soviet Studies* 20, no. 2 (1968): 245.

36. Ibid.

37. Ibid.

38. Ibid., pp. 245–46.

39. Kahn, *Hitler's Spies*, pp. 35–36.

40. Ibid., p. 36.
41. Ibid.
42. Ibid., p. 37.
43. Ibid.
44. Ibid.
45. Ibid.; Strong, *Men of Intelligence*, p. 10.
46. Witcover, *Sabotage*, p. 56.
47. Ibid., p. 70.
48. Ibid., p. 59.
49. Ibid., p. 60.
50. Ibid., pp. 65–66.
51. Ibid., p. 81.
52. Ibid., p. 80.
53. Ibid., pp. 108–9.
54. Ibid., p. 134.
55. Ibid., pp. 120–21, 134.
56. "Munitions Explosions Shake New York; Wreck $7,000,000 Jersey Storage Plant; Many Killed; Alarm and Damage Here," *New York Times*, July 30, 1916, pp. 1, 2.
57. Witcover, *Sabotage*, p. 152.
58. Ibid., p. 12; "Munitions Explosions Shake New York."
59. Witcover, *Sabotage*, p. 20.
60. Ibid., pp. 189–90.
61. Ibid., p. 193.
62. Ibid., p. 231.

3 Spies in the Great War: Eyes and Ears

1. Lee Kennett, *The First Air War 1914–1918* (New York: Free Press, 1991), p. 32.
2. Ibid., p. 37; Thomas G. Fergusson, *British Military Intelligence 1870–1914: The Development of a Modern Intelligence Organization* (Frederick, Md.: University Publications of America, 1984), p. 188.
3. Fergusson, *British Military Intelligence*, p. 188; Peter Mead, *The Eye in the Air: History of Air Observation and Reconnaissance 1785–1945* (London: Her Majesty's Stationery Office, 1983), p. 66.
4. Kennett, *First Air War*, p. 37.
5. Ibid., pp. 37–38.
6. Michael Occleshaw, *Armour Against Fate: British Military Intelligence in the First World War* (London: Columbus, 1989), p. 59.
7. David Kahn, *The Codebreakers: The Story of Secret Writing* (New York: Macmillan, 1967), p. 299.
8. Ibid., p. 305.
9. Occleshaw, *Armour*, pp. 55–56.
10. Ibid. p. 56.
11. Ibid.
12. Ibid., p. 57.
13. Ibid.
14. Kennett, *First Air War*, p. 32.
15. Mead, *Eye in the Air*, pp. 55–56.

16. Ibid., p. 56.

17. Ibid.

18. Wilhelm F. Flicke, *War Secrets in the Ether*, vol. 1 (Laguna Park, Calif.: Aegean Park Press, 1977), p. 23.

19. Ibid., pp. 23–24.

20. Robert Asprey, *The German High Command at War: Hindenburg and Ludendorff Conduct World War I* (New York: Morrow, 1991), p. 122.

21. Wilhelm F. Flicke, "The Early Development of Communications Intelligence," *Studies in Intelligence* 3, no. 1 (1959): 106.

22. W. Bruce Lincoln, *Passage through Armageddon: The Russians in War & Revolution, 1914–1918* (New York: Simon & Schuster, 1986), p. 64.

23. Naval Security Group Command, *Naval Cryptology in National Security*, (Washington, D.C.: NSGC, 1985), p. 4.

24. Ibid.

25. David Kahn, *Kahn on Codes: Secrets of the New Cryptology* (New York: Macmillan, 1983), p. 100; Flicke, "The Early Development of Communications Intelligence," p. 100.

26. Flicke, *War Secrets*, p. 5.

27. Lincoln, *Passage*, p. 71.

28. Flicke, *War Secrets*, p. 7.

29. Ibid., pp. 7–9.

30. Asprey, *German High Command*, p. 80.

31. Mead, *Eye in the Air*, pp. 74–75.

32. Ibid., p. 80.

33. Ibid.

34. Ibid., pp. 74–75.

35. Christopher Andrew, *Secret Service: The Making of the British Intelligence Community* (London: Heinemann, 1985), p. 86.

36. Ibid., p. 87.

37. Ibid., p. 94; Patrick Beesly, *Room 40: British Naval Intelligence 1914–1918* (New York: Harcourt Brace Jovanovich, 1982), p. 124.

38. Andrew, *Secret Service*, p. 89; Beesly, *Room 40*, p. 3.

39. Andrew, *Secret Service*, p. 89; Beesly, *Room 40*, pp. 4–5; David Kahn, *Seizing the Enigma: The Race to Break the German U-Boat Codes, 1939–1943* (Boston: Houghton Mifflin, 1991), pp. 15–30.

40. W. F. Clarke, "Room 40 O.B.," n.d., in Churchill College Archives Centre CLARKE/2, chap. 2; Andrew, *Secret Service*, p. 89.

41. Andrew, *Secret Service*, p. 90.

42. Ibid., p. 91.

43. Beesly, *Room 40*, p. 34.

44. Clarke, "Room 40 O.B.," chap. 3.

45. Andrew, *Secret Service*, pp. 91–92; Beesly, *Room 40*, p. 124.

46. Andrew, *Secret Service*, pp. 98–99.

47. Beesly, *Room 40*, p. 151.

48. Ibid., p. 155.

49. Ibid., pp. 155–56.

50. Ibid., pp. 160–61.

51. Ibid., pp. 161–62.

52. Ibid., p. 162.

53. Ibid.

54. Thomas R. Hammant, "Communications Intelligence and Tsarist Russia," *Studies in Intelligence* 22, no. 2 (1976): 32.

55. Ibid., p. 34.

56. Ibid.

57. Ibid., p. 35.

58. Ibid.

59. Ibid., pp. 35, 38.

60. Ibid., p. 38.

61. Henry F. Schorreck, "The Telegram that Changed History," *Cryptologic Spectrum*, Summer 1970, pp. 22–23.

62. Ibid., p. 26.

63. Ibid., p. 24.

64. Ibid., p. 25; William F. Friedman and Charles J. Mendelsohn, *The Zimmermann Telegram of January 16, 1917 and Its Cryptographic Background* (Washington, D.C.: War Department Office of the Chief Signal Officer, 1938), p. 6.

65. Schorreck, "The Telegram," p. 26; Friedman and Mendelsohn, *Zimmermann Telegram*, p. 6.

66. Schorreck, "The Telegram," p. 26.

67. Ibid.; Friedman and Mendelsohn, *The Zimmermann Telegram*, pp. 7–9.

68. Schorreck, "The Telegram," p. 27.

69. Ibid.

70. Ibid.

71. Ibid., p. 28.

72. Ibid.

73. Barbara W. Tuchman, *The Zimmermann Telegram* (New York: Ballantine, 1984), p. 146.

74. Schorreck, "The Telegram," p. 28.

75. Ibid., p. 29.

76. "Germany Seeks an Alliance Against Us; Asks Japan and Mexico to Join Her; Text of Her Proposal Made Public," *New York Times*, March 1, 1917, p. 1; Jules Witcover, *Sabotage at Black Tom: Imperial Germany's Secret War in America—1914–1917* (Chapel Hill, N.C.: Algonquin Books of Chapel Hill, 1989), p. 222.

77. Schorreck, "The Telegram," p. 29.

78. Ibid.

79. Ibid., p. 24.

80. Ibid.

4 Lenin's Spies

1. Central Intelligence Agency, *KGB and GRU* (Washington, D.C.: CIA, 1984), p. 1; W. Bruce Lincoln, *Red Victory: A History of the Russian Civil War* (New York: Touchstone, 1989), p. 33.

2. Central Intelligence Agency, *KGB and GRU*, p. 1; Lincoln, *Red Victory*, p. 33.

3. Central Intelligence Agency, *KGB and GRU*, p. 1.

4. Ibid.; Lincoln, *Red Victory*, pp. 38–39.

5. Central Intelligence Agency, *KGB and GRU*, p. 1.

6. Ibid.; William R. Corson and Robert T. Crowley, *The New KGB: Engine of Soviet Power* (New York: Quill, 1986), p. 35.

7. George Leggett, *The Cheka: Lenin's Political Police* (Philadelphia: Temple University Press, 1976), p. 19.

8. Ibid., p. 16.

9. Lennard D. Gerson, *The Secret Police in Lenin's Russia* (Philadelphia: Temple University Press, 1976), p. 21.

10. Ibid., p. 23; Leggett, *The Cheka*, p. 17.

11. Christopher Andrew and Oleg Gordievsky, *KGB: The Inside Story* (New York: Harper Collins, 1990), pp. 43–44.

12. Leggett, *Cheka*, p. 22; Gerson, *Secret Police*, p. 8.

13. Gerson, *Secret Police*, pp. 9–10.

14. Ibid., p. 10.

15. Ibid., pp. 10–11; Corson and Crowley, *New KGB*, p. 75.

16. Gerson, *Secret Police*, p. 11.

17. Ibid.

18. Ibid., p. 12.

19. Ibid., pp. 12–13; Leggett, *Cheka*, p. 23.

20. Gerson, *Secret Police*, p. 14.

21. Ibid., pp. 15–16.

22. Andrew and Gordievsky, *KGB*, p. 41.

23. Central Intelligence Agency, *KGB and GRU*, p. 4.

24. Ibid.

25. Andrew and Gordievsky, *KGB*, p. 56.

26. Ibid.

27. Ibid., p. 57.

28. Ibid., pp. 57–58.

29. Central Intelligence Agency, *KGB and GRU*, pp. 3–4.

30. Ibid., p. 4.

31. Ibid.

32. Ibid., pp. 2, 4–5.

33. Thomas Hammant, "Soviet COMINT and the Civil War," *Studies in Intelligence* 23, no. 2 (1979): 35. The article is a translation of Colonel Yu. Ural'skij, "The Organization and Combat Use of Radio Intelligence during Civil War," *Journal of Military History* (Moscow), no. 11 (1972).

34. Ibid., p. 36.

35. Ibid., pp. 37, 38.

36. Ibid., p. 38.

37. Ibid.

38. Ibid., pp. 38–39.

39. Ibid., p. 39.

40. Ibid.; Lincoln, *Red Victory*, pp. 223, 227–28.

41. Hammant, "Soviet COMINT and the Civil War," p. 39.

42. Ibid., pp. 39–40.

43. Ibid., p. 40.

44. Ibid.

45. Ibid.

46. Central Intelligence Agency, *KGB and GRU*, p. 5.

47. Gerson, *Secret Police*, p. 234.

48. Ibid., p. 231.

49. Ibid., pp. 234–35.

50. Central Intelligence Agency, *KGB and GRU*, p. 2.

51. Andrew and Gordievsky, *KGB*, pp. 72–73.

52. Ibid., p. 80.

53. Gerson, *Secret Police*, p. 236.

54. Andrew and Gordievsky, *KGB*, p. 87.

55. Gerson, *Secret Police*, p. 237.

56. Central Intelligence Agency, *KGB and GRU*, p. 2.

57. Ibid., p. 15.

58. Ibid.

59. Ibid.

60. Ibid., pp. 2, 16.

61. Leggett, *Cheka*, p. 301; John Dziak, *Chekisty: A History of the KGB* (Lexington, Mass.: Lexington Books, 1988), p. 15.

62. Central Intelligence Agency, *KGB and GRU*, p. 16.

63. Leggett, *Cheka*, p. 280; Andrew and Gordievsky, *KGB*, p. 51; Central Intelligence Agency, *The Trust* (Washington, D.C.: CIA, n.d.), p. 16.

64. Leggett, *Cheka*, p. 295; Central Intelligence Agency, *The Trust*, p. 16.

65. Leggett, *Cheka*, p. 296; Central Intelligence Agency, *The Trust*, p. 62.

66. Leggett, *Cheka*, p. 296; John Costello and Oleg Tsarev, *Deadly Illusions* (New York: Crown, 1993), p. 34; Central Intelligence Agency, *The Trust*, pp. 62–63.

67. Leggett, *Cheka*, p. 296; Andrew and Gordievsky, *KGB*, p. 96.

68. Andrew and Gordievsky, *KGB*, p. 96; Costello and Tsarev, *Deadly Illusions*, p. 34.

69. Andrew and Gordievsky, *KGB*, pp. 96–97; Costello and Tsarev, *Deadly Illusions*, p. 34.

70. Leggett, *The Cheka*, p. 296; Costello and Tsarev, *Deadly Illusions*, p. 35.

71. Andrew and Gordievsky, *KGB*, p. 97.

72. Andrew and Gordievsky, *KGB*, pp. 97–98; Natalie Grant, "Deception on a Grand Scale," *International Journal of Intelligence and Counterintelligence* 1, no. 4 (1986–87): 54, 55, 58.

73. Andrew and Gordievsky, *KGB*, pp. 98–99; Grant, "Deception on a Grand Scale," p. 56.

74. Costello and Tsarev, *Deadly Illusions*, p. 33.

75. Andrew and Gordievsky, *KGB*, pp. 99–100; Grant, "Deception on a Grand Scale," p. 63.

76. Andrew and Gordievsky, *KGB*, p. 100.

77. Ibid.; Grant, "Deception on a Grand Scale," p. 64; Central Intelligence Agency, *The Trust*, p. 26.

78. Andrew and Gordievsky, *KGB*, pp. 100–101.

79. Ibid., p. 101; Central Intelligence Agency, *The Trust*, p. 28; Costello and Tsarev, *Deadly Illusions*, p. 36.

80. Costello and Tsarev, *Deadly Illusions*, pp. 36–37.

81. Ibid., p. 39.

82. Ibid.; Phillip Knightley, "How the Russians Broke the Ace of Spies," *The Observer*, April 12, 1992, pp. 49ff. A skeptical view of Soviet archival material on the Reilly case is expressed in Robin Bruce Lockhart, "Reilly—A Hero or a Turncoat?" *The Observer*, April 26, 1992, p. 16.

83. Costello and Tsarev, *Deadly Illusions*, p. 40.

84. Ibid., p. 41; Grant, "Deception on a Grand Scale," pp. 68–69.

5 Spies Betweeen the Wars: 1919–1929

1. Robert G. Angevine, "Gentlemen Do Read Each Other's Mail: American Intelligence in the Interwar Era," *Intelligence and National Security* 7, no. 2 (1992): 6.

2. John Ferris, "Whitehall's Black Chamber: British Cryptology and the Government Code and Cypher School, 1919–1929," *Intelligence and National Security* 2, no. 1 (1987): 54.

3. A. G. Denniston, "The Government Code and Cypher School between the Wars," *Intelligence and National Security* 1, no. 1 (1986): 49; F. H. Hinsley, E. E. Thomas, C. F. G. Ransom, and R. C. Knight, *British Intelligence in the Second World War*, vol. 1 (New York: Cambridge University Press, 1979), p. 20.

4. Ferris, "Whitehall's Black Chamber," pp. 56–57; Christopher Andrew, *Secret Service: The Making of the British Intelligence Community* (London: Heinemann, 1985), p. 259; Hinsley et al., *British Intelligence*, p. 20.

5. Denniston, "The Government Code and Cipher School," p. 49; Andrew, *Secret Service*, p. 259.

6. Andrew, *Secret Service*, p. 260.

7. Ferris, "Whitehall's Black Chamber," pp. 69–70.

8. Ibid., p. 70.

9. Ibid., p. 64.

10. Ibid., p. 70.

11. Ibid., pp. 72–73; Andrew, *Secret Service*, pp. 260–61.

12. Ferris, "Whitehall's Black Chamber," pp. 70, 73.

13. Ibid., p. 73; Andrew, *Secret Service*, p. 261.

14. Ferris, "Whitehall's Black Chamber," p. 75; *The Treaties of Peace, 1919–1923*, vol. 2 (New York: Carnegie Endowment for International Peace, 1924), pp. 957–1022.

15. Ferris, "Whitehall's Black Chambers," pp. 73–74; Andrew, *Secret Service*, p. 261.

16. Andrew, *Secret Service*, pp. 261–62.

17. Ibid., p. 262.

18. Ibid.

19. Ibid.

20. Ibid., pp. 262–63.

21. Ibid., p. 268.

22. "The Daily Herald," *London Times*, August 19, 1920, p. 10.

23. Andrew, *Secret Service*, p. 268.

24. Ibid., p. 272.

25. Ibid., p. 273.

26. Ibid.

27. Ibid., pp. 273–274.

28. Ibid., p. 274.

29. Ibid.

30. A Selection of Papers Pertaining to Herbert O. Yardley, 1917–1950, SRH-038, RG 457, MRB, NARA; David Kahn, *Kahn on Codes: Secrets of the New Cryptology* (New York: Macmillan, 1983), p. 63.

31. James Bamford, *The Puzzle Palace: A Report on NSA, America's Most Secret Agency* (New York: Penguin, 1983), p. 6.

32. Ibid., pp. 6–7.

33. Nathan X. Woodeman, "Yardley Revisited," *Studies in Intelligence* 27, no. 2 (1983): 42; Bamford, *The Puzzle Palace*, p. 7; David Kahn, *The Codebreakers: The Story of Secret Writing* (New York: Macmillan, 1978), p. 352.

34. Army Security Agency, *Historical Background of the Signal Security Agency*, vol. 2: World War I (Washington, D.C.: ASA, 1946), pp. 74–76.

35. Ibid., 86–88.

36. Ibid., p. 86.

37. Ibid., pp. 79, 80.

38. Woodeman, "Yardley Revisited," p. 46.

39. Ibid., p. 47.

40. Bamford, *The Puzzle Palace*, p. 7.

41. Woodeman, "Yardley Revisited," p. 49.

42. A Selection of Papers Pertaining to Herbert O. Yardley, 1917–1950; Woodeman, "Yardley Revisited," p. 49; Kahn, *The Codebreakers*, p. 355.

43. Woodeman, "Yardley Revisited," p. 49; Kahn, *The Codebreakers*, p. 355; Angevine, "Gentlemen Do Read Each Other's Mail," p. 4.

44. Kahn, *The Codebreakers*, pp. 355–56.

45. Army Security Agency, *Historical Background*, vol. 2, p. 89n26.

46. Ibid., pp. 89–90.

47. Ibid., p. 73.

48. Ibid., pp. 94–97.

49. Ibid., pp. 99–102.

50. Kahn, *The Codebreakers*, p. 357: Army Security Agency, *Historical Background of the Signal Security Agency*, vol. 3 (Washington, D.C.: ASA, 1946), p. 92.

51. Kahn, *The Codebreakers*, p. 357.

52. Army Security Agency, *Historical Background*, vol. 3, pp. 97–98.

53. Ibid., pp. 111–12; Kahn, *The Codebreakers*, p. 358.

54. Herbert O. Yardley, *The American Black Chamber* (New York: Ballantine, 1981), pp. 187–200.

55. Ibid., p. 195.

56. Ibid., pp. 195–96.

57. Ibid., p. 196.

58. Kahn, *The Codebreakers*, p. 358.

59. Bruce Berkowitz, *Calculated Risks* (New York: Simon & Schuster, 1987), pp. 33–34.

60. Ibid., p. 34.

61. Ibid.; Kahn, *The Codebreakers*, p. 358.

62. Kahn, *The Codebreakers*, p. 358.

63. Ibid., pp. 358–59.

64. Army Security Agency, *Historical Background*, vol. 3, pp. 130–32; Chief Signal Officer, *French Codes Studied by MI-8 in 1921–1923* (Washington, D.C.: Signal Security Agency, 1945).

65. Kahn, *The Codebreakers*, p. 359.

66. Ibid.; "Naval Security Group History to World War II," 1971, SRH-355 (Part II) RG 457, MRB, NARA.

67. Army Security Agency, *Historical Background*, vol. 3, pp. 137–38.

68. William F. Friedman, "A Brief History of the Signal Intelligence Service," June 29, 1942, SRH-029, RG 457, MRB, NARA, pp. 6–8.

69. Avengine, "Gentlemen Do Read Each Other's Mail," p. 18; Kahn, *The*

Codebreakers, pp. 359–60; Friedman, "A Brief History of the Signal Intelligence Service," pp. 6–7.

70. Louis Kruh, "Stimson, The Black Chamber, and the 'Gentleman's Mail' Quote," *Cryptologia* 22, no. 2 (1988): 68; Army Security Agency, *Historical Background*, vol. 3, pp. 143–44.

71. Kahn, *The Codebreakers*, p. 360.

72. David Kahn, *Hitler's Spies: German Military Intelligence in World War II* (New York: Collier, 1985), p. 224; Heinz Hohne, *Canaris: Hitler's Master Spy* (New York: Doubleday, 1979), p. 155.

73. Wilhelm F. Flicke, *War Secrets in the Ether*, vol. 1 (Laguna Hills, Calif.: Aegean Park Press, 1977), pp. 81, 89.

74. Hohne, *Canaris*, pp. 153–54; Flicke, *War Secrets*, pp. 85, 89.

75. Flicke, *War Secrets*, p. 98.

76. J. W. M. Chapman, "No Final Solution: A Survey of the Cryptanalytical Capabilities of German Military Agencies, 1926–1935," *Intelligence and National Security* 1, no. 1 (1986): 18–20.

77. Kahn, *Hitler's Spies*, p. 225.

78. Chapman, "No Final Solution," p. 20.

6 Spies Between the Wars: 1930–1939

1. William F. Friedman, "Expansion of the Signal Intelligence Service from 1930–7 December 1941," December 4, 1945, SRH-134, 457, NARA, p. 1.

2. Army Security Agency, *Historical Background of the Signal Security Agency*, vol. 3 (Washington, D.C.: ASA, 1946), p. 183n10; James Bamford, *The Puzzle Palace: A Report on NSA, America's Most Secret Agency* (Boston: Houghton Mifflin, 1982), p. 27.

3. David Kahn, *The Codebreakers: The Story of Secret Writing* (New York: Macmillan, 1967), pp. 369–70; Ronald Clark, *The Man Who Broke Purple: The Life of Colonel William F. Friedman, Who Deciphered the Japanese Code in World War II* (Boston: Little, Brown, 1977), p. 16.

4. Kahn, *Codebreakers*, pp. 370–71; Clark, *Man Who Broke Purple*, p. 16.

5. Bamford, *Puzzle Palace*, p. 28; Clark, *Man Who Broke Purple*, p. 40.

6. Bamford, *Puzzle Palace*, pp. 29–31; John Patrick Finnegan, *Military Intelligence: An Overview, 1884–1987* (Arlington, Va.: U.S. Army Intelligence and Security Command, n.d.), pp. 49–50.

7. Finnegan, *Military Intelligence*, p. 50; Clark, *Man Who Broke Purple*, p. 121; Bamford, *Puzzle Palace*, p. 32.

8. Bamford, *Puzzle Palace*, p. 32.

9. Kahn, *Codebreakers*, p. 12; "Radio Station Marine Detachment, Peiping, China 1927–1935," SRH–178, RG 457, MRB, NARA; Captain Laurence F. Safford, "A Brief History of Communications Intelligence in the United States," March 27, 1952, SRH–149, RG 457, MRB, NARA, pp. 4–5.

10. Bamford, *Puzzle Palace*, p. 34.

11. Christopher Andrew, *Secret Service: The Making of the British Intelligence Community* (London: Heinemann, 1985), p. 352.

12. Ibid., p. 353.

13. Ibid., pp. 352–53.

14. Ibid., p. 332, 352–53; Christopher Andrew, "British Intelligence and the Breach with Russia in 1927," *Historical Journal* 25, no. 4 (1982): 957–64.

15. Andrew, *Secret Service*, p. 352.

16. F. H. Hinsley, E. E. Thomas, C. F. G. Ransom, and R. C. Knight, *British Intelligence in the Second World War*, vol. 1 (New York: Cambridge University Press, 1979), p. 52.

17. Ibid., pp. 52–53.

18. Ibid., p. 53.

19. Ibid.

20. Ibid.

21. Ibid., pp. 53–54.

22. Nigel West, *MI6: British Secret Intelligence Service Operations 1909–1945* (London: Weidenfeld & Nicolson, 1983), p. 45.

23. Ibid., p. 46; Wesley Wark, *The Ultimate Enemy: British Intelligence and Nazi Germany, 1933–1939* (Ithaca, N.Y.: Cornell University Press, 1985), p. 52.

24. West, *MI6*, p. 49.

25. Ibid., p. 55.

26. Ibid.; Hinsley et al., *British Intelligence*, p. 58; Frantisek Moravec, *Master of Spies: The Memoirs of General Frantisek Moravec* (New York: Doubleday, 1975), p. 58.

27. West, *MI6*, pp. 55–56; Hinsley et al., *British Intelligence*, p. 58.

28. Heinz Hohne, *Canaris: Hitler's Master Spy* (New York: Doubleday, 1979), pp. 4–5, 10.

29. Ibid., pp. 20–23.

30. Ibid., pp. 37, 39.

31. Ibid., p. 97.

32. Ibid., p. 136; David Kahn, *Hitler's Spies: German Military Intelligence in World War II* (New York: Macmillan, 1978), p. 226.

33. Hohne, *Canaris*, pp. 166–68.

34. Ibid., p. 180.

35. Ibid., pp. 184–85.

36. Ibid., pp. 185–86.

37. Ibid., p. 202.

38. Ibid., pp. 202–3.

39. Kahn, *Hitler's Spies*, pp. 178–79.

40. Ibid., p. 179.

41. Ibid., pp. 176, 184–87.

42. J. W. M. Chapman, "No Final Solution: A Survey of the Cryptanalytical Capabilities of German Military Agencies, 1926–35," *Intelligence and National Security*, 1, no. 1 (1986): 24.

43. Ibid.

44. Ibid.

45. Ibid., p. 35.

46. Ibid.

47. Simon Wolin and Robert M. Slusser, "The Evolution of the Soviet Secret Police," in Simon Wolin and Robert M. Slusser (eds.), *The Soviet Secret Police* (New York: Praeger, 1957), p. 15; John J. Dziak, *Chekisty: A History of the KGB* (Lexington, Mass.: Lexington Books, 1988), p. 61.

48. Robert Conquest, *The Great Terror: A Reassessment* (New York: Oxford University Press, 1990), pp. 3, 441; Kahn, *Codebreakers*, p. 640.

49. Christopher Andrew and Oleg Gordievsky, *KGB: The Inside Story* (New

York: Harper Collins, 1990), p. 173; Harry Rositzke, *The KGB: The Eyes of Russia* (Garden City, N.Y.: Doubleday, 1981), p. 62.

50. Andrew and Gordievsky, *KGB*, pp. 173–74.

51. Ibid., p. 174.

52. Ibid., pp. 178–79.

53. Ibid., p. 179.

54. Ibid., pp. 179–80.

55. Ibid., p. 180; Walter G. Krivitsky, *In Stalin's Secret Service* (Frederick, Md.: University Publications of America, 1985), pp. 16–18.

56. Andrew and Gordievsky, *KGB*, pp. 180–81.

57. Ibid., pp. 174–75.

58. Ibid., p. 175.

59. Ibid.

60. Ibid., pp. 175–76.

61. Ibid., p. 177.

62. Ibid., p. 178.

63. Ibid.; Rositzke, *KGB*, pp. 6–12.

64. Rositzke, *KGB*, pp. 10–12.

65. John Costello and Oleg Tsarev, *Deadly Illusions* (New York: Crown, 1993), p. 142.

66. Andrew and Gordievsky, *KGB*, pp. 182–83; Costello and Tsarev, *Deadly Illusions*, p. 198.

67. Andrew and Gordievsky, *KGB*, pp. 183–84; Costello and Tsarev, *Deadly Illusions*, p. 198.

68. Andrew and Gordievsky, *KGB*, p. 184.

69. Ibid., 196–97; Anthony Cave Brown, *"C": The Secret Life of Sir Stewart Menzies, Spymaster to Winston Churchill* (New York: Macmillan, 1987), p. 166.

70. Andrew and Gordievsky, *KGB*, p. 197.

71. Ibid., p. 198; Brown, *"C,"* p. 172; Phillip Knightley, *The Master Spy* (New York: Knopf, 1989), p. 36.

72. Andrew and Gordievsky, *KGB*, pp. 197–201; Knightley, *Master Spy*, pp. 36–37.

73. Knightley, *Master Spy*, pp. 45–46.

74. Andrew and Gordievsky, *KGB*, p. 203; Brown, *"C,"* pp. 174–75; Barrie Penrose and Simon Freeman, *Conspiracy of Silence: The Secret Life of Anthony Blunt* (New York: Vintage, 1988), p. 171; Costello and Tsarev, *Deadly Illusions*, p. 137.

75. Andrew and Gordievsky, *KGB*, p. 203; Penrose and Freeman, *Conspiracy*, p. 171.

76. Andrew and Gordievsky, *KGB*, p. 214; Costello and Tsarev, *Deadly Illusions*, p. 145.

77. Andrew and Gordievsky, *KGB*, pp. 212–13; Penrose and Freeman, *Conspiracy*, p. 138; Costello and Tsarev, *Deadly Illusions*, p. 145.

78. Andrew and Gordievsky, *KGB*, pp. 207–10.

79. Ibid., pp. 216–17; Penrose and Freeman, *Conspiracy*, p. 278.

80. Andrew and Gordievsky, *KGB*, p. 217.

81. Ibid., pp. 217–219; Costello and Tsarev, *Deadly Illusions*, pp. 200–201.

82. Andrew and Gordievsky, *KGB*, pp. 217, 219.

83. Ibid., pp. 216–217, 219.

84. Ibid., p. 220.

85. Ibid., pp. 221, 223; Knightley, *Master Spy*, pp. 53, 59–60.

86. Andrew and Gordievsky, *KGB*, pp. 228–29.

87. Ibid., p. 229.

88. Ibid., pp. 230–31; Rositzke, *KGB*, pp. 131–32.

89. Andrew and Gordievsky, *KGB*, pp. 230–31.

90. Kahn, *Hitler's Spies*, p. 116; Roy M. Stanley, *World War II Photo Intelligence* (New York: Scribner's, 1981), p. 43.

91. Kahn, *Hitler's Spies*, p. 116.

92. Ibid., pp. 116–17.

93. Ibid., pp. 117–18; Stanley, *World War II*, p. 43.

94. Kahn, *Hitler's Spies*, p. 118.

95. Ibid.; Stanley, *World War II*, p. 43.

96. Kahn, *Hitler's Spies*, p. 118.

97. Ibid., pp. 118–19.

98. Hinsley et al., *British Intelligence*, p. 28.

99. F. W. Winterbotham, *The Nazi Connection* (New York: Dell, 1978), p. 233.

100. Ibid.

101. Ibid.

102. Hinsley et al., *British Intelligence*, p. 28.

103. Winterbotham, *Nazi Connection*, pp. 233–34.

104. Ibid., p. 234.

105. Ibid., pp. 234–36; Hinsley et al., *British Intelligence*, pp. 28–29; Andrew, *Secret Service*, p. 468.

106. Winterbotham, *Nazi Connection*, pp. 238–39.

107. Ibid., p. 240.

108. Ibid., pp. 240–241.

109. Hinsley et al., *British Intelligence*, p. 29; Andrew, *Secret Service*, pp. 468–69.

110. Winterbotham, *Nazi Connection*, p. 242; Constance Babington-Smith, *Air Spy: The Story of Photo Intelligence in World War II* (New York: Harper & Brothers, 1957), pp. 10–11.

7 Intelligence and the Onset of War

1. Donald Lamb, *The Drift to War 1922–39* (New York: St. Martin's Press, 1991), p. 113.

2. Ibid., p. 173.

3. Douglas Porch, "French Intelligence and the Fall of France 1939–40," *Intelligence and National Security* 4, no. 1 (1989): 28; citing General Maurice Gauche, *Le deuxième bureau au travail (1935–1940)* (Paris: Dumont, 1955), p. 101.

4. Christopher Andrew, *Secret Service: The Making of the British Intelligence Community* (London: Heinemann, 1985), p. 391.

5. Anthony Adamthwaite, "French Military Intelligence and the Coming of War, 1935–1939," in Christopher Andrew and Jeremy Noakes (eds.), *Intelligence and International Relations 1900–1945* (Exeter, UK: Exeter University Publications, 1987), p. 192.

6. Andrew, *Secret Service*, p. 390.

7. Ibid., pp. 393–94; Wesley K. Wark, *The Ultimate Enemy: British Intelligence and Nazi Germany 1933–1939* (Ithaca, N.Y.: Cornell University Press, 1985), p. 103.

8. Andrew, *Secret Service*, pp. 394–95.

9. Ibid., pp. 395–96.

10. Ibid., p. 396.

11. Ibid.

12. Ibid., p. 397; Wark, *Ultimate Enemy*, p. 107.

13. Andrew, *Secret Service*, p. 397.

14. Ibid., p. 397.

15. Lamb, *Drift to War*, p. 239.

16. Anthony Cave Brown, *"C": The Secret Life of Sir Stewart Menzies, Spymaster to Winston Churchill* (New York: Macmillan, 1987), p. 190.

17. Ibid., pp. 190–91.

18. Ibid., p. 191; Andrew, *Secret Service*, p. 398.

19. Brown, *"C,"* pp. 192–93; Andrew, *Secret Service*, p. 398.

20. Andrew, *Secret Service*, p. 398.

21. Brown, *"C,"* p. 193.

22. Wark, *Ultimate Enemy*, pp. 67–68.

23. Adamthwaite, "French Military Intelligence," p. 192.

24. Andrew, *Secret Service*, pp. 416–17; Adamthwaite, "French Military Intelligence," p. 195.

25. D. Cameron Watt, "An Intelligence Surprise: The Failure of the Foreign Office to Anticipate the Nazi–Soviet Pact," *Intelligence and National Security* 4, no. 3 (1989), p. 512; William L. Shirer, *The Rise and Fall of the Third Reich: A History of Nazi Germany* (New York: Simon & Schuster, 1960), pp. 538–44.

26. Watt, "An Intelligence Surprise," pp. 518–19.

27. Ibid., pp. 520–21.

28. Ibid., p. 521.

29. Andrew, *Secret Service*, p. 424.

30. Ibid., pp. 424–25.

31. Lamb, *Drift to War*, p. 314.

32. Ibid.

33. Watt, "An Intelligence Surprise," p. 528.

34. Anthony Read and David Fisher, *The Deadly Embrace: Hitler, Stalin, and the Nazi Soviet Pact 1939–1941* (New York: Norton, 1988), pp. 89–91.

35. Watt, "An Intelligence Surprise," p. 529; Brown, *"C"*, p. 209.

36. Brown, *"C,"* p. 209.

37. Ibid.

38. Read and Fisher, *Deadly Embrace*, p. 110.

39. Adamthwaite, "French Military Intelligence," p. 198.

40. Ibid.

41. Barton Whaley, *Codeword Barbarossa* (Cambridge, Mass.: MIT Press, 1973), p. 13; Read and Fisher, *Deadly Embrace*, p. 621.

42. Whaley, *Codeword Barbarossa*, pp. 25–26.

43. Ibid., p. 32.

44. Read and Fisher, *Deadly Embrace*, p. 578; Shirer, *Rise and Fall*, p. 841.

45. Whaley, *Codeword Barbarossa*, pp. 33–34.

46. Ibid., pp. 109–10.

47. Ibid., pp. 39–40.

48. Ibid., pp. 43–45.

49. Ibid., pp. 107–8.

50. Ibid., p. 115, citing Anthony Eden, *The Reckoning*, vol. 2 (London: Cassell, 1965), p. 311.

51. Whaley, *Codeword Barbarossa*, p. 34.

52. Ibid., p. 67; Christopher Andrew and Oleg Gordievsky, *KGB: The Inside Story* (New York: Harper Collins, 1990), p. 262.

53. Read and Fisher, *Deadly Embrace*, p. 602.

54. Andrew and Gordievsky, *KGB*, pp. 264–65.

55. Ibid., p. 265.

56. Whaley, *Codeword Barbarossa*, p. 125.

57. Ibid., pp. 172–175.

58. Andrew and Gordievsky, *KGB*, p. 260.

59. Ibid.

60. Ibid., pp. 260–62.

61. Ibid., p. 262.

62. Ibid., pp. 264–65.

63. Whaley, *Codeword Barbarossa*, p. 126.

64. Roberta Wohlstetter, *Pearl Harbor: Warning and Decision* (Stanford, Calif.: Stanford University Press, 1962), pp. 349, 368.

65. Gordon W. Prange with Donald M. Goldstein and Katherine V. Dillon, *Pearl Harbor: The Verdict of History* (New York: McGraw-Hill, 1986), p. xxxi.

66. Ibid., pp. xxxi–xxxii.

67. U.S. Congress, Joint Committee on the Investigation of the Pearl Harbor Attack, *Pearl Harbor Attack*, pt. 15 (Washington, D.C.: U.S. Government Printing Office, 1946), p. 1852.

68. Wohlstetter, *Pearl Harbor*, p. 45.

69. Ibid., pp. 294, 298, 325.

70. U.S. Congress, Joint Committee on the Investigation of the Pearl Harbor Attack, *Pearl Harbor*, pt. 27 (Washington, D.C.: U.S. Government Printing Office, 1946), p. 56; W. H. Packard, "ONI Centennial," *Naval Intelligence Newsletter*, October 1982, pp. III-1-III-2.

71. Wohlstetter, *Pearl Harbor*, p. 284.

72. The Popov version is given in Dusko Popov, *Spy Counterspy: The Autobiography of Dusko Popov* (New York: Grosset & Dunlap, 1974), as well as John Masterman, *The Double-Cross System in the War of 1939 to 1945* (New Haven: Yale University Press, 1972). It would appear that much of Popov's account, including alleged meeting with J. Edgar Hoover at which Popov warned him of a possible attack on Pearl Harbor if negotiations failed, is less than fully believable. See Thomas F. Troy, "The British Assault on J. Edgar Hoover: The Tricycle Case," *International Journal of Intelligence and Counterintelligence* 3, no. 2 (1989): 169–209; B. Bruce–Briggs, "Another Ride on Tricycle," *Intelligence and National Security* 7, no. 2 (1992): 77–100.

73. Prange with Goldstein and Dillon, *Pearl Harbor*, pp. 309–10; John F. Bratzel and Leslie B. Rout, Jr., "Pearl Harbor, Microdots, and J. Edgar Hoover," *American Historical Review*, December 1982, pp. 1342–51.

74. Prange with Goldstein and Dillon, *Pearl Harbor*, p. 308. Other factors casting doubt on the thesis that the questionnaire was given Popov at Japanese request were the capabilities of Japanese intelligence on Hawaii and the im-

probability that the Japanese would inform Germany of their attack plans. On the sabotage motive see Bruce–Briggs, "Another Ride on Tricycle," p. 92.

75. Prange with Goldstein and Dillon, Pearl Harbor, pp. 273, 656; U.S. Congress, Joint Committee on the Investigation of the Pearl Harbor Attack, Pearl Harbor, pt. 12, pp. 261–62.

76. Wohlstetter, Pearl Harbor, pp. 187–88, Gordon W. Prange, At Dawn We Slept: The Untold Story of Pearl Harbor (New York: McGraw-Hill, 1981), p. 358; David Kahn, The Codebreakers: The Story of Secret Writing (New York: Macmillan, 1967), pp. 31–32.

77. Prange with Goldstein and Dillon, Pearl Harbor, p. 273.

78. Kahn, The Codebreakers, p. 32.

79. George O'Toole, Honorable Treachery: A History of U.S. Intelligence, Espionage, Covert Action from the American Revolution to the CIA (New York: Atlantic Monthly Press, 1991), pp. 368–69.

80. Wohlstetter, Pearl Harbor, pp. 189–90.

81. Ibid., p. 201; Department of Defense, The MAGIC Background of Pearl Harbor, vol. 4 (Washington, D.C.: U.S. Government Printing Office, 1977), p. A-118.

82. Prange, At Dawn We Slept, p. 419.

83. Kahn, The Codebreakers, pp. 40–41.

84. Ibid., pp. 43–44.

85. Ibid., pp. 52–53.

86. Ibid., pp. 53–54.

87. Kahn, The Codebreakers, pp. 1, 2.

88. Prange, At Dawn We Slept, p. 486; Department of Defense, The MAGIC Background, p. A-81; Wohlstetter, Pearl Harbor, p. 334.

89. O'Toole, Honorable Treachery, p. 378.

90. Prange, At Dawn We Slept, pp. 249–51.

91. Wohlstetter, Pearl Harbor, pp. 213–14. The quote is from CNO Admiral Harold R. Stark. Also see Ronald Lewin, The American Magic: Codes, Ciphers, and the Defeat of Japan (New York: Farrar, Straus, and Giroux, 1982), pp. 62–63; Prange with Goldstein and Dillon, Pearl Harbor, p. 274.

92. Wohlstetter, Pearl Harbor, p. 211.

93. Ibid., p. 379.

94. Ibid., pp. 379–80. It has been suggested that the Japanese task force did not maintain total radio silence, and task force signals were intercepted at least twice: by an oceanliner en route from Los Angeles to Honolulu and by a commercial press or wireless company from the northern Pacific region where ships rarely ventured. See Edward S. Barkin and L. Michael Meyer, "COMINT and Pearl Harbor: FDR's Mistake," International Journal of Intelligence and Counterintelligence 2, no. 4 (1988): 513–31. For a skeptical view of these claims see Prange with Goldstein and Dillon, Pearl Harbor, pp. 52–58.

95. O'Toole, Honorable Treachery, pp. 376–77; Kahn, The Codebreakers, p. 39.

96. Kahn, The Codebreakers, p. 41; Christopher Andrew, For the President's Eyes Only (New York: Harper Collins, 1995), pp. 120–21.

97. David Kahn, "The Intelligence Failure of Pearl Harbor," Foreign Affairs, 70, no. 5 (1991/92): p. 148.

98. Wohlstetter, Pearl Harbor, p. 354.

8 Spies and Counterspies

1. Christopher Andrew and Oleg Gordievsky, *KGB: The Inside Story* (New York: Harper Collins, 1990), pp. 270–71.

2. Ibid., p. 271.

3. Ibid.

4. Anthony Paul, "The Spy Who Loved Hanako," *Asia Week*, April 29, 1983, pp. 38–41.

5. Central Intelligence Agency, *The Rote Kapelle: The CIA's History of Soviet Intelligence and Espionage Networks in Western Europe, 1936–1945* (Washington, D.C.: University Publications of America, 1979), pp. 131–32; Armed Forces Security Agency, *Final Report on the "Rote Kappelle" Case (Third Reich)*, 1951, SRH–30, RG 457, MRB, NARA, p. 20.

6. John Costello and Oleg Tsarev, *Deadly Illusions* (New York: Crown, 1993), pp. 75, 77, 83.

7. Andrew and Gordievsky, *KGB*, p. 274; Armed Forces Security Agency, *"Rote Kapelle" Case*, pp. 20–26.

8. Armed Forces Security Agency, *"Rote Kapelle" Case*, pp. 7–8.

9. Ibid., pp. 20–26; Central Intelligence Agency, *Rote Kapelle*, pp. 133–34; Andrew and Gordievsky, *KGB*, p. 274.

10. Armed Forces Security Agency, *"Rote Kapelle" Case*, pp. 15–16; Andrew and Gordievsky, *KGB*, p. 275.

11. Andrew and Gordievsky, *KGB*, p. 276; Central Intelligence Agency, *Rote Kapelle*, p. xi; Heinz Hohne, *Codeword Direktor* (New York: Ballantine, 1982), pp. 3, 31.

12. Harry Rositzke, *The KGB: The Eyes of Russia* (Garden City, N.Y.: Doubleday, 1981), p.14; Central Intelligence Agency, *Rote Kapelle*, pp. 18–19, 87.

13. Rositzke, *KGB*, pp. 14–15; Central Intelligence Agency, *Rote Kapelle*, pp. 16, 24–25.

14. Rositzke, *KGB*, p. 15.

15. Ibid.

16. Ibid.

17. Ibid., p. 16.

18. Andrew and Gordievsky, *KGB*, p. 277.

19. Central Intelligence Agency, *Rote Kapelle*, pp. 165–66, 169.

20. Ibid., pp. 165–66; Nigel West, *MI6: British Secret Intelligence Service Operations 1909–1945* (London: Weidenfeld & Nicolson, 1983), pp. 115, 118.

21. Andrew and Gordievsky, *KGB*, p. 278; Central Intelligence Agency, *Rote Kapelle*, pp. 185–93; West, *MI6*, pp. 115, 118; Nigel West, *A Thread of Deceit: Espionage Myths of World War II* (New York: Random House, 1985), p. 59.

22. Andrew and Gordievsky, *KGB*, pp. 271–278; Central Intelligence Agency, *Rote Kapelle*, pp. 185–93.

23. Central Intelligence Agency, *Rote Kapelle*, pp. 166–67.

24. West, *MI6*, p. 73; Anthony Cave Brown, *"C": The Secret Life of Sir Stewart Menzies, Spymaster to Winston Churchill* (New York: Macmillan, 1987), pp. 213–19.

25. West, *MI6*, pp. 75, 239–47; Brown, *"C,"* p. 220.

26. West, *MI6*, pp. 81–82.

27. Ibid., p. 95.

28. Ibid., pp. 95, 141.

29. Ibid., p. 141; Nigel West, *Secret War: The Story of SOE, Britain's Wartime Sabotage Organization* (London: Hodder & Stoughton, 1992), pp. 35–36.

30. West, *MI6*, p. 142.

31. Ibid., p. 143.

32. Ibid.; West, *Secret War*, pp. 36–37.

33. West, *MI6*, pp.143–45.

34. Ibid., p. 237; West, *Secret War*, p. 42.

35. West, *MI6*, pp. 154–55.

36. Arnold Kramish, *The Griffin* (Boston: Houghton Mifflin, 1986), pp. 6, 8–12, 15–17.

37. Ibid., pp. 17–18.

38. Ibid., pp. 84, 99.

39. Ibid., pp. 112, 131–32.

40. R. V. Jones, *Reflections on Intelligence* (London: Mandarin, 1990), p. 284.

41. Richard Harris Smith, *OSS: The Secret History of America's First Central Intelligence Agency* (Berkeley: University of California Press, 1981), p. 1.

42. Nathan Miller, *Spying for America: The Hidden History of U.S. Intelligence* (New York: Paragon, 1989), pp. 277–78; Smith, *OSS*, p. 204; West, *MI6*, p. 222.

43. Smith, *OSS*, p. 204.

44. Anthony Quibble, "Alias George Wood," *Studies in Intelligence*, Winter 1966, pp. 69–70; West, *MI6*, p. 225; Smith, *OSS*, p. 219.

45. West, *MI6*, p. 225; Smith, *OSS*, p. 219; Quibble, "Alias George Wood," p. 75.

46. Smith, *OSS*, p. 219.

47. Ibid., p. 220; Quibble, "Alias George Wood," pp. 74–78; "Memoranda for the President: Boston Series," *Studies in Intelligence*, Winter 1965, p. 89.

48. Anthony Cave Brown, *The Last Hero: Wild Bill Donovan* (New York: Times Books, 1982), p. 285.

49. Ibid., pp. 286–89.

50. Kermit Roosevelt, *The Overseas Targets: War Report of the OSS (Office of Strategic Services)*, vol. 2 (New York: Walker, 1976), pp. 180–81.

51. Smith, *OSS*, p. 172.

52. Ibid., p. 166.

53. Ibid., pp. 179, 185.

54. Ibid., p. 225.

55. Roosevelt, *The Overseas Targets*, pp. 306, 309.

56. Ibid., p. 311.

57. Ibid., pp. 311–12.

58. Andrew and Gordievsky, *KGB*, p. 291.

59. Ibid., pp. 292–93.

60. Ibid., p. 294.

61. Ibid., p. 295.

62. Hugh Trevor-Roper, *The Philby Affair: Espionage, Treason, and the Secret Services* (London: William Kimber, 1968), pp. 28–29; Andrew and Gordievsky, *KGB*, pp. 295–96; Phillip Knightley, *The Master Spy: The Story of Kim Philby* (New York: Knopf, 1989), p. 110.

63. Kim Philby, *My Silent War* (New York: Grove Press, 1968), pp. 109–16; Andrew and Gordievsky, *KGB*, p. 297; Knightley, *The Master Spy*, pp. 124–25; Brown, *"C,"* pp. 620–22.

64. Andrew and Gordievsky, *KGB*, p. 300; Barrie Penrose and Simon Freeman, *Conspiracy of Silence: The Secret Life of Anthony Blunt* (New York: Vintage Press, 1988), pp. 250, 278–80.

65. Andrew and Gordievsky, *KGB*, p. 304.

66. Ibid.

67. Ibid., pp. 304–5.

68. Ibid., p. 311.

69. Michael Dobbs, "How Soviets Stole U.S. Atom Secrets," *Washington Post*, October 4, 1992, pp. A1, A36–A37.

70. Andrew and Gordievsky, *KGB*, p. 312.

71. Andrew and Gordievsky, *KGB*, p. 313; Robert Chadwell Williams, *Klaus Fuchs, Atom Spy* (Cambridge, Mass.: Harvard University Press, 1987), p. 39; H. Montgomery Hyde, *The Atom Bomb Spies* (New York: Ballantine, 1981), p. 101; Letter to James S. Lay, Jr., executive secretary, National Security Council, February 6, 1950, FBI File No. 65–58805, vol. 3, ser. 83–171.

72. Andrew and Gordievsky, *KGB*, p. 314; Williams, *Klaus Fuchs*, pp. 6, 22, 39.

73. Williams, *Klaus Fuchs*, p. 67.

74. Andrew and Gordievsky, *KGB*, p. 314; Hyde, *Atom Bomb Spies*, p. 105.

75. Hyde, *Atom Bomb Spies*, p. 107.

76. Andrew and Gordievsky, *KGB*, p. 315; Williams, *Klaus Fuchs*, p. 76; Letter to James S. Lay.

77. Williams, *Klaus Fuchs*, p. 78; Hyde, *Atom Bomb Spies*, p. 109; FBI Office Memorandum, To: The Director, From: Hugh W. Clegg and Robert J. Lamphere, Subject: FOOCASE–Espionage (R), Interviews in England with Fuchs, June 4, 1950, FBI File No. 65–58805, vol. 78, ser. 1, 396-1431, pp. 21–22.

78. Williams, *Klaus Fuchs*, p. 79; FBI Office Memorandum, Interviews in England with Fuchs, p. 32.

79. Williams, *Klaus Fuchs*, pp. 82–83.

80. Ibid., p. 84; Andrew and Gordievsky, *KGB*, p. 316; Ronald Radosh and Joyce Milton, *The Rosenberg File: A Search for the Truth* (New York: Vintage, 1984), p. 70; Rositzke, *KGB*, p. 37.

81. Dobbs, "How Soviets Stole U.S. Atom Secrets"; Vladimir Chikov, "How the Soviet Intelligence Service 'Split' the American Atom [pt. 1]," *New Times*, April 23–29, 1991, pp. 37–40; Vladimir Chikov, "How the Soviet Intelligence Service 'Split' the American Atom [pt. 2], *New Times*, April 30–May 5, 1991, pp. 36–39.

82. Dobbs, "How Soviets Stole U.S. Atom Secrets"; Chikov, "How the Soviet Intelligence Service 'Split' the American Atom [pt. 2]."

83. Chikov, "How the Soviet Intelligence Service 'Split' the American Atom [pt. 2]," p. 39.

84. David Kahn, *Hitler's Spies: German Military Intelligence in World War II* (New York: Macmillan, 1978), p. 332; William Breuer, *Hitler's Undercover War: The Nazi Espionage Invasion of the U.S.A.* (New York: St. Martin's Press, 1988), p. 142–44.

85. Kahn, *Hitler's Spies*, p. 332, Breuer, *Hitler's Undercover War*, p. 242.

86. Kahn, *Hitler's Spies*, p. 332.

87. Breuer, *Hitler's Undercover War*, pp. 148–50.

88. Kahn, *Hitler's Spies*, p. 333; Breuer, *Hitler's Undercover War*, pp. 241–42.

89. Breuer, *Hitler's Undercover War*, pp. 321–24.

90. J. C. Masterman, *The Double-Cross System in the War of 1939 to 1945* (New Haven, Ct.: Yale University Press, 1972), pp. 36–37; Kahn, *Hitler's Spies*, p. 367.

91. Masterman, *Double-Cross System* p. 38.

92. Ibid., pp. 39–41.

93. Ibid., p. 6.

94. Ibid., p. 63; "Masterman Revisited," *Studies in Intelligence* 18, no. 1 (1974): 27; Brown, "*C*," p. 307.

95. Masterman, *Double-Cross System*, pp. 114–15; F. H. Hinsley and C. A. G. Simkins, *British Intelligence in the Second World War*, vol. 4: *Security and Counterintelligence* (London: Her Majesty's Stationery Office, 1990), p. 114.

96. Masterman, *Double-Cross System*, p. 146; Michael Howard, *British Intelligence in the Second World War*, vol. 5: *Strategic Deception* (London: Her Majesty's Stationery Office, 1990), p. 121.

97. Masterman, *Double-Cross System*, p. 156; Howard, *British Intelligence*, vol. 5, pp. 120–21.

98. Howard, *British Intelligence*, vol. 5, p. 121; Masterman, *Double-Cross System*, pp. 160–61.

99. Brown, "*C*," p. 597; Howard, *British Intelligence*, vol. 5, p. 128.

100. Masterman, *Double-Cross System*, pp. 156–57; Brown, "*C*," p. 598.

101. Brown, "*C*," pp. 599–600.

102. Ibid., p. 600.

103. Ibid.

104. Kahn, *Hitler's Spies*, p. 313.

105. Ibid., p. 314.

106. David L. Thomas, "The Legend of Agent 'Max'," *Foreign Intelligence Literary Scene*, January 1986, p. 1.

107. Ibid., p. 5.

108. Ibid.

9   The Wrecking Crews

1. Callum MacDonald, *The Killing of SS Obergruppenführer Richard Heydrich* (New York: Free Press, 1989), p. 122.

2. David Stafford, "The Detonator Concept: British Strategy, SOE and European Resistance after the Fall of France," *Journal of Contemporary History* 10, no. 2 (1975): 192.

3. Ibid.

4. Ibid., p. 193; Nigel West, *Secret War: The Story of SOE* (London: Hodder & Stoughton, 1992), p. 1; E. H. Cookridge, *Set Europe Ablaze* (New York: Crowell, 1967), p. 2, citing J. R. M. Butler (ed.), *History of the Second World War Grand Strategy*, vol. 2 (London: Her Majesty's Stationery Office, 1957).

5. Stafford, "Detonator Concept," pp. 202–3; Charles Cruickshank, *SOE in Scandinavia* (New York: Oxford University Press, 1986), p. 59; M. R. D. Foot, *SOE: The Special Operations Executive 1940–46* (London: Mandarin, 1990), p. 301.

6. Stafford, "Detonator Concept," p. 206; Foot, *SOE*, p. 250.

7. West, *Secret War*, pp. 14, 22; Cookridge, *Set Europe Ablaze*, pp. 20–21.

8. West, *Secret War*, p. 31; Cookridge, *Set Europe Ablaze*, pp. 61–62.

9. Marcel Ruby, *F Section, SOE: The Story of the Buckmaster Network* (London: Leo Cooper, 1988), p. 10.

10. West, *Secret War*, p. 33; Ruby, *F Section*, p. 113.

11. West, *Secret War*, p. 33; Foot, *SOE*, p. 303; Ruby, *F Section*, p. 11.

12. West, *Secret War*, p. 35; Ruby, *F Section*, p. 114.

13. Ruby, *F Section*, p. 118–19.

14. Ibid., pp. 12–13.

15. Ibid., p. 121.

16. Ibid., p. 124.

17. West, *Secret War*, p. 92.

18. Ibid., pp. 92–93; Foot, *SOE*, pp. 179–80.

19. West, *Secret War*, p. 93.

20. Foot, *SOE*, p. 180.

21. West, *Secret War*, pp. 94–95.

22. Ibid., p. 95.

23. Ibid., p. 96.

24. Ibid., p. 98.

25. Ibid.

26. Ibid.

27. Ibid., p. 99.

28. Foot, *SOE*, p. 183.

29. Cruickshank, *SOE in Scandinavia*, p. 192.

30. Ibid., pp. 192–93.

31. Ibid., p. 197.

32. Ibid., pp. 119–20.

33. R. V. Jones, *The Wizard War: British Scientific Intelligence, 1939–1945* (New York: Coward, McCann & Geohegan, 1978), p. 307.

34. West, *Secret War*, p. 78; Cruickshank, *SOE in Scandinavia*, p. 198; Arnold Kramish, *The Griffin* (Boston: Houghton Mifflin, 1986), p. 167.

35. Foot, *SOE*, p. 298; Kramish, *Griffin*, p. 169.

36. Kramish, *Griffin*, p. 170.

37. Cruickshank, *SOE in Scandinavia*, p. 201.

38. Ibid., pp. 201–2.

39. Leslie B. Rout and John F. Bratzel, *The Shadow War: German Espionage and United States Counterespionage in Latin America during World War II* (Frederick, Md.: University Publications of America, 1986), p. 12; MacDonald, *The Killing*, p. 103.

40. MacDonald, *The Killing*, pp. 112–13; Frantisek Moravec, *Master of Spies: The Memoirs of General Frantisek Moravec* (New York: Doubleday, 1975), p. 195.

41. Moravec, *Master of Spies*, p. 196.

42. MacDonald, *The Killing*, p. 122.

43. West, *Secret War*, p. 89; Foot, *SOE*, pp. 279–80; Moravec, *Master of Spies*, pp. 203, 205.

44. Moravec, *Master of Spies*, p. 206; MacDonald, *The Killing*, p. 193.

45. Moravec, *Master of Spies*, p. 205; MacDonald, *The Killing*, pp. 186–87.

46. MacDonald, *The Killing*, pp. 176, 193, 197; Moravec, *Master of Spies*, p. 206.

47. West, *Secret War*, pp. 89–90; Moravec, *Master of Spies*, pp. 209–10.

48. West, *Secret War*, pp. 223, 226.

49. Kermit Roosevelt, *The Overseas Targets: War Report of the OSS (Office of*

Strategic Services) vol. 2 (New York: Walker, 1976), pp. 193–94; Cookridge, *Set Europe Ablaze,* p. 116.

50. Richard Dunlop, *Donovan: America's Master Spy* (New York: Rand McNally, 1982), p. 438.

51. West, *Secret War,* pp. 222–23.

52. Ibid., pp. 223, 231; R. Harris Smith, *OSS: The Secret History America's First Central Intelligence Agency* (Berkeley: University of California Press, 1981), p. 174.

53. Dunlop, *Donovan,* p. 438; Roosevelt, *The Overseas Targets,* p. 199.

54. William Colby, *Honorable Men: My Life in the CIA* (New York: Simon & Schuster, 1978), pp. 24–26.

55. Roosevelt, *The Overseas Targets,* pp. 199–200.

56. Ibid., p. 200.

57. Ibid., p. 205.

58. West, *Secret War,* pp. 224–25, 233.

59. Ibid., pp. 223, 226.

60. Ibid., p. 238.

61. Ibid.

62. Cruickshank, *SOE in Scandinavia,* p. 230.

10   Aerial Spies

1. Constance Babington–Smith, *Air Spy: The Story of Photo Intelligence in World War II* (New York: Harper & Brothers, 1957), p. 11.

2. Ibid., p. 13.

3. Ibid.

4. Ibid., p. 18.

5. Ibid., pp. 19–22; R. V. Jones, *The Wizard War: British Scientific Intelligence 1939–1945* (New York: Coward, McCann & Geohegan, 1978), p. 130.

6. Babington-Smith, *Air Spy,* p. 24.

7. Ibid.

8. Ibid., p. 36; F. H. Hinsley, E. E. Thomas, C. F. G. Ransom, and R. C. Knight, *British Intelligence in the Second World War,* vol. 1 (New York: Cambridge University Press, 1979), p. 104.

9. Babington-Smith, *Air Spy,* pp. 37–39.

10. Ibid., p. 42.

11. Ibid., p. 56; Hinsley et al., *British Intelligence,* p. 171.

12. Babington-Smith, *Air Spy,* p. 60.

13. Ibid., p. 70.

14. Ibid., p. 71.

15. Ibid.

16. Ibid., p. 72; Hinsley et al., *British Intelligence,* p. 184.

17. Babington-Smith, *Air Spy,* p. 72; Hinsley et al., *British Intelligence,* p. 185.

18. Babington-Smith, *Air Spy,* pp. 72–73.

19. Ibid., p. 73; Hinsley et al., *British Intelligence,* p. 186.

20. F. H. Hinsley, E. E. Thomas, C. F. G. Ransom, and R. C. Knight, *British Intelligence in the Second World War,* vol. 2 (New York: Cambridge University Press, 1981), p. 258.

21. Ibid., p. 260.

22. Ibid.

23. Ibid.

24. Ibid., pp. 260–61.

25. Babington-Smith, *Air Spy*, p. 99.

26. Hinsley et al., *British Intelligence*, vol. 2, p. 515.

27. Babington-Smith, *Air Spy*, p. 109.

28. Ibid., p. 111.

29. Ibid., pp. 113–14; Stephen W. Roskill, *The War at Sea, 1939–1945*, vol. 1: *The Defensive* (London: Her Majesty's Stationery Office, 1954), p. 609.

30. Peter Mead, *The Eye in the Air: History of Air Observation and Reconnaissance for the Army* (London: Her Majesty's Stationery Office, 1983), p. 206.

31. Ibid., pp. 215–16.

32. Ibid., p. 216.

33. David Kahn, *Hitler's Spies: German Military Intelligence in World War II* (New York: Macmillan, 1978), pp. 119–21.

34. Ibid., pp. 123, 127.

35. Ibid., p. 119.

36. Ibid.

37. Ibid., p. 120.

38. David Glantz, *Soviet Military Intelligence in War* (London: Frank Cass, 1990), pp. 21, 83.

39. Ibid., pp. 83–84.

40. Ibid., pp. 57–58.

41. Ibid., p. 121.

42. Ibid., p. 108; Alexander Werth, *Russia at War, 1941–1945* (New York: Carroll & Graf, 1984), pp. 405–7.

43. Glantz, *Soviet Military Intelligence*, pp. 108–9.

44. Ibid., pp. 158–59.

45. Ibid., p. 159.

46. Werth, *Russia at War, 1941–1945*, p. 680.

47. Glantz, *Soviet Military Intelligence*, p. 181.

48. Ibid., p. 192.

49. Ibid., p. 212.

50. Ibid.

51. Ibid., p. 215.

52. Ibid., pp. 213–14.

53. Ibid., p. 285.

54. Ibid., p. 287.

55. Ibid., pp. 284–85.

56. Ibid., p. 303.

57. Ibid., p. 305.

58. Ibid., pp. 343–44.

59. Ibid., p. 344.

60. Hinsley et al. *British Intelligence*, vol. 3, pt. 1, p. 362.

61. Ibid., p. 363; Jones, *Wizard War*, p. 332.

62. Hinsley et al., *British Intelligence*, vol. 3, pt. 1, p. 364; Babington-Smith, *Air Spy*, p. 212.

63. Hinsley et al., *British Intelligence*, vol. 3, pt. 1, pp. 366–67; Babington-Smith, *Air Spy*, pp. 207–8.

64. Hinsley et al., *British Intelligence,* vol. 3, pt. 1, p. 367.

65. Ibid., p. 369; Jones, *Wizard War,* pp. 340, 343; Babington–Smith, *Air Spy,* p. 209.

66. Hinsley et al., *British Intelligence,* vol. 3, pt. 1, p. 376.

67. Ibid., p. 382; Jones, *Wizard War,* p. 346; Babington-Smith, *Air Spy,* p. 212.

68. Babington-Smith, *Air Spy,* p. 213; Hinsley et al., *British Intelligence,* vol. 3, pt. 1, p. 385.

69. Hinsley et al., *British Intelligence,* vol. 3, pt. 1, p. 393.

70. Ibid., pp. 403–4; Babington-Smith, *Air Spy,* p. 215.

71. Hinsley et al., *British Intelligence,* vol. 3, pt. 1, pp. 413, 415.

72. Ibid., p. 421.

73. Jones, *Wizard War,* pp. 418–19.

74. Ibid., pp. 420–21.

75. Ibid., pp. 422–23.

11 Black Magic

1. James Bamford, *The Puzzle Palace: A Report on NSA, America's Most Secret Agency* (Boston: Houghton Mifflin, 1982), p. 41; "U.S. Navy Communication Intelligence Organization, Liaison and Collaboration, 1941–1945," October 8, 1945, SRH-197, RG 457, MRB, NARA, pp. 2–4.

2. David Kahn, "Roosevelt, Magic, and Ultra," *Cryptologia,* October 1992, pp. 293–94.

3. J. W. Bennett, W. A. Hobart, and J. B. Spitzer, *Intelligence and Cryptanalytic Activities of the Japanese during World War II* (Laguna Hills, Calif.: Aegean Park Press, 1986), pp. 3, 7, 11; Michael Barnhart, "Japanese Intelligence before the Second World War: 'Best Case' Analysis," in Ernest R. May (ed.), *Knowing One's Enemies: Intelligence Assessment before the Two World Wars* (Princeton, N.J.: Princeton University Press, 1984), p. 428; Signal Security Agency, "Japanese Signal Intelligence Service Third Edition," November 1, 1944, SRH–266, RG 457, MRB, NARA, pp. 5–7.

4. David Kahn, *Hitler's Spies: German Military Intelligence in World War II* (New York: Macmillan, 1978), pp. 173–75, 178–81, 185.

5. Ibid., pp. 169, 192–93.

6. F. H. Hinsley and Alan Stripp (eds.), *Codebreakers: The Inside Story of Bletchley Park* (New York: Oxford University Press, 1993), pp. v, xvii; Gordon Welchman, *The Hut Six Story: Breaking the Enigma Codes* (New York: McGraw-Hill, 1982), p. 10.

7. Welchman, *Hut Six Story,* p. 10.

8. David Kahn, *Seizing the Enigma: The Race to Break the German U-Boat Codes, 1939–1943* (Boston: Houghton Mifflin, 1991), pp. 92–93; Steven J. Heims, *John von Neuman and Norbert Weiner: From Mathematics to the Technologies of Life and Death* (Cambridge, Mass: MIT Press, 1980), p. 142; Thomas Parrish, *The American Codebreakers: The U.S. Role in Ultra* (Chelsea, Mich.: Scarborough House, 1991), pp. 165–66; Anthony Cave Brown, *"C": The Secret Life of Sir Stewart Menzies, Spymaster to Winston Churchill* (New York: Macmillan, 1987), p. 206.

9. Wesley K. Wark, "Cryptographic Innocence: The Origins of Signals Intelligence in Canada in the Second World War," *Journal of Contemporary History* 22

(1987): 645–46; N. K. O'Neill, *History of the CBNRC*, vol. 1 (Ottawa: Communications Security Establishment, 1987), p. 6.

10. Peter St. John, "Canada's Accession to the Allied Intelligence Community," *Conflict Quarterly* 4, no. 4 (1984): p. 10; David Kahn, "Introduction," in Herbert O. Yardley, *The American Black Chamber* (New York: Ballantine, 1981), p. xv; J. L. Granatstein, *A Man of Influence: Norman A. Robertson and Canadian Statecraft, 1929–1968* (Ottawa: Deneau, 1981), p. 181; Wark, "Cryptographic Innocence," p. 654.

11. St. John, "Canada's Accession to the Allied Intelligence Community," p. 11.

12. Christopher Andrew, "The Growth of the Australian Intelligence Community and the Anglo-American Connection," *Intelligence and National Security* 4, no. 2 (1989): 218–19.

13. David Kahn, *Seizing the Enigma: The Race to Break the German U–Boat Codes, 1939–1943* (Boston: Houghton Mifflin, 1991), pp. 37–38, 77, 209–10; Alan Stripp, "The Enigma Machine: Its Mechanism and Use," in Hinsley and Stripp, *Codebreakers*, p. 84.

14. Stripp, "The Enigma Machine," pp. 84–85.

15. Ibid., p. 86.

16. Ibid.

17. Josef Garlinski, *The Enigma War* (New York: Scribner's, 1979), p. 17; Kahn, *Seizing the Enigma*, pp. 57–59.

18. Kahn, *Seizing the Enigma*, p. 58; Richard A. Woytak, "The Origins of the Ultra-Secret Code in Poland, 1937–1938," *Polish Review* 23, no. 3 (1978): 82.

19. Kahn, *Seizing the Enigma*, p. 78.

20. Ibid., pp. 79–80.

21. Diana Payne, "The Bombes," in Hinsley and Stripp, *Codebreakers*, p. 134.

22. Brown, "*C*," p. 250.

23. Tommy J. Smith, *Ultra in the Battle of Britain: The Key to Success?* (Carlisle Barracks, Pa.: U.S. Army War College, 1980), p. 6.

24. Ibid.

25. F. H. Hinsley, E. E. Thomas, C. F. G. Ransom, and R. C. Knight, *British Intelligence in the Second World War*, vol. 1 (New York: Cambridge University Press, 1979), p. 177.

26. Ibid.

27. Ronald Lewin, *Ultra Goes to War* (New York: Pocket Books, 1978), pp. 80–81; Hinsley et al., *British Intelligence*, pp. 177–78.

28. Hinsley et al., *British Intelligence*, p. 176.

29. Lewin, *Ultra Goes to War*, p. 81.

30. Hinsley et al., *British Intelligence*, pp. 180–81.

31. Ibid., pp. 178, 180.

32. Ibid., p.179; Lewin, *Ultra Goes to War*, p. 83. The official history's statement contrasted sharply with that of F. W. Winterbotham in his *The Ultra Secret* (New York: Harper & Row, 1974), pp. 47–48.

33. Henry F. Schorreck, "The Role of COMINT in the Battle of Midway," *Cryptologic Spectrum*, Summer 1975, p. 3.

34. Ibid., p. 4; Edwin T. Layton with Roger Pineau and John Costello, *"And I Was There": Pearl Harbor and Midway—Breaking the Secrets* (New York: Morrow, 1985), p. 407.

35. Schorreck, "The Role of COMINT," p. 4; Dan Van der Vat, *The Pacific*

Campaign: World War II, The U.S.–Japanese Naval War 1941–1945 (New York: Simon & Schuster, 1991), p. 181.

36. Schorreck, "The Role of COMINT," p. 6.

37. Ibid.

38. Ibid.; Layton with Pineau and Costello, *"And I Was There,"* pp. 390, 392; Gordon W. Prange with Donald W. Goldstein and Katherine V. Dillon, *Miracle at Midway* (New York: McGraw–Hill, 1982), p. 48.

39. Schorreck, "The Role of COMINT," p. 7.

40. Ronald Lewin, *The American Magic: Codes, Ciphers and the Defeat of Japan* (New York: Farrar, Straus, and Giroux, 1982), p. 104.

41. Schorreck, "The Role of COMINT," p. 8.

42. Ibid.

43. Ibid.; Layton with Pineau and Costello, *"And I Was There"* p. 412.; David Kahn, *The Codebreakers: The Story of Secret Writing* (New York: Macmillan, 1967), p. 569.

44. Layton, *"And I Was There,"* pp. 405, 413.

45. Schorreck, "The Role of COMINT," p. 8.

46. Ibid.; Lewin, *American Magic*, p. 106.

47. Layton with Pineau and Costello, *"And I Was There,"* p. 422.

48. Schorreck, "The Role of COMINT," p. 9.

49. Ibid.

50. Ibid., pp. 9, 10; Prange with Goldstein and Dillon, *Miracle at Midway*, p. 72.

51. Schorreck, "The Role of COMINT," p. 11.

52. Layton with Pineau and Costello, *"And I Was There,"* p. 433; Lewin, *American Magic*, pp. 109–10.

53. Lewin, *American Magic*, p. 110; Kahn, *Codebreakers*, pp. 572–73.

54. Kahn, *Codebreakers*, p. 573.

55. Roger Pineau, "A Code Break and the Death of Admiral Yamamoto," *Naval Intelligence Professionals Quarterly*, Summer 1989, p. 3.

56. Ibid.

57. Ibid., p. 4.

58. Ronald H. Spector, *Eagle against the Sun: The American War with Japan* (New York: Vintage, 1985), p. 230; Kahn, *Codebreakers*, pp. 600–601.

59. Timothy P. Mulligan, "Spies, Ciphers and 'Zitadelle': Intelligence and the Battle of Kursk, 1943," *Journal of Contemporary History* 22, no. 2 (1987): 241.

60. Ibid., pp. 240–41.

61. Ibid.; on FISH, see F. H. Hinsley, "An Introduction to Fish," in Hinsley and Stripp, *Codebreakers*, pp. 141–48.

62. Mulligan, "Spies, Ciphers, and 'Zitadelle,' p. 241; F. H. Hinsley, E. E. Thomas, and C. F. G. Ransom, *British Intelligence in the Second World War*, vol. 2 (New York: Cambridge University Press, 1981), p. 624.

63. Mulligan, "Spies, Ciphers, and 'Zitadelle,'" p. 242; Hinsley et al., *British Intelligence*, vol. 2, pp. 625–26.

64. Mulligan, "Spies, Ciphers and 'Zitadelle,'" p. 243.

65. Ibid., p. 249; Ralph Erskine, "The Soviets and Naval Enigma," *Intelligence and National Security* 4, no. 3 (1989): 503; P. S. Milner Barry, "The Soviets and Ultra: A Comment on Jukes' Hypothesis," *Intelligence and National Security*, 3, 2 (1988): p. 250.

66. Geoff Jukes, "The Soviets and Ultra," *Intelligence and National Security* 3, no. 2 (1988): 239.

67. Mulligan, "Spies, Ciphers and 'Zitadelle,'" p. 250.

68. Ibid., p. 246.

69. Ibid.

70. Ibid.

71. Hinsley et al., *British Intelligence*, vol. 2, p. 627.

72. National Security Agency, *American Signal Intelligence in Northwest Africa and Western Europe* (Ft. Meade, Md., NSA, 19), p. 114.

73. A. Sinkov and Leo Rosen, To: Assistant Chief of Staff, G-2, Subject: Report of Technical Mission to England, April 11, 1941, in "Collection of Memoranda on Operations of SIS Intercept Activities and Dissemination 1942-45," SRH-145, RG 457, MRB, NARA.

74. Ibid.

75. Ibid.; Bradley F. Smith, *The Ultra-Magic Deals, and the Most Secret Special Relationship, 1940–1946* (Novato, Calif.: Presidio, 1993), pp. 55–56.

76. Smith, *Ultra-Magic Deals*, p. 74.

77. Ibid., pp. 58, 61; Sinkov and Rosen, "Report of Technical Mission to England."

78. Smith, *Ultra-Magic Deals*, p. 89.

79. Ibid., p. 120.

80. Ibid., p. 125.

81. Ibid.

82. Ibid., pp. 125–27; National Security Agency, *American Signal Intelligence*, p. 119.

83. Smith, *Ultra-Magic Deals*, pp. 127–28.

84. Ibid., p. 139.

85. Ibid., p. 140; National Security Agency, *American Signal Intelligence*, p. 123.

86. Smith, *Ultra-Magic Deals*, p. 142; Parrish, *American Codebreakers*, p. 96.

87. Smith, *Ultra-Magic Deals*, pp. 142–43.

88. Ibid., p. 149–50.

89. Ibid., p. 153.

90. "An Account of the Origins and Development of 3-US," June 11, 1945, in "Operations of the Military Intelligence Service War Department London (MIS WD London), SRH-110, RG 457, MRB, NARA, pp. 39–42; National Security Agency, *American Signal Intelligence*, p. 123.

91. "An Account of the Origins," p. 39.

92. Ibid., pp. 39–40.

93. Ibid., p. 39.

94. Kahn, *Seizing the Enigma*, p. ix.

95. Ibid., pp. 5–6; Dan Van der Vat, *The Atlantic Campaign: World War II's Great Struggle at Sea* (New York: Harper & Row, 1988), pp. 149, 171.

96. Jurgen Rohwer, "Allied and Axis Radio-Intelligence in the Battle of the Atlantic: A Comparative Analysis," in Walter T. Hitchcock (ed.), *The Intelligence Revolution: A Historical Perspective* (Washington, D.C.: Office of Air Force History, 1991), p. 79.

97. Ibid., pp. 79–85; John Winton, *Ultra at Sea: How Breaking the Nazi Code Affected Allied Naval Strategy during World War II* (New York: Morrow, 1988), p. 105.

98. Winton, *Ultra at Sea,* pp. 22–23; Rohwer, "Allied and Axis Radio-Intelligence," p. 81.

99. Kahn, *Seizing the Enigma,* pp. 104–12.

100. Ibid., pp. 125–26; John Pearson, *The Life of Ian Fleming* (New York: McGraw-Hill, 1966), p. 95.

101. Kahn, *Seizing the Enigma,* pp. 129–30.

102. Ibid., pp. 135–37.

103. Ibid., p. 137.

104. Ralph Erskine, "Naval Enigma: The Breaking of Heimisch and Triton," *Intelligence and National Security* 3 no. 1 (9188): 163–64.

105. Kahn, *Seizing the Enigma,* p. 148.

106. Ibid., pp 154–55.

107. Ibid., pp. 159, 161.

108. Ibid., p. 169.

109. Ibid., p. 182; Winton, *Ultra at Sea,* p. 24; Rohwer, "Allied and Axis Radio-Intelligence," p. 82.

110. Kahn, *Seizing the Enigma,* p. 183.

111. Ibid., pp. 214, 217; Rohwer, "Allied and Axis Radio-Intelligence," p. 83.

112. Winton, *Ultra at Sea,* p. 105; Rohwer, "Allied and Axis Radio-Intelligence," pp. 85, 88; Kahn, *Seizing the Enigma,* p. 212.

113. Winton, *Ultra at Sea,* p. 105; Kahn, *Seizing the Enigma,* p. 215.

114. Rohwer, "Allied and Axis Radio-Intelligence," p. 87; Winton, *Ultra at Sea,* p. 106; Kahn, *Seizing the Enigma,* pp. 216–17.

115. Kahn, *Seizing the Enigma,* pp. 190, 226; Van der Vat, *The Atlantic Campaign,* p. 310.

116. Kahn, *Seizing the Enigma,* p. 227.

117. Ibid., pp. 229–30.

118. Ibid., pp. 227, 245.

119. Ibid., pp. 245, 258.

120. Ibid., p. 264.

121. Ibid., pp. 259–60.

122. Erskine, "Naval Enigma," p. 162.

12 Knowing the Enemy

1. David Kahn, *Hitler's Spies: German Military Intelligence in World War II* (New York: Macmillan, 1978), pp. 42–63.

2. Ibid., p. 419.

3. Ibid., p. 420; David Thomas, "Foreign Armies East and German Military Intelligence in Russia 1941–45," *Journal of Contemporary History* 22 (1987): 262.

4. Kahn, *Hitler's Spies,* p. 429; E. H. Cookridge, *Gehlen: Spy of the Century* (New York: Random House, 1971), pp. 53–54; Thomas, "Foreign Armies East," p. 275.

5. Kahn, *Hitler's Spies,* p. 429; Cookridge, *Gehlen,* pp. 12, 14, 16; Heinz Hohne and Hermann Zolling, *The General Was a Spy* (New York: Coward, McCann & Geohegan, 1971), p. 6.

6. Kahn, *Hitler's Spies,* p. 429; Hohne and Zolling, *The General,* p. 6; Cookridge, *Gehlen,* p. 33.

7. Cookridge, *Gehlen,* p. 33.

8. Ibid., p. 37; Hohne and Zolling, *The General*, pp. 7–8.

9. Cookridge, *Gehlen*, pp. 41–42; Hohne and Zolling, *The General*, p. 8; Kahn, *Hitler's Spies*, p. 429.

10. Thomas, "Foreign Armies East," p. 263.

11. Hohne and Zolling, *The General*, p. 10; Cookridge, *Gehlen*, p. 59.

12. Kahn, *Hitler's Spies*, pp. 430–31; Hohne and Zolling, *The General*, p. 13; Reinhard Gehlen, *The Service: The Memoirs of Reinhard Gehlen* (New York: World, 1972), p. 43.

13. Hohne and Zolling, *The General*, p. 14.

14. Cookridge, *Gehlen*, p. 60; Hohne and Zolling, *The General*, pp. 14–16; Thomas, "Foreign Armies East," pp. 263–64; Kahn, *Hitler's Spies*, p. 433.

15. Kahn, *Hitler's Spies*, pp. 432–33; Hohne and Zolling, *The General*, pp. 14–15; Thomas, "Foreign Armies East," pp. 263–64.

16. Kahn, *Hitler's Spies*, p. 433; Hohne and Zolling, *The General*, p. 28; Thomas, "Foreign Armies East," pp. 264.

17. Kahn, *Hitler's Spies*, p. 433.

18. Hohne and Zolling, *The General*, p. 16; Thomas, "Foreign Armies East," p. 264.

19. Kahn, *Hitler's Spies*, p. 434.

20. Hohne and Zolling, *The General*, p. 23–24.

21. Ibid., p. 24.

22. Ibid., p. 20.

23. Ibid.

24. Kahn, *Hitler's Spies*, p. 431.

25. Ibid., pp. 418, 431; Hohne and Zolling, *The General*, pp. 28–29.

26. Thomas, "Foreign Armies East," pp. 281–82.

27. Ibid., p. 282.

28. Ibid.

29. Ibid., p. 283.

30. Ibid.

31. Ibid., pp. 283–84.

32. Ibid., p. 284.

33. Ibid.

34. Ibid., p. 287.

35. Ibid.

36. Ibid., p. 286.

37. Barry M. Katz, *Foreign Intelligence: Research and Analysis in the Office of Strategic Services 1942–1945* (Cambridge, Mass.: Harvard University Press, 1989), p. 5.

38. Ibid.

39. Robin Winks, *Cloak and Gown: Scholars in the Secret War, 1939–1961* (New York: Morrow, 1987), p. 72.

40. Bradley F. Smith, *The Shadow Warriors: O.S.S. and the Origins of the C.I.A.* (New York: Basic Books, 1982), p. 361.

41. Ibid., p. 371.

42. Winks, *Cloak and Gown*, pp. 104–5.

43. File of R&A Reports, Civil Reference Division, NARA; Katz, *Foreign Intelligence*, p. 18.

44. Katz, *Foreign Intelligence*, p. 18.

45. "National Socialist Germany," R&A 376A, M-1221, MRR, NARA.

46. "German Morale after Tunisia," June 25, 1943, R&A 933, M-1221, MRR, NARA.

47. "Possible Political Changes in Nazi Germany in the Near Future," August 10, 1943, R&A 1034, M-1221, MRR, NARA.

48. "Changes in the Reich Government," August 26, 1943, R&A 1130, M-1221, MRR, NARA.

49. "Effects of the Attempted Coup d'État on the Stability of the German Regime," July 24, 1944, R&A 2383, M-1221, MRR, NARA, p. 5.

50. "South Germany," September 22, 1944, R&A 2332, M-1221, MRR, NARA.

51. "Social Relations in Japan," March 19, 1942, R&A 259, M-1221, MRR, NARA.

52. "Japanese Labor: The Labor Union Movement," n.d., R&A 117, M-1221, MRR, NARA.

53. "Japanese Films: A Phase of Psychological Warfare," March 30, 1944, R&A 1307, M-1221, MRR, NARA.

54. "Japan's Cliques: The 'Batsu,'" March 7, 1942, R&A 226, M-1221, MRR, NARA.

55. Katz, *Foreign Intelligence,* p. 105.

56. Ibid.

57. Ibid., p. 106.

58. Ibid.

59. Ibid.

60. Ibid., p. 107.

61. Ibid.

62. Robert J. Young, "Spokesmen for Economic Warfare: The Industrial Intelligence Centre in the 1930s," *European Studies Review* 6, no. 5 (1976): 475.

63. Wesley K. Wark, *The Ultimate Enemy: British Intelligence and Nazi Germany, 1933–1939* (Ithaca, N.Y.: Cornell University Press, 1985), pp. 159–61; F. H. Hinsley, E. E. Thomas, C. F. G. Ransom, and R. C. Knight, *British Intelligence in the Second World War,* vol. 1 (New York: Cambridge University Press, 1979), pp. 30–31.

64. Young, "Spokesmen for Economic Warfare," p. 477; Wark, *Ultimate Enemy,* p. 163.

65. Young, "Spokesmen for Economic Warfare," pp. 478–79.

66. Ibid., p. 479.

67. Ibid., pp. 484–85.

68. Ibid., pp. 473, 481.

69. Hinsley et al., *British Intelligence,* pp. 100–101, 225–26.

70. Ibid., pp. 100, 289.

71. F. H. Hinsley, E. E. Thomas, C. F. G. Ransom, and R. C. Knight, *British Intelligence in the Second World War,* vol. 2 (New York: Cambridge University Press, 1981), pp. 129, 131–33.

72. Ibid., p. 138.

73. Ibid.

74. Ibid.

75. Ibid., p. 133.

76. Ibid.

77. Ibid., p. 134.

78. Ibid., pp. 134–35; Alexander Werth, *Russia at War, 1941–1945* (New York: Carroll & Graf, 1964), pp. 404–5.

79. F. H. Hinsley, E. E. Thomas, C. A. G. Simkins, and C. F. G. Ransom, *British Intelligence in the Second World War,* vol. 3, pt. 2 (New York: Cambridge University Press, 1988), p. 923.

13 New Adversaries

1. John Lewis Gaddis, *The United States and the Origins of the Cold War* (New York: Columbia University Press, 1972), pp. 263–64; Lynn Etheridge Davis, *The Cold War Begins* (Princeton, N.J.: Princeton University Press, 1974), p. 294.

2. Thomas F. Troy, *Donovan and the CIA: A History of the Establishment of the Central Intelligence Agency* (Frederick, Md.: University Publications of America, 1981), p. 255.

3. Ibid., pp. 302, 461–63.

4. Ibid., p. 464.

5. U.S. Congress, House Permanent Select Committee on Intelligence, *Compilation of Intelligence Laws and Related Laws and Executive Orders of Interest to the National Intelligence Community* (Washington, D.C.: U.S. Government Printing Office, 1983), p. 7.

6. Vladislav M. Zubok, "Soviet Intelligence and the Cold War: The 'Small' Committee of Information, 1952–53," Working Paper No. 4, Cold War International History Project (Washington, D.C.: Woodrow Wilson International Center for Scholars, December 1992), pp. 3–4; Christopher Andrew and Oleg Gordievsky, *KGB: The Inside Story* (New York: Harper Collins, 1990), p. 381.

7. Andrew and Gordievsky, *KGB*, p. 381.

8. Ibid., pp. 381–82.

9. Ilya Dzhirvelov, *Secret Servant: My Life with the KGB & the Soviet Elite* (New York: Harper & Row, 1987), p. 105.

10. "The Committee of Information ('K.I.'), 1947–1951," November 17, 1954, pp. 3–4; Australian Archives Canberra, CRS, A 6823/XR1/56. The paper is based on the debriefing of Soviet defectors Vladimir and Evdokia Petrov, who defected in 1954.

11. Ibid., pp. 3, 7.

12. Harry Rositzke, *The CIA's Secret Operations: Espionage, Counterespionage and Covert Action* (New York: Reader's Digest Press, 1977), pp. 17–21.

13. Rositzke, *CIA's Secret Operations*, pp. 19–20, 38.

14. Letter from H. M. McCoy to Chief of Staff, United States Air Force, 23 November 1948, Subject: Photographic Equipment for 1 May 1949 USSR Air Show, RG 341, entry 214, file 2-5400–99, MRB, NARA.

15. Letter from Colonel Malcolm D. Seashore, chief, Air Technical Intelligence Center, to AFOIN-C/AA, Subject: (Secret) Procurement and Development of Photographic Equipment for Air Attachés, 27 February 1952, RG 341, entry 214, file 2-22000–99, MRB, NARA.

16. "Air Intelligence Information Report 140-49: Soviet Air Day Show," July 19, 1949, RG 341, entry 214, file 2-8566, MRB, NARA.

17. W. Stuart Symington, "Memorandum for General Spaatz," April 5, 1948.

18. "Limit of Offshore Distance for Reconnaissance Flights in Pacific Areas," July 27, 1948, RG 341, entry 214, file 2-3003–99, MRB, NARA.

19. *Study on Electronic and Other Aerial Reconnaissance, Appendix B*, November 10, 1949, RG 341, entry 214, file 2-3003–99, MRB, NARA.

20. Routing and Record Sheet for Memorandum from Major General George C. McDonald, director of intelligence, WAF, to Director of Plans and Operations, April 23, 1948, Subject: Photographic Coverage—Chukotski Peninsula Airfields, RG 341, entry 214, file 3-3000–99, MRB, NARA.

21. "Memorandum for the Record," March 15, 1949, RG 341, entry 214, file 6700–99, MRB, NARA; Major General C. P. Cabell, director of intelligence, USAF, to Major General Budway, Alaskan Air Command, December 27, 1948, RG 341, entry 214, file 2-5400–99, MRB, NARA.

22. "Memorandum of Photographic Reconnaissance of USSR," RG 341, entry 267, file 2-10103, MRB, NARA.

23. "Memorandum for the Record," October 24, 1949, RG 341, entry 214, file 2-9600–99, MRB, NARA; Letter from Colonel A. Hansen, chief, Reconnaissance Branch, Air Intelligence Requirements Division, Directorate of Intelligence to Aeronautical Chart Service, Subject: Transmittal of Photo Intelligence Reports, October 25, 1949, RG 341, entry 214, file 2-9600–99, MRB, NARA.

24. Letter from Major General C. P. Cabell, director of intelligence, USAF, to Commanding General, Alaskan Air Command, Subject: ECM Ferret Program—Alaskan Air Command, July 26, 1948, RG 341, entry 214, file 2-3000–99 MRB, NARA.

25. *Study on Electronic and Other Aerial Reconnaissance, Appendix A.*

26. Letter from Richard Meyer, 1985.

27. Andy Thomas, "British Signals Intelligence after the Second World War," *Intelligence and National Security* 3, no. 4 (1986): 105–6.

28. Jeffrey T. Richelson, *American Espionage and the Soviet Target* (New York: Quill, 1988), pp. 120–26.

29. Letter from Arnold Ross, April 1, 1985.

30. Robert J. Donovan, *Tumultuous Years: The Presidency of Harry S Truman, 1949–1953* (New York: Norton, 1982), p. 98.

31. Ibid.

32. Ibid., p. 99.

33. Kenneth Condit, *The History of the Joint Chiefs of Staff: The Joint Chiefs of Staff and National Policy,* vol. 2: *1947–1949* (Washington, D.C.: Historical Division, Joint Secretariat, JCS, 1964), p. 526.

34. *Unit History of 3rd Radio Squadron Mobile, U.S. Air Force Security Service,* January 1 to December 31, 1950, SRH-139, RG 457, MRB, NARA.

35. Bradley F. Smith, *The Ultra-Magic Deals, and the Most Secret Special Relationship, 1940–1946* (Novato, Calif.: Presidio, 1993), p. 216.

36. J. L. Granatstein and David Stafford, *Spy Wars: Espionage and Canada from Gouzenko to Glasnost* (Toronto: Key Porter, 1990), p. 45.

37. Ibid.

38. Anthony Cave Brown, *"C": The Secret Life of Sir Stewart Menzies, Spymaster to Winston Churchill* (New York: Macmillan, 1987), pp. 686–87.

39. Smith, *Ultra-Magic Deals,* p. 218.

40. Ibid.

41. Ibid., pp. 218–19.

42. Christopher Andrew, "The Growth of the Australian Intelligence Community and the Anglo-American Connection," *Intelligence and National Security* 4, no. 2 (1989): 224; Granatstein and Stafford, *Spy Wars,* pp. 45–46; John Sawatsky, *Men in the Shadows: The RCMP Security Service* (New York: Doubleday, 1980),

p. 9n; Chapman Pincher, *Inside Story: A Documentary of the Pursuit of Power* (New York: Stein & Day, 1979), p. 157.

43. Andrew and Gordievsky, *KGB*, p. 370; Sawatsky, *Men in the Shadows*, pp. 72–74; Verne W. Newton, *The Cambridge Spies: The Untold Story of Maclean, Philby, and Burgess in America* (Lanham, Md.: Madison Books, 1991), p. 92; Robert Lamphere and Tom Schachtman, *The FBI–KGB War: A Special Agent's Story* (New York: Random House, 1986), pp. 32–34. Gouzenko was one of the most difficult defectors any Western intelligence or security service ever had to deal with. See John Sawatsky, *Gouzenko: The Untold Story* (Toronto: Macmillan, 1984).

44. Andrew and Gordievsky, *KGB*, p. 370; Sawatsky, *Men in the Shadows*, p. 80; Justice Robert Taschereau and Justice R. L. Kellock, *The Report of the Royal Commission* (Ottawa: Controller of Stationery, 1946), pp. 85, 447.

45. Andrew and Gordievsky, *KGB*, p. 370; Sawatsky, *Men in the Shadows*, p. 86; James Barros, "Alger Hiss and Harry Dexter White: The Canadian Connection," *Orbis*, Fall 1977, pp. 593–605; Robert Bothwell and J. L. Granatstein, *The Gouzenko Transcripts: The Evidence Presented to the Kellock–Taschereau Royal Commission of 1946* (Ottawa: Deneau, 1982), p. 98. Gouzenko told his interrogators that "an assistant secretary of the Secretary of State's Department was supposed to be implicated." Hiss had been assistant to the assistant secretary of state, then special assistant to the director of the Office of Far Eastern Affairs, then special assistant to the director of the Office of Special Political Affairs, and finally director of that office. See Granatstein and Stafford, *Spy Wars*, p. 64.

46. Andrew and Gordievsky, *KGB*, p. 370; Newton, *Cambridge Spies*, pp. 95, 128, 142, 216; Lamphere, *FBI–KGB War*, p. 36.

47. Andrew and Gordievsky, *KGB*, pp. 368–69.

48. Ibid., p. 374; Lamphere, *FBI–KGB War*, p. 82.

49. Andrew and Gordievsky, *KGB*, p. 373; David Martin, *Wilderness of Mirrors* (New York: Harper & Row, 1980), pp. 39–40; Peter Wright, *Spycatcher: The Candid Autobiography of a Senior Intelligence Officer* (New York: Viking, 1987), pp. 179–80, 182.

50. Andrew and Gordievsky, *KGB*, p. 374; Wright, *Spycatcher*, p. 181.

51. Federal Bureau of Investigation, *Summary Brief: Donald Duart Maclean, Guy Francis de Moncy Burgess, Harold Adrian Russell Philby*, November 5, 1955, p. 1.

52. Newton, *Cambridge Spies*, pp.136–37.

53. Ibid., p.147; Federal Bureau of Investigation, *Summary Brief: Donald Duart Maclean, Guy Francis de Moncy Burgess*, November 5, 1955 (revised August 10, 1956), pp. 15, 41; A. H. Belmont to L. V. Boardman, Subject: Donald Duart Maclean, Guy Francis de Moncy Burgess, Espionage-R, November 5, 1955, p. 4.

54. Newton, *Cambridge Spies*, p. 175; Federal Bureau of Investigation, *Summary Brief*, November 5, 1955, pp. 15, 41; A. H. Belmont to L. V. Boardman, Subject: Donald Duart Maclean, November 5, 1955, p. 4.

55. Newton, *The Cambridge Spies*, p. 160.

56. Andrew and Gordievsky, *KGB*, p. 377; Federal Bureau of Investigation, Subject: Donald Duart Maclean, Guy Francis de Moncy Burgess, June 19, 1951, FBI File Number 100-374183, Serial 1-175, pp. 108–10.

57. Barrie Penrose and Simon Freeman, *Conspiracy of Silence: The Secret Life of Anthony Blunt* (New York: Vintage, 1988), p. 324. Before arriving in the Far Eastern Department Burgess spent three months in the Foreign Office's covert

Information Research Department, responsible for black propaganda. Burgess undoubtedly provided the Soviets with details of the IRD's staff and operations. See Andrew and Gordievsky, *KGB*, p. 392.

58. Brown, *"C,"* p. 699; Andrew and Gordievsky, *KGB*, p. 393.

59. Newton, *Cambridge Spies*, pp. 81, 228.

60. Lamphere, *FBI–KGB War*, pp. 133–34; Robert Chadwell Williams, *Klaus Fuchs, Atom Spy* (Cambridge, Mass.: Harvard University Press, 1987), pp. 117–18.

61. Newton, *Cambridge Spies*, pp. 251–52; Andrew and Gordievsky, *KGB*, pp. 379–80; Lamphere, *FBI–KGB War*, pp. 151, 174–76. Elizabeth Bentley had also named a "Julius," whom she believed lived in the Knickerbocker Village complex in New York, where the Rosenbergs lived.

62. Andrew and Gordievsky, *KGB*, pp. 379–80. At the time the RAND Corporation had produced a 346-page study on space satellites. Rosenberg's ring included William Perl, an engineer at the NACA in Cleveland, where he worked on the atomic plane and other projects. It was thought he might have copied research reports on other projects. In 1953, when a new MiG fighter appeared in Korea, the Air Force noted that the MiGs had an unusual tail design similar to an American design developed from NACA antiturbulence research. Other members were Joel Barr (named in VENONA decrypts) and Alfred Sarant, who fled to the Soviet Union, changed their names, and became the chief engineer and chief designer respectively of an important Leningrad design bureau. See Lamphere, *The FBI–KGB War*, pp. 250, 298; William J. Broad, "How a Soviet Secret Was Finally Pierced," *New York Times*, June 26, 1984, pp. C1, C7.

63. Newton, *Cambridge Spies*, p. 322; Andrew and Gordievsky, *KGB*, p. 396.

64. Andrew and Gordievsky, *KGB*, p. 396.

65. Ibid., pp. 397–98.

66. Ibid.

67. Ibid., pp. 398–99; The National Cryptologic School, *On Watch: Profiles from the National Security Agency's Past 40 Years* (Fort George G. Meade, Md.: NCS, September 1986), p. 19. Both died in Moscow, Burgess in 1963 and Maclean in 1983.

68. Andrew and Gordievsky, *KGB*, pp. 399–400.

69. Newton, *Cambridge Spies*, p. 336; Martin, *Wilderness of Mirrors*, p. 54; Andrew and Gordievsky, *KGB*, p. 401; Kim Philby, *My Silent War* (New York: Dell/Grove, 1968), p. 197; Memorandum For: Chief of Staff [Deleted], Subject: Guy Francis De Moncy BURGESS, Central Intelligence Agency, June 18, 1951.

70. Brown, *"C,"* pp. 707–9.

71. Ibid., p. 710; Andrew and Gordievsky, *KGB*, pp. 401–2. In 1963 after a Soviet defector confirmed Philby's guilt he defected to the Soviet Union where he died in 1989.

72. Richard Hall, *The Rhodes Scholar Spy* (Sydney: Random House, Australia, 1991), pp. 104–5.

73. Ibid., p. 121.

74. Ibid., pp. 30–47, 172–73; Andrew and Gordievsky, *KGB*, pp. 374–75.

14 New Players

1. Roger Faligot and Pascal Krop, *La Piscine: The French Secret Service since 1984* (New York: Basil Blackwell, 1989), pp. 11–12, 15; P. L. Thyraud de Vosjoli, *Lamia* (Boston: Little, Brown, 1970), pp. 71–72.

2. De Vosjoli, *Lamia*, pp. 77–78.

3. Faligot and Krop, *La Piscine*, pp. 17–18.

4. Ibid., p. 22; De Vosjoli, *Lamia*, pp. 133–34; Roger Faligot, "The Plot to Unseat Qaddafi," *Middle East*, August 1981, pp. 32–36.

5. Heinz Hohne and Hermann Zolling, *The General Was a Spy* (New York: Coward, McCann & Geohegan, 1971), pp. 52–54, Mary Ellen Reese, *General Reinhard Gehlen: The CIA Connection* (Fairfax, Va.: George Mason University Press, 1990), p. 4; Reinhard Gehlen, *The Service: The Memoirs of General Reinhard Gehlen* (New York: World, 1972), p. 106.

6. Hohne and Zolling, *The General*, p. 54; Gehlen, *The Service*, p. 109.

7. Hohne and Zolling, *The General*, pp. 55–57; E. H. Cookridge, *Gehlen: Spy of the Century* (New York: Random House, 1972), pp. 117–18; Ian Sayer and Douglas Botting, *America's Secret Army: The Untold Story of the Counterintelligence Corps* (New York: Watts, 1989), p. 340.

8. Hohne and Zolling, *The General*, pp. 57–59; Reese, *General Reinhard Gehlen*, pp. 40–41; Sayer and Botting, *America's Secret Army*, p. 340.

9. Hohne and Zolling, *The General*, pp. 60–61.

10. Ibid., pp. 61–62.

11. Ibid., p. 62; Reese, *General Reinhard Gehlen*, pp. 47–48.

12. Hohne and Zolling, *The General*, pp. 62–63.

13. Ibid., pp. 64–65.

14. Ibid., p. 67.

15. Reese, *General Reinhard Gehlen*, pp. 72, 77; Gehlen, *The Service*, p. 126.

16. Reese, *General Reinhard Gehlen*, p. 88; Gehlen, *The Service*, p. 142.

17. Reese, *General Reinhard Gehlen*, pp. 90, 99–100, 106.

18. Ibid., pp. 106–7.

19. Ibid., p. 107.

20. Ibid., p. 107–8.

21. Ibid., p. 111.

22. Ibid., p. 108; Gehlen, *The Service*, p. 143.

23. Cookridge, *Gehlen*, p. 231; Hohne and Zolling, *The General*, pp. 116–21.

24. Hohne and Zolling, *The General*, p. 149.

25. Gehlen, *The Service*, pp. 162–63, 374.

26. Jefferson Adams, "Crisis and Resurgence: East German State Security," *International Journal of Intelligence and Counterintelligence* 2, no. 4 (1988): 497; "More on Mischa," *Foreign Report*, November 8, 1984, pp. 1–4.

27. Pierre de Villemarest, *Le Coup d'État de Markus Wolf: La guerre secrete des deux Allemagnes* (Paris: Stock, 1991), p. 95; Adams, "Crisis and Resurgence"; p. 497; "More on Misha."

28. Adams, "Crisis and Resurgence" p. 497; "More on Misha."

29. De Villemarest, *Le Coup d'État*, pp. 137–38; Norman M. Naimark, "'To Know Everything and to Report Everything Worth Knowing': Building the East German Police State, 1945–1949," (Washington, D.C.: Woodrow Wilson International Center for Scholars, 1994), p. 8.

30. Adams, "Crisis and Resurgence," pp. 496–97; J. A. Emerson Vermaat, "The East German Secret Service Structure and Operational Focus," *Conflict Quarterly*, Fall 1987, pp. 46–47.

31. Adams, "Crisis and Resurgence," p. 497.

32. William R. Corson and Robert T. Crowley, *The New KGB: Engine of Soviet Power* (New York: Quill, 1986), p. 254.

33. Ibid., pp. 254–55.

34. Ibid., pp. 255–56.

35. Samuel M. Katz, *Soldier Spies: Israeli Military Intelligence* (Novato, Ca.: Presidio, 1992), p. 41.

36. Central Intelligence Agency, *Foreign Intelligence and Security Services: Israel* (Washington, D.C.: CIA, 1977), p. 7.

37. Katz, *Soldier Spies*, pp. 14, 16.

38. Central Intelligence Agency, *Foreign Intelligence and Security Services: Israel*, p. 7; Katz, *Soldier Spies*, p. 12–13.

39. Ibid., p. 13; Richard Deacon, *The Israeli Secret Service* (New York: Taplinger, 1977), p. 39.

40. Katz, *Soldier Spies*, pp. 58–61.

41. Ian Black and Jeremy Morris, *Israel's Secret Wars: A History of Israel's Intelligence Services* (New York: Grove-Weidenfeld, 1991), p. 55; Katz, *Soldier Spies*, pp. 46–47.

42. Black and Morris, *Israel's Secret Wars*, p. 71; Katz, *Soldier Spies*, p. 46.

43. Katz, *Soldier Spies*, p. 47.

44. Stewart Steven, *The Spymasters of Israel* (New York: Macmillan, 1977), pp. 39–40.

45. Ibid., pp. 40–43; Black and Morris, *Israel's Secret Wars*, p. 25.

46. Black and Morris, *Israel's Secret Wars*, p. 78.

47. Stanley A. Blumberg and Gwinn Owens, *The Survival Factor: Israeli Intelligence from World War I to the Present* (New York: G. P. Putnam, 1981), pp. 154–55.

48. Steven, *Spymasters*, p. 31; Black and Morris, *Israel's Secret Wars*, pp. 83–84; Katz, *Soldier Spies*, p. 67.

49. Steven, *Spymasters*, pp. 32–33; Central Intelligence Agency, *Foreign Intelligence and Security Services: Israel*, pp. 7–8; Yossi Melman and Dan Raviv, *The Imperfect Spies: The History of Israeli Intelligence* (London: Sidgwick and Jackson, 1989), p. 56.

50. Melman and Raviv, *Imperfect Spies*, pp. 56–57, 74; Black and Morris, *Israel's Secret Wars*, pp. 72, 96–97.

51. Steven, *Spymasters*, pp. 36–37.

52. David Anthony Reynolds, "A Comparative Analysis of the Respective Roles and Power of the KGB and Chinese Intelligence/Security Apparatus in Domestic Politics," M.A. thesis, Boston University, February 1984, pp. 61–62.

53. John Byron and Robert Pack, *The Claws of the Dragon: Kang Sheng* (New York: Simon & Schuster, 1992), pp. 91–93, 95.

54. Ibid., pp. 99–102.

55. Ibid., pp. 17, 53, 57, 68–69.

56. Ibid., p. 103.

57. Ibid., pp. 112, 129.

58. Ibid., pp. 149, 155–56; Reynolds, "A Comparative Analysis," pp. 62–64; Warren Kuo, "CCP Wartime Secret Service and Underground Struggle, Part 1," *Issues and Studies*, August 1970, pp. 57–58.

59. Reynolds, "A Comparative Analysis," p. 65; Kuo, "CCP Wartime Secret Service, Part 1," p. 63.

60. Kuo, "CCP Wartime Secret Service, Part 1," p. 59.

61. Ibid.; Reynolds, "A Comparative Analysis," p. 64.

62. Reynolds, "A Comparative Analysis," p. 81.

63. Byron and Pack, *Claws of the Dragon*, p. 189.

64. Reynolds, "A Comparative Analysis," pp. 78–79.

15 Secret Wars

1. U.S. Congress, Senate Select Committee to Study Governmental Operations with Respect to Intelligence Activities, *Final Report, Book IV: Supplementary Detailed Staff Reports on Foreign and Military Intelligence* (Washington, D.C.: U.S. Government Printing Office, 1976), p. 28; Trevor Barnes, "The Secret Cold War: The C.I.A. and American Foreign Policy in Europe, 1946–1956, Part I," *Historical Journal* 24 no. 2 (1981): 412.

2. Thomas Powers, *The Man Who Kept the Secrets: Richard Helms and the CIA* (New York: Knopf, 1979), p. 30; Barnes, "The Secret Cold War," pp. 412–13.

3. U.S. Congress, Senate Select Committee, *Final Report, Book IV*, p. 29.; Barnes, "The Secret Cold War," p. 413.

4. "A Report to the National Security Council by the Executive Secretary on Office of Special Projects," June 18, 1948, NSC 10/2, pp. 1, 3.

5. U.S. Congress, Senate Select Committee, *Final Report, Book IV*, p. 30.

6. John Prados, *Presidents' Secret Wars: CIA and Pentagon Covert Operations from World War II through Iranscam* (New York: Quill, 1988), p. 33.

7. Prados, *Presidents' Secret Wars*, p. 55.

8. Ibid., pp. 40–41.

9. Ibid., pp. 41–42.

10. Ibid., pp. 42–43.

11. Ibid., pp. 43–44.

12. Ibid., pp. 55–56; Harry Rositzke, *The CIA's Secret Operations: Espionage, Counterespionage and Covert Action* (New York: Reader's Digest Press, 1977), p. 168.

13. Prados, *Presidents' Secret Wars*, pp. 56–57.

14. Ibid., p. 57.

15. Ibid., pp. 57–58; Rositzke, *CIA's Secret Operations*, pp. 168–69.

16. Roger Faligot and Pascal Krop, *La Piscine: The French Secret Service since 1944* (New York: Basil Blackwell, 1989), p. 75.

17. Ibid., pp. 77–78.

18. Powers, *Man Who Kept the Secrets*, p. 41.

19. Rositzke, *CIA's Secret Operations*, p. 171; John Ranelagh, *The Agency: The Rise and Decline of the CIA* (New York: Simon & Schuster, 1985), p. 227.

20. Rositzke, *CIA's Secret Operations*, pp. 170–71; Ranelagh, *The Agency*, p. 227.

21. Gregory F. Treverton, *Covert Action: The Limits of Intervention in the Postwar World* (New York: Basic Books, 1987), p. 44.

22. "A Report to the President by the National Security Council on the Position of the United States with Respect to Iran," June 27, 1951, NSC 107/2, pp. 1–2.

23. Ibid., p. 1; Prados, *Presidents' Secret Wars*, p. 93; Kermit Roosevelt, *Countercoup: The Struggle for Control of Iran* (New York: McGraw-Hill, 1979), pp. 3, 107, 119.

24. Roosevelt, *Countercoup*, pp. 1–2, 19.

25. Prados, *Presidents' Secret Wars*, p. 95.

26. Ibid., pp. 95–96; Treverton, *Covert Action*, p. 56.

27. Prados, *Presidents' Secret Wars*, pp. 96–97; Treverton, *Covert Action*, p. 66.

28. Prados, *Presidents' Secret Wars*, p. 97; Treverton, *Covert Action*, pp. 66–68.

29. Stewart Steven, *Spymasters of Israel* (New York: Macmillan, 1980), pp. 64–67; Samuel M. Katz, *Soldier Spies: Israeli Military Intelligence* (Novato, Calif.: Presidio, 1992), pp. 81–82; Ian Black and Benny Morris, *Israel's Secret Wars: A History of Israel's Intelligence Services* (New York: Grove-Weidenfeld, 1991), p. 108.

30. Katz, *Soldier Spies*, pp. 82, 85; Black and Morris, *Israel's Secret Wars*, p. 108.

31. Black and Morris, *Israel's Secret Wars*, p. 108.

32. Katz, *Soldier Spies*, p. 91.

33. Ibid., p. 89; Black and Morris, *Israel's Secret Wars*, p. 109.

34. Steven, *Spymasters of Israel*, p. 69; Katz, *Soldier Spies*, p. 92; Black and Morris, *Israel's Secret Wars*, p. 111.

35. Katz, *Soldier Spies*, p. 92.

36. Ibid., pp. 92–93.

37. Steven, *Spymasters of Israel*, pp. 75–82; Black and Morris, *Israel's Secret Wars*, pp. 111–13.

38. Martin Ebon, *The Soviet Propaganda Machine* (New York: McGraw-Hill, 1987), p. 100.

39. U.S. Department of State, "World Peace Council: Instrument of Soviet Foreign Policy," *Foreign Affairs Note*, April 1982.

40. U.S. Department of State, "World Federation of Trade Unions: Soviet Foreign Policy Tool," *Foreign Affairs Note*, August 1983; Central Intelligence Agency, "Soviet Covert Action and Propaganda," in U.S. Congress, House Permanent Select Committee on Intelligence, *Soviet Covert Action (The Forgery Offensive)* (Washington, D.C.: U.S. Government Printing Office, 1980), p. 80n29.

41. Central Intelligence Agency, "Soviet Covert Action and Propaganda," in U.S. Congress, House Permanent Select Committee on Intelligence, *Soviet Covert Action*, pp. 79, 80n29

42. Ebon, *The Soviet Propaganda Machine*, pp.101–2.

43. Central Intelligence Agency, "Soviet Use of Assassination and Kidnapping," February 17, 1964, p. 1; John Barron, *KGB: The Secret Work of Soviet Secret Agents* (New York: Reader's Digest Press, 1974), p. 311.

44. Central Intelligence Agency, "Soviet Use of Assassination and Kidnapping," p.3; Harry Rositzke, *The KGB: Eyes of Russia* (Garden City, N.Y.: Doubleday, 1981), p. 104.

45. "Specialized Soviet Assassination Weapons," *ONI Review* 9, no. 12 (1954): 510–12.

46. Ibid.

47. Ibid.

48. Central Intelligence Agency, "Soviet Use of Assassination and Kidnapping," pp. 19–20; Rositzke, *KGB*, p. 109.

49. Central Intelligence Agency, "Soviet Use of Assassination and Kidnapping," pp. 20–21; Rositzke, *KGB*, pp. 108–9.

50. Barron, *KGB*, pp. 315–16.

51. Ibid., pp. 316–17.

52. P. L. Thyraud de Vosjoli, *Lamia* (Boston: Little, Brown, 1970), pp. 255–56.

53. Faligot and Krop, *La Piscine*, pp. 157–59.

54. De Vosjoli, *Lamia*, p. 257.

55. Ibid., p. 261.

16 Superpower Espionage

1. Telegram from USAIRA, Moscow to Chief of Staff, U.S. Air Force, July 31, 1953, RG 341, entry 214, file 3-2900–99, MRB, NARA.

2. "Air Intelligence Information Report IR 40-53: Radar Signal Emanations," March 10, 1953, RG 341, entry 267, file 3-1000–99, MRB, NARA.

3. USAF, Directorate of Intelligence, *History of AFOIN-1, 1 July 1954 thru 31 December 1954*, RG 341, entry 214, file 5-530, MRB, NARA.

4. Philip Agee, *Inside the Company: CIA Diary* (New York: Stonehill, 1975), p. 68; Harry Rositzke, *The CIA's Secret Operations: Espionage, Counterespionage and Covert Action* (New York: Reader's Digest Press, 1977), p. 57.

5. Rositzke, *CIA's Secret Operations*, pp. 57–58.

6. Ibid., p. 60.

7. William Hood, *Mole* (New York: Norton, 1982), pp. 26, 104; Nigel West, *The Circus: MI 5 Operations, 1945–1972* (Briarcliff Manor, N.Y.: Stein and Day, 1983), p. 64.

8. Hood, *Mole*, pp. 63–64, 74, 127.

9. Ibid., pp. 170, 173, 251.

10. Vessie E. Hardy, *Historical Data Report for the 37th Radio Squadron Mobile, April 1, 1953 to June 30, 1953*, prepared for the Historical Office, 37th Radio Squadron Mobile, p. 2.

11. Interview.

12. Interview.

13. Duncan Campbell, *The Unsinkable Aircraft Carrier: American Military Power in Britain* (London: Michael Joseph, 1984), p. 154; Gabriel Marshall, "Chicksands—a rich legacy," *Spokesman*, July 1994, pp. 24–25.

14. Letter from Colonel Conrad J. Herlick, deputy, Commitments and Priorities, Operations and Commitments Division, Directorate of Operations, to the Director of Requirements DCS/D, Subject: (TS) Establishment of Ground Based ECM Unit in Turkey, October 2, 1951, RG 341, entry 214, file 2-23500–00, MRB, NARA; Wilham Dacko and Arthur Langenkamp, *Historical Data Report for Project Penn, January 1, 1953 through March 31, 1953*, Air Force Historical Office, Chap. 1.

15. Interview.

16. Marvine Howe, "U.S. and Turks Monitor Soviet at Isolated Post," *New York Times*, January 4, 1981, p. 7; Michael Getler, "U.S. Intelligence Facilities in Turkey Get New Attention after Iran Turmoil," *Washington Post*, February 9, 1979, p. A15; U.S. Congress, Senate Foreign Relations Committee, *Fiscal Year 1980 International Security Assistance Authorization* (Washington, D.C.: U.S. Government Printing Office, 1979), p. 365; U.S. Congress, House Committee on International Relations, *United States Military Installations and Objectives in Mediterranean* (Washington, D.C.: U.S. Government Printing Office, 1977), p. 39.

17. "How the U.S. Taps Soviet Missile Secrets," *Aviation Week & Space Technology*, October 21, 1957, pp. 26–27.

18. Ibid.

19. "Memorandum for the Record," June 19, 1951, RG 341, entry 214, file 2-20200–99, MRB, NARA.

20. *History of the 91st Strategic Reconnaissance Squadron, Medium, Photo, 1 October 1951 through 31 October 1951* (Yokota AB, Japan: 91st SRS, Medium, Photo, 1951), p. 30.

21. Letter from Carl Espe, Director of Naval Intelligence, to Major General J. A. Samford, Director of Intelligence, USAF, Subject: Request for Photography, May 25, 1954, RG 341, entry 214, file 4-1114–1290, MRB, NARA.

22. Campbell, *Unsinkable Aircraft Carrier*, pp. 127–28, 131.

23. Interview.

24. Thomas W. Lippman, "138 Reported Missing in U.S. Spy Flights," *Washington Post*, March 5, 1993, p. A28, "Flier's Remains Held By Russia, Family Says," *New York Times*, November 11, 1992, p. A19.

25. National Security Agency, "Incidents Involving U.S. Recon Missions," n.d.; Air Force Security Service, Air Force Special Communications Center, Special Research Study 1–59, "Review of Reactions to Reconnaissance Flights since 1952," January 27, 1959, p. 4; "Flier's Remains Held By Russia"; "Russians find bones of U.S. airman," *Washington Times*, September 15, 1994, p. A13.

26. National Security Agency, "Incidents Involving U.S. Recon Missions"; Air Force Security Service, Air Force Special Communications Center, "Resume of 'Incidents' or 'Shoot Downs' Related to U.S. Ferret Flights Near Communist Territory," September 14, 1956, p. 5; Department of State, "U.S. Note on Shooting Down of American Plane by Soviet MIG Aircraft," August 5, 1953; RG 59, Box 55, Civil Reference Division, NARA.

27. Department of State, "U.S. Note on Shooting Down of American Plane by Soviet MIG Aircraft"; "Flights of the Ferrets," *U.S. News & World Report*, March 15, 1993, pp. 44–45; William E. Burrows, "Beyond the Iron Curtain," *Air & Space*, August/September 1994, pp. 34–35.

28. Air Force Security Service, Air Force Special Communications Center, "Review of Reactions to Reconnaissance Flights since 1952," pp. 2–3; Richard Fitts (ed.), *The Strategy of Electromagnetic Conflict* (Los Altos, Calif.: Peninsula Press, 1980), p. 63; "Secrets of the Cold War," *U.S. News & World Report*, March 15, 1993, pp. 32–33.

29. John Ranelagh, *The Agency: The Rise and Decline of the CIA* (New York: Simon & Schuster, 1986), p. 289; CIA, *The Berlin Tunnel Operation*, [deleted]—*1956*, June 24, 1968, pp. 1–2.

30. Ranelagh, *The Agency*, p. 290.

31. Ibid., p. 291; CIA, *Berlin Tunnel Operation*, pp. 10, 11.

32. Ranelagh, *The Agency*, p. 293; CIA, *Berlin Tunnel Operation*, p. 6.

33. CIA, *Berlin Tunnel Operation*, p. 23; Ranelagh, *The Agency*, p. 294.

34. George Blake, *No Other Choice* (New York: Simon & Schuster, 1990), pp. 180–82; Ranelagh, *The Agency*, pp. 289, 295.

35. David Martin, *Wilderness of Mirrors* (New York: Harper & Row, 1980), p. 88.

36. Ibid., p. 75.

37. NSA document in the author's possession.

38. Oral history interview with Robert Amory, Jr., February 9, 1966, JFK Library, Cambridge, Mass., pp. 113–14.

39. A. J. Goodpaster, "Memorandum of Conference with the President, 0810, 24 November 1954," November 24, 1954, ACW Diary, Nov. 54, box 3, ACWD,

ACWF, DDE Papers as President, DDEL; Thomas Powers, *The Man Who Kept the Secrets: Richard Helms and the CIA* (New York: Knopf, 1979), p. 95; Ranelagh, *The Agency*, p. 313.

40. Ranelagh, *The Agency*, p. 312.

41. Ibid., p. 314.

42. Powers, *Man Who Kept the Secrets*, p. 96; "U.S. to Continue U-2 Flights over Soviet," *Aviation Week*, May 16, 1960, pp. 26–27; William E. Burrows, *Deep Black: Space Espionage and National Security* (New York: Random House, 1986), pp. 77–78.

43. Powers, *Man Who Kept the Secrets*, p. 96; "U.S. to Continue U-2 Flights over Soviet."

44. Dwight D. Eisenhower, *Waging Peace, 1956–1961* (Garden City, N.Y.: Doubleday, 1965), p. 41.

45. Jay Miller, *Lockheed U-2* (Austin, Tex.: Aerofax, 1983), p. 25.

46. Ibid., pp. 26–27.

47. Michael R. Beschloss, *Mayday: Eisenhower, Khrushchev and the U-2 Affair* (New York: Harper & Row, 1986), pp. 111–12; Chris Pocock, *Dragon Lady: The History of the U-2 Spyplane* (Shrewsbury, U.K.: Airlife, 1989), p. 25.

48. Beschloss, *Mayday*, p. 120; Rudolf Tamnes, *The United States and the Cold War in the High North* (Oslo, Norway: ad Notam, 1991), p. 12.

49. Pocock, *Dragon Lady*, p. 27.

50. Leonard Mosley, *Dulles: A Biography of Eleanor, Allen and John Foster and Their Family Network* (New York: Dial, 1978), p. 365; Miller, *Lockheed U-2*, pp. 26–30; Tamnes, *United States and the Cold War*, p. 128; Pocock, *Dragon Lady*, pp. 27–28.

51. Miller, *Lockheed U-2*, pp. 26–30; Mosley, *Dulles*, p. 368.

52. John Prados, *The Soviet Estimate*, pp. 45–46.

53. "Soviet Note No. 23," July 10, 1956, White House Correspondence General, 1956(3), box 3, John Foster Dulles Papers, White House Memoranda, DDEL.

54. Richard Bissell, Jr., interview with author, Farmington, Conn., June 6, 1984; Mosley, *Dulles*, p. 368.

55. Miller, *Lockheed U-2*, pp. 27, 30; Francis Gary Powers, *Operation Overflight* (New York: Holt, Rinehart & Winston, 1970), pp. 61–62; Beschloss, *Mayday*, pp. 147, 155.

56. Quoted in Ranelagh, *The Agency*, p. 317.

57. Powers, *Operation Overflight*, p. 46.

58. Ibid., p. 47.

59. Miller, *Lockheed U-2*, p. 30.

60. Pocock, *Dragon Lady*, pp. 45–46; Nick Cook, "How the CIA and RAF Teamed to Spy on the Soviet Union," *Jane's Defence Weekly*, August 7, 1993, pp. 11–15.

61. Miller, *Lockheed U-2*, p. 28; Interview with Richard M. Bissell, Jr., by Dr. Thomas Soapes, oral historian, DDEL, November 9, 1976, p. 47; Tamnes, *United States and the Cold War*, pp. 127–28.

62. Interview.

63. Rostizke, *CIA's Secret Operations*, pp. 58–59.

64. Ibid.

65. Ibid., pp. 59–60.

66. Ibid., p. 59.

67. West, *The Circus*, p. 64; Martin, *Wilderness of Mirrors*, p. 94.

68. Rositzke, *CIA's Secret Operations*, pp. 68–69.

69. Central Intelligence Agency, *Foreign Intelligence and Security Services: USSR* (Washington, D.C.: CIA, 1975), p. 6.

70. Ibid.

71. Ibid., pp. 6–7; Robert Conquest, *The Soviet Police System* (London: Bodley Head, 1968), p. 15.

72. Christopher Andrew and Oleg Gordievsky, *KGB: The Inside Story* (New York: Harper Collins, 1990), pp. 438–39.

73. Central Intelligence Agency, *Foreign Intelligence and Security Services: USSR* (Washington, D.C.: CIA, 1975), p. 69; Andrew and Gordievsky, *KGB*, pp. 442–43.

74. Andrew and Gordievsky, *KGB*, p. 444.

75. Ibid., p. 445.

76. Ibid., p. 450.

77. Thomas Whiteside, *An Agent in Place* (New York: Ballantine, 1983), pp. 47, 49.

78. Ibid., pp. 68–69.

79. Ibid., p. 71.

80. Ibid., p. 72.

17 Spies and Moles

1. David Wise, *Molehunt: The Secret Search for Traitors that Shattered the CIA* (New York: Random House, 1992), p. 24; Mary Ellen Reese, *General Reinhard Gehlen: The CIA Connection* (Fairfax, Va.: George Mason University Press, 1990), pp. 153–54.

2. Wise, *Molehunt*, pp. 24–25.

3. Reese, *General Reinhard Gehlen*, p. 144; Heinz Hohne and Hermann Zolling, *The General Was a Spy* (New York: Coward, McCann & Geohegan, 1971), pp. 245–50.

4. Reese, *General Reinhard Gehlen*, p. 143; Hohne and Zolling, *The General*, pp. 245–47.

5. Reese, *General Reinhard Gehlen*, p. 145.

6. Ibid., p. 146.

7. Ibid., p. 147.

8. Ibid., p.150; Hohne and Zolling, *The General*, p. 252.

9. Reese, *General Reinhard Gehlen*, p. 155.

10. Ibid., pp. 155, 159, 223n23.

11. Gordon Brook-Shepherd, *The Storm Birds: Soviet Post-War Defectors* (London: Weidenfeld & Nicolson, 1988), pp. 140–41; Oleg Penkovskiy, *The Penkovskiy Papers* (Garden City, N.Y.: Doubleday, 1965), pp. 30–31; Greville Wynne, *The Man from Odessa: The Secret Career of a British Agent* (London: Granada, 1983), p. 203. *The Penkovskiy Papers* was a CIA-constructed work based on, at most, information passed on by Penkovskiy, rather than being an actual memoir. Much of the book consists of commentary by Frank Gibney. Information from portions written by Gibney are cited as "Gibney, *Penkovskiy Papers*," while portions attributed to Penkovskiy are cited as "Penkovskiy, *Penkovskiy Papers*."

12. Penkovskiy, *Penkovskiy Papers*, pp. 29–31; Wynne, *The Man from Odessa*, p. 203; Gibney, *Penkovskiy Papers*, p. 7.

13. Brook-Shepherd, *The Storm Birds*, p. 142; Penkovskiy, *Penkovskiy Papers*, pp. 31, 52; Gibney, *Penkovskiy Papers*, p. 61.

14. Brook-Shepherd, *Storm Birds*, p. 145.

15. Jerrold L. Schechter and Peter S. Deriabin, *The Spy Who Saved the World: How a Soviet Colonel Changed the Course of the Cold War* (New York: Scribner's, 1992), pp. 28, 31, 35.

16. Ibid., p. 23.

17. Ibid., pp. 25, 39, 43, 47.

18. Ibid., p. 93.

19. Ibid., p. 159.

20. CIA Transcript, "Meeting #1 (London), 20 April 1961," 1961, p. 23.

21. Ibid.

22. Schechter and Deriabin, *Spy Who Saved the World*, p. 175.

23. Ibid., p. 185; Brook-Shepherd, *Storm Birds*, p. 135.

24. Schechter and Deriabin, *Spy Who Saved the World*, p. 191–92.

25. Ibid., p. 195.

26. Ibid., pp. 205, 354.

27. Ibid., pp. 225–26.

28. Ibid., p. 232.

29. Ibid., p. 441.

30. Raymond Garthoff, interview with author, Washington, D.C., August 18, 1993.

31. Schechter and Deriabin, *Spy Who Saved the World*, p. 351.

32. Ibid., p. 296; Nigel West, *The Circus: MI5, 1945–1972* (Briarcliff Manor, N.Y.: Stein and Day, 1983), p. 88.

33. Schechter and Deriabin, *Spy Who Saved the World*, p. 302; Brook-Shepherd, *Storm Birds*, p. 155.

34. Schechter and Deriabin, *Spy Who Saved the World*, pp. 354, 410; West, *The Circus*, pp. 88–89; Greville Wynne, *The Man from Moscow* (London: Hutchinson, 1967), p. 7.

35. Schechter and Deriabin, *Spy Who Saved the World*, p. 376.

36. Enclosure to Memorandum for: The Director of Central Intelligence, Subject: *MILITARY THOUGHT (TOP SECRET)*: "Some Thoughts on the Development of the Soviet Army Tank Troops," by Marshal of the Soviet Union, R. Malinovskiy, date illegible; Schechter and Deriabin, *Spy Who Saved the World*, pp. 376–377.

37. Garthoff interview; Richard Helms, Memorandum for the Director, Defense Intelligence Agency, Subject: Establishment of the TOP SECRET *Special Collection of Articles of the Journal "Military Thought" ("Voyennaya Msyl")* by the Ministry of Defense USSR, 8, November 1961, pp. 7–10.

38. Brook-Shepherd, *Storm Birds*, pp. 138–39.

39. Schechter and Deriabin, *Spy Who Saved the World*, p. 395.

40. ACSI-DSCC, Subject: Damage Assessment in the Case of Whalen (S), April 1965, p. 2.

41. Ibid.

42. Linda Hunt, *Secret Agenda: The United States Government, Nazi Scientists, and Project PAPERCLIP, 1945 to 1990* (New York: St. Martin's Press, 1991), pp. 196–97.

43. ACSI-DSCC, Subject: Damage Assessment in the Case of Whalen (S), p. 3; Hunt, *Secret Agenda*, pp. 203, 207.

44. ACSI-DSCC, Subject: Damage Assessment, pp. 3–4; Hunt, *Secret Agenda*, pp. 210–11.

45. Hunt, *Secret Agenda*, p. 212.

46. ACSI, U.S. Army, Memorandum for: Director, Defense Intelligence Agency, Subject: Administrative Investigation Concerning the Assignment of Lt. Colonel William Henry Whalen, USA (Retired) to J–2, JCS, February 1965.

47. ACSI-DSCC, Subject: Damage Assessment, pp. 13–14; Hunt, *Secret Agenda*, pp. 206–7.

48. ACSI-DSCO, "Damage Assessment of Classified Documents," 18 January 1965; ACSI, Army, Subject: Technical Assessment Re: Former Retired LTC William Henry Whalen (U), 8 April 1967.

49. ACSI-DSCC, Subject: Damage Assessment, p. 14.

50. Hunt, *Secret Agenda*, p. 213.

51. Ibid., p. 214.

52. Ibid., p. 215.

53. Ibid., p. 216.

54. Samuel M. Katz, *Soldier Spies: Israeli Military Intelligence* (Novato, Calif.: Presidio, 1992), p. 165; Ian Black and Benny Morris, *Israel's Secret Wars: A History of Israel's Intelligence Services* (New York: Grove-Weidenfeld, 1991), p. 228; Stanley A. Blumberg and Gwinn Owens, *The Survival Factor: Israeli Intelligence from World War I to the Present* (New York: Macmillan, 1985), p. 212.

55. Katz, *Soldier Spies*, p. 162.

56. Central Intelligence Agency, *Foreign Intelligence and Security Services: Israel* (Washington, D.C.: CIA, 1977), p. 18; Katz, *Soldier Spies*, p. 162.

57. Katz, *Soldier Spies*, p. 164.

58. Ibid., p. 165; Black and Morris, *Israel's Secret Wars*, p. 228; Blumberg and Owens, *Survival Factor*, pp. 213, 215.

59. Katz, *Soldier Spies*, pp. 165–66.

60. Ibid., p. 166.

61. Ibid.

62. Black and Morris, *Israel's Secret Wars*, p. 228; Katz, *Soldier Spies*, p. 167.

63. Katz, *Soldier Spies*, p. 167.

64. Black and Morris, *Israel's Secret Wars*, p. 228; Katz, *Soldier Spies*, p. 168.

65. Black and Morris, *Israel's Secret Wars*, pp. 228–29; Katz, *Soldier Spies*, pp. 168–69.

66. Dennis Eisenberg, Uri Dan, and Eli Landau, *The Mossad: Israel's Secret Intelligence Service* (New York: Signet, 1978), p. 116.

67. Yossi Melman and Dan Raviv, *The Imperfect Spies: The History of Israeli Intelligence* (London: Sidgwick & Jackson, 1989), p. 167.

68. Black and Morris, *Israel's Secret Wars*, p. 229; Melman and Raviv, *Imperfect Spies*, pp. 167–68; Katz, *Soldier Spies*, pp. 169–70.

69. Katz, *Soldier Spies*, p. 170; Melman and Raviv, *Imperfect Spies*, p. 168; Central Intelligence Agency, *Foreign Intelligence and Security Services: Israel*, p. 18.

70. Katz, *Soldier Spies*, p. 172; Black and Morris, *Israel's Secret Wars*, p. 197; Melman and Raviv, *Imperfect Spies*, p. 164.

71. Central Intelligence Agency, *Foreign Intelligence and Security Services: Israel*, p. 18; Katz, *Soldier Spies*, p. 172; Raviv and Melman, *Imperfect Spies*, p. 164.

72. Central Intelligence Agency, *Foreign Intelligence and Security Services: Israel*, p. 18; Katz, *Soldier Spies*, p. 172; Black and Morris, *Israel's Secret Wars*, p. 197.

73. Katz, *Soldier Spies*, pp. 172–73; Melman and Raviv, *Imperfect Spies*, pp. 164–65; Richard Deacon, *The Israeli Secret Service* (New York: Taplinger, 1977), pp. 143–44.

74. Katz, *Soldier Spies*, p. 173.

75. Eisenberg, Dan, and Landau, *Mossad*, p. 143.

76. Central Intelligence Agency, *Foreign Intelligence and Security Services: Israel*, p. 18.

77. Katz, *Soldier Spies*, p. 173.

78. Ibid.

79. Tom Mangold, *Cold Warrior: James Jesus Angleton: The CIA's Master Spy Hunter* (New York: Simon & Schuster, 1991), p. 71.

80. Mangold, *Cold Warrior*, p. 72; Brook-Shepherd, *Storm Birds*, p. 164, David Wise, *Molehunt: The Secret Search for Traitors that Shattered the CIA* (New York: Random House,1992), p. 22.

81. Wise, *Molehunt*, p. 40; Robin W. Winks, *Cloak and Gown: Scholars in the Secret War, 1939–1961* (New York: Morrow, 1987), pp. 328–29.

82. Wise, *Molehunt*, pp. 40–41; Winks, *Cloak and Gown*, p. 334.

83. Wise, *Molehunt*, p. 41.

84. Mangold, *Cold Warrior*, pp. 49–50.

85. Ibid., p. 57; Wise, *Molehunt*, p. 31.

86. Mangold, *Cold Warrior*, p. 75, Brook-Shepherd, *Storm Birds*, p. 169.

87. Roger Faligot and Pascal Krop, *La Piscine: The French Secret Service since 1944* (New York: Basil Blackwell, 1989), pp. 213–14.

88. Ibid., p. 214.

89. Mangold, *Cold Warrior*, p. 76.

90. Ibid., p. 89; Wise, *Molehunt*, p. 26.

91. Mangold, *Cold Warrior*, pp. 89–90.

92. Ibid., pp. 92, 94; Wise, *Molehunt*, pp. 101–2.

93. Mangold, *Cold Warrior*, p. 96; Wise, *Molehunt*, p. 98; Brook-Shepherd, *Storm Birds*, pp. 170–73.

94. Ladislav Bittman, *The Deception Game: Czechoslovak Intelligence in Soviet Political Warfare* (Syracuse, N.Y.: Syracuse University Research Corporation, 1972), p. 16.

95. Mangold, *Cold Warrior*, pp. 97–98, 100.

96. Ibid., p. 246.

97. Ibid.

98. Ibid., pp. 254–56.

99. Ibid., p. 263; Wise, *Molehunt*, p. 211.

100. Mangold, *Cold Warrior*, p. 341.

101. Brook-Shepherd, *Storm Birds*, pp. 181–82; Mangold, *Cold Warrior*, p. 163.

102. Wise, *Molehunt*, pp. 74–75, 76n, 142; Mangold, *Cold Warrior*, pp. 167–68.

103. Mangold, *Cold Warrior*, p. 171.

104. Ibid., p. 173.

105. Ibid., pp. 174–75.

106. Wise, *Molehunt*, p. 70.

107. Mangold, *Cold Warrior*, pp. 175, 183; Wise, *Molehunt*, p. 147; Samuel

Halpern and Hayden Peake, "Did Angleton Jail Nosenko?" *International Journal of Intelligence and Counterintelligence* 3, no. 4 (1989): 451–64.

108. Mangold, *Cold Warrior*, pp. 196, 201.

18 Technological Espionage

1. Michael R. Beschloss, *Mayday: Eisenhower, Khrushchev and the U-2 Affair* (New York: Harper & Row, 1986), p. 237; A. J. Goodpaster, "Memorandum for the Record," February 8, 1960, DDRS, 1981–623A.

2. Beschloss, *Mayday*, pp. 237–38; Jay Miller, *Lockheed U-2* (Austin, Tex.: Aerofax, 1983), p. 30.

3. Beschloss, *Mayday*, pp. 241–42; A. J. Goodpaster, "Memorandum for the Record," April 25, 1960, WHO St. Sec., Subject Series, Alphabetical Subseries, box 15, Intelligence Matters-14, March–May 1960, DDEL.

4. "U.S. to Continue U-2 Flights over Soviet," *Aviation Week*, May 16, 1960, pp. 26–27; Beschloss, *Mayday*, p. 241.

5. Nikita Khrushchev, *Khrushchev Remembers: The Last Testament* (New York: Bantam, 1976), p. 504.

6. Richard Bissell interview with author, Framington, Connecticut, March 16, 1984.

7. Robert L. Perry, *Origins of the USAF Space Program, 1945–1956* (Washington, D.C.: Air Force Systems Command, June 1962), p. 30.

8. Thomas White, Memorandum for Deputy Chief of Staff, Development, Subject: [deleted] Satellite Vehicles, 18 December 1952, RG 341, entry 214, file 2-36300–99, MRB, NARA; Merton E. Davies and William R. Harris, *RAND's Role in the Evolution of Balloon and Satellite Observation Systems and Related U.S. Space Technology* (Santa Monica, Calif.: RAND, 1988), pp. 14, 16.

9. Perry, *Origins*, p. 32; Merton Davies, interview with author, December 1, 1988, Santa Monica, Calif.

10. Perry, *Origins*, p. 41; Davies and Harris, *RAND's Role*, p. 57.

11. Davies and Harris, *RAND's Role*, p. 61.

12. Ibid.; Philip Klass, *Secret Sentries in Space* (New York: Random House, 1971), p. 87; Perry, *Origins*, pp. 42–43.

13. Office of the Director of Defense Research and Engineering, *Military Space Projects (Report No. 10)* (Washington, D.C.: Department of Defense, 1960), p. 1.

14. Interview; Andrew Goodpaster, interview with author, Washington, D.C., November 9, 1988; U.S. Congress, Senate Select Committee to Study Governmental Operations with Respect to Intelligence Activities, *Final Report, Book IV: Supplementary Detailed Staff Reports on Foreign and Military Intelligence* (Washington, D.C.: U.S. Government Printing Office, 1976), pp. 58–59.

15. Letter from Neil McElroy to President Dwight D. Eisenhower, January 29, 1959, DDRS 1982-001538; "Discoverer Aborted," *Aviation Week*, March 2, 1959, p. 27; "A Satellite Rocket is Fired on the West Coast," *New York Times*, March 1, 1959, pp. 1, 32.

16. "Frogman First on Scene," *New York Times*, August 12, 1960, p. 3; Richard Witkin, "Washington to Hail Retrieved Capsule in Ceremony Today," *New York Times*, August 13, 1960, pp. 1, 7.

17. Jeffrey Richelson, *America's Secret Eyes in Space: The U.S. Keyhole Spy Satellite Program* (New York: Harper & Row, 1990), p. 41.

18. Interview (anonymous source); Andrew Goodpaster, interview with author, November 9, 1988, Washington, D.C.

19. Richelson, *America's Secret Eyes in Space*, pp. 51, 68.

20. Klass, *Secret Sentries*, p. 106.

21. "Main Trends in Soviet Capabilities and Policies 1957–1962," NIE 11-4-57, November 12, 1957, pp. 26–27.

22. Lawrence C. McQuade, Memorandum for Mr. Nitze, Subj: But Where Did the Missile Gap Go? (Washington, D.C.: Assistant Secretary of Defense, International Security Affairs, May 31, 1963), pp. 7–8.

23. Ibid., pp. 9–10.

24. Ibid., pp. 10–11; "Main Trends in Soviet Capabilities and Policies 1960–1964," NIE 11-4-60, December 1, 1960, p. 52.

25. Fred Kaplan, *The Wizards of Armageddon* (New York: Simon & Schuster, 1983), p. 287.

26. Ibid.

27. Robert McNamara, interview with author, January 19, 1989, Washington, D.C.; John Newhouse, *War and Peace in the Nuclear Age* (New York: Knopf, 1989), p. 148.

28. McQuade, "Memorandum for Mr. Nitze," p. 14.

29. Jerrold L. Schechter and Peter S. Deriabin, *The Spy Who Saved the World: How a Soviet Colonel Changed the Course of the Cold War* (New York: Scribner's, 1992), pp. 273–74.

30. Ibid., p. 278.

31. McQuade, "Memorandum for Mr. Nitze," p. 15.

32. "Soviet Space Reconnaissance Systems," *ONI Review* 16, no. 12 (1961): 491.

33. Curtis Peebles, *Guardians: Strategic Reconnaissance Satellites* (Novato, Calif.: Presidio, 1987), p. 153.

34. Ibid.

35. Ibid., p. 154.

36. Ibid.

37. Ibid.

38. Klass, *Secret Sentries*, pp. 191–95.

39. Richelson, *America's Secret Eyes in Space*, p. 77.

40. Interview.

41. Central Intelligence Agency, "Soviet Military Strength," December 5, 1963, National Security File, NSC Meetings, vol. 1, Tab 1, 12/5/63, Box 1, LBJ Library, pp. 2–5.

42. Philip Klass, "Military Satellites Gain Vital Data," *Aviation Week & Space Technology*, September 15, 1969, pp. 55–61; interview.

43. CIA, "The Oxcart Story," p. 2; this is a typed version of an article with the same title by Thomas P. McIninch, which appeared in the CIA's *Studies in Intelligence* 15, no. 1 (1969). The typed version was released by the CIA in 1991. It is not clear whether there is any difference between the content of the typed article and the version that appeared in *Studies*.

44. CIA, "The Oxcart Story," p. 3.

45. Ibid.

46. Jay Miller, *The Lockheed A-12/YF-12A/SR-71 Story* (Austin, Tex.: Aerofax, 1983), p. 3; CIA, "The Oxcart Story," p. 9.

47. CIA, "The Oxcart Story," p. 21.

48. Miller, *The Lockheed A-12/YF-12A/SR-71 Story*, pp. 2, 5; Donald E. Fink, "U-2s, SR-71s Merged in One Wing," *Aviation Week & Space Technology*, May 10, 1976, p. 83; Bill Yenne, *SAC: A Primer of Modern Strategic Airpower* (Novato, Calif.: Presidio, 1985), p. 34.

49. Miller, *The A-12/YF-12A/SR-71 Story*, p. 2.

50. CIA, "The Oxcart Story," pp. 18–19.

51. Ibid., p. 19.

52. Ibid., pp. 19–21.

53. Ibid., p. 21.

54. Untitled memo, *DDRS* 1982-001583.

55. Martin Streetly, "US Airborne ELINT Systems, Part 3: The Boeing RC-135 Family," *Jane's Defence Weekly*, March 16, 1985, pp. 460–65.

56. Memorandum for Mr. Bill Moyers, assistant to the president, Subject: Weekly Report for the President, May 12, 1964; Duncan Campbell, *The Unsinkable Aircraft Carrier: American Military Power in Britain* (London: Michael Joseph, 1984), pp. 160–61; "British M.P. Accuses U.S. of Electronic Spying," *New Scientist*, August 5, 1976, p. 268.

57. James Bamford, *The Puzzle Palace: A Report on NSA, America's Most Secret Agency* (Boston: Houghton Mifflin, 1982), p. 209.

58. Ibid.

59. Eliot Marshal, "Senate Skeptical on SALT Verification," *Science*, July 27, 1979, pp. 373–76.

60. Hedrick Smith, "U.S. Aides Say Loss of Post in Iran Impairs Missile-Monitoring Ability," *New York Times*, March 2, 1979, pp. A1, A8.

61. Victor Marchetti and John Marks, *The CIA and the Cult of Intelligence* (New York: Laurel, 1980), p. 168.

62. Directorate of Collection, Office, ACS/Intelligence, Air Force, *History: Directorate of Collection, Office, ACS/Intelligence 1 July–31 December 1962*, n.d., p. 3.

63. Bamford, *Puzzle Palace*, p. 213.

64. Ibid., pp. 215–231.

65. Ibid., pp. 231–35.

66. Seymour Hersh, "Submarines of U.S. Stage Spy Missions Inside Soviet Waters," *New York Times*, May 25, 1975, pp. 1, 42.

67. Christopher Drew, Michael L. Millenson, and Robert Becker, "A Risky Game of Cloak-and-Dagger—Under the Sea," *Chicago Tribune*, January 7, 1991, pp. 1, 8–9.

68. Ibid.

69. Hersh, "A False Navy Report Alleged in Sub Crash," *New York Times*, July 6, 1975, pp. 1, 16.

70. Ibid.

71. Private information; Ed Offley, "Remembering the Scorpion," *The Virginia-Pilot/The Ledger-Star*, May 30, 1993, pp. C1, C8; Stephen Johnson, "A Long and Deep Mystery," *Houston Chronicle*, May 23, 1993, pp. 1A, 16A, 17A.

72. Peebles, *Guardians*, p. 155.

73. Ibid., pp. 155–157.

74. *The Soviet Space Program*, NIE 11-1-67, March 2, 1967, p. 7.

75. Ibid.

76. Peebles, *Guardians*, pp. 157–59, 225.

77. Ibid., p. 219.

78. Ibid., pp. 220–21; Desmond Ball, *Soviet Signals Intelligence (SIGINT)*: (Canberra: SDSC, Australian National University, 1989), pp. 99, 100; "Soviet ELINT Capabilities," *ONI Review* 15, no. 1 (1960): 13–14.

79. Peebles, *Guardians*, p. 221.

80. Letter to author from Bill Robinson, Project Ploughshares, March 8, 1993; Bob Gilmour, "Young Recruits Favored for Electronic Spy Work," *Edmonton Journal*, October 27, 1982, p. C5.

81. "Northernmost Weather Station Called Major Link for Espionage," *Toronto Globe and Mail*, January 12, 1974.

82. Robinson letter.

19 Crisis Intelligence

1. Dino Brugioni, *Eyeball to Eyeball: The Inside Story of the Cuban Missile Crisis* (New York: Random House, 1991), p. 207.

2. Ibid.

3. Michael Beschloss, *The Crisis Years: Kennedy and Khrushchev 1960–1963* (New York: Harper Collins, 1991), p. 4.

4. Brugioni, *Eyeball*, pp. 63, 72.

5. United States Intelligence Board, "The Military Buildup in Cuba," July 11, 1961, p. 1.

6. Brugioni, *Eyeball*, p. 80.

7. R. Jack Smith, *The Unknown CIA: My Three Decades with the Agency* (New York: Berkley, 1992), p. 179.

8. John Ranelagh, *The Agency: The Rise and Decline of the CIA* (New York: Simon & Schuster, 1986), p. 730. On McCone's background and his tenure as DCI, see Kenneth J. Campbell, "John McCone: An Outsider Becomes DCI," *Studies in Intelligence*, Summer 1988, pp. 49–60.

9. Brugioni, *Eyeball*, p. 80.

10. USAF Historical Division Liaison Office, *The Air Force Response to the Cuban Crisis, 1962* (Washington, D.C.: AFHDLO, n.d.) p. 54; Benjamin T. Harris, Office of the Secretary of Defense, Memorandum for the Chief of Operations, Operation Mongoose, Subject: End of Phase I, July 23, 1962, p. 4.

11. U.S. Senate Committee on Armed Services, *The Cuban Military Buildup* (Washington, D.C.: U.S. Government Printing Office, 1963), p. 6; John McCone, Memorandum for the File: Discussion in Secretary Rusk's office at 12 o'clock, 21 August 1962, in Mary S. McAuliffe (ed.), *CIA Documents on the Cuban Missile Crisis* (Washington, D.C.: CIA, 1992), pp. 21–23; John McCone, Memorandum: Proposed Plan for Action for Cuba, 21 August 1962, in McAuliffe, *CIA Documents*, pp. 31–32.

12. Peter S. Usowski, "John McCone and the Cuban Missile Crisis: A Persistent Approach to the Intelligence–Policy Relationship," *International Journal of Intelligence and Counterintelligence* 2, no. 4 (1988): 547–76; Brugioni, *Eyeball*, p. 96; National Security Action Memorandum No. 181, August 23, 1962; "The Military Buildup in Cuba," SNIE 85-3-62, September 19, 1962, p. 8; John McCone, "Soviet MRBMs in Cuba," 31 October 1962, in McAuliffe, *CIA Documents*, pp. 13–17.

13. Usowski, "John McCone and the Cuban Missile Crisis"; CIA, "Recent Soviet Military Activities in Cuba," p. 1.

14. Brugioni, *Eyeball*, p. 105.

15. Ibid., pp. 116, 118.

16. Ibid., p. 120; McCone, "Soviet MRBMs in Cuba"; CIA, "U-2 Overflights of Cuba, 29 August through 14 October 1962," 27 February 1963, in McAuliffe, *CIA Documents*, pp. 127–33.

17. Brugioni, *Eyeball*, p. 145; "Military Buildup in Cuba," p. 4.

18. "Military Buildup in Cuba," p. 82.

19. Brugioni, *Eyeball*, p. 146.

20. Ibid., pp. 149–50.

21. Ibid., p. 151; Victor Marchetti, interview with author, July 20, 1993, Herndon, Va.

22. Brugioni, *Eyeball*, pp. 153, 159–60.

23. Memorandum of Mongoose meeting held on Thursday, October 4, 1962, October 4, 1962.

24. Brugioni, *Eyeball*, p. 164; Richard Lehman, "CIA Handling of the Soviet Buildup in Cuba," in McAuliffe, *CIA Documents*, p. 101.

25. Usowski, "John McCone and the Cuban Missile Crisis," pp. 559–60; Brugioni, *Eyeball*, pp. 165, 167, 185.

26. Brugioni, *Eyeball*, pp. 197–98.

27. Ibid., pp. 201–2, 204.

28. John Hughes with A. Denis Clift, "The San Cristobal Trapezoid," *Studies in Intelligence* 36, no. 5 (1992): 60.

29. Brugioni, *Eyeball*, pp. 234, 251, 277.

30. Ibid., pp. 179, 251, 291, 385.

31. Private information.

32. Jerrold L. Schechter and Peter S. Deriabin, *The Spy Who Saved the World: How a Soviet Colonel Changed the Course of the Cold War* (New York: Scribner's, 1992), p. 335.

33. Ibid., p. 334.

34. Ibid., p. 335.

35. Ibid., pp. 334–35.

36. "Major Consequences of Certain US Courses of Action in Cuba," SNIE 11-19-62, October 20, 1962, pp. 7, 9.

37. Brugioni, *Eyeball*, p. 347.

38. Ibid., pp. 391–92, 399.

39. Central Intelligence Agency, "Soviet Bloc Shipping to Cuba," October 23, 1962, p. 2; Memorandum for the Director, Subject: Your Briefings of the NSC Executive Committee," November 3, 1962, in McAuliffe, *CIA Documents*, p. 353.

40. Assistant Chief of Staff, Intelligence, USAF, *Aerospace Forces in Cuba*, 1 November 1962 (revisions as of 14 November 1962), Supplement to Annex 1, Section 1.

41. Brugioni, *Eyeball*, pp. 423, 436–37, 452–53.

42. Ibid., p. 485.

43. Ibid., p. 512–13.

44. S. B. Frankel, Chief of Staff, DIA, To: Chairman, U.S. Delegation, Inter-American Defense Board, Subject: (U) Intelligence Briefings, 23 November 1962, pp. 7–8; Brugioni, *Eyeball*, pp. 536–37; "The Missiles Leave Cuba," *ONI Review* 17, no. 12 (1962): 511–12.

45. The White House, "Guidelines for the Planning of Cuban Overflights," November 30, 1962.

46. Ian Black and Benny Morris, *Israel's Secret Wars: A History of Israel's Intelligence Services* (New York: Grove-Weidenfeld, 1991), p. 211; Samuel M. Katz, *Soldier Spies: Israeli Military Intelligence* (Novato, Calif.: Presidio, 1992), pp. 181–82.

47. Black and Morris, *Israel's Secret Wars*, p. 211.

48. Ibid., pp. 210, 216; Katz, *Soldier Spies*, pp. 181–83.

49. Black and Morris, *Israel's Secret Wars*, p. 216.

50. Ibid.

51. Ibid., p. 217.

52. Ibid.

53. Ibid.

54. Ibid., p. 218; Katz, *Soldier Spies*, p. 188.

55. Black and Morris, *Israel's Secret Wars*, p. 224; Katz, *Soldier Spies*, p. 191.

56. Donald Neff, *Warriors for Jerusalem: The Six Days That Changed the Middle East* (New York: Simon & Schuster, 1984), pp. 201–3.

57. Ibid., p. 203.

58. Ibid., pp. 203–4; Ze'ev Schiff, *A History of the Israeli Army: 1874 to the Present*, (New York: Macmillan, 1985), p. 140.

59. Katz, *Soldier Spies*, pp. 190–91.

60. Black and Morris, *Israel's Secret Wars*, p. 230.

61. Ibid., p. 232.

62. Ibid.; Katz, *Soldier Spies*, p. 193.

63. CIA Board of National Estimates, Special Memorandum, "Czechoslovakia: The Dubcek Pause," June 13, 1968, pp. 1–2, 17–18.

64. Karen Dawisha, *The Kremlin and the Prague Spring* (Berkeley: University of California Press, 1984), p. 16.

65. Jiri Valenta, *Soviet Intervention in Czechoslovakia, 1968: Anatomy of a Decision* (Baltimore, Md.: Johns Hopkins University Press, 1979), pp. 11–12.

66. Ibid., pp. 15, 21, 23.

67. Christopher Andrew and Oleg Gordievsky, *KGB: The Inside Story* (New York: Harper Collins, 1990), p. 485; Dawisha, *The Kremlin and the Prague Spring*, p. 284.

68. Valenta, *Soviet Intervention*, pp. 124–25.

69. Ibid., p. 124; Dawisha, *The Kremlin and the Prague Spring*, pp. 279, 284.

70. Andrew and Gordievsky, *KGB*, pp. 482–83; Central Intelligence Agency, *KGB and GRU* (Washington, D.C.: CIA, 1984) p. 67.

71. Andrew and Gordievsky, *KGB*, p. 483.

72. Valenta, *Soviet Intervention*, pp. 125–27.

73. Ibid., p. 138.

74. Andrew and Gordievsky, *KGB*, pp. 483–84; Oleg Kalugin, *The First Directorate: My 32 Years in Intelligence and Espionage Against the West* (New York: St. Martin's Press, 1994) p. 106.

75. Andrew and Gordievsky, *KGB*, pp. 484–85.

76. Ibid., pp. 485–86.

77. Interview; *CIA: The Pike Report* (Nottingham: Spokesman Books, 1977), p. 140.

78. Interview.

79. Interviews.

80. *CIA : The Pike Report*, pp. 139–40; interview.

81. *CIA: The Pike Report*, p. 140.

82. Interview.

83. Cynthia M. Grabo, "The Watch Committee and the National Indications Center: The Evolution of U.S. Strategic Warning 1950–1975," *International Journal of Intelligence and Counterintelligence* 3, no. 3 (1989): p. 379.

20   The Technical Revolution Continues

1. Desmond Ball, *Pine Gap: Australia and the US Geostationary Signals Intelligence Satellite Program* (Sydney, Australia: Allen & Unwin, 1988), p. 73; Private information.

2. Robert Lindsey, *The Falcon and the Snowman: A True Story of Friendship and Espionage* (New York: Simon & Schuster, 1979), pp. 54–58.

3. Jeffrey Richelson, "The Canyon Program," unpublished paper, 1994.

4. Lindsey, *Falcon and the Snowman*, p. 57; Interview.

5. Desmond Ball, "The Rhyolite Program" (Canberra: Australian National University, 1982), mimeograph.

6. Interview.

7. Curtis Peebles, "The Guardians," *Spaceflight*, November 1978, pp. 381ff; Private information.

8. Interview; private information.

9. Interview; private information.

10. Peebles, "The Guardians," pp. 381ff; Interview.

11. Arms Control and Disarmament Agency, *Arms Control and Disarmament Agreements: Texts and Histories of Negotiations* (Washington, D.C.: ACDA, 1980), pp. 148–49.

12. Samuel L. Katz, *Soldier Spies: Israeli Military Intelligence* (Novato, Calif.: Presidio, 1992), p. 235.

13. Ibid., pp. 235–36.

14. Ibid., p. 236.

15. Ibid., p. 234.

16. Ian Black and Benny Morris, *Israel's Secret War: A History of Israel's Intelligence Services* (New York: Grove-Weidenfeld, 1991), p. 315.

17. Katz, *Soldier Spies*, p. 253.

18. Black and Morris, *Israel's Secret Wars*, p. 314.

19. Katz, *Soldier Spies*, p. 255.

20. Nicholas L. Johnson, *Soviet Military Strategy in Space* (London: Jane's, 1987), p. 92.

21. Ibid., pp. 92–93; Paul Stares, *The Militarization of Space: U.S. Policy, 1945–84* (Ithaca, N.Y.: Cornell University Press, 1985), pp. 140–41; "Soviets Launch Five Spy Satellites in Two Weeks," *New Scientist*, October 25, 1973, p. 260; Galia Golan, "Soviet Decisionmaking in the Yom Kippur War, 1973," in Jiri Valenta and William Potter (eds.), *Soviet Decisionmaking for National Security* (Boston: Allen & Unwin, 1984), pp. 185–217.

22. Johnson, *Soviet Military Strategy in Space*, pp. 92–93.

23. Paul Crickmore, *Lockheed SR-71 Blackbird* (London: Osprey,1986), pp. 161, 163; Office of History, 9th Wing, *History of the 9th Wing* (Beale AFB, Calif.: 9th Wing, 1993), p. xi; *CIA: The Pike Report* (Nottingham: Spokesman Books, 1977), p. 145.

24. Interview.

25. *CIA: The Pike Report*, p. 145.

26. Desmond Ball, *Soviet Signals Intelligence (SIGINT): Intercepting Satellite Communications* (Canberra: SDSC, Australian National University, 1989), p. 60.

27. Ibid., pp. 60–61.

28. Ibid., p. 60; private information.

29. Desmond Ball, *Australia's Secret Space Programs* (Canberra: Australian National University, 1988), pp. 11–12; Russell Spurr, "Enter the Spooks," *Far Eastern Economic Review*, February 25, 1977; "News Digest," *Aviation Week & Space Technology*, December 22, 1975, p. 38.

30. Ball, *Australia's Secret Space Programs*, p. 11.

31. Interview.

32. William E. Burrows, *Deep Black: Space Espionage and National Security* (New York: Random House, 1986), p. 227.

33. Interview.

34. Interview.

35. Interview.

36. Jeffrey T. Richelson, *America's Secret Eyes in Space: The U.S. Keyhole Spy Satellite Program* (New York: Harper & Row, 1990), pp. 126–28. John Noble Wilford, "Spy Satellite Reportedly Aided in Shuttle Flight," *New York Times*, October 20, 1981, p. C4.

37. James R. Janesick and Morley Blouke, "Sky on a Chip: The Fabulous CCD," *Sky & Telescope*, September 1987, pp. 238–42; Burrows, *Deep Black*, p. 244.

38. James R. Janesick and Morley M. Blouke, "Introduction to Charged Couple Device Imaging Sensors," in Kosta Tsipis (ed.), *Arms Control Verification: The Technologies that Make It Possible* (New York: Pergamon-Brassey's, 1985), p. 104; Curtis Peebles, *Guardians: Strategic Reconnaissance Satellites* (Novato, Calif.: Presidio, 1987), pp. 118–19.

39. Burrows, *Deep Black*, p. 247; interview.

40. Jeffrey Richelson, "The Satellite Data System," *Journal of the British Interplanetary Society* 37, no. 5 (1984): 226–28; James Bamford, "America's Supersecret Eyes in Space," *New York Times Magazine*, January 13, 1985, pp. 39ff; interview.

41. Interview.

42. Private information.

43. Richard Burt, "U.S. Plans New Way to Check Soviet Missile Tests," *New York Times*, June 29, 1979, p. A3.

44. Michael K. Burns, "U.S. Reactivating Bases in Turkey," *Baltimore Sun*, October 21, 1978, pp. 1, 23; Henry S. Bradsher, "U.S. Upgrades Spy Equipment at Turkish Sites," *Washington Star*, April 11, 1980, p. 7.

45. Burns, "U.S. Reactivating Bases"; Bradsher, "U.S. Upgrades Spy Equipment."

46. Burns, "U.S. Reactivating Bases."; Bradsher, "U.S. Upgrades Spy Equipment."

47. Dial Torgeson, "U.S. Spy Devices Still Running at Iran Post," *International Herald Tribune*, March 7, 1979, pp. A1, A8; Hedrick Smith, "U.S. Aides Say Loss of Post in Iran Impairs Missile-Monitoring Ability," *New York Times*, March 2, 1979, pp. A1, A8.

48. Torgeson, "U.S. Spy Devices Still Running at Iran Post."

49. Eliot Marshal, "Senate Skeptical on SALT Verification," *Science*, July 27, 1979, pp. 373–76; U.S. Congress, Senate Foreign Relations Committee, *Fiscal Year*

1980 International Security Assistance Authorization (Washington, D.C.: U.S. Government Printing Office, 1979), p. 366.

50. Smith, "U.S. Aides Say Loss of Post in Iran Impairs Missile-Monitoring Ability."

51. Cyrus Vance, *Hard Choices: Critical Years in America's Foreign Policy* (New York: Simon & Schuster, 1983), pp. 354–55.

52. "Cipher," *Defense Electronics*, March 1982, p. 30; Joint Intelligence Organization, *Fourth Annual Report, 1974, Part 2* (Canberra, Australia: JIO, 1974), p. 7.

53. Ball, *Australia's Secret Space Program*, p. 7; Duncan Campbell, "GCHQ's Lost Secrets," *New Statesman*, November 5, 1982, p. 5; Desmond Ball, "The US Naval Ocean Surveillance System (NOSIS)—Australia's Role," *Pacific Defence Reporter*, June 1982, p. 42.

21 Penetrations, Sunken Subs, and Sudden Death

1. John Barron, *KGB Today: The Hidden Hand* (New York: Reader's Digest Press, 1983), p. 428.

2. Ibid., pp. 428–29; Stansfield Turner, *Secrecy and Democracy: The CIA in Transition* (Boston: Houghton Mifflin, 1985), p. 50; David Martin, "A CIA Spy in the Kremlin," *Newsweek*, July 21, 1980, pp. 69–70; Myra McPherson, "The Good Neighbor Who Came in from the Cold," *Washington Post*, June 21, 1978, pp. B1, B4.

3. "Bonn Trades Spy for East German," *New York Times*, August 13, 1987, p. A6; William J. Eaton, "Soviet Journalist Gets 15 Years as Spy for West," *Los Angeles Times*, July 31, 1986, p. 5.

4. Central Intelligence Agency, *KGB and GRU* (Washington, D.C.: CIA, 1984), p. 58; Bill Gertz, "KGB General Reveals Exploits of Deep-Cover Agent in the U.S.," *Washington Times*, November 30, 1992, p. A7.

5. CIA, *KGB and GRU*, pp. 79–80; Thomas O'Toole, "South Africa's Spying Seen as Painful Blow to West," *Washington Post*, June 11, 1984, p. A10; "South African Officer Guilty of Spying," *New York Times*, October 30, 1983, p. A3.

6. Christopher Andrew and Oleg Gordievsky, *KGB: The Inside Story* (New York: Harper Collins, 1990), pp. 524–25.

7. Ibid., p. 526.

8. James Bamford, *The Puzzle Palace: Inside the National Security Agency, America's Most Secret Intelligence Organization* (New York: Penguin, 1983), pp. 506–7, 518–20.

9. "The Treason of Geoffrey Prime," *The Economist*, November 13, 1982, pp. 63–64.

10. Bamford, *Puzzle Palace*, pp. 522–23.

11. Ibid., p. 523.

12. Ibid., p. 512.

13. Ibid., pp. 512–14; Robert Lindsey, *The Falcon and the Snowman: A True Story of Friendship and Espionage* (New York: Simon & Schuster, 1979), pp. 54–63.

14. Turner, *Secrecy and Democracy*, p.64; Lindsey, *Falcon and the Snowman*, p. 54.

15. Harry Rositzke, *The KGB: The Eyes of Russia* (New York: Doubleday, 1981), p. 203.

16. Bamford, *Puzzle Palace*, p. 514; Rositzke, *KGB*, p. 202; Lindsey, *Falcon and the Snowman*, pp. 164–68.

17. Rositzke, *KGB*, pp. 203–4; Bamford, *Puzzle Palace*, pp. 520–21.

18. Rositzke, *KGB*, p. 204; Bamford, *Puzzle Palace*, pp. 521–22.

19. Bamford, *Puzzle Palace*, p. 522; Philip J. Klass, "U.S. Monitoring Capability Impaired," *Aviation Week & Space Technology*, May 14, 1979, p. 18.

20. Andrew Tully, *Inside the FBI* (New York: Dell, 1987), pp. 45, 48; George Lardner, Jr., "Spy Rings of One," *Washington Post Magazine*, December 4, 1983, pp. 60–65; Griffin Bell, *Taking Care of the Law* (New York: Morrow, 1982), p. 119; Henry Hurt, "CIA in Crisis: The Kampiles Case," *Reader's Digest*, June 1979, pp. 65–72; interview.

21. Turner, *Secrecy and Democracy*, p. 65.

22. *United States of America vs. William Peter Kampiles*, United States District Court, Northern District of Indiana, November 6, 1978, Direct Testimony of Donald E. Stukey, p. 805; Lardner, "Spy Rings of Ore,"; Curtis Peebles, *Guardians: Strategic Reconnaissance Satellites* (Novato, Calif.: Presidio, 1987), p. 120.

23. Lardner, "Spy Rings of One"; Peebles, *Guardians*, p. 120.

24. *United States of America vs. William Peter Kampiles*, Direct Testimony of Donald E. Stukey, p. 809.

25. Tully, *Inside the FBI*, p. 42.

26. *United States of America vs. William Peter Kampiles*, Direct Testimony of Leslie Dirks, pp. 10, 12.

27. Ibid., p. 13.

28. Interview.

29. Ruth Marcus and Joe Pichirallo, "Chin Believed Planted in U.S. as Spy," *Washington Post*, December 6, 1985, pp. A1, A22; Philip Shenon, "Former C.I.A. Analyst Is Arrested and Accused of Spying for China," *New York Times*, November 24, 1985, pp. 1, 31; Joe Pichirallo, "Ex-CIA Analyst Gave Secrets to China for 30 Years, FBI Says," *Washington Post*, November 24, 1985, pp. A1, A24.

30. Pichirallo, "Ex-CIA Analyst"; Stephen Engelberg, "30 Years of Spying for China Is Charged," *New York Times*, November 27, 1985, p. B8.

31. Pichirallo, "Ex-CIA Analyst"; "A Chinese Agent in the CIA?" *Newsweek*, December 2, 1985, p. 49.

32. Marcus and Pichirallo, "Chin Believed Planted in U.S. as Spy"; Philip Shenon, "U.S. Says Spy Suspect Had Access to Highly Classified Data," *New York Times*, January 3, 1986, p. A12; Michael Wines, "Bigger Role Laid to Suspected Spy," *Los Angeles Times*, November 28, 1985, pp. 1, 10; *United States of America vs. Larry Wu Tai Chin aka Chin Wu-Tai*, United States District Court, Eastern District of Virginia, Alexandria Division, January 2, 1986, Criminal No. 85-00263-A, pp. 2–3, 14.

33. Rositzke, *KGB*, p. 149; J. A. Emerson Vermaat, "The East German Secret Service Structure and Operational Focus," *Conflict Quarterly*, Fall 1987, p. 54.

34. Vermaat, "The East German Secret Service," p. 54.

35. Ibid.; Rositzke, *KGB*, p. 150.

36. Rositzke, *KGB*, p. 150; Vermaat, "The East German Secret Service," p. 54.

37. Werner Stiller with Jefferson Adams, *Beyond the Wall: Memoirs of an East and West German Spy* (New York: Brassey's, 1992), p. 115.

38. Vermaat, "The East German Secret Service," pp. 54–55; Steve Vogel, "'Mole' Who Doomed Brandt Tells How He Spied," *Washington Post*, July 1, 1993, p. A16.

39. Rositzke, *KGB*, p. 149; Stiller, *Beyond the Wall*, p. 99; Walter Laquer, "Coffee with 'Karla,'" *Washington Post*, September 29, 1991, pp. C1, C2.

40. "The Great Submarine Snatch," *Time*, March 31, 1975, pp. 20–27; Clyde W. Burleson, *The Jennifer Project* (Englewood Cliffs, N.J.: Prentice-Hall, 1977), p. 47; Roy Varner and Wayne Collier, *A Matter of Risk* (New York: Random House, 1977), p. 9; William J. Broad, "Russia Says U.S. Got Sub's Atom Arms," *New York Times*, June 20, 1993, p. 4.

41. "The Great Submarine Snatch"; Burleson, *Jennifer Project*, p. 18.

42. John Ranelagh, *The Agency: The Rise and Decline of the CIA* (New York: Simon & Schuster, 1986), p. 601.

43. "The Great Submarine Snatch"; Burleson, *Jennifer Project*, p. 18.

44. Burleson, *Jennifer Project*, p. 33; "The Great Submarine Snatch."

45. "The Great Submarine Snatch."

46. Ibid.; Varner and Collier, *A Matter of Risk*, p. 39.

47. "The Great Submarine Snatch"; Seymour Hersh, "Human Error Is Cited in '74 Glomar Failure," *New York Times*, December 9, 1976, pp. 1, 55.

48. "The Great Submarine Snatch"; Varner and Collier, *A Matter of Risk*, pp. 134.

49. "The Great Submarine Snatch"; Varner and Collier, *A Matter of Risk*, pp. 138–59.

50. Hersh, "Human Error Is Cited"; Burleson, *Jennifer Project*, pp. 112, 133.

51. Hersh, "Human Error Is Cited."

52. "CIA Raising USSR Sub Raises Questions," *FBIS-SOV-92-145*, July 28, 1992, pp. 15–16; CIA, "Burial at Sea," September 4, 1974.

53. John Barron, *MiG Pilot* (New York: Avon, 1981), pp. 169–86; Varner and Collier, *A Matter of Risk*, p. 26.

54. Barron, *MiG Pilot*, pp. 169–86.

55. Yossi Melman and Dan Raviv, *Imperfect Spies: The History of Israeli Intelligence* (London: Sidgwick & Jackson, 1989), pp. 200–201; Stanley A. Blumberg and Gwinn Owens, *The Survival Factor: Israeli Intelligence from World War I to the Present* (New York: G. P. Putnam, 1981), pp. 248–49; Michael Bar-Zohar and Eitan Haber, *The Quest for the Red Prince* (New York: Morrow, 1983) p. 129; Ian Black and Benny Morris, *Israel's Secret Wars: A History of Israel's Intelligence Services* (New York: Grove-Weidenfeld, 1991), pp. 269–70.

56. Blumberg and Owens, *Survival Factor*, p. 249; Bar-Zohar and Haber, *Quest for the Red Prince*, pp. 129–30; Black and Morris, *Israel's Secret Wars*, p. 270; Melman and Raviv, *Imperfect Spies*, p. 203.

57. Melman and Raviv, *Imperfect Spies*, p. 204; Black and Morris, *Israel's Secret Wars*, p. 276.

58. Bar-Zohar and Haber, *Quest for the Red Prince*, pp. 146–49, 153–54; Blumberg and Owens, *Survival Factor*, pp. 249–50; Stewart Steven, *Spymasters of Israel* (New York: Macmillan, 1980), pp. 270–71; Black and Morris, *Israel's Secret Wars*, p. 273; Samuel M. Katz, *Soldier Spies: Israeli Military Intelligence* (Novato, Calif.: Presidio, 1992), p. 229.

59. Katz, *Soldier Spies*, p. 232; Black and Morris, *Israel's Secret Wars*, p. 275; Bar-Zohar and Haber, *Quest for the Red Prince*, pp. 167–77.

60. Black and Morris, *Israel's Secret Wars*, p. 275; Bar-Zohar and Haber, *Quest for the Red Prince*, pp. 187–89; Blumberg and Owens, *Survival Factor*, pp. 250–51.

61. Melman and Raviv, *Imperfect Spies*, pp. 208–9; Bob Woodward, *Veil:*

The Secret Wars of the CIA 1981–1987 (New York: Simon & Schuster, 1987), pp. 244–45.

62. Black and Morris, *Israel's Secret Wars*, p. 276; Steven, *Spymasters of Israel*, p. 286.

63. Steven, *Spymasters of Israel*, p. 292; Bar-Zohar and Haber, *Quest for the Red Prince*, pp. 218–19. Aharon Yariv, former head of the AMAN acknowledged the assassination campaign in 1993. See David Hoffman, "Israel Confirms Assassinations of Munich Massacre Plotter," *Washington Post*, November 24, 1993, p. A10.

64. U.S. Congress, Senate Select Committee to Study Governmental Operations with Respect to Intelligence Activities, *Covert Action in Chile* (Washington, D.C.: U.S. Government Printing Office, 1976), pp. 1, 9.

65. Ranelagh, *The Agency*, p. 514; Seymour Hersh, *The Price of Power: Kissinger in the Nixon White House* (New York: Summit Books, 1983), p. 259.

66. U.S. Congress, Senate Select Committee to Study Governmental Operations with Respect to Intelligence Activities, *Alleged Assassination Plots Involving Foreign Leaders* (Washington, D.C.: U.S. Government Printing Office, 1976), p. 225.

67. U.S. Congress, Senate Select Committee to Study Governmental Operations with Respect to Intelligence Activities, *Covert Action in Chile* (Washington, D.C.: U.S. Government Printing Office, 1976), pp. 12–13; Central Intelligence Agency, "Report on CIA Chilean Task Force Activities, 15 September to 3 November 1970," November 18, 1970, p. 3; Hersh, *Price of Power*, p. 270.

68. U.S. Congress, Senate Select Committee to Study Governmental Operations with Respect to Intelligence Activities, *Alleged Assassination Plots Involving Foreign Leaders*, p. 227.

69. Central Intelligence Agency, "Report on CIA Chilean Task Force Activities, 15 September to 18 November 1970," pp. 5, 9, 10.

70. U.S. Congress, Senate Select Committee to Study Governmental Operations with Respect to Intelligence Activities, *Covert Action in Chile*, pp. 23–25.

71. Ibid., pp. 25–26; U.S. Congress, Senate Select Committee to Study Governmental Operations with Respect to Intelligence Activities, *Alleged Assassination Plots Involving Foreign Leaders*, pp. 226, 235–36; Ranelagh, *The Agency*, p. 517; Hersh, *The Price of Power*, pp. 281–82.

72. Hersh, *The Price of Power*, p. 286.

73. Ranelagh, *The Agency*, p. 518; U.S. Congress, Senate Select Committee to Study Governmental Operations with Respect to Intelligence Activities, *Alleged Assassination Plots Involving Foreign Leaders*, pp. 243, 45.

74. Ranelagh, *The Agency*, p. 518; U.S. Congress, Senate Select Committee to Study Governmental Operations with Respect to Intelligence Activities, *Alleged Assassination Plots Involving Foreign Leaders*, pp. 244–45.

75. U.S. Congress, Senate Select Committee to Study Governmental Operations with Respect to Intelligence Activities, *Alleged Assassination Plots Involving Foreign Leaders*, p. 254; U.S. Congress, Senate Select Committee to Study Governmental Operations with Respect to Intelligence Activities, *Covert Action in Chile*, pp. 29–31; John Prados, *Presidents' Secret Wars: CIA and Pentagon Covert Operations from World War II Through Iranscam* (New York: Quill, 1988), p. 320; Hersh, *Price of Power*, pp. 292–93.

76. Prados, *Presidents' Secret Wars*, p. 321.

77. Andrew and Gordievsky, *KGB*, p. 573; Vladimir Kuzichkin, *Inside the KGB: Myth and Reality* (London: Andre Deutsch, 1990), p. 312.

78. Andrew and Gordievsky, *KGB*, p. 573.

79. Ibid., pp. 573–74.

80. Kuzichkin, *Inside the KGB*, pp. 314–15; Andrew and Gordievsky, *KGB*, p. 574; Henry Bradsher, *Afghanistan and the Soviet Union* (Durham, N.C.: Duke University Press, 1985), pp. 117–18.

81. Michael Dobbs, "Secret Memos Trace Kremlin's March to War," *Washington Post*, November 15, 1992, pp. A1, A32.

82. Ibid.; Kuzichkin, *Inside the KGB*, pp. 315–16; Andrew and Gordievsky, *KGB*, p. 575; Edward R. Girardet, *Afghanistan: The Soviet War* (New York: St. Martin's Press, 1985), p. 12.

83. Andrew and Gordievsky, *KGB*, p. 575.

22 Elusive Truths

1. Samuel M. Katz, *Soldier Spies: Israeli Military Intelligence* (Novato, Calif.: Presidio, 1992), p. 225.

2. Ibid.

3. Ibid., pp. 240–41; Ian Black and Benny Morris, *Israel's Secret Wars: A History of Israel's Intelligence Services* (New York: Grove-Weidenfeld, 1991), p. 290.

4. Black and Morris, *Israel's Secret Wars*, p. 290; Stewart Steven, *The Spymasters of Israel* (New York: Macmillan, 1980), p. 297; "Agranat Commission Blames Elazar, Gonen, Zeira, 3 Others," *Jerusalem Post*, April 1, 1974, pp. 1, 13.

5. Katz, *Soldier Spies*, p. 241.

6. Ibid.

7. Ibid., p. 242; Black and Morris, *Israel's Secret Wars*, pp. 300–301.

8. Katz, *Soldier Spies*, p. 242; Steven, *Spymasters of Israel*, pp. 298–99, 299n; Janice Gross Stein, "The 1973 Intelligence Failure: Reconsideration," *Jerusalem Quarterly* 24 (1982): 41–54.

9. Katz, *Soldier Spies*, p. 242.

10. Black and Morris, *Israel's Secret Wars*, p. 302.

11. Ibid., p. 303.

12. Ibid., pp. 303–4.

13. Ibid., pp. 302, 304; Katz, *Soldier Spies*, p. 245.

14. Katz, *Soldier Spies*, p. 245; Black and Morris, *Israel's Secret Wars*, p. 297.

15. Katz, *Soldier Spies*, p. 246; Black and Morris, *Israel's Secret Wars*, pp. 296, 305.

16. Katz, *Soldier Spies*, p. 246; Black and Morris, *Israel's Secret Wars*, pp. 296, 305.

17. Katz, *Soldier Spies*, p. 246.

18. Ibid., p. 247; Black and Morris, *Israel's Secret Wars*, p. 308; Jacques Derogy and Henri Carmel, *The Untold Story of Israel* (New York: Grove Press, 1979), pp. 280–81.

19. Katz, *Soldier Spies*, p. 247; Black and Morris, *Israel's Secret Wars*, p. 308.

20. Katz, *Soldier Spies*, p. 247; Black and Morris, *Israel's Secret Wars*, pp. 307–8.

21. Derogy and Carmel, *Untold History of Israel*, p. 281.

22. Black and Morris, *Israel's Secret Wars*, p. 300; Steven, *Spymasters of Israel*, pp. 303–4; Seymour M. Hersh, *The Samson Option: Israel's Nuclear Threat and American Foreign Policy* (New York: Random House, 1991), pp. 225–40.

23. Black and Morris, *Israel's Secret Wars*, p. 318.

24. Daniel Callaghan, *Dangerous Capabilities: Paul Nitze and the Cold War* (New York: Harper Collins, 1990), p. 380.

25. John Ranelagh, *The Agency: The Rise and Decline of the CIA* (New York: Simon & Schuster, 1986), p. 492; R. Jack Smith, *The Unknown CIA: My Three Decades with the Agency* (New York: Berkley, 1992), p. 241.

26. Ranelagh, *The Agency*, pp. 493–94; Smith, *Unknown CIA*, p. 241; John Prados, *The Soviet Estimate: U.S. Intelligence Analysis and Russian Military Strength* (New York: Dial, 1982), p. 209.

27. Ranelagh, *The Agency*, p. 495.

28. Ibid., pp. 496–97; Lawrence Freedman, *U.S. Intelligence and the Soviet Strategic Threat*, 2nd ed. (Princeton, N.J.: Princeton University Press, 1986), p. 113; Smith, *The Unknown CIA*, p. 243.

29. Ranelagh, *The Agency*, p. 496–97; Freedman, *U.S. Intelligence*, p. 133; Prados, *Soviet Estimate*, pp. 217–18; Smith, *Unknown CIA*, p. 243.

30. Defense Intelligence Agency, *SS-19 ICBM System*, October 15, 1975.

31. Callaghan, *Dangerous Capabilities*, p. 378; Anne Hessing Cahn, "Team B: The Trillion Dollar Experiment," *Bulletin of the Atomic Scientists*, April 1993, p. 24. Pipes's views were spelled out in Richard Pipes, "Why the Soviet Union Thinks It Could Fight and Win a Nuclear War," *Commentary* 64, no. 1 (1977).

32. Team B, *Intelligence Community Experiment in Competitive Analysis: Soviet Strategic Objectives: An Alternative View: Report of Team "B,"* December 1976, p. 5.

33. Ibid., p. 47.

34. Ibid., pp. 19–20.

35. Ibid., p. 19.

36. *Soviet Forces for Intercontinental Conflict Through the Mid–1980s*, vol. 1: *Key Judgments and Summary*, NIE 11-3/8-76, December 1976, p. 9.

37. Ibid., p. 37.

38. Ibid.; the Backfire controversy continued into the 1980s. See Michael Gordon, "Pentagon Reassesses Soviet Bomber," *New York Times*, October 1, 1985, p. A8.

39. *Soviet Forces for Intercontinental Conflict*, p. 3.

40. Ibid., p. 22.

41. Ibid., p. 56.

42. For the evolution of Paul Nitze's views see Callaghan, *Dangerous Capabilities*; Strobe Talbott, *The Master of the Game* (New York: Knopf, 1988), and Paul Nitze, *From Hiroshima to Glasnost* (New York: Grove Weidenfeld, 1989).

43. Central Intelligence Agency, *Elites and the Distribution of Power in Iran*, February 1976, p. 5.

44. Ibid., pp. 51–54.

45. U.S. Congress, House Permanent Select Committee on Intelligence, *Iran: Evaluation of U.S. Intelligence Performance Prior to November 1978* (Washington, D.C.: U.S. Government Printing Office, 1979), pp. 6, 7; Central Intelligence Agency, *Iran in the 1980s*, August 1977, pp. i, iii.

46. Central Intelligence Agency, *Iran in the 1980s*, pp. iii–iv.

47. Central Intelligence Agency, *Iran in the 1980s,* October 5, 1977, p. 8.

48. U.S. Congress, House Permanent Select Committee on Intelligence, *Iran,* pp. 6, 7; Defense Intelligence Agency, DIAAPPR 195-78, "Iran: Renewal of Civil Disturbances," August 16, 1978, p. 9.

49. Central Intelligence Agency, "Iran: The Radicals in the Opposition," January 12, 1979, p. 2.

50. Zbigniew Brzezinski, *Power and Principle: Memoirs of the National Security Adviser 1977–1981* (New York: Farrar, Straus, and Giroux, 1983), pp. 366–67.

51. Ibid., p. 367; Ranelagh, *The Agency,* p. 649.

52. Stansfield Turner, *Secrecy and Democracy: The CIA in Transition* (Boston: Houghton Mifflin, 1985), p. 114.

53. Ibid., p. 115.

54. Ibid.

55. "The Shah's Illness and the Fall of Iran," *Studies in Intelligence,* Summer 1980, pp. 61–63.

23 A New Decade

1. Affidavit of Allan M. Power, Federal Bureau of Investigation, submitted to State and Northern District of California, City and County of San Francisco, October 16, 1983, pp. 1–2; "Partners in Espionage," *Security Awareness Bulletin,* August 1984, pp. 1–8; Linda Melvern, David Hebditch, and Nick Anning, *Techno-Bandits: How the Soviets Are Stealing America's High-Tech Future* (Boston: Houghton Mifflin, 1984), p. 242; "For Love of Money and Adventure," *Time,* October 31, 1983, pp. 39–40; Wallace Turner, "American Is Arrested on Charges of Selling Poland Missile Secrets," *New York Times,* October 18, 1983, pp. A1, A25; Howard Kurtz, "California Man Charged with Spying," *Washington Post,* October 18, 1983, pp. A1, A4; Howard Kurtz, "Spy Suspect Said to Possess More Missile Documents," *Washington Post,* October 19, 1983, p. A20; Thomas B. Allen and Norman Polmar, *Merchants of Treason: America's Secrets for Sale* (New York: Delacorte Press, 1988), p. 145; Department of Defense, *Soviet Acquisition of Militarily Significant Western Technology: An Update,* September 1985, p. 20.

2. Affidavit of Allan M. Power; "For Love of Money"; Turner, "American Is Arrested"; Kurtz, "California Man"; Kurtz, "Spy Suspect."

3. Central Intelligence Agency, *Foreign Intelligence and Security Services: USSR* (Washington, D.C.: CIA, 1975), pp. 68–69.

4. Ibid., p. 69; Bernard Gwertzman, "State Department Alters the Rules for Russians' Travel in U.S.," *New York Times,* November 20, 1983, pp. 1, 17; Steve Harvay, "Ban on Soviet Travel Is Map of Curiosities," *Los Angeles Times,* December 9, 1983, Metro, pp. 1, 2.

5. John Barron, *The KGB Today: The Hidden Hand* (New York: Reader's Digest Press, 1983), pp. 196–204; "Technology Transfer: An Introduction," *Security Awareness Bulletin,* February 1983, p. 9; Edward J. O'Malley and Lyle J. Thiesen, "Soviet Acquisition of U.S. and Western Technology," *Journal of Electronic Defense,* April 1983, pp. 35–40; Department of Defense, *Soviet Acquisition,* p. 20.

6. Allen and Polmar, *Merchants of Treason,* pp. 145–46.

7. Ibid., pp. 146, 161; Robert Lindsey, "Some Losers in Silicon Valley Said to Find Wealth in Spying," *New York Times,* October 23, 1983, pp. 1, 32.

8. Robert D. McFadden, "U.S. Says Bulgarian Suspect Bought Data on Atom Arms," *New York Times*, September 25, 1983, pp. 1, 6.

9. Ibid.; "Bulgarian Man Arraigned on Charges of Espionage," *Washington Post*, September 25, 1983, p. A13.

10. Jeff Gerth, "Ex-U.S. Sergeant Called Key Figure in Espionage Ring," *New York Times*, August 26, 1988, pp. A1, A10; Bill Gertz, "Ex-GI Held as Leader of Spy Ring for Soviets," *Washington Times*, August 26, 1988, pp. A1, A10; Robert J. McCartney, "Former U.S. Sergeant Held as Spy by Bonn," *Washington Post*, August 26, 1988, pp. A1, A18; Tyler Marshall, "Bonn Court Sentences Ex-GI for Spying," *Los Angeles Times*, June 7, 1990, p. A7.

11. Gerth, "Ex-U.S. Sergeant Called Key Figure in Espionage Ring"; Jeff Gerth, "American Passed Military Secrets since '74, Investigators Are Told," *New York Times*, August 27, 1988, pp. 1, 8; "NATO's Secrets Up for Sale," *Newsweek*, September 5, 1988, pp. 38–39; Tyler Marshall, "Bonn Court Sentences Ex-GI for Spying," *Los Angeles Times*, June 7, 1990, p. A7; Michael Isikoff, "Ex-Army Sergeant Held on Charges of Espionage," *Washington Post*, June 8, 1990, pp. A1, A6.

12. "On His Socialists' Secret Service," *The Economist*, November 27, 1982, pp. 43–44; Roger Faligot and Pascal Knop, *La Piscine: The French Secret Service Since 1944* (New York: Basil Blackwell, 1989) p. 279.

13. "On His Socialists' Secret Service"; "Goodbye to M," *The Economist*, November 20, 1982, pp. 31–32; Bryan Boswell, "Major Shake–up for French Spy Network," *The Weekend Australian*, November 20–21, 1982, p. 13; Paul Lewis, "Paris Spies: Shady Past of Agency," *New York Times*, September 23, 1985, p. A14; Pierre Marion, *La Mission Impossible: À la tête des Services Secrets* (Paris: Calmann, Levy, 1991), pp. 119–28.

14. Pierre Pean, *Secret d'État: La France du Secret, Les Secrets de la France* (Paris: Fayard, 1986), p. 193.

15. "On His Socialists' Secret Service"; "Goodbye to M"; Boswell, "Major Shake-up for French Spy Network"; Lewis, "Paris Spies."

16. Paul Lewis, "K.G.B. Figure Called a Spy for France," *New York Times*, January 8, 1986, p. 3; Oleg Kalugin, *The First Directorate: My 32 Years in Intelligence and Espionage Against the West* (New York: St. Martin's, 1994), pp. 203–4. Christopher Andrew and Oleg Gordievsky, *KGB: The Inside Story* (New York: Harper Collins, 1990), p. 662; Gordon Brook-Shepherd, *The Storms Birds: Soviet Post-War Defectors* (London: Weidenfeld & Nicolson, 1988) pp. 254–55.

17. Central Intelligence Agency, *Foreign Intelligence and Security Services: USSR*, p. 45.

18. Theirry Wolton, *Le KGB en France* (Paris: Bernard Grasset, 1986), pp. 248–49; Gordon Brook-Shepherd, *The Storm Birds: Soviet Post-War Defectors* (London: Weidenfeld & Nicolson, 1988), p. 257.

19. Andrew and Gordievsky, *KGB*, p. 622.

20. David Dickson, "Soviet High-Tech Spying Detailed in France," *Science*, April 19, 1985, p. 306; Michael Dobbs, "Soviets Angry at French Leak," *Washington Post*, April 2, 1975, pp. A21, A23; Philip Hanson, *Soviet Industrial Espionage: Some New Information* (London: Royal Institute of International Affairs, 1987), pp. 3, 10.

21. Andrew and Gordievsky, *KGB*, p. 622.

22. Ibid.; Hanson, *Soviet Industrial Espionage*, pp. 3–4, 10.

23. Brook-Shepherd, *Storm Birds*, pp. 264–265; "Throwing Out Moscow's Spies," *Newsweek*, April 18, 1983, pp. 36–39.

24. Wolton, *KGB en France*, pp. 254–55; Brook-Shepherd, *Storm Birds*, p. 261; Department of Defense, *Soviet Acquisition*, p. 20.

25. Andrew and Gordievsky, *KGB*, p. 622; Hanson, *Soviet Industrial Espionage*, p. 10.

26. Wolton, *KGB en France*, pp. 242, 244; Brook-Shepherd, *Storm Birds*, p. 261.

27. Brook-Shepherd, *Storm Birds*, pp. 253–54.

28. Ibid., pp. 263–64.

29. Andrew and Gordievsky, *KGB*, p. 583.

30. Nicholas L. Johnson, *The Soviet Year in Space 1989* (Colorado Springs: Teledyne Brown Engineering, 1990), pp. 27–37; Phillip S. Clark, "Aspects of Soviet Photoreconnaissance Satellite Programme," *Journal of the British Interplanetary Society* 36 (1983): 169–84.

31. Geoffrey Perry, "Soviet ELINT Satellites Cover the Globe," *Military Electronics/Countermeasures*, January 1983, pp. 38–48.

32. Desmond Ball, *Soviet Signals Intelligence (SIGINT)* (Canberra: SDSC, Australian National University, 1989), p. 24.

33. Ibid., pp. 48–51; David Kahn, "The Bugging of America," *Penthouse*, October 1984, pp. 69ff; William J. Broad, "Evading the Soviet Ear at Glen Cove," *Science*, September 1982, pp. 910–13; William Overend, "Soviet Consulate: Cow Hollow Intrigue," *Los Angeles Times*, July 28, 1985, pp. 1, 34–35; Desmond Ball, "Soviet Signals Intelligence (SIGINT): The Use of Diplomatic Establishments" (Canberra: SDSC Studies, Australian National University, 1987), pp. 1–27.

36. Ball, *Soviet Signals Intelligence (SIGINT)*, pp. 40–42.

35. Ibid., p. 95.

36. Andrew and Gordievsky, *KGB*, pp. 583–84.

37. Ibid., p. 588.

38. Christopher Andrew and Oleg Gordievsky, *Instructions from the Centre: Top Secret Files on KGB Foreign Operations 1975–1985* (London: Hodder & Stoughton, 1991), pp. 71–72.

39. Francis X. Clines, "Reagan Denounces Ideology of Soviet as 'Focus' of Evil," *New York Times*, March 9, 1983, pp. A1, A8; Andrew and Gordievsky, *Instructions*, p. 81; Don Oberdorfer, *The Turn: From the Cold War to a New Era* (New York: Touchstone, 1991), p. 23.

40. Andrew and Gordievsky, *KGB*, pp. 592–93.

41. Ibid., p. 593.

42. Private information; William E. Burrows, *Deep Black: Space Espionage and National Security* (New York: Random House, 1986), p. 172.

43. Private information; Burrows, *Deep Black*, p. 172.

44. Richard Burt, "Technology is Essential to Arms Verification," *New York Times*, August 14, 1979, pp. C1, C2; Murray Sayle, "KE 007: A Conspiracy of Circumstance," *New York Review of Books*, April 25, 1985, pp. 44–54; Kenneth J. Stein, "Cobra Judy Phased Array Radar Tested," *Aviation Week & Space Technology*, August 10, 1981, pp. 70–73; "X-Band Expands Cobra Judy's Repertoire," *Defense Electronics*, January 1985, pp. 43–44; Michael E. del Papa, *Meeting the Challenge: ESD and the Cobra Dane Construction Effort on Shemya Island* (Bedford, Mass.: Electronic Systems Division, Air Force Systems Command, 1979), pp. 1–3.

45. Sam Jameson, "747 Disclosure Costly to Japan's Security Effort," *Los Angeles Times*, September 19, 1983, pt. 1, pp. 1, 15; "On the Way to Securing a World Position? Japan's Intelligence Agencies and Their Activities," *Japan Quarterly*,

June 1982, pp. 159–62; personal communication from Owen Wilkes; Seymour Hersh, *"The Target is Destroyed": What Really Happened to Flight 007 and What America Knew About It* (New York: Random House, 1986), pp. 57, 60.

46. Hersh, *"The Target Is Destroyed,"* pp. 47–48; Keyes Beech, "Secret U.S. Base Keeps Eye on Far East," *Los Angeles Times,* January 20, 1980, p. 17.

47. Hersh, *"The Target Is Destroyed,"* pp. 57–58.

48. International Civil Aviation Organization, *Report of the Completion of the Fact-Finding Investigation Regarding the Shooting Down of Korea Airlines Boeing 747 (Flight KE 007) on August 1983* (Montreal: ICAO, May 28, 1993), pp. 1, 6, 48.

49. Hersh, *"The Target Is Destroyed,"* pp. 44, 45.

50. Ibid., p. 46.

51. Ibid., pp. 56–57.

52. Ibid., p. 61.

53. Ibid., p. 102; George Shultz, *Turmoil and Triumph: My Years as Secretary of State* (New York: Scribner's, 1993), pp. 361–62.

54. Shultz, *Turmoil and Triumph,* p. 362.

55. Hersh, *"The Target Is Destroyed,"* pp. 57, 60; Jameson, "747 Disclosure Costly to Japan's Security Effort."

56. National Security Decision Directive 102, "U.S. Response to Soviet Destruction of KAL Airliner," September 5, 1983.

57. Ibid.

58. Andrew and Gordievsky, *KGB,* p. 598; Shultz, *Turmoil and Triumph,* p. 373.

59. Oberdorfer, *The Turn* p. 65; Andrew and Gordievsky, *KGB,* p. 600.

60. Oberdorfer, *The Turn,* p. 65; Andrew and Gordievsky, *KGB,* pp. 599–600.

61. Andrew and Gordievsky, *KGB,* p. 600.

62. Oberdorfer, *The Turn,* pp. 65–66; Andrew and Gordievsky, *KGB,* p. 600; Bruce Blair, *The Logic of Accidental War* (Washington, D.C.: Brookings Institution Press, 1993), p. 181.

63. Oberdorfer, *The Turn,* pp. 66–67, 67n.

64. Andrew and Gordievsky, *KGB,* p. 602.

65. Ibid., pp. 601–2.

66. Ibid., pp. 604–5.

24   The Year of the Spy

1. Michael Dobbs, "Top Soviet Agent in London Defects; Britain Expels 25," *Washington Post,* September 13, 1985, pp. A1, A33; R. W. Apple, Jr., "K.G.B. Spy Defects and British Order 25 Russians Home," *New York Times,* September 13, 1985, pp. A1, A6.

2. Gordon Brook-Shepherd, *The Storm Birds: Soviet Post-War Defectors* (London: Wiedenfeld & Nicolson, 1988), pp. 271–73.

3. Ibid., p. 274; Christopher Andrew and Oleg Gordievsky, *KGB: The Inside Story* (New York: Harper Collins, 1990), pp. 522–23; Central Intelligence Agency, *Foreign Intelligence and Security Services: USSR* (Washington, D.C.: CIA, 1975), p. 41.

4. Andrew and Gordievsky, *KGB,* p. 2; Brook-Shepherd, *Storm Birds,* pp. 274–75.

5. Brook-Shepherd, *Storm Birds*, p. 276; Andrew and Gordievsky, *KGB*, pp. 567–570; "Spies: One for the West," *Newsweek*, September 23, 1985, p. 37, "What Russia Lost," *The Economist*, September 21, 1985, pp. 46–47.

6. Brook-Shepherd, *Storm Birds*, pp. 277–278; "Spies: One for the West."

7. Brook-Shepherd, *Storm Birds*, p. 270; "Spies: One for the West."

8. Murrey Marder, "Defector Told of Soviet Alert," *Washington Post*, August 8, 1986, pp. A1, A22; Leslie Gelb, "K.G.B. Defector Helped the C.I.A. Brief Reagan before Summit Talks," *New York Times*, August 9, 1986, pp. 1, 4.

9. Ronald Kessler, *Escape from the CIA* (New York: Pocket Books, 1991), pp. 15–16.

10. Central Intelligence Agency, "Vitaly Sergeyevich Yurchenko," November 8, 1985, p. 1.

11. Ibid., pp. 1–2.

12. Ibid., pp. 2–3; Central Intelligence Agency, *Foreign Intelligence and Security Services: USSR*, p. 46.

13. Central Intelligence Agency, "Vitaly Sergeyevich Yurchenko," pp. 2–3; Central Intelligence Agency, *KGB and GRU* (Washington, D.C.: U.S. Government Printing Office, 1984), p. 48.

14. Kessler, *Escape*, pp. 67, 70–71; David Wise, *The Spy Who Got Away* (New York: Random House, 1988), p. 18.

15. Kessler, *Escape*, p. 73; Bill Gertz, "Two Here Belong to Secret KGB Unit," *Washington Times*, pp. A1, A10; John Barron, "The KGB's Deepest Secret," *Reader's Digest*, November 1988, pp. 94–99.

16. David Wise, "Tinker, Tailor, Soldier—Victim," *Washington Post*, August 1, 1993, pp. C1, C2; Tom Mangold, *Cold Warrior, James Jesus Angleton: The CIA's Master Spy* (New York: Simon & Schuster, 1991), pp. 278–96; John Sawatsky, *For Services Rendered: Leslie James Bennett and the RCMP Security Service* (Garden City, N.Y.: Doubleday, 1982); "Forced-Out RCMP Officer Wasn't KGB Spy Ottawa Says," *Toronto Globe and Mail*, April 1, 1993, p. A4.

17. David Wise, *Molehunt: The Secret Search for Traitors that Shattered the CIA* (New York: Random House, 1992), p. 274.

18. Henry Hurt, *Shadrin: The Spy Who Never Came Back* (New York: McGraw-Hill, 1981), pp. 23, 38–51, 64–68.

19. Ibid., pp. 122–51.

20. Ibid., p. 206; Patrick E. Tyler, "Missing U.S. Agent Dead," *Washington Post*, October 30, 1985, p. A9.

21. The litany of errors made by the CIA in handling Yurchenko, clearly told from an FBI point of view, can be found in Kessler, *Escape*. On the problems of defectors, see Dmitry Mikheyev, "Defector's Problems in the West," *Studies in Intelligence*, Spring 1988, pp. 67–74.

22. "Did Yurchenko Fool the CIA?" *Newsweek*, November 18, 1985, pp. 34–39; Stephen Engelberg, "President Sees a Soviet 'Ploy' in 3 Defections," *New York Times*, November 7, 1985, pp. A1, A12; Stephen Engelberg, "Washington Ponders Yurchenko: A Troubled Spy or Actor?" *New York Times*, November 10, 1985, p. 20; Bob Woodward, "CIA Takes Serious Look at Theory that Yurchenko Was Double Agent," *Washington Post*, November 20, 1985, p. A35; Stephen Engelberg, "U.S. Aides Split on Yurchenko's Authenticity," *New York Times*, November 8, 1985, p. A10.

23. "Gates Calls '85 Defector Bona Fide," *Washington Post*, January 16, 1993, p. A7.

24. Kessler, *Escape*, p. 127.

25. Letter from Joseph E. DiGenova, United States Attorney, to Richard E. Hibey, Re: United States v. Jonathan Jay Pollard, February 9, 1987; Bob Woodward, *Veil: The Secret Wars of the CIA 1981–1987* (New York: Simon & Schuster, 1987), p. 447.

26. Kessler, *Escape*, p. 127.

27. Interview; Woodward, *Veil*, p. 448.

28. Woodward, *Veil*, pp. 448–49.

29. Woodward, *Veil*, p. 449; Susan Schmidt and Patrick E. Tyler, "Pelton Map Designation Held Wrong," *Washington Post*, May 31, 1986, pp. A1, A12.

30. Woodward, *Veil*, p. 451.

31. Wise, *The Spy Who Got Away*, pp. 19, 76–86, 131; Woodward, *Veil*, p. 425.

32. Wise, *The Spy Who Got Away*, pp. 68, 159.

33. Ibid., pp. 223–24, 226, 250.

34. Joe Pichirallo, "Retiree Kept Close CIA Ties," *Washington Post*, November 27, 1985, pp. A1, A10; Robin Toner, "Bail Denied Ex-CIA Worker in China Spy Case," *New York Times*, November 28, 1985, p. B8; Joe Pichirallo, "Ex-CIA Analyst Gave Secrets to China," *Washington Post*, November 24, 1985, pp. A1, A24.

35. "'Ministry of State Security' Set Up on Mainland China," *Issues and Studies*, July 1983, pp. 5–8; Nicholas Eftimiades, "China's Ministry of State Security: Coming of Age in the International Arena," *Intelligence and National Security* 8, no. 1 (1993): 23–43; "Chinese Official Said Exposer of CIA Turncoat," *Washington Post*, September 5, 1986, p. A18; Michael Wines, "Spy Reportedly Unmasked by China Defector," *Los Angeles Times*, September 5, 1986, pp. 1, 12; Daniel Southerland, "China Silent on Reported Defection of Intelligence Official," *Washington Post*, September 4, 1986, p. A30.

36. "Chinese Official Said to Be Exposer of CIA Turncoat"; Wines, "Spy Reportedly Unmasked by China Defector"; Thomas Allen and Norman Polmar, *Merchants of Treason: America's Secrets for Sale from the Pueblo to the Present* (New York: Delacorte, 1988), p. 302.

37. Kessler, *Spy vs. Spy*, pp. 202–3.

38. Allen and Polmar, *Merchants of Treason*, p. 22.

39. Ibid., pp. 22–23.

40. Ibid., pp. 264–65.

41. Ibid., pp. 111, 265.

42. Ibid., p. 266; John Barron, *Breaking the Ring: The Bizarre Case of the Walker Family Spy Ring*, (Boston: Houghton Mifflin, 1987), pp. 127–28.

43. Allen and Polmar, *Merchants of Treason*, p. 135; Howard Blum, *I Pledge Allegiance . . . The True Story of the Walkers: An American Spy Family* (New York: Simon & Schuster, 1987), p. 340; Ruth Marcus and Molly Sinclair, "Accused Spy Had Access to Nimitz's Burn Bag," *Washington Post*, May 25, 1985, pp. A1, A11.

44. Barron, *Breaking the Ring*, p. 201.

45. Central Intelligence Agency, *KGB and GRU*, p. 53; Barron, *Breaking the Ring*, p. 148.

46. Norman Polmar and Thomas Allen, "The Crypto Bandits," *Air Force Magazine*, June 1989, pp. 89–92; James M. Dorsey, "Walker Brought Soviet Subs Closer to U.S. Shores," *Washington Times*, April 8, 1987, pp. 1A, 8A.

47. For a more extensive analysis see David Kahn, "'Year of the Spy': Was U.S. Hurt?" *Newsday*, July 27, 1986, Ideas, pp. 1, 4.

48. Ian Black and Benny Morris, *Israel's Secret Wars: A History of Israel's Intelligence Services* (New York: Grove-Weidenfeld, 1991), p. 416; Wolf Blitzer, *Territory of Lies: The Exclusive Story of Jonathan Jay Pollard* (New York: Harper & Row, 1989), pp. 115, 133–34.

49. Allen and Polmar, *Merchants of Treason*, p. 283; Robert Pear, "Analyst Told 10 Years Ago of Working for Israeli Intelligence, Friend Says," *New York Times*, November 27, 1985, p. B8; Yossi Melman and Dan Raviv, *The Imperfect Spies: The History of Israeli Intelligence* (London: Sidgwick & Jackson, 1989), p. 324.

50. Government's Memorandum in Aid of Sentencing, *United States of America vs. Jonathan Jay Pollard*, United States District Court, District of Columbia, January 6, 1987, Criminal No. 86-0207, pp. 2, 3; Factual Proffer, *United States of America vs. Jonathan Jay Pollard*, United States District Court, District of Columbia, June 4, 1986, Criminal No. 86-0207, p. 1.

51. Blitzer, *Territory of Lies*, p. 3.

52. Factual Proffer, p. 2; Blitzer, *Territory of Lies*, p. 74; Government's Memorandum in Aid of Sentencing, pp. 24–25.

53. Blitzer, *Territory of Lies*, pp. 8, 77; Government's Memorandum in Aid of Sentencing, p. 25.

54. Central Intelligence Agency, *Foreign Intelligence and Security Services: Israel* (Washington, D.C.: CIA, 1977), p. 9; Black and Morris, *Israel's Secret Wars*, p. 418; Blitzer, *Territory of Lies*, p. 10.

55. Blitzer, *Territory of Lies*, pp. 11–12, 77.

56. Black and Morris, *Israel's Secret Wars*, p. 417; Government's Memorandum in Aid of Sentencing, p. 24.

57. Stanley A. Blumberg and Gwinn Owens, *The Survival Factor: Israeli Intelligence from World War I to the Present* (New York: G. P. Putnam, 1981), p. 272; Richard Halloran, "U.S. Offers Israel Plan on War Data," *New York Times*, March 13, 1983, pp. 1, 13; "How the Israelis Pulled It Off," *Newsweek*, July 19, 1976, pp. 42–47; Bob Woodward, "CIA Sought 3rd Country Contra Aid," *Washington Post*, May 19, 1984, pp. A1, A13; Bob Woodward, "Probes of Iran Deals Extend to Roles of CIA, Director," *Washington Post*, November 28, 1986, pp. A1, A33.

58. Woodward, "Probes of Iran Deals Extend to Roles of CIA, Director"; "Statement of Bobby Ray Inman on Withdrawing His Nomination," *New York Times*, January 19, 1994, p. A14.

59. Factual Proffer, p. 7; Joe Pichirallo, "Ex-Analyst Pleads Guilty to Spying for Israel," *Washington Post*, June 5, 1986, pp. A1, A37; Government's Memorandum in Aid of Sentencing, p. 26; Blitzer, *Territory of Lies*, p. 77.

60. Indictment, *United States of America vs. Jonathan Jay Pollard*, United States District Court, District of Columbia, June 4, 1986, Criminal No. 86-0207, pp. 27–29; Factual Proffer, pp. 4–5; Pichirallo, "Ex-Analyst Pollard Pleads Guilty to Spying for Israel"; Blitzer, *Territory of Lies*, pp. 90–91.

61. Wolf Blitzer, "Pollard: Not a Bumbler, but Israel's Master Spy," *Washington Post*, February 15, 1987, pp. C1, C2; Philip Shenon, "Spy Telling of Israeli Operations; Pelton Convicted of Selling Secrets," *New York Times*, June 6, 1986, p. A12; Blitzer, *Territory of Lies*, p. 95.

62. Government's Memorandum in Aid of Sentencing, p. 30; Blitzer, *Territory of Lies*, p. 97; Melman and Raviv, *Imperfect Spies*, pp. 329, 332.

63. Government's Memorandum in Aid of Sentencing, p. 31.

64. Blitzer, *Territory of Lies*, pp. 113–14, 165–66; "Pollard: Not a Bumbler"; Stephen Engelberg, "Israelis Drop Spy Unit, U.S. Says," *New York Times*, December 21, 1985, pp. 1, 6.

65. Blizter, "Pollard: Not a Bumbler"; Blitzer, *Territory of Lies*, pp. 113–14.

66. Goverment's Memorandum in Aid of Sentencing, pp. 47–48.

67. Philip Shenon, "Israel Denies Running Widespread Espionage Operation in U.S.," *New York Times*, June 2, 1986, p. A12.

68. Andrew Meisels, "Israeli Officer in Pollard Case Quits Key Post," *Washington Times*, March 30, 1987, pp. 1A, 10A; Victor Ostrovsky and Claire Hoy, *By Way of Deception: The Making and Unmaking of a Mossad Officer* (New York: St. Martin's Press, 1990), p. 268.

69. "Report of Rotenstreich-Tzur Committee on the Pollard Case; Communicated in English by the Prime Minister's Media Office" (Jerusalem: Government Press Office, May 27, 1987).

70. "Government Releases Eban Committee Report" (Jerusalem: Government Press Office, May 27, 1987), p. 8.

71. Wolf Blitzer, "Pollard Says Top Israeli Officials Authorized His Spying," *Jerusalem Post International Edition*, March 7, 1987, pp. 1–2; Melman and Raviv, *Imperfect Spies*, p. 341.

72. Blitzer, *Territory of Lies*, pp. 97–98.

73. Thomas L. Friedman, "Clinton Is Asked by Rabin to Cut Spy's Jail Term," *New York Times*, November 11, 1993, pp. A1, A7; Letter, Les Aspin to The President, December 27, 1993.

25 End of an Era

1. Sunday Times Insight Team, *Rainbow Warrior* (London: Hutchinson, 1986), p. 20; Michael King, *The Death of the Rainbow Warrior* (London: Penguin, 1986), p. 11.

2. Sunday Times Insight Team, *Rainbow Warrior*, pp. 161–163, 176; John Dyson, *Sink the Rainbow!* (London: Gollancz, 1986), pp. 91, 93; U.S. Army Intelligence and Threat Analysis Center, *Greenpeace: Repercussions in the French I&SS*, 1986, p. 3.

3. Sunday Times Insight Team, *Rainbow Warrior*, pp. 161, 163, 176; Dyson, *Sink the Rainbow*, pp. 93–94; U.S. Army Intelligence and Threat Analysis Center, *Greenpeace*, p. 3.

4. King, *Death of the Rainbow Warrior*, pp. 49–50; Sunday Times Insight Team, *Rainbow Warrior*, p. 188.

5. King, *Death of the Rainbow Warrior*, p. 74; Sunday Times Insight Team, *Rainbow Warrior*, pp. 205–7; "Killing of Agents Was Feared, Lange Says," *Los Angeles Times*, July 9, 1986, p. 9; Roger Faligot and Pascal Krop, *La Piscine: The French Secret Service since 1944* (New York: Basil Blackwell, 1989), p. 289.

6. King, *Death of the Rainbow Warrior*, p. 63; Sunday Times Insight Team, *Rainbow Warrior*, p. 207; Faligot and Krop, *La Piscine*, p. 289.

7. King, *Death of the Rainbow Warrior*, pp. 74–75; Faligot and Krop, *La Piscine*, p. 289.

8. Faligot and Krop, *La Piscine*, p. 289.

9. "Killing of Agents Was Feared"; Faligot and Krop, *La Piscine*, p. 290.

10. Faligot and Krop, *La Piscine*, pp. 290–92.

11. King, *Death of the Rainbow Warrior*, p. 48.

12. Faligot and Krop, *La Piscine*, pp. 292–93.

13. Ibid., p. 293.

14. Ibid., pp. 293–94.

15. "Killing of Agents Was Feared."

16. Edward Cody, "New Zealand Angered by Paris," *Washington Post*, December 15, 1987, p. A33; Edward Cody, "Chirac Frees French Agent on Election Eve," *Washington Post*, May 7, 1988, p. A16; "New Zealand Furious at French Spy Move," *Washington Times*, July 14, 1989, p. A2; "France Promotes an Officer Jailed in Greenpeace Sinking," *New York Times*, January 6, 1994, p. A7.

17. Walter Pincus and Mary Thornton, "U.S. to Orbit 'Sigint' Craft from Shuttle," *Washington Post*, December 19, 1984, pp. A1, A8–A9.

18. Edward H. Kolcum, "Night Launch of Discovery Boosts Secret Military Satellite into Orbit," *Aviation Week & Space Technology*, November 27, 1989, p. 29; private information.

19. James Gerstenzang, "Shuttle Lifts Off with Spy Cargo," *Los Angeles Times*, January 25, 1985, pp. 1, 11; "Final Launch Preparations Under Way for Signal Intelligence Satellite Mission," *Aviation Week & Space Technology*, November 6, 1989, p. 24.

20. William E. Burrows, *Deep Black: Space Espionage and National Security* (New York: Random House, 1987), pp. 304–5; *USAF Mishap Report 86-4-18-701* (Los Angeles: Space Division, June 8, 1986), pp. A-1, E-1; "Explosion Sequence Photos Depict Titan 34D Launch Failure," *Aviation Week & Space Technology*, November 3, 1986, p. 43.

21. Nigel Hawkes, Geoffrey Lean, David Leigh, Robin McKie, Peter Pringle, and Andrew Wilson, *Chernobyl: The End of the Nuclear Dream* (New York: Vintage, 1986), pp. 99–103.

22. Stephen Engelberg, "U.S. Says Intelligence Units Did Not Detect the Accident," *New York Times*, May 2, 1976, p. A9.

23. Hawkes et al., *Chernobyl*, p. 122.

24. "Meltdown," *Newsweek*, May 12, 1986, pp. 20–35; Boyce Rensberg, "Explosion: Graphite Fire Suspected," *Washington Post*, April 30, 1986, pp. A1, A17; Carl M. Cannon and Mark Thompson, "Threat to Soviets Grows, U.S. Spy Photos Indicate," *Miami Herald*, April 30, 1986, pp. 1A, 14A.

25. "Meltdown."

26. Ibid.

27. Robert C. Toth, "Satellites Keep Eye on Reactor," *Los Angeles Times*, May 2, 1986, p. 22.

28. "Meltdown"; Bernard Gwertzman, "Fire in Reactor May Be Out, New U.S. Pictures Indicate; Soviet Says Fallout Is Cut," *New York Times*, May 2, 1986, pp. A1, A8.

29. Philip M. Boffey, "U.S. Panel Calls the Disaster in the Ukraine the Worst Ever," *New York Times*, May 4, 1986, pp. 1, 20.

30. Serge Schmemann, "Soviet Mobilizes a Vast Operation to Overcome the Disaster," *New York Times*, May 19, 1987, p. A8.

31. Phillip S. Clark, "The Soviet Photoreconnaissance Satellite Programme 1982–1990," *Journal of the British Interplanetary Society* 44 (1991): 537–52.

32. Ibid.

33. Central Intelligence Agency, *KGB and GRU* (Washington, D.C.: CIA, 1984), p. 72.

34. Nicholas Johnson, *The Soviet Year in Space, 1988* (Colorado Springs: Teledyne-Brown Engineering, 1989), p. 42.

35. Jay Peterzell, *Reagan's Secret Wars* (Washington, D.C.: Center for National Security Studies, 1984), p. 9.

36. Joseph E. Persico, *Casey: From the OSS to the CIA* (New York: Viking, 1990), p. 225.

37. Carl Bernstein, "CIA's Secret Arms Aid to Afghanistan," *Chicago Sun-Times*, September 6, 1981, p. 1; Tim Weiner, "The CIA's Leaking Pipeline," *Philadelphia Inquirer*, February 28, 1988, pp. 1A, 12A; Peterzell, *Reagan's Secret Wars*, pp. 9, 10, 13; John Prados, *Presidents' Secret Wars: CIA and Pentagon Covert Operations from World War II through Iranscam* (New York: Quill, 1988), p. 359; Coll, "Anatomy of a Victory."

38. Bernstein, "CIA's Secret Arms Aid to Afghanistan."

39. Peterzell, *Reagan's Secret Wars*, p. 11.

40. Persico, *Casey*, p. 312.

41. Mohammad Youssaf, *The Bear Trap: Afghanistan's Untold Story* (London: Leo Cooper, 1992), p. 87; Robert Pear, "Arming the Afghan Guerrillas: A Huge Effort Led by U.S.," *New York Times*, April 18, 1988, pp. A1, A11; Bob Woodward and Charles R. Babcock, "U.S. Covert Aid to Afghans on the Rise," *Washington Post*, January 13, 1985, pp. A1, A30; Bob Woodward, *Veil: The Secret Wars of the CIA 1981–1987* (New York: Simon & Schuster, 1987), pp. 317–18.

42. Leslie H. Gelb, "U.S. Aides Put '85 Arms Supplies to Afghan Rebels at $280 Million," *New York Times*, November 28, 1984, pp. A1, A9; Woodward and Babcock, "U.S. Covert Aid to Afghans on the Rise"; Youssaf, *Bear Trap*, p. 85.

43. Coll, "Anatomy of a Victory."

44. Joanne Omang, "Secret Votes Give Afghans $300 Million," *Washington Post*, October 10, 1985, p. A16; "Leaks in the Pipeline," *Time*, December 9, 1985, pp. 50–51; David B. Ottaway, "Afghan Rebels to Get More Missiles," *Washington Post*, February 8, 1987, pp. A1, A28; "U.S. Aides Put '85 Arms Supplies to Afghan Rebels at $280 Million"; Woodward and Babcock, "U.S. Covert Aid to Afghans on Rise."

45. Bernard Gwertzman, "Stingers Aiding Afghans' Fight U.S. Aides Say," *New York Times*, December 13, 1986, pp. 1, 9; Ottaway, "Afghan Rebels to Get More Missiles"; "Afghan Transport Plane Downed by Guerrilla Force with a Missile," *New York Times*, February 10, 1987, pp. A1, A5; Pear, "Arming the Afghan Guerrillas."; David B. Ottaway, "Afghanistan Rebels Due More Arms," *Washington Post*, April 5, 1987, pp. A1, A19; James M. Dorsey, "Afghan Rebels Receive Hundreds of Stingers," *Washington Times*, March 25, 1987, p. 9A.

46. David B. Ottaway, "U.S. Missiles Alter War in Afghanistan," *Washington Post*, July 19, 1987, p. A16; David B. Ottaway, "Stingers Were Key Weapon in Afghan War, Army Finds," *Washington Post*, July 5, 1989, p. A2.

47. David B. Ottaway, "U.S. Widens Arms Shipments to Bolster Afghan Guerrillas," *Washington Post*, September 21, 1987, pp. A1, A7.

48. Yousaf and Adkin, *The Bear Trap*, pp. 189–90.

49. Tim Weiner, "U.S. Used Secret Global Network to Arm Afghans," *Philadelphia Inquirer*, February 29, 1988, pp. 1A, 8A.

50. Richard M. Weintraub, "New Arms Reaching Afghans," *Washington Post*, April 5, 1988, pp. A1, A19; Steve Coll, "In CIA's Covert Afghan War, Where to Draw the Line Was Key," *Washington Post*, July 20, 1992, pp. A1, A2.

51. William E. Burrows and Robert Windrem, *Critical Mass: The Dangerous Race for Superweapons in a Fragmenting World* (New York: Simon & Schuster, 1994), pp. 72–73.

52. Lally Weymouth, "Moscow's 'Invisible War' of Terror Inside Pakistan," *Washington Post*, March 13, 1988, pp. C1, C4.

53. Ibid.; James Morrison, "If the Soviets Leave, Will Afghans Notice?" *Washington Times*, pp. A1, A10.

54. Weymouth, "Moscow's 'Invisible War'"; Kamran Khan, "Afghan Guerrilla Leaders Killed by Kabul's 'KGB,'" *London Times*, November 3, 1985, p. 22; Aaron R. Einfrank, "Fleeing Afghans Terrorized Anew by KGB Surrogates in Pakistan," *Washington Times*, January 23, 1986, pp. 1A, 16A.

55. Weymouth, "Moscow's 'Invisible War'"; Khan, "Afghan Guerrilla Leaders Killed by Kabul's 'KGB'".

56. Einfrank, "Fleeing Afghans Terrorized."

26 A New World of Disorder

1. Bob Woodward, *The Commanders* (New York: Simon & Schuster, 1991), p. 206.

2. Ibid.

3. Ibid., p. 207.

4. Ibid., pp. 208, 216.

5. Ibid., pp. 218–19.

6. Interview.

7. Bill Gertz, "New Spy Satellite, Needed to Monitor Treaty, Sits on Ground," *Washington Times*, October 20, 1987, p. A5; Bob Woodward, *Veil: The Secret Wars of the CIA 1981–1987* (New York: Simon & Schuster, 1987), p. 221.

8. Douglas G. Armstrong, "The Gulf War's Patched-Together Air Intelligence," *Naval Institute Proceedings*, November 1992, pp. 109–11.

9. Office of the Deputy Chief of Staff for Intelligence, Annual Historical Review, *1 October 1990 to 30 September 1991*, 1993, pp. 4–10, 4–12.

10. Lon Rains, "Soviets Orbit Photo Satellite 48 Hours after Iraq Invasion," *Space News*, August 13–19, 1990, p. 4; "Soviet Recon Satellite Images Persian Gulf Area," *Aviation Week & Space Technology*, November 19, 1990, p. 24.

11. Armstrong, "The Gulf War's Patched-Together Air Intelligence," *Naval Institute Proceedings*, November 1992, pp. 109–11; Desmond Ball, *Intelligence in the Gulf War* (Canberra: SDSC, Australian National University, 1991), pp. 32, 35.

12. David A. Fulghum, "Key Military Officials Criticize Intelligence Handling in Gulf War," *Aviation Week & Space Technology*, June 24, 1991, p. 83.

13. Robert W. Ward et al., *Desert Storm Reconstruction Report*, vol. 3: C^3/Space and Electronic Warfare (Alexandria, Va.: Center for Naval Analyses, June 1992), pp. 6–19; U.S. Congress, House Committee on Armed Services, *Intelligence Successes and Failures in Operations Desert Shield/Storm* (Washington, D.C.: HCAS, 1993), p. 15.

14. Department of Defense, *Conduct of the Persian Gulf War, Final Report to Congress* (Washington, D.C: DOD, April 1992), C-14–C-15.

15. Elizabeth Shogren, "Hated Symbol of KGB Torn Down by Crowd," *Los Angeles Times*, August 21, 1991, pp. A1, A2.

16. David Remnick, "KGB Targeted for Major Reform," *Washington Post*, Au-

gust 27, 1991, pp. A1, A9; Serge Schmemann, "Yeltsin Says Elite K. G. B. Unit Refused to Storm His Office," *New York Times*, August 26, 1991, pp. A1, A12.

17. Central Intelligence Agency, "The Russian Security Services: Sorting Out the Pieces," September 1992, pp. vi, 3; "Primakov to Head Soviet Intelligence Unit," *Washington Post*, October 1, 1991, p. A16; Michael Parks, "Gorbachev Names a New Spymaster," *Los Angeles Times*, October 1, 1991, pp. A6, A7.

18. Central Intelligence Agency, "Russian Security Services," p. 3; Carey Goldberg, "New Soviet Spy Chief Wants No Cold War," *Los Angeles Times*, October 3, 1991, pp. A10–A11; Parks, "Gorbachev Names a New Spymaster"; Natalia Gevorkian, "The KGB: 'They Still Need Us,'" *Bulletin of the Atomic Scientists*, January/February 1993, pp. 36–38.

19. Goldberg, "New Soviet Spy Chief Wants No Cold War"; Parks, "Gorbachev Names a New Spymaster."

20. Bill Gertz, "KGB Halts Lookout for U.S. Nuclear Attack," *Washington Times*, November 28, 1991, p. A9.

21. Central Intelligence Agency, "Russian Security Services," p. vi.

22. Ibid., pp. vi, 6; Bill Gertz, "Russian Spies Remain in U.S. Despite KGB's Fall," *Washington Times*, November 15, 1992, p. A6.

23. "Cooperation with the Russian Intelligence Service," *FBIS-WEU-92-194*, October 6, 1992, p. 5.

24. Margaret Shapiro, "Ex-KGB, CIA Talk of Sharing," *Washington Post*, October 19, 1992, pp. A14, A22.

25. "FRG, Russian Intelligence Services Agree to Cooperate," *FBIS-WEU-93-029*, February 16, 1993, p. 13; "Russian Intelligence Service Head Visits," *FBIS-WEU-93-031*, February 18, 1993, p. 21; "Primakov Talks with CIA Director Woolsey in U.S.," *FBIS-SOV-93-116*, June 18, 1993, p. 10.

26. "GRU Head's Key Role in Afghanistan," *Jane's Defence Weekly*, August 19, 1989, p. 303.

27. William Drozdiak, "East Germany's Wolf: The Spy Who Came into the Fold," *Washington Post*, November 19, 1989, pp. A31–A32.

28. Anne McElvoy, "We Have the Videos," *The Spectator*, September 29, 1990, p. 8.

29. Drozdiak, "East Germany's Wolf."

30. John Tagliabue, "Fugitive German Spy Planning to Surrender," *New York Times*, November 7, 1989, p. A12.

31. Serge Schmemann, "Old Master Spy in East Berlin Tells Why He Backs Changes," *New York Times*, November 22, 1989, p. A14; John Tagliabue, "East Berlin Spy Returns to Germany," *New York Times*, October 18, 1991, p. A6.

32. Craig R. Whitney, "Ex-East German Spy Chief Says He Expects Conviction," *New York Times*, September 22, 1993, p. A5.

33. Ibid.; Steve Vogel, "'Mole' Who Doomed Brandt Tells How He Spied," *Washington Post*, July 1, 1993, p. A16.

34. Craig R. Whitney, "East German Spy Closes His Trial in Anger," *New York Times*, November 25, 1993, p. A9; Steve Vogel, "East German Spymaster Found Guilty of Treason," *Washington Post*, December 7, 1993, p. A16.

35. Peter B. de Selding, "Joxe: Spy Satellites Essential for France," *Space News*, May 13–19, 1991, pp. 1, 20.

36. Ibid.

37. Peter B. de Selding, "French Firm Outlines Helios' Complex Encryption Plan," *Space News*, May 31–June 6, 1993, p. 7; Peter B. de Selding, "Potential

Partners Give Helios Follow-on Cool Response," *Space News*, June 28–July 11, 1993, p. 5; "French Tally Savings in Helios-SPOT Work," *Space News*, March 12–18, 1993, p. 2.

38. Peter B. de Selding, "France to Provide Imagery to WEU," *Space News*, May 3–9, 1993, p. 9; Peter B. de Selding, "France Steps Up Its Military Space Activity, Spending," *Space News*, November 2–8, 1992, p. 21.

39. De Selding, "Potential Partners."

40. "France: Helios Program's Proposed All-Weather Reconnaissance Satellite Discussed," *JPRS-EST-92-004*, February 6, 1992, pp. 28–29; "Matra to Revise Helios Program, Proposes All-Weather Radar Detection Satellite," *JPRS-EST-92-004*, February 6, 1992, pp. 29–30; "France Gives DASA Nod for Prime Osiris Role," *Space News*, September 5–11, 1994, p. 2.

41. "Israeli Satellite Is 'Threat,' Say Arabs," *Jane's Defence Weekly*, October 1, 1988, p. 753; "Israel Launches Second Offeq," *Jane's Defence Weekly*, April 14, 1990, p. 678; Daniel Williams, "Israel Launches Satellite: Spy Role Rumored," *Los Angeles Times*, April 4, 1990, p. A9; Joel Brinkley, "Israel Puts a Satellite in Orbit a Day after Threat by Iraqis," *New York Times*, April 4, 1990, p. A6.

42. Neil Munro and Barbara Opall, "Israeli Spy Satellite May Be Imminent," *Space News*, March 11–17, 1991, p. 21; "Israel Launches Second Offeq," *Jane's Defence Weekly*, April 14, 1990, p. 678.

43. Yossi Melman, "Israel's Race into Space," *Washington Post*, May 17, 1992, p. C4.

44. David E. Sanger, "Tired of Relying on U.S., Japan Seeks to Expand Its Own Intelligence Efforts," *New York Times*, January 1, 1992, p. 6.

45. Maoaki Usui, "Group in Japan Recommends Spy Satellites," *Space News*, August 29–September 4, 1994, pp. 4, 21.

46. "Parlez-Vous Espionage?" *Newsweek*, September 23, 1991, p. 40.

47. Ibid.

48. Jay Peterzell, "When 'Friends' Become Moles," *Time*, May 28, 1990, p. 50; Michael Wines, "French Said to Spy on U.S. Computer Companies," *New York Times*, November 18, 1990, p. 4.

49. Memorandum for: Director/DR: Subject: DEST Collection Plan, 1991.

50. Ibid.

51. Peterzell, "When 'Friends' Become Moles."

52. Ibid.; Peter Schweitzer, *Friendly Spies: How America's Allies Are Using Economic Espionage to Steal Our Secrets* (New York: Atlantic Monthly Press, 1993), p. 145; "BND Reportedly Planning Industrial Espionage," *FBIS-WEU-94-014*, January 21, 1994, p. 10.

53. Private information.

54. Parks, "Gorbachev Names a New Spymaster"; Bill Gertz, "Russian Spies Remain in U.S. Despite KGB's Fall," *Washington Times*, November 15, 1992, p. A6; Bill Gertz, "Gates: China Has U.S. Missile Secrets," *Washington Times*, January 5, 1993, pp. A1, A10.

55. "Russia to Increase Military Aid, Maintain Espionage Center," *FBIS-LAT-93-114*, June 16, 1993, pp. 1–2; Bill Gertz, "Eavesdropping Complex in Cuba Being Upgraded," *Washington Times*, April 5, 1990, p. A4; Desmond Ball, *Soviet Signals Intelligence (SIGINT): Intercepting Satellite Communications* (Canberra: SDSC, Australian National University, 1989), pp. 61, 74–75.

56. See Seymour Hersh, *The Samson Option: Israel's Nuclear Arsenal and American Foreign Policy* (New York: Random House, 1991).

57. Don Oberdorfer, "North Koreans Pursue Nuclear Weapons," *Washington Post*, July 29, 1989, p. A9; John J. Fialka, "North Korea May Be Developing Ability to Build Nuclear Weapons," *Wall Street Journal*, July 19, 1989, p. A16; David E. Sanger, "Journey to Isolation," *New York Times Magazine*, November 15, 1992, pp. 28ff.

58. R. Jeffrey Smith, "N. Korea and the Bomb: High-Tech Hide-and-Seek," *Washington Post*, April 27, 1993, pp. A1, A11.

59. Sanger, "Journey to Isolation"; Paul Lewis, "U.S. Shows Photos to Argue Iraq Hides Nuclear Material," *New York Times*, June 27, 1991, p. A12; Bill Gertz, "Satellite Spots Iraq Burying Atomic Gear," *Washington Times*, July 10, 1991, pp. A1, A10.

60. "German Intelligence Probes Iranian Nuclear Program," *FBIS-NES-92-242*, December 16, 1992, p. 61.

61. Russian Foreign Intelligence Service, *Proliferation of Weapons of Mass Destruction*, 1993, Table of Contents. (Translated by Joint Publications Research Service).

62. Anthony Fainberg, *Stengthening IAEA Safeguards: Lessons from Iraq* (Stanford, Calif.: Center for International Security and Arms Control, Stanford University, 1993), p. 18.

63. Steve Coll, "U.S. Halted Nuclear Bid by Iran," *Washington Post*, November 17, 1992, pp. A1, A30; "BND Warns against Syrian Arms Program," *FBIS-WEU-92-231*, December 1, 1992, p. 14.

64. Private information; Neil Munro, "Intelligence Community Pushes Sensor Advances," *Space News*, September 6–12, 1993, p. 18.

Index

A-12 aircraft, 302–4
A-52, 83
A-54. *See* Thümmel, Paul
Abel, Richard F., 408
ABLE ARCHER, 385–87
Abu, Muhammad Najjar, 354
Abwehr (Germany), 77–78, 84–87, 96, 130
  Group II, 78
  problems of, 139–44
Active measures, 244
Adenauer, Konrad, 236
Administrative and Legal Work Department (China), 243*fn*
Advanced Telemetry System, 382
Adwin, Kamal, 354
AEFOXTROT. *See* Nosenko, Yuri Ivanovich
AELADLE. *See* Golitsyn, Anatoliy
Aerial reconnaissance, 16–17, 157–72
  American, 219–20, 260–62
  British, 31–34, 97–100, 157–63, 221
  French, 31–32, 97–100
  German, 31, 34, 37, 96–97, 163–64
  high-speed, high-altitude plane, 302–3
  navigational aids, 161
  in Six-Day War, 322–23
  Soviet, 164–69
Afghanistan, 411–15
  coup, 358–59
Agent 17. *See* Schluga, August
Agent C. *See* Menzies, Stewart

Ahcene, Ait, 254
AJAX, 248–50
Albert, Heinrich, 28–29
Alert, Canada (Soviet signal interception station), 309
Allavedelmi Hatosag. *See* State Security Authority (Hungary)
Allende Gossens, Salvador, 355–56
ALLIANCE, 130
All-Russian Extraordinary Commission for Combating Counterrevolution, Sabotage and Speculation. *See* Cheka (Russia)
AMAN (Israel), 282–83, 319–20, 322, 360–65
  Unit 8200, 332
Ames, Aldrich, 422*fn*
AMICOL, 130
Amin, Hafizullah, 358–59
Amos satellite, 425
Anders, Wladyslaw, 248
ANDREY, 292
Andries, Gerald, 405
Andropov, Yuri, 325, 374, 379–80
Angleton, James Jesus, 286, 289–90, 290*fn*, 291, 292*fn*
Anglo-Iranian Oil Company, 248–49
Anglo-Soviet trade negotiations, 67–68
Angooki Taipu A (Japan), 81
ANNA, 128
ANNE (Janet Chisholm), 276, 278

IIIb (Germany), 6, 19–21, 26–27. *See also* Abwehr (Germany)
Improved CRYSTAL, 418
Improved CRYSTAL Metric System, 418
India
espionage, industrial, 427
satellite reconnaissance, 425
INDIGO, 418
Indra, A., 325
Industrial Intelligence Centre (Great Britain), 104, 208–9. *See also* Ministry of Economic Warfare (Great Britain)
Inlow, Ronald, 330
Inman, Bobby Ray, 400
Innostranoye Otdel. *See* Foreign Department (Russia)
INO. *See* Foreign Department (Russia)
Institute for Economic Research (East Germany), 237
Institut für Wirtschaftswissenschaftliche Forschung (East Germany), 237
Intelligence, 111*fn*
economic, 197–98
future of, 430–31
industrial, 208–11
interpretation of, 360–72
misuse by military/political command, 25, 40–41, 327, 360–65
Intelligence Administration (China), 243*fn*
Intelligence Board (United States), Committee on Imagery Requirements and Exploitation, 330, 336
Intelligence Branch (Great Britain), 5
Intelligence Bureau (Germany), 6
Intelligence Department (China), 242–43
Intelligence Department of People's Liberation Army General Staff (China), 243
Intelligence Directorate (Russia), 59
INTERALLIE, 129–30
Inter-Allied Military Control Commission, 77–78
International Atomic Energy Authority, 429
International Federation of Resistance Fighters, 252
International Liaison Department (China), 243

International Organization of Democratic Lawyers, 252
International Organization of Journalists, 252
International Radio and TV Organization, 252
Inter-Republican Security Service (Soviet Union), 421
Inter-Services Intelligence Directorate (Pakistan), 412–13
INVENTOR, 148
Investigation Department (China), 243*fn*
Iran, 248–50, 370–72
nuclear program, 429
Iraq
nuclear program, 429–30
and Persian Gulf War, 417–20
IRONBARK, 277, 277*fn*
ISID. *See* Inter-Services Intelligence Directorate (Pakistan)
Israel
covert operations, 250–51
espionage
against Egypt, 284–85, 332–33
in Six-Day War, 319–23
against Syria, 239, 282–84
against United States, 398–403
espionage against
American, 400*fn*
Egyptian, 331–32
Soviet, 400*fn*
intelligence, misuse of reports, 360–65
intelligence organizations, 238–41
retaliation for Munich, 353–54
satellite reconnaissance, 425
Israeli Defense Forces, 240
Italy, espionage against, British, 66
Ivanov, 26
Ivashutin, Petr, 422
IVY BELLS, 393–94
IWF. *See* Institut für Wirtschaftswissenschaftliche Forschung (East Germany)
I Z Organization (Germany), 86

JA, 73
Jackson, Thomas, 40
Jacquier, Paul, 288*fn*
JADE/AMICOL, 130
Jaguar reconnaissance aircraft, 419
Jambroes, George, 149